WORK and FAMILY

Theory, Research, and Applications

Edited by
Elizabeth B. Goldsmith

*Originally published as
a special issue of the*
Journal of Social Behavior and Personality

SAGE PUBLICATIONS
The Publishers of Professional Social Science
Newbury Park   London   New Delhi

Copyright © 1989 by Select Press

All rights reserved. No part of this book may be reproduced or utilized in any form or by any means, electronic or mechanical, including photocopying, recording, or by any information storage and retrieval system, without permission in writing from the publisher.

For information address:

SAGE Publications, Inc.
2111 West Hillcrest Drive
Newbury Park, California 91320

SAGE Publications Ltd.
28 Banner Street
London EC1Y 8QE
England

SAGE Publications India Pvt. Ltd.
M-32 Market
Greater Kailash I
New Delhi 110 048 India

Printed in the United States of America

Library of Congress Cataloging-in-Publication Data

Main entry under title:

Work and family : theory, research, and applications / edited by
    Elizabeth B. Goldsmith.
        p.   cm.
    Bibliography: p.
    Includes indexes.
    ISBN 0-8039-3623-0. — ISBN 0-8039-3624-9 (pbk.)
    1. Work and family—United States.   I. Goldsmith, Elizabeth B.
HD4904.25.W69   1989
306.3'6'0973—dc20   89-6394
                                                                CIP

FIRST SAGE PRINTING, 1989

Contents

Foreword
by Douglas T. Hall — v

Preface
by Elizabeth B. Goldsmith — vii

SECTION I:
THE PRESENT STATE OF WORK AND FAMILY THEORY AND RESEARCH

Work and Family: A Review and Expanded Conceptualization
by Patricia Voydanoff — 1

The Intersection of Work and Family Roles: Individual, Interpersonal, and Organizational Issues
by Jeffrey H. Greenhaus — 23

The Urban Underclass and the Future of Work-Family Relations Research
by Robert F. Kelly — 45

Studying the Work-Family Connection: Atheoretical Progress, Ideological Bias, and Shaky Foundations for Policy
by Paul W. Kingston — 55

Re-thinking the Connections Among "Work and Family" and Well-Being: A Model for Investigating Employment and Family Work Contexts
by Marsha Kline and Philip A. Cowan — 61

A Systemic Perspective on Work and Family Units
by Jon Jankowski, Marnell Holtgraves, and Lawrence H. Gerstein — 91

SECTION II:
EFFECTS OF EMPLOYMENT AND UNEMPLOYMENT ON FAMILIES AND CHILDREN

Exosystem Influences on Family and Child Functioning
by Denise Daniels and Rudolf H. Moos — 113

Affective Response to Work and Quality of Family Life: Employee and Spouse Perspectives
by Sheldon Zedeck, Christina Maslach, Kathleen Mosier, and Linda Skitka — 135

Restructuring Work for Family: How Dual-Earner Couples with Children Manage
by Jeanne M. Brett and Sara Yogev — 159

Family Stress and Psychological Well-Being Among Employed and Nonemployed Mothers
by Neala S. Schwartzberg and Rita Scher Dytell — 175

Social Support and Resource Management of Unemployed Women
by Patricia S. Retherford, Gladys J. Hildreth, and Elizabeth B. Goldsmith — 191

SECTION III:
CAREER, JOB, AND FAMILY RESEARCH

Career Entry Influences on Social Networks of Young Adults
by Donna L. Sollie and Judith L. Fisher — 205

Gender Differences in the Prediction of Job Commitment
by Joe F. Pittman and Dennis K. Orthner — 227

Work/Family Concerns of University Faculty
by Jerelyn B. Schultz, Yonsuk L. Chung, and Chinella G. Henderson — 249

Lifestyle Patterns of University Women: Implications for Family/Career Decision Modeling
by Jan Cooper Taylor and Barbara A. Spencer   265

Night Shift Work: Job and Family Concerns
by Michael G. Weiss and Marsha B. Liss   279

SECTION IV:
CONFLICT RESOLUTION AND WORK/FAMILY CONFLICT RESEARCH

Some Antecedents and Consequences of Work-Family Conflict
by Ronald J. Burke   287

Managerial Conflict Resolution Styles: Work and Home Differences
by Joan Mills and Leonard H. Chusmir   303

A Gender-Role Perspective on Role Conflict, Work Stress and Social Support
by Esther R. Greenglass, Kaye-Lee Pantony and Ronald J. Burke   317

SECTION V:
TRANS-NATIONAL AND CROSS-CULTURAL RESEARCH STUDIES

Burning Out in Medicine: A Comparison of Husbands and Wives in Dual-Career Couples
by Dafna N. Izraeli   329

Mexican-American Professional Women: Role Satisfaction Differences in Single and Multiple Role Lifestyles
by Ruth E. Zambrana and Sandra Frith   347

Japanese and American Housewives' Attitudes Toward Employment of Women
by John W. Engel   363

Mothers Working Outside of the Home: Attitudes of Fathers and Mothers in Three Cultures
by Patsy Skeen, Ligaya Palang Paguio, Bryan E. Robinson, and James E. Deal   373

Selected Bibliography on Work and Family
by Elizabeth B. Goldsmith and Teryl A. Walters   383

Index of Names   397

Index of Subjects   411

Foreword

This is a goldmine of material on a topic of critical importance to society. I am tremendously impressed with the interdisciplinary nature of the contributions (psychology, sociology, business, social work, and others). This is the first time I have seen the problems attacked from such a rich array of conceptual perspectives, and with such a talented group of contributors. This is a major advance in getting our arms around the problems of work/family relationships.

I am also excited to see such a diversity of settings and populations studied here—urban workers, single parents, night shift workers, police, unemployed women, and others. I am struck by the consistent streams which show up in the findings across these varied settings

Related to the last point, the richness in cultural settings is also remarkable. It is gratifying indeed to begin to generalize beyond the U.S. and European experience.

All in all, this is a priceless resource for scholars and policymakers concerned about work/family relationships. Hopefully, it will be "must reading" in Washington for those responsible for creating a "kinder, gentler" world at home and in the work place.

> Dr. Douglas T. Hall
> Professor, Sloan School of Management,
> Boston University
> Co-author of *"The Two-Career Couple"*

Preface

The two most important life roles for the majority of people are work and family. With the increasing number of women entering the labor force, researchers from a variety of fields have turned their attention to investigating how individuals balance their work and family responsibilities.

This volume on work and family represents the latest theoretical and empirical work. For this endeavor, I was able to assemble a group of contributors from the forefront of the field and to welcome the contributions of several newcomers. It has been a pleasure to work with the authors and Rick Crandall, the editor of the *Journal of Social Behavior and Personality*. He deserves full credit for perceiving the need for a special issue on work and family and generously providing the guidance I needed as guest editor.

One of the volume's strengths is its inclusion of transnational and cross-cultural research. In addition, a wide range of income levels, career stages, lifestyles, and occupations are covered. Another progressive feature of the volume is its advancement of theory and its presentation of new models of work/family interactions.

Several themes are evidenced throughout the issue. The authors explore the topics of self-esteem, well-being, family and child functioning, marital satisfaction, parenting, role overload, job involvement, stress, conflict, absenteeism, career advancement, social support, depression, and time management within the context of the work/family interchange. A subject index has been provided for your convenience in locating key concepts.

The articles in this volume are grouped into five sections. The first section, in which the present state of work and family theory and research is discussed, starts with Patricia Voydanoff's thoughtful review and continues with three commentators' reactions and two theoretical articles. Voydanoff was asked to write the lead paper since she is a recognized expert in the work and family field, author of two books (1984, 1987), and is highly regarded by other work and family scholars. The commentators, Jeffrey Greenhaus, Robert Kelly, and Paul Kingston, were encouraged to not limit themselves strictly to the Voydanoff paper but to go beyond by adding their own unique perspectives. The second section is comprised of research articles on family and child-centered issues related to employment and unemployment. Research articles covering a diverse mix of career, job, and family topics are in section three. Section four covers conflict resolution and work/family conflict research. Transnational and cross-cultural research studies comprise section five. The volume concludes with a comprehensive bibliography.

I believe that this collection will stimulate a great deal of thought on the nature of the work and family interchange. I wish to express my appreciation to two of my colleagues at Florida State University, Colleen Sullivan for assistance in copy editing and Ed Augustyniak for the cover design. Finally, I want to heartily thank the reviewers and congratulate all the authors.

Elizabeth B. Goldsmith
Tallahassee, Florida

REFERENCES

Voydanoff, P. (1984). *Work and family*. Palo Alto, CA: Mayfield Publishing Company.

Voydanoff, P. (1987). *Work and family life*. Newbury Park, CA: Sage Publications, Inc.

Work and Family: A Review and Expanded Conceptualization

Patricia Voydanoff

Center for the Study of Family Development
300 College Park Avenue, Dayton, OH 45469-0001

This article reviews the development and current status of research on work and family life. An expanded conceptualization of the work/family interface is provided that suggests directions for future theoretical and empirical work. Further work needs to (1) view the work/family interface in the context of broad economic trends, (2) incorporate analyses of unpaid family and community work, (3) examine the implications of worker-earner role difficulties for families, and (4) acknowledge the importance of changing family structures for work and family life. In addition, policy research tends to be gender-linked and to neglect analyses of the effects of family-oriented personnel policies on families and employers. Addressing these limitations will increase understanding of the work/family interface and contribute substantially to policy development.

The editor's invitation to reflect on the current state of research on work and family for this special issue was most welcome. It provided an opportunity to assess in general terms a body of research that I have been working with for several years. In addition, in response to the call to stimulate reactions from others working in the field, I have suggested directions in which work and family research should move to extend our understanding of linkages between work and family.

I have structured my presentation in the following way. The first two sections review the development of the study of work and family and provide an overview of research areas that form the core of work/family research. The third section suggests ways in which the conceptualization of work/family research should be expanded and presents implications of this expanded conceptualization for research and policy analysis.

It is obviously impossible for such a brief article to review all of the research findings pertaining to work and family. Since much of this research was reviewed by Voydanoff (1987), this paper addresses general trends and issues. To avoid excessive duplication of the comprehensive bibliography, I have referenced research reviews where possible. In

©1988 Select Press

addition, the analysis is limited to studies of the recent situation in the United States, thereby omitting historical and cross-cultural research. Lastly, research areas bearing on work/family linkages such as consumer and family economics, social mobility, and demography must necessarily be neglected.

EARLY RESEARCH ON WORK/FAMILY ISSUES

Research on the work/family interface has evolved unevenly due to changes in behavior patterns and popular beliefs. During and since the Depression of the thirties, men's unemployment has been considered detrimental to family life; research over the years has documented pervasive effects in this area (Voydanoff, 1983a, 1983b). However, early studies attempting to examine the effects of men's employment on family life indicated that men did not see connections between their work and family lives (Aberle & Naegele, 1952; Dyer, 1964). Prior to the 1960's, limited research also was undertaken to document the presumed negative effects of maternal employment on children (Bronfenbrenner & Crouter, 1982).

Women's Employment

Large increases in wives' employment and recognition of the methodological limitations of earlier studies have led to more extensive and objective research on family life during and since the 1960's. In general, this research indicates that women's employment status per se has few direct and consistent effects on families and children. The most important factors affecting the relationship between maternal employment and child development include the age and sex of the child, quality of adult supervision, mother's job satisfaction, and mother's choice to work (Bronfenbrenner & Crouter, 1982; Hoffman, 1979; Moore & Sawhill, 1984; Moore, Spain, & Bianchi, 1984).

Several mediating factors also influence the effects of wife employment on marital relationships. For example, marital satisfaction is higher among employed wives who have high levels of education, are working out of choice, are working part-time, or receive support from their husbands. Wife employment is related to lower marital satisfaction for those with low incomes and those holding undesirable jobs. Similar factors affect the marital satisfaction of the husbands of employed women. In addition, employed women have more influence over financial decisions in their marriages and spend less time in family work than unemployed women (Miller & Garrison, 1982; Moore & Hofferth, 1979; Rallings & Nye, 1979; Szinovacz, 1984).

Increased wife employment among middle-class women also stimulated extensive research on two-career couples in which both husbands and wives are employed in professional or managerial occupations. This research began in the late 1960's and peaked in the late 1970's. The earlier studies focused on qualitative analyses of the benefits, strains, and trade-offs common to two-career families. Later research examines coping strategies used by these families to balance work and family demands. Other recent studies deal with relatively specific factors such as productivity, job seeking, geographic mobility, finances, and commuting (Gilbert, 1985; Gilbert & Rachlin, 1987; Hertz, 1986; Nicola & Hawkes, 1986; Piotrkowski, Rapoport, & Rapoport, 1987; Rapoport & Rapoport, 1978; Skinner, 1980; Voydanoff, 1987).

During this period, analysts also addressed the unpaid contributions of the wives of professionals and managers to their husbands' careers, through the "two-person career" in which wives have well-defined duties that are an integral part of their husbands' occupations (Papanek, 1973). These duties include entertaining business associates, attending work-related social functions, and making business contacts through volunteer work in the community. This assistance provides career advantages to husbands and creates status and prestige for the family. However, it also constrains wives' participation in the labor force because of demands on the wives' time, lack of control over time scheduling, geographic mobility, and the husbands' high levels of income (Voydanoff, 1987).

CURRENT WORK AND FAMILY RESEARCH

During the past decade the areas included in work/family research have expanded in several directions. The majority of early studies addressed male unemployment, female employment status, and two-career families, current topics are more diverse. An examination of recent reviews of work/family research reveals an emphasis on relationships between structural and psychological work role characteristics and work/family conflict, child rearing, and quality of family life. Other frequently reviewed topics include economic rewards and resources associated with work, effects of family on work, individual strategies for coordinating work and family roles, and employment policies that address work/family conflict (see e.g., Crouter & Perry-Jenkins, 1986; Galinsky, 1986; Moen, 1983; Mortimer & Sorensen, 1984; Nieva, 1985; Piotrkowski, Rapoport, & Rapoport, 1987; Statuto et al., 1984).

Economic Resources and Rewards

Research on social stratification, child development, and family life has investigated relationships between social class and family life for many years. Recently, several analyses of research on the work/family interface have examined the role of socioeconomic resources and rewards in relation to family life (e.g., Hoffman, 1984; Kanter, 1977; Moen, 1983; Mortimer and Sorensen, 1984; Piotrkowski, Rapoport, and Rapoport, 1987).

It is generally recognized that a minimum level of economic resources and security is necessary for family formation and stability. However, beyond this minimum, the relationship between economic resources and quality of family life is less clear. Scanzoni (1970, 1982) has suggested that occupational success is directly related to marital solidarity while Aldous, Osmond, and Hicks (1979) hypothesize that men who are moderately successful in their occupations are more likely to have satisfying marriages than those who are very successful or unsuccessful. Data from studies using different measures of occupational success indicate support for both hypotheses. Wives' employment status is used as a major variable in relation to quality of family life. However, the relationship between wives' occupational success and quality of family life is generally examined in relation to husbands' success rather than in absolute terms.

Structural and Psychological Characteristics of Work

As mentioned above, early studies of work/family linkages examined employment status in relation to family life. These studies dealt with the problem of unemployment among men and paid employment among women. During this period, however, other research areas, mainly organizational psychology and the sociology of work and leisure, were looking at the characteristics of work roles in relation to job satisfaction, stress, and quality of leisure. Studies of job satisfaction during this period focused on relationships between intrinsic and extrinsic job characteristics and job satisfaction and dissatisfaction. Job characteristics classified as extrinsic focus on the context or environment in which work is done and job features determined by external events or other people, for example, working conditions, relationships with co-workers, supervision, company policy and administration, pay, and job security. Intrinsic characteristics deal with the content and tasks involved in doing a job and opportunities for self expression and self actualization, for example, amount of responsibility, variety, skill, and autonomy; opportunities for personal growth and development; and feelings of pride and accomplishment (Locke, 1976; Mortimer, 1979). Similar job characteristics are used to assess relationships between occupational stress and health (see, for example, House et al., 1979; House et al., 1986; LaRocco, House, and French, 1980).

Studies of the effects of work on leisure concentrated on testing four types of linkages: spillover in which work role characteristics generalize into leisure roles; compensation in which those with dissatisfying work roles compensate by seeking satisfaction in leisure activities; opposition in which work roles conflict with the enjoyment of leisure activities; and segmentation in which work role characteristics and satisfactions are independent of leisure activities and satisfactions (Kabanoff, 1980; Staines, 1980). This research provides support for the spillover and compensation models under differing conditions; however, the research is limited by conceptual and methodological problems and the inability to establish causal direction.

Effects of Work on Family

Although work role characteristics had been examined in relation to work/family conflict and quality of family life prior to 1977, this type of research increased following Kanter's (1977) review and conceptualization of work and family as a research frontier. She discussed several ways in which work affects family life including absorption, time and timing, rewards and resources, occupational cultures, and emotional climate.

A relatively extensive body of research has examined relationships between structural and psychological aspects of work roles and work/family conflict and quality of family life. Structural characteristics of jobs most closely tied to family life include the timing and spatial location of work. Working long hours is associated with work/family conflict and strain; however, work hours generally are not significantly related to marital or family satisfaction. In addition, those working non-day shifts and weekends experience higher levels of work/family conflict. Those working on weekends also are more likely to report lower levels of marital/family satisfaction. However, working non-day shifts shows only a weak nonsignificant relationship to marital/family satisfaction. Thus, number and scheduling of work hours seem to have a more direct connection to work/family conflict and strain than to overall satisfaction with marriage and family life. The effects of work-related geographic mobility and travel on family life vary according to their extent and timing, family characteristics, and the availability and use of coping strategies and social supports (Voydanoff, 1987).

Psychological characteristics are associated with both positive and negative spillover into family life. Job demands create job stress which may influence family relationships as well as health. The following job demands are related to work/family conflict: role ambiguity, role conflict, intellectual and physical effort, rapid change, pressures for quality work, pressure to work hard and fast, and a heavy work load. Job involvement is related to work/family conflict and low marital satisfaction among male professionals and managers; however, job satisfaction and intrinsic work role characteristics generally show positive relationships with quality of family life (Voydanoff, 1987).

Effects of Family on Work

Research on the work/family interface has tended to focus on effects of work on family life; however, increasing attention is being given to ways in which family responsibilities and demands impact on work. The relationships under consideration are of two major types: (1) the influence of family responsibilities on labor force participation and job performance and (2) the effects of family structure demands and supports on work role performance.

Family responsibilities provide an important motivation for labor force participation and job performance among men and women. Since most men see the role of economic provider as their primary family role, having a job with adequate earnings is of crucial importance. The extent and timing of women's labor force participation over the life course varies according to economic need, constraints of husband's occupation, and family life-cycle stage. Limited data also suggest that family responsibilities increase married men's work hours, income, and involvement while married women's rates of absenteeism and turnover are comparable to those for men and unmarried women (Voydanoff, 1987).

Family structure and support also influence the extent to which workers find it difficult to meet the demands of work. Members of two-earner families, one-parent families, and families with young children are likely to experience work/family conflict and job tension (Kelly and Voydanoff, 1985; Voydanoff, 1988; Voydanoff and Kelly, 1984). In addition, spouse support has a direct positive relationship to job commitment (Orthner and Pittman, 1986).

Multiple Roles among Women

In recent years an extensive body of research has focused on the effects of performing multiple roles on mental and physical health. Most of this research is based on samples of women. As mentioned earlier, labor force participation by women has been thought by many to be harmful and disruptive to family life. A similar argument has been made regarding the combined effects of work and family roles on women's health and the quality of family life. In general, these studies indicate that performing multiple roles, that is worker, spouse, and parent, is *positively* related to physical and mental health. However, specific combinations of work and family roles are negatively related to health, for example, clerical workers who are married with children. Limited research suggests that characteristics associated with work and family roles are more strongly related to poor mental and physical health than are the number and constellation of roles. These characteristics include the perceived quality of the roles and the level of demands and responsibilities (Baruch, Biener, & Barnett, 1987; Crosby, 1987; Voydanoff, 1987).

Despite the body of literature on multiple roles and health, research examining the combined effects of work role characteristics and family demands on family life is relatively undeveloped. The few existing studies indicate that both work and family characteristics are related to perceived work/family conflict. These variables include work hours and schedule, workload pressure, role conflict and ambiguity, job involvement, job autonomy, time expectations at work, marital status, and number and ages of children (Voydanoff, 1987, 1988).

The Work/Family Life Cycle

The analysis of multiple roles has been extended by looking at how individuals coordinate the responsibilities associated with work and family roles over the life course. Both work and family roles consist of career stages which intersect at given points in the life course to form stages in a work/family life cycle. The stages are accompanied by varied demands, identities, rewards, histories, and projected futures. Analysis of the work/family life cycle reveals two major mechanisms used by indviduals and families to construct workable patterns of activities and relationships: work/family role staging and work/family role allocation.

Work/family role staging may be either simultaneous or sequential. In simultaneous staging individuals perform both work and family roles over the adult life course. Sequential staging involves shifting the extent of participation in work and family roles across stages in family and work careers. Sequential staging is the most common type of labor force participation among women. Most sequencing is an adjustment to demands associated with family career stages, especially childbearing. Employment rates decrease during pregnancy. However, by two years following a birth the employment rate has increased to 60 percent of its previous level (Waite, Haggstrom, & Kanouse, 1985). The extent to which employment rates are affected by childbearing varies according to the education, pre-birth labor force experience, and economic need of the mother (McLaughlin, 1982). The choice between early and late parenthood is a major element of role staging. This decision involves several trade-offs in the performance of work and family activities over the life course. Larger numbers of parents are selecting the advantages and disadvantages associated with having children at relatively later periods in their work/family life cycle than previously (Voydanoff, 1987).

Work/family role allocation ranges from traditional to symmetrical. In the most traditional pattern the husband is the major breadwinner and the wife performs most of the family work. Symmetrical role allocation involves a relatively interchangeable division of labor in which both husband and wife engage in earning outside the home and family work. Despite the need for symmetrical role allocation among employed women, its development has been slow. Although husbands of employed women have slightly increased the amount of time spent in family work in recent years, women still spend considerably more time than men do (Pleck, 1985; Szinovacz, 1984). Many men and some women resist major changes in the direction of symmetrical role allocation (Hood, 1983; Hunt & Hunt, 1987; Lein, 1979).

Combined Effects of Husbands' and Wives' Work Role Characteristics

In recent years researchers have recognized that it is necessary not only to understand relationships between work and family roles for either the husband or wife but also to examine the combined effects of husbands' and wives' work role characteristics on family life. Preliminary research has begun to address joint effects in terms of the amount and scheduling of work time, relative socioeconomic attainment of husbands and wives, work-related geographic mobility, and commuter marriage. The development of the concept of the family work day to determine the total number of hours that at least one spouse is at work is a first step in assessing how joint work hours and schedules affect the time spent in various family activities and quality of family life (Kingston & Nock, 1985, 1987; Nock & Kingston, 1987).

Studies of the effects of the relative success of husbands and wives on family life show mixed results. In general, wives' relative success is more likely to have negative effects on quality of family life when relative income is considered. Studies using occupational status as the indicator of success show few negative effects when wives have higher occupational status than their husbands (Hoffman, 1984; Piotrkowski, Rapoport, and Rapoport, 1987).

A few small-scale studies indicate that work-related moves in two-earner families have greater effects on women than men. In general, women are more likely to move to accommodate their spouses' job changes and transfers than men are. Such moves negatively affect wives' employment status, weeks worked, and earnings. However, limited research suggests that these effects have disappeared two years after the move (Voydanoff, 1987).

A recent alternative to career-related moves is a commuter marriage in which spouses work in different locations during the week and reunite on weekends. Commuter marriages are more successful when the jobs are located relatively close to each other, the separations are of short duration, both spouses are strongly career-oriented, at least one spouse has an established career, and the couples are older, married longer, and free from child rearing responsibilities (Voydanoff, 1987).

Family-Oriented Personnel Policies

Much analysis of the work/family interface addresses policy issues, especially family-oriented personnel policies. Some of this work uses research findings to articulate the need for more flexible personnel policies for working parents. Many studies of specific work/family issues, for example, the effects of geographic mobility on families, discuss policies and programs, such as transfer policies and relocation programs, that address that specific issue.

Other studies investigate the availability and provisions of various types of family-oriented personnel policies. Much of this work has been done by Columbia University researchers, Sheila Kamerman and Alfred Kahn, and by research organizations such as the Conference Board and Catalyst. Specific studies examine child care (Kahn & Kamerman, 1987) and parental leaves (Kamerman, Kahn, & Kingston, 1983; Catalyst, 1986; Zigler &Franks, 1988). Other studies assess several policy areas including child and dependent care, parental leaves, flexible work schedules, flexible benefit plans, employee counseling, and relocation assistance (Axel, 1985; Bureau of National Affairs, 1986; Economic Policy Council of UNA-USA, 1985; Galinsky, 1986; Kamerman & Kahn, 1987; Pleck, 1986). Although most research focuses on the United States, several studies have documented that Western European countries have more extensive family policies than the U.S. (Hewlett, Ilchman, & Sweeney, 1986; Kamerman & Kahn, 1981).

However, little work explicitly examines relationships between family-oriented personnel policies and quality of family life. The most extensive research looks at flextime. Two studies have documented that workers on flextime schedules spend more time with their children and spouses than those on traditional schedules (Winnett & Neale, 1980; Lee, 1983). A third study reports that flextime is most effective in reducing work/family strain among one-earner and childless families and has the least benefit for two-earner families with children (Bohen & Viveros-Long, 1981).

Discussion

This cursory review documents that the focus of early research on relationships between employment status and family life has shifted to a greater emphasis on the structural and psychological characteristics of jobs. In addition, two more complex models have emerged, one in which the combination of husbands' and wives' work role characteristics are considered and another in which an individual's performance of multiple work and family roles is assessed. The multiple role approach has been extended by examining the coordination of multiple roles over the life course, especially among women. Although some aspects of the work/ family interface are still more likely to be studied among either men or women, analyses are becoming more balanced, for example, studies of unemployment are beginning to include women. In addition, the analysis of policies and programs addressing work/family issues is underway.

Based on the review, we can conclude that work and family research lacks integrated theoretical grounding. Perhaps the most general theoretical framework reflected in the research is role strain and expansion theory. This approach is used most explicitly in studies of multiple roles among women. However, it also is compatible with other approaches such as role conflict and family stress. These approaches overlap when work and family role characteristics are viewed as stressors that may be alleviated through coping resources and behaviors. Role conflict, a concept used in role strain theory, is integral to the analysis of relationships between structural work role characteristics and family life. In addition, the family development framework is used when work/family relationships and processes are viewed over the work/family life cycle.

Although there is no integrated theory of work/family relationships, partial integrations are available. These include analyses of time-based, strain-based, and behavior-based aspects of role conflict (Greenhaus and Beutell, 1985), physical and psychological availability for family life (Mumola and Rollings, 1985), structural and psychological interfaces between work and family systems (Piotrkowski, 1979), and mechanisms for coordinating multiple roles over the work/family life cycle (Voydanoff, 1980, 1987).

AN EXPANDED CONCEPTUALIZATION OF WORK AND FAMILY

A critical assessment of the literature indicates that the topics generally included in work/family research reflect definitions of work and family that are too narrow. For example, the analysis of work is generally limited to paid work. Unpaid work either is not considered or is viewed as family work, a component of family life as a dependent variable. The analysis of family life focuses on nuclear families, especially husband-wife relationships. Single-parent families, extended family relationships and supports, and parent-child relationships are generally neglected. This section suggests ways in which these boundaries might be extended and discusses implications for work/family research.

Work and the Economy

Despite important implications for family life, research on work and family often neglects to examine the structure of the economy and the labor force. The economy consists of two markets, the product market and the labor market (Schervish, 1987). Goods and services are produced in the product market. Families create a demand for these goods and services through consumption expenditures. These expenditures are made possible by earnings derived from production activities. Jobs are provided to family members through the labor market. Labor provided to the economy is rewarded by wages and other benefits.

The structure and health of the economy determine the number and types of jobs that are available and their level of pay. The American economy is undergoing large-scale structural changes which have major effects on the size and structure of the labor force and earnings patterns. Recent analyses (Block, 1988; Bowman, 1988) conclude that the private sector is unable to provide jobs for all who need work. The greatest shortages are in relatively high-paying manufacturing jobs considered desirable by many American workers. Manufacturing jobs are decreasing in numbers because of automation and shifts to foreign countries. High technology jobs are not expected to replace basic manufacturing industries in terms of the number of jobs provided, the level and types of skills required, or geographic location.

Changes in earnings patterns are associated with economic climate and unemployment rates, the relative shift from manufacturing to low-wage service jobs, government policies, and the number of entrants into the labor force. Although adjusted family incomes generally rose from 1970 to 1986, some family types experienced decreases, namely, low-income female single parents and young families with heads under age 25 (Congressional Budget Office, 1988).

An additional aspect of the economy needs to be examined as part of the work/family interface—occupational segregation and the earnings gap between men and women. Women tend to be concentrated in relatively few occupations which are sex-typed as appropriate for women. In addition, women consistently earn less than men (Mortimer and Sorensen, 1984; Nieva and Gutek, 1981; Voydanoff, 1987). These patterns create serious problems for families dependent on women's earnings.

The Worker-Earner Role

The relationship between the economy and the family as institutions can be expressed on an individual level through the concept of the worker-earner role (Rodman & Safilios-Rothschild, 1984). This concept indicates that two roles are performed by one individual—the worker role in the economy and the earner role in the family. In the worker role, individuals produce goods and services; the earnings from this production provide economic support to families.

The concept of the worker-earner role documents an important linkage between working for pay and earning family income. However, the concept needs to encompass other dimensions of working and earning. For example, not all work is paid. Much unpaid work is devalued and invisible because of the tendency to define activities as work only when they are paid (Daniels, 1987). Unpaid family and community work is crucial to understanding the work/family interface. However, it has been relatively neglected in previous analyses (see Gerstel & Gross, 1987; Voydanoff, 1984, 1987, for exceptions). In addition, a recognition that some individuals are unable to fulfill the worker-earner role adequately is needed for a more comprehensive understanding of work/family linkages. For example, some individuals are unable to work and others earn insufficient incomes (Lupri, 1984; Rodman & Safilios-Rothschild, 1984).

Unpaid work. A great deal of research has examined patterns of unpaid family work, i.e., household work and child rearing. For example, many studies attempt to explain men's relatively low participation in family work, especially in two-earner families. These studies generally address the following hypotheses: time availability; relative power and earnings; and expectations, preferences, and sex role ideology (e.g., Coleman, 1988; Coverman, 1985; Ross, 1987; Spitze, 1986).

However, an analysis that links paid and unpaid work in the context of the worker-earner role shows promise for untangling some of the complexities associated with changing work and family roles among men and women. Some of this work uses the concept of the provider role. The provider role is comparable to the worker-earner role since the provider role in the family is assumed to be enacted through paid employment.

According to Scanzoni (1982), the extent to which the husband is successful in the provider role forms the basis of instrumental and expressive exchanges between husbands and wives in traditional families. When the husband is successful, his wife is motivated to perform her instrumental (family work) duties. This instrumental exchange of rights and duties leads to an exchange of expressive rights and duties, i.e., empathy, companionship, and affection. When wives become employed as junior partners in the provider role, the husband remains the "unique provider" and the exchange of instrumental rights and duties remains basically unchanged. Therefore, wives retain major responsibility for unpaid family work. It is only when wives become equal partners in the provider role that men should be expected to become equal partners in family work. Research based on this perspective documents complex reciprocal processes involved in the redefinition of the provider role and changes in the division of family work (Hood, 1983; Scanzoni, 1978; Statham & Larrick, 1986). Studies also indicate that male participation in family work is greater among co-provider families than main/secondary earner families (Perry-Jenkins & Crouter, 1987; Scanzoni, 1978).

Worker-earner role difficulties. Although problems associated with performing the worker-earner role have been documented in other literatures, this work needs to be integrated more fully into analyses of the work/family interface. These difficulties include unstable employment; inability to work because of physical disability, family responsibilities, or age; and employment accompanied by inadequate pay. Experiencing such difficulties is associated with decreased family stability and adjustment and increased tensions (Rodman & Safilios-Rothschild, 1984; Voydanoff, 1987; Voydanoff & Majka, 1988).

In addition, worker-earner role problems are closely tied to employment and income policy issues. When worker-earner role performance is inadequate, family income may be supplemented by transfer payments. Transfer payments differ with respect to whether eligibility and benefit levels are based on employment or economic need. Work-based benefits include pensions, Social Security, and Unemployment Insurance while programs such as AFDC and welfare are means-tested. Work-based programs generally provide more adequate benefits and are perceived as more respectable. Because of a generally weaker long-term attachment to the labor force, women are more likely to receive benefits from means-tested programs such as AFDC while men are more likely to be eligible for Unemployment Insurance (Pearce, 1986). Families dependent on transfer benefits often find it difficult to adapt to changes in policies determining eligibility and benefit levels (see e.g., Sarri, 1988, regarding the 1981 OBRA cuts in human service programs).

Family Structure

As with aspects of the work role discussed above, research that addresses important shifts in family structure and demands frequently is not included in analyses of the work/family interface. Two of the most important are one-parent families maintained by women and care of elderly family members. This relative neglect has led to gaps in knowledge about areas relevant to the work/family interface.

One-parent families maintained by women. Most writings on one-parent families maintained by women focus on their growth in the last two decades, their economic problems, and the question of whether welfare benefits encourage their development (see e.g., Garfinkel & McLanahan, 1986; Norton & Glick, 1986).

However, less is known about the effects of labor force participation and economic distress on the quality of family life among one-parent families. A few studies, based on small, nonrepresentative, middle-class samples, indicate few differences between employed and nonemployed single parents and between families with divorced and married employed mothers (Voydanoff, 1987). However, the data are too limited to permit generalization.

As with labor force participation, we know little about the effects of economic distress on family life among one-parent families. Most research on family life in one-parent families does not control for economic distress variables and almost none considers economic factors as major variables (Blechman, 1982; Gongla, 1982). However, one study finds that higher socioeconomic status, relatively high and stable incomes, and perceived security regarding future earnings and private transfers are positively related to adjustment following a divorce (Pett & Vaughn-Cole, 1986).

Care of elderly family members. Despite the extensive research in the work/family literature that addresses child care issues, this work generally has not been extended to incorporate issues associated with the care of disabled elderly family members. Both the number of elderly and the demand for family care of disabled elderly are increasing. Gerontological research has addressed family-related issues associated with elder care. These include objective and subjective aspects of burden among family caregivers, the difficulties experienced by middle-aged women caring for their elderly parents and adolescent children simultaneously, and differences in patterns of caregiving among the sons and daughters of elderly parents (see e.g., Brody, 1981; Horowitz, 1985; Montgomery, Gonyea, & Hooyman, 1985; Montgomery & Kamo, 1987; Montgomery, Stull, & Borgatta, 1985).

Only recently, however, has the paid employment of caregivers been investigated in relation to caregiving. This research indicates that significant minorities of caregivers, especially women, quit or consider quitting their jobs, rearrange work schedules, reduce work hours, or take time off without pay to care for elderly relatives (Brody, 1985; Brody, et al., 1987; Finch and Groves, 1983; Women's Bureau, 1986). Another study reveals that employed female caregivers continue to provide most of the help received by their disabled mothers (Brody and Schoonover, 1986). Being employed significantly reduces the hours of caregiving among sons but not daughters of elderly parents (Stoller, 1983). Although this work has important bearing on understanding and developing policy regarding the work/family interface, it has yet to be fully incorporated in this literature.

IMPLICATIONS

Expanding the conceptualization of work/family linkages to include topics such as the structure of occupations and earnings, occupational segregation, unpaid work, worker-earner role difficulties, one-parent families, and care of elderly family members extends our understanding of the work/family interface in three important ways.

A Broader Context

First, a consideration of the occupational and earnings structure provides a broader context in which to view work/family relationships on both the structural and individual levels. The structure of the economy has pervasive impacts on the types of jobs being created and eliminated. These trends influence the perceived need for family-oriented personnel policies, e.g., shortages have led to programs to attract nurses into hospital settings. This approach also highlights the need to incorporate research on worker-earner role difficulties and employment and income support policies into the work/family literature. These difficulties and associated policies, which have important bearing on the stability and quality of family life, often are derived from structural dislocations in the economy.

Local Communities

Second, incorporating the literature on unpaid work in the home and the community indicates the importance of the local communities in which families live and work. The work/family interface is tied not only to the structure of the economy but also to the nature of community relationships and institutions, e.g., schools, churches, human service organizations, kin networks, and social, recreational, and neighborhood organizations. For example, school schedules and programs are closely related to the ease with which working parents are able to accommodate work schedules and responsibilities. In addition, the strength and vitality of many of these community organizations depend on unpaid contributions of time and effort by community members. A deeper understanding of interrelationships among work, family, and community is needed to protect and extend the benefits derived by work organizations and families when communities are strong and healthy.

Gender Issues

Third, the analysis of occupational segregation, the earnings gap between men and women, and recent changes in family structure, such as the increase in one-parent families, reveals a need to expand the integration of gender issues into research on the work/family interface. These issues have been raised in the literature on women, work, and family; however, they have been relatively neglected by work/family researchers.

They point to areas in which the traditional model of work and family does not fit current conditions. This model views the structure of jobs from a perspective in which male workers are free from family responsibilities and women are secondary earners needing family-oriented personnel policies to accommodate their family responsibilities. When policies such as parental leave and part-time work are perceived as appropriate only for women, their use is accompanied by decreased opportunities for some types of advancement. This view reinforces occupational segregation and the earnings gap and makes it difficult for women maintaining families to do so adequately. An expanded conceptualization incorporating worker-earner role difficulties and one-parent families documents that these are family issues as well as women's issues.

Thus, although research on the work/family interface has made tremendous strides in the past decade, an expanded conceptualization of both work and family promises to extend our understanding of the importance of interrelationships among economies, workplaces, communities, families, and individuals.

CONCLUSION

This review and expanded conceptualization point to limitations and gaps that need to be addressed in future research. In addition, two issues involving policy research need to be addressed in further work: gender-based research and a lack of research on the effects of family-oriented personnel policies on families and employers.

Despite recent progress in reducing the extent to which examination of topics varies by sex, such differences still affect the nature and quality of research on the work/family interface. For example, most analyses of family-oriented personnel policies assume that policies such as flexible work schedules and parenting leaves are needed by and benefit middle-class working mothers. A broader conception that family-oriented personnel policies also could assist women in low-status jobs and men has yet to be accepted. Or, on another level, government policies such as tax credits for child care are assumed, without documentation, to benefit all families. In addition, gender is relevant for policies addressed to those experiencing difficulties in the worker-earner role. Previous analyses suggest that assumptions underlying income and employment policies such as welfare and Unemployment Insurance differ by the sex of those most likely to receive benefits. Preliminary research suggests that these assumptions have pervasive effects on family life, especially for families maintained by women.

A related concern involves the consequences of family-oriented personnel policies for employers and families. Despite a recent surge of interest among politicians and family advocates, little research documents the effects of these policies on employers or families. Employers are quick to ask whether family-oriented personnel policies increase productivity or reduce employment costs. Although preliminary small-scale studies do suggest that specific policies can improve productivity and lower costs, we need much better documentation before we can expect employers to adopt these policies on a large scale. In addition, it is important to understand the conditions under which these policies facilitate family activities and strengthen family relationships.

REFERENCES

Aberle, D., & Naegele, K. (1952). Middle-class fathers' occupational role and attitudes toward children. *American Journal of Orthopsychiatry, 22*, 366-378.

Aldous, J., Osmond, M., & Hicks, M. (1979). Men's work and men's families. In W. Burr et al. (Eds.), *Contemporary theories about the family*, Vol. 1 (pp. 227-259). New York: Free Press.

Axel, H. (1985). *Corporations and families*. New York: The Conference Board.

Baruch, G.K., Biener, L., & Barnett, R.C. (1987). Women and gender in research on work and family stress. *American Psychologist, 42*, 130-136.

Blechman, E.A. (1982). Are children with one parent at psychological risk? *Journal of Marriage and the Family, 44*, 179-195.

Block, F. (1988). Rethinking responses to economic distress. In P. Voydanoff and L.C. Majka (Eds.), *Families and economic distress* (pp. 190-205). Newbury Park: Sage.

Bohen, H., & Viveros-Long, A. (1981). *Balancing jobs and family life*. Philadelphia: Temple University.

Bowman, P.J. (1988). Post-industrial displacement and family role strains. In P. Voydanoff and L.C. Majka (Eds.), *Families and economic distress*, (pp. 75-96). Newbury Park: Sage.

Brody, E.M. (1981). "Women in the middle" and family help to older people. *Gerontologist, 21*, 471-480.

Brody, E.M. (1985). Parent care as normative family stress. *Gerontologist, 25*, 19-29.

Brody, E.M., Kleban, M.H., Johnsen, P.T., Hoffman, C., & Schoonover, C.B. (1987). Work status and parent care. *Gerontologist, 27*, 201-208.

Brody, E.M., & Schoonover, C.B. (1986). Patterns of parent-care when adult daughters work and when they do not. *Gerontologist, 26*, 372-381.

Bronfenbrenner, U., & Crouter, A.C. (1982). Work and family through time and space. In S.B. Kamerman & C.D. Hayes (Eds.), *Families that work* (pp. 39-83). Washington: National Academy Press.

Bureau of National Affairs. (1986). *Work and family: A changing dynamic.* Washington: Bureau of National Affairs.

Catalyst. (1986). *Report on a national study of parental leaves.* New York: Catalyst.

Coleman, M.T. (1988). The division of household labor. *Journal of Family Issues, 9*, 132-148.

Congressional Budget Office. (1988). *Trends in Family Income: 1970-1986.* Washington: GPO.

Coverman, S. (1985). Explaining husbands' participation in domestic labor. *Sociological Quarterly, 26*, 81-97.

Crosby, F.J. (Ed.). (1987). *Spouse, parent, worker.* New Haven: Yale University.

Crouter, A.C., & Perry-Jenkins, M. (1986). Working it out: Effects of work on parents and children. In M.W. Yogman & T.B. Brazelton (Eds.), *In support of families* (pp. 93-108). Cambridge: Harvard University.

Daniels, A.K. (1987). Invisible work. *Social Problems, 34*, 403-415.

Dyer, W. (1964). Family reactions to the father's job. In A. Shostak & W. Gomberg (Eds.), *Blue-collar world* (pp. 86-91). Englewood Cliffs, NJ: Prentice-Hall.

Economic Policy Council of UNA-USA. (1985). *Work and family in the United States: A policy initiative.* New York: United Nations Association of the U.S.A.

Finch, J., & Groves, D. (1983). *A labour of love.* Boston: Routledge & Kegan Paul.

Galinsky, E. (1986). Family life and corporate policies. In M.W. Yogman & T.B. Brazelton (Eds.), *In support of families* (pp. 109-145). Cambridge: Harvard University.

Garfinkel, I., & McLanahan, S.S. (1986). *Single mothers and their children.* Washington: Urban Institute.

Gerstel, N., & Gross, H.E. (Eds.). (1987). *Families and work.* Philadelphia: Temple University.

Gilbert, L.A. (1985). *Men in dual-career families.* Hillsdale, NJ: Lawrence Erlbaum.

Gilbert, L.A., & Rachlin, V. (1987). Mental health and psychological functioning of dual-career families. *The Counseling Psychologist, 15*, 7-49.

Gongla, P.A. (1982). Single parent families. *Marriage and Family Review, 5*, 5-27.

Greenhaus, J.H., & Beutell, N. (1985). Sources of conflict between work and nonwork roles. *Academy of Management Review, 10*, 76-88.

Hertz, R. (1986). *More equal than others.* Berkeley: University of California.

Hewlett, S.A., Ilchman, A.S., & Sweeney, J.J. (Eds.). (1986). *Family and work: Bridging the gap.* Cambridge: Balinger.

Hoffman, L.W. (1979). Maternal employment: 1979. *American Psychologist, 34*, 859-865.

Hoffman, L.W. (1984). Work, family and the socialization of the child. In R.D. Parke (Ed.), *Review of child development research*, Vol. 7: *The family* (pp. 223-282). Chicago: University of Chicago.

Hood, J.C. (1983). *Becoming a two-job family.* New York: Praeger.

Horowitz, M. (1985). Sons and daughters as caregivers to older parents. *Gerontologist, 25*, 612-617.

House, J.S., Strecher, V., Metzner, H.L., & Robbins, C.A. (1986). Occupational stress and health among men and women in the Tecumseh community health study. *Journal of Health and Social Behavior, 27*, 62-77.

House, J.S., Wells, J.A., Landerman, L.R., McMichael, A.J., & Kaplan, B.H. (1979). Occupational stress and health among factory workers. *Journal of Health and Social Behavior, 20*, 139-160.

Hunt, J.G., & Hunt, L.L. (1987). Male resistance to role symmetry in dual-earner households. In N. Gerstel & H.G. Gross (Eds.), *Families and work* (pp. 192-203). Philadelphia: Temple University.

Kabanoff, B. (1980). Work and nonwork. *Psychological Bulletin, 88*, 60-77.

Kahn, A.J., & Kamerman, S.B. (1987). *Child care: Facing the hard choices.* Dover, MA: Auburn House.

Kamerman, S.B., & Kahn, A.J. (1981). *Child care, family benefits, and working parents.* New York: Columbia University.

Kamerman, S.B., & Kahn, A.J. (1987). *The responsive workplace.* New York: Columbia University.

Kamerman, S.B., Kahn, A.J., & Kingston, P. (1983). *Maternity policies and working women.* New York: Columbia University.

Kanter, R.M. (1977). *Work and family in the United States.* New York: Russell Sage Foundation.

Kelly, R.F., & Voydanoff, P. (1985). Work/family role strain among employed parents. *Family Relations, 34*, 367-374.

Kingston, P.W., & Nock, S.L. (1985). The consequences of the family work day. *Journal of Marriage and the Family, 47*, 619-629.

Kingston, P.W., & Nock, S.L. (1987). Time together among dual-earner couples. *American Sociological Review, 52*, 391-400.

LaRocco, J.M., House, J.S., & French, Jr., J.R.P. (1980). Social support, occupational stress, and health. *Journal of Health and Social Behavior, 21*, 202-218.

Lee, R.A. (1983). Flextime and conjugal roles. *Journal of Occupational Behavior, 5*, 297-315.

Lein, L. (1979). Male participation in home life. *Family Coordinator, 28*, 489-495.

Locke, E.A. (1976). The nature and causes of job satisfaction. In M.D. Dunnette (Ed.), *Handbook of industrial and organizational psychology* (pp. 1297-1349). Chicago: Rand McNally.

Lupri, E. (1984). Comments—Bringing women back in. In M.B. Brinkerhoff (Ed.), *Family and work: Comparative convergence* (pp. 78-87). Westport, CT: Greenwood.

McLaughlin, S.D. (1982). Differential patterns of female labor-force participation surrounding the first birth. *Journal of Marriage and the Family, 44*, 407-420.

Miller, J., & Garrison, H.H. (1982). Sex roles: The division of labor at home and in the workplace. *Annual Review of Sociology, 8*, 237-262.

Moen, P. (1983). The two-provider family. In M.E. Lamb (Ed.), *Non-traditional families: Parenting and child development* (pp. 13-43). Hillsdale, NJ: Lawrence Erlbaum.

Montgomery, R.J.V., Gonyea, J.G., & Hooyman, N.R. (1985). Caregiving and the experience of subjective and objective burden. *Family Relations, 34*, 19-26.

Montgomery, R.J.V., & Kamo, Y. (1987). Caregiving issues: Differences between sons and daughters in parental caregiving. Paper presented at the annual meeting of the *Society for the Study of Social Problems.*

Montgomery, R.J.V., Stull, D.E., & Borgatta, E.F. (1985). Measurement and the analysis of burden. *Research on Aging, 7*, 137-152.

Moore, K.A., & Hofferth, S. (1979). Effects of women's employment on marriage. *Marriage and Family Review, 2*, 27-36.

Moore, K.A., & Sawhill, I.V. (1984). Implications of women's employment for home and family life. In P. Voydanoff (Ed.), *Work and family: Changing roles of men and women* (pp. 153-171). Palo Alto: Mayfield.

Moore, K.A., Spain, D., & Bianchi, S. (1984). Working wives and mothers. In B.B. Hess & M.B. Sussman (Eds.), *Women and the family: Two decades of change* (pp. 77-98). New York: Haworth.

Mortimer, J.T. (1979). *Changing attitudes toward work.* Scarsdale, NY: Work in America Institute.

Mortimer, J.T., & Sorensen, G. (1984). Men, women, work, and family. In K.M. Borman, D. Quarm, & S. Gideonese (Eds.), *Women in the workplace* (pp. 139-167). Norwood, N.J.: Ablex.

Mumola, D.E., & Rollings, A. (1985). Assessing the impacts of work on family dynamics. Paper presented at the annual meeting of the *Eastern Sociological Society*.

Nicola, J.S., & Hawkes, G.L. (1986). Marital satisfaction of dual-career couples: Does sharing increase happiness? *Journal of Social Behavior and Personality, 1*, 47-60.

Nieva, V.F. (1985). Work and family linkages. In L. Larwood, A.H. Stromberg, & B.A. Gutek (Eds.), *Women and work: An annual review*, Vol. 1 (pp. 162-190). Beverly Hills: Sage.

Nieva, V.F., & Gutek, B.A. (1981). *Women and work.* New York: Praeger.

Nock, S.L., & Kingston, P.W. (1987). *Time with children: The impact of couples' work schedules.* Unpublished paper.

Norton, A.J., & Glick, P.C. (1986). One parent families: A social and economic profile. *Family Relations, 35*, 9-17.

Orthner, D.K., & Pittman, J.F. (1986). Family contributions to work commitment. *Journal of Marriage and the Family, 48*, 573-581.

Papanek, H. (1973). Men, women and work: Reflections on the two-person career. *American Journal of Sociology, 78*, 852-872.

Pearce, D. (1986). Toil and trouble: Women workers and unemployment compensation. In B.C. Gelpi, N.C.M. Hartsock, C.C. Novak, & M.H. Strober (Eds.), *Women and poverty* (pp. 141-161). Chicago: University of Chicago.

Perry-Jenkins, M., & Crouter, A.C. (1987). Husbands' and wives' concepts of the "provider role." Paper presented at the annual meeting of the *National Council on Family Relations*.

Pett, M.A., & Vaughan-Cole, B. (1986). The impact of income issues and social status on post-divorce adjustment of custodial parents. *Family Relations, 35*, 103-111.

Piotrkowski, C.S. (1979). *Work and the family system.* New York: Free Press.

Piotrkowski, C.S., Rapoport, R.N., & Rapoport, R. (1987). Families and work. In M.B. Sussman & S.K. Steinmetz (Eds.), *Handbook of Marriage and the Family* (pp. 251-283). New York: Plenum.

Pleck, J.H. (1985). *Working wives/working husbands.* Beverly Hills: Sage.

Pleck, J.H. (1986). Employment and fatherhood: Issues and innovative policies. In M. Lamb (Ed.), *The father's role.* New York: Wiley.

Rallings, E.M., & Nye, F.I. (1979). Wife-mother employment, family, and society. In W.R. Burr et al. (Eds.), *Contemporary theories about the family*, Vol. 1. New York: Free Press.

Rapoport, R.N., & Rapoport, R. (1978). Dual-career families. *Marriage and Family Review, 1*, 1-12.

Rodman, H., & Safilios-Rothschild, C. (1984). Weak links in men's worker-earner roles. In M.B. Brinkerhoff (Ed.), *Family and work: Comparative convergence*. Westport, CT: Greenwood.

Ross, C.E. (1987). The division of labor at home. *Social Forces, 65*, 816-833.

Sarri, R.C. (1988). The impact of federal policy change on the well-being of poor women and children. In P. Voydanoff & L.C. Majka (Eds.), *Families and economic distress*, (pp. 209-231). Newbury Park: Sage.

Scanzoni, J. (1970). *Opportunity and the family*. New York: Free Press.

Scanzoni, J. (1978). *Sex roles, women's work, and marital conflict*. Lexington, MA: Lexington.

Scanzoni, J. (1982). *Sexual bargaining*. 2nd Ed. Chicago: University of Chicago.

Schervish, Paul. (1987). Family life and the economy. In F.H. Brigham, Jr. & S. Preister (Eds.), *Families, the economy, and the church* (pp. 9-19). Washington: U.S. Catholic Conference.

Skinner, D.A. (1980). Dual-career family stress and coping. *Family Relations, 29*, 473-480.

Spitze, G. (1986). The division of task responsibility in U.S. households. *Social Forces, 64*, 689-701.

Staines, G.L. (1980). Spillover versus compensation. *Human Relations, 33*, 111-129.

Statham, A., & Larrick, D. (1986). Changing family roles: Implications for married women's earnings. *Family Perspective, 20*, 13-25.

Statuto, C.M., Ooms, T., Brand, S., & Pittman, K. (1984). *Families in the eighties*. Washington: Family Impact Seminar Working Paper.

Stoller, E.P. (1983). Parental caregiving by adult children. *Journal of Marriage and the Family, 45*, 851-858.

Szinovacz, M.E. (1984). Changing family roles and interactions. In B.B. Hess & M.B. Sussman (Eds.), *Women and the family: Two decades of change* (pp. 163-201). New York: Haworth Press.

Voydanoff, P. (1980). Work/family life cycles. Paper presented at the Workshop on Theory Construction and Research Methodology, *National Council on Family Relations*.

Voydanoff, P. (1983a). Unemployment: Family strategies for adaptation. In C.R. Figley & H.I. McCubbin (Eds.), *Stress and the family*, Vol. II (pp. 90-102). New York: Brunner/Mazel.

Voydanoff, P. (1983b). Unemployment and family stress. *Research in the interweave of social roles: Jobs and families, 3*, 239-250.

Voydanoff, P. (1984). *Work and family: Changing roles of men and women*. Palo Alto: Mayfield.

Voydanoff, P. (1987). *Work and family life*. Newbury Park: Sage.

Voydanoff, P. (1988, in press). Work role characteristics, family structure demands, and work/family conflict. *Journal of Marriage and the Family, 50*.

Voydanoff, P., & Kelly, R.F. (1984). Determinants of work-related family problems among employed parents. *Journal of Marriage and the Family, 46*, 881-892.

Voydanoff, P., & Majka. L.C. (1988, in press). *Families and economic distress.* Newbury Park: Sage.

Waite, L.J., Haggstrom, G.W., & Kanouse, D.E. (1985). Changes in the employment activities of new parents. *American Sociological Review, 50,* 263-272.

Winett, R.A., & Neale, M.S. (1980). Modifying settings as a strategy for permanent, preventive behavior change. In P. Karoly & J.J. Steffan (Eds.), *Improving the long-term effects of psychotherapy* (pp. 407-437). New York: Gardner.

Women's Bureau. (1986). *Facts on U.S. working women: Caring for elderly family members.* Washington: U.S. Department of Labor.

Zigler, E., & Franks, M. (Eds.). (1988). *The parent leave crisis: Toward a national policy.* New Haven: Yale University.

The Intersection of Work and Family Roles: Individual, Interpersonal, and Organizational Issues

Jeffrey H. Greenhaus
*Department of Management and Organizational Sciences
Drexel University, Philadelphia, PA 19104*

Three broad research areas regarding work-family relationships were identified: the nature of the work-family interface; two-career relationships; and organizational responsiveness to work-family issues. It was suggested that future research address such issues as work-family conflict, daily transitions between work and family roles, the role of career orientation in two-career relationships, the relationship between two-career status and career accomplishments, and the implications of work-family interaction for career growth in organizational settings. The importance of examining theoretical models, applying diverse research methodologies, and developing valid measurement operations was emphasized.

This special issue of the *Journal of Social Behavior and Personality* undoubtedly reflects a heightened awareness of the interdependence of work and family roles in contemporary society. The recognition of this interdependence by scholars and practitioners has produced a considerable amount of research over the past twenty years. The lead article by Voydanoff (1989) provided an excellent overview of the research on work and family issues, and successfully demonstrated the historical underpinnings of the current research in the field.

The purpose of the present article is to emphasize several areas in which additional conceptualization and research are needed. In particular, I will focus on: (a) the interface between individuals' work and family roles, with an emphasis on the nature of work-family conflict; (b) the dynamics of two-career relationships; and (c) organizational responsiveness to the interdependence of work and family roles.

At the most fundamental level, Voydanoff (1989) clearly demonstrated the interdependence of work and family roles. She reviewed

©1988 Select Press

streams of research that examined the impact of work on family (e.g., the effects of job characteristics on the quality of family life) as well as the effects of family characteristics on work (e.g., the impact of family responsibilities on job performance). Voydanoff also showed how the study of work and family issues has expanded from an initial focus on men's unemployment, women's employment, and two-career couples to a much more diverse set of issues. She identified economic issues, structural and psychological characteristics of work, enactment of multiple roles, the work/family life cycle, combined effects of partners' work role characteristics, and family-oriented personnel policies as current areas of research endeavor.

Research in these areas has provided a great many insights into the intersection of work and family roles. For example, we have begun to develop an understanding—at least in general form—of the following phenomena:

- The positive and negative consequences of participation in multiple life roles.
- The antecedents and consequences of conflict between work and family roles.
- The role of coping and social support in ameliorating the negative effects of work-family conflict.
- The impact of job characteristics on the quality of family life.
- The impact of family characteristics and aspirations on career decisions.
- The determinants of quality of life in two-career relationships.

Despite these gains in recent years, there is a great deal more that we need to know about the interplay between the work and family domains. Hopefully, continued programmatic research will further our understanding of the phenomena identified above and will make inroads into other significant areas as well. In this article, I will address the need for additional research in three specific areas that encompass individual, interpersonal, and organizational perspectives.

First, there is a continued need to examine the many ways in which work and family roles interact. Our understanding of two-career relationships and organizational actions demand a more thorough understanding of the mechanisms by which work and family domains are interrelated. Within this broad area, I will examine the nature of work-family conflicts, the utilization of behavioral criteria of cross-role influence, the "daily transition" approach to the work-family interface, and the advantages of viewing work-family issues within a stress perspective.

Second, the prevalence of the two-career lifestyle in contemporary society (Sekaran, 1986) makes it imperative that we understand the sources of stress and resilience in two-career relationships. Within this context, I will address definitional issues that need to be resolved, the role of career orientation in two-career families, the relationship between two-career status and career accomplishments, and social and behavioral resources available to members of two-career families.

Third, I will address the need for organizations to recognize the interdependence of work and family roles and will identify the kinds of research questions that are required to support organizational practices and policies. I will propose an extension to Voydanoff's list of organizational responses to work-family issues, and will suggest changes in the fundamental way in which organizations should view the accomplishments and success of their employees.

THE WORK-FAMILY INTERFACE

Work-Family Conflicts

Work-family conflict is aroused by the presence of "role pressures from the work and family domains (that) are mutually incompatible in some respect" (Greenhaus & Beutell, 1985, p. 77). Three forms of work-family conflict were identified by Greenhaus and Beutell: (a) time-based conflict, in which the time demands of one role interfere with participation in the other role; (b) strain-based conflict, where the stress symptoms (e.g., fatigue, irritability) produced in one role intrude into the other role; and (c) behavior-based conflict, in which behaviors that are functional in one role are dysfunctional in the other role.

It is not difficult to understand why so much research has examined the causes and consequences of work-family conflict. The multiple role pressures experienced by women and men in today's society render work-family conflict virtually inevitable. Moreover, the impact of extensive work-family conflict on deteriorated satisfaction and quality of life (Kopelman, Greenhaus, & Connolly, 1983; Pleck, Staines, & Lang, 1980) provides an additional reason for understanding the dynamics underlying work-family conflict. Despite our considerable knowledge in this area, additional research is required in several directions. (See also Burke, this issue.)

First, future research must distinguish objective or sent role conflict from experienced or psychological role conflict (Kahn, Wolfe, Quinn, Snoek, & Rosenthal, 1964). In an objective sense, for example, a person whose work commitments preclude participation in a family activity experiences (time-based) work-family conflict. However, that situation may not necessarily produce psychological conflict for the focal person.

Psychological conflict depends not only on environmental pressures but also on the relative salience of work and family roles. For example, the person whose work commitment structurally "conflicts" with family activities may experience relatively little psychological conflict if the family role is not particularly important to his or her self-concept.

Therefore, models of work-family conflict should recognize the difference between objective and psychological conflict in order to examine the possibility that each type of conflict has somewhat different antecedents and consequences. Moreover, in order to examine this issue empirically, measurement operations should separately assess objective *and* psychological conflict. Many work-family conflict items either confound objective and psychological conflict (e.g., "My work schedule often conflicts with my family life") or focus exclusively on the degree of "internal" (i.e., psychological) conflict experienced between pairs of roles. Scales should be explicitly designed to assess each aspect of work-family conflict (objective and psychological) so that a more complete and balanced assessment of work-family conflict is possible.

We also need to understand why pressures from one particular role take precedence over pressures from another role. A person confronted with a Saturday morning business meeting (a work pressure) and a child's Saturday morning little league game (a family pressure) may choose to forego the baseball game (in which case work "interfered" with family), or may choose not to attend the business meeting (in which case family "interfered" with work). Which role takes precedence in a particular situation may well depend on the salience of each role to the focal person (Greenhaus & Beutell, 1985) as well as the negative sanctions associated with noncompliance with each role pressure (Gross, Mason, & McEachern, 1958). Yet we know very little about the decision process used by a focal person in the face of objective and psychological work-family conflict.

In this regard, Pleck (1977) has discussed gender differences in the permeability of boundaries between work and family roles. He suggests that social norms "permit" women to forego work activities in the face of family responsibilities (e.g., staying home with a sick child), whereas men are "permitted" to forego family activities in favor of work commitments (e.g., working late in the office). Despite the plausibility of such "asymmetrical permeability" (Pleck, 1977) of work and family roles for men and women, responses to work-family conflicts are likely to be situation specific and cut across gender.

It would be useful to recall Kahn et al.'s (1964) proposition that the intensity of role conflict is a direct function of the strength of the weaker of two opposing forces. According to this notion, conflict is heightened when both forces (work and family) are strong and nearly equal, and precedence is likely to be given to the stronger of the two forces. Therefore, it is important to understand the societal, interpersonal, and personal determinants of the strength of different role pressures. In this vein, scales that measure the directionality of the conflict (i.e., work interfering with family and family interfering with work) are necessary to shed light on the relative priority of roles, as a recent study by Wiley (1987) has demonstrated.

As noted earlier, three forms of work-family conflict have been identified in the literature. Although there is considerable evidence regarding the existence of time-based conflict and strain-based conflict, behavior-based conflict has not been subjected to extensive empirical scrutiny (Greenhaus & Beutell, 1985). A typical illustration of behavior-based conflict (Burke & Weir cited in Burke & Bradshaw, 1981) is an executive's logical, analytical, detached, and judgmental behavior that may be functional in the work domain, but is inappropriate and unappreciated when applied in the family domain. In a broader sense, behavior-based conflict occurs when any behavior is inappropriately transferred from one role to another.

Anecdotes aside, the prevalence of behavior-based conflict is uncertain. The existence of such conflict seems dependent on people's inability to "shift gears" when in transit between roles. Yet people's awareness of the need to change behaviors and their capacity and willingness to make such changes are as yet unresolved empirical questions. To the extent to which organizations retain their hierarchical, punitive qualities, and families continue to become more participative and expressive, there should be a pronounced tendency for employees to experience behavior-based conflict. Additional research in this area awaits the development of reliable and valid measures of behavior-based conflict.

Utilization of Behavioral Criteria

Much of the early research on the interdependence of work and family roles examined relationships between affective variables in each domain. Although these studies provided a number of interesting findings, it is time to expand the set of variables examined to determine the effects of role characteristics on *behaviors* in the other role.

Such research has already begun to provide a deeper understanding of the relationship between work and family roles. For example, Jackson and Maslach (1982) have shown how police officers' job burnout is associated with such home-related behaviors as difficulty in sleeping, absence from the home, and complaints about problems while at home. Barling and colleagues have demonstrated that employees' work experiences are related to wife abuse (Barling & Rosenbaum, 1986), children's behavior (Barling, 1986), and marital communications (Suchet & Barling, 1986).

Evidence regarding the impact of family variables on work role behaviors is also beginning to emerge. For example, young women's marital and family goals can affect a wide range of occupational and career decisions (Betz & Fitzgerald, 1987). In addition, two-career partners with children have been found to be more involved in their jobs than those without children (Gould & Werbel, 1983), and the number of children in a family has been associated with men's time involvement at work (Smith, 1983). In a somewhat similar vein, it has been found that men whose wives are employed outside the home work fewer hours (Parasuraman, Greenhaus, Rabinowitz, Bedeian, & Mossholder, in press) and are less involved in their jobs (Gould & Werbel, 1983) than men whose wives are not employed.

Additional research is needed to clarify the cross-role correlates of work and family involvements. Although affective variables (e.g., job satisfaction, marital satisfaction) should not be ignored, it is important to avoid using satisfaction measures as the *sole* indicator of work-family interdependence. Programmatic research in this area could profit from the development of behavioral taxonomies in the work and family domains that can be used to generate and test a series of hypotheses.

Daily Transitions As A Heuristic Framework

Every area of inquiry can benefit from the introduction of a different paradigm, if for no other reason than to encourage scholars to reexamine their assumptions, concepts, theories, and methodologies. The concept of daily transitions proposed by Hall and Richter (1988; Richter, 1984) promises to serve this function in the study of work-family relationships. Speaking of the interdependence of work and family domains, Hall and Richter suggest that "The best way to understand how the two domains affect each other is to look at them in their interface; that is, as they come into contact with one another....The point at which home and work come into contact with one another is when the employee is moving, either physically or psychologically, from one to the other" (Hall & Richter, 1988, p. 215).

The movement between work and home each morning and evening (the daily transition) is the major analytical concept with which Hall and Richter examine the general relationship between work and family roles. They go on to discuss daily transitions in terms of their source of initiation (self or other), the flexibility and permeability of the boundaries between the two domains, the styles with which people cross these boundaries (anticipatory, discreet, and lagged), and gender differences in transition styles.

The initial research on daily transitions has been based on a clinical methodology (Richter, 1984), and has generated a number of interesting findings and propositions relevant to personal and organizational functioning. Additional research utilizing a variety of methodologies is essential to examine the viability of the concept, the generalizability of the initial findings, and the development of additional hypotheses.

Work-Family Interactions within a Stress Perspective

An established body of research has examined the nature and outcomes of stress in the work domain (Brief, Schuler, & Van Sell, 1981; Cooper & Marshall, 1976; Ivancevich & Matteson, 1980). A generally unrelated area of inquiry has focused on nonwork sources of stress, most notably the effect of stressful life events on individuals' well-being (Holmes & Rahe, 1967; Johnson & Sarason, 1979). Greenhaus and Parasuraman (1986) have recently proposed a model of work-nonwork stress that illustrates the interplay of stressors and stress reactions between the work and nonwork domains.

Three linkages between stress and strain at the intersection of work and nonwork domains have been proposed (Greenhaus & Parasuraman, 1986). First, work stressors and nonwork stressors may produce extensive strain in an additive fashion. The experience of total life strain may increase as the amount of work-induced and nonwork-induced stress increases. Second, strain produced within one role can intrude into the other role and contribute to increased stress in the second role. Third, conflicts may occur at the interface of the work and nonwork domains because of the presence of incompatible demands and expectations arising from the two domains.

There are several advantages to viewing work and family issues within a stress perspective. First, the stress literature has historically emphasized the role of personal appraisal in the interpretation of a stimulus situation to explain individual differences in felt stress across similar objective environments. This view is consistent with the earlier distinction between objective role conflict and psychological role conflict, and researchers can learn much about this distinction from the literature on personal appraisal (Lazarus, 1966).

Second, a great deal is known about the behavioral, emotional, and physiological consequences of extensive stress (Brief et al., 1981; Ivancevich & Matteson, 1980). This knowledge can be incorporated into models of work-family conflict or, more generally, into models of work-family relationships to generate testable hypotheses.

Third, the stress literature has focused on the roles of personal resources (such as self-esteem and personal hardiness), social support, and coping responses as buffers against extensive stress. Many of the models and findings regarding these resources in the stress literature can be applied to work-family dynamics. In a more general sense, the primary usefulness of adopting a stress perspective is the existence of a paradigm (stressor-appraisal-stress-support and coping-strain-outcomes) that has proved useful to stress researchers. This may provide valuable insights into various aspects of the relationship between work and family roles.

A Positive Approach to Work-Family Interaction

Much of the research on the relationship between work and family roles has been somewhat negative in that it has emphasized the dysfunctional consequences of work-family interactions. Indeed, the very concept of work-family conflict refers to interference, a negative quality of the work-family interface. An examination of work-family issues within a stress perspective also has negative connotations. Although the positive consequences of the work-family relationship have occasionally been discussed (Kanter, 1977), it seems that very little of the research seeks to identify these positive linkages.

Perhaps some of the positive interdependencies are already known through the existing research. For example, if shiftwork is associated with high levels of work-family conflict (Staines & Pleck, 1984), then nonshift work schedules are by necessity associated with lower levels of conflict. However, it is possible that different factors are responsible for positive and negative cross-role consequences. This is a position similar to Herzberg's (1966) two-factor theory of work motivation that proposes that different work characteristics produce job satisfaction and job dissatisfaction. To use the previous example, it is possible that a nonshift work schedule prevents extensive work-family conflict, but does not, in and of itself, produce a high level of satisfaction with family life. Whether or not different factors are responsible for positive and negative work-family spillover is an empirical question. Additional research can provide insights into the work-family interface by focusing on the characteristics of the work or the family role that enrich experiences in the other role.

TWO-CAREER RELATIONSHIPS

Extensive research has been conducted on two-career relationships (Bryson, Bryson, & Johnson, 1978; Epstein, 1971; Rapoport & Rapoport, 1969, 1971; Sekaran, 1986). The study of two-career relationships is significant from a theoretical perspective because of the multiplicity of work and family roles that intersect in two-career families. The dominance of the two-career lifestyle in today's society adds a pragmatic dimension to the research effort. Despite recent advances in knowledge, a reevaluation of the definition of a two-career relationship is required, and a number of research questions need to be addressed.

The Definition of Two-Career Status

The definition of a two-career relationship necessarily hinges on the meaning of a career. The original (and still popular) definition of a two-career relationship requires that each partner in the relationship pursue a career rather than simply a job (Rapoport & Rapoport, 1969). A career is thought to involve high levels of work commitment and a developmental progression in the work role (Gupta & Jenkins, 1985; Rapoport & Rapoport, 1971; Sekaran, 1986). Hence, two-career status is reserved for those families in which each partner is not merely employed but is highly committed to a work role that provides (and demands) growth and progressive development. Those relationships in which one or both partners are involved in noninvolving, nondevelopmental work roles are often designated "dual-earner," "dual-income," or "two-paycheck" families (Sekaran, 1986).

It should be noted that the career concept has undergone rather dramatic revision in recent years. A career has been broadly defined as a pattern of work-related experiences that span the course of a person's life (Greenhaus, 1987). The key characteristic of a career perspective is an examination of work experiences *over time*. A person's work experiences need not be highly involving or engaging, upwardly mobile, or professional in nature to constitute a career (Greenhaus, 1987; Hall, 1976; Van Maanen & Schein, 1977). The application of such criteria as involvement, mobility, and/or professionalism simply excludes too many people whose cumulative work experiences can be examined and understood through a career perspective.

It is proposed that all classificatory distinctions among two-career, dual-earner, dual-income, and two-paycheck families be abandoned. Studies designed to examine "two-career relationships" should not be limited to elite samples of professionals or managers. The advantages of this expanded approach are two-fold. First, from a theoretical perspective, an inclusion of a broad spectrum of couples enables the researcher to examine the impact of such variables as work involvement/commitment, professionalism, and career growth on the dynamics of two-career relationships. The more circumscribed, rarified definition of two-career status would essentially preclude an examination of these questions because of the severe range restriction on these variables. Second, a broader view of two-career relationships should provide research findings that generalize to a larger segment of the population.

In sum, a broad view of two-career status will enable researchers to pose questions that might not ordinarily be considered if a more restrictive set of criteria were applied. In the following sections, a number of potentially significant research areas relevant to two-career relationships are identified.

Career Orientation

Each partner's career orientation can play a critical role in defining the nature of a two-career relationship. The concept of career orientation is broad and has been examined in a number of different ways. In one sense, career orientation refers to the significance or importance placed on the work role compared to other life roles. A person who is "career oriented" attaches a high level of salience to work and occupation. Some researchers have distinguished career oriented and family oriented partners in two-career relationships (Bailyn, 1970).

It is reasonable to expect that both partners' career orientations will interact to determine the interpersonal dynamics within a two-career relationship. For example, Hall and Hall (1979) suggested that couples in which both partners are career oriented may experience high levels of stress, especially if the partners also value their family and home life. A partner who is career oriented is likely to devote considerable time, effort, and energy to the work role, and may have little inclination to participate extensively in the family domain. When both partners in a relationship are career oriented, pressures on each partner will intensify in both the work domain - from one's own commitment to work - and in the family domain, from the partner's avoidance of family role activities (Greenhaus, Parasuraman, Granrose, Rabinowitz, & Beutell, in press). Not surprisingly, then, couples' marital satisfaction has been found to be especially low when both partners are strongly career oriented (Bailyn, 1970).

However, a recent study by Greenhaus et al. (in press) suggests that the impact of partners' career orientations on work-family dynamics may be more complex than anticipated. Contrary to prediction, they found that men in two-career relationships reported *low* levels of work-family conflict when both partners were highly involved in their respective jobs. They speculated that two partners who are highly job-involved may develop a mutual understanding and appreciation of each other's career needs and, as a consequence, relax mutual family role expectations, and reduce the level of conflict in the relationship. In contrast, men in two-career relationships reported *high* levels of work-family conflict when each partner placed a higher priority on his or her career than on the partner's career. Presumably, competition, jealousy, and inadequate communication may plague such relationships. The study revealed that the impact of partners' career orientations on work-family conflict seems to depend on the indicator of career orientation (job involvement versus career priority) that is examined.

In addition to their short-term effects, it is likely that changes in work and family orientation over time will affect the nature of a two-career relationship. Levinson, Darrow, Klein, Levinson, and McKee (1978) indicate that a reappraisal of one's role involvements tends to occur during transitional phases of adult development. They further indicate that midlife men who had been previously preoccupied with career issues are likely to reduce their involvement in work and increase the salience of the family role. In contrast, people whose earlier life structure was focused on family may seek future accomplishments and satisfactions in the work role.

Despite Levinson et al.'s (1978) persuasive arguments, additional research is needed to verify their conclusions. Moreover, gender differences in the shifts in role salience over time should be examined, especially in the context of two-career relationships. For example, it would be important to determine whether changes in role salience of two-career partners disrupt the equilibrium of the relationship, and to identify effective strategies used to cope with these changes. The typical cross-sectional research design will have to be replaced or supplemented by longitudinal studies to assess this phenomenon.

A related aspect of career orientation—the career anchor—may also play a significant role in two-career relationships. A career anchor has been viewed as the self-perceived cluster of talents, values, and motives that guides an employee in making suitable, congruent career decisions. Schein (1978) initially identified five dominant career anchors: managerial competence, technical-functional competence, creativity, autonomy, and security. Schein's (1985) reexamination of the concept revealed a number of other anchors, including "life-style integration," in which the primary concern is to balance and integrate career and family lives. It is reasonable to expect each partner's career anchor to influence the desired investments and benefits associated with work and family roles. There may be patterns of partners' career anchors that provide support and/or introduce stress into the relationship.

The Relationship Between Career Achievements and Family Life

Voydanoff (1989) reviewed two rival hypotheses regarding the relationship between occupational or career success and marital satisfaction, each of which has received empirical support. Scanzoni (1970, 1982) proposed a positive relationship between occupational success and marital quality, whereas Aldous, Osmond, and Hicks (1979) suggested an inverted-U shaped relationship in which marital satisfaction is higher at moderate levels of career success than at extremely low or extremely high levels of success.

A third perspective has emerged in a model of "career success/personal failure" advanced by Korman (1988; Korman & Korman, 1980; Korman, Wittig-Berman, & Lang, 1981). According to Korman and colleagues, career success may be accompanied by several things. These include a realization of the meaninglessness of material acquisitions, extensive role conflicts, feelings of powerlessness, guilt over surpassing parents' accomplishments, and strained affiliative relationships. All of these factors may produce feelings of personal and social alienation (i.e., "personal failure").

Korman's compelling analysis has the capacity to guide research and stimulate the development of hypotheses regarding the relationship between career success and personal and family adjustment. In an early test of portions of Korman's model, Greenhaus, Bedeian, and Mossholder (1987) found a negative relationship between work role success and marital adjustment for women but not for men. Moreover, success in the work role was most likely to detract from marital adjustment and quality of life for employees who worked in environments that produced extensive role conflicts and environments that were perceived to be inequitable.

Future research in this area should examine the impact of alternative indicators of career success (income, advancement, job performance, power, satisfaction) on multiple dimensions of family life. Adult life stage (Korman, 1988), the quality of the work environment (Greenhaus et al., 1987), the need for compromising one's values (LaBier, 1986), and family aspirations and goals can all be examined as moderators of the relationship between career success and personal/family failure. An examination of the "career success-personal failure" relationship would be especially revealing among two-career partners with different patterns of career orientation.

A related issue in need of further study is the impact of partners' relative level of career success on two-career relationships. Voydanoff (1989) reported that the negative impact of women's relative success on family life is more severe when salary is the indicator of success than when occupational status is the indicator of success. This is consistent with Staines, Pottick, and Fudge's (1986) finding that feelings of "breadwinner inadequacy" explain men's negative reactions to their wives' employment.

However, informal observation suggests that women's attainment of high levels of job performance, recognition, and job involvement may be more threatening to men (and perhaps more guilt-provoking to some women) than attainment of high salaries or occupational status. Moreover, many career-oriented, highly-educated women may react negatively when their husbands experience greater career success than they themselves do. Ultimately, it would appear that each partner's career and family orientation and each partner's level of self-esteem would determine the reactions to differential career success experienced by partners in two-career relationships. The determinants and consequences of competition, comparisons, and jealousy in two-career relationships clearly need further study.

Just as career accomplishments can influence the quality of family life, so may characteristics of the family system affect career accomplishments. On the one hand, Voydanoff (1989) reported that family responsibilities have been shown to increase married men's work hours, income, and job involvement. On the other hand, there is recent evidence that men whose wives are employed outside the home work fewer hours and are less satisfied with their jobs than men whose wives are not employed (Parasuraman et al., in press). It is possible that wives' employment produced more extensive family responsibilities for husbands who felt it necessary to reduce their time commitment to their own careers.

The impact of family role responsibilities on career accomplishments seems particularly salient for partners in two-career relationships on whose shoulders many family members' expectations fall. Decisions to reduce work hours, avoid extensive business travel, and forego promotions and relocations may all limit the opportunities for career accomplishments, especially if career success is defined as rapid advancement within an organization's hierarchy.

It is likely that the relationship between family involvement and career success is neither linear nor invariant across all situations. There are undoubtedly many moderators of this relationship that warrant close scrutiny. Again, an expanded definition of two-career status will enable researchers to identify the salient characteristics of each partner's career and family orientation that may influence the strength and direction of the association between family status and career accomplishments.

Social and Behavioral Resources in Two-Career Relationships

The literature clearly reveals the significance of social support in protecting people from the negative consequences of extensive stress (Cohen & Wills, 1985; Gore, 1986; House, 1981). Supportive relationships are also seen as critical social resources in dealing with work-family issues (Greenhaus & Parasuraman, 1986; Hall & Hall, 1979; Holahan & Gilbert, 1979; Rapoport & Rapoport, 1971; Suchet & Barling, 1986).

We need to know more about the facilitators of social support—especially spouse support—in two-career relationships. Why are some relationships more supportive than others? What role, if any, does a partner's self-esteem play in his or her willingness to provide support to a partner? Are highly career-oriented persons less willing to provide support to their partners than those less strongly committed to their work? Future research should examine these kinds of questions so that effective techniques for enhancing supportive relationships can be developed.

In a similar vein, the importance of coping behavior in ameliorating extensive stress is well documented (Kessler, Price, & Wortman, 1985; Lazarus & Launier, 1978; Pearlin & Schooler, 1978). The effectiveness of specific coping strategies depends on the nature of the stressor and the skills and resources of the individual (Burke & Belcourt, 1974; Newton & Keenan, 1985; Pearlin & Schooler, 1978). We need to examine the factors that encourage two-career partners to use alternative coping behaviors and the situational variables that affect the success of different coping strategies. For example, a woman's choice of coping strategies seems to be a function of the intensity of the conflict she confronts and her own sex-role orientation (Beutell & Greenhaus, 1983). The use of reactive coping strategies (Hall, 1972) is especially dysfunctional for women whose husbands are relatively dissatisfied with their own lives (Beutell & Greenhaus, 1982). The development of a contingency approach to coping effectiveness within two-career relationships seems especially important. The identification of linkages between social support and the utilization (and effectiveness) of different coping behaviors can provide valuable information in this regard.

ORGANIZATIONAL IMPLICATIONS AND REACTIONS

The interdependence of work and family lives has a significant impact on individual behavior in organizational settings and ultimately on organizational functioning itself. As noted earlier, family responsibilities can affect an employee's willingness to work long hours, travel extensively, accept greater job responsibilities, and seek promotions. Moreover, family responsibilities may intrude into the work domain and increase lateness, absenteeism, and preoccupation with family matters (Crouter, 1984). Additionally, family variables can be associated with strain (Cooke & Rousseau, 1984) and job dissatisfaction (Parasuraman et al., in press). The increasing representation of two-career couples and single heads of household in the workforce has posed a challenge to organizations to manage a generation of employees who are concerned about balancing their work and nonwork lives.

Despite the organizational consequences of work-family interdependence, employers have not always been quick to recognize the severity of the situation or to respond in a constructive manner. Hall and Richter

(1988) suggest that while some organizations are uncertain how to respond to work/family issues, other organizations are even unwilling to address work/family issues. The reasons for avoiding a serious consideration of these issues can be several. These could include the personal threat that these issues arouse in many executives (who themselves have suppressed their feelings about work and family), the nature of the organization's culture, the perception that work/family issues are a "woman's problem," the emphasis on short-term problems and solutions, and the inability to see the payoffs to an organization for resolving work/family dilemmas (Hall & Richter, 1988).

Voydanoff (1989) has identified a number of family-oriented personnel policies adopted by some organizations such as childcare, parental leaves, flexible work schedules, flexible benefits, employee counseling, and relocation assistance. She has correctly called for additional research to evaluate these policies from the perspectives of families and employers. Although family-oriented personnel policies can undoubtedly help ease the strain of juggling work and family responsibilities, organizations must also consider more fundamental changes in their structure, reward system, and culture to be truly responsive to contemporary work/family issues.

At the most basic level, an organization should expand its conception of what it takes to be a "successful" employee in its environment. Organizations must recognize the nonwork consequences of different career paths (Beutell & Greenhaus, 1986). It is likely that some jobs and career paths demand longer hours, require more extensive travel, and produce more stress than other jobs and career paths. For these reasons, career paths may differ in the extent to which they intrude into employees' family lives and also permit intrusion from family responsibilities. Organizations need to be aware of these differences and make this information available to employees so they can make career decisions compatible with their family responsibilities and their desired lifestyle.

This approach further requires organizations to sanction alternative career directions and to avoid pressuring employees to pursue the "one" route to career success. Some organizations have developed dual career ladders to reward productive employees for remaining in technical positions rather than entering management (for which they may have little real interest or talent). Similarly, employers should recognize, sanction, and reward alternative routes to "success" among employees who need to balance their work and family responsibilities.

Organizations need to recognize that family responsibilities (and the possibility of work-family conflict) may vary with employees' career and family stages. The early career, for example, is normally a time of intense job involvement and commitment as employees seek to establish themselves professionally and lay the groundwork for further achievement and advancement. Yet intense time and emotional involvement in work during the early career may produce extensive work-family conflicts for employees who also have heavy family responsibilities during this period of their lives (Greenhaus, 1987).

Bailyn (1980) has proposed an alternative "slow burn" approach to career development in which the early career years would require only moderate levels of job involvement with assignments that are less demanding and intrude less severely into employees' family lives. Then, over time, more challenge, responsibility, and involvement can be introduced as employees' family responsibilities begin to subside. Although career accomplishments and advancement are less rapid under this slow burn approach, it is hoped that employees will ultimately become more fully productive at a time when it is easier to balance their work and family lives (Greenhaus, 1987).

The adoption of a slow burn approach would require an organization to reconsider its conception of career development, the pace with which employees need to acquire and demonstrate work skills, and the contributions expected of relatively new employees. Even if an organization does not adopt this approach across the board, it can still offer this "career track" to those employees (women and men) with extensive family responsibilities.

In order to encourage organizations to pursue these practices, a number of research directions are required. First, we need to examine relationships between the characteristics of a job and the permeability of the boundary between that job and an employee's family life. What kinds of jobs intrude most severely (in terms of time and strain) into one's family life? For example, are there substantial differences in the potential for family intrusion between line positions and staff positions? Between jobs that involve boundary spanning or coordinating functions and those that do not? Research is also needed to identify the kinds of jobs that permit intrusion from the family role. Although each employee can shape his or her job to a significant degree, the potential for work-family conflict may still vary considerably across jobs and career paths.

Research also needs to examine the compatibility of the slow burn approach with individual and organizational well-being. It is important to know, for example, whether employees who avoid intense levels of work involvement during their early careers can still develop and grow in their careers over time. Are certain early experiences (e.g., a leadership role in a stressful and time-consuming project) so crucial that their absence permanently stalls an employee's career? Although early job challenge has been shown to facilitate subsequent career growth (Berlew & Hall,

1966), it is not clear whether a sufficiently challenging job need also involve extensive time, travel, and/or stress.

Even if the slow burn approach does no irreparable damage to an individual's career, it may detract from an organization's productivity. Research is needed to determine whether the pursuit of a "slower" career path has a significant negative impact on job performance, and whether additional staffing is required to compensate for possible performance deficiencies. On the positive side, the sanctioning of a more moderate level of work involvement may reduce burnout, increase employee commitment to the organization, and reduce turnover. This raises the larger issue regarding an organization's capacity to survive and prosper when its culture legitimatizes an employee's right to balance career and family involvements.

In a related vein, research needs to examine a range of practices assumed to facilitate career growth. For example, Hall and Hall (1979) question whether an employee's career growth really requires frequent relocation, a practice that may be more a matter of tradition than necessity. Hall and Hall indicate that other forms of training and development (simulations, short temporary assignments) may be just as satisfactory as frequent uprooting. Research is required to determine whether certain sacrosanct developmental experiences can be replaced by more family-compatible activities without loss of productivity and future career growth.

One particular practice that may enable employees to balance their work and family responsibilities is work-at-home. Technological advances may permit some employees whose jobs entail computer activities to perform a certain portion of their job duties on a terminal at home. Although at first glance this practice appears capable of solving a number of work/family problems, Shamir and Salomon (1985) suggest that employees who work at home may experience other stresses and strains and may develop feelings of social isolation. Future research should examine the relative benefits and costs associated with home-based work for different segments of the employee population.

In summary, organizations have a critical stake in the resolution of many different types of work-family issues. Extensive research is needed to develop and test theoretical models of work-family interaction that have implications for organizations and their employees. In addition, research is required to evaluate the effectiveness of a variety of organizational interventions (e.g., flexible work schedules, work-at-home programs) from multiple perspectives.

CONCLUSIONS

I have indicated three broad areas in which additional research is warranted. In a sense, the most basic of the areas concerns the nature of the work-family interface, since many findings in this area can be applied to studies of two-career relationships and organizational phenomena. I have also suggested a number of specific research questions that I believe deserve attention, although there are clearly many additional lines of research that can and should be pursued.

Regardless of its specific focus, research regarding work and family issues can be strengthened in three ways. First, research should continue to develop and test conceptual models of work-family relationships. As Voydanoff (1989) noted, there are a number of partially integrated models in existence. Whether these models are modified and extended, or whether new models are developed, the knowledge base regarding the interdependence of work and family roles will be enhanced primarily through programmatic, theoretically-oriented research.

Second, a diverse set of research methodologies should be pursued to test these theoretical models. Cross-sectional correlational studies can provide important insights, but can only take us so far. Longitudinal studies, experiments, quasi-experiments, and qualitative research all have their special advantages to bring to the study of work-family relationships. We should not be so tied to a particular methodology that we lose sight of the contributions that other approaches can make.

Finally, regardless of the particular methodology chosen, we should pay close attention to the validation of measures used to assess key concepts. Any empirical line of research is limited by the reliability and validity of its measurement operations. Schwab's (1980) suggestions regarding construct validity in organizational behavior have considerable merit in the study of work and family lives.

REFERENCES

Aldous, J., Osmond, M. W., & Hicks, M. W. (1979). Men's work and men's families. In W. R. Burr, R. Hill, F. I. Nye, & I. L. Reiss (Eds.), *Contemporary theories about the family* (Vol. 1, pp. 227-256). New York: Free Press.

Bailyn, L. (1970). Career and family orientations of husbands and wives in relation to marital happiness. *Human Relations, 23,* 97-113.

Bailyn, L. (1980). The slow-burn way to the top: Some thoughts on the early years of organizational careers. In C. B. Derr (Ed.), *Work, family, and the career* (pp. 94-105). New York: Praeger.

Barling, J. (1986). Fathers' work experiences, the father-child relationship and children's behaviour. *Journal of Occupational Behaviour, 7,* 61-66.

Barling, J., & Rosenbaum, A. (1986). Work stressors and wife abuse. *Journal of Applied Psychology, 71,* 346-348.

Berlew, D. E., & Hall, D. T. (1966). The socialization of managers: Effects of expectations on performance. *Administrative Science Quarterly, 11,* 207-223.

Betz, N. E., & Fitzgerald, L. F. (1987). *The career psychology of women.* Orlando, FL: Academic Press.

Beutell, N. J., & Greenhaus, J. H. (1982). Interrole conflict among married women: The influence of husband and wife characteristics on conflict and coping behaviors. *Journal of Vocational Behavior, 21,* 99-110.

Beutell, N. J., & Greenhaus, J. H. (1983). Integration of home and nonhome roles: Women's coping and conflict behavior. *Journal of Applied Psychology, 68,* 43-48.

Beutell, N. J., & Greenhaus, J. H. (1986). Balancing acts: Work-family conflict and the dual-career couple. In L. L. Moore (Ed.), *Not as far as you think: The realities of working women* (pp. 149-162). Lexington, MA: Lexington Books.

Brief, A. P., Schuler, R. S., & Van Sell, M. (1981). *Managing job stress.* Boston: Little, Brown.

Bryson, R. B., Bryson, J. B., & Johnson, M. F. (1978). Family size, satisfaction, and productivity in dual-career couples. *Psychology of Women Quarterly, 3,* 67-77.

Burke, R. J., & Belcourt, M. L. (1974). Managerial role stress and coping responses. *Journal of Business Administration, 5*(2), 55-68.

Burke, R. J., & Bradshaw, P. (1981). Occupational and life stress and the family. *Small Group Behavior, 12,* 329-375.

Cohen, S., & Wills, T. A. (1985). Stress, social support, and the buffering hypothesis. *Psychological Bulletin, 98,* 310-357.

Cooke, R. A., & Rousseau, D. M. (1984). Stress and strain from family roles and work-role expectations. *Journal of Applied Psychology, 69,* 252-262.

Cooper, C. L., & Marshall, J. (1976). Occupational sources of stress: A review of the literature relating to coronary heart disease and mental ill health. *Journal of Occupational Psychology, 49,* 11-28.

Crouter, A. C. (1984). Spillover from family to work: The neglected side of the work-family interface. *Human Relations, 37,* 425-442.

Epstein, C. F. (1971). Law partners and marital partners. *Human Relations, 24,* 549-564.

Gore, S. (1986). Perspectives on social support and research on stress moderating processes. *Journal of Organizational Behavior Management, 8*(2), 87-103.

Gould, S., & Werbel, J. D. (1983). Work involvement: A comparison of dual wage earner and single wage earner families. *Journal of Applied Psychology, 68,* 313-319.

Greenhaus, J. H. (1987). *Career management.* Hinsdale, IL: Dryden.

Greenhaus, J. H., Bedeian, A. G., & Mossholder, K. W. (1987). Work experiences, job performance, and feelings of personal and family well-being. *Journal of Vocational Behavior, 31,* 200-215.

Greenhaus, J. H., & Beutell, N. J. (1985). Sources of conflict between work and family roles. *Academy of Management Review, 10,* 76-88.

Greenhaus, J. H., & Parasuraman, S. (1986). A work-nonwork interactive perspective of stress and its consequences. *Journal of Organizational Behavior Management, 8*(2), 37-60.

Greenhaus, J. H., Parasuraman, S., Granrose, C. S., Rabinowitz, S., & Beutell, N. J. (in press). Sources of work-family conflict among two-career couples. *Journal of Vocational Behavior.*

Gross, N., Mason, W. S., & McEachern, A. W. (1958). *Explorations in role analysis: Studies of the school superintendency role.* New York: Wiley.

Gupta, N., & Jenkins, D. (1985). Dual-career couples. In T. W. Beehr & R. S. Bhagat (Eds.), *Human stress and cognition in organizations* (pp. 141-175). New York: Wiley.

Hall, D. T. (1972). A model of coping with role conflict: The role behavior of college-educated women. *Administrative Science Quarterly, 17,* 471-489.

Hall, D. T. (1976). *Careers in organizations.* Pacific Palisades, CA: Goodyear.

Hall, D. T., & Richter, J. (1988). Balancing work life and home life: What can organizations do to help? *Academy of Management Executive, 2,* 213-223.

Hall, F. S., & Hall, D. T. (1979). *The two-career couple.* Reading, MA: Addison-Wesley.

Herzberg, F. (1966). *Work and the nature of man.* Cleveland: World Publishing Company.

Holahan, C. K., & Gilbert, L. A. (1979). Conflict between major life roles: Women and men in dual-career couples. *Human Relations, 32,* 451-467.

Holmes, T. H., & Rahe, R. H. (1967). The social readjustment rating scale. *Journal of Psychosomatic Medicine, 11,* 213-218.

House, J. (1981). *Work stress and social support.* Reading, MA: Addison-Wesley.

Ivancevich, J., M., & Matteson, M. T. (1980). *Stress and work: A managerial perspective.* Dallas: Scott, Foresman.

Jackson, S. E., & Maslach, C. (1982). After-effects of job-related stress: Families as victims. *Journal of Occupational Behaviour, 3,* 63-77.

Johnson, J. H., & Sarason, I. G. (1979). Recent developments in research on life stress. In V. Hamilton & D. M. Warburton (Eds.), *Human stress and cognition* (pp. 205-233). New York: Wiley.

Kahn, R. L., Wolfe, D. M., Quinn, R., Snoek, J. D., & Rosenthal, R. A. (1964). *Organizational stress.* New York: Wiley.

Kanter, R. M. (1977). *Work and family in the United States: A critical review and agenda for research and policy.* New York: Russell Sage Foundation.

Kessler, R. C., Price, R. H., & Wortman, C. B. (1985). Social factors in psychopathology: Stress, social support, and coping processes. *Annual Review of Psychology, 36,* 531-572.

Kopelman, R. E., Greenhaus, J. H., & Connolly, T. F. (1983). A model of work, family, and interrole conflict: A construct validation study. *Organizational Behavior and Human Performance, 32,* 198-215.

Korman, A. K. (1988). Career success and personal failure: Mid- to late-career feelings and events. In M. London & E. M. Mone (Eds.), *Career growth and human resource strategies* (pp. 81-94). Westport, CT: Greenwood Press.

Korman, A. K., & Korman, R. W. (1980). *Career success/personal failure*. Englewood Cliffs, NJ: Prentice-Hall.

Korman, A. K., Wittig-Berman, U., & Lang, D. (1981). Career success and personal failure: Alienation in professionals and managers. *Academy of Management Journal, 24*, 342-360.

LaBier, D. (1986). *Modern madness*. Reading, MA: Addison-Wesley.

Lazarus, R. S. (1966). *Psychological stress and the coping process*. New York: McGraw-Hill.

Lazarus, R. S., & Launier, R. (1978). Stress-related transactions between persons and environments. In L. A. Pervin & M. Lewis (Eds.), *Perspectives in interactional psychology* (pp. 287-327). New York: Plenum.

Levinson, D. J., Darrow, C. N., Klein, E. B., Levinson, M. H., & McKee, B. (1978). *Seasons of a man's life*. New York: Knopf.

Newton, T. J., & Keenan, A. (1985). Coping with work-related stress. *Human Relations, 38*, 107-126.

Parasuraman, S., Greenhaus, J. H., Rabinowitz, S., Bedeian, A. G., & Mossholder, K. W. (in press). Work and family variables as mediators of the relationship between wives' employment and husbands' well-being. *Academy of Management Journal*.

Pearlin, L. I., & Schooler, C. (1978). The structure of coping. *Journal of Health and Social Behavior, 19*, 2-21.

Pleck, J. H. (1977). The work-family role system. *Social Forces, 24*, 417-427.

Pleck, J. H., Staines, G. L., & Lang, L. (1980). Conflicts between work and family life. *Monthly Labor Review, 103*(3), 29-32.

Rapoport, R., & Rapoport, R. N. (1969). The dual-career family: A variant pattern and social change. *Human Relations, 22*, 3-30.

Rapoport, R., & Rapoport, R. N. (1971). *Dual career families*. Middlesex, England: Penguin Books.

Richter, J. (1984). *The daily transitions between professional and private life*. Unpublished doctoral dissertation, Boston University.

Scanzoni, J. (1970). *Opportunity and the family*. New York: Free Press.

Scanzoni, J. (1982). *Sexual bargaining*. Chicago: University of Chicago.

Schein, E. H. (1978). *Career dynamics: Matching individual and organizational needs*. Reading, MA: Addison-Wesley.

Schein, E. H. (1985). *Career anchors: Discovering your real values*. San Diego: University Associates.

Schwab, D. P. (1980). Construct validity in organizational behavior. In B. M. Staw & L. L. Cummings (Eds.), *Research in organizational behavior* (Vol. 1, pp. 3-43). Greenwich: JAI Press.

Sekaran, U. (1986). *Dual-career families*. San Francisco: Jossey-Bass.

Shamir, B., & Salomon, I. (1985). Work-at-home and the quality of working life. *Academy of Management Review, 10*, 455-464.

Smith, S. J. (1983). Estimating annual hours of labor force activity. *Monthly Labor Review, 106*(2), 13-22.

Staines, G. L., & Pleck, J. H. (1984). Nonstandard work schedules and family life. *Journal of Applied Psychology, 69,* 515-523.

Staines, G. L., Pottick, K. J., & Fudge, D. A. (1986). Wives' employment and husbands' attitudes toward work and life. *Journal of Applied Psychology, 71,* 118-128.

Suchet, M., & Barling, J. (1986). Employed mothers: Interrole conflict, spouse support and marital functioning. *Journal of Occupational Behaviour, 7,* 167-178.

Van Maanen, J., & Schein, E. H. (1977). Career development. In J. R. Hackman & J. L. Suttle (Eds.), *Improving life at work: Behavioral science approaches to organizational change* (pp. 30-95). Santa Monica, CA: Goodyear.

Voydanoff, P. (1989). Work and family: A review and expanded conceptualization. *Journal of Social Behavior and Personality,* 1988, 3 (4), 1-22.

Wiley, D. L. (1987). The relationship between work/nonwork role conflict and job-related outcomes: Some unanticipated findings. *Journal of Management, 13,* 467-472.

The Urban Underclass and the Future of Work-Family Relations Research

Robert F. Kelly
Department of Sociology
Le Moyne College, Syracuse, NY 13214

It is argued that the literature generally recognized as constituting work-family relations research has failed to systematically integrate the concept of the urban underclass as an important part of its theoretical purview. Several potential explanations are developed for this failure. The paper then presents a brief descriptive analysis of the urban underclass in which the economic concepts of the informal economy and opportunity costs are central. Illustrations of work-family causal linkages deriving from previous analyses of the underclass are developed as examples of the benefits that should result from the proposed integration. Next, it is argued that work-family researchers should focus substantial attention on public policy issues in the 1990's. In particular, the impact of new federal workfare proposals on low income families are important. The paper concludes by leaving the topic of the underclass and developing a brief discussion of the two issues. The first is the politics of small birth cohorts. The second is the past acceptance of unnecessarily weak methodology. These two issues should significantly influence work-family research in the 1990's.

Soon social scientists will enter upon a new decade of research on work-family relations. Patricia Voydanoff's introductory essay to this special issue provides a well written and concise analytical review of research in this field with attention focused on work produced in the 1970's and 1980's. In addition to skillfully bringing together this large and growing literature, Voydanoff (1989) cogently argues that future achievements in work-family relations research will depend in large measure upon the research community's ability to expand upon current conceptualizations and theoretical systems. In the latter part of the essay, Voydanoff provides several illustrations of areas in which conceptual expansion is necessary. Two such illustrations included the need to better incorporate the role of unpaid work in work/family systems and the need to focus additional attention on the impact of the care of elderly family members on work/family relations when we conceptualize home based work.

©1988 Select Press

It is very much in the spirit of Voydanoff's call to expand the conceptualization of work-family relations, that I seek to develop the argument that the concept and the reality of the urban underclass need to be better understand and integrated in the theory of work-family relations. In this context, I present certain parameters for this integration as well as suggestions for the types of research that will be most needed in the future. In the paper's closing section, I shift my focus of attention and take up two issues that I believe will be central to work-family research in the 1990's, one political and the other methodological. While this discussion is not directly related to the discussion of the underclass that precedes it, it is my hope that each of the three discussions developed here will help to better focus work-family research in the coming decade.

Work-Family Research and the Underclass: The Needed Integration

Research that has come to be recognized as work-family research typically has dealt with the employment-family relations of professional workers, middle class service workers and blue collar industrial workers, especially those who have experienced cyclic or chronic spells of unemployment. This characterization of the implicit domain of work-family research is certainly supported by an examination of Voydanoff's discussions and bibliography. I would argue, however, that a parallel and similarly growing body of research should be integrated with the body of research reviewed by Voydanoff—namely research on work, welfare, the urban underclass and the urban informal or shadow economy. Most of this work/welfare research has been undertaken by economists and demographers in government, private or university based research organizations such as Rand, SRI, Mathematica, ABT, the Urban Institute, the Institute for Social Research at the University of Michigan and the Institute for Research on Poverty at the University of Wisconsin.

The public policy orientation of this research may, in part, account for its relative isolation from work-family relations research, which has been undertaken mainly by psychologists, sociologists and human developmentalists. It may also be the case, as Wilson has argued (1987, p.13), that in the late sixties and throughout the 1970's and 1980's, researchers generally avoided issues of ethnicity, long-term poverty and family structure due to the contentious and ideological climate occasioned by the Moynihan Report (1965). Such avoidance is, I argue below, damaging in the substantive field of work-family relations. Finally, because so much of the work and family behavior within the underclass is informal (e.g., informal labor markets, informal kinship and fictive kinship family systems), it is difficult to conceptualize using most social scientific concepts. These concepts typically focus on formally defined behavior (e.g., legal marriage, formally defined occupations). It is certainly more difficult methodologically to conduct research on these informal systems of behavior.

Whatever the origins of the relative autonomy of these two spheres of research, there are strong reasons to believe that without an integration of the two, current efforts at synthesis and theory development in work/family relations research are likely to be less fruitful than would otherwise be the case. Perhaps more importantly, without such an integrative expansion of the domain of work-family research, the validity and the power of what we, as social scientists, have to say on issues of public policy concerning work and family will be severely limited.

Before taking up this reformulation, a potential source of misinterpretation should be addressed. I am not faulting Voydanoff for excluding research on the urban underclass. Voydanoff has accurately portrayed the research literature commonly understood to constitute the work-family research studies. Indeed, there are several areas in which the review touches on issues that I will analyze below; for example, the relationship between the economic viability of young adults and family formation, the relative neglect of research on extended family relations, and the feminization of poverty vis à vis the formation and welfare status of single parent families. Rather, my point is that the work-family research literature, as currently understood, needs to be reformulated so as to more thoroughly incorporate the phenomenon of the urban underclass and the knowledge that has been produced about it.

The Underclass

The term "underclass" has been associated with a sufficient number of objectionable ideological connotations, that one is tempted to abandon its use altogether. Fortunately, in a recently published but already influential work, *The Truly Disadvantaged* (1987), Wilson has added substantial degrees of clarity to the term. The defining characteristics of the underclass are persistent poverty and welfare dependency among its women and dependent children. Erratic income patterns, street crime and marginality from formal labor markets mark its men (Wilson, 1987, p.8; Kelly, 1985,p. 160-161).

The term persistent poverty generally is defined either as long-term spells of poverty, five years or more consistently below the poverty level, or high incidences of poverty over a substantial period of time, eight of ten years spent below the poverty level. It is the persistent nature of the underclass's poverty that distinguishes its condition from that of the working poor who live close to the poverty level and periodically slip below it (Duncan, 1984; Bane & Ellwood, 1983). Research suggests that poverty of this type, perhaps 4-6% of the population, exists to a much greater extent than previously recognized (Bane and Ellwood, 1983), and that it has become increasingly concentrated in inner cities over the past three decades (Wilson, 1987, p. 46-62).

The underclass is not simply a longitudinal income category. There are behavioral correlates of persistent poverty—high levels of out-of-wedlock birth, low rates of marriage and remarriage, low levels of educational achievement, high crime rates (especially violent street crime) and low male labor force participation rates in the formal labor market. Research strongly suggests that these social dislocations are not isolated pathologies of specific types of individuals that are amenable to remedial and clinically oriented social services (Kelly, 1988). Rather, they are the result of structural transformations in the economy and the ecology of American urban labor markets. Employment requiring less than a high school diploma has become increasingly scarce in American inner cities over the past three decades (Wilson, 1987; Kasarda, 1985).

In response to such bleak economic prospects, inner city men, and to a less degree women, have been drawn to and/or have invented informal economies, that is, illegal or quasi-legal labor and consumer markets based on barter and exchange. A crucial characteristic of behaviors such as drug trade, auto theft and parts resale, loan sharking, numbers, fencing and mugging is that they provide substantial short-term incomes, albeit at significant physical risks as well as the long-term risk of imprisonment. Note, however, that in terms of opportunity costs, these apparent risks are lessened to the underclass participant in the informal economy because his expected wage in the formal economy is extremely low and his transaction costs, relative to his expected wage, are extremely high. An additional important attraction of the informal economy is that its sales and income tax rates are zero. Indeed, it is this near-zero tax rate that accounts in a large part for the high participation rates among the middle class in the informal economy.

Up to this point, what does this discussion imply for research on work-family relations? First, the range of classes about whom we ask questions concerning work-family relations needs to be expanded to include the urban underclass. Historically, and for the reasons that are not all together clear, this group has not been considered to be within the domain of work-family relations research. More importantly, this group's growth in the past three decades signals a major transformation, a dualization of the American class structure. Second, it follows that it is no longer sufficient to focus attention in work-family research on the formal economy when we conceptualize labor market and consumer market behaviors. Research suggests that the informal economy is large and probably expanding (Carson, 1984; *Business Week*, 1982), and that members of the underclass are heavy participants in the informal economy (Viscusi, 1983). Each of these propositions suggests the need for conceptual expansions that augment those set forth by Voydanoff.

Work-Family Causal Linkages

The economic structures and transformations discussed in the previous section have powerful impacts on underclass families. For example, Wilson and Neckerman have provided persuasive evidence that high rates of out-of-wedlock births among young black inner city women are not the result of increased fertility (indeed fertility rates are dropping in this group), but rather extremely low rates of marriage and remarriage (1987, p. 63-92). That is, although there are fewer births in this group, more out-of-wedlock children are being born because marriage is being avoided. Wilson and Neckerman demonstrate that the substantial decline in marriage/remarriage rates within this group is powerfully related to a marked decline in labor force participation rates among young cohorts of black men since the 1960's (1987, pp. 18, 89). That is, the pool of marriageable black men has declined as the concentration of the underclass and the expansion of the informal economy have progressed in the center cities of the United States.

In effect, an inner city woman living in a zone of concentrated poverty faces a marriage market in which propective spouses have erratic incomes, dangerous incomes and/or chronically low incomes. Under such circumstances, informal cohabiting rather than formal marriage is a rational course of action. Indeed, this dynamic is precisely what accounts for the high incidence of informal, fictive, and extended kinship structures in underclass neighborhoods (Stack, 1974; Hill, 1977; Kelly, 1985). Mothers, who have primary responsibility for children, expand the opportunity for the material well-being of their children by casting wide nets of reciprocal kinship bonds, rather than focusing their attention on economically unstable conjugal family bonds.

This abbreviated discussion of the relationships between male employment in the informal and formal labor markets, and fertility and marriage suggests several things. In terms of a causal analysis of underclass work and family behavior, a robust application of economic utility theory will advance our understanding of these behaviors. As a point of theoretical departure, the concept of opportunity costs, that is, the cost paid when one foregoes the benefits of one course of action in order to pursue another, should be prominent among the conceptual tools employed.

Economic utility theory and the concept of opportunity costs, however, are not sufficient as conceptual tools for the proposed integration of underclass and work-family research. It is also critical to integrate the concept of stress as a causal linkage in work-family relations among the underclass. Poverty, especially persistent poverty, is a powerful stressor associated with high rates of various mental and physical health problems, substance abuse, family violence and marital instability (Belle, 1982). Sociological and psychological theories of stress and adaptation to stress need to be used jointly with economic utility theory to develop comprehensive understandings of underclass work-family relations (Kelly, 1985).

In considering the use of economic utility and stress theories in relation to poverty and underclass populations, it is important to make explicit a general finding that has emerged from much governmental research on poverty programs undertaken during and after the War on Poverty. With relatively few exceptions, clinically oriented programs in the areas of criminal rehabilitation and job training based largely on a stress model of poverty impacts have been unsuccessful in improving the aggregate conditions of underclass populations (Kelly, 1985, 1988). By the same token, programs that focused both on improving the economic conditions of client population through job guarantees and income support, and reducing stress related conditions through clinically oriented program elements had much higher rates of success (Kelly, 1985). The inference that may be taken from this body of research is that improvement in economic status is a necessary condition for the success of clinically and family-systems oriented approaches to stress related problems in poor populations. The substantial success of the National Supported Work Demonstration is perhaps the best example of a program based on a synthesis of economic and stress-related theories that has resulted in a valuable public intervention among underclass populations (Hollister et al, 1984). Attention is next explicitly focused on public policy and work-family relations among the underclass.

Public Policy

The history of public policies intended to influence low-income families in the United States is complex and extremely difficult to interpret (Kelly, 1988; Patterson, 1982). However, two historical themes important to the integration of underclass research with work-family relations research should be made explicit. First, a gender-based division of labor exists in the major public institutions that seek to serve and to regulate the lives of the underclass. While there are exceptions, it is fair to generally characterize the urban criminal justice system as specializing in the men of the underclass and the urban public welfare system (AFDC) as specializing in the woman and dependent children of the underclass. This structural differentiation has yet to be comprehensively studied either historically or sociologically. To undertake such studies and to integrate their results with what we now know of gender-based differentiations and discrimination in the formal labor market and middle class family systems is an exciting and potentially fruitful task that awaits researchers and policy analysts in the 1990's. Indeed, the present research program on gender and work-family relations will be decidedly incomplete until this task begins.

Second, discussions of work, family and welfare in the United States have always been constrained by several ideological themes. There is a firmly entrenched American ideal that life on welfare for the able bodied person should be somewhat worse than life with the least attractive available job (the principle of least eligibility). This supports the constantly present distinction between the deserving poor and the undeserving poor. The deserving poor are defined typically as the object of individual calamities and tragedies that exempt them from the principle of least eligibility. Hence, they have a rightful claim to public assistance and private charity. The undeserving poor require the social control and management embodied in the income reporting and testing procedures, and the work requirements characteristic of American social welfare programs.

In many ways the issue of whether those who are referred to as the undeserving poor are truly undeserving has become politically irrelevant. The over-riding political reality is that a national commitment has been made to a welfare system that requires work in exchange for public income support. During the past decade, however, the work requirement issue has taken on a new dimension. Liberals have come to accept the reality of work requirements in the form of workfare programs. However, this acceptance has been conditioned by a recognition that work requirements, to be at all beneficial, must be implemented as components of programs that guarantee employment in jobs that provide at least some opportunity for upward mobility (jobs with internal job ladders) as well as some minimal level of individual and family income support. That is, this position accepts the notion of job requirements that derives from the concept of the undeserving poor, but it adds to it the concepts of job guarantees and income support. This position, a de facto political compromise, is in no small part the result of the promising findings of the National Supported Work Demonstration (Hollister et al., 1984) and the Youth Incentive Entitlement Pilot Project (Gueron, 1984). Each of these provided, and in some instances guaranteed, relatively high quality jobs as a form of income support in conjunction with the more therapeutically oriented counseling elements of these programs.

An employment requirements/jobs guarantees compromise is embodied in the recently enacted welfare reform legislation sponsored by Senator Daniel P. Moynihan and variations upon it that have already been implemented in states such as New York, Michigan, Massachusetts and New Jersey. The Federal legislation and the various state plans are important. First, they represent new tactics and strategies for dealing with the problems of the underclass. Second, they represent an unparalleled opportunity for researchers to understand the dynamics of work, family processes and public policy.

A key to comprehending the American public welfare system is that it is really fifty systems, one for each state. There are federal mandates and minimal requirements that must be met by each state for federal funding, but the states retain substantial discretion over the support levels, and the initiation and regulation of work programs related to their welfare systems. Hence, as the work requirements/job guarantee compromise referred to above is implemented in the 1990's, it is highly probable that there will be substantial variation among states and groups of states. Variations in program elements such as the nature of guarantees, the level of income support, and types of training and counseling, and their potential impact on family related variables such as fertility, marriage, remarriage, household composition, and health should be central topics in work-family research in the 1990's. In effect, multiple natural experiments will be occurring and we should not lose the opportunity to learn from them.

The preceding discussions of the underclass and work-family research has been necessarily truncated and schematic. It is hoped, however, that, in keeping with the tone set by Voydanoff, my discussion of the underclass and work-family relations will encourage the development of a more comprehensive and integrated body of work-family research. In the next section, I discuss two issues that are not directly related to the phenomenon of the underclass, but that hold a similar promise for expanding work-family research vistas in the 1990's.

Two Additional Projects for Future Work-Family Research

Small Birth Cohorts and the Politics of Work and Family. In the early 1990's, the smallest post-World War II birth cohorts will begin to mature into their first marriage and their initial full-time labor market commitments. Assuming that the formal economy does not enter a prolonged recession, these cohorts will be in an advantaged bargaining position in dealing with potential employers relative to the young adult baby boomers of the 1970's and 1980's.

If one makes the reasonable assumption that female labor force participation is not going to decline in the 1990's and, as a consequence, that the demands for family and child-related employer services/benefits will remain high, we will indeed be facing a unique political and economic situation. The young adults of the 1990's should be able to bargain from a more powerful position than previous cohorts of new workers. Will they take advantage of this situation? Will they organize independently or through increased unionization? Under what conditions will they be successful? How will employers in different sectors of the economy respond to these demands? These are fascinating and important questions that we, as researchers and policy analysts, need to prepare ourselves and our graduate and undergraduate students to address.

Methodology

It has become almost standard practice in many work-family research articles to excuse the use of poor convenience samples and mail-back questionnaires with extremely low response rates. There is a statement that research on work-family relations is still so new that most work is, by definition, exploratory. As a consequence, issues of sampling are not as central in work-family research as they are in other better-developed areas of research. As Voydanoff notes, the current body of work-family research dates at least from the 1960's. That is, we possess nearly three decades of research in this area. Hence, the implicit or explicit claim that the field is in its infancy simply no longer obtains. I would argue that editors, especially editors of journals that have clinical and applied orientations, and researchers guiding graduate students simply need to be more demanding with respect to the quality of samples and data that are deemed acceptable if the field of work-family research is to progress.

REFERENCES

Bane, M.J., & Ellwood, D.T. (1983). *Slipping into and out of poverty: The dynamics of spells* (Working Paper #1199). Cambridge, MA: National Bureau of Economic Research.

Belle, D. (Ed.) (1982). *Lives in stress.* Beverly Hills, CA: Sage.

Business Week (1982). *Answers that unveil the underground economy* (Harris Poll). October 11, p. 14.

Carson, C. S. (1984). The underground economy: An introduction. *Survey of Current Business, 64* (May and July).

Duncan, G. (1984). *Years of poverty, years of plenty.* Ann Arbor: Institute for Social Research, University of Michigan.

Gueron, J. (1984). *Lessons from a job guarantee: The youth incentive entitlement pilot project*. New York. Manpower Development Research Project.

Hill, R. (1977). *Informal adoption among black families*. Washington: The Urban League.

Hollister, R.G., Kemper, P., Maynard, R. (Eds.) (1984). *The national supported work demonstration*. Madison: University of Wisconsin Press.

Kasarda, J D. (1985). Urban change and minority opportunities. In P. Peterson (Ed.), *The new urban reality*. Washington: The Brookings Institution.

Kelly, R.F. (1985). The family and the urban underclass: An integrative framework. *Journal of Family Issues, 6*, 159-184.

Kelly, R.F. (1988). Poverty, the family and public policy: Historical interpretations and a reflection on the future. In P. Voydanoff and L.C. Majka (Eds.), *Families and Economic Distress*. Newbury Park: Sage.

Moynihan, D.P. (1965). *The Negro family: A case for national action*. Washington: U.S. Department of Labor.

Patterson, J.J. (1982). *America's struggle against poverty, 1900-1980*. Cambridge: Harvard University Press.

Stack, C. (1974). *All our kin*. New York: Harper and Row.

Viscusi, W. K. (1983). *Market incentives for criminal behavior* (paper 83-13). Durham, NC:Duke University, Center for the Study of Business Regulation.

Voydanoff, P. (1989). Work and family: A review and expanded conceptualization. In Goldsmith, E. (Ed.), Work and family: Theory, research, and applications. [Special issue]. *Journal of Social Behavior and Personality, 3 (4)*, 1-22.

Wilson, W.J. (1987). *The truly disadvantaged: The inner city, the underclass and public policy*. Chicago: University of Chicago Press.

Wilson, W. J., & Neckerman, K. (1987). Poverty and family structure: The widening gap between evidence and public policy issues. In W. J. Wilson, (Ed.), *The truly disadvantaged: The inner city, the underclass, and public policy*. Chicago: University of Chicago Press.

Studying the Work-Family Connection:
Atheoretical Progress, Ideological Bias, and Shaky Foundations for Policy

Paul W. Kingston
Department of Sociology
University of Virginia, Charlottesville, VA 22903

A review of the recent literature on the connections between work and family lives shows: 1) an increasingly sophisticated and subtle appreciation of these connections in diverse family types even if progress has largely been atheoretical, 2) some overinterpretation of how employment affects domestic life, and 3) the prevalence of a feminist ideology that constricts understanding of people's lives and of liberal policy prescriptions that are ungrounded in rigorous research.

Because the volume of research threatens to overwhelm us, the task of assessing all the research on the connections between work and family life is as daunting as it is necessary. As Voydanoff's paper so amply attests, scholars in this area have not lacked for energy. They have successfully established the importance of the topic, and increasingly sophisticated research substantially advances our understanding of family life in the contemporary United States. This is so even if the forest isn't always clearly visible through all the trees (or the twigs and leaves).

This research resists easy summary. Yet the signs of intellectual progress are clear. The days of asking whether women's employment is "bad" (or men's unemployment is "bad") are not long in the past, but they are surely over. As Voydanoff's review makes plain, researchers give much more than lip service to the fact that work (in and outside the home) and family life have many interrelated dimensions. This is the baseline of current research. We further know that the connections between work and family life take many forms and affect family members in varied ways. If the results of this research are complex, even messy, so too is the reality of family life.

While the sophistication of this research moved rapidly ahead, it barely kept pace with the changes in family structure, especially in the rise of the two-job family and the female-headed family. Social science literally had a challenge thrown up in its face—too obvious to ignore yet

©1988 Select Press

too complex for sweeping pronouncements ("*The* family has experienced..."). Subtlety and nuance in research were the necessary reaction to the very evident diversity in American family lives.

Voydanoff's review not only reflects this general development as it emerged in thousands of pages of journal articles and monographs, but also highlights many of the key findings of this collective effort. Even with her generous spirit (giving a nod to many of us toilers of the vineyard), both accomplishments and limitations of this effort are noted. At the same time she entices us to want more: evaluations of the quality of data and research techniques, suggestions for resolving apparently conflicting findings, and synthetic interpretations of diverse studies.

My intentions here are neither to summarize and comment on specific points of Voydanoff's own summary of this field nor to shoulder the burden of the "more" that remains to be done. The first task is unnecessary because the review informatively speaks for itself. In ducking the second task, I will claim the limitations of space, but honesty requires the profession of inadequacy as well. Rather, I would like to use Voydanoff's paper as a springboard for some general comments about 1) the intellectual process underlying research in this field, 2) the overinterpretations involved in attempting to debunk the "myth of separate worlds," and 3) the ideological constrictions and policy irrelevance of most of this research.

Step By Step

As a research topic, the field of work and family life has fairly well defined foci, but it was not born out of any unresolved theoretical problem nor has its progress been guided by any overarching theoretical perspective. The impetus seemed to be that the personal lives of so many researchers gave lie to the sanitized functional portrait of a gender-based division of labor. They perceived frustrations and problems—hence, early on, a somewhat narcissistic preoccupation with the difficulties in the lives of dual career families. In short order, however, researchers looked for problems in other family types and considered the connection between work and family lives in increasingly subtle lights.

Research advanced very incrementally, step by step down an atheoretical path. To be sure, this research has been guided by conceptual perspectives (e.g., role conflict) that ordered data in abstract terms, but it has lacked theory in the sense of systematically related general propositions. In the main, research in this field doesn't test theory or create it; it addresses questions framed by common sense like "How do job schedules affect marital happiness?" or "What factors affect the division of household chores?" Perhaps in answering these questions the researcher may allude to role theory or exchange theory, but it is difficult to believe that the design of the research or its central story is materially affected by such a "theoretical" gloss, much less that theory building is taking place.

Almost ritualistically, such a state of affairs is the cause of great lament, intellectual handwringing, and hortatory statements about the virtues of *theory*. At least this is so in my field of sociology. The drill is familiar in all subfields of this discipline: the lack of theory (meaning what?) is bemoaned, the mere descriptive nature of research is recounted, researchers nod in agreement (after all, theory is a good thing, the hallmark of science), and the field continues as before. Scholars appear to have a great tolerance for this cycle.

Even if scholars of the family may take some small comfort in the fact that their theoretical deficiencies are by no means unique, I believe a more active defense of the step-by-step, problem-driven approach is possible. The fact that our questions have roots in common concerns doesn't make them intellectually lesser, only more socially consequential. The act of chronicling what is happening in our society with the tools of rigorous social science is indispensible, especially because "common wisdom" is so often distorted. Moreover, the promise of theoretical explanation is empty in the absence of documented accounts of the reality that is to be explained.

While causal theory has had little role in this field, theory does exist in the weak sense of sensitizing concepts that give shape and focus to questions grounded in the common concerns that drive the field. Scholars will surely disagree about whether the absence of general causal theory is merely a sign of the field's immaturity or the reflection of an inherent impossibility, but the conceptual tools exist to analytically order diverse empirical findings in informative synthetic statements. For example, just think of how many aspects of work and family life can be profitably viewed through the conceptual prism of power relations.

The economists' invasion into family research represents a partial exception to my generalization about the atheoretical nature of this field. See, as a prominent example, Becker (1981). (Curiously, this approach is not considered in Voydanoff's review.) In brief, drawing on the suppositions of micro economics, proponents of the new home economics argue that the division of responsibilities within families represents the rationally calculated maximization of utility for the family unit (Berk, 1985). This explanation has the virtue of parsimony, and in some quarters it has an ideological appeal as well.

In my judgment this theoretical perspective flounders on both logical and empirical grounds, but this is not the place for a critique. I simply want to note that sociologists have attempted to translate this theory into falsifiable terms (no easy task), and have directly tested its explanatory power (e.g., Berk, 1985; England & Farkas, 1986; Ross, 1987). In doing so, they necessarily made more explicit the nature of competing sociological factors, but no integrated sociological theory has been advanced as a successful alternative. So far, the main effect of the economists' challenge has been to introduce a new sensitizing perspective that shapes research questions.

Myth for Myth

Talcott Parsons (Parsons & Bales, 1955) has taken it on the chin in study after study as researchers strive to discount what has been called the "myth of separate worlds"—the notion that family life and work life exist apart with little impact on each other (Kanter, 1977). Indeed, the thrust of most current research in this area is to detail how work and family are reciprocally linked. The connections are undeniably significant and extensive, but I fear that the point has been oversold. In effect, there has been a tendency to substitute the myth of inseparable worlds for the myth of separate worlds.

Consider, for example, the much-studied issue of the relation between wives' employment and marital happiness. Overall, employed wives seem happier, though this relation is conditioned by their motivations for work and their husband's attitude toward it (Spitze, 1988). Yet it is one matter to find a statistically significant coefficient and quite another to find a substantively important causal factor. Against the standard of explained variance, measures relating to employment don't go far— sometimes better than rolling dice but not by much. Whatever the ingredients of a happy marriage, they are not strongly linked to women's out of the home work.

Indeed, researchers find that work lives have small or no effects on many aspects of family life—subjective satisfaction, the division of domestic responsibility and labor, and child development. This is the statistical story in many of the articles cited in Voydanoff's review. Of course one could decry faulty measures, misspecified models and the like, but I think the honest reaction is to believe our results and recognize the considerable institutional autonomy of the work place and the family. They intrude on each other but are not seamlessly linked; their connections can be very intimate but are often very tenuous.

In part, this new myth has taken hold because the increasing participation of women in the labor force has been portrayed in overstated terms, seemingly implying that fundamental changes in family life would inevitably follow. True, at any one time, among married couples (even those with young children), two-job families outnumber the traditionalists with a male breadwinner and a female homemaker. However, primarily because so many women are in and out of the labor force or work part time, in only a quarter of all marriages do both the husband and wife work full-time, year-round. Many families thus live as one-and-a-fraction job families—an arrangement that permits only modest changes in traditional family life practices.

We should also recognize that issues relating to the connection between work and family life don't pertain to an increasing proportion of the population. Following the Census Bureau's definition of a family, 28 percent lived in a nonfamily household in 1986. Indeed, as family researchers seek to expand the scope of their view, they should give greater attention not only to families without a married couple (a point Voydanoff sensibly counsels) but also to all those people who don't reside in a family.

Remedying the "Problem"

Scratch just slightly beneath the surface of the regression coefficients and the other scientific armamentaria common to this research and you'll usually find a feminist at work—a feminist in the sense that she or he believes that most gender-related differences in the division of labor or the allocation of resources are undesirable, to be replaced by a more egalitarian order. (I like to think that I'm not exempt from this characterization.) A motivating impetus to this research, then, is to document the sense of "problem" defined by this ideology—e.g., the greater burden for housework borne by wives than husbands or the greater obstacle that family responsibilities impose on the career development of women than men.

My concern is not with the content of the ideology or even the desirability of value-driven research. Yet I do think that the ideological consensus in this field has created its own analytical blindspots. In particular, inequality is too readily interpreted as a social problem. The fact of the matter is that many women and men view the traditional, unequal division of domestic responsibilities as desirable or at least tolerable. It is perhaps possible to explain the persistence of this sentiment by referring to patriarchal ideology and practices, but we do little to understand the meanings people themselves attach to their lives by assuming that they express atavistic beliefs or that the quest for equality is a universal social solvent.

Often coupled with this broad feminist ideology is belief in the "need" for public and private policies that make it easier for families to accommodate the demands of their jobs and domestic lives. Thus, as family scholars become involved in the policy arena, it is fairly standard to hear their advocacy for such measures as government and employer-sponsored day care, flexitime, and more generous maternity leaves. As many others, I have promoted some of this "liberal/progressive" response, but candor should compel us to recognize that the link between research and prescription is quite tenuous.

For example, no one has accurately measured the demand for center care (many parents prefer care outside of centers) or show how its availability affects labor force participation. Moreover, no compelling research documents that center care has more positive effects than other care arrangements or is cost effective. In general, advocacy of care centers, especially on a subsidized basis, seems to reflect an ideological preference for a professional, systematically organized model of service delivery over market allocation.

Advocates of other policies on the liberal agenda must also guard against false advertising. The policies may seem humane and enjoy the support of workers, but as Voydanoff's review indicates, there's very little good evidence linking these policies to productivity (the necessary selling point to business) or to better family functioning.

To make our research relevant to policy, we need to go beyond documenting "problems" and systematically assess the impacts of initiatives designed to address them. At the same time debates about particular policies require a larger sense of social context. For that reason the challenge is to effectively synthesize and interpret what we know about American families.

REFERENCES

Becker, G. (1981). *A treatise on the family*. Cambridge, MA: Harvard.
Berk, S. F. (1985). *The gender factory*. New York: Plenum.
England, P., & Farkas, G. (1986). *Householders, employment, and gender: A social, economic, and demographic view*. New York: Aldine.
Kanter, R. (1977). *Work and family in the United States: A critical review and agenda for research and policy*. New York: Russell Sage.
Parsons, T., & Bales, R.F. (1955). *Family socialization and interaction process*. New York: Free Press.
Ross, C. (1987). The division of labor at home. *Social Forces, 65*, 816-833.
Spitze, G. (1988). Women's employment and family relations: A review. *Journal of Marriage and the Family, 50*, 595-618.

Re-Thinking the Connections Among "Work" and "Family" and Well-Being: A Model for Investigating Employment and Family Work Contexts

Marsha Kline
Philip A. Cowan
Department of Psychology
University of California, Berkeley, CA 94720

Researchers interested in the connection between employment and well-being treat families as shadowy organizations that somehow increase or decrease job stress and satisfaction. Family researchers tend to be similarly undifferentiated about the impact of employment conditions and patterns mediating the links between family work and individual, marital, and parental well-being. In this paper we propose a heuristic "multiple regression" model to describe how employment and family environments operate jointly to affect different indices of well-being, and we summarize, selectively, some of the research supporting the need for this model. We suggest that investigators: (a) avoid single unidimensional measures of well-being and adopt multiple measures reflecting individual, couple, parent-child and job domains; (b) consider work in both job and family contexts; (c) search for mechanisms to explain how work and well-being are interconnected; and (d) adopt a longitudinal perspective to describe dynamic transactional sequences in which work and well-being affect each other. In our four-step multiple regression model, well-being is considered to be a product of: (Step 1) involvement in employment and family work; (Step 2) moderator variables such as the meaning of work to the worker, couple relationship patterns and qualities, gender, and stage of life; (Step 3) interactions among variables; and (Step 4) prior levels of well-being (that is, well-being influences work which influences well-being over time). The goal of this paper is to promote studies by Industrial/ Organizational psychology and family researchers in which the joint impact of both employment and family work is viewed with complexity appropriate to the reality of individual and family life.

Authors' Notes: The authors' work on this paper was supported in part by grant R01-MH31109 from the National Institute of Mental Health. We would like to thank Sheldon Zedeck, Christina Maslach, and Carolyn Pape Cowan for their helpful comments on an earlier draft.

A widely produced poster depicts a map of the United States as seen by the inhabitants of Manhattan. According to this map, beyond the familiar New York skyline Easterners view the rest of the country as a wasteland terminating abruptly at the Pacific Ocean. Retaliatory maps from the Western perspective portray an enticing California coastline, with very little of interest between the Sierras and the Atlantic Ocean. The expanding research literatures on "work" and "family" suffer from similarly skewed vantage points.

From the frame of reference of researchers interested in employment, families are vaguely described organizations that sometimes produce job stress in employees (Bhagat, McQuaid, Lindholm, & Segovis, 1985; Cooke & Rousseau, 1983; Cooper, 1983; Hendrix, Ovalle, & Troxler, 1985; Martin & Schermerhorn, 1983). Or families may buffer work stress (Bhagat, 1983; Etzion, 1984; Seers, McGee, Serey, & Green, 1983). All that is usually recorded about the family life of employees is whether or not they are married and have children. We know very little about the quality of the workers' marriage, the joys and stresses in their relationships with their children, or their experiences of tension resulting from the complex demands of home life.

Family researchers show comparable disregard for the details of men's and women's job life. In most family studies, the variables used to represent job or career involvement are single indices describing whether mothers or fathers are employed, the extent of their employment (full- or part-time), or the number of hours they spend at the workplace. We rarely have data about the kind of job, the flexibility of working conditions, or the individual's perception of the broader relevance of work within his or her life.

Studies from the employment or family perspectives, like maps drawn from the viewpoints of inhabitants from particular regions, show one domain occupying the foreground, while the other is represented only in sketchy outline. The questions we raise in this review paper revolve around how employment and family patterns operate jointly to affect well-being. Past studies investigate whether working outside the home has a positive or negative connection to various aspects of women's well-being—their self-esteem, marital satisfaction, or parenting stress. Conversely, researchers ask whether being married, having a child, or experiencing family distress have a negative or positive bearing on individuals' job performance and satisfaction. In most of the recent empirical studies, even those that include data from both domains, we have almost no information about the mechanisms by which employment and family factors combine to influence men's and women's feelings of well-being at home and at the workplace.

Different kinds of models can be used to describe how work in family and employment contexts affects well-being. The simple, almost obvious assumption providing the focus for this paper is that conditions of family work and employment work interact. What happens at home alters the impact of the workplace, and what happens on the job alters the impact of work in the family setting. The question that we will explore in some detail is: how should we conceptualize this interaction? We are aware that simple bidirectional interaction models based on data obtained at one point in time can be too static, and may not accurately reflect the dynamic, transactional, phasic nature of the processes connecting the two domains (Zedeck, 1987). Our suggested strategy is to formulate a static interactional model first, and to expand it with a longitudinal approach, tracing how family events and employment events influence each other over time.

In addition to the difficulty of bridging disparate research traditions, the relative lack of system-oriented research linking family and employment appears to be due, in part, to an absence of models capable of integrating findings from *within* industrial and family perspectives. We will argue that understanding the joint impact of employment and family life on well-being requires a reformulation of the problem. Toward this end, we highlight four conceptual and methodological issues which, we believe, will begin to clarify the connections between employment and family life. After presenting these issues, we offer a four-step model with a selective review of research indicating that variables located within each step, and their interactions across steps, combine to help us understand how work in both employment and family life is related to well-being.

The conclusions of our review, then, are not derived solely by generalizing from the results of existing studies. Rather, we attempt to design a conceptual map of the territory that may help to explain some of the confusions and contradictions in the current literature. Our goal in organizing and critiquing past research is to describe pathways toward more fruitful exploration of the connections among employed work, family work, and well-being.

The Need for Differentiated, Multidomain Measures of Well-Being

Well-being is usually defined by satisfaction and effective functioning in major areas or domains of one's life. Job satisfactions and life satisfactions have been examined by researchers as primary contributors to perceived quality of life (well-being) for the worker population (Near, Rice, & Hunt, 1980; Orpen, 1978; Payton-Miyazaki, & Brayfield, 1976). Unfortunately, in our view, life satisfaction has usually been measured as a global index in which positives and negatives from many areas are simply summed to produce a single univariate dimension. Our first proposal for future research is that *well-being should be investigated in a more differentiated fashion that takes into account the domains in which it is experienced.*

There is evidence that individual, couple, parent-child, and employment domains are primary contributors to family members' well-being and that each contributes a unique portion of variance in the outcome (Baruch & Barnett, 1987; Cowan, Cowan, Heming, Garrett, Coysh, Curtis-Boles, & Boles, 1985; Goysh, 1984). Representative indicators of well-being in each domain include: (a) self-esteem (Andrews & Withey, 1974, 1976; Schmitt & Bedeian, 1982); (b) marital satisfaction; (c) parenting satisfaction; and (d) job satisfaction (Chacko, 1983; Near, Smith, Rice, & Hunt, 1984; Martin & Schermerhorn, 1983).

Although measures of well-being in different domains tend to be correlated (Cowan & Cowan, 1988a), there are good arguments for considering each domain separately. Arrangements of family or employment work may have different effects on each index of well-being. The strength as well as the direction of the connections between work and well-being vary from one domain to another. For example, high demands with rigid timetables at the office may have positive effects on an employee's self-esteem ("I'm a very important person") but negative effects on his or her marital relationship or enjoyment of parenting ("My wife and kids don't know me anymore"). Another example: visions of oneself as parent and spouse may lead to decisions about paid employment that increase well-being at home but decrease satisfaction and effectiveness on the job.

The Environmental Context of Work

It is necessary to reconceptualize the "work-family" polarity. Researchers and popular writers persist in contrasting work and family as if there were no work involved in family life and no important, primary relationships where one is employed. In line with Zedeck's (1987) analysis, *we propose a model of the individual in context, in which the place of employment and the home are environments that jointly affect the development of job satisfaction and of individual, marital, and parental well-being.*

Mechanisms Moderating the Connection Between Work and Well-Being

Another central characteristic of the interaction model we propose is *a concern for moving beyond validation of the global hypothesis that employment and family work are strongly related, to investigations of how they are connected.* The information that dual-earner partners have higher marital satisfaction than single-earner spouses (Fox & Hesse-Biber, 1984; Moen, 1982; Simpson & England, 1981) does not explain the processes or mechanisms creating the association. Although there are many moderators that influence the connections between work and well-being, we have singled out four with which to begin an exploration of how the connections are formed. These moderators represent primary internal, interpersonal, and biological/socialization[1] processes that are central to individual adaptation.

One neglected variable that moderates the impact of work on well-being is the psychological meaning that individuals assign to work both inside and outside the home. Paying attention to the meaning of work from the worker's perspective recognizes that each person's unique vantage point and biases are an important initial referent from which to examine their work choices and well-being. Workers comprise a diverse group; one person's challenge may be another person's stress. Variables that have been used repeatedly in the organizational literature to define the meaning of work include career salience, work values, and the amount of discretionary time spent on job-related matters (MOW International Research Team, 1987; Sekaran, 1983).

Researchers tend to study men's and women's work patterns separately, even when both spouses are included in their samples. This approach misses a second potentially important moderator of the connections between work and well-being—the couple relationship. In addition to the fact that the couple's *pattern* of work choices affects each partner's well-being, we will show that the *quality* of the couple relationship also has a direct effect on how men and women feel about each major aspect of their life. For example, the effect of a young mother's employment hours and conditions on her self-esteem and her job satisfaction may depend on the pattern of her own and her husband's career involvement and the quality of his psychological support for her working outside the home.

Gender is a third variable shaping the links between work and well-being. Biological and socialization effects operate together to produce important differences between men and women—differences that affect each individual and his or her relationships. Employment researchers tend to focus only on men, or to combine samples without analyzing for gender differences in mean trends or correlational patterns. Family investigators more often focus on women's employment choices as the pivotal influence on the quality of family life. We urge a concerted, systematic effort to describe similarities and differences between men and women in how work and well-being are connected; we need to understand how gender moderates these connections in family and employment contexts.

A fourth moderating influence of work on well-being is the life stage of the individual and family. Life stage is a shorthand designation for an individual's or family's position in the life cycle as determined by age and normative or non-normative life events (entering the work world, marrying, becoming parents, divorcing, retiring). Although a few studies of employment have focused on women at a particular life stage such as mothers with preschool or adolescent children (e.g., Gold & Andres, 1978a, 1978b), researchers have remained remarkably unconcerned with systematic exploration of work patterns across the life cycle.

Adopting a Longitudinal Perspective

Almost all studies that examine the impact of employment on individual or relationship well-being are conducted at a single point in time. For example, studies reporting that women who are employed outside the home have higher self-esteem than women who are full-time housewives (Haw, 1982; Pistrang, 1984) are interpreted as supporting the hypothesis that employment has beneficial effects on women. Given the single-time assessment design, however, it is equally plausible to interpret the data as showing that women with higher self-esteem are more motivated to seek employment outside the home.

Longitudinal research is necessary to establish antecedent-consequent sequences in the work-well-being connection and to turn static interactional models into dynamic transactional models. Only by following individuals and families over time can we describe the pathways by which family members move in and out of feelings of well-being in different domains of their life.

In sum, crucial conceptual issues to be addressed in our proposed model of employment and family well-being begin with: (1) a more differentiated assessment of well-being; (2) a simultaneous consideration of work in both job and family environments; (3) an emphasis on mechanisms and moderators that affect the connections between work and well-being; and (4) designs that encompass longitudinal assessments of husbands and wives in different life cycle phases and transitional periods. Our model is schematically represented in Figure 1. In essence, it proposes a "multiple regression" approach. At Step 1, simple correlations between well-being and conditions of work involvement in both family and employment settings are affected by Step 2 moderators such as 2a) meanings of work to the individuals, 2b) the pattern of spouses' work arrangements and the quality of the couple relationship, 2c) gender, and 2d) the life stage of the individual and/or the phase of family life. We have not included all the variables that could possibly influence employment-family connections (e.g., a test of the model should control for subjects' SES) but we have tried to select important, already-known correlates of well-being to be examined in concert.

The model has two additional steps. It seems very likely to us that

---

[1] *The third and fourth moderators to be discussed, gender and life stage, are determined by biological realities as well as cultural expectations; it is not important for present purposes that we distinguish the contributions of each.*

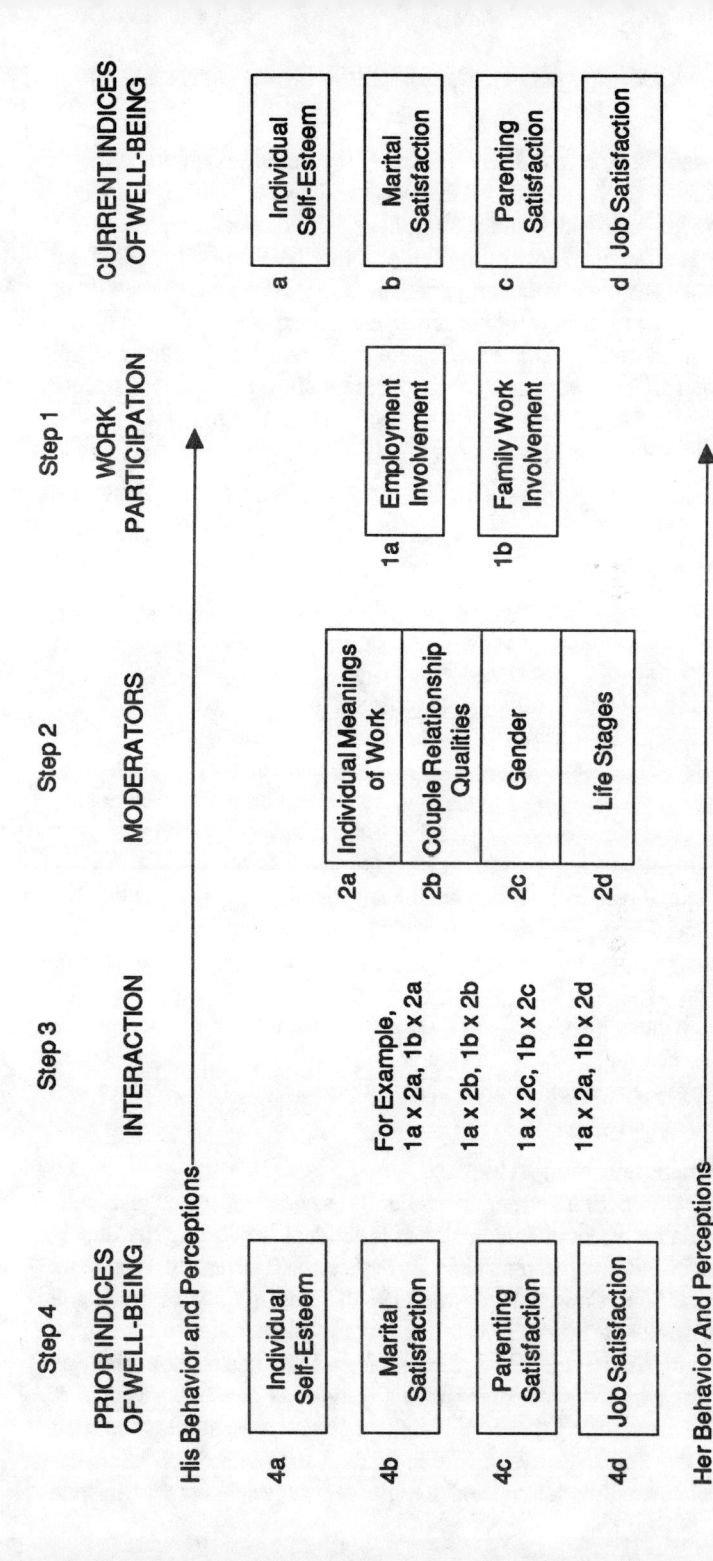

Step 4	Step 3	Step 2	Step 1	
PRIOR INDICES OF WELL-BEING	INTERACTION	MODERATORS	WORK PARTICIPATION	CURRENT INDICES OF WELL-BEING

His Behavior and Perceptions →

4a	Individual Self-Esteem	2a Individual Meanings of Work	1a Employment Involvement	a Individual Self-Esteem
4b	Marital Satisfaction	2b Couple Relationship Qualities	1b Family Work Involvement	b Marital Satisfaction
4c	Parenting Satisfaction	2c Gender		c Parenting Satisfaction
4d	Job Satisfaction	2d Life Stages		d Job Satisfaction

Interaction examples: For Example, 1a x 2a, 1b x 2a; 1a x 2b, 1b x 2b; 1a x 2c, 1b x 2c; 1a x 2a, 1b x 2d

Her Behavior And Perceptions →

FIGURE 1 A Proposed Model of Work and Well-Being with Moderators and Interaction Variables

Steps 1 and 2a, b, c, and d will interact (Step 3). For example, research designs and analyses are needed to determine how the meanings of work, different for men and women, may have important consequences for couples at different points in the life of a family. Finally, in Step 4 we suggest that the longitudinal properties of the model must take account of the fact that well-being is both a dependent and an independent variable. How work choices affect later well-being depends in part on how earlier well-being affected work choices. In the remaining sections of this paper we present evidence consistent with each step of our proposed model, with suggestions for further studies to fill in some important gaps in existing research.

STEP 1:
DIRECT LINKS BETWEEN WORK AND WELL-BEING

At its most descriptive level, work involvement refers to whether and how much time the person is employed or participates in family tasks, or what proportion of the work is done by each spouse. A more psychological measure of work involvement would be the salience of work to the individual, and how much investment he or she brings to family or employment tasks. Unfortunately, involvement has usually been assessed as a single global category or index, without attention to the nature of the working conditions, or to the fact that different aspects of employment and family settings elicit different levels of involvement.

Simple, direct correlations have been found by many investigators between well-being and involvement in employment or family work. Some attention has been paid to the cumulative or interactive impact of work in the two settings (e.g., the concept of role strain, Goode, 1960), but most researchers have conducted separate examinations of the correlations between employment or family work and the various aspects of well-being—self-esteem, marital satisfaction, parenting satisfaction, and job satisfaction.

Employment and Well-Being

Self-esteem. Employment and family researchers often use self-esteem as a representative indicator of individual well-being. Its importance lies in its demonstrated links with depression (Harter, 1984), general life satisfaction (Cowan & Cowan, 1988b), and quality of work life (Levine, Taylor, & Davis, 1984).

Although individual self-esteem has been evaluated for both men and women in studies of job environments (Levine et al., 1984; Martin & Schermerhorn, 1983; Schmitt & Bedelian, 1982), most studies focusing on employment with an eye toward individual and family well-being examine only the wife's self-esteem. Results generally suggest that, in spite of difficulties arising from increased role demands, wives and mothers derive benefits in self-esteem from working outside the home (Haw, 1982; Pistrang, 1984). Studies of men's employment and self-esteem have emphasized job competence and performance (e.g., Korman, 1974) rather than involvement. Available studies suggest that neither the quantity of occupational involvement (Keith, Goudy, & Powers, 1981) nor career salience (Sekaran, 1982) account for much of the variance in how men feel about themselves and their lives.

Marital satisfaction. Studies of employment and marital satisfaction have yielded less consistent findings than studies of self-esteem. Although researchers initially found the wife's employment to be associated with couple dissatisfaction (see Yogev, 1982, for a review), this conclusion has been questioned by studies using more sophisticated research designs. Recent studies indicate either no differences in marital happiness between single-earner and dual-earner families (see Moore, Spain, & Bianchi, 1984; Piotrkowski & Crits-Christoph, 1981), or higher marital satisfaction among dual-earner spouses (Simpson & England, 1981; Fox & Hesse-Biber, 1984; Moen, 1982). Conclusions about marital satisfaction from studies of men's employment are equally contradictory. Some investigators found no connection between men's employment time and marital satisfaction (Barling, 1984; Clark, Nye, & Gecas, 1978). Others found a link between greater employment time and marital unhappiness or increased work-family conflicts (Hoffman, 1984; Ridley, 1973).

Parenting satisfaction. In contrast with their emphasis on marital *satisfaction,* researchers focus on the *responsibilities* rather than the satisfactions of parenthood. The majority of studies focusing on work and parenting explore the effects of maternal employment on child development (Pistrang, 1984) or emphasize the impact of maternal role conflicts on parenting competence (Berheide, 1984). Yet, individual and family well-being may stem as much from parents' enjoyment of children as from their competence or conflicts in raising them.

In the few available studies, it appears that research on parenting resembles the self-esteem and marital research in its emphasis on *mothers'* employment. Mothers who work outside the home tend to have more positive parenting attitudes than those who are not employed (Hoffman, 1984), especially when they work part-time (Hoffman & Nye, 1974). In studies of families with nursery school and adolescent children conducted by Gold and her colleagues, couples with employed mothers expressed more satisfaction with the mothers' parenting role, and had lower child rejection scores, than couples with non-employed wives (Gold & Andres, 1978a, 1978b). By contrast, Bird and Bird (1984) reported equally high satisfaction with family roles for families with male-earner, dual-earner, and dual-career couples. However, the Birds' study combined marital and parenting satisfactions into one satisfaction measure; future researchers would do well to examine them separately. Krause's (1984) finding that working outside the home reduces marital stress but not parental stress for wives could be extended to investigate comparable effects of women's employment on marital versus parental satisfactions. Surprisingly, research on parenting rarely acknowledges the possibility that the age of the child or life stage of the parent may have a strong impact on each parent's satisfaction in the parenting role (see Step 2d and Step 3).

Job satisfaction. In industrial-organizational research, family contributions to job satisfaction are usually summarized by demographic data indicating only whether the subject is married or has children (e.g., Martin & Hanson, 1985; Nieva, 1984; Shaw, 1985). For example, it has been noted that married people report higher job satisfaction than unmarried people (Bersoff & Crosby, 1984).

Research on employment and job satisfaction from the family perspective has focused on whether men and women have jobs, how many hours each partner works, and whether the attempt to hold down a job and raise a family creates individual or marital stress (Rapoport & Rapoport, 1977). Family researchers tend to ignore each partner's enjoyment of work outside the family and its role as a buffer of stress or a source of social support. As family researchers ourselves, we cannot emphasize too strongly the point that a more differentiated picture of employed work, including type of job and working conditions, is essential to the understanding of job satisfaction and all of the other indices of individual and family well-being. For example, men in high-status jobs tend to show high levels of job satisfaction, but lower levels of satisfaction with marital and family life (Piotrkowski, Rapoport, & Rapoport, 1987). Moreover, satisfaction with intrinsic as compared with extrinsic aspects of the job may have different implications for family life. Only when we recognize that job satisfaction is multidimensional will it be possible to describe accurately the variables to which it is related.

The research summarized thus far certainly describes many simple correlations between employment and well-being, but there are many conflicting findings, and differences from one index of well-being to another. Our review of the research, reflected in the schematic model (Figure 1), suggests that *understanding the effects of involvement in paid work requires the simultaneous consideration of four or more aspects of well-being—individual, marital, parenting, and job satisfaction.*

Family Work and Well-Being

We will not provide an account of direct links between family work and each aspect of well-being as we have for employment research. Many fewer studies of this topic have been published. Moreover, the "who does what?" of household and childcare work is so inherently related to gender roles and expectations of husbands and wives that we will discuss family work primarily in Steps 2b and 2c of our model when we focus on couple relationships and gender as moderators of work-well-being connections. Here, we limit our presentation to a few general comments.

Like studies of employment, family-oriented research often emphasizes the quantity of parents' involvement in family work rather than the quality of their experiences. Studies document couples' division of household and childcare tasks (see Piotrkowski & Repetti, 1984; Pleck, 1985; Stein, 1984; Szinovacz, 1984) often using a single index of how equally or unequally partners share the labor of family life. Researchers generally assume that traditional female-centered family role arrangements are detrimental to women's well-being (e.g., Rossi, 1968). However, recent data suggest that well-being is attributable more to each partner's *satisfaction* with how family labor is divided than to the actual balance between his and her involvement in family tasks (Cowan & Cowan, 1988b).

Since families, like companies, are organizations (Zedeck, 1987), it is important to investigate the "organizational climate" in which family work occurs if we are to understand how it affects well-being both inside and outside the home. Just as some aspects of employment are more satisfying than others, household chores, decision-making, and childcare at home contribute differentially to well-being (Cowan & Cowan, 1988b), and the connection varies for different indicators (Kline, in preparation).

So far we have discussed well-being as if each of the major indices operates independently, but there is evidence that satisfaction or dissatisfaction generalizes across domains. For example, studies of the transition to parenthood indicate that individual and marital well-being predict both fathers' and mothers' parenting behavior and satisfaction (Cowan & Cowan, 1987; Grossman, Eichler, & Winickoff, 1980; Heinicke, 1984). Also, there may be "spillover" between marital dysfunction and job dissatisfaction (Bailyn, 1970; Ridley, 1973). *Research is urgently needed to identify situations in which work has independent effects on well-being, and situations in which a "domino effect" starts in one domain and spreads to every aspect of well-being.*

In sum, studies of employment and family work, and their simple correlations with well-being reveal a variety of trends, with some results flatly contradicting others. Employed wives seem to reap the most consistent benefits in self-esteem, but linkages between employment and marital, parenting, job, and family role satisfaction for men and women are far less clearly established. The remaining sections of this paper explore our hypothesis that *inconsistencies among studies may be attributable to the fact that important moderating variables have been ignored, and that these variables are affecting how work and well-being are connected.*

STEP 2: ESSENTIAL MODERATORS AND MECHANISMS

We have identified four of what is potentially a much longer list of variables to be considered in understanding the reciprocal relations between work and well-being at home and on the job: 2a) individually determined meanings of work; 2b) couple relationship quality and work patterns; 2c) gender effects; and 2d) life stage of the individual and family. That is, how an individual perceives his or her work, how he or she feels about a partner's work arrangements and how their combined schedules are negotiated, whether the individual is a man or a woman, and what phase of the life cycle the individual is facing may influence whether work at home or in the office has a positive or negative effect on well-being. Considering each of these variables, separately and together, will help us to move beyond the question of whether work has positive or negative effects, to the more differentiated question of what kinds of work have what kinds of effects on what kinds of people.

Step 2a: Individual Meanings of Work

Much of the work-family research literature relies on self-reports to provide measures of both independent and dependent variables, but researchers have not taken advantage of the strength of self-reports to provide a more differentiated view of what work means to the worker. It seems reasonable to assume that interpretations of work act as filters through which individuals interpret their experiences as stressful or enjoyable, appraisals that can affect their adaptation to work environments (Lazarus, Kanner, & Folkman, 1980).

Only a limited range of meanings of work has been explored systematically, primarily in connection with women's reasons for choosing to enter the labor force. Women differ in their view of employment as a voluntary choice or an economic necessity. In general, employed wives who prefer to work outside the home have higher self-esteem than their nonemployed counterparts (e.g., Moen, 1982; Ross, Mirowsky, & Huber, 1983). They also have happier marriages (e.g., Moore et al., 1984) and greater parenting satisfaction (Pistrang, 1984) than employed wives who do not desire to work outside the home. Stuckey and associates suggest that mothers who work outside the home, but prefer not to, express more negative feelings toward their preschool children (in Piotrkowski & Repetti, 1984).

The distinction between working "because I want to" and working "because I have to" is an important one in an individual's definition of the meaning of work. Economic necessity has been examined as a moderator of the link between employment and wives' well-being, and it shows different effects on different indices of well-being. Higher self-esteem (Sekaran, 1983; Warr & Parry, 1982), but lower marital satisfaction (Fuchs, 1971; Safilios-Rothschild, 1970) were found for employed wives who needed the income. It is plausible that the wives feel good about themselves for their contributions to needed family income, and angry at their husbands for having insufficient financial resources to allow them to stay home. Our model suggests that to clarify these findings it would be important to examine both self-esteem and marital satisfaction correlates in the same samples of women.

Research has barely begun to look beyond economic necessity to assess how other reasons for employment might affect wives' feelings about themselves and their lives. In one study, wives who returned to employed work after childbearing offered two kinds of reasons for their choice: (1) personal reasons such as boredom, depression, and exploration of new challenges; and (2) family reasons such as husbands' health problems, job insecurity, and financing private school education for the children. Some of the wives who returned to work achieved increased bargaining power with their husbands (Hood, 1983), a shift in marital power that could explain why they felt better about themselves but less satisfied with their marriage. Associations between paid work and well-being, then, are likely to vary with the meaning of the work and the type of well-being.

In contrast to women, men have not usually considered their involvement in paid work as a choice. Consequently, positive effects of employment on self-esteem or the marriage have been assumed and only the negative effects of unemployment have been investigated systematically. Researchers have shown great interest in the ramifications of men getting fired, laid off, or being unable to retain jobs (e.g., Elder, 1974). There is ample evidence that job loss has deleterious effects on men's self-evaluation and family relationships (see Hoffman, 1984; Liem & Liem, in press; Patterson, 1983; Voydanoff, 1984; Zvonkovic, Guss, & Ladd, 1988). We believe that studies of the meaning of work for men are long overdue.

There are some indications that men are not absolutely bound by the assumption that they will remain full time in the paid work force. A few are beginning to play a role as primary care parents while their wives work full time (Pruett, 1983; Radin, 1988; Russell, 1974). When these men re-enter the labor market, their reasons for why or where they work may color their sense of individual, marital, parental, and job-related well-being.

Reasons for choosing work are not the only important variables in determining what work means to individuals. What is lacking in research to date is attention to the more basic question of precisely what individuals consider to be "work" (does a toy inventor regard his or her job as "work?"). It is also necessary to pay more attention to the significance of particular work choices in individuals' lives—whether, for instance, they view a paid position as a temporary job or an important step along their career path.

Our examples have been drawn from employment because the meaning of family work for the individuals involved has yet to be examined. We know that family work allocations, and the processes by which decisions about family work are made have important repercussions for the marital relationship (Cowan & Cowan, 1988b). But family work tasks have been defined only by researchers. We have no indication of whether particular tasks are viewed as onerous or enjoyable by those involved in them (Does a father consider reading to his child as "work"?). *A central hypothesis derived from our discussion of Step 2a is that over and above variations in indices of well-being attributable to descriptions of home and employment work patterns, evaluations of the meaning of work will contribute significantly to our understanding of why some work patterns contribute positively to well-being while other work patterns contribute negatively.*

Step 2b: Work, Well-Being, and the Couple Relationship

Step 2b of our model moves away from an individual to a couple level of analysis. We are aware that marital satisfaction measures are limited to individual perspectives on the couple relationship, but we have noted above two truly dyadic effects of couplehood on the connection between work and well-being. First, the pattern of work choices is important because each partner's involvement or lack of involvement in work affects the other partner's well-being (Kline, in preparation). Second, the quality of the relationship, especially each partner's support for the other, affects how each evaluates satisfactions in the domains of family and employment life.

Employment, Well-Being, and the Couple.

(i). Pattern effects. Although Kessler and McRae (1982) found wives' employment associated with husbands' personal distress, other studies report no direct impact of wives' paid work on husband's individual well-being (Fendrich, 1984; Keith & Schafer, 1983, 1984). Studies of the impact of husbands' underemployment tend to find negative effects on wives' personal distress, though these effects are somewhat smaller and occur later than the effects on the husbands themselves (e.g., Liem & Liem, in press).

The marital well-being of husbands may be negatively affected when wives work outside the home (Burke & Weir, 1976), but more studies will be needed to establish whether this stereotype can be given the status of fact. Looking at husband-wife effects, Pond and Green (1983) and Barling (1984) found that wives are happier with marriage when their husbands are happier at work. By contrast, wives' employment satisfaction had no significant connection with their husbands' view of the marriage. Work may have different meanings for the men and women studied. For example, the men in Pond and Green's research described themselves as career-focused, while the women described themselves as having jobs rather than careers.

(ii). Relationship quality. The importance of couple relationship quality in understanding the work-well-being connection has been demonstrated from research that spans well-being domains and pertains predominantly to wife employment. In studies of marriage and work, relationship quality is assessed most frequently in terms of the support each partner shows the other. When husbands offer psychological and practical support to their employed wives, wives have higher self-esteem (Sekaran, 1983), marital happiness (Houseknecht & Macke, 1981; Moore et al., 1984; Staines, Pleck, Shepard, & O'Connor, 1978; Thomas, Albrecht, & White, 1984), family role satisfaction (Cowan & Cowan, 1987), and job satisfaction (Kline, in preparation). Wives are also happier with their marriages when their husbands give priority to family over employment (Bailyn, 1970; Dizard, 1968; Pleck, 1977). For example, Bailyn (1970) asked partners to rate themselves as more job-oriented or more family-oriented, and found that family-oriented wives were less happy with marriage when their husbands were job-oriented. Although wives' unhappiness was attributed to their husbands' emphasis on career rather than family, the orientation difference between husband and wife could also account for the wives' satisfaction, since partner differences in many areas of marriage are associated with conflict and declines in marital satisfaction (Cowan et al., 1985).

Like their wives, husbands benefit from having the support of their spouses (Dickie, 1987). Wives' support appears to help maintain marital satisfaction in the face of family strain associated with men's stressful job conditions (Belsky, Perry-Jenkins, & Crouter, 1985; Kelly & Voydanoff, 1985; Mortimer, 1980). While the role of "corporate wife," conjures a familiar image, how wives help to promote their spouses' careers, and the effects of the wives' behaviors on husbands have not been systematically explored. The effects may be specific to certain segments of society, since expectations for psychological support may be more prevalent in white-collar than in blue-collar marriages (Komarovsky, 1964).

Support is not the only important ingredient of marital well-being.

How partners communicate with each other—how they solve problems, resolve differences, and express feelings—is a strong determinant of how each will feel about the marriage, and how the partners behave toward each other in times of stress and relaxation (Cowan & Cowan, 1988a).

Family, work, well-being, and the couple. In the employment literature, working wives have been the focus of inquiry. In contrast, studies of family work have emphasized the relative participation, or lack of it, by the husband. In the Cowan and Cowan study of new parents (1988b), when fathers participated more in family work at 18 months postpartum, mothers had higher marital satisfaction and lower parenting stress. While the usual focus of these studies is on the impact of men's participation on the couple relationship, it is also the case that the quality of the marriage may affect the father's participation in family life. Men who were more satisfied with their marriage before the birth of a child were more likely to become directly involved in the tasks of child care two years later (Cowan & Cowan, 1987).

The question of support by one spouse for the other's work is considered as central in employment research, but has not been directly investigated by family researchers as far as we know. There is suggestive evidence in Coysh's dissertation (1983) that husbands who believed that their wives thought them competent as parents were more involved in their role as fathers. It seems to us that the issue of support of one spouse by another is as important in the area of family work as it is in the area of employment.

Following the literature, we have been discussing couple relationship effects on employment and family work separately, but there has been increasing interest in the connections between the two domains. In some studies, the extent of family work that husbands are doing appears to be unaffected by *whether* their wives are working outside the home (Fox & Nickols, 1983; Nickols & Metzen, 1982). In other studies, father involvement in childcare was influenced by couple employment *conditions*. Husbands were more involved in the daily tasks of looking after their children when they were employed fewer hours than other men and their wives were employed more hours than other women (Barnett & Baruch, 1988; Cowan & Cowan, 1987). Resolution of the differences between studies will probably require greater attention to the stage of family life at which the data are gathered (Step 2d).

One important question receiving relatively little research attention is how each spouse's job affects his or her partner's satisfaction with family roles, and how family responsibilities affect job satisfaction. Her employment may contribute to or detract from his satisfaction with parenting or family roles. For example, if her job involvement leads him to become more flexible in his hours so that he can spend more time with their child, he might find that his enjoyment of parenting increases. However, his job satisfaction might decrease.

The examples we have given suggest two general propositions. *First, when two individuals are involved in an intimate relationship, the combined pattern of their work choices, stresses, and satisfactions will explain variations in each partner's well-being. Second, the processes or transactions by which partners convey a sense of support for the other's job and family work will affect both individual and marital adaptation.*

Step 2c: Gender Differences

It is virtually impossible to draw general conclusions about work or about well-being without specifying whether a particular work role is occupied by a man or a woman. This unsurprising fact has not been given the attention it deserves in studies of employment, except in the implicit choices made by researchers to ask some questions only of women (how do you balance the tasks of job and childcare?) and others only of men (how is unemployment affecting you?). We see two important and quite different effects of gender on the results we have been discussing. First, there are widespread "main effects" at each step of our model, resulting from differences between men's and women's average scores or behaviors. Second, there are "moderator effects" resulting from the fact that gender appears to affect the patterns of correlations between work (e.g., involvement) and well-being.

Main effects. There are consistent indications of gender differences in levels of well-being. For example, self-esteem, especially when it is measured as a discrepancy between actual and ideal self-descriptions, tends to be higher for men than for women (Gough, Fioravanti, & Lazzari, 1982; Rossi, 1968). Sex differences in marital satisfaction may not be as widespread, but there is evidence in this domain, as well, that men may be more satisfied than women (see Spanier & Lewis, 1980).

Discrepancies also exist in satisfaction with the division of labor in the home. Again husbands are more satisfied than their wives (Cowan & Cowan, 1988b). These findings in which women show less satisfaction may be interpreted in a number of ways. Perhaps women are more honest in response to questionnaires and interviews than men. Perhaps they are more differentiated, noting discrepancies that men gloss over. Or, women may be reacting understandably to the reality of arrangements in both employment and family life that still favor men (Stafford, Backman, & Dibona, 1977; Szinovacs, 1984). However, not all gender differences favor men; wives have higher job satisfaction than their husbands (Burden &Googins, 1987). These gender differences in well-being as an "outcome" measure must be controlled for, or at the very least considered in interpretations of findings. Otherwise, there is a risk of obscuring real differences in the effects of work patterns in men and women.

In addition to sex differences in well-being, there are ubiquitous sex differences in patterns of work. Women's increasing participation in the paid work force is unreciprocated by men's involvement in the tasks of maintaining a home and family (Rapoport, Rapoport, & Streilitz, 1977). Thus, women are still doing the majority of housework and childcare in this country, and in many other countries as well (Pleck, 1985), despite the fact that the disparity between husbands' and wives' involvement in family tasks may be decreasing (Pleck, 1981). Women are also at a disadvantage at the office, where they have fewer promotion opportunities and earn only 60% as much as their male colleagues (Brown, Moon, & Zoloth, 1980; Lloyd & Niemi, 1980; Treiman & Hartmann, 1981). We have also suggested that there may be sex differences in the meaning of work, and in the reasons men and women make the choices they do. And within the couple relationship, men's work situations appear to be linked with women's well-being rather than the other way around (Boles, 1984; Pond & Green, 1983).

Moderator effects. Here we go beyond gender differences in average levels of the independent and dependent variables, to explore the possibility that gender affects the direction and magnitude of the correlations between work and well-being. As noted above, there are wide discrepancies between a pervasive egalitarian ideology and the actuality of family role arrangements and employment conditions for men and women. The fact that the burden of disappointed expectations falls unequally on men and women leads us to expect different patterns of connection between work and well-being for husbands and wives. The same conditions that place women's well-being at risk may enhance men's positive sense of themselves and their lives (Bernard, 1981; Rossi, 1968).

"Studies that have correlated measures of men's job and family satisfaction demonstrate consistently positive—if modest—associations (Rice, Near, & Hunt, 1980)....Studies of women's job satisfaction and marital solidarity have resulted in no clear pattern of findings" (Piotrkowski et al., 1987, pp. 266-267). For wives, job satisfaction is more consistently related to satisfaction with child-related rather than marital aspects of family life. The marital relationship may be less sensitive to wives' than to husbands' job satisfaction (Kemper & Reichler, 1976; Piotrkowski & Crits-Christoph, 1981). Thus, as our model suggests, the connections between employment and well-being vary for different indices of well-being depending upon whether men or women are being studied.

There is also evidence that patterns of *family* work and marital satisfaction have differential connections for each spouse. At 18 months after the birth of a first child, wives' marital happiness was highly correlated with husbands' participation in childcare tasks. But correlations between marital satisfaction and family work participation were not significant for the husbands (Cowan & Cowan, 1988b). In another study that considered involvement in both employment and household chores, more total work time was associated with higher marital adjustment for husbands and lower marital adjustment for wives (Pleck, 1981). This finding underscores the importance of gender differences in work patterns as moderators of men's and women's well-being. His total work time is likely to be represented by more hours of employment and her total work time by more chores in the home.

Given that there are gender differences in well-being, employment and family work (main effects), and in the correlations between work and well-being (moderator effects), our model suggests that *every study of employment and well-being must include a male-female comparative context*. We realize that some of the differences between men's and women's employment and family roles are so large that it will not be possible to provide matched comparison groups in each study. For example, because of markedly unequal participation in family work, the impact of flextime employment poses a qualitatively different issue for men and women (Ronen, 1981). Nevertheless, the impact of flextime must be considered in light of this difference. It cannot be ignored in the interests of simplifying our research designs and reports.

Step 2d: Individual and Family Life Stages

Step 2d in the model implicates individual and family life stages as critical moderators of the connection between work and individual well-being. It has been suggested that a woman's life stage relates to her personal satisfactions more than her age or the number of roles she manages simultaneously (Hall, 1975). Until recently, women's job activities and pressures declined at each stage of childrearing, only to increase again when they had older children. But even when women re-enter the labor force immediately after having children, the ingredients of well-being may change markedly over time. Similarly, it is unlikely that the connections between work conditions and well-being remain stable for men as they move from their initial career choices through the planning of their retirement.

Paid work probably changes in both salience and meaning at each stage of family life. Hood (1983) showed that women's age of re-entry into the work force after having children had implications for both spouses. A midlife "blooming" for wives coinciding with a midlife shift toward family priorities for husbands led, in some cases, to intensified marital problems. Couples with entrenched sex-role ideologies had a particularly difficult time adapting. Thus, meanings of work (2a)—different for men and women (2c)—may have different effects on the couple relationship (2b) at different points in the family life cycle (2d).

We are aware of very few systematic studies of employment or family work and well-being that examine the impact of life stages, or that follow individuals and families over time (Benin & Nienstadt, 1985; Hall, 1975). In this section, we will focus our examples on the transition to parenthood because it is a time of life that highlights dilemmas about the coordination of employment and family life. Longitudinal studies of the transition to parenthood indicate that a couple's division of labor tends to become more traditional (differentiated and gender specific) after the birth of a first child (Belsky, Lang, & Rovine, 1985; Cowan & Cowan, 1981; McHale & Huston, 1985). But there are different changes for men and women at different periods of the transition (Cowan & Cowan, 1988b). From late pregnancy to 6 months postpartum, men do more of some household tasks, such as shopping and meal preparation, while doing less of many others. From 6 to 18 months they increase their involvement in some aspects of childcare—though it never approaches an equal division with women's involvement (Pleck & Rustad, 1980).

In addition to the main effects of the life cycle on levels of work involvement and well-being, there are moderator effects described by the fact that connections between family work and well-being change systematically over time. Cowan and Cowan (1988b) found that in pregnancy there were no significant correlations, for men or women, between marital satisfaction or self-esteem and men's involvement in family tasks. For women, these correlations increased markedly at 6 months postpartum and again at 18 months postpartum. Women with higher self-esteem and marital satisfaction tended to have husbands who were more involved in family tasks. For men, the correlations between household and/or childcare involvement and well-being were statistically significant at 6 months postpartum, but the connections disappeared when their babies were 18 months old. Like the time-lapse representations of DNA in the formation of living cells, we find that life cycle changes strengthen some bonds while weakening other bonds between aspects of work and well-being. In this example we can also see that gender and life cycle effects interact (2c x 2d). We will discuss the implications of this kind of interaction effect in the following section of this paper.

Special circumstances of families with young children may lead to different effects of employment on well-being than those generally cited in the literature. As we noted above, although employed women generally have higher self-esteem than their nonemployed counterparts, part-time employment appears to be most beneficial for the self-esteem of mothers with young children (Booth, Johnson, & White, 1984; Cowan & Cowan, 1985; Keith & Schafer, 1984). Employment and marital satisfaction are also linked in ways that seem specific to early parenthood. A study conducted two decades ago found that, in contrast to other parent subgroups, couples with preschoolers were happier in their marriages if the wives did not choose employed work (Orden & Bradburn, 1969). Social values may have changed in our society; mothers with small children no longer work only out of necessity. Other findings also support the position that the presence of youngsters may strain a marriage due to the increased difficulty of handling the competing demands of employment and family work (Hill, 1981; Szinovacz, 1984). A connection has been cited between the presence of children under 6 years and work-family role strain (Kelly & Voydanoff, 1985), but the role strain has not been specifically linked to marital adjustment.

The importance of incorporating a family life cycle perspective in work and well-being research is underscored by evidence that mothers with young children report higher positive and negative spillover of family to work life than either fathers or mothers with older children report (Crouter, 1984). The direction of effects may depend on factors such as role strain, work hours, or the couple relationship—which are likely to be especially important moderators of well-being during the early years of family formation. For example, consider husbands' and wives' work hours in the context of the couple relationship. We can expect different outcomes for couples who each work 9-5 than for couples in which one partner is employed from 7-4 and the other partner works an evening shift. The first of these patterns may present more problems associated with care of the children, while the latter schedule could pose serious dilemmas for the marital relationship, and for the maintenance of intimacy and communication. Patterns associated with the well-being of individual young parents may not prove beneficial for the couple, and patterns that benefit the couple may place additional strain on one or both partners.

We have been focusing on the transition to parenthood, but the general points we are making suggest the need for two kinds of research at various phases of the life cycle. First, *it will be necessary to identify the life stages of subjects in studies of employment and family life, and not to combine them into heterogeneous samples. Second, within each life phase, it will be necessary to examine the special meanings of employment and family work, how they interact, and how the different life changes of men and women affect their relationship and in turn shape the nature of the connections between work and well-being.* Only with careful comparisons of work well-being connections at various life stages will we be able to determine when we can make general statements and when we must limit what we say to specific periods in the life of an individual or family.

The moderators in Step 2 (a,b, c, d) of this model begin to tease out some of the intraindividual, interpersonal, and societal influences on the direct effects of work on well-being that were examined in Step 1. Understanding consistent connections between work and well-being, and their variations, requires indentifying which moderators are operating in a given circumstance. Inclusion of variables representing individual (meanings of work), couple (relationship quality), and family (gender and life stage) levels of analysis adds depth and context to our knowledge of how work life affects behavior and satisfaction.

STEP 3: INTERACTIONS AMONG STEPS OF THE MODEL

The examples we have given in Steps 1 and 2 almost always suggest the possibility that well-being is a product of many variables operating at the same time. Within each step we need to pay more attention to the separate and joint effects of employment and family work, and to the possibility that each may be linked differently to different indices of well-being. So far, our between-step analysis of conceptual issues suggests that individual meanings of work, couple relationship work patterns and quality, gender, and life stage may each contribute unique variance in individual differences to *levels* of work involvement or levels of well being. In essence this moderator effect already signifies the presence of an interaction—for example, that high levels of work could have different effects depending on whether employment is seen as a job or a career.

But work meaning as a moderator may not function independently of the other moderator variables we have been discussing. Let us take the case of married women who work outside the home either because they want to or because they have to. Under conditions of high support from their spouse, marital satisfaction should remain high regardless of their reasons for working. If economic conditions dictate their choice of paid work, they may maintain a positive view of the marriage even if husbands want them to remain at home. The "worst case" should occur when they want to be employed, but their husbands are opposed. If our hypotheses are correct, we would see an interaction between 2a and 2b.

It is possible that the impact on the marriage of what work means and how supportive each spouse is would be different for men and women (2a x 2b x 2c). Furthermore, we know that the meaning of wives' employment to husbands changes with the age of the youngest child, such that men are increasingly supportive of their wives working outside the home as their children grow older (Eyland, Lapsley, & Mason, 1983). This fact may produce a simple main effect in level of marital satisfaction, or we may find that differences between spouses in the meaning of work have different effects for men and women at different family stages, depending on the existing level of couple communication or satisfaction with the marriage (2a x 2b x 2c x 2d).

These examples have focused only on one index of well-being, marital satisfaction. As we have been suggesting throughout this paper, there may be different interaction patterns for different indices of well-being (1 x 2a x 2b x 2c x 2d). The well-being of men and women in their parenting roles, for example, may bear the brunt of the struggles involved in balancing jobs, home-related work, and family relationships (Fischer, 1980; Rapoport et al., 1977).

In simple multiple regression equations, it is assumed that variables are additive. Interactive effects must be given a separate test, and this test would occur at Step 3 of our model. We are not claiming that all studies would reveal five-way interactions, or expecting that all moderator variables will be assessed in every study. Our model does suggest that reports of simpler studies should be aware of the limits of generalization of their findings until the potential interactions have been determined. The focus on interactions is necessary because it is clear that main effects models do not do justice to the complexity of the findings.

STEP 4:
PRIOR WELL-BEING IN LONGITUDINAL PERSPECTIVE

Finally, we must make clear that our emphasis on longitudinal studies is not simply addressed to the issue of examining changes in work and well-being at different family stages. Cross-sectional studies can certainly document life-cycle trends. Longitudinal studies become necessary in the determination of the direction of effects. Too often, single time assessments are interpreted as providing evidence of the effect of work on well-being when the causal influence may just as well occur in the opposite direction. In the multiple regression model we are proposing that the influence of earlier levels of well-being on subsequent outcomes must be factored into the well-being equation.

Having come this far with the multiple regression model, we should emphasize that we are using it as a heuristic to organize the conceptual connections among the variables that affect the links between work and well-being. Once we view findings from a longitudinal perspective, it becomes increasingly clear that the connections among work and family and well-being may involve more circular and dynamic processes than the linear multiple regression model implies. We offer Figure 1 as a first approximation to the models that will eventually emerge when employment and family researchers begin to take a more differentiated and integrated collaborative perspective on the problems that concern both camps.

SUMMARY AND CONCLUSIONS

Despite a growing consensus that one's employment and one's family are interrelated environments that jointly explain variations in individual well-being, facets of employment and family work have yet to be investigated in an integrated fashion. Past research examined disparate aspects of individual, couple, parental, and job well-being without assessing the overlaps among domains of family process. The result has been a unidimensional portrait of the individual, as sketchy in detail as the posters of New York and California drawn from similarly biased perspectives. Fleshing out what lies between requires a reformulation of "work" as activities occurring at home and on the job. It also mandates systematic exploration of the events and relationships in both environments that moderate the connections between work and well-being, and that explain differences between husbands and wives. In order to provide a comprehensive theory, we must first integrate personal and interpersonal perspectives so that spouses' activities, perceptions, and experiences over time can be understood in a family context. The steps in our model represent a first approximation of the complex picture that will ultimately emerge in the study of work and well-being.

We have proposed a model that makes the systematic assumption that activities and relationships in job and family environments are important, simultaneous contributors to well-being. Furthermore, the model examines multi-levels of well-being from the vantage point of several domains of life that contribute to general life satisfaction: individual, marital, parental, and job.

We find that well-being is closely tied to all of the components of the model. First, work events or conditions inside and outside the home, and the stresses associated with them, must be considered if we are to understand variations in well-being (Step 1). Next, several moderators can be included to begin differentiating work-well-being connections. The subjective meaning of work in people's lives must be accounted for in specific fashion, in order to determine people's motivations for seeking employment, and their personal goals and values with respect to their work environments (Step 2a). Furthermore, the couple relationship must be included in models of employment and family life: how each partner's job settings and goals influence the other partner's well-being, and how the relationship between the two partners affects the direct connections between work and well-being must be taken into consideration (Step 2b). Gender differences in normative social roles and meanings of work can contribute to our understanding of how employment influences individual adaptation (Step 2c). Individual and family life stage will also be connected to work and family environments and satisfactions over the course of the life cycle (Step 2d). None of the variables discussed will affect well-being in a vacuum. Therefore, interconnections are expected among all components of the model, including work settings and the meaning of work, couple relationships, gender, and family life stage (Step 3). Finally, using longitudinal designs to account for the levels of well-being each individual brought to a given situation may explain more about subsequent work decisions and outcomes, and their impact on personal adjustment (Step 4).

To advance empirical understanding in these directions, researchers must look beyond their own perspectives to fill in the details of the structure and meaning family members give to work from both the industrial/organizational and family-oriented vantage points. The challenge for the future is to clarify the benefits and costs involved in employment, housework, and childcare responsibilities that influence and are influenced by family outcomes. This information is eagerly awaited by mental health professionals, organizations, and by couples themselves.

REFERENCES

Andrews, F.A., & Withey, S.B. (1974). Developing measures of perceived life quality. *Social Indicators Research, 1,* 1-26.

Andrews, F.A., & Withey, S.B. (1976). *Social indicators of well-being in America: The development and measurement of perceptual indicators.* New York: Plenum.

Bailyn, L. (1970). Career and family orientation of husbands and wives in relation to marital happiness. *Human Relations, 23,* 97-113.

Barling, J. (1984). Effects of husbands' work experiences on wives' marital satisfaction. *Journal of Social Psychology, 124,* 219-225.

Barnett, R.C., & Baruch, G.K. (1988). Correlates of father's participation in family work. In P. Bronstein & C. Cowan (Eds.), *Fatherhood today: Men's changing role in the family.* New York: Wiley.

Baruch, G.K., & Barnett, R.C. (1987). Role quality and psychological well-being. In F.J. Crosby (Ed.), *Spouse, parent, worker: On gender and multiple roles.* New Haven, CT: Yale University Press.

Belsky, J., Lang, M.E., & Rovine, M. (1985). Stability and change in marriage across the transition to parenthood: A second study. *Journal of Marriage and the Family, 47,* 855-865.

Belsky, J., Perry-Jenkins, M., & Crouter, A.C. (1985). The work-family interface and marital change: Across the transition to parenthood. *Journal of Family Issues, 6,* 205-220.

Benin, M.H., & Nienstedt, B.C. (1985). Happiness in single- and dual-earner families: The effects of marital happiness, job satisfaction, and life cycle. *Journal of Marriage and the Family, 47,* 975-984.

Berheide, C.W. (1984). Women's work in the home: Seems like old times. *Marriage and Family Review, 7,* 37-55.

Bernard, J. (1981). The good provider role: Its rise and fall. *American Psychologist, 36,* 1-12.

Bersoff, D., & Crosby, F. (1984). Job satisfaction and family status. *Personality and Social Psychology Bulletin, 20,* 19-83.

Bhagat, R. (1983). Effects of stressful life events on individual performance and effectiveness and work adjustment processes within organizational settings: A research model. *Academy of Management Review, 8,* 660-671.

Bhagat, R., McQuaid, S., Lindholm, E., & Segovis, J. (1985). Total life stress: A multimethod validation of the construct and its effects on organizationally valued outcomes and withdrawal behaviors. *Journal of Applied Psychology, 70,* 202-214.

Bird, G.A., & Bird, G.W. (1984). Satisfaction in family, employment, and community roles. *Psychological Reports, 55,* 675-678.

Boles, A.J., III. (1984). *Predictors and correlates of marital satisfaction during the transition to parenthood.* Unpublished doctoral dissertation, University of California, Berkeley.

Booth, A., Johnson, D.R., & White, L. (1984). Women, outside employment, and marital instability, *American Journal of Sociology, 90,* 576-583.

Brown, R., Moon, M., & Zoloth, B. (1980). Occupational attainment and segregation by sex. *Industrial and Labor Relations Review, 33,* 506-517.

Burden, D.S., & Googins, B. (1987). *Boston University balancing job and homelife study: Managing work and family stress in corporations.* Boston University School of Social Work.

Burke, R.J., & Weir, T. (1976). Relationship of wives' employment status to husband, wife, and pair satisfaction. *Journal of Marriage and the Family, 38,* 279-287.

Chacko, T.I. (1983). Job and life satisfactions: A causal analysis of their relationship. *Academy of Management Journal, 26,* 163-169.

Clark, R.A., Nye, F.I., & Gecas, V. (1978). Work involvement and marital role performance. *Journal of Marriage and the Family, 40,* 9-22.

Cooke, R.A., & Rousseau, D.M. (1983). Relationship of life events and personal orientations to symptoms of personal strain. *Journal of Applied Psychology, 68,* 446-458.

Cooper, C.L. (1983). Identifying stressors at work: Recent research developments. *Journal of Psychosomatic Research, 27,* 369-376.

Cowan, C.P., & Cowan, P.A. (1981, April). *Couple role arrangements and satisfaction during family formation.* Paper presented at the meeting of the Society for Research in Child Development, Boston.

Cowan, C.P., & Cowan, P.A. (1985, April). *Parents' work patterns, marital and parent-child relationships, and early child development.* Paper presented at the meeting of the Society for Research in Child Development, Toronto.

Cowan, C.P., & Cowan, P.A. (1987). A preventive intervention for couples becoming parents. In D.F.Z. Boukydis (Ed.), *Research on support for parents and infants in the postnatal period.* Norwood, NJ: Ablex.

Cowan, C.P., & Cowan, P.A. (1988a). Changes in marriage during the transition to parenthood: Must we blame the baby? In G.Y. Michaels & W.A. Goldberg (Eds.), *The transition to parenthood: Current theory and research.* Cambridge: Cambridge University Press.

Cowan, C.P., & Cowan, P.A. (1988b). Who does what when partners become parents: Implications for men, women, and marriage. In M.B. Sussman & R. Palkovitz (Eds.), The transition to parenthood. *Marriage and Family Review, 12,* 105-132

Cowan, C.P., Cowan, P.A., Coie, L., & Coie, J.D. (1978). Becoming a family: The impact of a first child's birth on the couple's relationship. In W.B. Miller & L.F. Newman (Eds.), *The first child and family formation.* Chapel Hill, NC: Carolina Population Center.

Cowan, C. P., Cowan, P.A., Heming, G., Garrett, E., Coysh, W.S., Curtis-Boles,

H., & Boles, A. J. (1985). Transitions to parenthood: His, hers, & theirs. *Journal of Family Issues, 6*, 451-481.

Coysh, W. (1983). Men's role in caring for their children: Predictive and concurrent correlations of father involvement. Unpublished doctoral dissertation, University of California, Berkeley.

Crouter, A.C. (1984). Spillover from family to work: The neglected side of the work-family interface. *Human Relations, 37*, 425-442.

Dickie, J.R. (1987). Interrelationships within the mother-father-infant triad. In P.W. Berman & F.R. Pedersen (Eds.), *Men's transitions to parenthood: Longitudinal studies of early family experience.* Hillsdale, NJ: Erlbaum.

Dizard, J. (1968). *Social change in the family.* Chicago: University of Chicago Press.

Elder, G.H., Jr. (1974). *Children of the great depression.* Chicago: University of Chicago Press.

Etzion, D. (1984). Moderating effect of social support on the stress-burnout relationship. *Journal of Applied Psychology, 69*, 615-622.

Eyland, A., Lapsley, H., & Mason, C. (1983). The attitude of husbands to working wives. *Australian Journal of Social Issues, 18*, 282-289.

Fendrich, M. (1984). Wives' employment and husbands' distress: A meta-analysis and a replication. *Journal of Marriage and the Family, 46*, 871-879.

Fischer, K.W. (1980). A theory of cognitive development: The control and construction of hierarchies of skills. *Psychological Review (1987)*, 477-531.

Fox, K.D., & Nickols, S.Y. (1983). The time crunch: Wife's employment and family work. *Journal of Family Issues, 4*, 61-82.

Fox, M.F., & Hesse-Biber, S. (1984). Problems and strategies for dual-worker families. *Woman at work* (Ch. 8). Palo Alto, CA: Mayfield.

Fuchs, R. (1971). Different meanings of employment for women. *Human Relations, 24*, 495-499.

Gold, D., & Andres, D. (1978a). Developmental comparisons between adolescent children with employed and nonemployed mothers. *Merrill-Palmer Quarterly, 24*, 243-254.

Gold, D., & Andres, D. (1978b). Relations between maternal employment and development of nursery school children. *Canadian Journal of Behavioral Science, 10*, 116-129.

Goode, W.J. (1960). A theory of role strain. *American Sociological Review, 41*, 483-496.

Gough, H.G., Fioravanti, M., & Lazzari, R. (1982). Some implications of self versus ideal congruence on the revised adjective checklist. *Journal of Consulting Psychology, 44*, 1214-1220.

Grossman, F., Eichler, L., & Winickoff, S., et al. (1980). *Pregnancy, birth and parenthood.* San Francisco: Jossey-Bass.

Hall, D.T. (1975). Pressures from work, self, and home in the life stages of married women. *Journal of Vocational Behavior, 6*, 121-132.

Hall, R.H. (1986). *Dimensions of work.* Beverly Hills, CA: Sage.

Harter, S. (1984). Developmental perspectives on the self system. In N. P. Mussen (Ed.), *Handbook of Child Psychology.* New York: Wiley

Harvey, A.S. (1984). The context of discretionary activities. In M.D. Lee and R.N. Kanungo (Eds.), *Management of work and personal life: Problems and opportunities.* New York: Praeger.

Haw, M.A. (1982). Women, work and stress: A review and agenda for the future. *Journal of Health and Social Behavior, 23*, 132-144.

Heinicke, C. (1984). Impact of prebirth parent personality and marital functioning on family development: A framework and suggestions for further study. *Developmental Psychology, 20*, 1044-1053.

Hendrix, W.H., Ovalle, N.K., II, & Troxler, R.G. (1985). Behavioral and psychological consequences of stress and its antecedent factors. *Journal of Applied Psychology, 70*, 188-201.

Hill, M.S. (1981). Patterns of time use. Survey Research Center, University of Michigan (mimeo).

Hoffman, L.W. (1984). Work, family, and the socialization of the child. In R. Parke (Ed.), *Review of child development research* (Vol. 7: *The family*). Chicago: University of Chicago Press.

Hoffman, L.W., & Nye, F.I. (1974). *Working mothers*. San Francisco: Jossey-Bass.

Hood, J.C. (1983). *Becoming a two-job family*. New York: Praeger.

Houseknecht, S.K., & Macke, A.S. (1981). Combining marriage and career: The marital adjustment of professional women. *Journal of Marriage and the Family, 43,* 651-661.

Keith, P.M., & Schafer, R.B. (1983). Employment characteristics of both spouses and depression in two-job families. *Journal of Marriage and the Family, 45,* 877-884.

Keith, P.M., & Schafer, R.B. (1984). Role behavior and psychological well-being: A comparison of one-job and two-job families. *American Journal of Orthopsychiatry, 54,* 137-155.

Keith, P.M., Goudy, W.J., & Powers, E.A. (1981). Employment characteristics and psychological well-being in two-job families. *Psychological Reports, 49,* 975-978.

Kelly, R.F., & Voydanoff, P. (1985). Work/family strain among employed parents. *Family Relations, 34,* 367-374.

Kemper, T.D., & Reichler, M.L. (1976). Work integration, marital satisfaction, and conjugal power. *Human Relations, 29,* 929-944.

Kessler, R.C., & McRae, J.A., Jr. (1982). The effect of wives' employment on the mental health of married men and women. *American Sociological Review, 47,* 216-227.

Kline, M. (in preparation). *Employment, family work, and well-being among couples with preschoolers*. Doctoral dissertation, University of California, Berkeley.

Komarovsky, M. (1964). *Blue-collar marriage*. New York: Random House.

Korman, A.K. (1974). *The psychology of motivation*. Englewood Cliffs, NJ: Prentice-Hall.

Krause, N. (1984). Employment outside the home and women's psychological well-being. *Social Psychiatry, 19,* 41-48.

Lazarus, R.S., Kanner, A.D., & Folkman, S. (1980). Emotions: A cognitive-phenomenological analysis. In R. Plutchik & H. Kellerman (Eds), *Theories of emotion*. New York: Academic Press.

Levine, M.F., Taylor, J.C., & Davis, L.E. (1984). Defining quality of working life. *Human Relations, 37,* 81-104.

Liem, R., & Liem, J.H. (in press). The psychological effects of unemployment on workers and their families. In D. Dooley & R. Catalano (Eds.), Social costs of economic stress. *Journal of Social Issues*.

Lloyd, C., & Niemi, B. (1980). *The economics of sex differentials*. New York: Columbia University Press.

Martin, J.K., & Hanson, S.L. (1985). Sex, family wage-earning status, and satisfaction with work. *Work and Occupations, 12,* 91-109.

Martin, T.N., & Schermerhorn, J.R., Jr. (1983). Work and nonwork influences on health: A research agenda using inability to leave as a critical variable. *Academy of Management Review, 8,* 650-569.

McHale, S.M., & Huston, T.L. (1985, April). The transition to parenthood in parallel and companionate marriages. Paper presented at the meeting of the Society for Research in Child Development, Toronto.

Model, S. (1981). Housework by husbands: Determinants and implications. *Journal of Family Issues, 2,* 225-237.

Moen, P. (1982). The two-provider family: Problems and potentials. In M.E. Lamb (Ed.), *Non-traditional families: Parenting and child development*.

Hillsdale, NJ: Erlbaum.
Moore, K., Spain, D., & Bianchi, S. (1984). Working wives and mothers. *Marriage and Family Review, 7,* 77-98.
Mortimer, J.T. (1980). Occupation-family linkages as perceived by men in the early stages of professional and managerial careers. In *Research in the interweave of social roles: Men and women* (Vol. 1). Greenwich, CT: JAI.
MOW International Research Team (1987). *The meaning of working.* New York: Academic Press.
Near, J.P., Rice, R.W., & Hunt, R.G. (1980). The relationship between work and nonwork domains: A review of empirical research. *Academy of Management Review, 5,* 415-429.
Near, J.P., Smith, C.A., Rice, R.W., & Hunt, R.G. (1984). A comparison of work and nonwork predictors of life satisfaction. *Academy of Management Journal, 27,* 184-190.
Nickols, S.Y., & Metzen, E.J. (1982). Impact of wife's employment upon husband's housework. *Journal of Family Issues, 3,* 199-216.
Nieva, V.F. (1984). Work and family roles. In M.D. Lee & R.N. Kanungo (Eds.), *Management of work and personal life: Problems and opportunities.* New York: Praeger.
Orden, S.R., & Bradburn, N.M. (1969). Working wives and marriage happiness. *American Journal of Sociology, 74,* 392-407.
Orpen, C. (1978). Work and nonwork satisfaction: A causal-correlational analysis. *Journal of Applied Psychology, 63,* 530-532.
Patterson, G. (1983). Stress: A change agent for family process. In N. Garmezy & M. Rutter (Eds.), *Stress, coping, and development in children.* New York: McGraw-Hill.
Payton-Miyazaki, M., & Brayfield, A.H. (1976). The good job and the good life: Relation of characteristics of employment to general well-being. In A.D. Biderman & T.F. Drury (Eds.), *Measuring work quality of social reporting.* Beverly Hills, CA: Sage.
Piotrkowski, C.S., & Crits-Christoph, P. (1981). Women's jobs and family adjustment. *Journal of Family Issues, 2,* 126-147.
Piotrkowski, C.S., & Repetti, R.L. (1984). Dual-earner families. *Marriage and Family Review, 7,* 99-124.
Piotrkowski, C.S., Rapoport, R.N., & Rapoport, R. (1987). Families and work. In M.B. Sussman & S.K. Steinmetz (Eds.), *Handbook of marriage and the family.* New York: Plenum.
Pistrang, N. (1984). Women's work involvement and experience of new motherhood. *Journal of Marriage and the Family, 46,* 433-436.
Pleck, J.H. (1977). The work-family role system. *Social Problems, 24,* 417-427.
Pleck, J.H. (1981, August). *Changing patterns of work and family roles.* Paper presented at the meeting of the American Psychological Association, Los Angeles.
Pleck, J.H. (1985). *Working wives/working husbands.* Beverly Hills, CA: Sage.
Pleck, J.H., & Rustad, M. (1980). *Husbands' and wives' time in family work and paid work in the 1975-76 study of time use.* Wellesley, MA: Wellesley College Center for Research on Women.
Pond, S.B., & Green, S.B. (1983). The relationship between job and marriage satisfaction within and between spouses. *Journal of Occupational Behavior, 4,* 145-156.
Pruett, K.D. (1983, April). *Two-year followup of infants of primary nurturing fathers in intact families.* Paper presented to the World Congress in Infant Psychiatry, Cannes, France.
Radin, N. (1988). Primary caregiving fathers of long duration. In P. Bronstein & C.P. Cowan (Eds.), *Fatherhood today: Men's changing role in the family.* New York: Wiley.
Rapoport, R., & Rapoport, R.N. (1977). *Dual-career families re-examined.* New

York: Harper Colophon.

Rapoport, R., Rapoport, R.N., & Streilitz, A. (with Kew, S.) (1977). *Fathers, mothers, and society: Towards new alliances.* New York: Basic Books.

Rice, R.W., Near, J.P., & Hunt, R.G. (1980). The job-satisfaction/life-satisfaction relationship: A review of empirical research. *Basic and Applied Social Psychology, 1,* 37-64.

Ridley, C.A. (1973). Exploring the impact of work satisfaction and involvement on marital interaction when both partners are employed. *Journal of Marriage and the Family, 35,* 224-237.

Ronen, S. (1981). *Flexible working hours.* New York: McGraw-Hill.

Ross, C.E., Mirowsky, J., & Huber, J. (1983). Dividing work, sharing work, and in-between: Marriage patterns and depression. *American Sociological Review, 48,* 809-823.

Rossi, A. (1968). Transition to parenthood. *Journal of Marriage and the Family, 30,* 26-39.

Russell, C. (1974). Transition to parenthood: Problems and gratifications. *Journal of Marriage and the Family, 36,* 294-302.

Safilios-Rothschild, C. (1970). The influence of the wife's degree of work commitment upon some aspects of family organization and dynamics. *Journal of Marriage and the Family, 32,* 681-691.

Schmitt, N., & Bedelian, A.G. (1982). A comparison of LISREL and two-stage least squares analysis of a hypothesized life-job satisfaction reciprocal relationship. *Journal of Applied Psychology, 67,* 806-817.

Seers, A., McGee, G.W., Serey, T.T., & Green, G.B. (1983). The interaction of job stress and social support: A strong inference investigation. *Academy of Management Review, 26,* 273-284.

Sekaran, U. (1982). An investigation of the career salience of men and women in dual-career families. *Journal of Vocational Behavior, 20,* 111-119.

Sekaran, U. (1983). How husbands and wives in dual-career families perceive their family and work worlds. *Journal of Vocational Behavior, 22,* 288-302.

Shaw, L.B. (1985). Determinants of the increasing work attachment of married women. *Work and Occupations, 12,* 41-57.

Simpson, I.H., & England, P. (1981). Conjugal work roles and marital solidarity. *Journal of Family Issues, 2,* 180-204.

Spanier, G.B., & Lewis, R.A. (1980). Marital quality: A review of the 70's. *Journal of Marriage and the Family, 42,* 825-840.

Stafford, R., Backman, E., & Dibona, P. (1977). The division of labor among cohabiting and married couples. *Journal of Marriage and the Family, 39,* 43-57.

Stahnes, G.L., Pleck, J.H., Shepard, L.J., & O'Connor, P. (1978). Wives' employment status and marital adjustment. *Psychology of Women Quarterly, 3,* 90-120.

Stein, P.J. (1984). Men in families. *Marriage and Family Review, 7,* 1143-1162.

Szinovacz, M.E. (1984). Changing family roles and interactions. *Marriage and Family Review, 7,* 163-201.

Thomas, S., Albrecht, K., & White, P. (1984). Determinants of marital quality in dual-career couples. *Family Relations, 33,* 513-521.

Treiman, D.J., & Hartmann, H.I. (1981). *Women, work, and wages: Equal pay for jobs of equal value.* Washington, DC: National Academy Press.

Voydanoff, P. (1984). *Work and family.* Palo Alto, CA: Mayfield.

Warr, P., & Parry, G. (1982). Paid employment and women's psychological well-being. *Psychological Bulletin, 91,* 498-516.

Yogev, S. (1982). Happiness in dual-career couples: Changing research, changing values. *Sex Roles, 8,* 593-605.

Zedeck, S. (1987, August). Work, family, and organizations: An untapped research triangle. Paper presented at the meeting of the American Psychological Association, New York City.

Zvonkovic, A.M., Guss, T., & Ladd, L. (1988).. Making the most of job loss: Individual and marital features of underemployment. *Family Relations, 37,* 56-61.

A Systemic Perspective on Work and Family Units

Jon Jankowski
Marnell Holtgraves
Lawrence H. Gerstein

*Department of Psychology, Ball State University
Muncie, IN 47306*

Traditionally, Employee Assistance Programs (EAPs) have focused almost exclusively on the individual troubled worker. With the rising incidence of family-related employee difficulties, however, EAPs are placing more emphasis on interventions designed to help both workers and their families. Given this shift in focus, we introduce a systemic conceptualization to describe the structural relationship between work and family units. Case scenarios are used to illustrate this conceptualization. A theoretical rationale, based on Bayer and Gerstein's (1988) bystander-equity model of supervisory helping behavior, is also discussed in terms of altruistic actions that might be used by members of these two units. Finally, we suggest some directions for future systemic organizational interventions and research on the work-family system interaction. We suspect that the successful implementation of the interventions described should result in decreased costs associated with maintaining and replacing troubled employees.

Past and Current Roles of Employee Assistance Programs

Not surprisingly, the number of Employee Assistance Programs (EAPs) has increased from 5,000 in 1979 to between 9,000 and 12,000 in 1984 (Stackel, 1987). Most of this growth has occurred primarily in the past three years. Historically, EAPs were instituted to curb alcoholism in the workplace. As such, interventions were focused almost exclusively on the individual troubled employee. Recently, however, this focus has shifted. In fact, Dr. Harry Brownlee, a designer of EAPs, has suggested that family problems are now the most common worker difficulties (based on

---

Authors' Note: We wish to thank Gregory Bayer for his comments on an earlier version of this paper. Please note that a coin flip was used to establish the order for the second and third authors. Correspondence about this article should be addressed to Jon Jankowski or Lawrence H. Gerstein.

©1988 Select Press

levels of incidence) followed by child and adolescent problems, general psychological concerns, and substance abuse (Stackel, 1987).

Given this shift in employee difficulties, it follows that EAPs are recognizing the importance of offering family intervention to their troubled workers. EAP investigators are also realizing the significance of focusing on the impaired employee's family situation. Stackel (1987), for instance, provides a revealing case study to illustrate the relationship between impaired work behavior and family dynamics. In this case, the employee's spouse has become increasingly depressed to the point of possible hospitalization. Throughout this ordeal, it appears that the worker has begun abusing alcohol as a coping strategy to deal with the depression. Stackel argues that, traditionally, EAPs would most likely intervene in this situation after the employee's alcohol abuse adversely affected his/her work behavior. Currently though, Stackel suggests that EAPs should pursue some form of early family intervention to prevent further difficulties, undue employee and organizational stress, and expensive hospitalizations for troubled employees.

The Need for Family Interventions

Based on the brief discussion just presented, family counseling within an EAP context may be the logical choice in a number of situations. The average corporate executive, for example, is transferred or faced with a change of jobs every three to four years (Wagner & DeMunn, 1979). This situation, coupled with a typical executive's unhealthy preoccupation with work and excessive amount of time spent on the job, can take its toll on family life (Kanter, 1977). This can also lead to deteriorated job performance that may filter down through all levels of the organizational hierarchy (Wagner & DeMunn, 1979). Further difficulties can arise if the relocated executive is part of a dual-career couple. A spouse's unemployment could have a devastating impact on the marital relationship, especially when this causes financial problems. Even if both spouses are employed, there is research suggesting that dual-career couples experience greater degrees of stress due to work overload (Price-Bonham & Murphy, 1980), strain resulting from conflicting family and work-role expectations (Cooke & Rousseau, 1984), and dissatisfaction because of the limited amount of time they can devote to parenting (Knaub, 1986). Researchers have discovered that single parents struggle with similar difficulties (Ihinger-Tallman, 1986).

While it appears that the interaction between family life and work behavior may sometimes be negative, research also suggests that this is not necessarily the case. LaRocco, House, and French (1980), for instance, report that family roles provide a social support system which can buffer the impact of employees' work stressors. Moreover, Thoits (1982) argues that this support system can reduce the level of strain experienced by the worker. When an individual's work roles and family roles are in conflict, however, this conflict can lead to unhealthy marital adjustment, poor role performance, and other types of negative consequences (Blood & Wolfe, 1960; Jones & Butler, 1980). This suggests that while family roles may help reduce stress, these same roles could contribute to stress for the working individual. Such a situation warrants some type of EAP intervention targeted at the family rather than just the employee. Other family factors that may contribute to an employee's impaired job performance include the family's ethnic and cultural values, and the quality of the emotional and motivational climate at home (Kanter, 1977).

Illness, or death that produces a complicated bereavement within an employee's family, can necessitate an intervention at the family system level as well. During times of crisis like these, an individual's usual coping mechanisms are frequently insufficient and "...people tend to feel anxious and upset, not just because of the particular event that precipitated the crisis but because of their apparent helplessness in dealing with it" (Lewis & Lewis, 1986, p.98).

A sense of helplessness is also quite common when spouse or child abuse occurs in a family. Employees faced with this problem would certainly benefit from an EAP referral that involved some form of family counseling. Organizations would profit from this type of intervention as well. It is estimated that businesses lose from three to five billion dollars each year as a result of absenteeism due to spouse abuse (Engelken, 1987). Ninety-five percent of these abusers are employed males with 20 percent earning $40,000 or more per year (Engelken, 1987). Estimates of the number of women who will be battered this year range from four to six million (Engelken, 1987). In light of these statistics, it seems that some form of family intervention would be mutually beneficial for all concerned parties.

While child abuse may not result in the same kind of organizational costs, it is a blatant example of poor parenting skills that can adversely affect an employee's work and home life. Abusing parents, for example, are often summoned by school officials or social service agencies, and may even be required to miss work because of court appearances. Other less severe disruptions in a worker's family life (e.g., inharmonious relationships with children) can also negatively impact on job performance. Normal tasks that must be mastered during various developmental stages of the family life cycle, for instance, may cause unexpected stress placing families at risk. In fact, "...[m]any families come to the attention of an EAP counselor because of their difficulties in dealing with changes brought about by new developments in the family's life cycle" (Lewis & Lewis, 1986, p. 103). Such family problems generally evolve due to poor communication skills, low self-esteem, insufficient anger control, sexual dysfunction, substance abuse, financial difficulties, impaired parenting skills, and job related stress (Myers, 1985). Once again, given the fact that marriage and family discord is the most frequently cited employee problem (Myers, 1985), there seems to be a strong need to focus on the family system within the context of EAPs.

THE WORK AND FAMILY SYSTEM

This need to focus on a system rather than a particular individual is consistent with the current theoretical framework in psychology which conceptualizes various situations (e.g., family behavior, the process of psychotherapy, workplace communities) in terms of a systemic or holistic point of view (Bopp & Weeks, 1984; Wynne, McDaniel, & Weber, 1986). From this perspective, a system is defined as a complex of component parts that mutually interact with one another (Goldberg & Goldberg, 1985). Following from this, systems theorists stress the pluralistic and interactive effect of variables as they relate to different events. As such, these persons argue that a symptom (problem) in one individual can be perceived as evidence of dysfunction in one or more systems in which the individual operates.

Although additional randomized empirical studies are needed, research has supported the general efficacy of family systems interventions across many types of clinical problems. Structural family therapy (Minuchin, 1974), for instance, has been found to be effective when treating families with children and adolescents who display anorexia nervosa, diabetes, or chronic asthma (Liebman, Minuchin, Baker, & Rosman, 1974; Minuchin et al., 1975; Minuchin et al., 1978). This approach has also proved to be effective when working with adult substance abusers (Stanton, Todd, & Associates, 1982; Stanton & Todd, 1976; Stanton & Todd, 1978). In fact, some writers (Gurman & Kniskern, 1981) have even argued that this approach is the treatment of choice for substance abusers and persons who experience psychosomatic disorders.

We believe, like other investigators (Borwick, 1986; Ford & Ford, 1986; Friedman, 1986), that principles of systems theory can also be applied to the workplace, particularly EAPs. As alluded to earlier, an employee's family and work unit may influence each other in a systemic way (Friedman, 1986). Realizing that every family problem does not affect the behavior of other individuals in all contexts, we still contend that social systems in which a person operates may interact, especially through the employee whose behavior has been labeled dysfunctional. Ford and Ford (1986) describe this interdependence by likening tolerance of substance abuse in the workplace to a surrogate family that enables an individual to avoid family responsibilities. In the remainder of this paper, we will extend this idea to illustrate how a work group can be conceptualized systemically and, more importantly, how transactions that occur between families and work units through the employee can be operationalized from this nonlinear view of causality. To clarify our discussion, we will first present two case scenarios. Each of these scenarios (illustrated in Figure 1) is conceptualized from Minuchin's (1974) structural form of family systems therapy. In specific, Minuchin's constructs are employed to assess the structural features of transactions between family members and workers highlighted in the scenarios.

Scenario 1: The Home Situation

As shown in the center and left side of Figure 1, Mrs. Identified Patient lives with her mother, husband, and two children (her son from a previous marriage and her step-daughter). Her mother moved in with the family two months ago when Mrs. Patient's father passed away. Mrs. Patient misses her father terribly and wants to help her mother through this difficult transition period as much as possible. She and her mother, however, are experiencing conflict stemming from their differing opinions on the way children should be raised. Her mother is a cool, detached, unemotional woman with a rational explanation for everything. She believes that parents should establish strict rules that children "should follow to the letter." Mrs. Patient wants a different kind of relationship with her children. She believes that by providing a loving atmosphere with respect and emotional support, her children will automatically turn out right.

Mrs. Patient is also experiencing role conflict with her husband due to a role reversal which took place seven months ago when he lost his job. Shortly after his dismissal, she was promoted to a middle management position in the factory where she had worked for several years. Her husband has been unsuccessful in finding permanent employment, and so, for the first time in their marriage, she is providing the major financial support for the family. Her new position necessitates her spending more time away from home. Yet, her husband has not assumed more of the domestic responsibilities, and she is afraid to ask, fearing this may damage his self-concept even more. Recently, arguments between them have resulted in violence, and Mrs. Patient has missed numerous days from work because she did not want her co-workers to see her cuts and bruises.

Mrs. Patient's son and step-daughter are also reacting to the stresses

FIGURE 1 Mrs. I. Dentified Patient's Role in Her Work and Family Systems

within the family. Both of the children's grades in school have dropped, and she is finding them increasingly combative and difficult to discipline. They also resent her spending longer periods away from home and asking them to assume more responsibility for household chores. Each child tends to be more sympathetic with their biological parent's situation as evidenced by Mrs. Patient's son working evenings and weekends in a gas station to supplement the family's income, while her step-daughter becomes angrily defensive when Mrs. Patient expresses irritation over her husband's lack of support.

Case Assessment: Scenario 1

Based on Minuchin's (1974) structural theory, this family has poorly defined boundaries within the family system. Few rules of conduct or power distribution have been established since each parent is aligned with and enmeshed with their own child, yet, relatively disengaged from each other. Also, weak generational boundaries exist in that Mrs. Patient is too intimidated by her mother and step-daughter to be an effective disciplinarian. The recent changes in the family structure resulting from her husband's unemployment, her advancement, and her father's death have created coping problems for Mrs. Patient's family. Mrs. Patient and her husband were raised to believe family problems should stay within, and be resolved by, the family. Consequently, they are unaccustomed to seeking outside assistance which typifies their rigid inter-system boundaries.

Scenario 2: The Work Situation

As shown in the center and right side of Figure 1, Mrs. Patient is also experiencing conflicts at work. She frequently disagrees with the strict, authoritarian rule which upper-management believes is necessary to maintain production levels. Having worked years alongside the employees she now supervises, she is more sympathetic with their views when disputes between them and upper-management erupt. She believes that taking the needs and values of the employees into consideration will foster an atmosphere of cooperation and increased production. Upper-management, in contrast, continually reminds her that the factory is not a charitable organization, and profit is "the name of the game."

Mrs. Patient is experiencing role conflict with the man who was her direct supervisor prior to her promotion. He now resents being supervised by a woman, and believes he would have been given the middle-management position if it were not for their company's newly established policy of hiring and advancing women. Mrs. Patient's previous position will not be refilled. Yet her former supervisor and this person's staff refuse to assume any additional work or responsibility. Because of this, and Mrs. Patient's recent absenteeism, several of Mrs. Patient's loyal co-workers have had to work overtime and on weekends in an effort to maintain production levels. As a result, opposing factions have evolved within the factory and employee absenteeism and accidental injuries have increased.

Mrs. Patient feels extreme frustration and anxiety over her home and work situations. Her best efforts have been unsuccessful in resolving the numerous difficulties she experiences in both systems. As a means of coping, she has drastically increased her alcohol consumption and started taking a prescription tranquilizer. While these substances provide some momentary relief, the overall impact has been decreased productivity and effectiveness on her part. This and her frequent absenteeism has been noticed by upper-management who is beginning to suspect she is not suitable for a managerial position. In her last evaluation, she received a severe reprimand and warning that she would be demoted or fired if she were not able to resolve her difficulties within a reasonable amount of time.

Case Assessment: Scenario 2

Again, based on Minuchin's (1974) structural model, this work system has poorly defined boundaries and inadequate rules of conduct or power distribution. Mrs. Patient and her former supervisor are each aligned with and enmeshed with certain employees, yet relatively disengaged from each other. Also, weak generational boundaries exist in that Mrs. Patient is too intimidated by upper-management and other employees to be an effective manager. The recent role restructuring which took place with Mrs. Patient's advancement has created problems with which she is unable to cope. Upper-management's handling of the situation by issuing a reprimand and warning rather than a referral to the factory's EAP typifies this factory's rigid inter-system boundaries. Mrs. Patient has been labeled as having a substance abuse problem which is "causing" the numerous difficulties within this factory.

An Analysis of Mrs. Patient's Family-Work System

These scenarios illustrate the need for a more holistic understanding of a troubled employee's subsystems (Borwick, 1986; Friedman, 1986). The fact that Mrs. Patient is experiencing similar difficulties at home and at work may exacerbate her feelings of helplessness and despair since there is no role in which she feels truly competent. She may, for example, overreact to a conflict at work because she recently experienced a similar conflict at home. Given the impact each of these system has on the other, it would seem pointless to design an intervention without taking both systems into account. For example, if Mrs. Patient received counseling for her difficulties at work without receiving some form of family counseling, the intervention may be destined for failure. Her dysfunctional family and work systems are not entirely independent of each other. EAPs, therefore, could increase their effectiveness by designing interventions that identify, clarify, and treat an individual's dysfunctional interfacing systems.

The scenarios just presented clearly illustrate the parallels between work group behavior and family interactions. Obviously, Mrs. Patient enacted the same role in her work and family units and was a member of two similarly functioning systems. Although this similarity was illustrated in our scenarios to clearly suggest parallels between work and family systems, the systemic structure of each of these units is not always the same. Family concepts (e.g., roles, boundaries, power, & tasks) used to understand family systems can be applied, however, to the work unit (Borwick, 1986), and the interaction of this unit with the family system. The impact that Mrs. Patient's work and family unit had on each other, for example, seems apparent when recognizing the similarities in roles, boundaries, and relationships depicted in each unit.

Inter-Role Conflict for the Worker and Family Member

Research on the interaction between these two systems attests to the importance of conceptualizing the workplace and impaired employee from a systemic perspective. In a study investigating family and work role expectations (Cooke & Rousseau, 1984), 200 teachers were used when collecting questionnaire and interview data. The results generally supported a model of inter-role conflict. Specific to family influence, inter-role conflict increased as individuals married and had children. Also, as workers married and had children, family demands seemed to interact with work-role expectations to increase the individuals level of perceived work overload and strain.

Similar results were obtained in another study on inter-role conflicts. When assessing 28 dual-career couples in terms of specific roles, Holahan and Gilbert (1979) reported that, in general, couples felt the most conflict in their professional and self-roles, professional and parent roles, and self and parent roles. Somewhat different results were found in a study designed to investigate the competing pressures of work and family roles (Kopelman, Greenhaus, & Connelly, 1983). Kopelman et al. (1983) did discover that employees who experienced conflict at work felt job dissatisfaction, and persons who felt conflict in their family experienced dissatisfaction at home. But, these investigators also discovered that inter-role conflict did not result in job or family dissatisfaction.

Overall, these studies lend partial support to Greenhaus and Beutell's (1985) model of inter-role conflict. This model suggests the presence of three factors that could contribute to a worker-family member role conflict. These include problems related to time (role overload, work schedule conflicts, lack of time spent with spouse or children), emotional strain (work-family stress, level of support from partner), and incompatible behaviors (work-family role expectations).

WORK UNITS AS A FAMILY SYSTEM

Thus far, we have discussed the influence that various work and family roles may have on job and home conflicts. As such, we have provided one possible conceptualization of the systemic interactions between family and work units. We will now present some similarities in how families behave and how work units operate by examining the process, interactions, and dynamics of families and/or systems when encountering stressors (Borwick, 1986). According to Hill (1949), stressors vary from family to family, but can be viewed as discrete events, such as death, or on-going demoralizing events such as nonsupport or alcoholism. In his A B C-X model of family stress, Hill proposes that various events and hardships (A) combine with a family's resources for coping (B) and a family's perception of the seriousness of an event (C) leading to a crisis (X). Since introducing this model, Hill's concept of family stress has been broadened to include normative family events or transitions like childbearing and retirement (McCubbin, Joy, Cauble, Comeau, Patterson, & Needle, 1980). It also has been expanded to encompass family hardship due to work-related stressors such as problems arising from females (wives) being employed outside the home (McCubbin et al., 1980).

Extrapolating Hill's A B C-X model of family stress to work units results in viewing such a unit as a family system with at least one member who is impaired (e.g., Mrs. Identified Patient in Figure 1). More specifically, the A component of Hill's model represents work group tension, conflict, or a particularly difficult situation facing the work unit. The B factor, in comparison, symbolizes a work group's resources including their skills, degree of social support and other forms of assistance that they have available to meet the demands of a difficult work situation. As with a troubled family, the troubled work unit has many resources (B) at its disposal. For example, communication skills have been shown to be an important resource, with communication clarity being a discriminator between healthy and unhealthy families (Doane, 1978). Rarely, however, are such resources pooled to bring about changes in the dysfunctional work unit. Rather, the tendency has been to identify or perceive (C) the impaired employee as *the* problem, isolate him or her from the work unit, and engage this person in a constructive confrontation or, if necessary, offer him or her individual treatment.

As discussed in our two scenarios, Hill's C factor may also operate in a work unit as it does in a family. In a family, perceptions about the seriousness of the event or problem can vary from member to member (e.g., Mrs. Patient's perception of the family problem versus her mother's viewpoint). This may be true in an industrial environment as well. For instance, supervisors often have markedly different perceptions than their supervisees as to what constitutes a problem (e.g., the importance of considering the employee's needs and values). In our second Scenario, this is illustrated by the discrepancy between Mrs. Patient's perception of the factory situation and that of her supervisors. Additionally, supervisors might view profit as the only essential factor, whereas employees may see this as a disregard for their needs. Both of these situations, plus those that could arise from differences in employee's perceptions about problems, suggest that a work unit can function like a family system.

Hill's final factor in his model, the X component, represents a family crisis in the original application and a dysfunctional work unit in our adaptation. Analagous to the identified patient in a dysfunctional family, a troubled worker, like Mrs. Identified Patient in Scenario 2, could be offering his or her primary work group an opportunity for change by making it possible for the group to resolve a crisis situation (e.g., work-related accidents, peer conflict) in a new way (e.g., constructive confrontation). By continuing to identify and isolate an impaired employee as "the problem," the supervisor, work group, and EAP miss a chance to treat the entire dysfunctional work unit. If the unit is not ignored and treated, there is a greater likelihood of preventing the recurrence of a vicious cycle that involves "farming out" all troubled workers and treating them and "their" problems, and then returning these persons to the same untreated dysfunctional system or work unit (Baum-Baicker, 1984).

Clearly, an intervention that was designed to help the work unit (e.g., strengthen the relationship between Mrs. Patient and upper-management and/or restructure her interactions with her former supervisor) would lessen the possibility of maintaining a dysfunctional system. Kormanski (1988) in his article on using group development theory in business and industry, offers a number of group interventions that may be useful in this regard. Obviously, there may be instances where it is critical to first assist the impaired employee before helping the work unit. When an employee is actively psychotic, dangerous to others, or in severe substance abuse withdrawal, it would seem necessary to offer care to the troubled person prior to the work group.

Assessing the Work System

Before initiating a work unit intervention, we believe it is necessary to identify and assess various interpersonal stressors and tensions within the work group. This could be accomplished through the development of a worker's observation checklist similar to the Spouse Observation Checklist designed by Wills, Weiss, and Patterson (1974). Such a device could be used to investigate pleasing and displeasing behavior displayed by all members of a work unit. The unit's general level of adjustment could also be assessed through instruments based on family adjustment tests. Imig and Imig's (1985) Family Effectiveness Scale, for example, could be adapted to assess work unit effectiveness. The three basic factors measured by this instrument would be revised to reflect managerial efficacy (e.g., each of us wants to tell the others what to do), work unit cohesion-regard (e.g., we often praise or compliment one another), and work unit cohesion-involvement (e.g., we do many things together). Clearly, the information gathered as a result of administering such devices would be valuable to EAPs in that staff could tailor their interventions to the particular needs of a troubled work unit.

Data on irritants/stressors that may be unrelated to the interpersonal dynamics of work units (e.g., a corporate-wide policy concerning allowable scrap amounts) may be of importance to EAPs as well. These data could reveal information about various features of the corporate culture (e.g., if Mrs. Patient's factory can be described as a cool and aloof environment). To collect these data, it would be necessary for EAPs to rely on another tool constructed to assess non-relationship stressors exhibited by troubled work units. As a prototype, we suggest that the Hassles Scale (Kanner, Coyne, Shaefer, & Lazarus, 1981) be adapted to measure potential everyday work hassles that contribute to feelings of stress.

Not surprisingly, some investigators believe that a particular employee's hassles or feelings of stress can affect the entire work unit (e.g., conflict that results from Mrs. Patient's relationship with her husband). Friedman (1986), for instance, indicates that a change in leadership, a personal problem that affects a leader, or a significant promotion or retirement can result in organizational stress. Baum-Baicker (1984) also states that: 1) if workplace stress is generated through the mismatching of individual needs and organizational demands, and 2) if such stress is coped with through alcohol abuse, and 3) if alcohol abuse can be viewed as an interaction between the employee and his or her environment, then 4) others in the workplace will be adversely affected. Baum-Baicker claims as well that this sequence of events suggests a strong need to treat the entire work group. Regardless of the validity of Baum-Baicker's argument, it is hard to disagree with the idea that work units, like family systems, are influenced when one member abuses alcohol. Thus, we think that it is advantageous for the "alcoholic work system" to be treated and not just the identified troubled employee.

A NEW TREATMENT PERSPECTIVE FOR EAPs

As stated earlier, this new treatment perspective is not consistent with the traditional EAP approach of identifying, isolating, and treating just the impaired worker—persons who commonly experience alcohol problems. It is also at odds with the widely endorsed procedure of returning such persons to unhealthy systems or work units. We contend that this shift in focus is not only necessary, but critical given the fact that alcohol usage is highly rampant in the American workplace. Sending a recovering substance abusing employee back into a system, like Mrs. Patient's work group, where alcohol consumption is prevalent, and peer pressure and enabling behaviors common, severely hinders this person's chances for successful treatment. Again, analogous to treating one family member and then returning this individual to a dysfunctional family system, it may be myopic and potentially destructive to provide treatment for only the impaired employee and not the entire work unit (Friedman, 1986).

Treating the alcohol abuser's work unit is consistent with the current emphasis of alcohol rehabilitation programs of including the abuser's family in the counseling process (Royce, 1981). This suggestion is even more compelling when considering the amount of time employees spend with their "work family" (e.g., playing softball after work) as compared to their actual family. We suspect, like others (Friedman, 1986), that it is fairly typical for employees to interact more frequently with their work unit "family members" than their "home life family members." This is based on societal and workplace demands that stem from being divorced, living in a dual-career marriage, or desiring to succeed as an executive (e.g., to advance in today's economy and a highly competitive business climate these persons must work long hours). Even "average" workers often work overtime by choice or requirement for additional income. They also work longer hours to avoid being replaced by the numerous persons who could easily step into their jobs.

Persons might also spend more time with their work family as a way to avoid being with their natural family. This assumption seems plausible given the research cited earlier on the pervasiveness of family problems among members of the workforce. All in all, we believe that individuals are spending a larger portion of their lives with their work unit families. Assuming this is accurate, it seems important that EAPs include the impaired employee's dysfunctional work unit/family system in the treatment.

General support for this recommendation can be found in Levinson's (1972) writings. Although he previously focused on the problems and symptoms of the individual troubled worker, Levinson came to realize that the managerial methods utilized by an organization had a major impact on the mental health and functioning of its employees. In fact, Levinson (1972) states that, "individuals are necessarily members of families" (p. 3) and that every work group has its own process that can be referred to as a system. Based on such beliefs, Levinson posited as we did, that to prevent employee impairments, one must understand and intervene in the dysfunctional organizational system. This view is contrary, however, to a perspective endorsed by others (Lasch, 1977) who see such interventions as the medicalization of the helping process, or as an invasion and usurption of the family's rights and functions. It is our contention though, that certain families and individuals need outside assistance like an EAP intervention to cope with or resolve their difficulties.

The Bystander-Equity Model and the Work-Family System

While we have supported the claim that troubled employees can indeed be viewed as part of dysfunctional work units/family systems, it is still necessary to understand the interpersonal dynamics involved in initiating a healthy helping process in these systems and the role of helping in human nature. Although there is no specific model addressing the work/ family system helping process, there is research on why family members may assist each other. Sociobiologists, for instance, explain human prosocial behavior through the concept of the fittest genes hypothesis (Hamilton, 1964; Trivers, 1971; Trivers & Hare, 1976). This hypothesis suggests that the key to the evolution of a particular species is linked to the survival of genes shared by relatives rather than genes shared by two unrelated members of a group. An animal, for example, is expected to save offsprings or other relatives, as opposed to non-family members, in order to preserve the genes of kinship. According to Hoffman (1981), genetic altruism is also a basic biological drive for humans. Empathy has been viewed in terms of genetics as well (Matthews, Batson, Horn & Rosenman, 1981). Consequently, sociobiologists would most likely maintain that the helping process is influenced first by a vested interest in preserving shared genes (e.g., other family members), and second by the inherent characteristics of the potential helper.

Given the many changes in the traditional human family structure (e.g., blended families) and the "non-relatedness" of employees, perhaps a more comprehensive or refined model is needed to explain the work/ family system helping process. We believe that the bystander-equity model of supervisory helping behavior (Bayer & Gerstein, 1988) offers useful information when trying to understand this process. Basically, according to this model, supervisors or co-workers help impaired employees as a function of the clarity and severity of the person's problem, characteristics of the troubled worker and supervisor, and the costs connected to helping. Bayer and Gerstein argue that each of these variables interact to affect potential helpers' (e.g., supervisors or co-workers) willingness to assist troubled workers. These theorists also suggest that these helpers will be more likely to offer assistance when the balance of rewards to costs in their work group is inequitable. To illustrate some of Bayer and Gerstein's constructs, we will now discuss various features of the Scenarios presented earlier.

In Scenario 2, for instance, Mrs. Identified Patient seems to have similar characteristics to the employees she supervises by virtue of having worked with them for five years. While this should, based on Bayer and Gerstein's (1988) model, facilitate helping, Mrs. Patient's dissimilarities with the upper-management staff and her frequent contacts with them should inhibit altruism in her particular work situation. Thus, Mrs. Patient would probably be perceived as an outsider by persons affiliated with her work and management units. This perception should reduce the degree to which potential helpers experience what Bayer and Gerstein termed "we-ness." Limited feelings of "we-ness," according to these theorists, results in less willingness to help someone like Mrs. Patient.

The probability of Mrs. Patient receiving assistance might also be reduced by the quality of communication in her work unit. As mentioned, some of Mrs. Patient's colleagues felt resentment about her promotion causing communication difficulties in her work unit. Consequently, Mrs. Patient and the upper-management staff were probably unclear (clarity of the situation) about the cause of her recent problem. This situation, coupled with the fact that it seemed difficult to recognize the problems in Mrs. Patient's work system, suggests that Mrs. Patient's impairments and especially those of her workers were not viewed as severe. Furthermore, these problems failed to generate the necessary amount of arousal that results, according to Bayer and Gerstein (1988), in helping.

Levels of arousal in Mrs. Patient's work unit were also reduced by the various struggles for independence and dependence that existed throughout Mrs. Patient's factory system (e.g., employees vs. management; upper-management vs. Mrs. Patient's leadership style; Mrs. Patient vs. her former supervisor). Since Bayer and Gerstein contend that perceived dependency between helper and victim generates arousal, it follows, that potential helpers in Mrs. Patient's work unit would not experience enough arousal to initiate the helping process.

Along with this, the costs for helping Mrs. Patient were probably too high; a situation, according to Bayer and Gerstein (1988), that results in limited assistance. It is conceivable, for instance, that Mrs. Patient's former supervisor perceived the costs of helping as too great given the threat from his lost power. It is also possible that this person's leadership style promoted discord and turmoil keeping the focus on Mrs. Patient and ensuring this individual's power.

Mrs. Patient's family system can be evaluated in terms of Bayer and Gerstein's bystander-equity model also. In general, family members might view helping behavior as extremely costly, particularly in terms of emotional costs. In contrast, fellow employees may not experience helping as being emotionally costly (Friedman, 1986). Additionally, families might be too enmeshed to recognize when their members need help. In other words, enmeshed families may be unable to clearly identify when a family member needs assistance.

This appears to be the situation in Mrs. Patient's family. As we discussed in Scenario 1, the boundaries in Mrs. Patient's family were rather unclear. This was particularly apparent with respect to the boundaries involving Mrs. Patient's children, spouse, and mother. (Note the similarity of this situation with the poorly defined boundaries in Mrs. Patient's work unit, e.g., boundaries between supervisees, Mrs. Patient, & upper-management staff). This was also the case with Mrs. Patient's husband and his daughter.

We contend that because of these ambiguous and unclear boundaries, members of Mrs. Patient's family would experience minimal levels of arousal. Since Bayer and Gerstein (1988) predict that helping only occurs under high levels of arousal, it appears that members of Mrs. Patient's family might underestimate the severity of a family member's problem and not offer assistance.

An unwillingness to help in Mrs. Patient's family may also be related to characteristics of potential helpers and victims in her family. The perpetual power struggles and squabbles in Mrs. Patient's family could have eroded her family's sense of "we-ness." Such struggles might have also contributed to unhealthy family alliances that, in turn, inhibited the helping process in her family.

TREATING MRS. PATIENT'S FAMILY AND WORK UNITS

Given the dynamics of Mrs. Patient's work and family systems, it is interesting to speculate about how she or others might receive help. Traditionally, there would be three possible actions that would result in assistance offered to Mrs. Patient or her co-workers. First, Mrs. Patient might seek out her EAP on her own. This is unlikely, since Mrs. Patient's company is generally unsupportive of persons who refer themselves to the EAP. Second, Mrs. Patient's supervisor or physician may refer her or her entire work unit to the EAP. This is also unlikely, given the overall negative attitude of Mrs. Patient's company toward EAPs. Because of this attitude, we suspect that Mrs. Patient's company would overlook her dysfunctional work unit and thus contribute to perpetuating her unit's inability to operate effectively.

The third action might involve Mrs. Patient's family. It is possible that someone in Mrs. Patient's family could initiate an EAP referral for her or for her entire family system. This action also seems unlikely. As stated earlier, there is an insufficient amount of arousal in Mrs. Patient's family to activate a helping response or to stimulate the family's desire to change.

If, however, help was initiated, and Mrs. Patient's family received family therapy, we suspect that Mrs. Patient would be seen as a scapegoat. This suggests that Mrs. Patient's family would probably be more supportive if she received counseling alone. We believe that this option would perpetuate Mrs. Patient's dysfunctional family system. Similarly, if Mrs. Patient's family participated in therapy without her work unit, we think that her dysfunctional work system would still be able to affect her family situation.

Given the shortcomings of each of the intervention strategies just discussed, we would strongly recommend an intervention designed to address Mrs. Patient's work and family systems holistically. First, the upper-management staff would need to perceive Mrs. Patient's difficulties as symptoms of a troubled person within a dysfunctional work unit. As a step in this direction, each member of management could be given the Behavioral Index of Troubled Employees (BITE) (Bayer & Gerstein, in press) to determine their beliefs about behaviors suggestive of impaired workers. This 23-item questionnaire is composed of four distinct, valid, and reliable factors known as: Resistance (R), Acrimoniousness (A), Industriousness (I), and Disaffection (D). In Scenario 2, for instance, Mrs. Patient exhibited symptoms related to Industriousness (e.g., decreased productivity), Resistance (e.g., absenteeism), and Acrimoniousness (e.g., disputes with former supervisor). Results of administering the BITE could be used to structure supervisory training sessions on how to identify impaired employees (Gerstein, 1988; Gerstein & Bayer, 1988).

Next, the upper-management staff would need to contact their EAP to help restore Mrs. Patient's dysfunctional work system to a healthy unit. The EAP, in turn, would assess the interpersonal dynamics (using the scales mentioned earlier) of the work group and construct a systemic intervention to modify the particular roles, boundaries, and alignments of Mrs. Patient's work unit.

The EAP staff would also need to evaluate the structural relationships inherent in Mrs. Patient's family system. This information would be used to intervene at the family level and to change the unique covert and overt transactions occurring between Mrs. Patient's work and family units. Ideally, the EAP staff would perceive the mutual interaction and impact of the two dysfunctional units as part of an overall problematic system, and design interventions that reduced problems inherent in Mrs. Patient's organization.

This approach to working with Mrs. Patient's family, work unit, and entire organization is consistent with the notion that family systems' principles can be used to design interventions for employment groups (Borwick, 1986; Friedman, 1986). The intervention used, however, must be tailored for work groups adapted from those that are often utilized by family therapists (Borwick, 1986). It is imperative that EAP staff understand this, since families typically seek treatment while work groups do not. Families may benefit from interventions that might not be permitted in a bureaucratic, profit driven, quasi-legal work environment. Moreover, work units may be less motivated to participate in treatment, and potentially less emotionally invested in their co-workers' recovery.

Given this, before intervening, EAP personnel and consultants need to become familiar with an organization's structure and climate, recognize that they are helping a work system and not a family (Borwick, 1986), and understand that they must establish close contact with key members of the work unit (Friedman, 1986). When intervening, it is important that these persons teach employees a systemic way of considering relationships and identifying patients. They should work with personnel as high up the organizational hierarchy as possible, avoid restructuring established relationships (Friedman, 1986), and offer support and a method for integrating supervisors and employees into the organizational system (Borwick, 1986). It is critical that these helpers develop short-term and problem-focused solutions to assist work systems (Borwick, 1986). Finally, it is imperative that EAP personnel go to great lengths to protect the anonymity of the troubled employee(s), so that this person is not labeled deviant by his or her peers or superiors. Establishing a confidentiality rule in a work group that is participating in an intervention program might be one solution to this potential problem.

CONCLUSION

This article integrated a number of findings and concepts to explain family and work systems, and the structural relationship between these groups. A theoretical rationale for considering this relationship was presented in terms of a systemic analysis of various roles, boundaries, sources of power, and alignments found in families and work units. Throughout this paper, we have argued that such an analysis symbolizes a change of perspective in how EAP personnel and organizations can perceive impairments in the workforce. We also suggested that this shift represents a move away from treating individual workers who may be impaired to helping an entire work unit or an interfacing work-family system.

Obviously, further research is needed to investigate the validity and importance of this shift in thinking. Studies that examine the effect of holistic interventions on work units, families, and interactions between the two are needed. Research on the similarities between family and work systems (e.g., roles, boundaries) is needed as well, as are data on how these two systems relate to each other. It would also seem useful to gather information on the applicability of the bystander-equity model of supervisory helping behavior to transactions involving members of work and family systems. Finally, research is needed on the effects of training work units to use systemic concepts when evaluating the performance and satisfaction of their employees.

Although research must be conducted to substantiate the validity of the theoretical shift we have proposed, we suspect that a successful systemic intervention with a work and family system would result in many benefits to organizations. Such an intervention should decrease the number of EAP referrals from a particular work unit, reduce employee turnover, and lessen the possibility of the reemergence of worker worker and work group symptoms. This type of intervention would also appear to be preventive in that employees and supervisors would become educated sooner about the dynamics of their group and the potential employee problems that could emerge. Given these benefits, it seems rather apparent that implementing a systemic treatment and conceptual model in the business world should decrease the costs associated with maintaining and replacing troubled workers.

REFERENCES

Baum-Baicker, C. (1984). Treating and preventing alcohol abuse in the workplace. *American Psychologist, 39*, p. 454.

Bayer, G., & Gerstein, L. (in press). Supervisory attitudes about impaired workers: A factor analytic study of the Behavioral Index of Troubled Employees (BITE) *Journal of Applied Behavioral Sciences.*

Bayer, G., & Gerstein, L. (1988). An adaptation of models of prosocial behavior to supervisor interventions with troubled employees. *Journal of Applied Social Psychology, 18*, 23-37.

Blood, R., & Wolfe, D. (1960). *Husbands and wives.* New York:Macmillan.

Bopp, M. & Weeks, G. (1984). Dialectical metatheory in family therapy. *Family Process, 23*, 49-61.

Borwick, I (1986). The family therapist as business consultant. In L. Wynne, S. McDaniel, & T. Weber (Eds.), *Systems consultation: A new perspective for family therapy* (pp. 423-440). New York: Guilford Press.

Cooke, R., & Rousseau, D. (1984). Stress and strain from family roles and work-role expectations. *Journal of Applied Psychology, 69*, 252-260.

Doane, J. (1978). Family interaction and communication deviance in disturbed and normal families: A review of the research. *Family Process, 17*, 357-376.

Engelken, C. (1987). Employee assistance: Fighting the cost of spouse abuse. *Personnel Journal, 6*, 31-34.

Ford, J. D., & Ford, J. G. (1986). A systems theory analysis of employee assistance programs. *Employee Assistance Quarterly, 2*, 37-48.

Friedman, E. (1986). Emotional process in the marketplace: The family therapist as consultant with work systems. In L. Wynne, S. McDaniel, & T. Weber (Eds.), *Systems consultation: A new perspective for family therapy* (pp. 398-422). New York:Guilford Press.

Gerstein, L. (1988). *The bystander-equity model of supervisory helping behavior: Future research on the prevention of employee problems.* Paper presented at the NIAAA Research Conference on Alcohol and the Workplace: Integrating Perspective on Prevention and Intervention, Jekyll Island, GA.

Gerstein, L., & Bayer, G. (1988). *Psychology and the future of EAP research.* Paper presented at the Annual Meeting of the American Psychology Association, Atlanta, GA.

Goldberg, I., & Goldberg, H. (1985). *Family therapy: An overview.* (2nd ed.) Monterey: Brooks/Cole.

Greenhaus, J., & Beutell, N. (1985). Sources of conflict between work and family roles. *Academy of Management Review, 10*, 76-88.

Gurman, A., & Kniskern, D. (1981). Family therapy outcome research: Knowns and unknowns. In A. Gurman & D. Kniskern (Eds.), *Handbook of family therapy.* New York: Brunner/Mazel.

Hamilton, D. (1964). The genetic evolution of social behavior, I & II. *Journal of Theoretical Biology, 7*, 1-52.

Hill, R. (1949) *Families under stress.* New York: Harper and Row.

Hoffman, M. (1981). Is altruism part of human nature? *Journal of Personality and Social Psychology, 40*, 121-137.

Holahan, C., & Gilbert, L. (1979). Conflict between major life roles: Women and men in dual-career couples. *Human Relations, 32*, 451-457.

Imig, D., & Imig, G. (1985). Influences of family management and spousal perceptions on stressor pile-up. *Family Relations, 34*, 227-232.

Ihinger-Tallman, M. (1986). Member adjustment in single parent families: Theory building. *Family Relations, 32*, 215-221.

Jones, A., & Butler, M. (1980). A role transition approach to the stresses of organizationally-induced family role disruption. *Journal of Marriage and the Family, 42*, 367-376.

Kanner, A., Coyne, J., Shaefer, C. & Lazarus, R. (1981). Comparison of two modes of stress measurement: Daily hassles and uplifts versus major life events. *Journal of Behavior Medicine, 4*, 1-39.

Kanter, R. (1977). *Work and family in the United States: A critical review and agenda for research and policy.* New York: Russell Sage Foundation.

Knaub, P. (1986). Growing up in a dual-career family: The children perceptions. *Family Relations, 32*, 431-437.

Kopelman, R., Greenhaus, J., & Connelly, T. (1983). A model of work, family, and interrole conflict: A construct validation study. *Organizational Behavior and Human Performance, 32*, 198-215.

Kormanski, C. (1988). Using group development theory in business and industry. *Journal of Specialists in Group Work, 13*, 30-43.

LaRocco, J., House, J., & French, J. (1980). Social support, occupational stress, and health. *Journal of Health and Social Behavior, 21*, 202-218.

Lasch, C. (1977). *Haven in a heartless world.* New York: Basic Books.

Levinson, H. (1972). *Organizational Diagnosis.* Cambridge, Massachusetts: Harvard University Press.

Lewis, J. & Lewis, M. (1986). *Counseling programs for employees in the workplace.* Monterey: Brooks/Cole.

Liebman, R., Minuchin, S., Baker, L., & Rosman, B. (1974). An integrated treatment program for anorexia nervosa. *American Journal of Psychiatry, 131*, 432-436.

Matthews, K., Batson, C., Horn, J., & Rosenman, R. (1981). The heritability of emphatic concern for others. *Journal of Personality, 49*, 237-247.

McCubbin, H., Joy, C., Cauble, A., Comeau, J., & Patterson, J., & Needle, R. (1980). Family stress and coping. *Journal of Marriage and the Family, 42*, 855-871.

Myers, D. (1985). *Employee problem prevention and counseling: A guide for professionals.* Westpoint, Conn: Quorum.

Minuchin, S. (1974). *Families and family therapy.* Cambridge, MA:Harvard University Press.

Minuchin, S., Baker, L., Rosman, B., Liebman, R., Milman, L., & Todd, T. (1975). A conceptual model of psychosomatic illness in children. *Archives of General Psychiatry, 32*, 1031-1038.

Minuchin, S., Rosman, B., & Baker, L. (1978). *Psychosomatic families.* Cambridge, MA: Harvard University Press.

Price-Bonham, S., & Murphy, D. (1980). Dual career marriages: Implications for the clinician. *Journal of Marriage and the Family, 6*, 181-188.

Royce, J. (1981). *Alcohol problems and alcoholism.* New York: Free Press.

Stackel, L. (1987). EAPs in the workplace. *Employment Relations Today, 3*, 289-294.

Stanton, M., & Todd, T. (1976). *Some outcome results and aspects of structural family therapy with drug addicts.* Paper presented at the Society for Psychotherapy Research. San Diego.

Stanton, M., & Todd, T. (1978). Some outcome results and aspects of structural family therapy with heroin addicts. In D. Smith, S. Anderson, M. Buxton, T. Chung, N. Gottlieb & W. Harvey (Eds.), *A multicultural view of drug abuse.* Cambridge, MA: Shenkman.

Stanton, M., & Todd, T., & Associates. (1982) *The family therapy of drug abuse and addiction.* New York: Guilford.

Thoits, P. (1982). Problems in the study of social support. *Journal of Health and Social Behavior, 23*, 145-158.

Trivers, R. (1971). The evolution of reciprocal altruism. *Quarterly Review of Biology, 46*, 35-57.

Trivers, R., & Hare, H. (1976). Haplodiploidy and the evolution of the social insects. *Science, 191*, 249-263.

Wagner, B., & DeMunn, E. (1979). Preventing casualties in the executive family. *Management World, 8,* 10-12.

Wills, T., Weiss, R., & Patterson, G. (1974). A behavioral analysis of the determinants of marital satisfaction. *Journal of Consulting and Clinical Psychology, 42,* 802-811.

Wynne, L., McDaniel, S., & Weber, T. (eds.). (1986). *Systems consultation: A new perspective for family therapy.* New York: Guilford Press.

Exosystem Influences on Family and Child Functioning

Denise Daniels
Rudolf H. Moos
*Social Ecology Laboratory,
Department of Psychiatry and Behavioral Sciences
Stanford University Medical Center, Stanford, CA 94305*

*Veterans Administration Medical Center
3801 Miranda, Palo Alto, CA 94304*

> *Parental experiences outside the family, such as work environments and extrafamilial social networks, can influence family and child functioning. These exosystem factors may have a direct impact on parental functioning and the family environment and they may indirectly influence child functioning through their impact on parents and family life. This report examines parental exosystems and paths by which they exert their influences in a representative sample of 133 families. Fathers' work stressors and social resources, and mothers' extrafamilial social networks were associated with specific aspects of parental functioning and the family environment. In turn, parental functioning and the family environment were related to child functioning. For example, fathers' positive work relationships were associated with positive family relationships and, in turn, with fewer child adjustment problems. Mothers' activities with friends were related to higher self-esteem, which was associated with positive family relationships and better child functioning.*

Recently, Bronfenbrenner (1986) outlined how social systems and settings outside the family, such as the child's school and parents' circle of friends, can affect the family environment and child functioning. Bronfenbrenner distinguished between mesosystem and exosystem influences on child development. The mesosystem refers to childrens' experiences in different settings (i.e., family, school, peer group) and their effect on each other and on the child. The exosystem refers to the effects of parents' experiences outside the family (i.e., work, social networks) on

---

Authors' Note: The research was supported in part by NIMH Grant MH16744, the William T. Grant Foundation, NIAAA Grants AA02863 and AA06699, NIAMD Grant AR20610, and Veterans Administration Medical Research Funds. We wish to thank Nancy Bovee and Bernice Moos for their help in collecting, organizing, and analyzing the data, and Ruth Cronkite, Aaron Ebata, and Ralph Swindle for their assistance in formulating the issues and commenting on the manuscript.

©1988 Select Press

family life and the child. This report focuses on exosystem influences (quality of parental work environment and social network) on family and child functioning and on the idea that these influences may operate indirectly through parental functioning. We expect that parental and family adaptation will be enhanced when parents have cohesive and less stressful work environments and larger and closer extrafamilial social networks. In turn, better parental and family adaptation will be associated with improved child adjustment.

Parent Work Environment and Family and Child Functioning

In the area of parental work, most prior research has focused on maternal employment status and work-family conflict (see Bronfenbrenner, 1986; Reppetti, 1987). In general, maternal employment does not detract from family life and child functioning. In some circumstances, family life (Baruch, Biener, & Barnett, 1987) and children (Bronfenbrenner, Alvarez, & Henderson, 1984) may benefit. However, when maternal employment leads to work-family time and role conflict, there may be an increase in family conflict (Pleck & Stains, 1982), more stressors for husbands (Kessler & McCrae, 1982), and a negative impact on family members (Reppetti, 1987).

A more promising line of research involves an assessment of the characteristics and processes in both women's and men's work environments that may be linked to parental and family functioning (Baruch, et al., 1987); Reppetti, 1987; Voydanoff, 1987). Support from coworkers and supervisors, job involvement and autonomy, and work demands can influence parental functioning (Baruch, et al., 1987; Billings & Moos, 1982a, 1982b; Kohn & Schooler, 1982). They may affect family and child functioning as well. Although compensatory (Bergermaier, Borg, and Champoux, 1984) and no-relationship models (Kanter, 1977) have been proposed, most studies suggest that there is some direct carryover between work and family. Specifically, work stressors may erode family and child adaptation, whereas work support and satisfaction may enhance them.

Piotrkowski & Katz (1983) noted that fathers in a high conflict work environment experienced more tension in family relationships. Jackson and Maslach (1982) found that male police officers who experienced more job stress reported less marital satisfaction and involvement in family matters. In addition, job satisfaction has been linked to low family conflict and high marital and family satisfaction in a national sample of male professionals and managers (Voydanoff, 1987). In a study of 285 father-son pairs in Germany, Schneewind (1986) used path analysis to demonstrate a link between fathers' restrictive work environment and high control and low intellectual climate in the family. In turn, high family control and low family intellectual climate were related to the fathers' authoritarianism and an external personality style among their sons.

Research on working mothers also indicates that women who have better work environments tend to report more favorable family relationships and better child adaptation. For example, Reppetti (1987) found that unpleasant and demanding work climates among woman bank employees were associated with more family conflict and less family cohesion. Soliman and Mayseless (1982) reported a correlation between mothers' work satisfaction and fewer psychological problems among Israeli children referred to a mental health clinic. Although characteristics of mothers and fathers have not been included in these studies, they may mediate or act as a connecting factor in relationships between work environment and family and child functioning.

Parent Social Networks and Family and Child Functioning

Parent's social networks and extrafamilial support systems are another primary exosystem influence on family and child functioning (Cochran & Brassard, 1979). A few studies point to the benefits of parent support systems on family and child functioning, particularly for at risk populations (Bronfenbrenner, 1986). For example, Crnig, Greenberg, Ragozin, Robinson, & Baskam (1983) report that mothers of premature and full-term infants who experienced support from friends are more satisfied with parenting and that support from friends moderates stressors in predicting infant responsiveness to parents. In contrast, parents who are isolated from formal and informal support systems are more likely to abuse their children (Belsky, 1980). There is an extensive body of research linking social support to better individual functioning, especially among mothers (Belsky, 1984; Billings & Moos, 1982b; Gottlieb, 1981). This suggests the likelihood of direct or indirect associations between extrafamilial support and better family relationships and child functioning.

Exosystem Influences Through Parental Functioning

Parental work environment and extrafamilial support systems both affect parental functioning which, in turn, is related to the family environment and child functioning. Parental functioning is likely to be a link or mediator in some aspects of exosystem-family and child relationships. For example, work stressors are associated with parental depression, physical symptoms, and lack of self-esteem (Billings & Moos, 1982a). These, in turn, are related to high family conflict, low family cohesion and expressiveness, and poorer psychological adjustment among children in the family (Billings & Moos, 1983; Holahan & Moos, 1987). Thus, it is important to examine the way in which parental exosystem affects parental self-esteem and depression.

Bronfenbrenner (1986) has commented on the importance of inves-

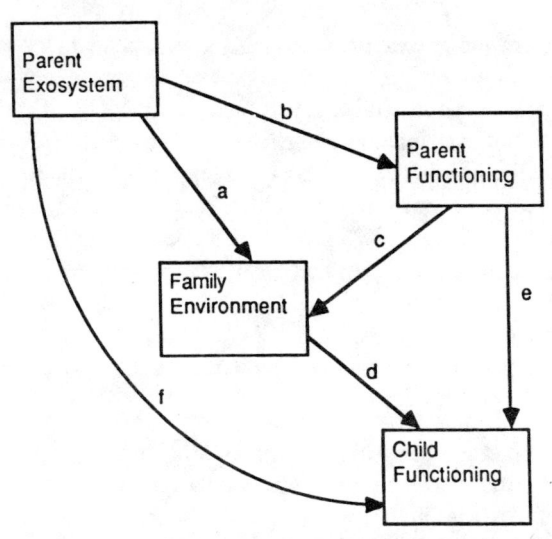

FIGURE 1 Path Model Depicting the Role of Parent Functioning in Exosystem, Family Environment, and Child Functioning Connections

tigating "both links in the presumed causal chain: (a) the influence of employment on parental functioning and (b) the effect of the induced change in family processes on the behavior and development of the child" (p.735). Prior work has focused on the direct impact of the parental exosystem on the family environment and child functioning, but has not examined the idea that extrafamilial influences may affect family and child adaptation through their influence on parental functioning.

In this study we use a conceptual model (Figure 1) to examine possible causal relationships among parent exosystem, parent functioning, family environment, and child functioning. The model is adapted from Belsky (1984) and Schneewind (1986) to include both direct and indirect paths from exosystem to family and child functioning. Parental work environments and extrafamilial social networks affect the family environment either directly (path a) or indirectly through parental functioning (paths b and c). For example, a stressful work environment may be carried over into family interactions even though it does not influence parental functioning (path b). Alternatively, a cohesive work environment may enhance parent self-esteem, which may lead to less family conflict.

The model also includes both direct and indirect paths from exosystems to child functioning. The indirect paths, which are more likely, may take place through the family environment (paths a and d) or through parental functioning (paths b and e). For example, positive work relationships may lead to a more cohesive family environment and, in turn, to better child adjustment (path a and d). Alternatively, parents who are more socially isolated may become more depressed which, in turn, can lead to more child psychosocial problems (paths b and e). Finally, although exosystems are not likely to affect child functioning directly, the model does allow for this path (f), because there may be direct links in some circumstances (Cochran & Brassard, 1979). For example, children often have direct experiences with their parents' friends.

Summary and Study Goals

Prior studies suggest that parental work environments and social networks may have important links to family and child functioning. However, these studies have used a limited set of work-related and social network variables and have neglected fathers' and mothers' social networks. Furthermore, there is little or no information about how parental exosystems are linked to family and child functioning. This study broadens the focus of prior research by examining both father's and mother's work environments and social networks, both the family environment and child functioning, and both direct and indirect paths from exosystems to family and child adjustment. More specifically, we address two related sets of questions:

(1) Are positive work relationships, fewer work stressors, closer social ties, and more social network activities related to better family and child functioning? We examine these associations separately for fathers and mothers.

(2) How are exosystem influences associated with family and child functioning? Do extrafamilial factors influence the family environment directly or do such influences take place through parental functioning? Do extrafamilial factors have any direct influence on the child or do they influence child adjustment indirectly through their effect on parental functioning and the family environment? Again, we examine these questions separately for mothers and fathers using the model shown in Figure 1.

METHOD

Sample

The sample is a subset of 133 families with at least one child and one working parent who were drawn from a larger, randomly selected panel of 424 families and adults residing in the San Francisco Bay Area. The sampling procedure for the larger sample of 424 adults and families involved randomly selecting a street segment from census tracts in the Bay Area and randomly selecting a household from each street segment. If a telephone number was available, an adult family member was contacted by phone and asked to participate. Alternative households within the same census tract were contacted if the telephone number was not available, disconnected, or the family declined to participate. Inventories were sent to each family agreeing to participate. Of families contacted initially, 86.9% agreed to participate and 84.0% of them provided complete data. Of these 424 families, 133 had at least one child and one working parent. (For more details on the overall sample, see Billings & Moos, 1983.)

Of the 133 families, 97 are two-parent families and 36 are single parent families (33 mothers and three fathers). Thus, there are a total of 130 mothers. Their average age was 35.4 years (ranging from 21 to 52 years) and they were relatively well educated (mean = 13.8 years). All 33 single mothers were working, as were 57 of the 97 married mothers. Mother occupation and work environments were quite varied, ranging from factory workers to office jobs to electrical engineers. The average Duncan (Stevens & Featherman, 1981) socioeconomic scores for mothers was 47.5 (SD=18.5) which is equivalent to a medical/dental technician, manager of a variety store, or telephone service person.

The 100 fathers ranged in age from 24 to 56 years (mean = 35.4 years). They were also quite well educated (mean = 14.8 years). The majority of fathers were working full-time in occupations spanning the labor industry, including sales, clerical work, managers, technicians, engineers, teachers, and doctors. (Only two fathers were working part-time.) The average Duncan socioeconomic status score was 56.8 (SD=22.0) which corresponds to occupations such as a librarian, construction manager, or railroad conductor.

There are a total of 110 Caucasian and 20 noncaucasian families. Sixty-two are one child families, 52 are two child families, and 19 have three or more children. The children range in age from 1 to 18 years with a mean of 10.5 years (SD=7.1).

Measures

Both mothers and fathers provided information on their work environment, social network outside the family, family environment, and personal functioning. Mothers and single fathers reported on child psychosocial functioning. In each domain, dimensions tapping life stressors and social resources were selected. The instruments used to assess these dimensions were drawn from the Health and Daily Living Form, the Family Environment Scale, and the Work Environment Scale. Each of these measures has been widely used and has adequate reliability and validity.

Work Environment. The Work Environment Scale (WES, Moos, 1986) provided two summary indices. The *Work Relationship Index* is a

27-item index of the quality of social relationships at work based on three WES subscales: peer cohesion, supervisor support, and involvement and commitment to work (Holahan & Moos, 1983). This index has high internal consistency (Cronbach's Alpha = 0.88). The *Work Stressors Index* is a 36-item index based on four WES subscales: high work pressure and supervisor control and lack of autonomy and clarity (Alpha = 0.77; Billings & Moos, 1982b).

Parental Social Network. The Health and Daily Living Form (HDL, Moos, Cronkite, Billings, & Finney, 1984) was used to assess parent social networks. *Activities With Friends* is based on the sum of yes responses to 12 activities with friends in the last month, such as athletics with a friend, had a long talk with a friend, went to a club or organization, and went to a party (Alpha = 0.73). Quality of social relationships is tapped using a two item scale, *Close Relationships*, reflecting number of close friends and number of people that can be counted on for real help in time of trouble.

Family Environment. We examined resources and stressors in the family environment. Our family resource dimension is based on the *Family Relationship Index* from the Family Environment Scale (FES; Moos & Moos, 1986). This index is composed of three FES scales: high cohesion and expressiveness and low conflict (Alpha = 0.89; Holahan & Moos, 1983). Another family resource measure is *Family Social Connectedness* which is based on the mean of two FES subscales: intellectual-cultural orientation and active-recreational orientation (average Alpha =0.73). Family stressors is based on the *Family Arguments* index from the HDL. The score is a count of yes responses to 14 items about family disagreements, such as arguments about friends, relatives, politics, money, sex, and so on (Alpha = 0.75).

Parent Functioning. To tap parental functioning, we looked at physical symptoms, depressed mood, and self-esteem. *Physical Symptoms* is the sum of yes responses to 12 items, such as headaches, felt weak all over, poor appetite, and indigestion (Alpha = 0.80). *Global Depression* is the sum of 18 five-point items, such as felt sad or blue, poor appetite or weight loss, loss of energy, loss of interest, crying, and feeling sorry for oneself. For each item, respondents indicate how often they experience a symptom from "never" (0) to "often" (4) (Alpha = 0.92). *Self-Esteem* is based on six items rated on five-point scales: ambitious, assertive, confident, dominant, outgoing, and successful. For each item, respondents indicate how characteristic an item is of them from "not at all" (0) to "quite accurately" (4) (Alpha = 0.77).

Child Functioning. The HDL was used to assess three indices of child functioning. *Child Physical Health Problems* is the number of yes responses to eight physical problems (allergies, anemia, asthma, colds or coughs, headaches, over- or underweight, serious physical problem, and stomach aches or indigestion). *Child Adjustment Problems* is the number of five psychological (anxiety, feeling sad or blue, nail biting, nightmares, and mental or emotional problems) and three behavior problems (academic problems at school, discipline problems at school, and problems getting along with other children) for all children living in the family (Alpha = 0.61; Holahan & Moos, 1987). *Child Multiproblem Index* is a dichotomous variable which taps whether children in the family have five or more of the eight physical and the five psychological problems and/or all three of the behavior problems. (All three of the child functioning indices show little relation to child age and gender; Daniels, Moos, Billings, & Miller, 1987).

RESULTS

Descriptive Information

Table 1 shows means and standard deviations for the work, social network, family environment, parental functioning, and child functioning variables. The means and standard deviations are comparable to those for the larger community sample (Moos et al., 1984). There are only two significant mean differences between fathers' and mothers' reports. As noted in Table 1, mothers report more physical symptoms and depression than fathers.

As shown in Table 1, husband-wife correlations for work relationships and work stressors tend to be low and nonsignificant, which reflects the fact that they are in different work environments. On the other hand, because husbands and wives share some of the same friends, they show moderate agreement on the social network indices. Husbands and wives agree even more highly on characteristics of the family environment and child functioning. Since only one parent provided the only report of child functioning in the current sample, Table 1 presents husband-wife agreement correlations on the child functioning indices from another sample (Billings et al., 1987). Inter-parent correlations are significant for the parental functioning indices of physical symptoms and depression but not for self-esteem.

Associations Between Father Exosystem Influences and Family and Child Functioning

As shown in Table 2, all correlations between father work environment and family environment are significant. Fathers who have more positive relationships at work and fewer work stressors have more positive family relationships, higher family social connectedness, and fewer fam-

TABLE 1 Descriptive Information for Father and Mother Reports of Work Environment, Social Network, Family Environment, Parent Functioning, and Child Functioning

Variables	Father Report Mean	SD	Mother Report Mean	SD	Father-mother r
Work Environment					
Positive Work Relationships (0-9 scale)	6.10	2.21	6.06	1.83	.22
Work Stressors (0-9 scale)	3.94	1.41	3.91	1.45	-.04
Social Network					
Number of Close Relationships	7.10	6.75	6.62	6.88	.46*
Activities with Friends	4.86	2.86	4.95	2.66	.29*
Family Environment					
Positive Family Relationships (0-9 scale)	6.52	1.43	6.66	1.23	.56*
Family Social Connectedness	5.03	1.94	5.43	1.89	.56*
Family Arguments (number of 14)	2.92	2.65	2.89	2.30	.42*
Parent Functioning					
Physical Symptoms (number of 12)	1.50	2.23	2.43[+]	2.60	.47*
Depressed Mood (0-72 scale)	15.70	11.12	19.10[+]	11.51	.26*
Self-Esteem (0-24 scale)	14.89	3.92	14.67	4.32	.15
Child Functioning					
Child Physical Health Problems (number of 8)			1.10	1.09	.60*[a]
Child Adjustment Problems (number of 8)			1.22	1.42	.54*[a]
Child Multiproblem Index (% yes)			6.8%		.48*[a]

+ Mother mean significantly higher than father mean, $p<.05$.
* $p<.05$
a Based on N=68 in another sample (Billings et al., 1987).

TABLE 2 Father Exosystem Variables Related to Family and Child Functioning

	Father Work Environment		Father Social Network	
	Positive Work Relationships	Work Stressors	Close Relationships	Activities With Friends
Family Environment (Father Reports)				
Positive Family Relationships	.41*	-.34*	-.01	.06
Family Social Connectedness	.31*	-.21*	.13	.36*
Family Arguments	-.32*	.26*	-.04	-.04
Child Functioning (Mother Reports)				
Child Physical Problems	-.12	.05	-.10	-.24*
Child Adjustment Problems	-.11	.11	-.08	-.02
Child Multiple Problems	-.07	.06	-.15	-.13

*$p<.05$

ily arguments. In general, the significant correlations in Table 2 replicated when fathers' experience at work were associated with mothers' reports of family relationships, family social connectedness, and family arguments.

As expected, there are only weak associations between fathers' work environment and child functioning (Table 2). In addition, fathers' positive work relationships and fewer work stressors were somewhat related to mothers' reports of better child functioning ($p<.10$).

In general, fathers' social network is independent of the family environment and child functioning, except that fathers who participated in more activities with friends reported more family social connectedness and had children with fewer physical problems.

Associations Between Mother Exosystem Influences and Family and Child Functioning

Unlike fathers' work environment, mothers' work environment showed little association with family adaptation (Table 3). Positive work relationships are associated with fewer family arguments, but there are no associations between mothers' work environment and child functioning.

Mothers' social networks—having closer social ties and more activities with friends—are associated with more family social connectedness. These same relationships were found using father reports of family social connectedness ($r = .16$ with closer social ties and $r = .28$ with activities with

TABLE 3 Mother Exosystem Variables Related to Family and Child Functioning

	Mother Work Environment		Mother Social Network	
	Positive Work Relationships	Work Stressors	Close Relationships	Activities With Friends
Family Environment (Mother Reports)				
Positive Family Relationships	.08	.07	.08	.10
Family Social Connectedness	.17	.02	.22*	.36*
Family Arguments	-.18*	.02	-.08	.09
Child Functioning (Mother Reports)				
Child Physical Problems	.09	-.15	-.18*	-.26*
Child Adjustment Problems	-.05	-.03	-.11	.00
Child Multiple Problems	-.09	-.12	-.09	-.10

*$p<.05$

friends). In turn, mothers' close relationships and activities with friends are associated with fewer physical problems.

The Role of Parental Functioning in Exosystem Connections

We have shown some associations between father work environment and family functioning as well as between mother social network and family functioning. We now examine the role of parental functioning in exosystem-family and child relationships by conducting bivariate correlations and selected path analyses using the model we presented in Figure 1.

Associations between parental functioning and exosystem, family, and child functioning. By referring back to Figure 1, one can view the possible relationships between parent functioning and exosystem, family, and child functioning variables. Table 4 shows the bivariate correlations between exosystem factors and parental functioning (path b in the model) and between parental functioning and the family environment (path c) and child functioning (path e). For fathers, positive work relationships are associated with fewer physical symptoms, lower depression, and higher self-esteem. Work stressors are associated with more physical problems, greater depression, and lower self-esteem.

For mothers, more social network resources are associated with less depression and higher self-esteem. Among mothers, functioning is not related to the work environment, except that work stressors are linked to

TABLE 4 Parent Functioning Variables Related to Exosystem, Family and Child Functioning[+]

	Father Functioning			Mother Functioning		
	Phy. Symp.	Depression	Self-Esteem	Phy. Symp.	Depression	Self-Esteem
Exosystem Dimensions						
Positive Work Relationships	-.41*	-.47*	.28*	-.10	-.06	-.04
Work Stressors	.34*	.41*	-.18*	.09	-.04	.20*
Close Relationships	.06	-.17	.08	-.14	-.18*	.21*
Activities with Friends	-.16	-.07	.14	-.10	-.30*	.21*
Family Environment						
Positive Family Relationships	-.29*	-.39*	.19*	-.38*	-.45*	.28*
Family Social Connectedness	-.22*	-.04	.15	-.24*	-.32*	.28*
Family Arguments	.37*	.46*	-.15	-.13	.22*	-.08
Child Functioning						
Child Physical Problems	.19*	.21*	-.07	.17*	.27*	-.22*
Child Adjustment Problems	.28*	.31*	-.15	.20*	.24*	-.02
Child Multiple Problems	.22*	.42*	-.20*	.06	.18*	-.13

* $p<.05$
+ Father functioning is correlated with father reports of exosystem dimensions and family environment and mother reports of child functioning. Mother functioning is correlated with mother reports of exosystem dimensions, family environment, and child functioning.

higher self-esteem. Both father and mother functioning, particularly physical symptoms and depression, are related to less positive family relationships, less family social connectedness, and more family arguments, as well as to more child physical, adjustment, and multiple problems.

Although not presented in the table, we identified expected relationships between family environment and child functioning (path d in the model). For example, both parent's reports of more family arguments were significantly related to more child adjustment problems, whereas better family relationships (as reported by both the father and mother) were significantly related to fewer child physical problems.

Selected path analyses: The role of parent functioning in exosystem, family, and child functioning relationships. We next conducted selected path analyses to determine the extent to which father work environment and mother social network are related to the family environment and child functioning indirectly through their influences on parent functioning. We examined each path using the model presented in Figure 1, which depicts possible causal relationships among parent exosystem, parent functioning, family environment, and child functioning.

With our multivariate data set, numerous sets of exosystem and parent-family-child connections are possible. Thus, we selected three sets of parent-family-child stressors and resources based on their conceptual relation to each other (e.g., parent physical problems and child physical problems were grouped in the same set) and on the empirical results shown in Tables 2-4 (i.e., the variables had to show a meaningful pattern of relationships to begin with). Using these two criteria, we grouped the variables in three sets: (1) parent self-esteem, positive family relationships, and child adjustment problems, (2) parent depression, family arguments, and child multiple problems, and (3) parent physical symptoms, family social connectedness, and child physical problems.

The first set is based on the idea that parent self-esteem is conceptually related to the child adjustment index, that parent self-esteem and child adjustment show a significant pattern of associations with positive family relationships, and that self-esteem and positive family relationships are social resource dimensions. The second set is based on similar ideas: parent depression is conceptually closest to the child multi-problem index, both these variables show a pattern of relationship to family arguments, and depression and family arguments tap stressor dimensions. The third set matches parent physical problems with child physical problems. It uses the family social connectedness scale, which showed a significant association with parent physical problems and conceptually is linked to physical activities.

We examined these three sets of parent-family-child variables in the path model with father positive work relationships and work stressors and with mother close relationships and activities with friends. For these 12 selected analyses, standardized partial regression coefficients were determined for each path in the model.

Father work environment and family and child functioning. Of the six path diagrams for fathers, three showed that father work environment had a direct impact on family functioning, which, in turn, influenced childrens' adjustment. The other three indicated that father work environment influenced the family environment and child functioning through its impact on the fathers' functioning. Two path models with standardized partial regression coefficients are shown to illustrate these two types of connections (Figures 2 and 3).

Figure 2 shows that father positive work relationships are directly

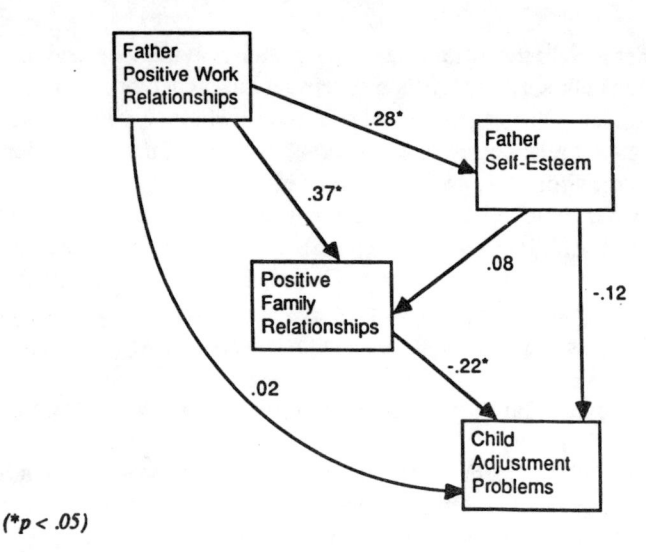

FIGURE 2 Path Model Depicting a Direct Connection from Father Work Environment to Family Environment which, in turn, is related to child functioning

(*p < .05)

related to positive family relationships which, in turn, are related to fewer adjustment problems for children. In addition, positive work relationships are associated with higher father self-esteem, but father self-esteem does not mediate the influence of work on family or child functioning. Two other sets of variables (not shown) followed a similar pattern in that aspects of fathers' work settings were associated with family and child functioning.

Figure 3 shows a different pattern. Here, father work stressors have an indirect impact on more family arguments and child multiple problems through their connection to father depression. The other two path models (not presented) showed that father functioning indirectly mediated between work and family and child functioning.

Mother social network, family environment, and child adaptation. Turning to the findings for mothers, the standardized partial regression coefficients again showed evidence for both an influence of mother social network on child adjustment through its impact on the family environment and an influence of her social network on child problems mediated through her functioning. Figure 4 shows that mothers' close social ties modestly enhance family social connectedness which, in turn, is associated with fewer physical problems for children.

The standardized partial regression coefficient in Figure 5 points to an indirect influence of mother activities with friends on positive family

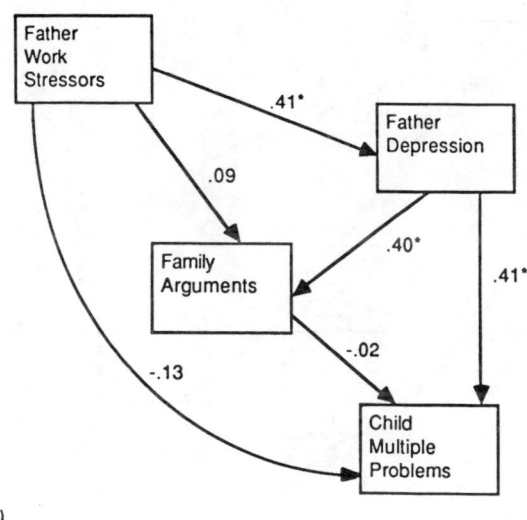

[Figure 3: Path diagram with the following paths:
- Father Work Stressors → Father Depression: .41*
- Father Work Stressors → Family Arguments: .09
- Father Work Stressors → Child Multiple Problems: -.13
- Father Depression → Family Arguments: .40*
- Father Depression → Child Multiple Problems: .41*
- Family Arguments → Child Multiple Problems: -.02]

(*p < .05)

FIGURE 3 Path Model Depicting an Indirect Influence of Father Work Environment on Family and Child Functioning Through Father Functioning

relationships mediated by increased mother self-esteem. In turn, positive family relationships were associated with fewer child adjustment problems. Two other path models (not presented) pointed to a mediating influence of mother functioning.

DISCUSSION

This study examined connections between parental experiences outside the family (or exosystems) and the family environment and child adaptation. It also examined how exosystems may exert their influence on the family and child through their effects on parental functioning. The study encompassed both father and mother exosystems, and includes both stressor and social resource dimensions in work, social network, and family environment. Father work environment and mother extrafamilial social network were related to the family environments both directly, and indirectly through parental functioning. Parental stressors and resources outside the family appear to affect child functioning indirectly through their influence on both the family environment and parental functioning.

Father Exosystem Influences

The fathers' work environment was connected to both family and child functioning. It influenced child functioning through its effect on

128   WORK AND FAMILY: THEORY, RESEARCH, AND APPLICATIONS

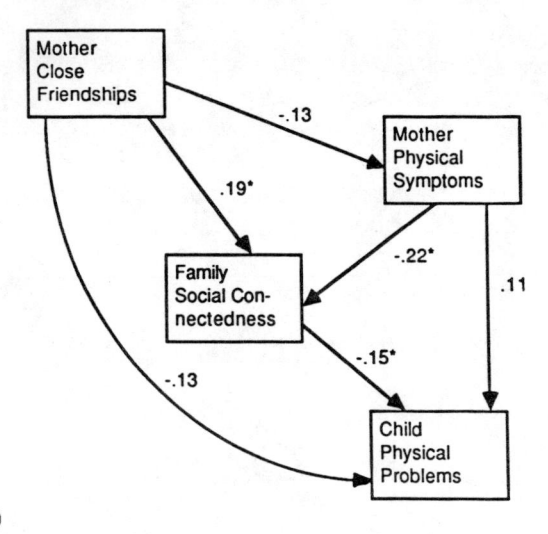

(*p < .05)

FIGURE 4   Path Model Depicting a Direct Connection from Mother Extrafamilial Social Network to Family Environment which, in turn, is related to child functioning

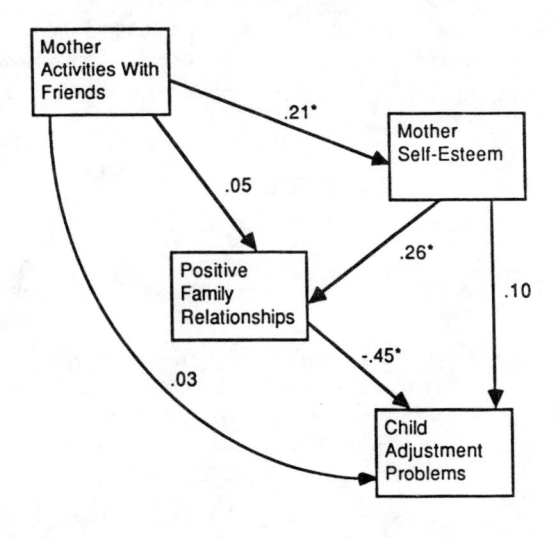

(*p < .05)

FIGURE 5   Path Model Depicting an Indirect Influence of Mother Extrafamilial Social Network on Family and Child Functioning Through Mother Functioning

family functioning. Positive work relationships and fewer work stressors for fathers were associated with positive family relationships, more family social connectedness, and fewer family arguments. In turn, better family functioning fostered child adaptation. Path models examining the interconnections between father work environment, father functioning, family environment, and child functioning showed evidence for direct impact of favorable father work environments on improved family functioning which, in turn, fostered child adaptation. Specifically, we identified an indirect impact of father work stressors on family conflict and child adjustment problems through father dysfunction. Thus, our results show evidence for both direct and indirect connections among father work environment, father functioning, family environment, and child functioning.

Although we found relatively strong connections between father work environment and the family environment, we noted little association between father extrafamilial social networks and family or child functioning. This suggests a "no relationship" model in that fathers tend to separate their non-work extrafamilial social relationships and activities from their family and home life. This conclusion is supported by the fact that father work environment and social network variables showed little or no relationship with each other. Furthermore, none of the father's non-work social network variables were related to father functioning.

Mother Exosystem Influences

In contrast to the findings for fathers, mother work stressors and resources showed little overall association with family or child functioning, while her extrafamilial social network did. (As with father's, mother's work and social network characteristics were not correlated with each other.) Mothers who had closer friendships and who engaged in more activities with friends reported more family social connectedness. In addition, mothers with more extrafamilial social resources had higher self-esteem and were less depressed. Better mother functioning was associated with more positive family relationships and fewer family stressors, and, in turn, with better child adaptation.

In our sample, the overall pattern of results suggests that working mothers separate their work and family life. The mothers' work environment was not linked to family or child functioning. In this respect, work-family environment links may be more complicated for working mothers than for working fathers. Processes in the work environment may also have different effects on single mothers than on married mothers. We examined preliminary work-family correlations separately for each group. For married mothers the correlations were more consistent with those of married men; better work relationships were significantly associated with better family relationships, family connectedness, and fewer family arguments. Although our sample of single mothers was small (N = 33), positive work relationships showed no association to the family environment. In fact, a more stressful work environment for single mothers was linked to somewhat better functioning among their children.

Piotrkowski & Katz (1983) noted that the socioeconomic status of working mothers is an important consideration in work-family associations (see also Piotrkowski & Crits-Christoph, 1981). Accordingly, we examined preliminary correlations between work environment and family and child functioning for lower versus higher socioeconomic status mothers. Among higher socioeconomic status women, positive work relationships were related to higher family social connectedness, fewer family arguments, and fewer child adjustment and multiple problems. Among lower class mothers, however, less positive work relationships and more work stressors were related to better child functioning. Piotrkowski & Katz (1983) also found that job demands among lower class mothers were related to higher school achievement among their adolescent children. Stressful or demanding work environments may be stimulating and enhance family and child functioning among some lower class and single mothers. This possibility is consistent with our finding that work stress was positively related to higher self-esteem among mothers. In addition, less positive work relationships were linked to fewer adjustment problems in children of lower class mothers. A less involving and cohesive work milieu may sometimes lead to better child functioning because the mother has more energy for family and child interaction (see Moos & Fuhr, 1982, for an example of how a highly engaging work setting reduced a mother's involvement with her adolescent daughter).

Father and Mother Exosystem

Our study points to at least four valuable areas for future research. To begin, the extent and direction of exosystem influences, such as the work environment may depend on the life circumstances of the parents, such as their marital and socioeconomic status. Thus, a stressful or demanding work environment may have different effects for low versus high socioeconomic status mothers or for single versus married mothers. Second, because work and social network characteristics show different links to family life and child functioning for both mothers and fathers, research should examine both interactive and cumulative influences of mother and father exosystem factors on family and child functioning.

A third area is a focus on mediating variables between parental exosystems, the family environment, and child functioning. In this study, parental self-esteem, depression, and physical symptoms all contributed to the links between exosystems and family and child functioning. Other areas of parental functioning, parental attitudes, parental personality traits, and parenting characteristics may be important in mediating both work and social network connections to family and child functioning. For example, although the mother's work environment may not affect overall family climate, it may influence more specific parent-child interactions. Prior studies have shown relationships between mothers' work environment and better interaction with children, such as praising, smiling, laughing, teaching, and playing (Harrell & Ridley, 1975; Hoffman, 1983), more positive attitudes toward child rearing (Alvarez, 1985; Schneewind, 1986), and less strain on the marital relationship and ability to parent (Belsky, Perry-Jenkins, Crouter, 1985).

Our study and others to date have been cross-sectional. Longitudinal studies may provide information about the direction of effects between parental exosystems and family and child functioning. To evaluate the role of parental functioning in exosystem family and child connections, we used a path model displaying possible causal relationships. This path model was drawn from a conceptual framework developed by Bronfenbrenner and others (Belsky, 1984; Schneewind, 1986). For heuristic purposes, we assumed unidirectional effects from exosystem to parent, family, and child functioning. However, family life has been shown to effect the work milieu (Brett, 1989; Crouter, 1984) and child functioning is known to effect parent functioning, which can change the family environment and possibly even parental exosystem factors. Overall, future research should be directed toward the development of a comprehensive model that encompasses both positive and negative influences of exosystem factors on the family, as well as the reciprocal effects of family and child functioning on parental exosystems.

REFERENCES

Alvarez, W. F. (1985). The meaning of maternal employment for mothers and their perceptions of their three-year-old children. *Child Development, 56,* 350-360.

Anderson-Kulman, R. E., & Paludi, M. A. (1986). Working mothers and the family context: Predicting positive coping. *Journal of Vocational Behavior, 28,* 241-253.

Baruch, G. K., Biener, L., & Barnett, R. C. (1987). Women and gender in research on work and family stress. *American Psychologist, 42,* 130-136.

Belsky, J. (1980) Child maltreatment: An ecological integration. *American Psychologist, 35,* 320-335.

Belsky, J. (1984). The determinants of parenting: A process model. *Child Development, 55,* 83-96.

Belsky, J., Perry-Jenkins, M., & Crouter, A. C. (1985). The work-family interface and marital change across the transition to parenthood. *Journal of Family Issues, 6,* 205-220.

Bergermaier, R., Borg, I., & Champoux, J. E. (1984). Structural relationships among facets of work, nonwork, and general well being. *Work and Occupations, 11,* 163-181.

Billings, A. G., & Moos, R. H. (1982a). Social support and functioning among community and clinical groups: A panel model. *Journal of Behavioral Medicine, 5,* 295-311.

Billings, A. G., & Moos, R. H. (1982b). Work Stress and the stress-buffering roles of work and family resources. *Journal of Occupational Behavior, 3,* 215-232.

Billings, A. G., & Moos, R. H. (1983). Comparisons of children of depressed and nondepressed parents: A social-environmental perspective. *Journal of Abnormal Child Psychology, 11,* 215-232.

Billings, A. G., & Moos, R. H., Miller, J. J., & Gottlieb, J. E. (1987). Psychological adaptation in juvenile rheumatic disease: A controlled evaluation. *Health Psychology, 6,* 343-359.

Brette, J., & Yogev, S. (1988). Restructuring work for family: How dual-earner couples with children manage. In E. Goldsmith (Ed.), Work and family: Theory, research, and applications. [Special issue]. *Journal of Social Behavior and Personality, 3* (4), 159-174.

Bronfenbrenner, U. (1986). Ecology of the family as a context for human development: Research perspectives. *Developmental Psychology, 22,* 723-742.

Bronfenbrenner, U., Alvarez, W. F., & Henderson, C. R. (1984). Working and watching: Maternal employment status and parents' perceptions of their three-year-old children. *Child Development, 55,* 1362-1378.

Cochran, M.M., & Brassard, J. (1979). Child development and personal social networks. *Child Development, 50,* 601-616.

Crnig, K.A., Greenberg, M. T., Ragozin, A. S., Robinson, N. M., & Baskam, R. B. (1983). Effects of stress and social support on mothers and premature and fullterm infants. *Child Development, 54,* 209-217.

Crouter, A.C. (1984). Spillover from family to work: The neglected side of the work-family interface. *Human Relations, 37,* 425-442.

Daniels, D., Moos, R. H., Billings, A. G., & Miller, J. J. (1987). Psychological risk and resistance factors among children with chronic illness, healthy siblings, and healthy controls. *Journal of Abnormal Child Psychology, 15,* 295-308.

Gottlieb, B. H. (1981). *Social networks and social support.* Beverly Hills, CA: Sage.

Harrell, J., & Ridley, C. A. (1975). Substitute child care, maternal employment, and the quality of mother child interaction. *Journal of Marriage and the Family, 37,* 556-564.

Hoffman, L. W. (1963). Mother's enjoyment of work and effects on the child. In F.I. Nye & L.W. Hoffman (Eds.) *The employed mother in America.* (pp. 95-105) Wesport, Conn.: Greenwood Press.

Holahan, C. J., & Moos, R. H. (1982). Social support and adjustment: Predictive benefits of social climate indices. *American Journal of Community Psychology, 10,* 403-415.

Holahan, C. J., & Moos, R. H. (1983). The quality of social support: Measures of family and work relationships. *British Journal of Clinical Psychology, 22,* 157-162.

Holahan, C. J., & Moos, R. H. (1987). Risk, resistance, and psychological distress: A longitudinal analysis with adults and children. *Journal of Abnormal*

Psychology, 3-13.
Jackson, S., & Maslach, C. (1982). After-effects of job-related stress: Families as victims. *Journal of Occupational Behavior, 3*, 66-77.
Kanter, R.M. (1977). *Work and family in the United States: A critical review and agenda for research and policy.* New York: Russell Sage.
Kessler, R. C., & McCrae, J. A. (1982). The effects of wives' employment on the mental health of men and women. *American Sociological Review, 47*, 216-227.
Kohn, M. L., & Schooler, C. (1982). Job conditions and personality: A longitudinal assessment of their reciprocal effects. *American Journal of Sociology, 87*, 1257-1286.
Moos, R. H. (1986a). Work as a human context. In S.M. Pallack & R.O. Porloff (Eds.), *Psychology and work: Productivity, change, and employment.* (pp. 9-52) Washington, DC: American Psychological Association.
Moos, R. H. (1986b). *Work Environment Scale manual.* Palo Alto, CA: Consulting Psychologist Press.
Moos, R. H., Cronkite, R. C., Billings, A. G., & Finney, J. W. (1984). *Health and Daily Living Form manual.* Palo Alto, CA: Social Ecology Laboratory, Veterans Administration and Stanford University Medical Centers.
Moos, R., & Fuhr, R. (1982). The clinical use of social-ecological concepts: The case of an adolescent girl. *American Journal of Orthopsychiatry, 52*, 111-122.
Moos, R.H., & Moos, B.S. (1984). The process of recovery from Alcoholism: III. Comparing functioning in families of alcoholics and matched control families. *Journal of Studies on Alcohol, 45*, 111-118.
Moos, R.H., & Moos, B.S. (1986). *Family Environment Scale manual - Second Edition.* Palo Alto, CA: Consulting Psychologist Press.
Piotrkowski, C.S., & Crits-Christoph, P. (1981). Women's jobs and family adjustment. *Journal of Family Issues, 2*, 127-147.
Piotrkowski, C.S., & Katz, M.H. (1982). Indirect socializations of children: The effects of mothers' jobs on academic behavior. *Child Development, 53*, 1520-1529.
Piotrkowski, C.S., & Katz, M. H. (1983). Work experience and family relations among working-class and lower-class families. *Research in the Interweave of Social Roles: Jobs and Families, 3*, 187-200.
Pleck, J.H., & Stains, G. L. (1982). Work schedules and work-family conflict in two-earner couples. In J. Aldous (Ed.), *Two paychecks: Life in dual-earner families.* Beverly Hills, CA : Sage.
Reppetti, R.L. (1987). Linkages between work and family roles. In S. Oskamp (Ed.) *Family processes and problems: Social psychological aspects.* Newbury Park, CA: Sage.
Schneewind, K.A. (1986). Contextual approaches to family systems research: The macro/micro puzzle. Presented at the *Conference on Family Systems and Life Span Development.* Max Planck Institute for Human Development and Education, Berlin, West Germany.
Soliman, P., & Mayseless, O.B. (1982). Correlates between mother's employment, father's involvement and child's mental health. *Israel Journal of Psychiatry and Related Sciences, 19*, 121-127.
Stevens, G., & Featherman, D.L. (1981). A revised socioeconomic index of occupational status. *Social Science Research, 10*, 364-395.
Voydanoff, P. (1987). *Work and family life.* Newbury Park, CA :Sage.

Affective Response to Work and Quality of Family Life: Employee and Spouse Perspectives

Sheldon Zedeck
Christina Maslach
Kathleen Mosier
Linda Skitka

*Department of Psychology
University of California at Berkeley, Berkeley, CA 94720*

The affective variables of job satisfaction and burnout, as experienced in an employing organization, were studied with respect to their relationship to the quality of life in a family organization. Affective measures were obtained from employees working in social services, whereas the assessment of the quality of life was obtained from their spouses. Results indicated that the employee group was generally dissatisfied and burned out, but that these variables did not relate to their self-reported performance assessments. However, the employees' affective responses were related to spousal reports of problems in the family and home life. Relationships between the employee affective responses and the spouse perceptions of family life revealed that the spouse perceptions were more highly related to employees' satisfaction with extrinsic aspects of the work, and with emotional exhaustion and depersonalization components of burnout, than with intrinsic satisfaction or personal accomplishment. These results can be understood in terms of two types of interpersonal communication between employee and spouse; that which is episodic and public (extrinsic satisfaction) vs. chronic or private (intrinsic satisfaction).

Family and employing organizations are considered to be the two most central institutions that impinge on the life of an individual (Mortimer, Lorence, & Kumka, 1986). Traditionally, researchers have focused on only one of these spheres, to the general exclusion of the other. However, current researchers are beginning to recognize the natural relationship that exists between the employing organization and family experiences, and are starting to establish empirically the precise nature of

---

Authors' Note: The authors acknowledge the support of the participant union members and the Institute of Industrial Relations, University of California at Berkeley, in the conduct of the research described in this paper.

the connections between the two spheres. For example, behavior in a work situation is influenced by outside factors such as stressful family situations (Bhagat, McQuaid, Lindholm, & Segovis, 1985), a person's familial role (Kanter, 1977), and the degree of satisfaction with non-work life (Crosby, 1984). Conflict between work and family has also been related to turnover (Bray, Campbell, & Grant, 1974; Ross & Zander, 1957) and to job satisfaction (Nieva, 1979). Evidence has also been obtained to document the impact of work variables on an individual's home and family life (see Burke & Bradshaw, 1981; Burke & Greenglass, 1987 for reviews). Job demands and job stress, for example, can negatively impact marital and life satisfaction (Burke, Weir, & Du Wors, 1981; Jayaratne, Chess, & Kunkel, 1984), family experiences (Burke & Weir, 1981; Burke, Shearer, & Deszca, 1984), and spousal well-being (Burke, Weir, & Duwors, 1980a,b).

Our recent research has established an initial link between affective reactions to work and the impairment of certain aspects of an individual's family life. In one study, employees' level of job burnout was reflected in their interactions with their spouse and children (Jackson & Maslach, 1982). In a second study, satisfaction with job and family congruence was related to employees' health and mood as well as to structural job conditions (Jackson, Zedeck, & Summers, 1985). The current study was designed to replicate and extend this earlier research by exploring the relationship between an employee's affective reaction to the job and his or her family life. In particular, the study examined the implications of both job satisfaction and job burnout for the quality of family life.

Job Satisfaction. Job satisfaction is generally considered to be a multidimensional affective response to one's job (Locke, 1976; Smith, Kendall, & Hulin, 1969; Weiss, Dawis, England, & Lofquist, 1964). It is dependent on both externally-controlled factors (such as pay, promotion, supervision, recognition, working conditions and other facets of work), and on factors intrinsic to the work itself (e.g., ability utilization, opportunity for learning or achievement, difficulty, autonomy, and responsibility). This distinction between intrinsic and extrinsic satisfaction provides a finer assessment of the job satisfaction construct and its relationship to meaningful variables. For example, such extrinsic factors as pay and promotion may have more of an impact on a family's well-being than would the employee's intrinsic sense of autonomy or responsibility. However, because there has been almost no research on the relationship between either of the job satisfaction components and family variables, the current study investigated the intrinsic-extrinsic satisfaction distinction on an exploratory basis.

The antecedents of job satisfaction have traditionally been explored with reference to other employee and work-related variables, such as mentally challenging but not physically tiring work, appropriate work conditions and rewards for work, and supportive agents within the workplace (Locke, 1976). Similarly, studies of the effects of job satisfaction have concentrated on such work outcomes as performance, job burnout, turnover, absenteeism, and organizational commitment. However, some studies have found links between job satisfaction and personal outcomes such as self-confidence (Herzberg, Mausner, & Snyderman, 1959), physical and mental health (Burke, 1969/1970; Herzberg et al., 1959; Kornhauser, 1965) and attitudes toward other areas of life (Kornhauser, 1965; Iris & Barrett, 1972). Surprisingly, the only outcome listed above that has not been empirically and strongly linked to job satisfaction is performance (Locke, 1976).

Job Burnout. Burnout is a syndrome of emotional exhaustion, depersonalization, and feelings of reduced personal accomplishment, which can occur among individuals who work extensively with other people in a service relationship (Maslach, 1982; Maslach & Jackson, 1986). A key aspect of burnout is increased feelings of emotional exhaustion. As emotional resources are depleted, workers feel they are no longer able to give of themselves at a psychological level. Another aspect of burnout is the development of depersonalization—that is, negative, cynical attitudes and feelings about the people with whom one works. A third aspect of burnout is reduced personal accomplishment, which refers to the tendency to evaluate oneself negatively, particularly with regard to one's work with other people.

Burnout has been studied most extensively among employees in the human services sector, such as social workers, nurses, teachers, and mental health workers. This research has shown that the occurrence of burnout, in one or more of its forms, is linked to a number of negative behavioral outcomes, both for the individual employee and for the people with whom he or she works. For example, burnout has been linked to greater dissatisfaction, either with the job in general or with specific aspects of the job (Burke et al., 1984; Jayaratne et al., 1986; Maslach & Florian, 1988). Burnout also has been related to a variety of job withdrawal behaviors, including the intention to quit one's job and actual turnover (Burke et al., 1984; Jackson & Maslach, 1982; Jackson, Schwab, & Schuler, 1986; Lazaro, Shinn, & Robinson, 1984; Maslach & Jackson, 1984). In addition, burnout has been linked to poor job performance (Nowack & Hanson, 1983) and poor health (Belcastro & Gold, 1984; Burke et al., 1984; Jayaratne et al., 1986).

Family Life and Affective Reactions to Work

One of the most consistently documented relationships between employing and family organizations is that of job satisfaction and overall non-work life. Satisfied workers tend to be more satisfied with life in general (Near, Rice, & Hunt, 1978; Rice et al., 1980). In fact, Crosby (1984) concluded that the best predictor of job satisfaction is a full life outside of the work environment.

It seems logical, but is less-well defined, that marital and familial components of non-work life also would be related to an individual's job satisfaction. In fact, some research indicates that contentment with one's job is correlated with family satisfaction (Schneider & Dachler, 1978), with marital relationship quality (Pahl & Pahl, 1971), and with the quality of the work/home relationship (Evans & Bartolomè, unpublished in Burke & Bradshaw, 1981). On the basis of extensive interviews with workers and their families, Piotrkowski (1978) identified job satisfaction as a critical factor for a positive interface between work and family spheres. Individuals who were satisfied with their jobs were more emotionally and interpersonally available to their families. Conversely, spousal or family satisfaction with an employee's job also has been shown to be related to employee job satisfaction (Dyer, 1956; Guest & Williams, 1973; Pahl & Pahl, 1971).

A few analyses have revealed hints that particular components of job satisfaction may be related to family or non-work life in different ways. Chacko (1983), for example, found evidence for a direct link from work satisfaction to life satisfaction when extrinsic job elements, such as supervision, pay, and promotion were considered. His data also suggested that the direction of influence is reversed (i.e., life satisfaction affects work satisfaction) for intrinsic job elements, such as satisfaction with work itself, authority, and responsibility (see also Kemper & Reichler, 1976).

Much like job satisfaction, the impact of burnout is not limited to the boundaries of the job. Although the sources of this type of stress may be largely work-related, the effects may be felt in non-work areas of life as well. The employee who is feeling emotionally drained, cynical about people, and negative about himself or herself is not likely to shed these feelings as soon as he or she leaves the job and goes home. As a result, relations with both family and friends may be impaired—an hypothesis for which there is some supportive evidence. Workers who experience higher levels of burnout report that the job has a negative impact on their family life (Burke et al., 1984) and that they are less satisfied with their marriages (Jayaratne et al. 1984). Independently, spouses of more burned-out workers describe the quality of their family life in more negative terms

(Jackson & Maslach, 1982). Other data that speak to the link between burnout and family life are analyses of demographic variables, which indicate that employees who are married or who have children experience less burnout (Maslach & Jackson, 1985).

Current Research

In general, the empirical studies of affective reactions to work and their relationship to family variables have been limited. Most investigations have directed attention only to male employees and their families. Generally only the employee's perspective of work and home life has been measured. Following the lead of earlier research (Jackson & Maslach, 1984; Jackson et al., 1985), the current study obtained two perspectives on this issue. The affective responses were obtained from the employee, but the impact of the job on family and home life was studied by obtaining responses from the employee's spouse.

As indicated, most studies in the employing organization and family arena have limited their samples to male employees. Because females are entering the workforce in increasing numbers, it has become increasingly important to examine their reactions to work, and the impact of their work experiences on aspects of family life. In addition, some studies have documented sex differences in affective responses to work and in the nature of the carryover of that work to the family (e.g., Holahan & Gilbert, 1979; Sekaran, 1983). This study extends previous research by considering a sample of workers who are predominantly female, but with a sufficient sample of men to allow for comparison. Not only does this sample allow us to examine female employees, but also the neglected perspective of male spouses.

Particular attention was given to the difference between intrinsic and extrinsic job satisfaction, because of the earlier suggestion that these might be differentially related to family life. The relationship between satisfaction and actual job performance was also assessed, to determine (1) if performance and satisfaction are related (as assumed to be by early researchers), and (2) how performance is related to burnout and family life.

METHOD

Subjects

The participants in this study were a non-random sample of 1057 members of a statewide union for public service employees and their spouses (or partners). These employees were located in offices throughout the state, where they provided a variety of social services for clients. The modal tenure of these employees was 10 to 14 years, but it ranged from less than six months to more than 25 years. With regard to college education, 22% actually graduated from a four year college, 9% had some graduate coursework, and 7% had received a graduate degree (e.g., MA or Ph.D.).

The current sample represents those couples where both the employee and his or her spouse (partner) responded to a union solicitation for research participation. The employee sample was composed of 818 females and 257 males, with the spouse sample having the reverse sex composition. Thus, this sample is one of predominantly female employees and male spouses, which is in marked contrast to other studies of work-family relationships. Most of the respondents (62%) were between 35 and 50 years of age. The ethnic composition of the sample was 62% Caucasian, 18% Hispanic, 7% Black, and 5% Asian.

Over 89% of the respondents reported that they were married to their partner, 7% were unmarried but living together, and the remainder reported that they were presently separated or getting a divorce. On the average, couples had been together 18.2 years. Sixty-four percent of the couples had children living in the home; 28% had one child, 24% had two children, 8% had three children, 3% had four children, and the remaining had more than four children still living at home.

Procedure

Data were collected via questionnaires distributed to approximately 4000 union members and their spouse/partners. The questionnaire was designed in conjunction with union leaders, and the union handled the printing and distribution of these surveys. After the initial mailing, a reminder card was sent out. Although more than 1075 employees returned completed questionnaires, the sample of 1075 represents those employees whose spouse also received a spousal questionnaire and for whom an employee and spouse/partner could be matched. (Questionnaires were number coded so that respondents could remain anonymous but matched.) Employees and spouses/partners were asked to complete their distinct questionnaires independently and then to mail them back to the investigators (separate envelopes were provided for the employee and spouse). Based on pretests, the average length of time for completing the questionnaire was 45-60 minutes for employees and 20-30 minutes for spouses. Based on the number of questionnaires distributed, the return rate for both the spouse and employee samples was approximately 25%. This percentage response rate is an underestimate since the number of employees who were married is unknown.

Instruments

Employee Measures. In addition to providing the demographic information summarized above, employees responded to a twenty-five page questionnaire that probed their performance, reactions to work, health, organizational climate, and so forth. This paper will focus only on the affective reactions to work, specifically the perceived job satisfaction and experienced burnout of the employee. Job satisfaction was measured using the short form of the Minnesota Satisfaction Questionnaire (MSQ; Weiss et al., 1964), which taps two components of job satisfaction—(1) Intrinsic Satisfaction (IS; the feelings of competence and pleasure derived from inherent aspects of one's work, such as the chance to be creative, independent, or to make use of one's abilities); and (2) Extrinsic Satisfaction (ES; satisfaction derived from elements outside the work itself and out of the employee's control, such as compensation, job security, or recognition). A general satisfaction (GS) score is also obtained, based on all 20 questions on the MSQ (the Intrinsic and Extrinsic Satisfaction component are formed by using 18 of the 20 questions). Median reliability coefficients for the subscales are .86 and .80 for intrinsic and extrinsic satisfaction, respectively, and .90 for general satisfaction (Weiss et al, 1964).

The Maslach Burnout Inventory (MBI; Maslach & Jackson, 1981) was also used to assess the employee's affective response to the job. The MBI yields scores on three subscales: (1) Emotional Exhaustion (EE; high scores indicate feelings of emotional over-extension and being worn out by one's work; the worker is no longer able to give of himself or herself at the psychological level); (2) Depersonalization (D; high scores reflect a tendency to describe an unfeeling or impersonal response towards recipients of one's care or service and negative cynical attitudes and feelings about clients); and (3) Personal Accomplishment (PA; low scores reflect feelings of incompetence or ineffectiveness at work). High scores on the Emotional Exhaustion and Depersonalization scales, and low scores on the Personal Accomplishment scale indicate burnout. Cronbach internal consistency estimates of reliability are .90 for EE, .79 for D, and .71 for PA (Maslach & Jackson, 1986).

Two other questions that were asked of the employee and analyzed in the present paper pertain to self-reported performance indices: (1) "are you meeting your department's/office's performance standard?" (1 = "yes;" 2 = "no") and (2) an 11-point scale of the degree to which the employee was above, at, or below standard, where "1" represented "25% or more above standard," "6" represented "at standard," and "11" represented "25% or more below standard."

Spouse/Partner Measure

The spouse/partners in this study were asked questions that assessed: (1) happiness with own job, (2) happiness with employee's job, (3) desire for the employee to change occupation, (4) affect of employee's work on home life, and (5) kind of effect work has on home life. In addition, the questionnaire incorporated items from three domains adapted from Jackson and Maslach (1982) and Jackson et al. (1985), (6) five questions on how employee work is brought home, (7) 14 questions on family life, and (8) 5 questions on the quality of employee's relationship with children. Finally, there was (9) a single question on the extent to which employee's work causes children emotional distress, and (10) a single question on the extent to which employee's work causes spouse emotional stress. Each of these questions was responded to on 5-point scales where the first, third, and fifth points were anchored with descriptors.

RESULTS AND DISCUSSION

As indicated, there are two samples studied in this research—an employee sample and a spouse sample. Within each sample, a different set of variables was examined.

Employee Sample

For the employee sample, the main variables of interest were three satisfaction measures (IS, ES, and GS) and three burnout measures (EE, D, and PA). Table 1 provides the means and standard deviations for each of the above variables for the employee sample. Examination of the satisfaction results, and comparison with norms provided by Weiss et al. (1964), reveal that the employee group is relatively low on each of the facets of satisfaction. The MBI results indicate higher than average levels of burnout for the employee group. Comparison to normative data for social service workers indicates that the present sample has somewhat greater burnout with respect to EE and D, but average levels of reduced PA.

The performance data indicate that most employees saw themselves as meeting standards (92%) and as generally being between 10-15% above standard. The correlation between these two measures is .48 (n = 916, $p < .01$). (This correlation is restricted, given the disproportionate percentage of those who indicated they were meeting the standard—92% responded "yes".) Given the restriction, most of the following results and discussion will focus on only the second performance measure, the degree of meeting the standard.

There were high intercorrelations between the satisfaction facet scores (see Table 1). The intercorrelations among the burnout measures are somewhat lower. The correlations between the burnout measures and satisfaction measures reveal moderate to strong relationships (r's range from .22 to .60). In general, those who were more satisfied had less emotional exhaustion and depersonalization, but experienced more per-

TABLE 1 Means, Standard Deviations, and Correlations Among Employee Variables

Variable	N	Mean	SD	(1)	(2)	(3)	(4)	(5)	(6)	(7)	(8)
(1) General Satisfaction (GS)	962	61.71	13.52	—							
(2) Intrinsic Satisfaction (IS)	970	42.59	9.01	.94	—						
(3) Extrinsic Satisfaction (ES)	1013	15.93	5.30	.83	.61	—					
(4) Emotional Exhaustion (EE)	1003	26.47	13.75	-.60	.52	-.54	—				
(5) Depersonalization (D)	991	11.08	7.56	-.50	.49	-.38	.65	—			
(6) Personal Accomplishment (PA)	973	34.16	8.98	.39	.44	.22	-.28	-.30	—		
(7) Meeting Performance Standard (MPS)	1026	1.06	.24	-.14	-.13	-.10	.18	.13	-.06	—	
(8) Level of Standard (LOS)	920	3.79	2.38	-.15	-.20	-.07	.17	.13	-.15	.48	—

Note: All correlations are significant at the $p < .01$ level, except for $r = -.06$, which is significant at $p < .05$.

sonal accomplishment. These results indicate that there is some overlap between the concepts of satisfaction and burnout. This overlap has been found in other research (Burke et al., 1984; Jayaratne et al., 1986; Maslach & Florian, 1988; Maslach & Jackson, 1982, 1984; Rigger, Godley, & Hafer, 1984; Ursprung, 1986). There is, however, a reasonable amount of variance yet to be explained.

The correlations between the satisfaction and burnout measures and the performance data indicate modest to low correlations. The highest correlations are between intrinsic satisfaction and the degree to which the standards were met, and between emotional exhaustion and the performance measures of meeting the standard and the degree to which the standard was met. Extrinsic satisfaction had the lowest correlations with the two performance measures. In general, the results indicate that those who were less emotionally exhausted and who had greater intrinsic interest were reporting better performance.

The above set of results indicates that, in general, the employees were relatively dissatisfied and burned out, but perceived themselves as above average performers. Furthermore, consistent with the literature, there were low correlations between employee satisfaction and performance, and the correlations between performance and burnout were also low. Consequently, though a relatively dissatisfied and burned out group was studied, the pattern of correlations with performance suggests similarity to employee groups studied in the literature who were not negatively impacted by their work.

Spouse Sample

Examination of the means and standard deviations of the questions answered by the spouses reveals that, in general, the average values are the midpoints of each scale, and the variances are sufficiently high to indicate the full ranges of the scales were used. The latter result indicates heterogeneity among the spouse respondents in their perceptions of the effect of the employee's work on home, family, and children.[1]

In general, the spouses were happy with their own job, were happy to neutral with the employee's job, believed that the employee's work had a moderate effect on home life, and perceived the effect to range from beneficial to detrimental. Furthermore, spouses reported the employees frequently came home physically exhausted. With regard to family life, the results indicate that the employees spend time with their family, were interested in family matters, had friends who were not associated with work, performed non-job-related activities on days off, and were present

---

[1] *The table of means and standard deviations for the spouse variables is available from the first author.*

during family or holiday celebrations. With regard to relationships with children, employees were perceived to be involved in children's activities. Finally, an employee's work was perceived to cause no emotional distress for children, but some distress for the spouse.

Analysis of correlations within and between particular sets of the spouse variables reveals higher correlations among the variables within a set than the correlations between variables in one set and another set. These correlational results suggest that the results are *not* due to method bias that is common to much self-report, survey research. The correlations make sense from both a convergent and discriminant validity perspective.[2]

There is a low correlation (r = .12, n = 859, p < .01) between the spouse's happiness with own job and happiness with employee's job. Thus, we can conclude that there is little relationship between satisfaction with one's own job and satisfaction with a spouse's job. There is a strong correlation between happiness with the employee's job and the desire for the employee to change occupations (r = .48, n = 1025, p < .01) such that those who were unhappy with the employee's job had a greater desire for the employee to change. There was no relationship, however, between happiness with "own" job and desire for the employee to change. The latter result suggests, again, that one's own job satisfaction has little, if any, relationship with the spouse's job.

There is a strong correlation (r = .50, n = 1032, p < .01) between how large an effect the work had on home life and the kind of effect, such that those who perceived a large effect saw it as a very detrimental effect. Among the set of variables that reflect the impact of work brought home, there appears to be consistency, such that the intercorrelations among the five variables range from .39 to .71 (all r's are significant). This means that those spouses who indicated the employees came home feeling exhausted also indicated the employees came home angry, complaining about work, and were anxious and not cheerful.

Among the set of 14 variables that reflect family life, there are, again, expected consistencies. For example, those spouses who indicated the employees spent time with the family also indicated the employees were more interested in family matters (r = .52, n = 1006, p < .01). Those employees who were perceived to often lose their temper were also those who were perceived to often get angry at their spouse or children (r = .59, n = 1007, p < .01). Those spouses who indicated employees spent days off doing non-job-related work also indicated the employees generally were present during holiday or family celebrations (r = .50, n = 1017, p < .01).

---

[2]*The full set of correlations is available from the first author.*

Likewise, those employees who were reported to be interested in family matters were also reported to be present during holiday or family celebrations ($r = .26$, $n = 1008$, $p < .01$). Finally, many of the variables in this set were not correlated or at best had low correlations. For example, there was no correlation between whether the spouse told the employee about family problems and whether the employee was absent during holiday or family celebrations.

Among the set of five variables that pertain to children, there is, again, consistency. Those employees who were reported to be very involved in children's activities were perceived by the spouse to be emotionally close to the children ($r = .43$, $n = 634$, $p < .01$), whereas the less the perceived closeness between the employee and the children, the more the children went to the spouse for help with their problems ($r = .38$, $n = 629$, $p < .01$).

The above correlational results suggest that the spouses perceive particular patterns of behavior in the employees. These patterns are consistent and expected; problems in one aspect of family life behavior are perceived to carry over to other aspects.

To gain additional insight into the set of spousal questions, a principal components analysis was conducted. Application of the criteria that meaningful factors exist when eigenvalues are greater than one and factor loadings are .30 or greater resulted in five factors with three or more items per factor. These five factors explained 48.6 percent of the variance. Factor 1 (11 items) is generally composed of the items that deal with work brought home (6a-6e; see Table 2) as well as the individual items that deal with the effect of the job on home life. Factor 2 (6 items) is composed of items that deal with family relationships (8a-8e). Factor 3 (3 items) deals with the patience of the employee and spouse. Factor 4 (3 items) deals with involvement with family celebrations and days off activities. Factor 5 (4 items) deals with family life activities and friends.[3] Overall, the principal components analysis does not shed much light on the interconnections among the 31 items, though it tends to confirm the grouping as presented in Table 2. Because the current study is exploratory, the results and discussion to follow will focus on the individual questions.

Overall, the spouse sample reports problems in family and home spheres. Whereas the spouse's own satisfaction generally is not related to his or her satisfaction with the employee's job, the issue of concern is whether links can be established between employee satisfaction/burnout and the spouse's perceptions of home and family spheres. These relationships are reported and discussed in the next section.

---

[3] *The full set of principal components results is available from the first author.*

Spouse-Employee Variable Relationships

The major focus for this research is the relationship between employee reports of satisfaction and burnout and spouse views of the impact of the employee's work on the spouse and the family. Table 2 presents the correlations for these relationships. In general, there are a number of significant correlations in Table 2, though most are low to moderate. Of particular interest is the comparison of the relationship between the two facets of employee satisfaction—intrinsic and extrinsic—and each of the spouse variables.

For the set of spouse variables, extrinsic satisfaction was more highly correlated with a spouse variable than was intrinsic satisfaction for 20 of the 31 spouse variables. Thus, it appears that employee extrinsic satisfaction has a more associative link with spouse perceptions than occurs for intrinsic satisfaction. Extrinsic aspects of satisfaction reflect supervision, pay, opportunities for advancement, and praise received. These are beyond the direct control of the employee. When they function, they are readily public. In contrast, intrinsic aspects of satisfaction reflect aspects of the work itself—the variety, responsibility, autonomy, and the like. Attitudes towards these may be harder to communicate and can be kept private. The above relationships suggest that it is the extrinsic, public aspects that are being picked up by the spouse. It is these areas that may be influencing what the employee is communicating and making known to others, and thus serving as cues to the spouse. The underlying dynamic in the employee satisfaction-spouse perception link may be interpersonal communications.

Examination of the burnout results also presents a clear pattern. In general, the spouse variables were more highly related to emotional exhaustion, less so to depersonalization, and least to sense of personal accomplishment. The consequences of increased burnout for the family appear to be largely in terms of increased emotional distress of family members, with little or no relationship to how the employee spends his or her time, or to relationships with people outside of the family. Thus, another conclusion is that the different means of expressing burnout can be differentiated by spouse views of family, home, and children behavior. If we treat emotional exhaustion to depersonalization to personal accomplishment on a continuum from relatively external to internal markers of burnout, then these results can be interpreted to suggest that external factors inherent to the employee's job are those that are perceived by a spouse and related to spouse views of family and home spheres. This interpretation is consistent with the satisfaction results where it was found that satisfaction with extrinsic aspects of work was related more strongly to spouse perceptions than was intrinsic satisfaction.

TABLE 2 Correlations Among Employee and Spouse Variables

| Variables | LOS | Satisfaction |||| Burnout ||| R^2 |
		IS	ES	GS	EE	D	PA	
(1) Happiness with own job	-.03	.07**	.07**	.08*	-.05	-.05	.08*	.10
(2) Happiness with employee's job	-.11*	.34*	.39*	.40*	-.42*	-.23*	.11*	.22
(3) Desire for occupation change	.06**	-.32*	-.31*	-.35*	.36*	.23*	-.13*	.13
(4) Effect of job on home life	.12*	-.24*	-.29*	-.30*	.36*	.22*	-.10*	.15
(5) Kind of effect	.12*	-.33*	-.36*	-.40*	.42*	.28*	-.14*	.22
(6) Work brought home								
(6a) Physically exhausted	.03	-.25*	-.28*	-.30*	.47*	.25*	-.09*	.23
(6b) Angry	.09*	-.31*	-.41*	-.40*	.48*	.31*	-.15*	.26
(6c) Complains about work	.08*	-.33*	-.41*	-.41*	.45*	.29*	-.14*	.25
(6d) Cheerful	-.06**	.24*	.26*	.28*	-.33*	-.21*	.15*	.12
(6e) Tense or anxious	.10*	-.30*	-.37*	-.37*	.49*	.30*	-.12*	.26
(7) Family life								
(7a) Employee's time with family	-.07**	.20*	.17*	.21*	-.27*	-.21*	.09*	.08
(7b) Employee loses temper	-.02	-.17*	-.19*	-.20*	.22*	.17*	-.14*	.06
(7c) Spouse loses temper	.02	-.03	-.04	-.05	.01	.02	-.02	.00
(7d) Employee interested in family matters	-.06*	.10*	.12*	.12*	-.15*	-.09*	.03	.03
(7e) Spouse tells employee about family problems	.00	.02	.00	.01	.02	.00	.00	.00

(7f) Employee has friends	-.02	.15*	.09*	.14*	-.14*	-.11*	.11*	.03
(7g) Spouse has friends	.05	.04	.05**	.05**	-.04	-.05	.03	.00
(7h) Sharing of friends	-.01	.08*	.04	.07**	-.07**	-.02	-.02	.01
(7i) Friends not associated with work	-.06**	.00	-.04	-.02	.01	-.03	.07**	.01
(7j) Employee has activities outside home	-.04	-.02	-.05	-.04	-.06	-.04	.06**	.02
(7k) Days off, employee prefers to stay home	-.02	-.01	.01	-.01	.00	.05	-.02	.01
(7l) Days off, employee does non-job-related activities	-.03	.07**	.13*	.10*	-.09*	-.01	.01	.02
(7m) Employee angry at spouse/children	.03	-.17*	-.16*	-.20*	.22*	.13*	-.11*	.06
(7n) Employee present during holiday/family celebrations	-.05	.10*	.10*	.12*	-.09*	-.07**	.05**	.02
(8) Children relationships								
(8a) Employee involved in children's activities	-.03	.05	.10*	.08*	-.07**	-.06	-.05	.02
(8b) Agreement on discipline of children	.04	.09**	.15*	.12*	-.16*	-.10*	.01	.03
(8c) Children seek help from employee	-.13	.06	.04	.04	.02	-.01	-.01	.01
(8d) Children's emotional attachment to spouse	.05	.04	.07**	.06	-.06	.00	.00	.01
(8e) Children's emotional attachment to employee	-.12*	.12*	.09*	.12*	-.03	-.03	.04	.02
(9) Effect of employee's work on children's emotional stress	.14*	-.26*	-.30*	-.31*	.38*	.20*	-.05	.17
(10) Effect of employee's work on spouse's emotional stress	.12*	-.33*	-.37*	-.39*	.44*	.29*	-.13*	.23

* = $p < .01$; ** = $p < .05$.
R^2 = Variance explained by combination of IS, ES, EE, D, and PA.

Consideration of the relationship between employee performance and spouse views reveals that the correlations between degree to which the employee's performance was above, at, or below standard, and the 31 spouse variables were generally zero or low (r's ranged from .00 to -.14). Thus, in contrast to the satisfaction and burnout results, employee performance has little relationship to spouse perceptions of family and home spheres. Consequently, we find that employee performance is not a strong correlate of employee satisfaction or spouse perceptions.

To this point, we have examined patterns across the 31 spouse variables and the employee variables. Particular relationships of interest in Table 2 include the relationship between spouse's satisfaction with the employee's job and the employee's satisfaction and burnout. As seen in Table 2 (row 2), there is a higher correlation between spouse satisfaction with the employee's job and with employee's extrinsic satisfaction than with intrinsic satisfaction. With regard to burnout, the less emotional exhaustion and the less depersonalization felt by the employee, the higher the spouse's satisfaction with the employee's job. In contrast, there was a low relationship with sense of personal accomplishment.

We see a specific example of the situation where the employee's behavioral reaction to his or her work (i.e., the way clients are dealt with) is related to the spouse's satisfaction with the job. But the satisfaction is not related to any strong degree to the employee's sense of accomplishment or meaningfulness of work. This is partial confirmation of the conclusion that spouse's satisfaction is not as highly impacted by employee intrinsic satisfaction as by extrinsic satisfaction. Again, the cues for the spouse may be the more extrinsic or tangible aspects of the employee's job than intrinsic factors. The employee may talk about his or her clients, but not about the challenge or variety in the work. Furthermore, the relationship between employee's performance and spouse satisfaction with employee's job is low. In summary, examination of row 2 in Table 2 shows that spouse satisfaction with an employee's job is more highly related to affective measures than to behavioral, performance measures.

Other particular relationships of interest pertain to the correlations between the home and family variables and employee responses (rows 6a-6e in Table 2). Examination of "work brought home" variables indicates that those employees who were less satisfied with their jobs and who were experiencing emotional exhaustion or depersonalization were perceived to come home more physically exhausted, angry, complaining, non-cheerful and tense. Personal accomplishment and performance indices yielded low correlations. This same pattern is repeated for the family life variables (rows 7a-7n). In general, those employees who were less satisfied on all three facets had spouses who indicated that the work had detrimental effects on home life. Again, there is a stronger relationship for extrinsic than intrinsic satisfaction and for emotional exhaustion than for other burnout facets.

Examination of the relationships between the employee variables and children relationship variables (Table 2, rows 8a-8e) generally show zero to low correlations. Thus, the employee's job may not be related to how they are perceived to be interacting with their children. However, the employee's satisfaction and burnout are related to perceptions of the work and its causative impact on spouse's and children's distress (rows 9 and 10).

Table 2 also reports the squared multiple correlation for the relationship between each spouse variable and a set of employee variables. That is, each spouse variable was regressed on five of the employee variables; IS, ES, EE, D, and PA.[4] These multiple correlations (squared) indicate the extent to which spouse variables can be explained by a *set* of affective data. In general, the results reveal that the "work brought home" variables (rows 6a through 6e) were the most predictable from the employees' affective responses (generally, about 25% of the variance was explained).

Much of the above suggests that extrinsic satisfaction and emotional exhaustion are the more important variables. As a test of the power of extrinsic satisfaction as an important explanatory variable, a hierarchical multiple regression analysis was undertaken whereby variables were entered in the following order: (1) a set of background data (number of children, education, job tenure, race, age, and sex), (2) intrinsic satisfaction, and (3) extrinsic satisfaction. The purpose of the hierarchical analysis was to determine whether extrinsic satisfaction explained a significant percentage of variance in the spousal variables after controlling for the background information *and* intrinsic satisfaction. Results generally support the influence of extrinsic satisfaction. For the 20 situations in which ES correlated with spousal variables to a greater extent than did IS, 16 showed a significant increment in explained variance for extrinsic satisfaction; the amounts of additional variance ranged from 1 to 16 percent. (The results also indicate that significant variance in spousal variables can be explained *after* controlling for background information; thus, any main effects that may be found for sex, age, and the like are not too insightful for the present purposes.)

For the burnout components, another hierarchical multiple regression analysis was undertaken to study the impact of emotional exhaustion

---

[4] *GS was excluded from the multiple correlation analysis since it is a linear function of IS and ES.*

as an explanatory variable. In this hierarchical analysis, variables were entered in the following order: (1) background information, (2) personal accomplishment, (3) depersonalization, and (4) emotional exhaustion. This order was chosen to determine if EE explained spousal variable responses after controlling for background information and after taking into account the other burnout components (PA and D). Results showed that for 21 of the 31 spousal variables, EE explained a significant increment (percentage increases ranged from 1 to 16 percent). These results are, again, consistent with the extrinsic satisfaction findings reported above.

CONCLUSION

Family Life and Affective Reactions to Work

This study examined the relationship between employee views toward their work, as measured by satisfaction with their job and burnout, and spousal perceptions of the employee's work and impact on family life. The obtained relationships support the notion that there is "spillover" between the work and family spheres in which the experiences in one sphere have a direct influence on the other (see Champoux, 1978; Staines, 1980; and Zedeck, 1987, for reviews of the spillover, compensation, and segmentation models). In addition, the general results suggest that an employee's satisfaction with extrinsic aspects of work is more highly related to spousal perceptions of the work's impact on family life than is found with the employee's intrinsic satisfaction.

Differential Influence of Extrinsic and Instrinsic Satisfaction

The results suggest that there are differences between intrinsic and extrinsic satisfactions and the way in which they relate to family variables. Whereas intrinsic satisfaction is characterized by internal analyses of the work by the employee (does he/she find meaning, significance, sense of accomplishment, and the like from performing the work), extrinsic satisfaction is characterized by externally controlled aspects of the work (rewards that are fulfilling to the individual). In a sense, the distinction is one of private, internal vs. public, external mechanisms for analysis of one's work environment. The fact that extrinsic satisfaction is more highly related to spousal perceptions of the employee's work can be explained by the public vs. private hypothesis. That is, it is more likely that an employee will discuss with another individual (the spouse) that which is public to begin with. At the end of the work day, the employee will discuss what took place at work, such as the interactions with the supervisor, the unusual events that occurred with the clients or in the work space, the praise or criticism received, etc. Furthermore, extrinsic satisfaction factors such as pay and rewards are likely to be brought up as matters of family budgets, bills, vacations, etc. are discussed with the spouse. It is relatively less likely that an employee will discuss, at the end of the work day, the meaningfulness of the work, the intrinsic satisfaction derived from helping a client, etc.

In part, the above suggests that the explanation for the results can be attributed to communication dynamics between the employee and spouse. Another explanation centers on frequency of events that merit discussion with others. For example, the meaningfulness of one's work is more likely to be discussed when one chooses to enter an occupation or when one is first employed with an organization. Unless the work becomes so intolerable as to cause the employee to seek new employment or a change of careers, the discussion of the work per se is likely to diminish as one's time in the job increases. On the other hand, events that deal with rewards, supervision, work environment and other such extrinsic factors are likely to be affected each day. Thus, the more episodic events are likely to have a greater impact on others and send cues to the spouse/partner than are the chronic aspects of the work.

Causality

One of the concerns with the type of research described in this study is the attribution of causal relationships with a correlational design. Whereas the above explanation suggests that what happens at work impacts the spousal view, there is an alternative that is plausible. Spousal reactions to one's own job, environment, role in the family, and attitudes towards children's development may influence the spouse to raise particular issues in discussions with the employee spouse. As a consequence, the employee picks up the cues that identify the aspects of the home life that are important to the spouse and, in turn, primarily discusses aspects of the work that are perceived to impact the home life. For example, if the spouse "complains" about the employee's low income or insufficient time spent with the children, the employee can respond with how the conditions of the work do not allow time or provide significant income. Thus, that which the employee chooses to discuss is that which can "defend" or rationalize the employee's situation vis-à-vis the home. Obviously, more attention in the future needs to be given to the causal relationship between the variables studied in this research project as well as who is the initiator of the discussion of the issues. Does the employee raise problems of the work first or does the spouse first raise the perceptions of the home environment?

Nature of Sample

It was pointed out in the introduction that the sample used in this study, unlike most studies in this research area, consisted primarily of a female employee/male spouse sample. While there were some significant differences in correlations between affective reactions to work and family life variables by sex, when sex was entered in a hierarchical regression analysis as part of an interaction term, multiple regression analyses with burnout or satisfaction measures as predictors indicated no significant interaction effects. Thus, there were no major sex differences in the relationship between burnout and satisfaction and family life variables.

Link Between Satisfaction and Burnout

This study concentrated on the affective variables of burnout and job satisfaction. As indicated, the results revealed moderate to strong relationships (r's ranged from .22 to .60) among those two sets of affective measures. The question arises as to whether the two responses are overlapping. The multiple correlational results in Table 2 indicate that there is a slight increment in explained variance when the set of measures is analyzed as compared to when only the single best predictor (which most often was EE) is included in the analysis. This result would suggest that there is little gain in including both types of measures. Nevertheless, the conclusion presently reached is that there is a need for both measures.

A basic tenet of the job satisfaction literature is that poor working conditions lead to greater dissatisfaction with the job (Herzberg et al. 1959). If so, then it is plausible to assume that stressful working conditions would also lead to job dissatisfaction. Since burnout is hypothesized to be a personal response to specific stressors on the job, it should also be linked to job dissatisfaction. Several studies, which have each used different measures of "job dissatisfaction," have all found data to support the link between burnout and job dissatisfaction (Burke et al., 1984; Jayaratne et al., 1986; Maslach & Florian, 1988; Maslach & Jackson, 1982, 1984; Rigger et al., 1984; Ursprung, 1986). The correlations have ranged from about .20 to .50, a range similar to the one found in this study. The fact that the correlations are not stronger may reflect differences in assessment techniques (e.g., global satisfaction vs. satisfaction with specific facets of the job; single-item questions vs. standardized and normed scales; questions that emphasize affect vs. behavior; and other such methodological issues). The overall pattern of findings, however, does lead to the conclusion that there are conceptual links between burnout and job dissatisfaction with sufficient unexplained variance to suggest that there is a certain degree of distinctiveness between the two concepts.

The specific nature of the link between burnout and job satisfaction remains open to speculation. An implicit assumption in some of the research (see Maslach & Jackson, 1986) is that burnout causes a drop in job satisfaction—i.e., that job dissatisfaction is an affective outcome of burnout. This contrasts with an assumption that the causal relationship is reversed, and that job dissatisfaction causes burnout. Yet another plausible explanation is that burnout and job dissatisfaction are both caused by a third variable, such as poor working conditions. In this case, the possibility arises that burnout and job dissatisfaction are actually the same phenomenon. Previous research has not directly tested these alternative explanations for the link between burnout and job satisfaction. The correlations between burnout and job dissatisfaction are not strong enough to support the claim that they are completely overlapping concepts. Yet they are sufficiently large to reject the alternative that the phenomena are completely different. Additional research studies will need to be designed to provide a more direct test of these competing hypotheses. For present purposes, they are treated as relatively independent and each is examined in relationships with other variables of interest.

In conclusion, this research has demonstrated that affective variables in one environment are related to quality of life in another environment. Though there are links between the two environments, much variance still remains unexplained. Future research should focus on the complex interplay between the variables within and between environments, and in addition, extend the examination to leisure, community, and other environments that are meaningful to the individual.

REFERENCES

Belcastro, P. A., & Gold, R. S. (1972). Teacher stress and burnout: Implications for school personnel. *Journal of School Health, 53*, 404-407.

Bhagat, R. S., McQuaid, S. J, Lindholm, S., & Segovis, J. (1985). Total life stress: A multimethod validation of the construct and its effects on organizationally valued outcomes and withdrawal behaviors. *Journal of Applied Psychology, 68*, 43-48.

Bray, D. W., Campbell, R. J., & Grant, D. L. (1974). *Formative years in business: A long term AT&T study of managerial lives.* New York: John Wiley.

Burke, R. J. (1969/1970). Occupational and life strains, satisfaction, and mental health. *Journal of Business Administration, 1*, (Winter), 35-41.

Burke, R. J., & Bradshaw, P. (1981). Occupational and life stress and the family. *Small Group Behavior, 12*, 329-375.

Burke, R. J., & Greenglass, E. R. (1987). Work and family. In C. L. Cooper & I. T. Robertson (Eds.), *International Review of Industrial and Organizational Psychology.* New York: John Wiley.

Burke, R. J., Shearer, J., & Deszca, G. (1984). Burnout among men and women in police work: An examination of the Cherniss model. *Journal of Health and Human Resources Administration, 7*, 162-188.

Burke, R. J., & Weir, T. (1981). Impact of occupational demands on non-work experiences. *Group and Organization Studies, 6*, 472-485.

Burke, R. J., Weir, T., & Duwors, R. E. (1980a). Work demands on administrators and spouse well-being. *Human Relations, 33*, 253-278.

Burke, R. J., Weir, T., & Du Wors, R. E. (1980b). Perceived Type A behavior of husbands' and wives' satisfaction and well-being. *Journal of Occupational Behavior, 1*, 139-150.

Chacko, T. I. (1983). Job and life satisfactions: A causal analysis of their relationships. *Academy of Management Journal, 26*, 163-169.

Champoux, J. E. (1978). Perceptions of work and nonwork: A re-examination of the compensatory and spillover models. *Sociology of Work and Occupations, 5*, 402-422.

Crosby, F. (1984). Job satisfaction and domestic life. In M. D. Lee & R. N. Kanungo (Eds.), *Management of work and personal life.* New York: Praeger.

Dyer, W. G. (1956). A comparison of families of high and low job satisfaction. *Marriage and Family Living, 18*, 58-60.

Guest, D., & Williams, R. (1973). How home affects work. *New Society, 9*, 14-19.

Herzberg, F., Mausner, B., & Snyderman, B. (1959). The motivation to work. New York: John Wiley.

Holahan, C. K., & Gilbert, L. A. (1979). Conflict between major life roles: Women and men in dual-career couples. *Human Relations, 32*, 451-467.

Iris, B., & Barrett, G. V. (1972). Some relations between job and life satisfaction and job importance. *Journal of Applied Psychology, 56*, 301-304.

Jackson, S. E., & Maslach, C. (1982). After-effects of job-related stress: Families as victims. *Journal of Occupational Behavior, 3*, 63-77.

Jackson, S. E., Schwab, R. L., & Schuler, R. S. (1986). Toward an understanding of the burnout phenomenon. *Journal of Applied Psychology, 71*, 630-640.

Jackson, S. E., Zedeck, S., & Summers, E. (1985). Family life disruptions: Effects of job-induced structural and emotional interference. *Academy of Management Journal, 28*, 574-586.

Jayaratne, S., Chess, W. A., & Kunkel, D. A. (1984). Burnout: Its impact on child welfare workers and their spouses. *Social Work, 31*, 53-59.

Kemper, T. D., & Reichler, M. L. (1976). Work integration, marital satisfaction, and conjugal power. *Human Relations, 29*(10), 929-944.

Kornhauser, A. W. (1965). *Mental health of the industrial worker: A Detroit study.* New York: John Wiley.

Lazaro, C., Shinn, M., & Robinson, P. E. (1984). Burnout, job performance, and job withdrawal behaviors. *Journal of Health and Human Resources Administration, 7*, 213-234.

Locke, E. A. (1976). The nature and causes of job satisfaction. In M. D. Dunnette (Ed.), *Handbook of industrial and organizational psychology.* Chicago: Rand McNally.

Maslach, C. (1982). *Burnout: The cost of caring.* Englewood Cliffs, NJ: Prentice-Hall.

Maslach, C., & Florian, V. (1988). Burnout, job setting, and self-evaluation among rehabilitation counselors. *Rehabilitation Psychology, 2*, 85-93.

Maslach, C., & Jackson, S. E. (1981). Maslach Burnout Inventory (research ed.). Palo Alto, CA: Consulting Psychologists Press.

Maslach, C., & Jackson, S. E. (1986). *Maslach Burnout Inventory* (2nd ed.). Palo Alto, CA: Consulting Psychologists Press.

Maslach, C., & Jackson, S. E. (1982). Burnout in health professions: A social psychological analysis. In G. Sanders and J. Suls (Eds.), *Social psychology of health and illness* (pp. 227-251). Hillsdsale, NJ: Erlbaum Press.

Maslach, C., & Jackson, S. E. (1984). Patterns of burnout among a national sample of public contact workers. *Journal of Health and Human Resources Administration. 7*, 189-212.

Maslach, C., & Jackson, S. E. (1985). The role of sex and family variables in burnout. *Sex Roles, 12*, 837-851.

Mortimer, J. T., Lorence, J., & Kumka, D. S. (1986). *Work, family and personality: Transition to adulthood.* Norwood, NJ: Ablex Publishing Co.

Near, J. P., Rice, R. W., & Hunt, R. G. (1978). Work and extra-work: Correlates of life and job satisfaction. *Academy of Management Journal, 21*, 248-264.

Nieva, V. F. (1979). *The family's impact on job-related attitudes of men and women: Report of work in progress.* Paper presented at the meeting of the American Psychological Association, New York.

Nowack, K. M., & Hanson, A. L. (1983). The relationship between stress, job performance, and burnout in college student resident assistants. *Journal of College Student Personnel, 24*, 545-550.

Pahl, J. J., & Pahl, R. E. (1971). *Managers and their wives: A study of career and family relationships in the middle class.* New York: Viking.

Piotrkowski, C. S. (1978). *Work and the family system.* New York: The Free Press.

Rigger, T. F., Godley, S. H., & Hafer, M. (1984). Burnout and job satisfaction in rehabilitation administrators and direct service providers. *Rehabilitation Counseling Bulletin, 27*, 151-160.

Ross, I. E., & Zander, A. (1957). Need satisfaction and employee turnover. *Personnel Psychology, 10*, 327-338.

Schneider, B., & Dachler, H. P. (1978). *Work, family and considerations in understanding employee turnover intentions.* College Park, MD: University of Maryland.

Sekaran, U. (1983). Factors influencing the quality of life in dual-career families. *Journal of Occupational Psychology, 56*, 161-174.

Smith, P. C., Kendall, L. N., & Hulin, C. L. (1969). *The measurement of satisfaction in work and retirement.* Chicago: Rand McNally.

Staines, G. L. (1980). Spillover versus compensation: A review of the literature on the relationship between work and nonwork. *Human Relations, 33*, 111-129.

Ursprung, A. W. (1986). Incidence and correlates of burnout in residential service settings. *Rehabilitation Counseling Bulletin, 29*, 225-239.

Weiss, D. J., Dawis, R. V., England, G. W., & Lofquist, L. H. (1964). Construct validation studies of the Minnesota Importance Questionnaire. *Minnesota Studies in Vocational Rehabilitation, XVIII.*

Zedeck, S. (1987). *Work, family, and organizations: An untapped research triangle.* Paper presented at the meeting of the American Psychological Association, New York.

Restructuring Work for Family:
How Dual-Earner Couples with Children Manage

Jeanne M. Brett
Organization Behavior, Kellogg Graduate School of Management
Northwestern University, Evanston, IL 60208

Sara Yogev
Center for Urban Affairs and Policy Research
Northwestern University, Evanston, IL 60208

This study proposes and tests alternative models of the conditions under which dual-earner, professional couples with children living at home, restructure their work in order to accommodate family needs. Seventy-six such couples where at least one spouse was a professional in advertising, law, or accounting participated in the study. The results showed that women restructure more than men. Men and women in occupations that allow flexibility and control over time restructured more than those in less flexible occupations. Aside from occupation, different factors are associated with restructuring for men and women. For instance, men who were restructuring the most had low self-efficacy and so did their wives, but there was no relationship between restructuring and self-efficacy for women.

The influx of women into the work force has already had a substantial impact on family life. This study investigates whether the movement of women into professional occupations is also affecting some of the traditional means by which professional work is done. The study proposes and tests alternative models of the conditions under which dual-earner, professional couples with children restructure their work in order to accommodate needs of the family.

The purpose of this study is fourfold: 1) to determine whether professional couples with children are managing the inevitable conflicts be-

---

Authors' Notes: This research was supported by the Office of Naval Research-Organizational Effectiveness Research Group, Contract N00014-83-K-0049. We would like to thank Ellen Galinsky, Barbara Gutek, Douglas T. Hall, Lawrence James, Laura Lein, Joseph Pleck, Graham L. Staines, Ilan Solomon, as well as anonymous reviewers and the editors for helpful comments on an earlier version of this paper. Melissa Ferrall and Barbara Dornbush provided able research assistance. A version of this paper was presented at the Annual Meeting, American Psychological Association, Atlanta, Georgia, August, 1988.

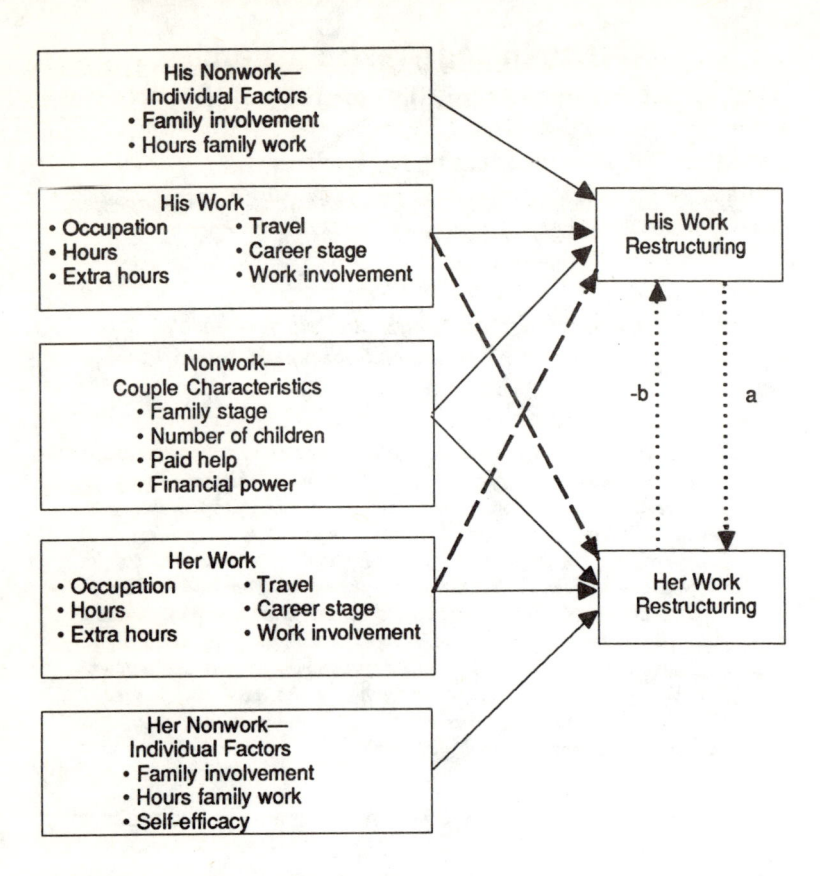

160   WORK AND FAMILY: THEORY, RESEARCH, AND APPLICATIONS

```
┌─────────────────────────────┐
│ His Nonwork—                │
│ Individual Factors          │
│  • Family involvement       │
│  • Hours family work        │
└─────────────────────────────┘
┌─────────────────────────────┐
│ His Work                    │
│  • Occupation  • Travel     │
│  • Hours       • Career stage│
│  • Extra hours • Work involvement│
└─────────────────────────────┘
┌─────────────────────────────┐
│ Nonwork—                    │
│ Couple Characteristics      │
│  • Family stage             │
│  • Number of children       │
│  • Paid help                │
│  • Financial power          │
└─────────────────────────────┘
┌─────────────────────────────┐
│ Her Work                    │
│  • Occupation  • Travel     │
│  • Hours       • Career stage│
│  • Extra hours • Work involvement│
└─────────────────────────────┘
┌─────────────────────────────┐
│ Her Nonwork—                │
│ Individual Factors          │
│  • Family involvement       │
│  • Hours family work        │
│  • Self-efficacy            │
└─────────────────────────────┘

           His Work Restructuring
              -b ↕ a
           Her Work Restructuring
```

FIGURE 1   Two Models of Restructuring

tween work and family by restructuring work, (2) to identify under what conditions professionals restructure work, (3) to test whether there are cross-over effects, i.e., from one spouse's conditions of work to the other spouse's restructuring, and (4) to determine whether these effects are direct or mediated by the other spouse's restructuring.

THE MODELS

The solid and dashed lines in Figure 1 show the direct effect model where one spouse's restructuring is affected directly by conditions in his or her own work and nonwork environments, and by conditions in the other spouse's work environment, as well as characteristics of the couple. For example, when the husband's job requires a great deal of travel, the wife may have to restructure her own work to handle family responsibilities. The solid and dotted lines show the indirect effect model where one spouse's restructuring is affected directly by conditions in his or her own work and nonwork environments, but only indirectly by factors in the other spouse's work and nonwork environments. This model implies that the effect of his work conditions on her restructuring is mediated by the effect of his restructuring on hers. For example, the more he travels, the less restructuring he does, and the more restructuring she does.

Previous research has documented direct effects of conditions of work on aspects of life outside of work. For example, Pleck (1983) reported that the level of family work done by husbands is inversely related to their hours of paid work. Near, Rice, and Hunt (1980), after reviewing 350 work-life satisfaction studies, concluded that increases in the quality of work would have a significant effect on perceived quality of life and life attitudes. They found that characteristics of the workplace including type of occupation, job characteristics, and even just being employed were correlated with life satisfaction. Other researchers have found cross over effects of one spouse's work on the other's psychological well-being. Bailyn (1971, p. 103) concluded, "marriages of men whose exclusive or primary emphasis is on their careers to women who themselves place store on integrating career with their family lives are not very happy." Jackson, Zedeck, and Summers (1985) reported that spouses of employees having difficulty making physical and emotional adjustments to their shift work are dissatisfied with the shift worker's job. Yogev and Brett (1985) found that husbands were taking greater responsibilities at home when their wives were psychologically involved with their work. These studies have identified effects of work on family and of one spouse's work on the other's attitudes and behaviors, but they have not identified whether the nature of the effect is direct or indirect.

HYPOTHESES

Restructuring

The models in Figure 1 make different predictions about the relationship between husband and wife's restructuring. No relationship is hypothesized in the direct effect model in Figure 1. In the indirect effect model, arrows a and b indicate that husband and wife's restructuring are reciprocal causes of each other. In our previous research (Yogev & Brett, 1985) we found that symmetry was the dominant pattern of work and family involvement for dual-earner couples. Here we hypothesized a symmetric, positive relationship between his work restructuring and hers (arrow a). The more he restructures the more she does. We hypothesized a negative relationship between her restructuring and his (arrow b). The more she does, the less he does. The rationale for the negative relationship is that social norms and sex role stereotypes are such that even in dual-earner couples, the wives take the greater responsibility for the children (Pleck, 1983).

Conditions of Work

Occupation. Because occupations differ in the amount of work that can be done working alone versus interacting with others, we hypothesized that occupations which emphasize individual work will be more amenable to restructuring.

Normal work hours. We hypothesized that the longer hours a person worked the less restructuring he or she would be doing.

Extra work hours. We hypothesized that those working extra hours (e.g., weekends and evenings) would be restructuring less than those who do not, though their spouses might be restructuring more.

Travel. We hypothesized that those traveling for business would be restructuring less, but that their spouses might be restructuring more.

Career Stage. We hypothesized that professionals in the establishment stage of a career (Hall & Nougaim, 1968) are most likely to be restructuring their work since it coincides with the period when people are also establishing families.

Work involvement. We hypothesized that the lower the psychological involvement in work (Lodahl & Kejner, 1965), the fewer reservations about flouting norms, and the more likely restructuring.

Nonwork-Individual Factors

Family involvement. We hypothesized that the greater the family involvement (Yogev & Brett, 1985), the more likely an individual would be to restructure work.

Hours of family work. We hypothesized that parents who are spending the most time in housework and childcare activities will be the ones doing the most restructuring at work in order to have time to do so.

Self-efficacy. Following Bandura (1977), self-efficacy in our model is a cognitive evaluation— an indicator of feelings of personal mastery of one's life. We hypothesized that those professionals who perceive that they are effective in managing their lives are less likely to engage in restructuring. People who have a sense of self-efficacy "bounce back from failure; they approach things in terms of how to handle them rather than worrying about what can go wrong" (New York Times, 1988).

Nonwork-Couple Characteristics

Family stage. Family dynamics change with the changing stages of the family. We hypothesized that couples with young children, regardless of the ages of other children, will have more intense family needs that interfere with work and will, therefore, restructure more.

Number of children. We hypothesized that more children would put greater demands on parents and cause more restructuring.

Paid help with housework and childcare. Professionals may not have a great deal of time to devote to family, but their time-consuming work does provide significant financial resources to pay for help with housework and childcare. We hypothesized that the more hired help the couple has the less they will restructure.

Financial power. Financial power in the family refers to the proportion of the family's financial resources provided by each spouse. Following an economic rationale, we hypothesized that the spouse with the lowest financial power would be doing the most restructuring, since restructuring might jeopardize future salary growth.

METHOD

Respondents

The target population was dual-earner couples, with at least one spouse employed by an advertising agency, a law firm or an accounting firm, and who had children living at home. We selected these three occupations because we wanted to study professionals whose jobs potentially required that they work nights, weekends, early mornings, and travel.

We used a multipronged approach to identify lists of potential respondents, including contacts through law and accounting firms and advertising agencies in the Chicago area, and business school alumni. We determined eligibility by sending letters with return postcards to potential respondents prior to mailing questionnaires. The eligibility rate within the lists ranged between 20 and 30 percent. The response rates among eligibles varied from 47 percent to 74 percent.

This study reports data from 76 couples. Average age was 35; years married, 10; number of children, 1.7; education, professional degree; race, white; family stage, youngest child between 13 months and 3 years old; work hours per day, 9; years with current firm, 5 and one-half. The major differences between men and women had to do with career stage (men, "advancing"; women, "getting established"), and income (men $66,893; women $37,046).

Because of the methods used to identify respondents for the study, we were concerned that this sample of professional couples might somehow be unique. For this reason, we compared our respondents to dual-career couples studied by other researchers. Our respondents' demographics compare favorably to those of Rapoport and Rapoport (1971) with regard to education and income; Hertz (1983) with regard to income; Piotrkowski and Crits-Cristoph (1981) with regard to hours of work per week; Haas (1982) and Nicola and Hawkes (1986) with regard to occupation; and

Bebbington (1973) and Leslie and Leslie (1977) with regard to number of children.

Measures

Work restructuring. The measure of work restructuring was developed particularly for this research. We were interested in both permanent and temporary arrangements at work in order to accommodate family. Respondents were asked the following seven questions:
1. Are your hours of arrival and departure dictated by family schedule?
2. Do you structure your hours at work in order to be at home at certain times?
3. Do you limit the number of evenings per week that you work in the office?
4. Do you limit your weekend work at the office?
5. Do you limit your travel or structure it?
6. Do you make special, one-time arrangements at work in order to attend a child's activity?
7. Do you make any special, one-time arrangements at work in order to accommodate your spouse's needs?

Answers were coded first for content, e.g., "Yes, I leave at 5 p.m. to pick up children at daycare"; "I avoid weekends in the office by staying late evenings"; etc. The resulting content code was then sorted by two different people into six categories: permanent reduction of schedule for children (10 points); regular rescheduling to accomodate spouse (8 points); regular rearrangement of work (6 points); temporary rearrangement for a special event (4 points); unexplained restructuring (3 points); restructuring for personal leisure time (0 points). (The categorized content code is available from the authors.) These categories define a continuum ranging from no restructuring for family, through temporary rearrangement of work for family, to permanent reduction in availability at the office. Respondents' scores were calculated by summing their weighted answers and dividing by the number of questions that were relevant to their work situation.

Occupation. One member of each couple was employed in law, accounting or advertising. We coded occupations as follows: 1) law; 2) accounting; 3) managerial, e.g., account managers in advertising and other managerial functions; 4) other professional, e.g., doctors, psychotherapists, college professors; 5) all other, including white collar, technical; clerical; sales.

Normal work hours. This was measured by asking arrival and departure times at work during a period of normal work load.

Extra work hours. This was measured as the sum of answers to three questions: When your workload is heavy how many times per month do you stay late at the office? When your workload is normal how many times per month do you stay late at the office? How often do you go into the office in the morning earlier than your normal arrival time?

Travel. Each respondent was asked how many nights per year he/she traveled for business.

Career stage. Career stage (Hall, 1976) was measured by asking subjects to choose among seven statements:
- ... focusing my ideas about the type of work I really want to do and that is personally satisfying.
- ... focusing on developing new skills to deal with new opportunities.
- ... focusing on getting firmly established in my occupation.
- ... focusing on advancing in my occupation.
- ... focusing on maintaining the occupational position I have already achieved, despite competition from others; technological change, etc.
- ... focusing on letting up; concentrating on factors beyond work, e.g., family friends, activities.

Work involvement. This construct was measured by the sum of answers to three questions from Hackman and Lawler's (1971) short version of the Lodahl and Kejner (1965) scale.

Family involvement. Family involvement was measured with 11 questions from a previous study (Yogev & Brett, 1985). Questions include: a great satisfaction in my life comes from being a parent; I am very much involved personally with my family member's lives; nothing in life is as important as being a spouse. Response choices were 5 point Likert scales ranging from strongly agree through neutral to strongly disagree.

Hours of family work. Hours of family work is the sum of the number of weekday and weekend hours were spent doing family work, including housework, childcare and finances.

Self-efficacy. Perceptions of self-efficacy were measured by the sum of answers to four questions asking in the last month how often have you felt.
- ...confident about your ability to handle personal problems?
- ...that you were effectively coping with important changes that were occurring in your life?
- ...things were going your way?
- ...that you were on top of things?

Answer choices included: never, almost never, sometimes, fairly often, very often. These questions were based on a scale developed by Cohen, Kamarck and Mermelstein (1983).

Family stage. Family stage was based on the age of the youngest child, according to Rodgers (1964). Categories were: 0-12 months; 13 months to 3 years; 3 years, 1 month to 6 years; 6 years, 1 month to 12 years; 12 years, 1 month to 18 years.

Number of children. Number of children was determined from the parents' listing of initials and ages of children.

Help with housework and childcare. Help with family work was measured by asking whether there was paid help to do 8 different housework and 12 different childcare tasks on a regular basis.

Financial power. Financial power was operationalized as the proportion of the family's income earned by the husband.

Analysis

The first step in evaluating the hypotheses is to determine whether there is a reciprocal relationship between the spouses' restructuring. The appropriate analysis is two-stage least squares (James & Singh, 1978).

If no reciprocal relationship is found, the direct effects model in Figure 1 is tested with correlational analysis and hierarchical regression. For the latter analysis, variables are grouped into four categories: his work, her work, his nonwork, her nonwork. The nonwork category contains both individual characteristics and couple characteristics. The latter are the same for both spouses and are entered into the equation only once. The equation predicting his restructuring enters the variables in the following sequence: 1) his work; 2) his nonwork; 3) her work; 4) her nonwork. The order is reversed for predicting her restructuring. Analysis stops when the increase in prediction from adding variables is not significant. The Gocka (1973) technique for mixed-mode variables is used to generate a single coefficient for occupation, a categorical variable.

RESULTS

Men and Women's Restructuring–Testing the Models

Both men and women were restructuring work for family. Women were restructuring significantly more than men (t=2.31, p < .05). On a scale ranging from 0 to 15, women averaged 8.80 (sd 4.75), while men averaged 7.11 (sd 4.18).

The correlation between his and her restructuring was .11 and not significant. A correlation of this magnitude suggests that the direct effect model, and not the indirect effect model, accounts for any correlations between conditions of each spouse's work and nonwork on restructuring. However, because the indirect effect model hypothesizes a positive reciprocal relationship between his restructuring and hers (arrow a), and a negative reciprocal relationship between her restructuring and his (arrow b)—it is possible that the low positive correlation was the result of these two effects canceling each other. In order to test this possibility, we ran the two-stage least squares analysis. There were no significant reciprocal effects. These results provide definitive evidence that the indirect model does not account for the data.

Men's Restructuring

Table 1 presents the correlations among the independent and dependent variables. Men's restructuring was significantly correlated with conditions of their work and nonwork, as well as conditions of the wife's work and nonwork. Work variables that predicted men's restructuring included occupation and career stage. The occupational averages in the first column of Table 2 show that male managers do the least restructuring, while male professionals: doctors, psychotherapists, do the most. Also as predicted, men in the establishment stage of their career were restructuring more, though this was not because they had young children. The correlation between career stage and family stage was not significant. Men's restructuring was not related to the number of hours they worked per day, the number of extra work activities they were engaged in, the frequency of their traveling, or their psychological involvement in work.

Nonwork variables that predicted men's restructuring included help with housework and childcare and self-efficacy. Interestingly, the more paid help the family was receiving with housework and childcare, the more restructuring the men were doing. This finding, which was counter to our hypothesis, suggests that men who are doing more restructuring see the need for more paid help. Self-efficacy for the men was strongly and negatively correlated with restructuring. Those doing the most restructuring felt the least self-efficacious. For the men there was a real psychological cost associated with restructuring, although it is not clear whether the psychological cost preceded restructuring or vice versa.

Financial power, family stage, number of children, family involvement, and hours spent in housework and childcare were not correlated with restructuring.

There were four significant cross over correlations predicting men's restructuring: her occupation, her extra work activities, her career stage, and her self-efficacy. The occupational averages in Table 2 help interpret the correlation between her occupation and his restructuring. Husbands of women lawyers were doing the most restructuring; husbands of women managers and professionals the least. The sign of the significant relationship between her extra work hours and his restructuring was in the direction opposite that hypothesized. Her extra work activities seemingly should place an additional burden on him to restructure. The results showed that the more extra work activities she was doing, the less restructuring he was doing. Husbands were, however, restructuring more when their wives were in the establishment stage of their careers. Finally, the correlations show that husbands may be restructuring in response to

TABLE 1 Correlations Between Conditions of Work and Non Work for 76 Dual-Earner Couples

Variable	1	2	3	4	5	6	7	8	9	10	11	12	13	14	15	16	17	18	19	20	21	22	23	24	25	26
1. His restructuring	—																									
2. Her restructuring	.11	—																								
3. His occupation[a]	.37**	.09	—																							
4. Her occupation[b]	.21*	.17	.55**	—																						
5. His work hours	-.01	.02	-.02	-.12	—																					
6. Extra work hours	-.06	-.06	-.06	.04	-.24*	—																				
7. Travel	.10	.23*	.07	.01	.02	.11	—																			
8. Career stage	-.26**	-.04	-.11	-.12	.10	.20	.01	—																		
9. Work involvement	-.08	-.01	.05	-.06	.07	.22*	.02	.28*	—																	
10. Family involvement	.04	.00	-.04	-.09	.24*	-.26**	.29**	-.02	-.17	—																
11. Family work	.05	.06	.09	.14	.11	-.13	.07	.07	-.01	.09	—															
12. Self-efficacy	-.42**	-.10	-.26**	-.16	-.10	.06	-.03	.42**	.01	-.10	.04	—														
13. Family stage	-.02	-.30**	.12	.09	-.07	.13	-.19	-.05	-.04	-.14	-.27**	-.20	—													
14. No children	.04	-.17	.21*	.00	-.04	.04	-.08	.02	-.04	.08	.18	-.17	.34**	—												
15. Paid help	.22*	-.10	.08	.05	.28	-.14	-.02	.15	.26**	.22**	-.08	.05	-.20*	-.17	—											
16. His % family income	.13	.12	.05	.04	.14	.08	.23*	.00	.18	.08	-.10	-.21*	.06	.10	.21*	—										
17. His occupation[a]	.24*	.42**	.25**	.17	-.22*	-.12	.21*	-.18	-.22*	-.06	.15	-.20*	-.12	-.03	-.05	-.06	—									
18. Her occupation[b]	.31**	.33**	.27**	.17	-.26**	-.10	.21*	-.37**	-.27**	-.08	.16	-.29**	-.10	.03	-.10	-.10	.78**	—								
19. Her work hours	.10	.05	-.03	-.15	-.05	-.02	-.13	.00	-.13	-.12	-.03	-.04	-.18	-.02	.10	-.26**	-.06	.10	—							
20. Extra work hours	-.34**	-.31**	-.20	-.17	-.07	.15	-.07	.11	-.05	-.02	-.03	.32**	.08	.03	.04	-.16	-.36**	-.24*	.07	—						
21. Travel	-.15	-.15	-.09	.06	.04	-.01	-.17	-.10	-.01	-.04	-.20*	-.10	-.04	-.19	.16	-.17	-.14	-.14	.06	.05	—					
22. Career stage	-.28**	-.11	-.10	.08	.00	.03	-.14	.29**	-.07	-.02	.09	.36**	-.02	.00	.06	-.34**	-.29**	-.35**	.04	.32**	.10	—				
23. Work involvement	.08	-.26**	.08	.16	.06	.06	-.21*	.11	.17	-.07	-.35**	.00	.30**	.10	.14	-.06	-.31**	-.36**	.05	.21*	.00	.20	—			
24. Fam involvement	-.08	-.03	-.23**	.03	-.10	-.10	-.06	-.21	-.18	.23*	.13	.13	-.08	-.14	-.13	.07	-.10	.02	-.16	-.12	.01	-.08	-.32**	—		
25. Family work	-.05	.23*	-.11	-.04	.08	-.01	.04	-.07	-.08	.13	.12	.13	-.27**	-.02	.04	.23*	.16	.13	-.03	-.01	-.06	-.08	-.22*	.19	—	
26. Self-efficacy	-.22*	-.05	-.19	-.14	-.11	.03	-.05	.44**	.04	.03	.03	.74**	-.15	-.05	.09	-.26**	-.17	-.34**	-.08	.27**	.01	.43**	.01	.19	-.07	-.15	—

$*p \leq .05; **p \leq .01.$
[a]Gocka technique his restructuring means used.
[b]Gocka technique her restructuring means used.

TABLE 2   Work Restructuring by Occupation

	Men's Occupations			Women's Occupations		
	Husbands' Restructuring	Wives' Restructuring	N	Husbands' Restructuring	Wives' Restructuring	N
Law						
Mean	7.81	8.84	27	10.80	8.60	31
SD	3.80	4.76		4.40	4.11	
Accounting						
Mean	7.81	7.92	8	6.95	6.87	6
SD	3.97	4.26		5.35	3.93	
Management						
Mean	5.19	8.78	23	7.23	5.84	20
SD	4.03	4.86		4.42	3.43	
Professional						
Mean	10.75	11.22	6	9.96	5.90	9
SD	2.41	3.82		5.00	4.87	
Other						
Mean	6.90	8.10	12	5.79	6.21	10
SD	4.85	5.53		3.36	4.60	

their wives' feelings of low self-efficacy.

Table 3 presents the results of the hierarchical regression analyses in which his work variables, his nonwork variables, and her work, and nonwork variables were entered in subsequent blocks. Twenty-two percent of the variance in his restructuring could be accounted for uniquely by knowledge of his occupation, the degree to which the family had paid help with housework and childcare, and his feelings of self-efficacy. There were no unique effects of her work conditions, or her self-efficacy on his restructuring, despite the significant correlations. This result is due to the similarity between the conditions of her work and of his, and between her and his feelings of self-efficacy.

In summary, men who do the most restructuring are in professions where they have control over their own daily schedule, are in the establishment stage of career development, have paid help with housework and childcare, but feel as though they are not handling things well. Their wives tend to be lawyers who are just getting established in their careers. Nevertheless, they are limiting their own extra work activities, and, like their husbands, feel as though they are not handling their lives well. Thus, the husband's restructuring may be occurring when working conditions make it most feasible and when neither spouse feels he or she is managing well the events of their complicated work family situations.

TABLE 3   Results of Hierarchical Regression Analyses

Conditions of Work and Nonwork	Beta Coefficients	
	Husband's Restructuring	Wives' Restructuring
His Occupation	.25*	
Work hours	-.10	
Extra work hours	.04	
Travel	.06	
Career stage	-.09	
Work involvement	-.17	
Family involvement	-.07	
Family work	.08	
Self-efficacy	-.36**	
Family Stage	-.05	
No of Children	-.02	
Paid Help	.31*	
His % Family Income	-.02	
Her Occupation		.31**
Work hours		.06
Extra work hours		-.20
Travel		-.10
Career stage		.09
Work involvement		-.14
Family involvement		
Family work		
Self-efficacy		
	R = .60**	R = .49**
	adjR2 = .22	adjR2 = .17
	F change = 2.26*	F = 3.56**

*$p < .05$; **$p < .01$.

Women's Restructuring

Women's restructuring was significantly correlated with conditions of their work and nonwork, and of their husbands' work. Work variables that predicted women's restructuring included occupation, extra work hours, and work involvement. The occupational averages in Table 2 show that women lawyers were restructuring the most, and women in the "other" category, the least. As predicted, women doing many extra work activities and those highly involved in their work were doing significantly less restructuring than those doing fewer extra activities and those less involved. Women's restructuring was not related to the number of hours worked per day, travel, or career stage.

Nonwork variables that predicted women's restructuring included family stage and hours of family work. As predicted, women with young children were doing more restructuring than those with older children. Women who were spending more time in housework and childcare were also doing more restructuring. Number of children, family involvement, help with housework and childcare, and women's self-efficacy were not associated with restructuring.

There were two significant cross over correlations, where his work variables predicted her restructuring. As shown by Table 2, wives of professional men were doing the most restructuring; wives of accountants, the least. Consistent with our prediction, when the husband was traveling, the wife was doing more restructuring.

Seventeen percent of the variance in her restructuring could be accounted for by simply knowing her occupation. (See Table 3.) Due to intercorrelations between characteristics of wife and husband's working conditions, there were no unique effects of his work conditions, or his self-efficacy on her restructuring.

In summary, the results show that women who are restructuring the most are lawyers who are relatively uninvolved with work and who have young children. Their husbands are professionals, or men whose work requires travel. These women are limiting their extra work activities and are doing more at home with housework and childcare than those doing less restructuring. For these women, restructuring is consistent with the fulfillment of traditional sex roles.

DISCUSSION

This study was designed to answer four questions. The first was whether professional couples with children are managing inevitable work-family conflicts by restructuring work. The results show clearly that both men and women are restructuring work to accommodate family and that this restructuring is systematically related to conditions of work and nonwork.

The second purpose of the study was to identify conditions associated with restructuring. The two primary predictors of restructuring are sex and occupation. Occupations that allow the professional to schedule his or her own time are associated with more restructuring. Not surprisingly, women are restructuring more than men.

The third and fourth questions were whether there were cross over effects from conditions of his work and nonwork to her restructuring and vice versa and if these effects were direct or mediated by the other spouse's restructuring behavior. The results showed no consistent pattern of restructuring within a couple. Her level of restructuring does not predict his; his does not predict hers. The direct model in Figure 1 has the best fit with the data. The cross-over effects, for example his traveling and her restructuring, and her early career and his restructuring are direct effects, not mediated by the other spouse's restructuring behavior.

One explanation for why there is no consistent relationship between spouses' restructuring is that, aside from occupation, different factors are associated with restructuring for men and women. Men's restructuring is predicted by low self-efficacy, paid help with housework and childcare, wives who are just getting established in their own careers, who are limiting their own extra work activities, and who also feel low self-efficacy. Women's restructuring is predicted by early family stage, low work involvement, and doing more housework and childcare.

It is possible that the men who are restructuring have low self-efficacy because they feel they are losing on both fronts: work and family. Their reference group at work may consist of men who are married to homemakers and are more successful (Pfeffer & Ross, 1982). At home they may see themselves again as less adequate compared to their wives who are working full-time and still doing the majority of family work (Pleck, 1983; Berardo, Shenan, & Leslie, 1987). Thus, compared to other men, they may be doing a lot of restructuring, but when it comes to home, they are only doing their share.

Another explanation for this finding is that men who are actively restructuring work in order to accommodate family are violating traditional sex role stereotypes. When a man violates traditional sex roles through participation in "feminine" household tasks, his self-esteem may suffer (Keith & Schafer, 1980).

This study, of course, cannot determine why men who restructure feel low self-efficacy: whether they feel inadequate, overloaded, guilty, or in too much opposition to traditional sex role stereotypes. The important contribution here is that restructuring for men is not associated with a psychologically healthy outlook on life.

The study design also cannot sort out causal order among conditions of work and family, attitudes, and restructuring. While conditions of work and family are likely to be primary causes, attitudes and restructuring, may be causes or effects of each other.

The study does show conclusively that men who are restructuring are part of a couple who have rather different characteristics from couples in which women are restructuring. When men are restructuring, he is most likely to be a professional, while she is a lawyer. They hire help for family work, are in the establishment career stage, and feel that they are not coping well with their lives.

When women are restructuring, in contrast, there is no negative relationship with self-efficacy. These are women with young children who have limited their extra work hours and have reduced their psychological involvement in work. We speculate that many of these women have made conscious choices. They want careers, but they want families, too. So they are willing to make accommodations. While restructuring work may mean they advance on a slower career track than others (Bailyn, 1977), they appear to be willing to pay this price in order to maintain traditional sex roles and have a career.

The relatively low financial power of the women in this study coupled with the finding that financial power is not related to restructuring, provides evidence against an economic explanation for restructuring. Indeed the results of the study emphasize the importance of studying dual-earner couples as a work-family system where economic reality gives way to psychological considerations.

The relationship between occupation and restructuring for both men and women is an important finding of the study. The causal variable seems to be flexibility and control over one's workday. Occupations in which individuals schedule their own time, are more amenable to work restructuring. Future research might investigate what trade-offs there might be between say working as a lawyer in a corporate environment where there is little flexibility regarding working hours, but little unpredictable evening and weekend work, versus working as a lawyer in a law firm, where hours might be flexible, but much less predictable.

A limitation of this study is that we only included professionals working full-time. In collecting the data, we found that women professionals, but not men, were restructuring by working part-time. We have data from too few couples where the wife was working between 20 and 35 hours a week (11 couples) to do a formal analysis of differences between their restructuring and that of couples where the wife was working full-time.

In considering the implications of these results, it is important to keep in mind that social norms regarding women's employment, and perhaps with regard to men's family involvement, are changing rapidly. Since attitudinal changes frequently follow rather than lead behavioral change, it is quite possible that when we collected our data in 1986, we captured behavioral changes, e.g., men's restructuring, and not the attitudinal ones, e.g., self-efficacy. A replication of this study might find quite a different relationship between men's restructuring and their level of self-efficacy. Similarly a replication of this study may find significantly higher levels of restructuring in occupations, like management, where restructuring is currently low. Just the fact that restructuring is occurring will, over the long term, begin to change norms about what is and what is not legitimate behavior.

REFERENCES

Bailyn, L. (1971). Career and family orientations of husbands and wives in relation to marital happiness. *Human Relations, 23*, 97-113.

Bailyn, L. (1977). Involvement and accommodation in technical careers: An inquiry into the relation to work at mid-career. In J. Van Maanen (Ed.), *Organizational careers*. London: Wiley.

Bandura, A. (1977). Self-efficacy: Toward a unifying theory of behavioral change. *Psychological Review, 84*, 191-215.

Bebbington, A. (1973). The function of stress in the establishment of the dual-career family. *Journal of Marriage and the Family, 35*, 530-537.

Berardo, D.H., Shehan, C.L., & Leslie, R. G. (1987). A residue of tradition: Jobs, careers and spouse's time in housework. *Journal of Marriage and the Family, 49*, 381-390.

Cohen, S., Kamarch, T., & Mermelstein, R. (1983). A global measure of perceived stress. *Journal of Health and Social Behavior, 24*, 385-396.

Gocka, E.F. (1973). Stepwise regression for mixed mode predictor variables. *Educational and Psychological Measurement, 33*, 310-325.

Haas, L. (1982). Determinants of role-sharing behavior: A study of egalitarian couples. *Sex Roles, 8*, 747-760.

Hackman, R., & Lawler, E. E. (1961). Employee reactions to job characteristics. *Journal of Applied Psychology, 55*, 259-286.

Hall, D. T. (1976). *Careers in organizations*. Pacific Palisades, CA: Goodyear.

Hall, D. T., & Nougaim, K. (1968). An examination of Maslow's need hierarchy in an organizational setting. *Organizational Behavior and Human Performance, 3*, 12-35.

Hertz, R. (1983). *Dual-career couples in the corporate world*. Doctoral Dissertation, Northwestern University, Evanston, Illinois.

Jackson, S. E., Zedeck, S., & Summers, E. (1985). Family life disruptions: Effects of job-induced structural and emotional interference. *Academy of Management Journal, 28*, 574-586.

James, L.R., & Singh, B. K. (1978). An introduction to the logic, assumptions and basic analytic procedures of two-stage least squares. *Psychological Bulletin, 85*, 1104-1122.

Keith, P.M., & Schafer, R.B. (1980). Role strain and depression in two job families. *Family Relations, 29*, 485-488.

Leslie, G., & Leslie, E. (1977). *Marriage in a changing world*. New York: Wiley.

Lodahl, T., & Kejner, M. (1965). The definition and measurement of job involvement. *Journal of Applied Psychology, 49*, 24-33.

Near, J. R., Rice, R., & Hunt, R. (1980). The relationship between work and nonwork domains: A review of empirical research. *Academy of Management Review, 5*, 415-429.

The New York Times, April 5, 1988.

Nicola, J.S., & Hawkes, G.R. (1986). Marital satisfaction of dual-career couples: Does sharing increase happiness? *Journal of Social Behavior and Personality, 1*, 47-60.

Nock, S.L., & Kingston, P.W. (1984). The family work day. *Journal of Marriage and the Family, 46*, 333-343.

Olson, D.H., Russell, C.S., & Sprenkle, D.H. (1980). Marital and family therapy: A decade review. *Journal of Marriage and the Family, 42*, 973-993.

Piotrkowski, C.S., & Crits-Christoph, P. (1981). Women's jobs and family adjustment. *Journal of Family Issues, 2*, 126-147.

Pfeffer, J., & Ross, J. (1982). The effects of marriage and a working wife on occupational and wage attainment. *Administrative Science Quarterly, 27*, 66-80.

Pleck, J. (1983). Husband's paid work and family roles: Current research issues. In H. Lopata and J. Pleck (Eds.), *Research in the interweave of social roles: Women and men, 3*. Greenwich, CT: JAI Press.

Price-Bonham, S., Murphy, D. (1980). Dual-career marriages: Implications for the clinician. *Journal of Marital and Family Therapy, 6*, 181-188.

Rapoport, R. and Rapoport, R. (1971). *Dual-career families*. New York: Viking.

Rodgers, R.H. (1964). Toward a theory of family development. *Journal of Marriage and the Family, 26*, 262-270.

Yogev, S., & Brett, J. M. (1985). Patterns of work and family involvement among single and dual-earner couples. *Journal of Applied Psychology, 70*, 754-768.

Family Stress and Psychological Well-Being Among Employed and Nonemployed Mothers

Neala S. Schwartzberg, Ph.D.

Psychology Department, C.W. Post College
Long Island University 11548

Rita Scher Dytell, Ph.D.

Psychology Department
College of Mount St. Vincent, Riverdale, NY 10471

Scales of family stress as well as outcome measures of depression, self-esteem, and psychological disturbance were completed by 94 employed and 68 nonemployed mothers. These two groups did not differ on any measure of psychological well-being, and family stress was a significant predictor of well-being for both groups. However, stress arising from their family roles accounted for a greater proportion of the variance on all outcome scores among nonemployed mothers compared to their employed counterparts. Moreover, scores on these psychological health consequences were predicted by different family stresses depending on employment status. Although overload, and lack of emotional support were important predictors of psychological well-being for both groups, only nonemployed women were sensitive to the stresses of nonchallenge, and conflicting demands within their family roles. The results indicated that employment status moderates the impact of family stress on psychological well-being, and underscores the importance of distinguishing between the magnitude of a stressor and its potency in accounting for these outcomes.

There is little debate over the importance of a woman's family role to her psychological health, but there is considerable debate over whether the effects of combining family roles with a paid occupational role will be beneficial or detrimental. Moreover, despite evidence that the stresses experienced within the family differ, depending on employment status, the issue of the importance of those stresses in determining emotional health is still unresolved. What do employed and nonemployed mothers experience as stressful within their families, and how do these stresses affect psychological well-being?

©1988 Select Press

Women and the Family

The primacy of family roles, especially that of wife and mother, has been assumed in the literature (See Barnett & Baruch, 1985; 1987). The stresses and satisfactions arising from those roles have been found to be an important influence on women's psychological well-being (Dytell & Schwartzberg, 1986; Stewart & Salt, 1981). Married women appear to have better psychological health than unmarried women (Ensel, 1986; Thoits, 1984; Vanfossen, 1986). But the quality of their experiences within the family may be a crucial moderator. Gove, Hughes and Style (1983) have concluded that the affective quality of a marriage is important in determining mental health among married women. Aneshensel (1986) has found that women who are married but experience high levels of marital stress do not have an advantage relative to unmarried women. Women with a high degree of marital strain were about as likely to be depressed as were unmarried women. Thus, it is not being married per se which is beneficial to a woman's psychological well-being but being in a satisfactory relationship. The quality of a relationship cannot be inferred from marital status alone (Ensel, 1986).

Research on the effects of motherhood is less encouraging. Verbrugge (1984) reported that the best physical health was found among employed married mothers, and parenthood was associated, although weakly, with good health. Whether the effect of parenthood was ultimately positive or negative was contingent on the age and number of children. Having preschoolers, or numerous children was associated with health problems. Barnett and Baruch (1985), however, found that the role of mother was related to overload and anxiety, regardless of employment status.

Many women are wives and mothers, but growing numbers of women are also workers. Some researchers have reported that employed women are physically healthier (Verbrugge & Madans 1985), report less depression (Thoits, 1984), and greater psychological health and self-esteem (Baruch & Barnett, 1986; Kessler & McCrae, 1981) than do nonemployed women. Given the potential of work and family to benefit women psychologically and physically, it would be logical to suggest that combining both work and family roles could confer even greater psychological health. However, both research and theory are equivocal.

Some have argued (see Aneshensel & Pearlin, 1987; Barnett & Baruch, 1987) that combining work and family roles leads to overload because women committed primarily to their family roles experience strain and conflict when the responsibilities of the role of paid employee is added. Employed women do put in a longer "work" day when paid and unpaid work are combined (Pleck, 1985). Moreover, family obligations increase with parenthood, and this increase is greater for women than for men (Aneshensel, Frerichs & Clark, 1981). Although employed mothers would therefore be expected to experience greater stress and concomitant strain reactions than housewives, Aneshensel and Pearlin (1987) found no difference between employed and nonemployed women in depression. Moreover, Barnett and Baruch (1985) found that a woman's sense of overload and role conflict comes from the role of mother, and not of worker. Mothers, regardless of their employment status reported greater stress. Thus, these studies provide little support for the notion that dual roles are detrimental to a woman's psychological well-being.

In contrast, holding both family and employment roles ties individuals into two major social networks which can act as alternative sources of social and psychological gratification (Gove & Tudor, 1973; Thoits, 1984). Baruch and Barnett (1986) have found that the psychological well-being of employed wives was influenced by the quality of their experiences in both of their roles. Housewives who are tied into only one social network have been found to experience more psychological distress, suggesting that the singular focus of their lives put them in a position of higher risk. However, support for this notion is mixed (Thoits, 1984)

Role Occupancy Versus Quality of Experience

Aneshensel (1986) has noted that most studies treat stress as an implicit concomitant of social roles rather than studying the actual stressors occurring within those roles. When research has investigated the experiences within roles, subjectively experienced stressors have been found to be important in understanding and predicting psychological outcomes. For example, perception of spousal support and acceptance (Aneshensel, 1986; Vanfossen, 1986) has been important. Role "captivity," i.e., the extent to which individuals feel locked into their role (Pearlin, 1983), perceived conflict between roles (Krause & Geyer-Pestello, 1985) and the quality of experience within a given role (Barnett & Baruch, 1985; Baruch & Barnett, 1986) have all been found to be important variables. Thus, it is not always possible to predict if a role, or even a combination of roles, will be onerous solely on the basis of the conditions that can be easily and objectively observed. If it is not the roles themselves, but the stresses and satisfactions experienced within them which influence psychological well-being, then questions about the way employed and nonemployed women perceive their family roles become crucial.

Interactions Between Social Roles

Social roles are not experienced in isolation from one another. Research demonstrates that the stresses and satisfactions of family roles experienced by women differ, depending on whether or not the women are employed. Housewives have reported feeling unappreciated for work done in the home, bored with household chores, and lonely for the company of adults (Aneshensel & Pearlin, 1987). Ferree (1984) reported that housewives were more likely than employed women to describe life as free and easy, and less hectic. Employed women were more likely to describe life as rewarding, interesting and enjoyable. Thus, the psychological health of mothers appears to be shaped by a different combination of stresses, depending on their employment status.

There are also some indications that employment status may influence the strength of the association between family role stresses and depression, with nonemployed women showing greater sensitivity (Baruch, Biener, & Barnett, 1987). Tension in the family role has also been found to be associated with high blood pressure among housewives, but not employed women (Hauenstein, Kasl & Harburg, 1977).

The stresses perceived to exist within her family roles influence a woman's psychological well-being. However, several aspects of this relationship, between stress and well-being, depend on whether or not these roles are combined with the role of paid worker. The fact of employment or nonemployment may alter both the amount and kind of stresses experienced, as well as the impact of those stresses on psychological health. The question to be addressed is not primarily whether employed mothers experience greater or poorer psychological well-being or greater or lesser levels of stress. It is to investigate the specific sources and magnitudes of family stress among employed and nonemployed mothers, and the relevance of these stresses to psychological well-being. The present research was conducted to address those issues.

METHOD

Procedure

Questionnaires were distributed to every second, third, and fourth grade student in all three elementary schools of a suburban New York school system. One third of the questionnaires were addressed to the male, and two-thirds were addressed to the female parent. Completed questionnaires were returned to the school in sealed envelopes. A total of 70% of the questionnaires were returned. The data from the males are reported elsewhere (Dytell & Schwartzberg, 1988; Schwartzberg & Dytell, 1989).

Sample

The sample was composed of working- and middle-class families. A chi-square analysis showed that the distribution of husband's occupation among employed and unemployed women was similar ($X^2=4.63$, df=6, p>.10). The husbands were primarily professional, technical or managerial (50%), service (18%) or blue-collar (20%). Among the employed wives, 41% were in professional, technical or managerial positions, 35% were clerical workers, and 15% were service workers.

Employed women were defined as those working outside the home on a regular basis for at least six months. Nonemployed women were those who reported not working outside the home at all. Only women currently married with at least one elementary-school-age child living at home were included in this study. The total sample was made up of 94 employed mothers and 68 nonemployed mothers.

The two groups did not differ in age or years married, but they did differ on the number of children and age of youngest, with employed women having significantly fewer and older children than nonemployed women. (See Table 1).

Questionnaire

The questionnaire elicited information on background characteristics (age, years married, number and ages of children), family stresses, and psychological well-being (depression, self-esteem, and psychological disturbance).

Family stress was assessed through an 18-item, 7-point Likert Family Stress Scale with 8 subscales. The internal consistency (alpha coefficient) for the full scale in the current sample of mothers was .82. The subscales were: role insignificance (3 items, r=.61), role overload (2 items, r=.62), conflicting demands (2 items, r=.66), role ambiguity (2 items, r=.41), nonchallenge (3 items, r=.41), lack of emotional support from spouse (2 items, r=.61), and lack of task sharing (2 items, r=.73). All items were scored so that a higher score reflected greater stress.

Although new, the Family Stress Scale is composed of dimensions found to be important in other research (e.g., role conflict, overload, spousal support), and parallels occupational stresses reported by Dytell, Pardine, and Napoli (1985) (e.g., ambiguity, nonchallenge, and conflicting demands). In previous research with female teachers (Dytell & Schwartzberg, 1986), scores on the Family Stress Scale were moderately and significantly correlated with lowered self-esteem (r=-.478), heightened levels of depression (r=.485), psychological disturbance (r=.614), and physical illness (r=.308). Among fathers (Dytell & Schwartzberg, 1988) Family Stress Scale scores again correlated moderately and significantly with self-esteem (r=-.38), and psychological disturbance (r=.49).

There were three indices of psychological well-being. Psychological disturbance was measured with the Langner 22-item screening scale (Langner, 1962). The scale correlates .71 with psychiatrists' judgments of impairment (Langner, 1962), and is also sensitive to subclinical levels of distress (Kessler, Price & Wortman, 1985).

Self-esteem was measured by the Rosenberg (1965) 10-item scale scored in the direction of higher self-esteem. Rosenberg found a reproducibility of 92%, and alpha coefficients of .85 and higher have been reported (Dean, 1986; Vanfossen, 1986).

Depressed mood was measured using an 8-item index derived from the Zung scale (Zung, 1965). This scale, which was part of the basis for CES-D Scale (Ensel, 1986), correlated .70 with the MMPI depression scale, and differentiated depressed patients from controls as well as patients before and after treatment (Zung, 1965; Zung, Richards & Short, 1965).

RESULTS

The results of this study are reported in three parts. T-tests were used on the measures of psychological well-being and family stress to reveal differences between groups. Stepwise regression analyses were done to compare differences between employed and nonemployed mothers on the relative impact of family stress on psychological outcomes. And finally, stepwise regression analyses explored differences within each group in the relationship between family stressors and strain outcomes.

Family Stress and Psychological Well-being

The results of the t-tests on measures of family stress and psychological well-being are summarized in Table 1. Employed and nonemployed women did not differ on any of the outcome measures, on total family stress, or on the specific component stresses of role insignificance, overload, conflicting demands, role ambiguity, nonchallenge, and lack of task sharing. Employed and nonemployed women differed only on the two emotional support stresses, with housewives reporting less support from their children than employed mothers (t=-2.70, df=155, p<.01), and employed mothers reporting less support from their spouse (t=2.20, df=155, p<.05) than nonemployed mothers.

Between Group Regression Analyses

The question of whether employment status has an effect on the stress-strain relationship was investigated through a series of hierarchical regression analyses. In each analysis the number of children and age of youngest was entered into the equation as the first step in order to remove their effects, since employed and nonemployed women differed on these variables. This step did not account for a significant proportion of variance in any of the analyses. In the second step a specific stress component was entered into the equation, in the third step employment status (a dummy variable) was entered, and in the fourth and final step, the

TABLE 1 Means and Standard Deviations for Employed and Nonemployed Mothers

	Employed (n=94)		Nonemployed (n=68)		
	Mean	SD	Mean	SD	T-Value
Demographics					
Age	35.93	4.02	36.07	4.66	-0.20
Years Married	13.85	4.47	13.76	5.15	0.11
Number of Children	2.48	0.70	2.99	1.26	-2.99**
Age of Youngest	6.47	2.47	4.90	2.64	3.84***
Family Stress Scale[a]					
Role Insignificance	2.76	1.09	2.69	1.28	0.35
Overload	3.94	1.73	3.61	1.55	1.28
Conflicting Demands	4.08	1.76	4.50	1.55	-1.60
Role Ambiguity	2.76	1.31	2.79	1.20	-0.14
Nonchallenge	3.21	1.19	3.41	1.30	-0.96
Lack of Support-Child	1.94	0.99	2.43	1.23	-2.70**
Lack of Support-Spouse	2.29	1.38	1.87	1.05	-2.20*
Lack of Task Sharing	3.12	1.67	2.90	1.78	0.81
Total Family Stress	54.21	15.57	54.52	13.71	-0.13
Outcomes					
Self-Esteem	43.01	6.68	41.22	6.82	1.62
Depression	24.11	8.22	23.69	8.20	0.32
Psychological Disturbance	3.19	3.47	3.43	4.08	-0.39

[a] *Individual stresses were equalized for number of items comprising scale. Total stress score is the total of all scale items.*

*$p < .05$; **$p < .01$; ***$p < .001$.

interaction of the family stress by employment status (the cross-product of the stress by the dummy variable of employment) was added to the direct effects.

Although these analyses indicated whether the main effects of family stress and employment status explained a significant amount of variance in well-being, the primary purpose was to investigate whether or not the addition of the cross-product term significantly increased the amount of variance accounted for in psychological well-being. A significant increment in explained variance due to the addition of the interaction term meant that the direct effects of family stress were different, depending on employment status. If employment status made no difference in the strength of the relationship between stress and outcome then the interaction term would not account for any additional variance.

Table 2 summarizes only those analyses which yielded significant

TABLE 2 Family Stresses as Predicators of Psychological Well-Being: Between Group Hierarchical Regression with Significant Interaction Terms

	Outcomes					
	Self-Esteem		Depression		Psychological Disturbance	
Step-Variable Added[a]	Incremental Variance	F	Incremental Variance	F	Variance	F
2. Total Stress	.228	40.11***	.320	61.78***	.220	37.09***
+ 3. Employment Status	.009	1.64	.000	0.01	.002	0.42
+ 4. Stress x Status	.034	6.29*	0.21	4.81*	.016	2.79
2. Nonchallenge	.080	12.25***	.079	11.95***	.043	6.20*
+ 3. Employment Status	.009	1.37	.001	0.07	.002	0.25
+ 4. Stress x Status	.380	6.11*	.022	3.35	.016	2.33
2. Lack of Support	.119	19.46***	.172	29.16***	.171	29.22***
+ 3. Employment Status	.024	4.04*	.004	0.71	.012	2.10
+ 4. Stress x Status	.026	4.41*	.011	1.90	.002	0.32

[a]In step 1 the variables of age of youngest and number of children were residualized to control for their effects.
*p < .05; **p < .01; ***p < .001.

interaction effects. Direct effects due to family stress, entered in the second step, were found but the importance of these stresses for psychological well-being is considered more fully in the stepwise analyses to follow. Direct effects for employment, added in the third step, were found to be significant only in the analyses with nonchallenge as a predictor.

The results indicate that the effects of total family stress on self-esteem and depression differ depending on employment status. The zero-order correlations between total family stress and these outcomes indicated that total family stress was more highly correlated with lowered self-esteem among nonemployed women (r=-.636) than among employed women (r=-.406; z=-1.97, p=.0488), and more highly correlated with heightened levels of depression among nonemployed (r=.657) than employed mothers (r=.487; z=2.67, p=.0076). For psychological disturbance the interaction term was of borderline significance (p<.10) and the difference in the correlation between total stress and this outcome was not significant; employed mothers (r=.457), and nonemployed mothers (r=.520) were equally sensitive to total family stress.

The only two specific family stresses which interacted with employment status were nonchallenge, and lack of emotional support from spouse. Nonemployed mothers were more affected by these stresses than employed mothers. Nonchallenge was moderately associated with self-esteem among nonemployed (r=-.496), but was not correlated with self-esteem among employed women (r=-.143). The difference between the correlations was significant (z=-2.46, p=.0138). Lack of spousal support was significantly correlated with lowered self-esteem among both groups. Although the correlation was higher among nonemployed (r=-.510) than employed mothers (r=-.367) this difference was not significant. For the stress of nonchallenge, the interaction term for the outcome of depression was of borderline significance, and nonemployed mothers were again more sensitive to this stress (r=.446) than employed mothers (r=.147; z=2.04, p=.0414). Thus, total family stress, and the specific stress of nonchallenge had a greater effect on the self-esteem and depression scores of nonemployed mothers than employed mothers.

Within Group Regression Analyses

Although the above analyses indicated that the relationship between family stress and well-being was stronger for nonemployed women, these results do not indicate the pattern of stresses which predict psychological well-being within these two groups of mothers. In order to determine which stresses influenced self-esteem, depression, and psychological disturbance, separate stepwise multiple regression analyses were performed for employed, and nonemployed mothers. Regression analyses were used because the specific family stresses were moderately intercorrelated and regression analysis partials out these intercorrelations.

These analyses were performed in two stages. In stage one, stepwise regression analyses were done for each outcome using the variables of total family stress, number of children, and age of youngest. Total family stress accounted for a significant proportion of the variance in self-esteem (16%), depression (24%) and psychological disturbance (21%) among employed women. Total family stress also accounted for significant amounts of self-esteem (40%), depression (43%), and psychological disturbance (27%) among nonemployed women (See Table 3). Number of children and age of youngest did not emerge as predictors in any of these analyses.

Having found that total family stress accounted for significant proportions of variance in self-esteem, depression, and psychological distur-

TABLE 3 Family Stresses as Predictors of Psychological Well-Being: Between Group Hierarchical Regression with Significant Interaction Terms

	Zero Order Correlation	Intercept	Incremental Variance	R	Beta	R^2	t-value
Employed Mothers							
Self-Esteem							
Total Family Stress	-.406	52.676	.165	.406	-.406	.165	-3.97***
Follow-up Analysis		50.833		.462		.214	
Overload	-.371		.156		-.322		-3.02**
Lack of Support-Child	-.319		.057		-.250		-2.35*
Depression							
Total Family Stress	.487	10.450	.237	.487	.487	.237	4.99***
Follow-up Analysis		13.295		.558		.311	
Overload	.440		.233		.340		3.19**
Lack of Support-Spouse	.388		.079		.315		2.95**
Psychological Disturbance							
Total Family Stress	.457	-2.40	.209	.457	.457	.209	4.60***
Follow-up Analysis		.145		.509		.259	
Lack of Support-Spouse	.520		.259		.509		5.19***

184

Nonemployed Mothers

Self-Esteem						
Total Family Stress	-.636	58.015	.404	.636	-.636	.404	-6.16***
Follow-up Analysis		57.445		.722		.521	
Lack of Support-Spouse	-.510		.305		-.302		-2.71**
Overload	-.441		.112		-.378		-3.83***
Nonchallenge	-.496		.104		-.367		-3.36**
Depression						
Total Family Stress	.657	2.082	.432	.657	.657	.432	6.70***
Follow-up Analysis		2.367		.690		.476	
Lack of Support-Spouse	.481		.266		.282		2.41*
Conflicting Demands	.466		.129		.404		3.91***
Nonchallenge	.446		.081		.324		2.83**
Psychological Disturbance						
Total Family Stress	.520	-.506	.271	.520	.520	.271	4.64***
Follow-up Analysis		.690		.407		.166	
Lack of Support-Spouse	.379		.166		.407		3.27**

*$p < .05$; **$p < .01$; ***$p < .001$.

bance, a second set of stepwise regression analyses were conducted using the specific stresses which comprised the Family Stress Scale. Again, neither age or number of children accounted for a significant proportion of variance in any of the equations, although number of children showed a nonsignificant tendency ($p<.10$) to predict depression scores among both employed and nonemployed mothers. As predicted, the specific component stresses which accounted for the outcomes scores differed depending on employment status.

Among employed women the two crucial stresses were a lack of support from spouse and overload. Lack of support from spouse predicted depression and psychological disturbance and overload predicted self-esteem and depression. In addition, lack of support from children accounted for a significant proportion of variance in self-esteem. Among nonemployed women emotional support from spouse was a signficant predictor of all outcomes, but nonchallenge significantly predicted two of the outcomes, depression and self-esteem. Overload was also a significant predictor of self-esteem, and conflicting demands also predicted depression. Although both employed and nonemployed mothers were affected by a lack of spousal support and overload, only nonemployed mothers were affected by conflicting demands, and nonchallenge, and only employed mothers were affected by a lack of support from children.

These results indicate that the psychological well-being of employed and nonemployed mothers are shaped by somewhat different family stresses. The analyses also indicate that nonemployed mothers are affected by a greater number of stresses, and that these stresses account for a greater proportion of the outcomes. Consistent with the results of the hierarchical regression analyses reported above, housewives are more sensitive than employed mothers to family stress.

DISCUSSION

These findings have demonstrated that employed and nonemployed mothers do not report differences either on the total amount of family stress, or the specific subscales of family stress, including overload. The research finding that employed women spend more hours in work, paid and unpaid combined (Pleck, 1985; Shehan, 1984), would suggest that employed women would experience, and report a greater sense of subjective overload. Theories of multiple roles also suggest that adding the role of worker would provoke role strain as women attempt to satisfy the demands of work and family (See Baruch, Biener & Barnett, 1987). However, Anderson-Kulman and Paludi (1986), and Barnett and Baruch (1985) found that occupancy of the role of employee did not predict overload. The sense of overload came from being a mother, a role shared by all the women in this study.

The similarity in stress levels found in this research is consistent with the notion that a mother's role in the family is fairly similar, regardless of whether or not it is combined with other roles, such as employee. Mothers change linens, buy children's clothes, clean the oven, dust and vacuum, cook and do laundry (Krausz, 1986). Moreover, the women in this study were all married with children in the elementary grades, making similar levels of family stress even more likely. Women in very different circumstances (e.g., single parents, parents with children living out of the home) may have reported levels of stress different from those in the present research. Investigation of other role configurations (e.g., volunteer worker and parent and spouse), and their impact on family stress and psychological well-being would also be of value.

On two of the stresses, the emotional support subscales, there was a difference between employed and nonemployed mothers. Employed mothers reported less support from their spouse than nonemployed mothers, while the latter reported less support from their children. The reason for this is unclear. Vanfossen (1986) noted that having an appreciative spouse who is helpful and gives of himself may be particularly salient to employed wives who are faced with the demands of both job and family roles. This suggests that such women may more closely monitor the level of support they receive from their spouse and as a result may be more critical of the level of support they do receive. Alternatively, employed mothers may actually receive less emotional support from their spouses. Unfortunately there is no way to distinguish between these hypotheses based on the present data. Further research with more objective measures of spousal support would be helpful in clarifying the reason for the difference in reported levels.

In contrast, nonemployed mothers reported less support from their children than employed mothers. Nonemployed women had more, and younger, children than employed women. It is likely that they spent more time with those children regardless of their ages. Research has shown that mothers of preschool children are involved in one disturbance every 15 to 20 minutes (Fawl, 1963). Mothers closely monitor the behavior of their children and frequently issue commands and express disapproval (Minton, Kagan, & Levine, 1971). Nonemployed women may therefore experience a greater number of negative parent-child interactions, and the lower levels of support reported by nonemployed mothers may be a result of this greater number of aversive interactions. Future investigations should be directed to the study of variables (e.g., family demographics, quality of interactions, expectations) which affect family stress.

Despite the similarity of stress levels, the importance of those stresses in predicting psychological outcomes differed as a function of employment status, with employed women being less sensitive to family sources of stress. This both supports and clarifies the notion that multiple roles protect individuals by providing alternative sources of gratification. Employment and access to an additional network does not directly influence psychological well-being. Employed and nonemployed women had similar levels of self-esteem, depression and psychological disturbance. Holding another major role, however, did reduce women's sensitivity to the stresses within their family roles, and therefore their dependence on those roles for their psychological well-being. Their self-esteem, and depression became less determined by family stress, and the stresses and satisfactions accompanying their work role would now influence these outcomes (Dytell & Schwartzberg, 1986).

These findings also underscore the importance of distinguishing between magnitude, and impact of stresses. The levels of reported stress did not change with, and were not reduced by employment, rather the subjective importance and influence of those stresses were altered. Employed and nonemployed women were equally likely to feel that their family role was not challenging and was characterized by conflicting demands; however, only nonemployed women were affected by this perception. Employed women reported less stress than nonemployed women arising from a lack of support from their children, but they were more affected by this stress. It was a significant predictor of their self-esteem.

This study does have certain limitations. The sample was restricted to intact suburban families and can not be generalized to other groups. Moreover, the internal consistency of some of the subscales could be improved, and such improvements might lead to stronger relationships between those stresses and psychological well-being. Nonetheless, role configuration (i.e., parent and spouse; parent and spouse and worker) did not seem to influence the magnitude of family stresses within the present sample. But role configuration did affect the importance of those family stresses for psychological outcomes. The role of worker may provide its own independent stresses, but holding that role not only influenced the specific kinds of stress which affected psychological well-being, but it also reduced the psychological impact of stresses experienced within the family.

REFERENCES

Anderson-Kulman, R.E., & Paludi, M.A. (1986). Working mothers and the family context: Predicting positive coping. *Journal of Vocational Behavior, 28*, 241-253.

Aneshensel, C.S. (1986). Marital and employment role-strain, social support, and depression among adult women. In S.E. Hobfoll (Ed.), *Stress, social support, and women*. Washington, DC: Hemisphere Publishing Corp.

Aneshensel, C.S., Frerichs, R.R., & Clark, V.A. (1981). Family roles and sex differences in depression. *Journal of Health and Social Behavior, 22*, 379-393.

Aneshensel, C.S., & Pearlin, L.I. (1987). Structural contexts of sex differences in stress. In R.C. Barnett, L. Biener, and G.K. Baruch (Eds.), *Gender and stress*. New York: Free Press.

Barnett, R.C., & Baruch, G.K. (1987). Social roles, gender, and psychological distress. In R.C. Barnett, L. Biener, and G.K. Baruch (Eds.), *Gender and stress*. New York: Free Press.

Baruch, G.K., & Barnett, R. (1986). Role quality, multiple role involvement, and psychological well-being in midlife women. *Journal of Personality and Social Psychology, 51*, 578-585.

Baruch, G.K., Biener, L., & Barnett, R.C. (1987). Women and gender in research on work and family stress. *American Psychologist, 42*, 130-136.

Dean, A. (1986). Measuring psychological resources. In N. Lin, A. Dean, & W. Ensel (Eds.), *Social support, life events, and depression*. Orlando: Academic Press.

Dytell, R.S., Pardine, P., & Napoli, A. (1985). *Importance of occupational and nonoccupational stress among professional men and women*. Paper presented at the meeting of the Eastern Psychological Association, Boston.

Dytell, R.S., & Schwartzberg, N.S. (1986). *Work and family stress and strain outcomes among male and female teachers*. Paper presented at the Eastern Psychological Association convention, New York.

Dytell, R.S., & Schwartzberg, N.S. (1988). *Interaction of work and family stress on fathers in single and dual-earner families*. Eastern Psychological Association convention, Buffalo.

Ensel, W.M. (1986). Measuring depression: The CES-D scale. In N. Lin, A. Dean, and W.M. Ensel (Eds.), *Social support, life events, and depression*. Orlando: Academic Press.

Fawl, C.L. (1963). Disturbances experienced by children in their natural habitat. In R. Barker (Ed.), *The stream of behavior*. New York: Appleton-Century-Crofts.

Ferree, M.M. (1984). Class, housework, and happiness: Women's work and life satisfaction. *Sex Roles, 11*, 1057-1074.

Gove, W.R., Hughes, M., & Style, C.B. (1983). Does marriage have positive effects on the psychological well-being of the individual? *Journal of Health and Social Behavior, 24*, 122-131.

Gove, W.R., & Tudor, J. (1973). Adult sex roles and mental illness. *American Journal of Sociology, 78*, 812-835.

Hauenstein, L.S., Kasl, S.V., & Harburg, E. (1977). Work status, work satisfaction, and blood pressure among black and white women. *Psychology of Women Quarterly, 1*, 334-349.

Kessler, R.C., & McCrae, J.A. (1981). Trends in the relationship between sex and psychological distress: 1957-1976. *American Sociological Review, 46*, 443-452.

Kessler, R.C., Price, R.H., & Wortman, C.B. (1985). Social factors in psychopathology: Stress, social support, and coping processes. *Annual Review of Psychology, 36*, 531-572.

Krause, N., & Geyer-Pestello, H.F. (1985). Depressive symptoms among women employed outside the home. *American Journal of Community Psychology, 13*, 49-64.

Krausz, S.L. (1986). Sex roles within marriage. *Social Work*, 457-463.

Langner, T.S. (1962). A twenty-two item screening scale of psychiatric symptoms indicating impairment. *Journal of Health and Human Behavior, 3*, 269-276.

Minton, C., Kagan, J., & Levine, J. (1971). Maternal control and obedience in the two-year-old. *Child Development, 42*, 1873-1894.

Pearlin, L.I. (1983). Role strains and personal stress. In H.B. Kaplan (Ed.), *Psychosocial stress: Trends in theory and research*. New York: Academic Press.

Pleck, J.H. (1985). *Working wives/working husbands*. Beverly Hills, CA: Sage Publications.

Rosenberg, M. (1965). *Society and the adolescent self-image*. Princeton, NJ: Princeton University Press.

Shehan, C.L. (1984). Wives' work and psychological well-being. *Sex Roles, 11*, 881-899.

Stewart, A.J., & Salt, P. (1981). Life stress, life-styles, depression, and illness. *Journal of Personality and Social Psychology, 40*, 1063-1069.

Thoits, P.A. (1984). *Multiple identities: Explaining gender and marital status differences in distress*. Paper presented at the Self and Identity Conference, Cardiff, Wales.

Vanfossen, B.E. (1986). Sex differences in depression; The role of spouse support. In S.E. Hobfoll (Ed.), *Stress, social support, and women*. Washington, DC: Hemisphere Publishing Corporation.

Verbrugge, L.M. (1984). *Women, work, and health*. Paper presented in the symposium "Health prospects for American women," American Association for the Advancement of Science, New York.

Verbrugge, L.M., & Madans, J.H. (1985). Women's roles and health. *American Demographics, 7*, 36-39.

Zung, W.A. (1965). A self-rating depression scale. *Archives of General Psychiatry, 12*, 63-70.

Zung, W.W.K., Richards, C.B., & Short, M.J. (1965). Self-rating depression scale in an outpatient clinic. *Archives of General Psychiatry, 13*, 508-515.

Social Support and Resource Management of Unemployed Women

Patricia S. Retherford
Gladys J. Hildreth
*School of Home Economics, Louisiana State University
Baton Rouge, LA 70808*

Elizabeth B. Goldsmith
*Department of Home and Family Life, College of Home Economics
Florida State University, Tallahassee, FL 32306*

This paper describes an investigation of 216 unemployed women in regard to their resource use and social support network. The data suggests that unemployed women seek and successfully receive assistance from relatives and friends. Parents were significantly more likely to give aid than other relatives, friends, or spouse's parents. Emotional support was received significantly more often than financial or information support. A significant association ($p<.05$) was found between expenditures for food and the number of earners in a family.

The work and family interchange literature by its very name presupposes that an individual is actively involved in the two major life spheres of work and family. What happens when a person loses one of these significant life roles by becoming unemployed? What adjustments do they make in their consumption patterns? Who do they turn to for help? Is the help there when they need it? Nearly all previous research studies on the effects of unemployment on consumption and on the family have been gathered from unemployed male populations only. The purpose of this article is to explore these questions from the unemployed women's perspective.

The newfound interest in the effects of women's unemployment has emerged from the growing recognition of the important contribution women make to the labor force and the significant economic contribution

Authors' Note: This work was supported, in part, by the Louisiana Agricultural Experiment Station.

©1988 Select Press

they make in providing for their families (Moen, 1989). There is also an increased public awareness of the economic struggles of many families headed by female single parents. These problems are exacerbated when women are unemployed. The federal government records numbers of males and females unemployed, but there is very little data on how women actually adjust their way of living to accommodate the loss of income and status that unemployment implies. According to Voydanoff (1987) the little research that has been done on women and unemployment has been on married women's unemployment which indicates that women's response to unemployment is similar to that of men and that women are less negatively affected than men. She concludes that more work must be done before we can adequately describe and understand the effects of wives' unemployment and other aspects of economic distress on family life. This statement could be expanded to include single women as well as married women. Since most of the previous research has focused exclusively on men during the 1930's Depression or the more recent recession of the 1970's, the unique contribution of this paper is its investigation into how women cope with unemployment, not as wives of unemployed men but as workers and providers in their own right.

Social Support and Resource Management

Unemployment is characterized as a crisis event. It is apparent that families utilize resources from within the family unit and its social networks as well as from formal organizations in times of crisis. Except for psychological impairment, research indicates that families seek help from friends and relatives more often than from outside organizations (Croog, Lipson, & Levine, 1972; Lin, Simeone, & Kuo, 1979; Lindenthal, Thomas, & Myers, 1971; Lopata, 1978; Unger & Powell, 1980). Hill (1970) in his three generational study points out the particular importance of parents as providers of social support.

There is a sizable body of literature on social support. One of the most comprehensive books on the subject is Work Stress and Social Support by House (1983) in which the many varied definitions of social support are examined. A generally agreed upon definition is one by Lin, Simeone, Ensel, and Kuo (1979). They define social support as support accessible to an individual through social ties to other individuals, groups, and the larger community. Pinneau (1975) distinguishes between three different types of social support: (1) tangible, e.g., money, (2) appraisal or information, e.g., informing an unemployed person about a new job opportunity, and (3) emotional support, e.g., building up a person's self-esteem.

The role of social support in protecting people against the adverse effects of unemployment was first studied in the 1930's Great Depression. Bakke (1940) reported that extrafamilial relationships were important for sustaining family stability because they provided emotional support and encouragement, financial assistance, job leads, and social pressure to maintain the integrity of the family. More recently, Cobb and Kasl (1977) and Gore (1978) found that high levels of social support tended to protect male industrial workers from the adverse effects of long term unemployment. Findings from a 1975 study by Caplan, Cobb, French, Harrison, and Pinneau of over 2,000 males in 23 occupations reinforced the importance of social support to employed and unemployed workers.

Caplan (1982) who has written extensively on the topic of social support sees the family as a primary source of self validation during a time of crisis. He has found that family members often recount past accomplishments and extoll the abilities of the unemployed person thus serving to bolster their self-esteem and lessen feelings of helplessness and ineffectiveness. In the 1978 Gore study, unemployed men who perceived lack of emotional support from their families were more prone to depression and physical illness. It can be concluded that the social network is one of the major resources available to families experiencing unemployment (McCubbin, Joy, Cauble, Comeau, Patterson, & Needle, 1980). Unemployment has also been shown to have consequences not just for the unemployed individual, but for all family members (Moen, 1983).

Although most of the research points to the family as the main source of social support, it has also been shown that friends can provide support. In Hanlon's (1981) study of unemployed municipal and state workers, friends provided practical help and support in the form of information related to job search, unemployment benefits, and government services. In a Swedish study, Tietjen (1985) found that, for single mothers, friends were the most important source of personal support. Adams (1968) found that when individuals have support from their primary networks, whether it be family or friends or a combination of both, it provided a basis for better communication and interaction between the individual and formal institutions. So the notion of social support has implications not just for families and family facilitators but also for large organizations such as relief agencies, companies, labor unions, and government agencies.

Another aspect of the effects of unemployment on the individual and the family has to do with the practical changes families have to make to adjust to reduced incomes and uncertain financial futures. Some minimum of economic resources is necessary for family maintenance and stability.

Research indicates that although men may experience more stress related to unemployment, women, especially those who head families, actually experience more economic deprivation (Cohn, 1977; Hefferan, 1983; Johnson, 1978). Women who are heads of families are particularly vulnerable to financial stress due to job loss since many women hold low paying, low skill jobs where turnover is high and work is more subject to seasonal or cyclical variations in the economy. Family type (i.e., single vs. multiple-earner families) has been identified as a factor in managerial behavior during times of financial stress (McCubbin et al., 1980; Moen, 1980).

In an analysis of spending behavior during the Depression, Bakke (1940) traced family adjustment to reduced income. In the early weeks of unemployment he observed reduced spending for recreation, various luxuries, and social contact expenses. As the situation continued, some essentials were replaced, and recreation and social contact expenditures were further reduced.

More recent studies have shown that reductions are made in housing, food, clothing, transportation, and recreation during times of financial hardship (Briar, 1978; Nicholson & Corson, 1976). Food, entertainment, gasoline, and home energy costs were areas targeted for spending reductions by most of the unemployed workers and their spouses in a study by Larson (1984). He suggested that the appearance of gasoline and home energy costs on more recent lists of reduced expenditures reflected the high cost of these items and also a greater awareness of energy conservation since the earlier Depression studies.

Because little is know about how women cope with unemployment, one purpose of the present study was to explore the nature of interaction between unemployed women and their family and friendship networks. The importance of the social support provided by family and friends during a person's unemployment has been documented by Adams (1968), Bakke (1940), Caplan (1982), Caplan et al. (1975), Gore (1978), Hanlon (1981), McCubbin et al. (1980), and Tietjen (1985). A second purpose was to assess changes in household spending for food and energy and relate these to family type based on the findings of Larson (1984), Briar (1978), Nicholson and Corson (1976), McCubbin et al. (1980), and Moen (1980). The previous research suggests the following hypotheses.

H1: There is a positive relationship between assistance sought by unemployed women and assistance received from relatives.

H2: There is a positive relationship between assistance sought by unemployed women and assistance received from friends.

H3: Unemployed women who are the only earner in the family will reduce spending for utilities and gasoline more than unemployed women in a family with more than one earner.

H4: Unemployed women who are the only earner in the family will reduce spending for food more than unemployed women in a family with more than one earner.

H5: Earner status is associated with type of assistance received from the primary support network (parents, relatives other than parents, friends and spouses' parents). Unemployed women who are the only earner in the family will receive more types of assistance than unemployed women in families with more than one earner.

METHOD

Subjects

The subjects were 216 women applicants at the Job Service Offices in the State Department of Employment Security in nine parishes in Louisiana. These nine parishes had been identified as having consistently maintained a rate of unemployment higher than the national average since 1984. The sample was obtained from a data set on families experiencing unemployment in Louisiana during late 1985 and early 1986. The study of unemployed families in Louisiana was designed to investigate the impact of a period of unemployment on family life and to determine the importance of the social support network as a coping resource. There were 606 individuals in the total sample: 390 males and 216 females. The research was supported by the U.S. Department of Agriculture and was administered through the Louisiana Agricultural Experiment Station and the School of Home Economics at Louisiana State University in Baton Rouge. This article presents the women's data only.

The subjects ranged in age from 17 to over 60. Slightly over half (54.7%) were in the 17-29 years of age category. The racial composition of the sample was 53.1% black, 45.5% white, and 1.4% Hispanic. Educational levels ranged from less than a high school education to graduate school diploma. Single women made up 35.8% of the sample, 39.1% were married, and the remainder were divorced (14.9%), separated (7.4%), or widowed (2.8%). Most of the women were in professional, clerical, sales, or service occupations. Sixty-nine percent of the subjects reported that they had been unemployed for six months or less.

Procedure

On data collection days each woman entering the office was asked by a member of the research team to complete a questionnaire. Records were kept of the race and estimated age of those who refused to participate. Ninety women who were asked to fill out a questionnaire refused. Their average estimated age was 35, 36 were white, and 54 were black. The 216 who agreed to participate, therefore, represented 70% of those who were approached. Each subject was guaranteed anonymity and signed a statement of consent in accordance with the procedure established at Louisiana State University by the Human Subjects Committee.

Instrument

Each subject completed the Effects of Unemployment questionnaire which was developed for the survey conducted by the Louisiana Agricultural Experiment Station. In addition to demographic items the questionnaire contained a variety of items measuring behavioral reaction to unemployment. Only a portion of these were used in the present study.

The instrument was pilot tested in East Baton Rouge Parish with a sample of 117 unemployed men and women applying for unemployment assistance. Adjustments were made in the final instrument and in data collection procedures based on results of the pilot test. Two scales from the Effects of Unemployment questionnaire were used for analysis for the present study: the two subscales of the Consumption Cutbacks Scale measured the extent to which individuals change spending patterns during a period of unemployment (Hanlon, 1981). Two energy consumption questions were added to the original Hanlon scale. A five-point, Likert-type response format was used ranging from "spent a great deal less" to "spent a great deal more" for each item. The food and energy subscales consist of the following items: "To what extent have you changed your spending on: 1) food; 2) eating out in restaurants; 3) fuel, light, and power; and 4) gasoline."

The Scope of Assistance Scale measures the amount of assistance received from relatives and friends during a period of unemployment. Hanlon (1981) constructed the measure from a content analysis of prior research on unemployed individuals and from open-ended responses concerning assistance from primary groups in a pilot study of unemployed workers. The scale is composed of 15 items reflecting 3 assistance types: financial aid, information services, and moral support. For each item there are four possible responses for source of assistance: parents, other relatives, friends, and spouse's parents.

Analyses

The data were analyzed using chi-square analysis, split plot analysis of variance, and the Cochran Q test. The chi-square technique was used to determine if significant differences existed for hypothesized relationships between: (1) seeking and receiving assistance from the primary support group; and, (2) changes in expenditure for food and number of earners, where the two categories of earner status were sole earner and not sole earner. The split plot ANOVA tested the influence of earner status on source of assistance and type of assistance.

TABLE 1   Chi-Square Analysis of the Relationship Between
Seeking and Receiving Assistance from Relatives

		Received Assistance		Totals
		Yes	No	
	Yes	65[a] (77%)	19 (23%)	84
Sought Assistance	No	13 (11%)	101 (88%)	114
	Totals	78	120	198

$X^2 = 88.179; p < .001$

[a] Numbers in parentheses are the row percentages. Thus, 77% of those women who sought assistance, received assistance, while only 11% of those who did not seek assistance received it.

RESULTS

Based on the chi-square analysis results, a positive relationship was found between seeking and receiving assistance from both relatives and friends. Hypothesis one, a positive relationship between assistance sought by unemployed women and assistance received from relatives, was supported by the chi-square analysis shown in Table 1. While 77% of those women who sought assistance from relatives received it, only 11% of women who did not seek assistance from relatives received it.

Hypothesis two, a positive relationship between assistance sought by unemployed women and assistance received from friends, was supported by the chi-square analysis shown in Table 2. While 73% of those women who sought assistance from friends received it, only 6% of women who did not seek assistance from friends received it.

Over half (54%) of the women spent less on gasoline and utilities yet this was not significantly related to earner status. Therefore, hypothesis three, that unemployed women who are the only earner in the family will reduce spending for utilities more than unemployed women in a family with more than one earner, is not supported.

Hypothesis 4, that unemployed women who are the only earner in the family will reduce spending for food more than unemployed women in a family with more than one earner was supported. (See Table 3.) More than half (55%) of the women cut down on spending for in-home consumption. Seventy-three percent of the women spent less on eating out in restaurants.

TABLE 2   Chi-Square Analysis of the Relationship Between Seeking and Receiving Assistance from Friends

		Received Assistance Yes	Received Assistance No	Totals
Sought Assistance	Yes	30 (73%)[a]	11 (26.8%)	41
Sought Assistance	No	10 (6%)	141 (93%)	151
	Totals	40	152	192

$X^2 = 86.583; p < .001$

[a] Numbers in parentheses are the row percentages. Thus, 73% of those women who sought assistance, received assistance, while only 6% of those who did not seek assistance received it.

TABLE 3   Chi-Square Analysis of the Relationship Between Earner Status and Changes in Spending for Food

		Spent More or Somewhat More	Spent Same	Spent Less or Somewhat Less	Totals
Earner Status	Sole Earner	10 (17.8%)[a]	7 (12.5%)	39 (69.6%)	56
Earner Status	Not Sole Earner	18 (22.7%)	22 (27.8%)	39 (49.3%)	79
	Totals	28 (20.7%)	29 (21.5%)	78 (57.8%)	135

$X^2 = 6.303; p < .05$

[a] Numbers in parentheses are the row percentages. Thus, 17.8% of sole earners spent more or somewhat more on food, while 69.6% spent less or somewhat less.

TABLE 4 Frequency of Response by Type[a] of Assistance and Sources[b] of Assistance for Sole Earners and Not Sole Earners

	Sole Earners				Not Sole Earners			
	Type				Type			
Source	1	2	3	Total	1	2	3	Total
1	25	27	21	73	49	56	42	147
2	12	15	7	34	27	36	35	98
3	19	20	20	59	30	42	37	109
4	5	6	6	17	15	19	15	49
Total	61	68	54	183	121	153	129	403

[a]Types of assistance: 1=financial 2=emotional 3=information
[b]Sources of assistance: 1=parents 2=relatives 3=friends 4=spouse's parents.

It was hypothesized that earner status is associated with type of assistance received from parents, relatives other than parents, friends, and spouse's parents. Sole earners will receive more types of assistance than individuals in multiple-earner families. Responses by type of assistance and source of assistance are give in Table 4.

A Cochran's Q analysis for sole earners revealed a significant interaction between source and type of assistance (Q = cSSAB = 3.32, df = 6, p < .001). Parents were more likely to provide emotional and financial support than the other sources of help. From friends, the type of help was more likely to be informational and emotional. The main effect of source of assistance was significant at p < .001 (Q = cSSB = 74.05, df = 3). Regardless of types, parents were more likely to provide assistance than were relatives, friends, or spouse's parents. These findings also held true for unemployed women who were not the sole earner (Q = cSSB = 101.11, df = 3, p<.001).

The split plot analysis of variance revealed no significant differences between women who were sole earners and women who were not sole earners for either source of support or type of support. Therefore hypothesis five was not supported.

The split plot analysis revealed a significant difference for the main effect of source of assistance (F(3,1529) = 60.55, p < .0001). In agreement with the Cochran's Q analysis, parents were significantly more likely to give aid than relatives, friends, or spouse's parents. Type of support was also significant (F(2,1529) = 4.66, p < .01). Emotional support was received significantly more often than either financial or informational support.

DISCUSSION

The present study supports the notion that the social network is perceived as a viable resource during times of unemployment. Positive relationships were found between seeking assistance and receiving assistance from both relatives and friends. Single-earner women were much more likely to ask for help than women in multiple-earner families. Previous research has indicated the need for examining family type and coping responses in crisis situations (McCubbin et al., 1980; Moen, 1980). The current findings provide much needed empirical evidence concerning coping responses among unemployed women.

The types of social support available through the primary network had been previously categorized as emotional, tangible, and appraisal or informational by Pinneau (1975). In this study the unemployed women were more likely to receive emotional support than the other two types.

It was expected that the number of earners would also be related to types of support. Sole earners are likely to have fewer resources for moderating unemployment than families in which more than one earner is available. However, this study found no relationship between type of assistance received and the number of earners in a family. The relationship between earner status and source of assistance was also not verified. Although few other studies on earner status for women and types of assistance from family and friends have been reported in the literature, research on marital status and types of support indicates that differences exist (Tietjen, 1985).

Consistent with previous research, parents were the most common source of help. Hill's (1970) study of three generations produced evidence that parents often provide support to grown children in need. Most of the women surveyed in this study were 39 or younger. Slightly over half were between the ages of 17 and 29. The majority of women in this study had a network of support composed of parents, other relatives, and friends who lived within an hour's travel from them (mother, 58%; father, 49%; other relatives, 77%; friends, 86%). Regular interaction with all segments of the network was reported by over one-half of the sample. After parents, friends were the next most likely source of emotional support. Tietjen (1985) also found friends to be important support providers for unemployed women. In addition, as was found by Hanlon in 1981, the type of help friends gave was primarily informational.

Examination of resource management within households revealed a significant association between number of earners and spending for foods but not for energy expenditures. Over half of the women reduced spending for food, eating out in restaurants, gasoline, and utilities. Briar (1978) and Larson (1984) reported reductions in spending for food in their research on unemployment families. Larson (1984) also reported reductions in spending for gasoline and utilities by unemployed workers. Having other family members enter the labor force is a common method of coping with income loss stemming from unemployment (Moen, 1983; Unger & Powell, 1980). Single earners, lacking that option, are more likely to be forced to reduce expenditures for basic necessities as income dwindles.

The results of this study have several research implications. Research on women's experiences with unemployment is in the preliminary stage. The present study provides indications of variability among women who are unemployed. The focus of future investigation should be on efforts to extend understanding about the nature of the variability. It is known that sex and family type are related to the poverty cycle (Moen, 1983). Those women who are chronically unemployed are more likely to be heads of household and to be in the early stages of child-bearing. Single-earner women in the present study exhibited greater seeking of assistance behavior than those who were not the sole earner. Confirmation of seeking behavior for women who are experiencing unemployment is a necessary step for expanding knowledge about unemployment among females. Apparently, unemployment for women signals a need at least as great as has been documented for men (Briar, 1978; Gore, 1978). An investigation of the type of assistance-seeking behavior is a logical part of future study of assistance-seeking behavior. Unemployed women experience need and many request help from the primary support network. Future studies which focus on type of assistance sought and type received will furnish valuable information about exchange of resources in a time of crisis. Similarly, the association between source of assistance and seeking behavior should be part of future research.

Longitudinal studies might examine the relationship between number of earners and the timing of resource allocation. Most of the women in this study had been unemployed for less than six months. Since Cobb and Kasl (1977) found that an important stressor is not job loss per se but how long the worker is unemployed, it would be useful in a future study to see if unemployed women's social network assistance and resource use change over longer periods of unemployment. Knowledge of family type and the sequence of behavior regarding management of resources would be valuable in evaluating efficiency in resource allocation.

It was established in the present study that single earners are more likely to reduce expenditures for food than women in multiple-earner families. It is probable that household spending in other areas changes as well as a function of earner status.

Replication and extension are needed to expand understanding of help-seeking behavior by unemployed women. The importance of emotional support has been reported in many types of stressful situations (Gore, 1978; Unger, 1980; Tietjen, 1985). It is possible that not only the perception of the situation by the primary support network, but also resources available in the network for response limit the type of reaction possible. Additionally, the composition and the scope of the network may have an impact on type of response. It is conceivable, given the pervasiveness of the unemployment situation in Louisiana at the time of data collection, that regardless of the type of family surveyed, resources in the family environment were limited. Possibly, the primary support network was also experiencing economic deprivation. In that case, emotional support may have been the only type of support available to give. Some people may also not have a family or friend network available, especially if they are new to an area. One of the limitations of this study is that the data were collected in a single state. A nationwide study would provide a more generalizable data set.

The results of this study have implications for family facilitators. In areas of high unemployment, programs and individual counseling should emphasize the importance of family and friends as resources for unemployed women. The special needs of sole earner families deserve additional attention. As Adams (1968) noted, knowledge and support from family and friends can provide a basis for better interaction between individuals and formal institutions. Clearly, a continued understanding of resource availability and resource allocation is basic to developing problem-solving strategies in high unemployment areas.

More needs to be known about unemployed women and the effects of their unemployment on the total family system. As Moen, (1983) noted, unemployment has consequences for all family members. Fortunately for the women in this study the social support network consisting of family and friends provided much needed assistance in a time of financial uncertainty and stress.

REFERENCES

Adams, B. N. (1968). *Kinship in an urban setting*. Chicago: Markham.

Bakke, E.W. (1940). *Citizens without work*. New York: Yale University Press.

Briar, K.H. (1978). *The effects of long-term unemployment on workers and their families*. San Francisco: R and E Research Associates, Inc.

Caplan, R.D., Cobb, S., French, J.R.P., Harrison, R.V., & Pineau, S.R. (1975). *Job demands and worker health*. U.S. Dept. of Health, Education and Welfare, HEW Publication No. (NIOSH) 75-160.

Caplan, G. (1982). The family as a support system. In H. McCubbin, E. Cauble, & J. Patterson (Eds.), *Family stress, coping, and social support* (pp. 200-220). Springfield, IL: Charles C. Thomas.

Cobb, S., & Kasl, S. (1977). *Termination: The consequences of job loss*. U.S. Dept. of Health, Education and Welfare, HEW Publication No (NIOSH) 77-224.

Cohn, R.M. (1977). *The consequences of unemployment on evaluation of self*. Unpublished doctoral dissertation, University of Michigan, Ann Arbor.

Croog, S.H., Lipson, A., & Levine, S. (1972). Help patterns in severe illness: The role of kin network, non-family resources, and institutions. *Journal of Marriage and the Family, 34*, 32-41.

Gore, S. (1978). The effect of social support in moderating the health consequences of unemployment. *Journal of Health and Social Behavior, 19*, 157-165.

Hanlon, M.D. (1981). Determinants of primary group assistance during unemployment. *Journal of Sociology and Social Welfare, 8*, 623-637.

Hefferan, C. (1983). Unemployment: The effects on family income and expenditures. *Family Economics Review, 1*, 2-9.

Hill, R. (1970). *Family development in three generations*. Cambridge, MA: Schenkman Publishing Company.

House, J.S. (1983). *Work stress and social support*. Reading, MA: Addison-Wesley.

Johnson, B.L. (1978). Women who head families: Their numbers rise, income lags. *Monthly Labor Review, 101* (2), 32-37.

Larson, J.H. (1984). The effect of husband's unemployment on marital and family relations in blue-collar families. *Family Relations, 33*, 503-511.

Lin, N., Ensel, W., Simeone, R.,, & Kuo, W. (1979). Social support, stressful life events, and illness: A model and an empirical test. *Journal of Health and Social Behavior, 20*, 108-119.

Lindenthal, J.J., Thomas, C.S., & Myers, J.K. (1971). Psychological status and the perception of primary and secondary support from the social milieu in time of crisis. *Journal of Nervous and Mental Disease, 153*, 92-98.

Lopata, H. (1978). Contributions of extended families to the support systems of metropolitan area widows: Limitations of modified kin network. *Journal of Marriage and the Family, 40*, 355-366.

McCubbin, H., Joy, C., Cauble, E., Comeau, J., Patterson, J., & Needle, R. (1980). Family stress and coping: A decade review. *Journal of Marriage and the Family, 42*, 855-871.

Moen, P. (1980). Measuring unemployment: Family considerations. *Human Relations, 33*, 183-192.

Moen, P. (1989). Unemployment, public policy, and families: Forecasts for the 1980s. *Journal of Marriage and the Family, 45*, 751-760.

Nicholson, W., & Corson, W. (1976). A longitudinal study of unemployment insurance exhaustees. Princeton, NJ: Mathematics, Inc.

Pinneau, S. (1975). *Effects of social support on psychological and physiological stress.* Unpublished doctoral dissertation. University of Michigan, Ann Arbor

Tietjen, A.M. 1985) The social networks and social support of married and single mothers in Sweden. *Journal of Marriage and the Family, 47*, 489-496.

Unger, D.G., & Powell, D.R. (1980). Supporting families under stress: The role of social networks. *Family Relations, 29*, 566-574.

Voydanoff, P. (1984). Unemployment: Family strategies for adaption. In P. Voydanoff (Ed.), *Work and family: Changing roles of men and women* (pp. 61-72). Palo Alto, CA: Mayfield Publishing Company.

Voydanoff, P. (1987). *Work and family life.* Newbury Park, CA: Sage Publications, Inc.

Career Entry Influences on Social Networks of Young Adults: A Longitudinal Study

Donna L. Sollie
Family and Child Development, 203 Spidle Hall
Auburn University, Auburn, Al 36849

Judith L. Fischer
Texas Tech University, Lubbock, TX 79409

During young adulthood men and women acquire new roles which impact on their interactions with social network members who provide social support. The longitudinal design of this study allowed an examination of how the transition to work is related to changes in social network structure and function. More specifically, using a longitudinal research design, the social networks of young adults in the beginning stages of their careers were examined using such descriptors as network size, contact, commitment, gives/receives, affective and instrumental exchanges, and profits. Across the three time periods studied, career stage, time, and gender interacted in various ways with each other as influences on network size, gives/receives, and affectionate behaviors. Partial effects of career entry appeared in group by relationship interactions for commitment and affectionate behaviors. Although a number of interactions were significant, the mean differences showed the impact of career entry on contact with friends, overall gives/ receives, for transition men on affectionate behaviors, and in subtle patterns on profit.

During the young adult years, changes in roles and statuses occur at a fairly rapid pace. One of the major transitions during these years is graduation from college and beginning a career. Other changes revolve around intimate relationships as young adults make decisions about marriage and parenthood and begin to redefine their roles and relationships to family members and friends. These types of transitions reflect changes in two major arenas of life: work and family roles. Although work and family roles are important elements of most people's lives, researchers have only recently turned their attention to the relationships between these two roles. This paper provides an exploratory analysis of the impact of career entry on the individual's social support network, focusing on changes in interactions with family members and friends who form these social networks.

©1988 Select Press

Work and family roles are now major roles for both men and women, and handling the strains associated with both types of roles can be stressful (Pleck, 1977). Voydanoff (1985) views both work and family roles from a career perspective, indicating that the combined demands from these roles have an impact on individual well-being. In the early stages of a career, individuals are establishing themselves as full members of an occupation and thus high work involvement is common (Hall & Hall, 1979). At the same time, changes in family roles and responsibilities are also occurring, and since networks affect well-being by providing support for important roles and social identities (Hirsch, 1981; Kahn & Antonucci, 1980), maintaining network involvement is also important. By looking at changes in social network composition and function of young adults as they enter careers, we may obtain a better understanding of how young adults in the early stages of career development structure and utilize their social networks and how these networks serve supportive functions for both work and family roles.

The onset of a new job or career brings about changes in the social network structure (Monroe, 1983), and thus has implications for how individuals adapt during this transition period. Stueve and Gerson (1977) found in their study of life stage effects on men's networks that the stage of the life cycle influenced both family and friend social network composition. Work by Leslie and Anderson (1986) suggests that being involved in a career is likely to influence how social network sectors are structured. Other research has found that major transitions during young adulthood, including both career and marriage, are thought to rekindle kin ties (Monroe, 1983; Shulman, 1975). Thus, there are likely to be changes in both network composition and the types of interactions with network members as a result of early career demands. Since social support can reduce work stress (House, 1981), it is important to identify changes in social networks that have implications for the availability of social support during the stressful stages of career entry.

The effects of women's career or work involvement on family involvement has only recently begun to be identified. There is some evidence that women's (but not men's) career commitment may be detrimental to marital adjustment (Ladewig & McGee, 1986), although this effect may be mitigated by factors such as the husband's own career involvement and support of his wife's career. In their review of the literature on women, work, and family stress, Baruch, Biener, and Barnett (1987) reported that the work setting provides a set of social ties for women. In general, employment tends to have a positive impact on such factors as women's well-being and self-esteem. Furthermore, accessibility of work colleagues may enhance opportunities for the exchange of supportive behaviors with these members of the social network. Particularly as we see increases in career tracking for women, the friend-family-career connection is becoming more important to study.

During young adulthood, then, men and women experience new roles which change their interactions with social network members. Therefore, it would be expected that young adults who have recently moved into the adult world of work or career operate in social networks which differ in composition and behavioral interactions from those network sectors in place prior to work or career involvement. These changes have implications for the extent of social support experienced by these young adults in transition. Since the importance of supportive social networks in dealing with stress has been extensively documented, learning more about the types of changes that occur in individual's support networks has implications for well-being, particularly during periods of life change.

Perhaps the aspect of social networks that has received the most attention is social support, with an extensive literature focusing on the identification of the supportive functions that social networks serve for the network members (Caplan, 1974; Cobb, 1976; Hirsch, 1980; Tolsdorf, 1976). More recently, researchers have recognized the need to distinguish between different types of network support and attention has turned to identifying typologies of the resources or supportive behaviors that characterize interactions among network members (Antonucci & Depner, 1982; Barrera & Ainlay, 1983; Hirsch & Jolly, 1982; House, 1981; Mitchell & Trickett, 1980; Moos & Mitchell, 1982). Unfortunately, these typologies vary in both their categorizations of the types of supportive behaviors provided as well as in the terminology used to identify the categories. There are some consistencies across these categorizations, such that most typologies of social support include emotional or affective support through love, comfort, and reassurance of worth, instrumental support through sharing information, providing guidance and advice, and sharing activities, and material support in the form of goods, money, services or other tangible support. During periods of life cycle change and stress, individuals may rely on their social network to provide different types of supportive resources, and they may also structure these networks such that desired supportive resources are more readily available (cf., Schultz & Rau's review, 1985). In this study, the focus is on exploring how the factor of career stage may influence aspects of the social network, particularly the network size, amount of time spent together, commitment to network members, and affective and instrumental supportive behavior exchanges that characterize the social networks of young men and women in transition.

Since the gender role literature has consistently identified women as oriented toward affective and socioemotional needs, and men as instrumental and task-oriented, we expect to see differences in how young men and women structure their social networks. As noted above, life-cycle transitions have been found to alter social network structure, with young adults moving toward greater kin involvement, and with women more likely to be the kin-keepers (Bahr, 1976: Booth, 1972). However, as more women are moving into the work world, this pattern may change.

The literature suggests that during the young adult years, social networks are in a state of transition. As individuals become involved in careers, changes in both social network composition as well as the types of interactions with social network members occur. Factors such as gender and the sector of the social network also have an influence on network composition. The focus in this study is the impact of early career stage on social network factors. For the purposes of this study, career stage refers to two distinct groups, the transition group of those who are about to graduate from college and begin their work careers, and the career group composed of those who are currently in the initial stages of their work career. Both groups were studied over a two year time period. Social network sector refers to the type of relationship with network members, and includes friend relationships and kin relationships. We expect that there will be significant changes over the two year time period studied, and that there will be interactions among the variables of gender, career stage, and network sector. Although literature in this area is sparse, we expect that there will be an interaction of career stage by network sector such that the transition respondents will report greater numbers of friends and fewer kin relations than those already involved in careers. It is thought that during college years friends provide a supportive network somewhat supplanting kin ties. But when young adults graduate from college and move into jobs, they often leave behind many of the friendships of college. The work of Rose (1984) and Monroe (1983) indicates that such factors as physical separation, new jobs, and interactions with dating and marital partners influence network sector composition. Changes in amount of contact with network members will follow a similar pattern, with transition respondents reporting decreasing contact with friends over time. It is also expected that women will show stronger affective ties to the network, particularly to the kin network sector, than will men, and that men will demonstrate stronger instrumental ties to the social network. The sex role literature generally indicates women's more prominent participation in affective dimensions of relationships and men's greater involvement with instrumental aspects of relationships. Other aspects of the social network, including commitment levels and profit in relationships, will be examined on an exploratory basis.

METHODS

Sample

A random sample of 1600 graduates and potential graduates of a large southwestern university, using gender and major as delimiting criteria, was contacted in 1982 to participate in research requiring completion of an interview and questionnaire about their social networks. It was anticipated that the large number of letters sent would supply the desired research sample of 100 males and 100 females from each graduating class. Four hundred twenty-two young men and women volunteered for the study with approximately equal numbers of men and women and graduates and graduates-to-be. Distributions of the sample across academic majors closely resembled the target percentages in the random sampling procedure. The vast majority of respondents are Caucasians.

The design for this study called for two levels of gender and two levels of career stage which yielded four subgroups. In order to meet the purposes of this study, selection of subjects into subgroups was based on whether the respondents met certain criteria for career status, age, and nonmissing data. To insure that participants had similar on-time graduations from college, ages of participants were restricted to 21-26 years of age. The transition group consisted of graduating college seniors (with initial data collection occurring during the spring of the year of graduation), and the career group consisted of career-involved postgraduates (with initial data collection occurring for this group approximately two years after college graduation). All of the career group were employed in professional or managerial careers, and only a fourth of the college seniors were employed (all at part-time work). Volunteers who failed to meet these criteria were eliminated from this study. Among those who graduated from college in 1980, 77% were in careers two years later at time 1. For those who graduated in 1982 and for whom there was information at time 3, 67% were in careers two years after graduation.

From the larger sample, participants were selected who had responded to the interview and questionnaire at all three testing times. Equal numbers (20 of each) of men and women in the career and transition groups were chosen. Members of the career group were 1980 graduates who were involved in careers at all three times. Members of the transition group were students at time 1 who were all involved in careers by time 3 (but not necessarily at time 2). In previous research (Fischer, Sollie, Sorell & Green, in press) marital status was a significant factor at time 1, therefore the groups were composed of equivalent numbers of single, engaged, and marrieds at each time. At time 1, 11 of 20 were single in each group and 9 were either engaged or married with a higher number of marrieds than engaged. At time 3, 7 of 20 in each group were single and

13 were engaged or married. These Ns were too small for meaningful analyses of possible marital status effects. If more than 20 participants met the criteria for inclusion in a group, the first 20 were selected for the study. In the analyses, a few cases of missing data appeared (reflected in the degrees of freedom reported in the results), but Ns per group never dropped below 19.

Procedures

Participants completed a questionnaire and responded to a face-to-face or telephone interview. The last part of the questionnaire asked respondents to list all members of their social networks (up to 50) and to indicate this person by initials, gender, and by relationship to the respondent. A member of the network was defined as one with whom there was a personal relationship, one who was known by name, and one who was seen at least once a year (Tolsdorf, 1976). The interview procedure obtained detailed information about behaviors exchanged with each network member. Following completion of the questionnaire and interview, respondents received $5 as a token of appreciation for their participation at each of the three testing times.

In order to assess the test-retest reliability of this procedure of obtaining information on social networks, the network task was given to 77 undergraduates at the same southwestern university and repeated two weeks later. Results showed that network size correlated significantly across the two testing times ($r(70) = .91, p < .001$). The N was reduced by missing data at time 2 of this assessment.

Approximately 9-12 months after the first testing the procedures were repeated and constituted the time 2 testing. Approximately 12 to 15 months later a third testing took place with the same procedures and variables. This third testing was labeled time 3. For most participants the third interview was two years after the first interview, thus the transition group was then two years out of college just as the career group had been when first interviewed. Dropouts among men (45%) were more numerous than dropouts among women (29%), and many dropouts occurred as a result of the highly mobile nature of the sample. A comparison of Time 1 scores of dropouts with nondropouts found few significant differences and these were related to the differential dropout rates of men and women, including such variables as masculinity, number of male friends, and amount of affection exchanged. Only nondropouts were included in this study.

MEASURES

Size

Network size is one of the structural social network variables that is consistently assessed in the literature (Israel, 1982). Network size was determined by recording the total number of individual members listed in each respondent's social network and could include up to 50 social network members. Previous research (Fischer et al., 1988) indicated that the sector of the social network, either family or friend, constituted an important distinction. Therefore, the network sector was distinguished as kin or friend. Kin size consisted of the total number of network members related to the respondent through biologic ties or marriage. Fiances were designated as kin for purposes of this study. Friend size was calculated by recording the total number of relationships identified by the respondent as "friend." In addition to kin and friends, there were network members, such as coach, minister, co-worker, who did not fit the kin or friend designation. These other network members were omitted from the study for the following reasons: they comprised only 12% of the social networks of these participants and missing data on the other relationships would have seriously lowered the Ns in some of the subgroups.

Relationship Contact

Contact with social network members was determined by asking respondents how often they had seen each network member during the past year based on a 30 day month. An average monthly frequency of contact for each of the three relationships was computed by dividing the total relationship contact sum by the appropriate measure of relationship size.

Commitment

Respondents were asked to identify on a six point scale, from 1=not at all to 6=extremely strong commitment, how committed they were to remaining in each relationship. Scale values were selected to purposely force respondents to make fine distinctions between higher commitment values, thus, 4=strong commitment and 5=very strong commitment. Kin and friend commitment levels were obtained by dividing the total score for each type of relationship by the appropriate measure of relationship size.

Overall Gives/Receives

Respondents were asked to carefully identify resources actually exchanged with network members in eight areas: money, goods, affection, comfort, information, activity, opinion, and evaluation. These areas were derived from the literature on social support functions that networks serve (see earlier discussion), and from Foa's theory and research (Foa, 1971; Foa & Foa, 1974) identifying resources that are exchanged in interpersonal relationships. Respondents were given the following definitions of each category:

1) Money—to give or receive money in the form of change, bills, checks, or use of credit card;

2) Goods— to give or receive some tangible item such as fruit, a meal, a tape or a record, clothing, presents of any kind;
3) Affection—to give or receive expressions of affection, verbally or nonverbally (e.g., hug, kiss, shared confidence, or secret, person remains near you);
4) Information—to give or receive factual information;
5) Opinion—to give or receive opinions about weather, other people, sports, politics; opinions do not have to relate to person or self;
6) Evaluation—to give or receive positive or negative feedback on something you or the other is doing, thinking, or feeling;
7) Activity—to give or receive activities such as going to a movie, a sporting event, or going shopping or playing tennis; and,
8) Comfort—to give or receive sympathy or comfort when something has upset you.

For each network member the respondent indicated which behaviors were given to the other and which were received from the other in that relationship. A score of one was recorded for each behavior given and each behavior received. For example, if one or more of the behaviors listed under comfort were given in that relationship a score of 1 was assigned. If none of the comfort behaviors were given a score of zero resulted. Similar assignments were made for the comfort receives and the gives and receives for each of the other eight areas of exchange. Overall gives/receives for kin was calculated by adding all the gives and receives for kin and dividing by the number of kin. Overall gives/receives for friends was computed in the same manner, adding all the gives and receives for friends and dividing by the number of friends. Scores could range from 0 to 16.

Instrumental and Affectionate Behaviors

Instrumental and affective behavior exchanges have been consistently identified in the literature as the salient exchanges between network members (Barrera & Ainlay, 1983; Mitchell & Trickett, 1980). Leslie and Grady's (1985) variables, termed emotional support and instrumental support, used definitions nearly identical to ours.

Since the literature points to the importance of reciprocity in social support relationships (Caplan & Killilea, 1976; Cobb, 1976), in this study, affectionate and instrumental behaviors reflected both giving and receiving. Affectionate behaviors were designated by combining the two gives and two receives in the areas of affection and comfort as defined above. Instrumental behaviors were designated by combining the two gives and two receives of information and activity as defined above. The number of gives and receives in the affectionate behaviors area was summed across members in the network sector and divided by the network sector size, thus controlling for different network sector sizes. For example, kin affectionate behaviors were calculated as kin affectionate gives (on comfort and affection) plus kin affectionate receives divided by kin size. Instrumental behaviors were computed in similar fashion. Scores could range from 0 to 4.

Profit

Profit in relationships was measured by subtracting the average gives across the eight exchange areas (equivalent to costs) from the average receives across the same eight exchange areas (equivalent to rewards). Positive scores reflect overbenefitted relationships (receives exceed gives) while negative scores reflect underbenefitted relationships (gives exceed receives). A score of zero represents an equitable relationship. Separate profit scores were calculated for kin and friend network sectors.

Although analyses involving network size, contact and commitment were based on the total network, exchange behaviors were described for only the first twenty members of a respondent's social network. Pilot data revealed minimal changes in reported behaviors beyond the twentieth network member such that gives and receives appeared nearly identical regardless of the relationship of the network member to the respondent. It appeared that the respondents were unable or unwilling to discriminate among network members who appeared in the last 30 of network members listed. Mean size of the overall network was 31.19 with a S.D. of 13.06. Kin comprised 36% of the total network size and 45% of the first 20 network members, friends were 52% of the total network and 45% of the first 20 network members listed, while others were 12% of the total and 10% of the first 20.

Comparisons were made of the percentages of kin, friends, and others in the total social network versus the first 20 network members at time 1. Eighty-six percent of all kin were in the first 20 network members listed, 14% were in the remaining 30 network members listed. Sixty-two percent of all friends were in the first 20 while 48% were among the last 30. Sixty-seven percent of all others were in the first 20 and 43% were in the last 30.

At times 2 and 3 new friends and kin appeared in the social networks of the respondents. New friends and kin at time 2 were defined as those who had not been listed at time 1. New friends and kin at time 3 were those not listed at either times 1 or 2. At time 2, 16% of the kin listed were new and 41% of the friends listed were new. At time 3, 13% of kin listed were new and 39% of friends listed were new. Thus, kin composition remained relatively stable across two years, but friends changed with more than a third of friends at each time new to the social network. In analysis of variance of group, gender, time and network sector on percent new in the social network, there was a significant group by time interaction (F(1,68) = 7.90, p < .01). The greatest change in the social network occurred from time 1 to time 2 for the transition group with 33.5% of the social network composed of new members, a significantly greater percentage (Tukey, p < .05) than that of the career group at time 2 (M = 23.5%). The transition and career groups at time 3 were in between with 24.5 and 28.0 percent new members respectively.

RESULTS

The research questions of this study were tested by analyses of variance with both between and within components on the dependent variables. Between factors were group (transition vs. career) and gender (male and female); within factors were time (time 1, time 2 and time 3) and network sector (kin and friend). Results for each dependent variable are reported below. As a guide to the results section, if career entry has an effect, then there should be group by time interactions with the transition group's scores different at time 2 or 3 (or both) from time 1 scores. The transition group's scores at time 1 should be different from the career group's scores at time 1. If career entry has effects on family which are different from effects on friends, then there should be a group by network sector by time interaction such that time 2 and 3 scores for the transition group are different from time 1 scores and these vary according to network sector. In addition, the transition group should be different from the career group at time 1, and variations by family and friend would be seen across time. Gender effects may appear as main effects or these may interact with other variables. Table 1 presents means for all the dependent variables broken down by all the independent variables. Subsequent tables present means for specific comparisons related to results of the analyses of variance.

Network Size

The result for network size found a significant group by time interaction (F(2,152) = 3.72, p < .05) but this effect was modified by a three way interaction of group by gender by time (F(2,152) = 3.56 p < .05). Table 2 presents the means with comparison on this and subsequent means conducted by Tukey's test with p set at .05. The difference at time 3 between men and women in the transition group was significant and this difference approached significance at time 2. There were no differences among men and women in the career group. A trend was seen for career group network sizes to diminish across time. Transition group women's network size increased at time 2 but decreased at time 3. These findings

TABLE 1   Means on Dependent Variables by Group, Gender, Time, and Network Sector

Independent Variable	*Size*	*Contact*	*Commit*	*Give/Rec.*	*Aff.*	*Instr.*	*Profit*
TIME 1 KIN							
Transition							
Male	8.60	66.64	5.55	12.60	3.50	3.18	.342
Female	10.70	73.34	5.72	13.04	3.49	3.52	.517
Career							
Male	11.15	52.94	5.33	10.22	2.58	3.06	.088
Female	11.60	62.28	5.44	12.94	3.36	3.60	.521
TIME 1 FRIENDS							
Transition							
Male	14.65	136.63	3.96	10.50	2.15	3.56	.063
Female	18.00	91.53	4.37	11.29	2.84	3.43	.138
Career							
Male	15.10	52.45	4.14	8.90	1.68	3.42	.033
Female	18.70	59.43	4.36	11.82	2.94	3.49	-.085
TIME 2 KIN							
Transition							
Male	8.85	44.19	5.57	13.47	3.40	3.72	.351
Female	13.70	77.05	5.63	12.86	3.28	3.62	.362
Career							
Male	10.95	60.99	5.52	11.10	2.64	3.33	-.004
Female	10.60	86.58	5.44	13.67	3.58	3.72	-.013
TIME 2 FRIENDS							
Transition							
Male	14.30	85.90	3.92	10.47	1.90	3.76	.110
Female	19.00	90.06	4.30	11.53	2.37	3.58	-.024
Career							
Male	14.15	53.09	4.14	8.50	1.33	3.53	.060
Female	13.60	76.01	4.56	12.78	2.98	3.86	-.062
TIME 3 KIN							
Transition							
Male	10.05	60.91	5.46	11.42	2.61	3.41	.221
Female	13.30	61.78	5.65	13.04	3.22	3.62	-.017
Career							
Male	12.90	55.08	5.29	11.90	2.77	3.51	.224
Female	10.95	61.02	5.56	13.62	3.22	3.77	.109
TIME 3 FRIENDS							
Transition							
Male	10.35	54.40	4.43	9.21	1.32	3.65	-.043
Female	16.80	66.38	4.20	10.88	2.14	3.48	-.149
Career							
Male	12.70	61.88	4.42	10.40	1.94	3.71	-.126
Female	13.15	74.41	4.71	12.69	3.00	3.62	.149

network size increased at time 2 but decreased at time 3. These findings show a partial impact of career entry on network size. Additional significant effects were found: friends were more numerous than kin overall ($F(1,76) = 14.17$, $p < .001$; M friends = 15.04 and M kin = 11.11). However, this effect was modified by an interaction between time and network sector ($F(2,152) = 11.33$, $p < .001$). The greater number of friends than kin was significant at both times 1 and 2 but not at time 3. The great similarity in numbers of friends and kin at time 3 came about through a significant decrease in friend size over time and a nonsignificant increase in kin size over time. At time 1 there were 10.51 kin and at time 3 there were 11.80 kin; conversely, at time 1 there were 16.61 friends but 13.25 friends at time 3. There were no interactions involving network sector and group, thus, career entry did not have an impact on the composition of the social network in these interactions of time and network sectors.

Contact

Contact referred to the number of days per year the network member was seen by the respondent. For this variable there was a significant main effect of time ($F(2,152) = 4.16$, $p < .05$) that was modified by interaction effects on time with group ($F(2,152) = 9.59$, $p < .001$) and time with gender ($F(2,152) = 4.40$, $p < .01$). In addition, there was a significant group by time by network sector interaction ($F(2,152) = 6.45$, $p < .01$). Means for the group by time by network sector interaction are in Table 2. When participants were in college, friends were seen most frequently, somewhat less frequently by time 2 and even less frequently at time 3. Indeed, at times 1 and 2, friends were seen significantly more frequently than kin on the part of the transition group. By time 3 this group saw friends and kin about equally as often. Seeing kin and friends equally often was the norm for the career group where there were no significant mean differences at any time period for this group between kin and friends. The time effect and the group by time effect were largely due to the great amount of friend contact on the part of the transition group at time 1. The gender by time effect found that men followed the pattern of decreasing contact across time (Ms = 77.16, 61.04, and 58.07, respectively) but women increased contact with social network at time 2 and decreased contact to below time 1 levels by time 3 (Ms = 71.65, 82.43, and 65.90, respectively). Only the mean comparison between women at time 2 (M = 82.43) and men at time 3 (M = 58.07) was significant. Although there was not a significant interaction of gender, time, network sector and group, examination of the means indicated that the high degree of friend contact on the part of the women at time 2 was attained by transition women compared to career women (M = 90.06 vs M = 76.01). In sum, career entry appeared to have an impact on contact with friends, decreas-

TABLE 2 Means for Network Size, Contact and Commitment in Three Way Interactions

	Time 1	Time 2	Time 3
NETWORK SIZE[1]			
Transition			
Male	11.62	11.58	10.20[a]
Female	14.35	16.35	15.05[a]
Career			
Male	13.12	12.55	12.80
Female	15.15	12.10	12.05
CONTACT[2]			
Transition			
Kin	69.99	60.62[b]	61.34
Friend	114.08	87.98[b]	60.39
Career			
Kin	57.61	73.78	58.05
Friend	55.94	64.55	68.15
COMMITMENT[3]			
Male			
Kin	5.44[c]	5.54[e]	5.61[h]
Friend	4.05[ci]	4.03[ej]	4.42[g]
Female			
Kin	5.58[d]	5.54[f]	5.61[h]
Friend	4.37[di]	4.43[fj]	4.45[h]

[1] *Means which differ by 4.54 are significantly different, $p < .05$. Matching superscripts indicate means which are significantly different.*

[2] *Means which differ by 25.40 are significantly different, $p < .05$. Matching superscripts indicate meaningful significant differences. Not indicated are the significant differences for Time 1, Transition group Friend scores which are significantly different from all other scores.*

[3] *Means which differ by .34 are significantly different, $p < .05$. Matching superscripts indicate meaningful significant difference.*

ing it for men and increasing it for women 1 year after the transition, but decreasing contact for both men and women two years later.

Commitment

The degree of commitment to a relationship was assessed with higher values reflecting greater commitment. In the analysis with commitment as the dependent variable, network sector turned out to be an important factor with a main effect of network sector ($F(1,75) = 288.97$, $p < .001$)

and with interactions of network sector with group (F(1,75) = 6.18, p < .05), with time (F(2,150) = 3.23, p < .05) and with gender and time (F(2,150) = 3.57, p < .05). There were large and unvarying commitments to kin. What changed with time were the commitments to friends, with these being significantly greater at time 3 than at time 1 (Ms = 4.21, 4.23, 4.44 for friends at times 1, 2, and 3, respectively; the commitments to kin across time were 5.51, 5.54, and 5.49, respectively). The group by network sector interaction found significant differences only between kin and friends within each group; the interaction appeared to come about in a greater difference between kin (M = 5.60) and friend (M = 4.20) commitment for the transition group than for the career group where the kin (M = 5.43) and friend (M = 4.39) difference was less. The gender by time by network sector interaction again found large and unvarying commitments to kin for men and women. Variations in friend commitment were seen between men and women at times 1 and 2. These means are in Table 2 and show men's commitment at times 1 and 2 to be less than women's commitment to friends. With respect to impact of career entry, the findings for commitment show none of the expected group by time or group by time by network sector interactions; rather, there was a slight difference between the transition and career groups overall on kin and friend commitments.

The foregoing variables, size, contact, and commitment, describe aspects of the social network which did not necessarily involve social exchange. The variables to be discussed below, overall gives/receives, affectionate and instrumental exchanges, and profit in the relationship, all refer to aspects of exchange. The overall gives/receives described the exchanges across all eight areas of exchange measured: money, goods, affection, comfort, information, activity, opinion, and evaluation. The affectionate behaviors measured gives and receives in the areas of affection and comfort alone while the instrumental behaviors measured gives and receives in the areas of information and activity alone. Profit referred to the degree that receives outweighed gives across all eight areas.

Overall Gives/Receives. There were six significant effects in the analysis with overall gives/receives as the dependent variable: gender (F(1,74) = 24.81, p < .001); network sector (F(1,74) = 58.34, p < .001); group by gender (F(1,74) = 7.18, p < .01); group by time (F(2,148) = 9.90, p < .01); group by gender by time (F(2,148) = 5.00, p < .01); and group by time by network sector (F(2,148) = 3.48, p < .05). The three way interactions of group by gender by time and group by time by network sector will be the primary focus of the results in this section. These interactions modified all the other findings and interactions of group with time are important to examine for the possible effects of career entry. Table 3 presents the means which correspond to these interactions. As seen in Table 3, at all times, women reported higher overall gives/receives than men, but this was significant only within the career group. In particular, career group men were very low on overall gives/receives, significantly lower than transition group men at both times 1 and 2. Over time, the career group men increased while the transition group first increased and then, by time 3, decreased. The changes across time were nonsignificant however within each group. In the second part of Table 3, the results show that across time, the transition group's scores were stable from time 1 to time 2 but there was a significant decrease in overall gives/receives between times 2 and 3. On the other hand, the career group's scores between times 1 and 3 showed significant increases. According to the means, there was a crossover in both kin and friend scores such that at times 1 and 2 the career group was lower than the transition group, but at time 3 the career group was higher than the transition group. The difference between the career and transition groups for friends at time 3 was significant. The difference between the career and transition groups for kin at time 1 was significant. To summarize, there were effects of career entry as seen in the scores of the transition group but these were interwoven with effects across time for the career group as well.

Affectionate Behaviors

There were eight significant effects in the analysis of variance with affectionate behaviors as the dependent variable: gender ($F(1,74) = 21.88$, $p < .001$); group by gender ($F(1,74) = 3.97, p < .05$); time ($F(2,148) = 5.47$, $p < .01$); group by time ($F(2,148) = 9.72$, $p < .001$); group by gender by time ($F(2,148 = 4.73, p < .01$); network sector ($F(1,74) = 87.63, p < .001$); group by network sector ($F(1,74) = 4.46$, $p < .05$); gender by network sector ($F(1,74) = 7.65, p < .001$).

First, the three way interaction of group by gender by time will be presented, then the interactions of group by network sector and gender by network sector will be cited. Table 3 contains the means for the three way interaction. At times 1 and 2 career men were significantly lower than career women on affectionate behaviors with network members. The scores of career men contributed to the significant interactions of group by gender and group by time in that career men over all times were lower than career women (Ms = 2.16 vs. 3.18) and the career group at time 1 was significantly lower than the transition group at time 1 (Ms = 2.62 vs. 3.22). Across time, the three way interaction means found men in the transition group significantly higher on affectionate behaviors at time 1 than at time 3; indeed, the men's scores contributed to the transition group showing a significant decline in affectionate behaviors from time 1 to time 3 (Ms =

3.22 vs. 2.33) while the career group had a nonsignificant gain from time 1 to time 3 (Ms = 2.62 vs. 2.72).

Turning to the interactions of group and gender with network sector, it was found that kin were more involved in affectionate behavior exchanges than friends for both the transition (Ms = 3.25 vs 2.15) and the career group (Ms = 3.02 vs. 2.29). The interaction appeared to come about in the greater difference seen in the kin vs. friends scores of the transition group than the career group. With respect to the gender by relationship interaction, again kin were more involved in affectionate behavior exchanges than friends for both men (Ms = 2.91 vs. 172) and women (Ms = 3.36 vs 2.71). In this case, friend behaviors were significantly lower for men than for women, while kin behaviors did not differ significantly across men and women. For affectionate behaviors, the effects of career entry were modest and appeared for transition men such that by time 3 the affectionate behaviors of transition men were very low.

Instrumental Behaviors

There were two significant effects for instrumental behavior exchanges: time ($F(2,148) = 6.62$, $p < .01$) and gender by network sector ($F(1,74) = 7.10$, $p < .01$). Across time there were significant increases in instrumental behaviors from time 1 to times 2 and 3 (Ms = 3.41, 3.64, and 3.60, respectively). The two way interaction of gender by network sector found men with kin particularly low in instrumental behavior exchanges: the average for these men was 3.37, significantly lower than the mean for men with friends (3.64), the mean for women with kin (3.60), and the mean for women with friends (3.58). The results for instrumental behaviors found no effects of career entry.

Profit

There were two significant effects in the analysis when profit was the dependent variable: network sector ($F(1,74) = 14.83$, $p < .001$); and group time by network sector ($F(2,148 = 3.14$, $p < .05$). Overall, relationships with kin provided overbenefitting to the respondents while relationships with friends were equitable (Ms = .224 vs. .005). Table 3 provides the means which correspond to the three way interaction. In general, time contributed to a decline in overbenefitting with kin. This decline occurred more rapidly in the career group such that at time 2 the transition group and the career group were significantly different. Across time, relationships with friends hovered about the equity point but there was more volatility (albeit, nonsignificant) in the transition group in that the slight overbenefitting at time 1 became a slight underbenefitting at time 2 for this group. With no significant within group differences across time, the impact of career entry appeared in more subtle ways for profit in relationships.

TABLE 3 Means for Overall Gives/Receives, Affectionate Behaviors and Profit for Three Way Interactions

	Time 1	Time 2	Time 3
OVERALL GIVES/RECEIVES[1]			
Transition			
Male	11.55[a]	11.97[c]	10.32
Female	12.16	12.20	11.96
Career			
Male	9.56[ab]	9.80[cd]	11.15[e]
Female	12.38[b]	13.22[d]	13.16[e]
OVERALL GIVES/RECEIVES[2]			
Transition			
Kin	12.82[fk]	13.16[hp]	12.25[jp]
Friend	10.91[f]	11.01[ho]	10.06[jno]
Career			
Kin	11.55[gkl]	12.35[i]	12.73[l]
Friend	10.32[gm]	10.59[i]	11.52[mn]
AFFECTIONATE BEHAVIORS[3]			
Transition			
Male	2.82[q]	2.65	1.96[q]
Female	3.16	2.82	2.68
Career			
Male	2.13[r]	1.92[s]	2.36
Female	3.15[r]	3.28[s]	3.11
PROFIT[4]			
Transition			
Kin	.43	.36[t]	.10
Friend	.10	.04	-.10
Career			
Kin	.30	-.01[t]	.17
Friend	-.02	.00	.01

[1] Means which differ by 2.01 are significantly different, $p < .05$.
[2] Means which differ by .91 are significantly different, $p < .05$.
[3] Means which differ by .82 are significantly different, $p < .05$.
[4] Means which differ by .36 are significantly different, $p < .05$.

Note: Matching superscripts indicate meaningful significant differences.

DISCUSSION

As Pleck (1977) has noted, work and family constitute major roles for men and women, with inherent strains in simultaneously handling these two roles. Voydanoff (1985) suggested that a clearer understanding of the relationships between work and family might be enhanced by viewing both of these areas of life from a career perspective, with each having certain stages and some of these stages being more demanding than others. The initial stage of career development is particularly demanding, and individuals may find that they have less time for family and friends, even though they may be in more need of support from these social network members as they are experiencing a number of life transitions. In this study, the impact of career stage on social network structure and function was examined in an effort to identify the types of supportive functions served by the network sectors of family and friends. By selecting respondents who were just beginning work, and comparing them to respondents who had been in their careers for a couple of years, and by studying these individuals over time, we were able to identify how young adults in transition structured and utilized their social networks.

In this study, social networks differed considerably depending on gender and career stage. The picture which emerged from the results indicated that being further along in one's career is likely to result in a somewhat smaller network, and that changes in network contact begin in the early stages of career involvement. Over time, the number of friends in the network decreases and the amount of time spent with friends also declines significantly. Interestingly, however, commitment to friends increased significantly over time, which seems to reflect the need to more actively maintain friend relationships once career and family demands have begun to have more influence in one's life. A similar pattern for kin commitment was not seen, which remained relatively high across all the time periods.

The types of interactions with network members were influenced by career stage, network sector, and gender. In general, kin exchanges were higher than friend exchanges, and women in the career group reported higher gives and receives than career men. Across time, the career group increased exchanges with friends in comparison to the transition group. The transition group was more stable over time, suggesting that those somewhat further along in their careers experience an increase in need and thus level of involvement with network members. Those further along in their careers are also more likely to have added marital and parental roles to their repertoire, and these new roles and related role expectations undoubtedly influence patterns of interaction with network members.

A closer look at the types of behaviors exchanged reflects several interesting gender differences. As expected, men reported lower affectionate behaviors than women, and the men in the transition group showed a decrease in the level of affectionate behaviors over time. Overall, affectionate exchanges were higher with kin than friends. Interestingly, there were significant increases in instrumental behaviors across time. Exchanges of instrumental behaviors were consistently high and similar for women with both kin and friends and for men with friends, but men's instrumental exchanges with kin were significantly lower. In general, women tended to be higher on commitment, on overall gives and receives, and on affectionate behaviors. These gender differences reflect traditional cultural patterns of women assuming responsibility for maintaining kin ties through affective involvement and may additionally reflect a greater role overload for women who are trying to balance the demands of marriage, parenthood, and career, and thus have a need for more instrumental exchanges with network members. Gender differences also suggest that for men, friendships provide a more important source of instrumental support than family, and this type of support may be related to career concerns.

Relationships with friends were likely to be equitable, whereas the respondents indicated that their relationships with kin were more likely to result in the respondent being overbenefitted. This difference in equity in kin relationships very likely reflects a pattern identified by Schutz and Rau (1985), in which young adults are more likely to rely on friends for emotional and instrumental support, which is reciprocated, and on parents or other kin for material support, which is not necessarily reciprocated.

Of particular interest was the change over time of the friends who comprised the friendship network. At each time period studied, more than a third of the friends identified were new to the social network. These new friends were very likely work colleagues who were also identified as part of the friendship network. The addition of these friends may be an important source of both instrumental and affective support as individuals adjust to their work setting and face the challenges of initial career development.

Future studies should address to what extent the network is influenced by the addition of work colleagues, and how support from friends who are also colleagues differs from that of other friends. Attention also should be paid to the influence of marital and parental status on both social network interactions and career development. Continued longitudinal research is necessary to more closely examine the interactions of the three young adult "careers" of marriage, parenthood, and work.

In sum, the transition to work and the early years of career development are characterized by a reorganization of social networks, such that there is a partial withdrawal from friends and an increase in kin contact among both men and women, as well as a solidifying of kin relationships through affective involvement. Over time, entering a career impacts on the amount of contact with friends, the overall gives/receives with network members, affectionate behaviors for transition men, and patterns in profit in kin and friend relationships. Although kin composition within the network remained relatively stable over time, friends who were in the network changed, with more than a third of friends at each time new to the social network. The increased commitment to friends reflects the importance of these new relationships and perhaps the difficulty of maintaining friendships in the face of competing work and family demands. These patterns suggest that as young adults are faced with the demands of beginning their careers, they both create and maintain social networks that provide them with instrumental and affective supports.

REFERENCES

Antonucci, T., & Depner, C. (1982). *Social support and informal helping relationships.* Thomas A. Wills (Ed.), Basic Processes in Helping Relationships. (pp. 233-254). NY, Academic Press.

Bahr, H. M. (1976). The kinship role in a contemporary community: Perceptions of obligations and sanctions. F. Ivan Nye (Ed.), *Role Structure and Analysis of the Family* (pp. 97-112). Beverly Hills, CA: Sage.

Barrera, M., Jr., & Ainlay, S. (1983). The structure of social support: A conceptual and empirical analysis. *Journal of Community Psychology, II*, 133-143.

Baruch, G. K., Biener, L. & Barnett, R. C. (1987). Women and gender in research on work and family stress. *American Psychologist, 42*, 130-136.

Booth, A. (1972). Sex and social participation. *American Sociological Review, 37*, 183-195.

Caplan, G., & M. Killilea. (1976). *Support systems and mutual help.* NY: Gurne and Stratton.

Cobb, S. (1976). Social support as a moderator of life stress. *Psychosomatic Medicine, 38*, 300-314.

Fischer, J. L., Sollie, D. L., Sorell, G., & Green, S. (in press). Marital status and career stage influences on social networks of young adults. *Journal of Marriage and the Family.*

Foa, U. G. (1971). Interpersonal and economic resources. *Science, 171*, 345-351.

Foa, U. G., & Foa, E. B. (1974). *Societal structures of the mind.* Springfield, IL: Charles C. Thomas.

Hall, F. S., & Hall, D. T. (1979). *The two-career couple.* Reading: Addison-Wesley.

Hirsch, B. (1980). Natural support systems and coping with major life changes. *American Journal of Community Psychology, 8*, 159-172.

Hirsch, B. (1981). Social networks and the coping process: Creating personal communities. B. Gottlieb (Ed.), *Social networks and social support.* (pp. 149-170). Beverly Hills, CA: Sage.

Hirsch, B., & Jolly, E. A. (1982). Role transitions and social networks: Social support for multiple roles. Vernon L. Allen and Evert Van de Vliert (Eds.), *Role transitions: Explorations and expectations.* (pp. 39-51). NY, Plenum.

House, J. S. (1981). *Work stress and social support.* Reading MA: Addison-Wesley.

Israel, B. A. (1982). Social networks and health status: Linking theory, research and practice. *Patient Counseling and Health Education, 4,* 65-79.

Kahn, L., & Antonucci, C. (1980). Convoys over the life course: Attachment, roles and social support. Paul B. Baltes and Orville G. Brim (Eds.), *Life span development and behavior.* Vol. 3. (pp. 253-286). NY: Academic.

Ladewig, B.H., & McGee, W. (1986). Occupational commitment, a supportive family environment, and marital adjustment: Development and estimation of a model. *Journal of Marriage and the Family, 48,* 821-829.

Leslie, A., & Anderson, A. (1986). The social networks of employed couples: The role they play in coping with stress. Paper presented to the Annual Conference of the National Council on Family Relations, Dearborn, MI.

Leslie, L., & Grady, K. (1985). Changes in mothers' social networks and social support following divorce. *Journal of Marriage and the Family, 47,* 663-673.

Mitchell, R., & Trickett, E. (1980). Social networks as mediators of social support. *Community Mental Health Journal, 16,* 27-44.

Monroe, S. M. (1983). Social support and disorder: Toward an untangling of cause and effect. *American Journal of Community Psychology, 11,* 81-97.

Moos, R. H., & Mitchell, E. (1982). Social network resources and adaptation: A conceptual framework. Thomas A. Wills (Ed.), *Basic Processes in Helping Relationships.* (pp. 213-230). New York: Academic.

Pleck, J. H. (1977). The work-family role system. *Social Problems, 24,* 417-427.

Rose, S.M. (1984). How friendships end: Patterns among young adults. *Journal of Social and Personal Relationships, 1,* 267-277.

Schulz, R., & Rau, M. T. (1985). Social support through the life course. In Sheldon Cohen and S. Leonard Syme (Eds.), *Social Support and Health.* New York: Academic.

Shulman, N. (1975). Life-cycle variations in patterns of close relationships. *Journal of Marriage and the Family, 35,* 813-821.

Stueve, C., & Gerson, K. (1977). Personal relations across the life-cycle. In C. S. Fischer (Ed.), *Networks and Places: Social Relations in the Urban Settings.* New York: Free Press.

Tolsdorf, C. (1976). Social networks, support and coping: An exploratory study. *Family Process, 15,* 407-417.

Voydanoff, P. (1985). Work/family linkages over the life course. *Journal of Career Development, 12,* 23-32.

Gender Differences in the Prediction of Job Commitment

Joe F. Pittman
Department of Family and Consumer Studies
University of Utah, Salt Lake City, UT 84112

Dennis K. Orthner
Human Services Research Laboratory, School of Social Work
University of North Carolina, C B 3550, Chapel Hill, NC 27599-3550

This paper examines similarities and differences in the ways in which job commitments are made among men and women in a hierarchical work organization dominated by male values. Familial, social, personal and organizational variables were factor analyzed, and three factors were produced: sense of fit between the work organization and the self/family, organizational support of families, marital satisfaction, and job commitment. Path models using these factors were specified. Job commitments for both genders were significantly and positively predicted by "fit" and by organizational support. Evidence was found, however, for the idea that the work-family interface is more stressful for women than men. Refinements to the model developed for women workers were proposed based on gender differences in the relations between work and family variables.

Although a majority of American women are involved in the work force, the majority of working women occupy jobs traditionally assigned to females and characterized by low power, prestige and pay. Fox and Hesse-Biber (1984) assert that much of this distribution of jobs can be attributed to the outcomes of sex role socialization. Women are moving in increasing numbers into more powerful and prestigious positions traditionally assigned to men. It has been recognized for some time that the effects of such moves on their personal and family lives often differ from those for men (Pleck, 1977; Poloma & Garland, 1971). For example,

Authors' Note: The data presented in this paper were collected under contract to the Department of the Air Force. The findings presented and their interpretation are those of the authors and do not necessarily represent the official view of the Department of the Air Force.

©1988 Select Press

regardless of the time spent by each gender in the work place, wives far exceed husbands in the time spent in household tasks and child care (Farkas, 1976; Berk & Berk, 1979). Pleck's (1985) study of this time difference indicates that its size seems to vary with a combination of factors including gender, time spent in the work role, and to a lesser degree, liberalism in sex role orientation. Similarly, as women enter positions that demand greater investments of time and energy, or as women become increasingly motivated to achieve, marital relationships can become more conflicted and stressful (Berger, Foster & Wallston, 1978; Rice, 1979).

The potential for conflict between work and family roles among employed persons is great. Both roles require time and energy commitments that may be difficult to reconcile. The primacy of job commitments for men, and family commitments for women, has become part of our folklore and our social science (Bernard, 1981; Rabinowitz & Hall, 1977). It has been recently suggested that these role conflicts are beginning to lessen and that men are relaxing their work commitments as family considerations are increasing in importance (Juster & Stafford, 1985). Likewise, employed women are relaxing some of their own work and family stress by putting less emphasis on family roles and identifying more with their work organizations. This trend has resulted in husband's support for wife employment becoming less important than other sources of support in the work commitments of employed women (Orthner, 1980).

The current study builds on several points that arise from the above findings. If men and women have different experiences in their work and family roles, and if these two role sets fit together in meaningfully different ways for the two sexes, then perhaps there are also differences in the elements that need to be considered before the job commitments of each gender can be understood. The present study focuses on the prediction of job commitment in separate samples of men and women with a special emphasis on gender differences. It is guided by two basic questions. The first is whether males and females working in a traditional work organization dominated by masculine values view their work environment differently. The second question extends the search for theoretically meaningful differences in the ways antecedent conditions combine to predict the job commitments of men and women. As the relations between the worlds of work and family have become better understood, it has become increasingly important to recognize the complexity of their interaction (Kanter, 1977). Recent thinking in the emerging paradigm of human ecology (cf. Bronfenbrenner, 1979) argues for recognizing the impact on ongoing experience of increasingly removed spheres of social structure and process.

In an examination of the interface between work and the family, this recognition can be translated into an exploration of domains of experience relevant to both social spheres. These include perceptions of immediate personal experience, family relationships, social support, and the organizational environment. This multidimensional approach is increasingly seen in recent studies on the work-family interface as researchers build organizational, familial, social and personal factors into their models (Kelly & Voydanoff, 1985; Orthner & Pittman, 1986; Voydanoff & Kelly, 1984). The current study combines this strategy with the search for gender differences by observing how variables representing organizational, familial, social and personal characteristics are perceived by each gender and by examining how these factors are related to reports of job commitments.

METHOD

Sample

The data presented in this study were collected in 1984 as part of a larger study of Family Support Centers in the Air Force. Probability samples of Air Force members and spouses assigned to nine installations worldwide were surveyed. The total number of individuals identified for the study exceeded 9,000. The response rate for the mailed surveys was 58%. Analyses conducted for present purposes were based on subsamples of the original dataset. First, only Air Force members were considered, meaning that spouses and adolescent children were excluded from the study. Second, the sample was limited to members who had served fewer than ten years, allowing a focus on the years during which career commitments were assumed to be forming. The final sample used in the present study consisted of 1,037 respondents of whom 851 were males and 186 were females.

Measures

This study builds on a previous research finding that organizational, familial, social, and personal variables combine to predict the career commitments of employed persons (Orthner & Pittman, 1986). Our current focus on gender differences extends two research questions. First, do male and female members of an organization differ on variables that predict job commitment? Second, do these variables fit together in comparable or different patterns when applied to the prediction of the job commitments of each gender? Answering these questions requires beginning with a set of variables common to the two genders. Twelve variables were identified that reflect perceptions of organizational, familial, social and personal conditions. In this section operationalizations and gender differences for each variable are reported.

Organizational Variables. Four of the twelve variables deal with members' perceptions of the organization or the work environment. Since the authors were primarily interested in the work-family interface, the relevant perceptions dealt with the connection between the organizational environment and the family. The variables measured included: (a) perceived organizational responsiveness to families [4 items],[1] (b) knowledge of the availability of support programs intended to enhance family life [12 items], (c) satisfaction with 16 family support programs that each respondent might have experienced [16 items], and (d) the perception that the military organization is a good environment for rearing children [1 item]. None of these variables revealed significant gender differences.

Family variables. Three family variables were identified. The first assessed marital satisfaction [2 items]. Female respondents tended to be less satisfied with their marriages than were male respondents. The second family variable tapped the perceived support workers received from their spouses for making a career of the military [2 items]. No gender differences in spousal support were found. Finally, a single item tapped the extent to which respondents valued their spouses' opinions about the career decisions they were attempting to make. Females were slightly less likely to value their spouses' opinions than were males, suggesting that women may desire to be more independent in their career decisions than men.

Social variables. Social networks were evaluated through ratings on a five point scale of the likelihood that each of nine types of people (e.g., friends, parents, job supervisor, mental health personnel) would be sought out for help if the need ever arose. Women reported more extensive functional networks than did men.

Personal variables. Four variables tapped the domain of personal feelings. A three item composite which evaluated general satisfaction with the work organization, satisfaction with the quality of life made possible by the organization, and satisfaction with the respondent's current assignment was labelled morale. The intent to pursue a career in the organization was assessed with a single item. A single global satisfaction item indicated the respondent's general satisfaction with life. Finally, personal adjustment was a composite of nine items indicating the frequency with which selected positive and negative emotions were experienced (e.g., boredom, security, anger, hopefulness). Women respondents tended to report slightly lower personal adjustment and were somewhat

---

[1] *To conserve space, the authors have omitted specific wording of items used to measure variables. In addition, information on the reliability of variables is excluded from the text. This information is available upon request from the senior author.*

less certain about their intent to pursue a career in the organization.

Analysis Strategy The analysis process consisted of three steps. First, ten of the twelve variables were factor analyzed using principal components analysis with varimax rotation. Two variables, morale and the intent to pursue a career in the organization were withheld from the factor analysis because they were conceptually defined as the dependent factor, job commitment. Factor scores were constructed by summing the actual values of the variables that produce loadings exceeding a predetermined cutoff point.[2] In the second step of the analysis process, multiple regression was used to predict job commitments for each gender. Finally, secondary regression models were specified to permit the development of path models through which indirect effects on job commitments could be assessed independently for male and female workers.

RESULTS

Samples Comparisons

The present study is organized around an examination of gender differences in a sample of male and female Air Force members. Such a strategy must begin with a comparison of the genders on background variables (see Table 1). Although comparable on most demographic indicators, several relevant contrasts were noted. First, male respondents had been married somewhat longer than females, perhaps partly because men were also slightly more likely to be in a first marriage than were women. Although actual family income was not measured, assessments of the perceived adequacy of family income in meeting family needs indicated that women viewed their family income to be more adequate than did men. This finding may be due in part to differences in the employment of members' spouses. The typical married male member belonged to a family structured along traditional lines, with wives either unemployed or involved in part-time work. Conversely, the modal married female member belonged to a nontraditional, dual-career military family. These same gender patterns are often seen in corporate work environments (Fernandez, 1986).

Factor analysis yielded three factors for the full sample.[3] Five variables loaded on the first factor, which was labelled, "fit between the work organization and the self/family." This sense of "fit" was most powerfully

---

[2] *The standard cutoff of 0.40 was used to determine which variables loaded on a given factor. Summing the values of high loading variables allows the derived factors to intercorrelate, making the expectation of interrelations among the factors testable by multiple regression.*

[3] *Results of the factor analysis, statistics on derived factors, their reliability and intercorrelations are available upon request from the senior author.*

TABLE 1 Descriptive Statistics on Background Variables for Males and Females with Gender Differences Indicated

Variable	Males (n = 851) Mean	S.D.	Females (n = 186) Mean	S.D.	p-Level[a]
Age	26.36	3.57	26.32	3.34	
Years married	3.94	2.74	3.19	2.03	***
Number of children[b]	1.30	.91	1.11	.84	*
Years in Air Force	5.06	2.32	4.73	2.24	
Education level	3.05	.96	3.04	.83	
Socioeconomic status[c]	3.24	1.29	3.19	1.09	
Income adequacy	2.65	.63	2.92	.65	***

Variable	% Yes	(n)	% Yes	(n)	p-Level[d]
First marriage?	90.5	766	82.1	151	**
Parent?	71.8	611	66.7	95	
Race - white?	78.8	671	76.9	143	
Rank - officer?	19.0	162	14.5	27	
Live on base?	33.1	281	18.4	34	***
Spouse employed?	46.1	388	94.0	173	***
(Part-time civilian)	17.7	149	6.0	11	
(Full-time civilian)	18.5	156	9.8	18	
(Full-time military)[f]	9.9	83	78.3	144	

[a] Gender differences tested with Oneway ANOVA.
[b] Calculated for parents only.
[c] Socioeconomic status (derived by factor analysis) combines education level and rank. Only SES was used in the analysis.
[d] Gender differences tested with Chi-square.
[e] Reflects dummy code for dual career military families used in analysis.
* $p < .05$; ** $p < .01$; *** $p < .001$.

indicated by two individual level variables: personal adjustment and satisfaction with life. In addition, perceived responsiveness of the work organization to families,[4] the quality of the organizational environment as

---

[4] The variable, "perception of organizational responsiveness to families," loaded on both the first and third factor. It was decided to treat this complex loading as a simple loading on the first factor, the fit between organization and self/family. This decision was based on the following two considerations. First, this strategy prevents a spuriously high correlation between the two factors due simply to the shared variable. Second, the loading on the first factor is relatively large (0.53) compared to the loading for the third factor, which barely exceeded the cutoff (0.42).

a child rearing milieu and level of spousal support for one's career commitments loaded positively on this factor. This combination of personal, organizational and familial variables suggests that "fit" is a multidimensional phenomenon. Factor two was named marital satisfaction and is indicated by two strongly and positively loading variables: marital satisfaction and the tendency to value the opinions of one's spouse.

The third factor was labelled "organizational supportiveness." This factor appears to be a community assessment consisting of organizational and social variables. Knowledge of and satisfaction with available family support programs loaded on this factor along with the size of respondents' functional social networks.

Since the specific interest of the study was to examine the gender differences in the prediction of job commitments, separate path models were constructed, for each gender. A single model in which gender was entered as an independent variable would provide considerable relevant information, but such a strategy would not allow the examination of patterns of results more idiosyncratic to the two genders. Even though different patterns are expected for the genders, the underlying structure of the model was expected to be consistent across the genders. Therefore, only one theoretical ordering of the variables in the model needs to be specified.

Path Models

The variables included in a path model can be classified as either endogenous or exogenous. Exogenous variables are temporally or logically prior to the other variables in the model. For the present study, ten variables were identified and used as exogenous, control variables. These include: the number of years already committed to the organization, the status of being part of a dual career couple (both spouses full-time with the Air Force), the level of spousal employment (not employed, part-time, full-time), the proximity of residence to the organizational setting (on versus off the base), socioeconomic status (a composite of education and rank), the perceived adequacy of family income, race (white versus nonwhite), years married, first versus later marriage, and parental status (children living at home versus not).

Endogenous variables are expected to be the recipients of effects in the path model, but they may also affect other variables. When it affects other variables, an endogenous variable is treated as an independent variable; when it is the recipient of effects, it is treated as a dependent variable. Before a path model can be conducted, a "causal ordering" must be specified among the endogenous variables, based on logical or theoretical reasoning, to justify when a variable will be treated as dependent or independent. The models developed for this study required ordering only the three derived factors. First, the supportiveness of the organizational setting was defined as the most "distal" to job commitment on purely logical grounds. It seemed more reasonable to assert that the sense of fit between an organization and self/family as well as the feeling of marital satisfaction would be affected by a characteristic of an organization, its supportiveness, rather than the reverse.

The remaining variables were more difficult to order since there is little reason to assert that marital satisfaction will affect, but not be affected by, the fit between one's work organization and oneself/family. Nevertheless, a unidirectional causal flow is assumed in the specification of a fully recursive path model (Pedhazur, 1982). Thus, the following argument was advanced: since job commitment is the variable of final interest, the sense of fit in the work organization would seem to be a more "proximate" predictor of such commitments. For the purposes of the present analysis, therefore, marital satisfaction was considered a predictor of job commitment and fit, while fit was defined as a predictor only of commitment.

Prediction of Male Job Commitments

Regression equations for each stage of the analysis were estimated twice, once to obtain estimates of the effects of all predictors in a simultaneous regression and then to estimate the effects of only the reliable predictors identified in the first procedure. Beta weights for both full and restricted models are presented in Table 2. Figure 1 illustrates the combined results of the restricted models.

Among men, two of the derived factors were found to play a significant role in the prediction of job commitment. The sense of fit between the organization and one's self and family had by far the greatest effect, but the perception of the organization's supportiveness was also significant to job commitments. Greater fit and higher levels of organizational supportiveness were associated with greater commitment. Three background factors also affected job commitments. The years already in the organization were positively related to the likelihood of continued commitment. In addition, respondent's socioeconomic status and the perceived adequacy of their family income were each positively related to reports of job commitment. Forty percent of the variance in job commitments was explained by the five significant predictors. Using a formula to test the significance of the difference between regression models (Netter & Wasserman, 1974, p. 264) no significant difference was found in the explanatory power of the restricted model compared to the full model, which indicates that the five variable model is a good fit with the data.

TABLE 2 Beta Weights for Full and Reduced Regressions Used in the Path Model of Male Job Commitments (n=851)

	Job Commitment Full	Job Commitment Reduced	Work & Self/Family Fit Full	Work & Self/Family Fit Reduced	Marital Satisfaction Full	Marital Satisfaction Reduced	Organizational Support Full	Organizational Support Reduced
Work & Self/Family Fit	.58***	.57***						
Marital Satisfaction	-.03		.29***	.29***				
Organizational Support	.06*	.07*	.21***	.21***				
Race	-.02		-.06		.06		-.05	
Location of Residence	.01		.04		.12***	.12***	.10**	.09**
First Marriage?	-.05		.02		.04		.03	
Dual Military Couple?	.01		-.01		-.01		.03	
Socioeconomic Status	.09**	.09***	.06		.05		-.14***	-.16***
Parental Status	.00		.06		-.07*		.02	
Income Adequacy	.07*	.07*	.24***	.24***	.07*	.09**	.08*	.08*
Years of Service	.07*	.10***	.01		-.06		-.01	
Spouses' Employment	-.01		.10**	.08*	-.07		-.07	
Years Married	.02		-.00		.05		-.02	
Multiple R	.64	.63	.47	.45	.22	.16	.21	.19
R Square	.40	.40	.22	.21	.05	.03	.04	.04

*p < .05; **p < .01; ***p < .001.

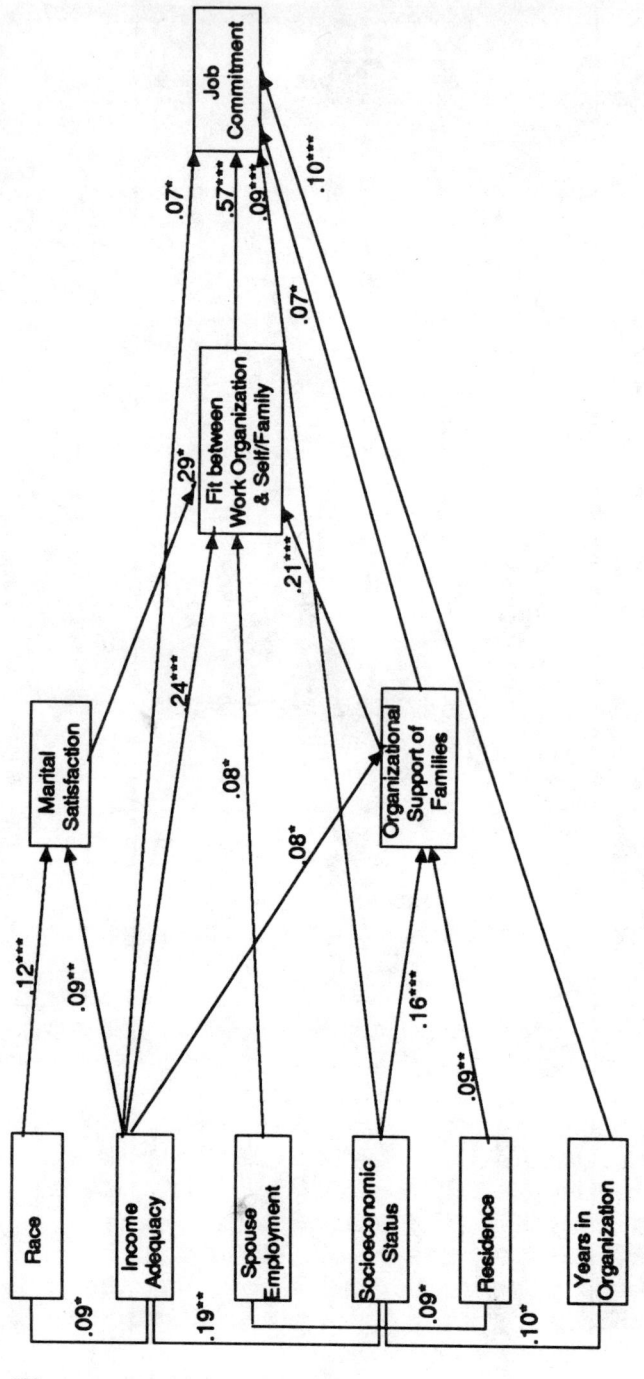

FIGURE 1 Path Model Predicting Job Commitments of Males

*p < .05; **p < .01; ***p < .001

Additional analysis permits identification of indirect effects on job commitment. A second regression took as the criterion variable the sense of fit between the organization and one's self/family. The two derived factors considered more "distal" to job commitment and the background variables were entered in the equation. Four significant predictors produced a good fitting model explaining 21% of the variability in fit. The best predictor was marital satisfaction. More satisfying marriages were associated with better fit. Perceived organizational supportiveness was also a positive predictor. Finally, two background variables positively affected male workers' perceptions of fit: family income and having wives who were relatively more involved in the labor force.

The third equation estimated for the male sample regressed marital satisfaction on organizational supportiveness and the background variables. While organizational supportiveness did not affect marital satisfaction, race, parenthood, and adequacy of family income did yield significant parameter estimates. When the restricted model was computed, however, the effect of parenthood was not significant. Therefore, a second restricted model was computed which regressed only race and income adequacy on marital satisfaction. Only 3% of the variance in marital satisfaction was explained by the two significant predictors. Marital satisfaction was somewhat greater among white males and among respondents who felt their family income was more sufficient in meeting family needs.

The final regression for the male model found three background variables produced a good fitting model of perceived supportiveness, explaining 4% of its variability. Socioeconomic status was negatively related to the perception of supportiveness. Perhaps respondents at lower SES levels were more likely to use the support services of the organization and thus to have their opinions shaped by the experience. Being a resident of the organizational environment (living on base as opposed to away from the base) was a positive predictor of the perception of organizational supportiveness, lending support to the idea that experience may relate to the perception. Finally, a more adequate income seemed to translate into a perception of greater organizational supportiveness.

A complete elaboration of all indirect effects identified by this path model would be a very large task and would produce results of doubtful utility. Several indirect effects, however, are worthy of note. Computing interpretable indirect effects involves summing the products of the parameter estimates along the identified paths of interest. The effect of marital satisfaction, for example, passes through the sense of fit between organization and self/family and proceeds to job commitment (I.E. = 0.29 X 0.57 = 0.17). A change of one standard deviation in marital satisfaction produces a 0.17 standard deviation change in job commitment because of

TABLE 3   Beta Weights for Full and Reduced Regressions Used in the Path Model of Female Job Commitments (n=186)

	Job Commitment		Work & Self/Family Fit		Marital Satisfaction		Organizational Support	
	Full	Reduced	Full	Reduced	Full	Reduced	Full	Reduced[a]
Work & Self/Family Fit	.63***	.62**						
Marital Satisfaction	-.23***	-.24***	.18*	.17*				
Organizational Support	.12*	.12*	.26***	.24***	-.16*	-.17		
Race	-.01		.04		.00		-.04	
Location of Residence	-.03		-.05		-.11		.10	
First Marriage?	.10		.05		-.15		.04	
Dual Military Couple?	.05		-.03		.01		-.02	
Socioeconomic Status	-.00		.06		.06		-.16*	
Parental Status	-.13*	-.14*	.02		-.11		-.05	
Income Adequacy	-.08		.28***	.29***	.08		.14	
Years of Service	-.01		.12		-.25*	-.19*	-.07	
Spouses Employment	-.09		.06		.12		-.04	
Years Married	.04		.05		.14		.07	
Multiple R	.70	.69	.47	.43	.36	.25	.25	
R Square	.49	.47	.22	.18	.13	.06	.06	

[a]Because the overall F-ratio for the full model was not significant, no reduced model was computed for women's perceptions of the organizational environment.
*p < .05; **p < .01; ***p < .001.

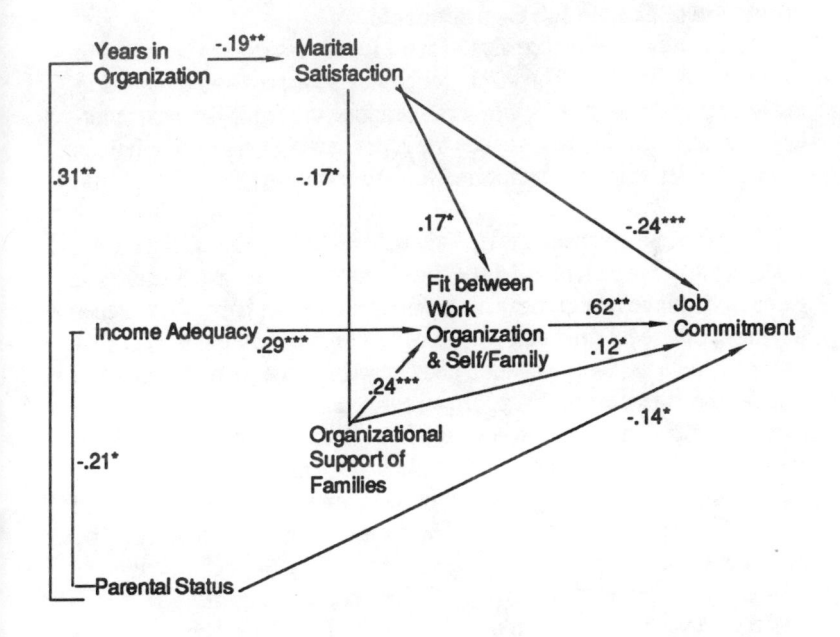

```
                    -.19**
    Years in  ─────────────→ Marital
    Organization              Satisfaction

.31**              -.17*
                              .17*                    -.24***
                              Fit between
                              Work              .62**      Job
    Income Adequacy ─────→    Organization  ──────→   Commitment
                    .29***    & Self/Family   .12*
                         .24***
                              Organizational
-.21*                         Support of                 -.14*
                              Families

    Parental Status
```

*$p < .05$; **$p < .01$; ***$p < .001$.

FIGURE 2 Path Model Predicting Job Commitments of Females

the mediating effects of the sense of fit between organization and self/family.

In addition to its direct effect on job commitment, perceptions of organizational supportiveness also has an indirect effect through the factor reflecting "fit" (I.E. = 0.21 X 0.57 = 0.11). A change of one standard deviation in perceived organizational supportiveness indirectly affects a 0.11 standard deviation change in job commitment above its direct effect of 0.07 standard deviations.

The importance to the male sample of the provider role is repeatedly seen in this analysis. The perceived adequacy of family income was a positive and significant predictor in each of the equations estimated. A conservative estimate of the indirect effect of income adequacy can be made by summing only the products of the four indirect paths that involve the endogenous variables. The indirect effect produced was 0.10.

Prediction of Female Job Commitments

The results of the path analysis for the female sample are presented in Table 3 and Figure 2. The same underlying structure was assumed to operate for male and female workers, therefore, the original causal ordering was used for the endogenous variables, even though the relations among the variables were expected to vary enough to justify a separate model.

The first procedure regressed all endogenous and exogenous variables on job commitment. All three endogenous variables and the status of parenthood played a significant role among women workers. As was true for males, the best predictor of job commitments was the sense of fit between one's work organization and oneself/family. Also like the male sample, the organization's supportiveness was a positive predictor of job commitments. Unlike the males, however, a negative relation between marital satisfaction and job commitment was found for women. Furthermore, parenthood was negatively related to job commitment for female workers. These four variables accounted for 47% of the variability in job commitments.

The perception of fit between the organization and oneself/family was the criterion factor for the second regression. The results indicated that, as for the male sample, "fit" was greater for women with more satisfying marriages and with more positive perceptions of the organization's supportiveness. Fit was also positively affected by the belief that family income was sufficient to meet family needs. These variables explained 18% of the variance in fit.

The third regression took marital satisfaction as the criterion variable. Two predictors explaining 6% of the variance in satisfaction were obtained. Years with the organization and its perceived supportiveness were each negatively related to marital satisfaction. For a woman, longer tenure in a work setting organized around traditional male values may place increasing stress on the marriage, thus eroding satisfaction. The negative relation between organizational supportiveness and marital satisfaction suggests that women with less satisfying marriages are those that are most likely to use and appreciate the supportive services available. If valid, this argument would suggest that the causal ordering between these two variables is misspecified in the women's model.

The final stage of analysis involved regressing the perception of organizational supportiveness on the background factors. The resulting F-ratio for the analysis was not statistically significant. Consequently, no restricted model was constructed.

Computation of interpretable indirect effects reveals some of the complexity of the model. For instance, not only does organizational supportiveness have a direct effect on job commitment, but its indirect effects follow three paths (see Figure 2). Its primary indirect influence is mediated by the fit between the organization and self/family, but two lesser paths of opposite sign pass through marital satisfaction. The total indirect effect for organizational supportiveness is 0.17. In addition to its direct effect, therefore, a one standard deviation change in perceived supportiveness would be associated with an indirect change of almost one-fifth of a standard deviation in job commitment.

Marital satisfaction was negatively related to job commitment along the direct path (-0.24), but the indirect path through the fit dimension was positive (0.11). The overall effect for women (-0.13) is the sum of these paths. While more satisfying marriages may be associated with lower job commitment, they also result in a more comfortable fit between organization and self/family, which, in turn, has an enhancing effect on job commitment.

The indirect effect of perceived income adequacy for women was mediated by the fit between organization and self/family and came to 0.18. Thus while no direct relation was found for women between income adequacy and job commitment, its indirect effect for women workers was roughly comparable to its total effect for males.

DISCUSSION

This study was organized around two sets of research questions. The first asked if there are differences in the ways men and women view their work environment. Very few differences were found. Women tended to have support networks that were larger and they seemed more willing to use them. This attitude apparently contributed to a more positive view of the organization's supportiveness. Broadening the perspective to include family factors, however, revealed evidence to suggest that a much greater level of marital stress exists among the working women of the sample than among the working men. Women reported less marital satisfaction and tended to value the opinion of their spouses less than their male counterparts when career decisions were being made. Further, women revealed a greater likelihood of divorce in their past and of a dual career marriage in their present. The primary differences between the genders, then, appear to be family based rather than being founded on perceptions of the work environment unique to each gender.

The second research question focused more directly on the work-family interface and asked if characteristics of the work place and the family combine differently for women and men to affect their job commitments. Given the similarity in perceptions of the organizational environment and the considerable differences in the family lives of the male and female samples, the fact that women tended to report somewhat lower levels of job commitment suggested that the work-family interface might be important. Indeed, a number of substantial differences were found in the ways work environments and personal/family factors affect job commitments. Equally interesting, however, are the considerable similarities, which will be briefly reviewed first.

Regardless of gender, the sense of fit between the work organization and oneself/family is fundamental to job commitment. There appears to be an exchange at the root of this finding. The more comfortable the fit, the more likely it is that the job will be viewed as a positive contributor to a high quality of life. When career decisions have to be made, a commitment to the organization could be seen as an exchange for the quality of life the job is believed to make possible. Another common finding is seen in the importance to job commitments of the organization's perceived supportiveness. Among males and females, a supportive environment directly enhances the likelihood of commitment while it also seems to magnify the perception of fit with the organization. Finally, both genders show a positive relation between marital satisfaction and the feeling of fit within the organization. It is hard to tell from the current study whether the effect is unidirectional (from family to work) or bidirectional.

In spite of these important similarities in the prediction of job commitments among the two genders, it is apparent that some fundamental differences also exist. These differences were the initial targets of the present investigation. Therefore, the remainder of the discussion will attempt to review these differences, to explain them in the context of the data available, and to consider their consequences.

First, the time already committed to an organization appears to have different effects on the two genders. Among men, years of service tend to enhance their commitment to their jobs. In the military, as in many corporate environments, the organization is structured around hierarchical and traditional male values. The work and family lives of males seem to fit well with this structure. For the women in the present sample, length of service lacks the positive effect on career commitments and, instead, seems to be a detriment to marital satisfaction. The organizational structure, thus, seems to enhance males' careers while being neutral to women's careers but detrimental to their family lives over time.

Although the quality of marriage does not appear to impact the job commitments of males directly, among women an apparent negative linkage between these variables was found. As the model reads, increases in marital satisfaction correspond to decreases in job commitment. If one accepts these findings at face value, one might conclude that work and marriage are less compatible for women than for men. Given the research on the nature of family time and home maintenance responsibilities (e.g., Pleck, 1985), there is some reason to accept this interpretation. As a woman's investment in her marriage (and presumably in her family and home) increases, she may increasingly perceive her marital and family roles as conflicting with those of the work place. However, an alternate interpretation is also consistent with the data if the implied causal direction shown in the model can be questioned. This alternative interpretation would also be consistent with other findings of the model.

Rather than greater marital satisfaction producing lower job commitment, perhaps greater job commitment among women affects their evaluations of the marital relationship. Aldous, Osmond and Hicks (1979) suggest, with respect to males' employment, that job satisfaction and marital satisfaction may be related in a curvilinear fashion with lower levels of marital satisfaction being associated with the extremes of job satisfaction. It seems only a small step to assert that marital satisfaction might be related in the same curvilinear fashion to job commitment. Furthermore, because military members can terminate their employment after each four year tour, most workers with extremely low job commitment have probably already left, leaving only those with moderate to high commitment. Consequently, the effect obtained with such restrictions would tend to be linear and negative.

If this interpretation is correct, the causal structure of the women's model should read: (a) greater marital satisfaction enhances the sense of fit between the organization and the self/family, (b) greater fit enhances the level of job commitment, but (c) high level of job commitment undermines marital satisfaction, perhaps because of a sense of poorer fit due to the loss of "balance" between work and family roles. The implications of the alternative interpretations differ dramatically. If greater marital satisfaction leads to weaker job commitment, then the often practiced tendency to hire unmarried women or women not heavily invested in marriage makes good business sense. If, on the other hand, the circular model is accurate, the wisest corporate policy is to provide supports for the marriages of women employees. Indeed, this support would be best supplied in proportion to the level of job commitment evidenced, as those with the greatest commitments would also be those with the most stressed marriages.

Another gender difference revealed in these models also appears relevant to the discussion of the relations between marital satisfaction and job commitment. The marital satisfaction of males is not related to the organization's perceived supportiveness, while a negative relation is seen for females between organizational supportiveness and marital satisfaction. Again the proposed causal ordering appears to be suspect. The authors' original reasoning assumed that the perceived supportiveness of a work organization would have an average positive effect in the marriages of all workers, which leads to the proposed causal ordering. In other words, it was reasoned that supportiveness would lead to greater satisfaction. The results suggest, however, that supportiveness, while having positive import for job commitments and for the sense of fit between the organization and the self/family, may not relate to marital satisfaction except in the case of marital stress. To test this idea, additional analyses were conducted with the sample of female workers.

Although respondents might have utilized a variety of family support programs (e.g., day care, financial counseling, adolescent programs), only two were specifically targeted at enhancing the quality of marriage. The hypothesis was tested that female respondents with greater marital stress (operationalized as lower marital satisfaction) have more contact with those programs designed to enhance the quality of marriages (i.e., marital counseling and marriage enrichment), but the same level of contact with other programs. A oneway ANOVA was conducted with the independent factor being use versus nonuse of each program. The results provided some support for the expectation. Marital counseling ($F = 11.0$, $p < 0.01$) was used more by the maritally distressed, but other programs were not. The results for enrichment programs approached statistical significance but did not reach it ($F = 1.9$, $p = .17$). The second hypothesis tested whether perceptions of the work organization's supportiveness were related to the use of these two marriage oriented programs. The results of the oneway analyses revealed that the organization was thought to be significantly more supportive by those respondents who had used marital counseling ($F = 14.8$, $p < 0.001$), and marriage enrichment ($F = 9.1$, $p < 0.01$).

These analyses were not intended to show simply that more maritally distressed women use more counseling services. Such results would hardly be surprising. Rather, these results help build the case that, at least among women employees, the use of marital support services results in enhanced perceptions of the supportiveness of the organization among the more distressed women who take advantage of the services. Thus, the empirical linkage between organizational supportiveness and marital satisfaction seems to be misspecified. Among employees (probably both males and females) who do not use marital support services, there seems to be no connection between organizational support and marital quality. However, among those who do use these support services, perceptions of organizational support are enhanced.

One apparent "gender difference" seems to be less a true discrepancy than an idiosyncrasy in the operation of job commitments on men's and women's perceptions of the adequacy of their family income and job commitment. The ostensible difference is seen in the pervasive importance of income adequacy for males compared to its focused effect among females. Not only are the men's job commitments directly influenced by their attitudes about their income, but their views of the organization's supportiveness, its fit with self and family, and even marital quality are affected. Among women, adequacy of income is directly relevant only to the sense of fit between organization and self/family. Nevertheless, the actual total effect of income adequacy on job commitments in each model is equivalent. Thus, while income adequacy is widely significant in the male model, the effect size is small in most cases. Women place heavy emphasize on the sense of fit between the organization and self/family, which is itself considerably affected by the feeling that the money earned is adequate.

This discrepancy in the operation of income adequacy may reflect contrasting identification with the provider role. Males may feel that their adequacy as a provider is indicated by their income. This idea is supported by the nonsignificant correlation between level of spousal employment and adequacy of income. Whether his wife works full-time, part-time, or not at all, a male's perception of income adequacy rests primarily in his own contribution to the family income. Women could be expected to enter careers for reasons other than a commitment to a traditionally male provider role. Nevertheless, the level of income plays a significant role in the perception of a good fit between the work organization and self/ family, which enhances the likelihood of commitment to the job.

Although four characteristics of respondent's marriages and families were included as background variables, only one produced a significant effect in either model. Parental status and job commitment played a small, though significant, negative role in the prediction of women's job commitments. Apparently enough young mothers in the sample found that being a parent invokes enough role conflict between the traditional family role and the nontraditional work role to produce a small average disinclination in the female sample to remain committed to the job.

Conclusions and Caveats

This study began with the idea that there may be important differences in the ways men and women form their work commitments due to differences in the fit between their respective work and family lives. While a preponderance of findings reveal no differences in perceptions of the work organization or in the ways work variables affect commitments, several findings support the idea that the work-family interface differs importantly for the two genders. Indeed, while years on the job had only positive effects on men's job commitments, among women, longer tenure on the job appeared to be associated with greater marital stress. Job commitments and marital quality showed no direct linkage among men. For women, the negative connections between marital satisfaction and job commitments, on the one hand, and perceptions of the organization, on the other, suggest that women have less opportunity to insulate their family life from their work life. This interpretation is consistent with Pleck's (1977) hypothesis that work demands intrude into the family lives of women more than men.

While the great similarity in the two models supports the underlying assumption that the basic process "causing" job commitments is shared across genders, several modifications were proposed for the female model based on the apparent differences in the interaction of work and family domains. Specifically, the causal flow from marital satisfaction to job commitment should probably be reversed, creating a circular process with marital satisfaction enhancing the fit between work and family, which then enhances the probability of job commitment. This, in turn, feeds back to marital satisfaction negatively if job and family commitments get "out of balance."

It was also proposed that the direction of the linkage between marital satisfaction and perceptions of the organization's supportiveness should be reversed. In families with less stressed marriages, there is probably no linkage between these two variables (as in the male model). However, as marital quality is strained due to the intrusion of work demands into the family lives of women, use of family support services increases which tends to enhance the perception of the supportiveness of the organization.

A few caveats should be pointed out with respect to the interpretation and generalization of the results of the present study. First, while the models presented have been constructed from variables originating in organizational, familial, social and personal domains, it would be a gross oversimplification to suppose that all variables relevant to the prediction of job commitments have been incorporated. The fact that the models presented are not "complete" means that interpretation of the models must proceed with caution. For instance, while we found the sense of fit between the organization and the self/family best predictor of job commitments for both genders, other better predictors may exist that were not included. This line of reasoning is particularly important when interpreting indirect effects. Any change to the model would change the value of parameter estimates, and therefore, the indirect effects as well, since they are constructed from the parameter estimates obtained. Moreover, changes in the model could introduce other mediating relations which would also provide added paths through which the indirect effects could be transmitted. Consequently, the models presented here must be viewed as a limited rather than as a full explanation of job commitments among men and women.

A second caveat pertains to the generalization of the given findings to the population at large. Because the data presented here were obtained from a military population, care must be taken in generalizing the results to any non-military population. There are several points of similarity between the present sample and many non-military samples. For instance, the frequency with which families are transferred make many military and corporate families more comparable. Similarly, the rise in the number of women in a traditionally male occupation makes a military sample comparable to many male dominated professions. There are also many demonstrated similarities between the organizational culture of the Air Force and large, civilian corporations (Ouchi, 1982; Schein, 1985). However, there are substantive differences that make the military setting unique and that potentially limit the generalizability of findings to non-military families. More research is certainly needed to further examine the findings of the present investigation.

REFERENCES

Aldous, J., Osmond, M.W., & Hicks, M.W. (1979). Men's work and men's families. In W. R. Burr, R. Hill, F.I. Nye & I.L. Reiss (Eds.), *Contemporary theories about the family* (Vol. 1) (pp. 227-256). New York: Free.

Berger, M., Foster, M., & Wallston, B.S. (1978). Finding two jobs. In R. Rapoport & R.N. Rapoport (Eds.), *Working couples,* New York: Harper & Row.

Berk, R. A., & Berk, S. F. (1979). *Labor and leisure at home.* Beverly Hills, CA: Sage.

Bernard, J. (1981). The good-provider role: Its rise and fall. *American Psychologist, 36,* 1-12.

Bronfenbrenner, U. (1979). *The ecology of human development: Experiments by nature and design.* Cambridge, MA: Harvard University.

Farkas, G. (1979). Education, wage rates, and the division of labor between husband and wife. *Journal of Marriage and the Family, 38,* 473-483.

Fernandez, J. P. (1986). *Child care and corporate productivity: Resolving family/work conflicts.* Lexington, MA: D. C. Heath.

Fox, M. F., & Hesse-Biber, S. (1984). *Women at work.* Palo Alto, CA: Mayfield.

Juster, F. T., & Stafford, F. P. (Eds.). (1985). Time, goods, and well-being. Ann Arbor, MI: Institute for Social Research.

Kanter, R. M. (1977). *Work and the family in the United States: A critical review and agenda for research and policy.* New York: Russell Sage.

Kelly, R. F., & Voydanoff, P. (1985). Work/family role strain among employed parents. *Family Relations, 34,* 367-374.

Netter, J., & Wasserman, W. (1974). *Applied linear statistical models.* Homewood, IL: Richard D. Irwin.

Orthner, D. K. (1980). *Families in blue: A study of married and single parent families in the Air Force.* Washington, DC: Department of the Air Force.

Orthner, D.K., & Pittman, J. F. (1986). Family contributions to work commitment. *Journal of Marriage and the Family, 48,* 573-581.

Ouchi, W. (1982). *Theory Z.* New York: Avon Books.

Pedhazur, E. J. (1982). *Multiple regression in behavioral research* (2nd. Ed.). New York: Holt, Rinehart, & Winston.

Pleck, J. H. (1977). The work-family role system. *Social Problems, 24,* 417-427.

Pleck, J. H. (1985). *Working wives, working husbands.* Beverly Hills: Sage.

Poloma, M. M., & Garland, T. N. (1971). The married professional woman: A study in the tolerance of domestication. *Journal of Marriage and the Family, 33,* 531-540.

Rabinowitz, S., & Hall, D. T. (1977). Organizational research on job involvement. *Psychological Bulletin, 84,* 265-288.

Rallings, E.M., & Nye, F.I. (1979). Wife-mother employment, family, and society. In W. R. Burr, R. Hill, F.I. Nye & I.L. Reiss (Eds.), *Contemporary theories about the family* (Vol. 1) (pp. 203-226). New York: Free.

Rice, D. G. (1979). *Dual-career marriage: Conflict and treatment.* New York: Free.

Schein, E. H. (1985). *Organizational culture and leadership.* San Fransisco: Josey-Bass.

Voydanoff, P., & Kelly, R. F. (1984). Determinants of work related family problems among employed parents. *Journal of Marriage and the Family, 46,* 881-892.

Work/Family Concerns of University Faculty

Jerelyn B. Schultz
Family and Consumer Sciences Education
Iowa State University, Ames, IA 50011

Yonsuk L. Chung
Department of Home Management
Songsim College of Women, Buchun City, Korea

Chinella G. Henderson
Division of Home Economics
Alabama A & M University, Normal, AL 35762

Data from questionnaires and interviews were integrated to provide more complete insights into the work/family concerns experienced by 60 faculty at a large midwestern land-grant university. Content analyses of interview data provided information on the nature of faculty members' work/family concerns. Results of analyses of variance showed that sex, age and number of children, and employment status of spouse affected some work/family interface index scores. Pearson product moment correlation analyses indicated that some consistency was found between responses to questionnaire and interview items.

Recent social and demographic changes in American society have resulted in increased attention on the relationships between work and family life. Both husband and wife work outside the home in over one half of all American marriages today. By 1990 it is predicted that only one-fourth of two-parent families will have a nonemployed parent. The growing number of dual-income families combined with the rise in the number of single-parent families indicates that more and more individuals are confronted with both work and family responsibilities. Thus, the relationships between work and family are being examined from a number of different perspectives.

A number of studies (Herman & Gyllstrom, 1977; Keith & Schafer, 1980; Pleck, Staines, & Lang, 1980; Dubois, 1981; Voydanoff & Kelly 1984, 1985; Greenhaus & Beutell, 1985; Schultz & Henderson, 1985; Gupta & Jenkins, 1985) have found that many individuals experience conflicts in combining work and family responsibilities. Voydanoff and

---
©1988 Select Press

Kelly (1984) have suggested that the most important types of work/family conflicts for employed parents are income inadequacy and time shortages. Income inadequacy was termed an economic-based conflict by Felstehausen, Glosson, and Couch (1986).

The shortage of time also was identified as a basis of work/family conflicts by Greenhaus and Beutell (1985) in a review of the literature. Along with time-based conflicts, Greenhaus and Beutell suggested that individuals experience strain-based and behavior-based conflicts in balancing work and family life. Strain-based conflicts exist when stress in one role influences one's performance in another role. Several sources of time-based conflicts also result in strain-based conflicts. Behavior-based conflicts occur when the specific behavior required by one role makes it difficult to fulfill the requirements of another. A number of factors associated with aspects of work have been found to be related to work/family conflicts. Using data from the Quality of Employment Survey conducted by the University of Michigan, Pleck, Staines, and Lang (1980) found that the work-related factors most strongly associated with work/family conflicts were the number of hours worked, frequency of overtime, assignment to an afternoon shift, and physical or psychological demands of work. In a study of two-income families' role strain and depression, Keith and Schafer (1980) identified the number of hours per week spent at work as the most important factor in explaining work/family conflicts. Similar variables such as excessive work time, schedule conflicts, and fatigue were cited by Voydanoff and Kelly (1984, 1985) and Schultz and Henderson (1985) as leading to work/family conflicts. The number of hours commuted per week and the inflexibility of work schedules were identified by Greenhaus and Beutell (1985) as other work factors associated with time-based work/family conflicts.

Along with time-related factors, ambiguity and/or conflicts within and among roles, low levels of leader support and interaction facilitation, the rate of work environment changes, the mental concentration required at work, and stress in communication were found to be positively related to strain-based work/family conflicts by Greenhaus and Beutell (1985). Furthermore, Gupta and Jenkins (1985) found in their review of literature that pressure for mobility, travel, and the rigidity of organizational norms and expectations were variables related to role conflicts.

Research examining work/family concerns has identified that sex, the presence of younger children, and employment status are important factors related to work/family conflicts. Studies by Voydanoff and Kelly (1984, 1985) have found that female working parents with younger children at home experience the greatest degree of conflict between work and family life. Large family size, conflicts within the family, and low spouse support also have been found to be positively related to time-based and strain-based work/family conflicts (Greenhaus & Beutell, 1985).

According to research by Voydanoff and Kelly (1984), other family-related demands associated with work/family conflicts include experiencing three or more important family changes such as divorce, death, and new relationships; increased expenses; or being a member of a family in which the wife's occupational status is higher than the husband's. Along with experiencing important family changes, having an unemployed spouse and being a female single-parent were found to be related to economic-based work/family conflicts. In addition, managing household tasks, finding quality day care, and managing time and energy have been identified as being related to work/family conflict situations (Felstehausen, Glosson, & Couch, 1986).

Resources and strategies for coping with work/family conflicts have been identified in the literature. Gutek, Nakamura, and Nieva (1981) suggested that providing flexible working hours, adopting the concept of shared jobs and team work, and providing greater legitimacy to part-time jobs are policies that could be beneficial for the worker who has family responsibilities. Higher income levels, job satisfaction, not marrying early, and time management skills were identified as resources used to cope with time-based work/family conflicts by Voydanoff and Kelly (1984). They also found that a longer length of time between marriage and the birth of the first child, achieving job tenure, higher levels of education, and husbands having a higher level of occupational status were resources used to deal with economic-based work/family conflicts.

Schultz and Henderson (1985), in their review of the literature, identified time, money, and energy management strategies to reduce work/family conflicts for individuals who combine work and family roles. Along with time, energy, and money management strategies, Gupta and Jenkins (1985) suggested that seeking flexible occupations and work hours, alternating the partner who gives primary emphasis to work versus family roles, and careful timing of family role demands as well as mutual support, understanding, consideration, and cooperation may help alleviate conflicts between work and family life. Although a number of studies on work/family conflicts were found in the literature, none examined these conflicts for university faculty and most used a single method of data collection. Herman and Gyllstrom (1977), Pleck, Staines, and Lang (1980), Keith and Schafer (1980), and Voydanoff and Kelly (1984, 1985) conducted studies using self-report questionnaire data. Data also have been collected on work/family conflicts using interview procedures. Dubois (1981), Pierre (1984), and Crouter (1984) used interviews to collect in-depth data on problems associated with combining work and family responsibilities.

Jick (1983) and Denzin (1978) have advocated the use of multiple data collection methods in the social sciences. The use of multiple methods including both quantitative and qualitative approaches is usually described as convergent methodology or triangulation (Jick, 1983). Triangulation is broadly defined by Denzin (1978, P. 291) as "the combination of methodologies in the study of the same phenomenon." Jick stated that triangulation allows researchers to be more confident of their results and uncovers the deviant or off-quadrant dimensions of a phenomenon. In spite of these advantages, studies using a triangulation of methods to address the work/family interface have not appeared until recently. In conjunction with questionnaires, Felstehausen, Glosson, and Couch (1986) conducted in-depth semi-structured interviews to describe more adequately the nature of the reciprocal relationships between work and the home. The data from the questionnaire and interview schedules, however, have been only reported separately thus far.

Although recent attempts have been made to use triangulation methods in the study of work and family conflicts, no research studies were found that actually reported results using multiple data collection procedures. Therefore, this research study was designed to provide more complete insights into the work/family interface problems of university faculty and to integrate data obtained from questionnaires and interviews.

Specific objectives were to:

1. Identify the work/family concerns or problems experienced by university faculty.

2. Determine the degree to which selected demographic variables affect the work/family concerns experienced by faculty.

3. Investigate the consistency of responses to items dealing with work/family concerns on a structured questionnaire and a semi-structured interview.

METHOD

Sample

The sample for this study consisted of 60 faculty members at a midwestern land-grant university. These faculty members had volunteered to be interviewed as part of a larger study on work and family (Schultz & Chung, 1986). For the larger study, a stratified random sample of 204 faculty members was drawn. The bases for stratification were sex and college in which the faculty member held academic rank. A questionnaire was mailed to each of the 204 faculty members and a total of 140 (68.6%)

completed the questionnaire, 60 of whom agreed to be interviewed. These faculty members were contacted by telephone to confirm their participation in the second phase of the study and to establish an appointment for the interview. Semi-structured interviews were conducted by researchers in each faculty member's office.

Of the faculty participating in the interviews, 43.4% held the rank of professor, 18.3% the rank of associate professor, and 38% the rank of assistant professor. Tenure had been achieved by 70% of the faculty interviewed, and the mean salary of participants was $38,200. The academic division of the faculty members interviewed was distributed as follows: 21.7% agriculture, 6.7% business, 6.7% design, 16.7% education, 6.7% engineering, 20% home economics, 10% science and humanities, and 11.7% veterinary medicine. The average percentage of appointment for each job activity performed by faculty was 63% for teaching and advising, 20% for research, and 16.8% for administration, extension, or other. The mean class teaching load per semester of faculty interviewed was 5.5 hours. Of this group, 38.3% worked with both undergraduate and graduate students, 36.7% worked entirely with undergraduates, and 23.3% worked with graduates.

The sex distribution for participating faculty members was 51.7% male and 48.3% female. The age of faculty members interviewed was distributed as follows: 45% under 40 years of age; 21.7%, 40-49; and 33.3%, 50 years of age or older. Most of this group were white (98.3%), married (80%), and described their health as good or excellent (96.7%). Almost half of the participants' (46.6%) households contained two or fewer members. Twenty percent of those interviewed did not have any children, 40% had one or two children, and 35% had three or more children. The age of participants' children was distributed in the following way: 15% preschool age or younger, 15% elementary school age, 20% high school or college age, and 16.7% adult.

The average number of hours per week spent doing household tasks by wives was 20.1 hours, by husbands 9.7 hours, and by children 4.0 hours. Over half of the interviewee's spouses were employed, 48.3% full-time and 11.7% part-time. Respondents were asked to describe the extent to which their spouse's job had deterred them from considering another job. Of the respondents whose spouse was employed full-time or part-time, 58% indicated that their spouse's job had not been a deterrent, whereas 41.7% reported their spouse's job had been a major or minor deterrent.

Instrumentation

The questionnaire contained a work-related information instrument and a demographic information instrument. Data related to work performance and participation in professional organizations were obtained by the work-related information instrument. Questions on the demographic information instrument were designed to ascertain selected demographic characteristics, home and family variables, and employment background of the respondent's spouse. University records were used to collect information on salary, rank, and year of last promotion.

A semi-structured interview schedule was developed to more comprehensively investigate the diversity of work/family issues confronting faculty. The questions contained in the interview schedule were as follows: positive and negative effects of the job on personal and family life, positive and negative effects of personal and family life on the job, family support systems, division of household tasks, time management strategies, methods of coping with schedule conflicts, major personal and family life events, and other problems related to the work/family interface.

Data Analysis

Descriptive statistics including frequencies, percentages, and means were used for all questionnaire items. Content analyses were performed to examine the narrative portions of the interview schedule. Following the method outlined by Berelson (1954), two major units of analysis were used: words and themes. The results are reported using logical analysis as described by Patton (1980). Frequency distributions and percentages were then computed for responses to each question. Each response to a question was given a numeric value of 1. Next, seven work/family interface index scores were computed by summing the coded value of responses for questions related to the positive and negative effects of the job on personal and family life, the positive and negative effects of personal and family life on the job, family support systems, time management strategies, and methods of coping with schedule conflicts. A similar method was used by Crouter (1984) to create positive and negative spillover indices.

One-way analyses of variance were conducted to examine how the demographic variables of sex, number and age of children, and spouse support affected the work/family interface index scores. These variables were selected because they have been consistently found in the research literature (Voydanoff & Kelly, 1984, 1985) to be factors resulting in work/family conflicts. Pearson product moment correlation analyses were used to examine the degree of consistency between responses to questionnaire and interview items assessing similar work and family variables.

RESULTS AND DISCUSSION

Results of the content analyses of the interview data regarding spillover between work and family, family support systems, the division of household tasks, time management strategies, methods for coping with work/family conflicts, and other aspects of the work/family interface will be discussed first.

Spillover from job to family. Respondents were asked to indicate both the positive and negative effects of their job on their personal and family life. Seven different positive effects were reported including "a better self-concept" (66.7%), "increased income" (31.7%), "good benefits for family" (30%), "personal growth" (20%), "social access" (13.3%), and "flexibility of job" (11.7%). In the case of negative effects, 61.7% of the faculty members indicated "less time for family" and 36.7% reported "stress carry over." These data support earlier findings about both time-based conflicts and strain-based conflicts being associated with the work/family interface (Pleck, Staines, & Lang, 1980; Keith & Schafer, 1980; Voydanoff & Kelly, 1984, 1985; Schultz & Henderson, 1985; Greenhaus & Beutell, 1985; Gupta & Jenkins, 1985).

Spillover from family to job. Respondents also were asked to report both the positive and negative effects of their personal and family life on their job. A large majority of the faculty interviewed (90%) reported "a supportive environment" as a positive effect of their personal and family life on their job. The supportive nature of family relationships also was found to be an important aspect related to positive spillover from family to job by Crouter (1984). Over half of the respondents (58.3%) identified no negative effects of their family and personal life on the job. However, "not enough time for work" (25%), "absenteeism" (10%), and "stress carryover" (10%) were reported by some faculty members as negative spillover effects.

Family support systems. The interviewed sample was asked to identify individuals who assisted with household or family tasks. Of this group of faculty, over half of the faculty (51.7%) reported that they did not have any family support systems outside of their immediate family. Housekeeper (21.7%), relative (21.7%), yard worker (6.7%), and friends (6.7%) were mentioned respectively as sources of support.

Division of household tasks. Faculty interviewed were asked to describe how household tasks were divided among family members and to indicate which household tasks they would like to eliminate from their responsibilities. Of the respondents, 21.7% indicated that household tasks were divided equally, 31.7% divided along traditional lines, 28.3% shared all household tasks, and 18.3% were done by one person. Examination of responses to this question for married faculty revealed that over 60%

reported a joint division of household tasks. Earlier studies have found that joint housekeeping roles were positively related to nontraditional gender role values (Seccombe, 1986) and to the employment status of women (Maret & Finlay, 1984). Maret and Finlay also reported some change toward greater sharing of household tasks for both employed and nonemployed women.

Among the household tasks, "cleaning the house" (30%), "yard work" (11.7%), and "dishwashing" (13.3%) were most frequently mentioned as tasks faculty members wanted to eliminate from their household responsibilities.

Time management strategies and methods for coping with conflicts. Respondents were asked to indicate the time management strategies they used to balance job and personal or family life. Seven different time management strategies were identified. These were "getting up early" (21.7%), "buying prepared foods" (6.7%), "placing less emphasis on cleanliness" (25%), "staying up late" (25%), "eating out more" (18.3%), "following a strict schedule" (36.7%), and "cooking in quantity" (11.7%). The time management strategies most frequently used were to follow a strict schedule, to stay up late, and to place less emphasis on cleanliness. Following a strict schedule and staying up late are time management strategies that may place a greater burden on faculty members and lead to more stress. Lowering standards, including the placement of less emphasis on cleanliness, has been identified as a time management skill that can be used to successfully balance work and family responsibilities (Gupta & Jenkins, 1985; Schultz & Henderson, 1985).

Interviewees were asked to identify the methods they used in coping with schedule conflicts between their work and personal or family life. Respondents identified "giving first priority to work" (26.7%), "compromising with one's spouse" (25%), and "eliminating after work meetings" (16.7%) most frequently. Gupta and Jenkins (1985) also suggested compromising with one's spouse as a strategy that can be used to alleviate dual-career stress.

Other aspects of work/family concerns. Over half of the faculty interviewed (57.9%) indicated that their personal and family life was more important than their job, while 29.8% reported that their personal and family life and their job were equally important. No major changes in personal and family life during the past 5 years were reported by 26.7% of the respondents. Birth (23.3%), death (21.7%), moving (20%), and children leaving home (16.7%) were mentioned as the major family-life changes faculty members had experienced. Family life changes such as death and birth of a child were found to be associated with time-based and economic-based work/family conflicts by Voydanoff and Kelly (1984).

Faculty members were asked to indicate whether or not they can turn personal and family life concerns off once they reach the job. Responses were distributed as follows: 38.3% "yes," 35% "no," and 16.7% "sometimes." Respondents observed eight work/family problems as occurring among their faculty colleagues. These include marital problems (31.7%), child care concerns (30%), an overload of outside activities (15%), problems with teenage children (13.3%), divorce (8.3%), caring for elderly parents (8.3%), financial problems (6.7%), and alcoholism (5%). Marital and child care problems were most frequently observed as work/family problems by respondents. Marital problems such as divorce were found to be important family changes related to both time-based and economic-based work/family conflicts by Voydanoff and Kelly (1984). Felstehausen, Glosson, and Couch (1986) identified child care concerns, such as finding quality day care, as problems associated with the work/family interface.

Demographic Variables and Work/Family Concerns

One-way analyses of variance were used to determine the effects of sex, age and number of children, and employment status of spouse on the seven work/family interface index scores (see Table 1). The results of the analyses revealed that sex was a significant main effect for the index scores on family support systems, time management strategies, and coping methods. Female faculty members reported they used more family support systems to assist them with household or family tasks as well as more time management strategies to balance job and personal life than their male counterparts. In addition, female faculty members used more methods for dealing with schedule conflicts between work and personal or family lives. Several studies (Herman & Gyllstrom, 1977; Dubois, 1981; Kelly & Voydanoff, 1984, 1985) have found that women perceived greater conflicts between work and family roles than men. This may provide a partial explanation for these results in the present study. Women may need more support systems, time management strategies, and coping methods to balance work and family responsibilities because they have continued to assume major responsibility for child care and household task completion.

The age of a faculty member's children significantly affected the negative spillover index scores of both job-to-family and family-to-job. Faculty members whose children were preschool age or younger reported higher levels of negative spillover from both job-to-family and family-to-job. This result is consistent with earlier studies by Keith and Schafer (1980), Crouter (1984), Pierre (1984), Kelly and Voydanoff (1984, 1985), Greenhaus and Beutell (1985), and Schultz and Henderson (1985). These

TABLE 1 Effect of Demographic Variables on Work/Family Interface Index Scores

		Support Systems		Time Mgt. Strategies		Schedule Conflicts		Positive Spillover Job-to-Fam.		Negative Spillover Job-to-Fam.		Positive Spillover Fam.-to-job		Negative Spillover Fam.-to-job	
Demographic Variables	N	Mean	F	Mean	F	Mean	F	Mean	F	Mean	F	Mean	F	Mean	F
Sex															
Male	31	.35	5.99*	1.12	9.07**	.64	7.29**	1.51	3.46	.94	.45	.94	.88	.39	.65
Female	29	.79		1.79		1.03		1.96		1.03		.86		.51	
Age of children															
Under preschool	9	.67		1.67		1.22		2.30		1.44		1.00		1.02	
Elementary	9	.78	1.60	1.56	1.04	1.00	2.36	2.40	2.70	1.89	3.00*	1.00	1.68	.67	7.76**
High school & college	12	.17		1.50		.67		1.70		.92		.83		.09	
Adult	10	.60		1.00		.60		1.40		.80		1.00		.40	
Number of children															
None	15	.80		1.53		.80		1.33		1.00		.73		.20	
1 or 2	24	.58	1.51	1.50	.27	1.00	1.89	2.20	5.89**	.96	.04	.96	3.27**	.54	1.65
3 or more	21	.38		1.33		.67		1.50		1.00		.95		.52	
Employment of spouse															
Full time	29	.69		1.62		.90		1.79		.93		1.00		.38	
Part time	7	.29	1.63	1.85	1.40	1.29	4.91*	2.14	0.77	.86	.93	1.00	3.27**	.57	1.44
Not employed	12	.33		1.17		.50		1.58		1.17		.83		.75	

*$p < .05$ **$p < .01$

studies found that the presence of younger children was an important factor in producing work/family conflicts. The positive spillover index scores from both job-to-family and family-to-job were influenced by the number of children of respondents. Faculty members who had one or two children reported more positive effects of their job on their personal and family life than those with no children or three or more children. This result is somewhat inconsistent with Keith and Schafer's (1980) findings. They found that men and women who had more children at home experienced greater work/family strain than persons with fewer or no children at home.

The employment status of the respondent's spouse resulted in a significant difference in index scores dealing with coping methods and positive spillover from family-to-job. Faculty members whose spouse was employed full-time or part-time used more coping methods to deal with schedule conflicts between work and personal or family life and reported more positive effects of family life on the job than faculty members whose spouse was not employed. Research (Dubois, 1981; Crouter, 1984; Voydanoff & Kelly, 1984, 1985; Gupta & Jenkins, 1985; Schultz & Henderson, 1985) has found that employment status of the spouse is a factor related to the experiencing of a greater number of work/family conflicts. This may partially explain the present study's results regarding the relationship between spouse's employment status and the number of coping methods used. Individuals who have experienced greater conflicts may use more coping methods to balance work and family life.

Questionnaire and Interview Consistency

Pearson product moment correlation analyses were used to examine whether or not the four index scores of spillover based on interview responses were consistent with faculty members' responses to questionnaire items assessing the same aspects of work/family spillover (see Table 2). Significant positive relationships were found between responses to interview and questionnaire items regarding both the positive and negative effects of personal and family life on one's job ($r=.31$, $r=.26$, respectively). Faculty who indicated more examples of positive and negative spillover from family-to-job in the interview also reported on the questionnaire that their personal and family life more frequently influenced their job performance. Only one significant correlation was found between questionnaire and interview items assessing the influences of one's job on personal and family life. Faculty members who reported that their job more frequently influenced their family life in a negative way on the questionnaire gave more examples of negative effects of the job on family life during the interview.

TABLE 2 Correlations between Questionnaire and Interview Items Assessing Work and Family Spillover

Questionnaire Items	Work/Family Interface Index Scores[a]			
	Positive Spillover Job-to-Fam.	Negative Spillover Job-to-Fam.	Positive Spillover Fam.-to-Job	Negative Spillover Fam.-to-Job
Has your personal/family life influenced your job performance in a positive way?	.17	-.36**	.31**	.05
Has your personal/family life influenced your job performance in a negative way?	.14	.43**	-.16	.26*
Has your job influenced your personal/family life in a positive way?	.12	.12	.47**	.01
Has your job influenced your personal/family life in a negative way?	.12	.28*	-.14	.06

[a] Work/Family interface index scores derived from interview data.

* $p < .05$; ** $p < .01$.

Other correlations presented in Table 2 provide additional insights into the consistency of responses to items in the interview and questionnaire. Two significant correlations were found between interview items assessing spillover from job-to-family and questionnaire items assessing the influence of personal and family life on the job. Faculty members who reported more negative instances of spillover from their work life to their family life were less likely to respond that their family life influenced their job performance in a positive way (r=-.36). These same faculty were more likely to report that their family life influenced their job in a negative way (r=.43). A similar result was found regarding positive spillover from family-to-job and the positive influences of the job on personal and family life. Faculty who provided more specific examples of how their family influenced their job in a positive way during the interview also responded that their job more frequently influenced their family life in a positive way during the interview (r=.47). These significant correlations as well as the responses of faculty members to the interview items suggest that to some extent faculty members are aware of the reciprocal relationships between work and family in their lives.

TABLE 3   Correlations between Hours Spent Doing Household Tasks and the Division of Household Tasks

Task Division Pattern	Hours in Household Tasks		
	Wife	Husband	Child
One person does all	.10	-.13	—
Divided equally	.02	.38**	.14
Divided traditionally	.19	-.10	-.09
All tasks shared	-.20	-.25*	-.11

* $p < .05$
** $p < .01$

The consistency between responses to the questionnaire item on the number of hours per week family members spent doing household tasks and to interview questions on household task division and use of family support systems also was examined using Pearson product moment correlations (see Table 3). The results showed that time spent on household tasks by the husband was positively correlated with a pattern of household tasks being divided equally. The more hours husbands spent on household tasks the more likely faculty members were to report an equal division of household tasks. A significant negative correlation was found between the number of hours husbands spend in household tasks and a pattern of sharing all tasks. These significant relationships suggest that the hours per week that husbands spend doing household tasks reflect in part how tasks are shared within the home. However, more research is needed in order to get a clearer picture of whether it is the number of tasks or the amount of time spent in tasks that faculty members are referring to when they respond that tasks are divided equally, traditionally, or shared.

The relationship between the total number of hours per week each family member spent doing household tasks and the index score on family support systems was not statistically significant ($r=-.04$). The fact that over half of the respondents (51.7%) do not have family support systems outside of their immediate family may have resulted in the lack of a significant correlation between responses to these items.

CONCLUSIONS AND IMPLICATIONS

Several conclusions can be made based upon the results of this study. First, faculty members identified several concerns related to the combining of work and family life. "Less time for family" and "stress carry over," time-based and strain-based conflicts, were indicated by faculty as negative aspects of combining work and family responsibilities. The general types of work/family concerns experienced by faculty are consistent with studies addressing these same issues for other occupational groups. Second, sex, age and number of children, and employment status of spouse affected some of the work/family concerns experienced by faculty. Female faculty members and dual-earner couples tended to use more coping or time management strategies in balancing work and family responsibilities. The presence of younger children also resulted in more reported work and family conflicts. As was found in other studies, these demographic variables also appear to influence the work/family concerns experienced by faculty members. Third, although some consistency was found between responses to the questionnaire and responses to the interview, less than 20% of the total variance in responses is explained. Faculty members who were interviewed stated that they had not really considered all the possible impacts of work on family and family on work when they responded to the questionnaire. The questionnaire sensitized them to the concept and they began to look at their daily lives with this in mind. By the time of the interview, they had begun to more fully realize the interrelationships between work and family life.

For researchers interested in investigating the work/family interface, these results point to an area of inquiry that deserves further attention. This preliminary effort to triangulate data on the work/family concerns of faculty from two sources, a questionnaire and an interview, suggests that responses to questions on the problems faced may not be consistent across time. The time at which a person responds and the particular problems encountered or not encountered that day appear to affect responses. In addition, comments during the interview from respondents suggest that many faculty members may not even have thought about the reciprocal relationships between work and family life. More indepth qualitative data collection strategies such as daily logs combined with interview and questionnaire data appear to be necessary. It is also recommended that similar studies be conducted with different samples to determine whether responses to questions on work/family concerns using multiple methods are more or less consistent among other occupational groups. Studies on individuals involved in less time demanding positions may result in different findings. Work/family concerns may be more consistent over time. It is only through triangulation of data from these different sources that a more differentiated, accurate, and complete picture of the work/family interface for a variety of occupational groups will emerge.

For family practitioners, the results of the present study indicate that individuals in professional positions, such as university faculty members, need assistance in learning how to combine work and family responsibilities. They appear to have limited support systems outside their immediate family and do experience both time-based and strain-based conflicts.

Possible topics that might be included in work/family education or counseling efforts are: restructuring role performance, increasing efficiency, reducing self-imposed standards, delegating household responsibilities to others within and outside the family, compartmentalizing certain work and family responsibilities, and developing emotional support systems within and outside the immediate family. Because of the time-based conflicts experienced, these sessions should be planned at the work site and during the work day whenever possible.

REFERENCES

Berelson, L.B. (1954). Content analysis. In G. Lindzey (Ed.), *Handbook of social psychology* (pp. 488-522). Reading, MA: Addition-Wesley.

Crouter, A.C. (1984). Spillover from family to work: The neglected side of the work-family interface. *Human Relations, 37,* 425-447.

Denzin, N.K. (1978). *The research act* (2nd Ed.). New York: McGraw-Hill.

Dubois, L.M. (1981). Career and family in mid-life men and women (Doctoral dissertation, Adelphi University, 1981). *Dissertation Abstracts International, 42,* 812-877.

Felstehausen, G., Glosson, L.R., & Couch, A.S. (1986). *A study to determine the relationship between the workplace and the home.* Lubbock: Texas Tech University.

Greenhaus, J.H., & Beutell, N. J. (1985). Sources of conflict between work and family roles. *Academy of Management Review, 10*(1), 76-80.

Gupta, N., & Jenkins, C.D., Jr. (1985). Dual-career couples: Stress, stressors, strains, and strategies. In T. A. Beehr & R.S. Bhagat (Ed.), *Human stress and cognition in organization: An integrated perspective.* New York: John Wiley & Sons.

Gutek, B. A., Nakamura, C. Y., & Nieva, V. F. (1981). The interdependence of work and family roles. *Journal of Occupational Behavior, 2*(1), 1-16.

Herman, J. B., & Gyllstrom, K. K. (1977). Working men and women: Inter-and intra-role conflict. *Psychology of Women Quarterly, 1*(4), 319-333.

Jick, T. D. (1983). Mixing qualitative and quantitative methods: Triangulation in action. In J.V. Maanen, *Qualitative methodology.* Beverly Hills: Sage Publications.

Keith, P. M., & Schafer, R. B. (1980). Role strain and depression in two-job families. *Family Relations, 29,* 483-488.

Maret, E., & Finlay, B. (1984). The distribution of household labor among women in dual-career families. *Journal of Marriage and Family, 46,* 357-363.

Patton, M.O. (1980). *Qualitative evaluation methods.* London: Sage Publications.

Pierre, T. W. (1984). Adressing work and family issues among extention personnel. *Journal of Home Economics,76.* 42-47.

Pleck, J.H., Staines, G.L., & Lang, L. (1980). Conflicts between work and family life. *Monthly Labor Review, 103,* 29-31.

Schultz, J. B., & Chung, Y. L. (1986). *Impact of home and family satisfaction on job satisfaction and productivity of faculty*. Paper presented at the American Vocational Association Annual Meeting, Dallas, TX.

Schultz, J. B., & Henderson, C. (1985). Family satisfaction and job performance: Implications for career development. *Journal of Career Development, 12*(1), 33-47.

Seccombe, K. (1986). The effects of occupational conditions upon the division of household labor: An application of Kohn's theory. *Journal of Marriage and Family, 48,* 839-843.

Voydanoff, P., & Kelly, R. F. (1984). Determinants of work-related family problems among employed parents. *Journal of Marriage and Family, 46,* 881-892.

Voydanoff, P., & Kelly, R. F. (1985). Work/family role strain among employed parents. *Family Relations, 34,* 367-374.

Lifestyle Patterns of University Women: Implications for Family/Career Decision Modeling

Jan Cooper Taylor
Department of Home Economics
Mississippi State University, Mississippi State, MS 39762-5765

Barbara A. Spencer
Department of Management
Mississippi State University, Mississippi State, MS 39762-5765

This study investigated the lifestyle orientations of career women and the influence of these lifestyles on family/career decisions, actions and attitudes. Ninety-three professional, university-employed women responded to 16 hypothetical career-family dilemmas by indicating the likelihood that a woman would accept a financially rewarding, but demanding promotion. Four decision cues, husband's assistance with the household, her career aspirations, husband's approval, and family income, were present or absent in each decision. At the end of the decision modeling exercise, attitudinal and descriptive questions were asked. The data were analyzed by calculating within subject regression equations, between subject analyses of variance, and Duncan's multiple-range tests. Results suggest that career aspirations are most influential in the decision dilemmas, followed by spouse approval, assistance with family maintenance tasks, and finances. No differences among lifestyles are evident for marital and job satisfaction. Women did differ in time spent on their careers and in household chores. Further research is indicated.

Working mothers acknowledge both the joys and the demands of combined employment and family responsibilities. For career women, the demands can be especially high. Advancement in a profession may require a weekly work commitment which exceeds 40 hours as well as overnight travel. Meanwhile, family needs must also be satisfied. Despite these challenges, however, most professional women are confident that both roles can be managed well (Baron, 1987).

Authors' Note: We gratefully acknowledge the assistance of J. William Rush in the development of this study.

1988 Select Press

Although much research has described the conflicts and stresses that can result from the assumption of these dual roles (Kilpatrick, 1982; Miller, 1985; Schultz & Henderson, 1985; Voydanoff, 1985), the reality is that women are choosing non-traditional lifestyles in ever-increasing numbers. The purpose of the present study is to examine the effect of these diverse lifestyle commitments on women's family/career decisions, actions, and attitudes.

Related Research

Career women who are also wives and mothers must find ways to balance work and family roles (Benin & Nienstedt, 1985; Poloma & Garland, 1971; Rapoport & Rapoport, 1976). Unless adequate support is available, these women may have to make tradeoffs in order to meet all demands in the allotted time. Responses to this time crunch may range from simply ignoring home maintenance tasks to passing up a promotion at work.

For the woman with high career aspirations, the range of alternatives available to achieve this balance may depend on both her personal lifestyle orientation and the level of support provided by her husband. The first factor, lifestyle orientation, refers to the dimensions of life that are most highly valued by an individual (Regan & Roland, 1985). Valued dimensions will be prioritized over other activities should a tradeoff be required. Thus, a woman's lifestyle orientation may affect the way she allocates her time (both at work and in the home), and it may influence certain types of career decisions.

The second factor, spousal support, has three components: emotional support (the husband's attitude toward his wife's career); domestic support (the husband's help with household and child care); and, economic support (the husband's ability to meet family financial needs). Each of these components has been shown to relate to women's career and family decisions.

First, the husband's approval or disapproval of his wife's career endeavors appears to have implications for two areas. Studies by Arnott (1972) and Houseknecht and Macke (1981) indicate that the husband's attitude seems to have an important impact on family adjustment at home. Also, Orthner and Pittman (1986) and Chusmir (1986) found higher job commitment among individuals whose spouses were perceived to be career supportive. Thus a woman whose husband approves of her career may be more apt to focus her efforts there.

The husband's involvement in household chores and child care is also a form of support. Most husbands and wives believe that husbands of employed wives, compared to husbands whose wives do not work, should do more household tasks (Ferber, 1982). Yet most activities to maintain the household and provide child care are handled by wives (Araji, 1977; Bryson, Bryson, Licht, & Licht, 1976; Condran & Bode, 1982; Holmstrom, 1972). Berardo, Shehan, and Leslie (1987) found that women, on the average, completed 79% of all housework including child care. Although women in dual career families spent only half the time that full-time housewives spent on household tasks, this was still almost triple the amount of time that dual career husbands spent in household tasks. Further, the researchers suggested that professional women with high career commitment may be jeopardizing their careers as they attempt to maintain traditional household and child care responsibilities.

Finally, the husband's financial support of the family must be considered. Working by choice and for personal satisfaction received attention in the studies of professional women in the 1970s. Both Astin (1984) and Gerson (1986) have pointed out that changing economic conditions in the eighties have forced more and more women to seek employment. Moreover, Chusmir (1986) reports that a negative correlation exists between a woman's job commitment and her husband's level of earnings. Thus, if the husband can financially support the family's lifestyle with ease, a woman may be less inclined to devote high levels of time to spend with family concerns.

The preceeding studies suggest that women may make different career decisions in the presence or absence of various forms of spousal support. The effects of this support may also be moderated by personal lifestyle orientation. It seems logical that women who prioritize dissimilar life values will also make different career decisions. For example, women who prioritize career over family may be more likely than others to accept a promotion requiring more time and travel, even with limited spousal support. In contrast, women who value family first, despite their own high career aspirations, may be more apt to refuse such a promotion if spousal support is lacking. Therefore, the following hypothesis can be proposed:

> H1: Lifestyle orientation will moderate the effects of spousal support and career aspirations on women's career decisions.

Just as lifestyle orientation affects career related decisions, it can also be expected to influence family/home decisions. For example, women who prioritize family first may spend more time on household chores and with children than would women who value their career most highly. In contrast, the latter women would likely spend more time on career related tasks than would the former. Hence, we hypothesize the following:

> H2: The amount of time devoted to household, child care, and career related tasks will vary among women with different lifestyle orientations.

Finally, between 1970 and 1980 a significant increase in the number of college females who preferred career-prioritized lifestyles was reported (Regan & Roland, 1985). The researchers speculated that increased competition between career-oriented spouses, who also desired family life, could result in lowered career aspirations and reduced spousal support for career-oriented women. Extending this logic, we may expect this anticipated conflict to manifest itself in lower marital and/or job satisfaction among women in career-oriented lifestyles. In contrast, women who value family first may be expected to report higher levels of satisfaction in these areas. This leads to the third hypothesis:

H3: Marital and job satisfaction will vary among women with different lifestyle orientations.

METHOD

How can the criteria used by women when they are making a career decision be determined? Although it would be ideal for the researcher to be present during the actual decision process, this is seldom possible. Another approach might be to ask the decision maker to recall her decision making process. However, Slovic and Lichtenstein (1971) and Stahl and Zimmerer (1984) found that most decision makers have rather poor insight into their own multiple criteria decision process. For these reasons, a decision exercise was constructed to simulate the career decision process. This methodological approach is advantageous because the information that participants incorporate into their decisions can be controlled and differences among women with diverse lifestyle orientations can be more easily highlighted.

Questionnaire

The decision modeling exercise used in this study was based on behavioral decision theory research. This method has been used in numerous business decision modeling studies (Butler & Cantrell, 1984; Lane, Murphy, & Marques, 1982; Spencer & Butler, 1987; Stahl & Harrell, 1981; Zedeck, 1977). It requires participants to make decisions about a particular issue that is defined by specific "cues."

In this exercise, women were asked to make decisions involving hypothetical family/career conflicts. Each decision scenario was defined by the presence (labeled yes) or absence (labeled no) of four cues: (1) the woman's career aspirations; (2) the husband's approval of employment; (3) his help with household and child care tasks; and, (4) his economic status. Based on these cues, each participant rated the likelihood that a woman would accept a managerial position that demanded more time and energy while providing greater prestige and pay (see appendix).

The questionnaire included 20 career decisions, with the first four introducing the format and the remaining 16 decisions used in the analysis. This format resulted in a fully-randomized, full-factorial design with 2 X 2 X 2 X 2 = 16 combinations of mutually orthogonal cues.

Other attitudinal and descriptive questions including age, marital status, number of children, level of education, and estimated hours devoted to home, career, and children were asked. Job satisfaction and marital satisfaction were measured with single-item Likert-like scales ranging from 1 (very unsatisfied) to 5 (very satisfied).

Lifestyle orientation was measured by asking each respondent to prioritize the importance of six values: career, family, recreation, religion, community participation, and participation in activities in the national and international arena. This variable, constructed by Regan and Roland (1985), was based in part on items from the Cornell Values Study (Goldsen, Rosenberg, Williams, & Suchman, 1960). Based on their prioritized values, subjects were categorized into five lifestyles: (a) family-accommodated in which family was prioritized first and career, second; (b) family-directed in which family was valued first and any value except career, second; (c) career-accommodated in which career provided the greatest satisfaction and family was chosen second; (d) career-directed in which career was prioritized first and any value except family, second; and, (e) other-directed in which any value except career or family was prioritized first.

Subjects

A random sample of 200 female employees at a southern university was selected from all women in the three highest of eight EEO employment categories at the university. These categories were (a) executive, administrative and managerial; (b) faculty; and, (c) professional nonfaculty. Each category reflected clear requirements for significant education or specialized skills which would be common for career-oriented women. It was expected that these women would be in a unique position to respond to factors which influence career decisions when family, personal and career plans are in conflict.

Data Analysis

One hundred questionnaires were returned through campus mail for a return rate of 50%. Of these, seven were omitted from analysis due to missing data. As the first step of the analysis, each individual's lifestyle commitment was determined following the procedures established by Regan and Roland (1985). Each respondent was categorized as following a family-directed (FD), family-accommodated (FA), career-directed (CD), career-accommodated (CA), or other-directed (OD) lifestyle.

Next, each respondent's career decisions were regressed onto the four orthogonal cue values (n = 16). The basis for using regression coefficients to reflect the cues' importance is that these coefficients indicate a change in the career decision (dependent variable) per unit of change in each orthogonal cue (independent variable). This procedure produced 93 within-subject regression equations.

The consistency of each participant's decisions was determined by the magnitude of the R^2 s associated with each regression model (Stahl & Harrell, 1981). Based on this logic, low R^2's indicate random decision making. Therefore, if the R^2 associated with an individual regression model did not reach significance at the .05 level, that participant was to be excluded from further analysis. The relative importances of the four decision cues for remaining respondents were determined by a between-subjects one-way analysis of variance and Duncan's multiple-range ordering of the means of the regression coefficients (Butler & Cantrell, 1984). Family and personal data for each lifestyle orientation were also analyzed using a between-subjects one-way analysis of variance and Duncan's multiple-range ordering test.

RESULTS

The women in the sample ranged from 22 to 65 years with a mean age of 40 years. Nearly half (49.5%) were in their first marriage. The never married group included 11.8% of the sample, while 15.1% were divorced/single, 19.4% were divorced/remarried, and the remaining 5% were either widowed or living together. Nearly two-thirds of the respondents were mothers. The average number of children was 1.33 with ages ranging from 3 months to 40 years.

Respondents had achieved high educational training, which was expected since professional and career involved women were targeted for the study. Doctoral degrees were held by 35.5% of the women, master's degrees by 37.6%, bachelor's degrees by 15.1%, associate's degrees by 3.2%. Some college coursework had been completed by the remaining 7.5%.

Women in the FD lifestyle (family first, any value but career second) composed 14% of the sample. Family-accommodated (family first, career second) women constituted 50.5%, CA (career first, family second) women made up 12%, and OD (neither career nor family first) women composed 16%. The smallest proportion of the sample was 7.5%, which was the CD (career first, any value but family second) group.

Decision Modeling and Lifestyle

All 93 regression models produced R^2's which were significant at the .05 level. The R^2's for this group ranged from .58 to .96 with a mean of .85.

TABLE 1 Lifestyle Influence on Career Decision Modeling

		Mean Decision Cue Weights			
Lifestyle	n	Career Aspirations	Husband's Approval	Husband's Assistance	Finances
Family-Directed	13	1.702[a]	1.356[a]	.567[b]	.048[c]
Family-Accommodated	47	1.528[a]	1.180[b]	.652[c]	-.075[d]
Career-Directed	7	1.857[a]	1.357[b]	.357[c]	-.179[d]
Career-Accommodated	11	1.955[a]	.977[b]	.705[b]	-.409[c]
Other-Directed	15	1.792[a]	1.092[b]	.708[c]	-.242[d]

Note. Means in the same row with different subscripts differ significantly at $p < .05$.

This pattern indicates that all participants consistently applied the four decision cues across scenarios. Based on the high reliability of all responses, all 93 sample participants were included in further analysis.

Table 1 shows how lifestyle patterns affected the prioritization of the four cues in deciding to accept a hypothetical managerial position. As shown in this table, the weights of the four cues differed only slightly across lifestyle groups. Thus, hypothesis 1 received only limited support.

For three groups, family-accommodated, career-directed, and other-directed, the Duncan's multiple-range test indicated significant differences between all four cues. In each of these groups, the hypothetical career decisions were most influenced by career aspirations. The second most influential factor was husband's approval. Assistance with household chores and family income ranked third and fourth in influence. Decisions made by women in the family-directed lifestyle (n = 13) were most influenced by two factors, career aspirations ($\hat{C}$ = 1.702) and husband's approval ($\hat{C}$ = 1.356), which were not significantly different from each other. Assistance with household tasks ($\hat{C}$ = .567) and family income ($\hat{C}$ = .048) were signficantly different from the first two cues and from each other.

Women in the final lifestyle pattern, career-accommodated (n = 11), also weighted career aspirations ($\hat{C}$ = 1.955) most heavily. In this model, however, there were no significant differences between the next two factors, husband's approval ($\hat{C}$ = .977) and assistance with household responsibilities (^C = .705), in making career decisions. The least influential factor for the career-accommodated in this exercise was family income (^C = -.409).

Hypothesis 2 predicted that women in dissimilar lifestyle patterns would utilize their time in different ways. This hypothesis was supported (see Table 2). Career-directed women reported an average of 55.75 hours per week in career related activities. Women in this lifestyle pattern differed significantly from women in all other lifestyles. Family-accommodated women reported the fewest hours (43.1) per week in career activities.

Hours spent in weekly household chores varied significantly between family-directed women and women in two additional lifestyle patterns, career-directed and other-directed ($p < .05$). Family-directed women averaged 23 hours in weekly household maintenance while career- and other-directed women averaged 11.38 and 7.79 hours per week, respectively.

While the amount of time devoted to child care did not vary significantly across lifestyles, interestingly, the number of children did. Women in family-accommodated and family-directed lifestyle patterns had significantly more children than those in career-directed, career-accommodated, and other-directed lifestyles. Among both family-oriented lifestyles, however, fewer than two children were the average.

There were no significant differences among women in the five lifestyles in either marital satisfaction or job satisfaction; therefore, hypothesis 3 was not supported. Women who reported the status of their marital relationship generally reflected fairly high levels of marital satisfaction. In each lifestyle pattern, over half of the women who responded to this question reported their marriages as very happy or pretty happy. Similarly, job satisfaction among women was not significantly different among the five lifestyles. The majority of women reported that they were very satisfied or satisfied with their current work situation.

DISCUSSION

The first hypothesis stated that lifestyle orientation would moderate the effects of social support and career aspirations on women's career decisions. Contrary to what one might expect, very few variations in the weights placed on these career decision criteria were evident among the five lifestyles. As might be expected, career-directed and career-accomodated women placed the most value on a woman's career aspirations in making a decision to accept a more prestigious and lucrative position. Not anticipated, however, was the same prioritization of career aspirations by family-directed and family-accommodated women. Of all the groups,

TABLE 2 Personal and Family Characteristics by Lifestyle

Variables	FD	FA	CD	CA	OD	F
Job Satisfaction	3.69	3.89	3.50	4.00	3.47	.88
Marital Satisfaction	3.67	4.39	3.50	4.25	4.22	1.39
Age	43.69	39.44	39.88	39.67	39.40	.66
Number of Children	1.85^a	1.72^a	.38^b	.67^b	.60^b	6.54***
Hours Spent on Her Career Weekly	45.00^b	43.10^b	55.75^a	46.83^b	49.29^b	5.03**
Hours Spent on Housework Weekly	23.00^a	15.69^{a,b}	11.38^b	15.25^{a,b}	7.79^b	2.76*
Hours Spent on Child Care Weekly	17.44	23.35	12.50	18.25	9.80	.76

Note: Means in the same row with different subscripts differ significantly at $p < .05$. [a] FD = family-directed; FA = family-accommodated; CD = career-directed; CA = career accommodated; OD = other-directed.
*$p < .05$. **$p = .001$. ***$p = .0001$.

these women, who prioritized family or family and career, might be expected to weigh spousal support most heavily in order to maintain the centrality or consistent operation of the family. Yet, career aspirations were designated first.

The family-directed women did appear to make one concession to family issues in making career decisions, however. This group gave first priority not only to career aspirations but also to the husband's approval when rating the likelihood that a woman would accept a career advancement.

In the family-accommodated, career-directed, and other-directed lifestyles, husband's approval was the second most influential factor in career decisions. Variations in the second prioritization occurred in two lifestyles. For FD women, who had two first-place choices, the husband's assistance with child care and household tasks ranked as the second most influential factor. For CA women two factors, husband's approval of her career and his assistance with household maintenance, were equal in influence as a second priority in career decisions. For the three remaining lifestyles, FA, CD, and OD, husband's assistance with household and child care responsibilities was the third factor in influencing career decisions.

Studies present conflicting views about the importance of financial status in the decision to work for career women (Chusmir, 1986; Rapoport & Rapoport, 1976). The findings of this study do not suggest straightforward answers for the issue. Career women in this study, irrespective of lifestyle priorities, considered family finances last in the hypothetical decision making process. However, for four lifestyles, family finances were negatively related to the decision to accept career advancement. That is, when family financial conditions based on husband's income alone were viewed as satisfactory, these women (FA, CD, CA, and OD) were slightly less supportive of the decision to accept the career advancement.

While family-oriented women might be more likely to attempt to reduce career-family conflicts by refusing a career advancement, it is surprising that women in both career-oriented lifestyles were less supportive of the career advancement when husbands' income comfortably supported the desired lifestyle. We can speculate that career-oriented women think that women who face increased family-career competition should consider family first. Another explanation may indicate that finances and subsequently, a comfortable lifestyle which develops from this financial situation, are desired by career women and indeed, even among these highly career committed women, not working sometimes appears attractive. This explanation is consistent with Chusmir (1986), who suggests that changing economic conditions necessitate both spouses working to maintain their desired lifestyle.

We may speculate on why there were so few differences in factors affecting career decisions among women with different lifestyle priorities. A number of explanations may be offered. First, women may have given responses on the basis of what they feel should be the "right" or expected response. This is, however... a typical concern with self-report research. A second explanation could relate to the four cues selected for the decision exercise. Though based on research evidence, these cues are not the only factors that may impact career decision making. Given that the study narrowed its focus to only four cues, some vital criteria may be missing in this exercise skewing results. Future research should examine this possibility in a more naturalistic setting. Third, this sample may be unusually career oriented. In all lifestyles, however, the women averaged more hours per week in their career endeavors than the benchmark 40 hours per week. A fourth explanation may stem from the age of the present sample (average age in the study was 40 years). With their children growing up, many of these women may be in a position to re-focus their energies on their careers. Thus they may be quite sensitive to the career aspiration factor.

The second hypothesis which focused on women's prioritization of time was supported by these results. The number of hours women spent on weekly career activities was significantly different across groups. Note, however, that only one lifestyle, CD, varied significantly from other lifestyles. Because there were so few women in this pattern, caution must be used in interpreting these results. In the CD pattern, most of the women are single, either never married or divorced. That these career-directed women spent significantly more hours each week involved in their careers may be related to fewer demands on their time.

FD women reported spending significantly more hours on weekly household chores than CD and OD women. The average hours FD women spent in housework was 23 per week. When this number is added to the average number of hours they spent on child care (17.44) each week, it becomes evident that FD women are basically maintaining the equivalent of two full time jobs. This may explain why the FD women in this sample judged the husband's emotional support to be just as important as the woman's career aspirations in making family/career decisions.

A large number of weekly hours for combined housework and child care responsibilities were also reported by FA (39.04) and CA (33.50) women, which is consistent with significant home and family commitments reported by other employed and professional women (Berardo, Shehan, & Leslie, 1987; Yogev, 1981). Career-directed and other-directed women spent the least amount of time on child care and housework. With fewer children on the average, these groups may not have as many household tasks to perform. They may also seek others to do household maintenance for them.

The final hypothesis, which dealt with marital and job satisfaction, was not supported. In spite of the differences in mean hours spent on career, household tasks, and child care each week, women in these lifestyles did not differ signficantly in either marital or job satisfaction. In fact many women who were married reported high levels of satisfaction with their relationship. Across lifestyles women also reported high levels of satisfaction with their current employment. Although a limitation of this finding is the use of single-item measures for these variables, it may also mean that Regan and Roland (1985) were too negative in their predictions. Rather than competing, career spouses may be enjoying fuller, though more hectic lives as suggested in earlier studies of dual-career couples (Rapoport & Rapoport, 1976). Further research is needed to examine this issue.

This study, while limited to 93 academic women in the southern region, offers insight into the criteria that women prioritize in making career/family decisions. Although the career-family dilemmas in the decision modeling exercise were hypothetical, the consistent prioritization of career aspirations suggests that professional women recognize the importance of personal career aspirations in attempting to fulfill career goals. In addition, it appears that many of these women would seek to pursue their career goals despite limited support from their husbands. Yet they appear to be satisfied with their employment and their marriages. As Baron (1987) has suggested, this may mean that today's career women are prepared to do whatever it takes to manage both roles well.

To what extent women will continue to expend the time and energy needed to realize both family and career satisfaction is a continuing question. To what degree spouses, employers, and society, in general, will assume more supportive roles for career women continues to be debated. Whatever solutions emerge, there is a need to explore the connections between work and family. Furthermore, it may be that the strong career aspirations of women in diverse lifestyles will provide the motivation to develop new strategies and policies to enhance these connections.

REFERENCES

Araji, S. K. (1977). Husbands' and wives' attitude-behavior congruence on family roles. *Journal of Marriage and the Family, 39,* 309-320.

Arnott, C. C. (1972). Husbands' attitude and wives' commitment to employment. *Journal of Marriage and the Family, 34,* 673- 684.

Astin, H. S. (1984). The meaning of work in women's lives: A sociopsychological model of career choice and work behavior. *Counseling Psychologist, 12*(4), 117-126.

Baron, A. S. (1987). Working partners: Career-committed mothers and their husbands. *Business Horizons, 30*(5), 45-50.

Benin, M. H., & Nienstedt, B. C. (1985). Happiness in single- and dual-earner families: The effects of marital happiness, job satisfaction, and life cycle. *Journal of Marriage and the Family, 47,* 975-984.

Berardo, D. H., Shehan, C.L., Leslie, G. R. (1987). A residue of tradition: Jobs, careers, and spouses' time in housework. *Journal of Marriage and the Family, 49,* 381-390.

Bryson, R. B., Bryson, J. B., Licht, M. H., & Licht, B. G. (1976). The professional pair: Husband and wife psychologists. *American Psychologist, 31*(1), 10-16.

Butler, J. K., Jr., & Cantrell, R. S. (1984). A behavioral decision theory approach to modeling dyadic trust in superiors and subordinates. Psychological Reports, 55, 19- 28.

Chusmir, L. H. (1986). Increasing women's job commitment: Some practical answers. *Personnel, 63*(1), 41-45.

Condran, J., & Bode, J. (1982). Rashomon, working wives, and family division of labor: Middletown, 1980. *Journal of Marriage and the Family, 44,* 421-426.

Ferber, M. (1982). Low-market participation of young married women: Cause and effects. *Journal of Marriage and the Family, 44,* 457-468.

Gerson, K. (1986). What do women want from men? Men's influence on women's work and family choices. *American Behavioral Scientist, 29,* 619-634.

Goldsen, R. K., Rosenberg, M., Williams, R. M., Jr., & Suchman, E. A. (1960).

What college students think. Princeton, NJ: Van Nostrand.

Holmstrom, L. L. (1972). *The two-career family.* Cambridge, MA: Schenkman.

Houseknecht, S. K., & Macke, A. S. (1981). Combining marriage and career: The marital adjustment of professional women. *Journal of Marriage and the Family, 43,* 651-661.

Kilpatrick, A. (1982). Job change in dual career families: Danger or opportunity? *Family Relations, 31,* 363-368.

Lane, D. M., Murphy, K. R., & Marques, T. E. (1982). Measuring the importance of cues in policy capturing. *Organizational Behavior and Human Performance, 30,* 231-240.

Miller, J. V. (1985). The family-career connection: A new component for career development programs. *Journal of Career Development, 12*(1), 8-22.

Orthner, D. K., & Pittman, J. F. (1986). Family contributions to work commitment. *Journal of Marriage and the Family, 48,* 573-581.

Poloma, M. M., & Garland, T. N. (1971). The married professional woman: A study in the tolerance of domestication. *Journal of Marriage and the Family, 33,* 531-540.

Rapoport, R., & Rapoport, R. N. (1976). *Dual-career families re-examined: New integrations of work and family.* New York: Harper Colophon Books.

Regan, M. C., & Roland, H. E. (1985). Rearranging family and career priorities: Professional women and men of the eighties. *Journal of Marriage and the Family, 47,* 985-992.

Schultz, J. B., & Henderson, C. (1985). Family satisfaction and job performance: Implications for career development. *Journal of Career Development, 12*(1), 33-47.

Slovic, P., & Lichtenstein, S. (1971). Comparison of Bayesian and regression approaches to the study of information processing in judgment. *Organizational Behavior and Human Performance, 6,* 649-744.

Spencer, B. A., & Butler, J. K., Jr. (1987). Measuring the relative importances of social responsibility components: A decision modeling approach. *Journal of Business Ethics, 6,* 573-577.

Stahl, M. J., & Harrell, A. M. (1981). Modeling effort decisions with behavioral decision theory: Towards an individual differences model of expectancy theory. *Organizational Behavior and Human Performance, 27,* 303-325.

Stahl, M. J., & Zimmerer, T. W. (1984). Modeling strategic acquisition policies: A simulation of executives' acquisition decisions. *Academy of Management Journal, 27*(2), 369-383.

Voydanoff, P. (1985). Work/family linkages over the life course. *Journal of Career Development, 12*(1), 23-32.

Yogev, S. (1981). Do professional women have egalitarian marital relationships? *Journal of Marriage and the Family, 43,* 865-871.

Zedeck, S. (1977). An information processing model and approach to the study of motivation. *Organizational Behavior and Human Performance, 18,* 47-77.

APPENDIX

This questionnaire asks you to make career choices for women in different situations. The decisions you make will be for research purposes only. Your participation is voluntary and all information will remain confidential. You may withdraw or refuse to answer any question at any time; however, our research efforts are dependent on your cooperation and we hope that you will be able to answer all the questions.

Please circle the response which best describes your decision for each of the following situations.

Situation #1

Sue Jones has been offered a management position that provides more money and prestige, but requires longer work days and overnight travel. Several pros and cons include...
—her husband shares the housekeeping and parenting chores....No
—her husband's pay alone can easily support their lifestyle...Yes
—she has high career aspirations...No
—her husband approves of her career endeavors...No

Decision #1

With these factors in mind, what are the chances that Sue will accept this position?

| No Chance | Slight Chance | Moderate Chance | Strong Chance | Very Strong Chance |

Night Shift Work: Job and Family Concerns

Michael G. Weiss
Marsha B. Liss

*Department of Psychology
California State University, San Bernardino
5500 University Parkway, San Bernardino, CA 92407-2397*

Research on night shift work and its effects upon workers and their families has been scarce and often limited in scope. The present study sought to examine job satisfaction, social life and family interactions of night shift workers. Subjects were 100 female and 102 male night shift workers who completed a 31 item questionnaire entitled "Night Workers' Lifestyle Survey." Night shift workers generally had favorable attitudes toward their work and perceived their social lives as adequate. The workers also described their family relationships (including time spent with their children and in what activities, childcare issues, and marital concerns). Analysis of the data revealed patterns between the job satisfaction family variables. Future research directions and adjustment issues are outlined.

The changing harsh economic realities of the 1980's have focused attention on alternative family lifestyles and occupational choices. One such occupational choice is night shift work defined as employment between 7 pm and 7 am (Finn, 1981). As of 1980, shift workers represented 16% of the work force or 10 million Americans (Presser & Cain, 1980). Research in the area of night shift work is scarce, often narrow in scope and presenting conflicting findings. For instance, Finn (1981) noted that there is limited data on the effects of shift work on employees and their families. This article presents the results of a survey of night shift workers' job satisfaction, social relationships and family concerns.

There are many reasons why people work night shifts. Among these reasons are: incentives of higher wages compared to day time work, the ability to moonlight during the day, convenience for students who must work while attending college, and a more relaxed pace at work. Night work also accommodates individuals who, because of their cyclical biological rhythms, consider themselves "night people" (Folkard, Minors and Waterhouse, 1985). Night work may also be preferred by those indi-

©1988 Select Press

viduals who use their unusual schedules as an accommodation to (or avoidance of) family responsibilities. The drawbacks to night shift work fall into three general categories: health, family and social life. In 1981, Finn wrote "night shift workers feel out of step in terms of their minds and bodies, families and social lives, and routines of the rest of their community."

Social life can also be hindered by night work, as workers cannot attend evening functions with friends who work during the day (Maurice, 1975). While night work limits extensive friendships, it increases camaraderie and loyalty within the work group (Finn, 1981). In addition, there is a greater sense of work companionship along with conflicts in other non-work related social relationships because of the time constraints (Walker, 1966). On the other hand, Folkard, Minors and Waterhouse (1985) found that while night workers' friendships are work-based, they spend more social and relaxation time with families than with friends. Folkard et al. believe this is due to the willingness of families to spend time together during "odd" or inconvenient hours.

Night work interferes with the time that adults usually spend with their families, the hours between dinner and bedtime (Walker, 1966). In a study by Maurice (1975), sixty-six percent of the workers indicated that shift work interfered with family life more than any other area. This is especially critical in families with young children. Walker (1966) reports that night shift work intensifies the time pressures on young married people due to their poor time management practices. As more young families realize the need for two incomes and enter the work force, childcare for night workers becomes an issue. Until recently this issue has not been examined by researchers. Presser and Cain (1980) indicate that night shift workers tend to have preschool age children and many of these couples share the childcare responsibilities. Furthermore, many of the parents have split shift schedules allowing the children to be with each parent for portions of the day but not providing for times when the entire family can be home (Morgan, 1981). There is some evidence that night workers rely on childcare provided by relatives more than day workers do (Presser, 1986). Relatively little is known, however, about how these young families coordinate family life. Presser (1984) noted that most studies of night shift workers focused solely or predominantly on male workers. This is a serious limitation in the previous research since the responsibility to make childcare arrangements is usually incumbent upon the mother. As a result, most of the earlier studies were unable to fully address the childcare concerns. In the present study, an equal proportion of males and females participated and provided a base to begin examination of childcare needs.

The present study examined the various issues of concern to night workers and the special adjustments their families must make. In particular, the study sought to explore issues of parenting and family obligations as well as job satisfaction and time organization. The motivations and tensions contributing to and arising from night shift work were examined.

METHOD

Subjects

The subjects were 100 females and 102 males ranging in age from 18 to 67 (median = 31; mean = 35). The sample was 75% Anglo, 8% black, and 7% Hispanic. The majority of the subjects (68%) were married, 10% were divorced and 22% had never married. Subjects varied by education level: 21% had at most a high school diploma, 61% had some college or less, while 18% had a B.A. or higher. While subjects' income ranged from between 0 - $10,000 and $45,000 - $50,000, mean income was $15,000 - $20,000 (s.d. = 1.673). Approximately 15% earned less than $10,000 and 15% earned more than $25,000.

Materials

A 31-item questionnaire entitled "Night workers' lifestyle survey" was designed for the study. The final form of the questionnaire was based on pilot testing with a sample of night shift workers and psychology students for ease of comprehension and appropriateness. The questionnaire included the following sections: a) demographic information; b) lifestyle questions (current childcare arrangements, satisfaction with current arrangements, number of hours and meals spent with child, type of family activities); c) sleeping and eating patterns; d) shift schedule issues (length of night shift employment, perceived advantages and disadvantages, ease of rescheduling of work hours); and e) attitudes about night work by the subject and family members. The questionnaire consisted of both forced choice and open-ended items.

Sampling and Procedure

Workers from a total of 14 sites participated in the study. Some of the sites sampled are found in both large and small communities while others were more limited to the service area. Those sites found in most communities included newspaper offices, hospitals, telephone companies, fire departments, all-night restaurants, and service stations. Those sites which were more unique to the study's geographic area included military bases and university campuses (in particular custodial workers).

Experimenters initially contacted site supervisors to obtain permission to contact their employees. A variety of questionnaire distribution methods were used. In some cases, materials were distributed in person (but not collected) to the employees at their work stations, group meeting rooms or lounges; in other cases the questionnaires were distributed in employee pay envelopes. Participants either returned the questionnaires anonymously by depositing them in sealed envelope at a designated place at the worksite or returned them to the experimenters by mail. A cover letter accompanied the questionnaire outlining the study's purpose, instructions, emphasis on confidentiality, and the voluntary nature of their participation. Return rate was approximately 80%. The high rate of return may be attributed to the relatively low frequency with which night shift workers are asked questions about their special needs as night workers and their interest in being more involved in work-related decision-making.

RESULTS

Plan of Analysis

Correlations were performed on scaled variables and Chi-Square analyses were performed on categorical variables. Few demographic variables yielded any significant findings; therefore, discussion of demographics is limited to those exceptional cases. Due to the large size of the correlation matrix and corresponding number of spurious significant findings, analyses were limited to those suggested by the literature and hypothesized above.

General Attitudes Toward Night Work

Overall only 10% of the subjects disliked night work. The remainder were evenly divided between liking night work somewhat and liking it a lot. By breaking subjects into two occupation categories in terms of reasons for working at night and for level of enjoyment of night work shed light on this distinction. The first of these occupation categories, comprising 39.6% of the sample, included the direct service providers (nurses, psychiatric technicians, telephone operators); the second category, comprising 57.4% of the sample, consisted of general service providers (firefighters, police, military personnel, custodians and non-health care delivery hospital personnel). As illustrated in Table 1, most direct service providers (95%) had a preference for night work whereas most general service providers (60%) work at night because of mandatory shift schedules (X^2=164.81, df=56, p<.0001). Direct service providers enjoy working at night, where as the general service providers do not enjoy night work (X^2=63.46, df=28, p<.0001).

Social Concerns

Almost half of the subjects believe that their social lives are adequate, while almost 1/3 believe their social lives are inadequate. There

TABLE 1 Direct and General Service Providers' Reasons for Night Shift Work

| | Occupational Category | |
Reason	Direct Service Provider	General Service Provider
Personal Preference	95	40
Mandatory Shift Schedule	5	60

Note: The values represent percentages of subjects in each occupational category.

was no relationship between marital status and perceived adequacy of social life. There was a relationship between enjoyment of night work and assessment of the adequacy of social life ($r=.39$, $p<.0001$). Specifically, people who do not like night work also find their social lives inadequate (85.7%). Those who enjoyed night work somewhat, felt their social lives were adequate (55.4%), or inadequate (31.8%); whereas those who enjoyed night work were more likely to report that their social lives were adequate (50%), or very adequate (30.7%). More direct service providers felt their social lives were adequate when compared with general service providers ($X^2 = 54.27$, $df=28$, $p<.0021$). Most of the subjects believed that their adult family members either like (46.8%) or have adjusted (13.6%) to the subjects' night work schedules while 39.6% dislike the schedules. The majority of the subjects (56%) would not be interested in changing their schedules.

Family Relationships

Night workers are available for their children during the children's waking hours although they are not home during bedtime preparation and sleeping hours. They reported spending an average of 5.7 hours on a workday and 12.6 hours on non-workdays with their children. The most common activities that parents engaged in with their children were home entertainment (43.6%), family outings (43.1%), and errands (38.1%). In addition, some families also went to school activities (29.7%), amusement parks (26.2%), and sports events (23.3%). It is interesting to note that the only significant sex differences in the data set were found in relation to the types of activities in which fathers and mothers engaged with their children. Compared with fathers, mothers did more errands ($X^2= 8.93$, $df=1$, $p<.003$), school activities ($X^2=4.07$, $df=1$, $p<.04$), and sports events ($X^2=4.15$, df=1, p. < 04). More workers felt it was difficult (31.6%; $X^2=32.99$, df=4, p<.001) to rearrange their work schedules to attend special functions or appointments with their children compared to those who could rearrange their schedules (27.3%); 41.1% felt that the ability to rearrange their schedules varied day to day. Some parents (59.5%) did not adjust their work schedules when children were on vacation, while others did (30.4%); the remaining parents where only able to adjust their schedules on an occasional basis. The parents ate approximately 8.7 meals a week with their children. Parents believed that their children were evenly divided between wanting the parents to stay home at night (38.5%) and liking their parents' night work schedules (44%); the remainder (17.5%) felt their children did not have strong opinions on this subject.

Childcare

The most common provider of childcare for parents in all occupations was the spouse (59.3%), ($X^2=104.95$, df=72, p<.006). The next most common childcare provider was a hired babysitter (14.3%). A wide variety of alternative childcare plans were used by the remaining families, including day care centers. A majority of these individuals were pleased with their childcare provider (86.2%, $X^2=22.8$, df=1, p<.001). When children are sick one of the parents stays home with the child (79%) and 21% rely on another relative to take care of the child.

DISCUSSION

Several overall conclusions are evident from the results. Job and social life satisfaction are related to motivations for working at night. Occupation appears to be a determinant of satisfaction with both night shift work and social lives. Although night shift workers find it difficult, they attempt to adjust their schedules to meet family obligations. Night shift workers generally rely on family members for the provision of childcare.

On a simplistic level, being satisfied with night shift work is directly related to the individual's motivation for this type of work. Those individuals not wanting to work at night perceive their social lives more negatively. The cause and effect relationship between these variables is unclear; the question remains as to whether the dislike for night work precedes or is the result of dissatisfaction with social lives.

The number of people who would not change their work shift schedules is evidence of the number and variety of functions which night shift work serves. Some of these functions are the ease of relying on other family members for childcare, financial incentives and job opportunities, or social life accommodations. It is hypothesized that one function night shift work may serve in some families is a form of escape from or avoidance of obligations and tensions while in other families it is an unavoidable inconvenience. The factors which promote either path to night work are important for future examination. Furthermore, one variable cited by Staines and Pleck (1986) and which should be studied in future research is schedule flexibility. Staines and Pleck report that those workers with more flexibility in their schedules suffer fewer negative disturbances in their family lives. Further work is needed to examine how people who work at night accommodate their social relationships and community obligations.

While it might initially appear that night work would interfere with family life, it now appears that there is a greater opportunity for daytime family interactions where a larger amount of time is spent with family members. The night worker is employed and away from the family during the sleeping hours rather the higher intensive waking hours. In contrast to daytime workers, parents may then be able to participate with their children in school related excursions or extra-curricular activities without taking time off from work. The data regarding amount of time spent with children supports Staines and Pleck's work (1984). They found that other nonstandard variable shift work parents spent more time in the home than other parents while at the same time experiencing great conflicts between work and family. The family member who may be most inconvenienced is the spouse or significant other. As noted earlier, absence from the home may be a form of adaptation to or avoidance of family conflict. Future research should focus on the influences of rotating shifts, variable shifts, swing and graveyard shifts on family and social adjustments and attitudes towards night work.

The results support previous findings that parents use one another and other relatives as childcare providers (Presser, 1984). This is especially true when one or more children are sick and there are limited resources available to care for the child (Liss & Weiss, 1985). Despite the increased number and success of hospital-based evening childcare programs (Adolf & Rose, 1985), other industries and employers have not yet addressed the childcare needs of the night worker. The present data indicate that there are employees for whom night time childcare is a needed commodity. Night care programs might be designed based on those which have achieved success in Sweden since 1978 (Khan, 1984). In addition, flexible schedules are associated with increased job and family satisfaction; this finding needs to be considered in establishing work environment.

Another overall conclusion is that night workers do not comprise a singular class of individuals but rather are a diverse group with many needs, interests and concerns. Further research should break down the population of night shift workers into its subgroups. At that point analysis could more effectively outline the impact of night work on job satisfaction, social life and family interactions. Given the current economic situation, shift work and two income families will continue to be a reality for many Americans.

REFERENCES

Adolf, B., and Rose, K. (1985). *The employer's guide to childcare: Developing programs for working parents*. New York: NY, Praeger.

Finn, P. (1981). The effects of shift work on the lives of employees. *Monthly Labor Review, 104*, 31-34.

Folkard, S., Minors, D. S., and Waterhouse, J. M. (1985). Chronobiology shift work: Current issues and trends. *Chronobiogia, 12*, 31-54.

Khan, G.B. (1984). Childcare programs in Sweden for children with shift-working parents. *Early Child Development and Care, 17*(4), 307-317.

Liss, M. B., and Weiss, M. G. (1985, March). *Childcare: A needs assessment*. Paper presented at the meeting of the International Symposium on Parenting Issues, Chicago, IL.

Maurice, M. (1975). *Shift work*. Geneva, International Labor Office.

Morgan, J. N. (1981). Childcare when parents are employed. In M. S. Hill, D. H. Hill and J. N. Morgan (eds.), *Five thousand American families—Patterns of economic progress*, Vol. IX, 441-456. The University of Michigan, Institute for Social Research.

Presser, H. (1984). Job characteristics of spouses and their work shifts. *Demography, 21*, 575-589.

Presser, H. (1986). Shift work among American women and childcare. *Journal of Marriage and the Family, 48*, 551-563.

Presser, H., and Cain, V. (1980). Shift work among dual-earner couples with children. *Science, 219*, 876-878.

Staines, G. L., and Pleck, J. H. (1984). Nonstandard work schedules and family life. *Journal of Applied Psychology, 69*, 515-523.

Walker, J. (1966). Frequent alternation of shifts on continuous work. *Occupational Psychology, 40*, 215-225.

Some Antecedents and Consequences of Work-Family Conflict

Ronald J. Burke
Faculty of Administrative Studies, York University
4700 Keele Street, North York, Ontario M3J 1P3

This paper reports a study of work-family conflict and its relationship with antecedent and outcome variables. Eight hundred and twenty-eight men and women in police work provided data using questionnaires. Ratings of work-family conflict were weakly correlated with demographic antecedents but strongly correlated with work setting characteristics, social support, levels of work and non-work stress and several outcome measures. A research model received considerable empirical support. This presumed that work-family conflict leads to negative outcomes, and was caused by levels of subjective work and non-work stress resulting from work setting and non-work conditions.

It has only been in the past decade that researchers have become interested in work and family (Burke & Greenglass, 1987). Several forces have come together to highlight the work-family interface (Nieva, 1985; Gutek, Repetti & Silver, 1988). These include: the influx of women into the workforce, new life-styles which integrate work, family, and leisure in different ways, increases in single-parent families and increases in dual-career couples. There is also greater realization that events in one sphere are likely to influence, and be influenced by, events in another sphere, the open systems concept (Kanter, 1977).

Kanter (1977) identified five aspects of the structure and organization of work life that seemed most important in shaping and influencing the family. These were: the relative absorptiveness of an occupation, time and timing—the effects of work hours and work schedules, rewards and resources, the job as a socializer of world view, and the emotional

---

Author's Note: This research was supported in part by the Faculty of Administrative Studies, York University, and the Social Science and Humanities Research Council. The study would not have been possible without the cooperation of administrators at the Ontario Police College. I would like to thank the individuals who participated by providing data, and acknowledge the assistance of my colleagues, Gene Deszca and Jon Shearer in the development of the questionnaire, Jacob Wolpin in the analysis of the data, and Dorothy Zavitz for preparing the manuscript.

©1988 Select Press

climate of work. She also identified three ways in which family patterns impacted on work systems. These were: membership in ethnic groups and families representing certain cultural traditions, the situation of the "corporate wife" and her impact on her husband's career opportunities, and ways in which the family situation can define work orientation, motivation, abilities, emotional energy and demands people bring to the work place.

One aspect of the work-family interface that has received research attention is the conflict an individual may experience between these two roles. Greenhaus and Beutell (1985) recently reviewed this literature. They define work-family conflict as "a form of interrole conflict in which the role pressures from the work and family domains are mutually incompatible in some respect. That is, participation in the work (family) role is made more difficult by participation in the family (work) role" (p. 77). They identified three sources of work-family conflict: time, strain, and behavior. That is, any role characteristic that affects a person's time involvement, strain, or behavior within a role can produce conflict between that role and another role. *Time-based conflict* included concepts such as excessive work time, role overload, schedule conflict, inflexibility of schedules, marital status, presence of children, and family size. *Strain-based conflict* involved work and family stress, negative emotional spillover, and supportiveness of partner. *Behavior-based conflict* resulted from incompatibilities between the role behaviors required in one sphere and behaviors in another sphere. The most common example would involve the male managerial stereotype emphasizing competitiveness, aggressiveness and the control of emotions being in conflict with the supportive, expressive behaviors expected between family members. Their model provides a useful framework for identifying potential antecedents of work-family conflict.

Empirical studies of work-family conflict have also been undertaken. Kopelman, Greenhaus and Connelly (1983) provide a theoretical model for describing the relationship between role conflicts at work, in the family and between the two, as well as satisfaction at home, at work and with life in general. They define work conflict as the extent to which an individual experiences incompatible role pressures within the work domain, and family conflict as the extent to which incompatible role pressures are experienced within the family. For both types of conflict, the model postulates that incompatibility may arise from multiple role senders, one role sender, or a lack of fit between the focal person and role requirements. The model also includes interrole conflict which is described as the extent to which a person experiences pressures within one role that are incompatible with pressures from another role. In two studies which tested the theoretical model, Kopelman and his colleagues (1983) report strong links between domain conflict and domain satisfaction, i.e., work conflict and job satisfaction, and between domain satisfaction and life satisfaction. The investigators, however, failed to find a significant relationship between interrole conflict and domain satisfaction.

Holahan and Gilbert (1979), in one of the few studies of its kind, investigated conflict between specific pairs of work and family roles and its relationship to attitudinal, self-concept and satisfaction variables. Focusing directly on relevant life roles (Professional, Spouse, Parent, and Self as Self-Actualized Person) rather than on time demands, Holahan and Gilbert constructed six scales to measure conflict between specific pairs of roles (e.g., Professional vs. Parent). In a study of 28 dual career couples, they investigated the relationship between being a parent and various role conflicts. They report that Professional vs. Self roles were associated with the greatest conflict for both non-parent and parent groups with Professional vs. Parent, and Self vs. Parent roles as equally conflict-related for the parent group as was Professional vs. Self conflict. Thus, the addition of the parent role resulted in additional conflict between each role and those in most conflict, namely Professional vs. Self. They also found that career aspirations were positively correlated with role conflict for females in dual career couples but negatively correlated with role conflict in males.

In addition to accumulating research findings which serve to increase our understanding of work-family conflict, it is also important to begin developing and testing more comprehensive models which include both antecedents and consequences of work-family conflict. Unfortunately, little attention has so far been devoted to this need. Both Van Sell (1984) and Greenhaus and Parasurawan (1987) have made a start in this direction. They have proposed integrative frameworks for understanding the relationship among individual, family, and work setting characteristics, work and family demands and rewards, work-family conflict, and a variety of work and family outcomes. While useful, the complexity and comprehensiveness of these specific models make them impossible to test empirically.

The present study will focus on work-family conflict. It will first examine potential antecedents and consequences of work-family conflict. It will then consider the usefulness of a model of work-family conflict that examines hypothesized relationships among several variables simultaneously. This research model, shown in Figure 1, builds on Van Sell (1984) and Beutell and Parasurawan (1987) but was simplified so that it could be tested with data that were available. Thus it both adds

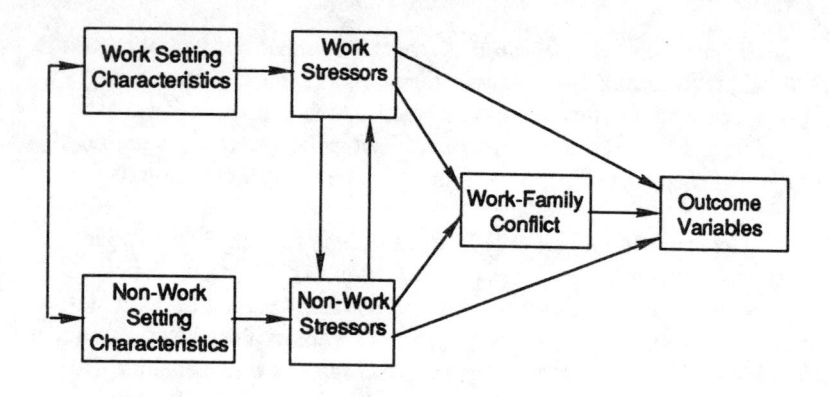

FIGURE 1   Research Model

to the accumulating research findings on work-family conflict and moves in the direction of examining a more comprehensive model for understanding sources and consequences of work-family conflict.

The model proposes that work setting characteristics (e.g., lack of autonomy, work load, supervision) lead to sources of experienced work stress (bureaucratic interference, lack of fulfillment). At the same time, life setting characteristics (e.g., lack of social support) give rise to particular non-work stressors (e.g., difficulties in relationship with spouse). These sources of stress influence each other as well as have an effect on work-family conflict. Finally the model proposes direct effects of work stressors, non-work stressors and work-family conflict on a wide variety of individual-level outcome measures. Because this is the first time the model has been studied empirically, this research is exploratory. The model specifies a causal sequence and some connections between variables, but there is not yet an empirical or theoretical basis for explicitly ruling out other connections. Our objective is to discover which of its direct effects are supported, assuming that the causal sequence is as shown in Figure 1.

METHOD

Respondents

Respondents were 828 men and women employed in police work (738 males, 62 females, and 28 who did not indicate their sex). Table 1 presents some of the characteristics of the sample. The sample was mostly male (92%), working shifts (84%), married (68%), had a high

TABLE 1 Demographic Characteristics of Police Sample (N = 828)

	N	%			N	%
1. Age:			**6. Married:**			
21-27	346	43.4	Yes	534	68.2
28-35	177	22.2	No	253	31.8
36-43	156	19.6			
44-50	86	10.8	**7. Work Shifts:**		
Over 50	32	4.0	Yes	585	83.8
2. Sex:			No	113	16.2
Males	738	92.2			
Females	62	7.7	**8. Rank:**		
3. Years in Policing:			4th to 2nd class Constable	345	45.9
Less than one	173	21.7	1st class Constable	240	31.1
1-5	203	25.4	Corporal or Sergeant	123	15.9
6-15	235	29.4	Staff Sergeant	21	2.7
16-25	152	19.0	Inspector	14	1.8
Over 25	36	4.5	Superintendent	7	.9
4. Size of Force:			Deputy Chief	5	.6
Less than 15	78	9.8	Chief	8	1.0
16-50	172	21.7			
51-150	188	23.7	**9. Years in Present Job:**		
151-450	147	18.5	Less than one	251	31.5
Over 450	280	26.2	1-5	305	38.3
5. Education:			6-15	190	23.9
Less than Gr.12	113	14.2	16-25	5	5.7
Gr.12 or 13	398	50.1	Over 25	5	.6
Comm. Coll.	185	28.3			
BA	90	11.3			
MA	6	.8			
PhD	3	.4			

school education (50%), and were in the early stage of their police careers. Thus, about half the sample had been in police work five years or less and were in the lowest ranked constable jobs (4th to 2nd class).

Procedure

Respondents were attending various educational offerings related to police work. An administrator at the Ontario Police College approached various classes and asked respondents to cooperate in the research by returning a completed questionnaire to him. Participation was voluntary and anonymous. Almost all individuals asked to participate did so (more than 90%).

Measures

All variables in the research model (see Figure 1) were assessed by multi-item measures which are described below.

Work-Family Conflict

The potential impact of one's job and job demands on nine areas of personal, home, and family life were examined (see Burke, Weir & DuWors, 1979, for sample items): *Relationship with Spouse*, 5 Items; *Preoccupied and Tired*, 5 Items; *Reduced Social Life*, 6 Items; *Relationship with Children*, 6 Items; *Family and Home Life*, 6 Items; *Weekends and Vacations*, 4 Items; *Self-Development*, 4 Items; *Health and Safety*, 4 Items; and *Exemplary Behavior*, 3 Items. These were combined into a single measure since the nine areas were positively and significantly intercorrelated (a = .92).

Antecedents of Work-Family Conflict

Work-Setting Characteristics. Cherniss (1980) identified eight work-setting characteristics to be precursors of the negative attitude changes constituting burnout. These characteristics were: *Orientation*, 3 Items; *Workload*, 6 Items; *Stimulation*, 4 Items; *Scope of Client Contacts*, 3 Items; *Institutional Goals*, 3 Items; *Autonomy*, 3 Items; *Leadership and Supervision*, 9 Items; and *Social Isolation*, 3 Items. A total score was obtained by combining the scores on the eight measures (a = .86).

Social Support. This was assessed by five items. A total score was obtained by combining these items (a = .48).

Work Stressors. Cherniss (1980) identified five sources of stress as antecedents of burnout. These included: *Doubts about Competence*, 3 Items; *Problems with Clients*, 5 Items; *Bureaucratic Interference*, 5 Items; *Lack of Stimulation and Fulfillment*, 3 Items; and *Lack of Collegiality*, 4 Items. The above were combined into a total score (a = .88).

Non-Work Stressors. Non-work stressors were assessed using a 10 item scale similar to the Schedule of Recent Experiences developed by

Holmes and Rahe (1967). Individuals indicated whether they had experienced a particular event during the past year, and if it did occur, how upsetting they felt the experience of that event was. Events included: serious difficulties in my relationship with spouse and death of a close friend or relative. The internal consistency reliability of this scale was modest ($a = .45$) as expected.

Consequences of Work-Family Conflict

Seven consequences or outcomes of work-family conflict were considered:

Work Alienation. Cherniss identified six areas of negative attitude change in his work and emotion concept. These were: *Reduced Work Goals,* 2 Items; *Reduced Personal Responsibility for Outcomes,* 2 Items; *Less Idealism/Greater Realism,* 3 Items; *Emotional Detachment,* 2 Items; Work *Alienation,* 3 Items; and *Greater Self-Interest,* 4 Items. These were combined into a total score ($a = .84$).

Psychological Burnout. The Maslach Burnout Inventory (MBI), developed by Maslach and Jackson (1981), was used as a measure of psychological burnout. This instrument measures three constructs: *Emotional Exhaustion,* 9 Items; *Depersonalization,* 5 Items, and *Lack of Personal Accomplishment,* 8 Items. These were combined to form a composite measure ($a = .89$).

Job Satisfaction. This was measured using six items. These items, developed by Quinn and Shepard (1974), were combined into a total score ($a = .77$).

Intention to Turnover. This was measured using two items ($a = .68$).

Psychosomatic Symptoms. Respondents indicated how often they experienced 18 physical conditions. These were combined into a total score ($a = .86$).

Negative Affective States. Five negative feeling states (Cobb, Brooks, Kasl & Connelly, 1966) were examined: *Impulse to Aggression,* 4 Items; *Anger-Irritation,* 7 Items; *Insomnia,* 2 Items; *Depression,* 7 Items; and *Overt Aggression,* 4 Items. These were combined into a single measure ($a = .83$).

Physical Health and Life Style. Police officers provided self-reports of their physical health and life style behaviors. Eight items were used: Regular Exercise, Alcohol Consumed, Coffee Drunk, Cigarettes Smoked, High Blood Pressure, Heart Attack, Days Ill Last Six Months, and Currently Taking Medication. These eight items were combined into a single measure. The internal consistency reliability of this index measure was modest ($a = .44$) as expected.

Individual Characteristics

Type A Behavior. Type A Behavior was assessed using a 14-item scale developed and validated by Bortner (1969) and Bortner and Rosenman (1967). Individuals rated themselves on 14 seven-point scales anchored by bi-polar objectives (e.g., Never late—Casual about appointments. Fast: eating, walking, etc. — Slow about things).

Demographic Variables. These included a standard array of demographic characteristics such as age, sex, marital status, level of education, current police rank, and years in police work.

Analysis Plan

Two levels of analysis, each employing different statistical procedures, were used. First, bi-variate statistical techniques, e.g., zero-order correlation, were employed to study the general pattern of relationships between the variables. Second, multi-variate statistical techniques, e.g., regression analysis, were used to examine the relationship of several predictors simultaneously. Non-recursive structural equation models (two-stage least squares) involving an independent system of linear equations were also employed as appropriate.

A set of simultaneous structural equations was created to examine the relationship between work and non-work sources of stress. Structural-equation models include three broad classes of variables: endogenous variables, exogenous variables, and disturbances. Endogenous variables, as their name implies, are determined within the model, and may be influenced by other endogenous variables, by exogenous variables, and by disturbances. Exogenous variables, in contrast, are treated as "givens": they may appear as causes in the model, but not as effects. Disturbance variables, sometimes termed errors or errors in equations, represent the aggregated omitted causes of the endogenous variables and play a role similar to that of the error variable in the general linear model. Disturbance variables are taken to be independent of the exogenous variables in the model.

With cross-sectional data, however, these equations can only be solved if extremely stringent assumptions are made about the effects of exogenous variables on both dependent variables. In particular, if the effect of work stress on non-work stress is to be estimated, we must specify in advance the numerical magnitude of the effect that at least one exogenous variable has on work stress. This is usually done by assuming that a given exogenous variable has no effect on non-work stress, but only upon work stress. That is, this variable is an identifier of work stress. In a similar way, an identifier of non-work stress is located.

TABLE 2 Antecedents of Work-Family Conflict

Antecedents	Work-Family Conflict
Demographic Characteristics	
Marital Status	.18*
Age	-.02
Sex	.01
Rank	-.05
Education	.05
Type A	.16*
Work Setting Characteristics	
Cherniss Work Setting	.61*
Shiftwork	-.23*
Lack of Social Support	.43*
Work Stress	.60*
Non-Work Stress	.32*

* $p = .001$

RESULTS

Antecedents of Work-Family Conflict

Table 2 presents correlations between various antecedents of work-family conflict (e.g., demographic, work setting, experienced stress, social support) and the measure of work-family conflict. The following comments are offered in summary. First, demographic characteristics were generally unrelated to work-family conflict. Married police officers and police officers exhibiting stronger Type A behavior reported more work-family conflict. Second, police officers reporting less social support also reported greater work-family conflict. Third, work setting characteristics were significantly related to work-family conflict. Police officers working shifts, and reporting a more negative work setting (Cherniss composite measure) also reported greater work-family conflict. Fourth, police officers reporting a greater number of stressful non-work events or demands in the preceding year also reported greater work-family conflict.

Table 3 indicates the correlations between the measure of work-family conflict and various organizational and individual consequences. The following comments are offered in summary. First, police officers reporting greater work-family conflict were less satisfied with their jobs and had greater intentions to leave police work. Second, police officers reporting greater work-family conflict also reported greater psychologi-

TABLE 3   Consequences of Work-Family Conflict

Consequences	Work-Family Conflict
Work Outcomes	
Job Satisfaction	-.40*
Intention to Turnover	.30*
Work Alienation and Burnout	
Maslach Burnout Inventory	.60*
Cherniss Negative Attitude Change	.54
Emotional and Psychological Well-Being	
Psychosomatic Symptoms	.46*
Negative Feeling States	.47*
Physical Health and Life Style	.25*

* $p = .001$

cal burnout and work alienation. Third, police officers reporting greater work-family conflict reported more psychosomatic symptoms and more negative feeling states. Finally, police officers reporting greater work-family conflict were also more likely to engage in negative life style behaviors and report poorer physical health.

Testing a Comprehensive Model

Zero-Order Correlations. Table 4 presents the means, SDs and correlations between the variables in the research model (Figure 1). The following comments are offered in summary. First, the various antecedents of work-family conflict were significantly intercorrelated. Second, the six outcomes were also significantly intercorrelated. Although interesting in their own right, zero-order correlations do not inform about the process whereby feelings of work-family conflict are addressed and how they lead to negative outcomes. Consequently, we performed a series of path analyses which included the paths specified in Figure 1.

Path Analyses. Seven different path analyses were undertaken using the research model shown in Figure 1. Each analysis examined a different outcome variable (e.g., job satisfaction, psychosomatic symptoms, negative affective states, psychological burnout (MBI), work alienation, intention to turnover and physical health) while holding the other variables in the research model constant.

Figure 2 shows the statistically significant relationships (standardized beta coefficients) present when predicting psychosomatic symptoms. Work-family conflict, work stressors and non-work stressors were

TABLE 4   Means, Standard Deviations, and Intercorrelations Among Variables in the Research Model

Variable	Mean	SD	2	3	4	5	6	7	8	9	10	11	12
1. Work-Family Conflict	163.5	44.7	.61	.43	.60	.32	-.40	.46	.47	.54	.60	.30	.25
2. Work Setting Characteristics	127.0	23.11		.40	.76	.23	-.57	.38	.35	.66	.64	.38	.25
3. Lack of Social Support	13.9	4.90			.43	.16	-.29	.29	.38	.38	.45	.20	.19
4. Work Stressors	76.7	14.73				.22	-.53	.41	.42	.73	.66	.40	.28
5. Non-Work Stressors	1.7	1.53					-.20	.29	.30	.21	.23	.15	.23
6. Job Satisfaction	23.8	5.21						-.41	-.40	-.58	-.55	-.70	.30
7. Psychosomatic Symptoms	37.2	9.11							.59	.45	.54	.32	.51
8. Negative Affective States	84.5	18.60								.44	.50	.32	.33
9. Psychological Burnout (NAC)	65.2	12.87									.63	.43	.32
10. Psychological Burnout (MBI)	66.1	18.95										.40	.33
11. Intention to Turnover	2.3	.67											.29
12. Physical Health	12.6	3.05											

All correlations were statistically significant (.05).

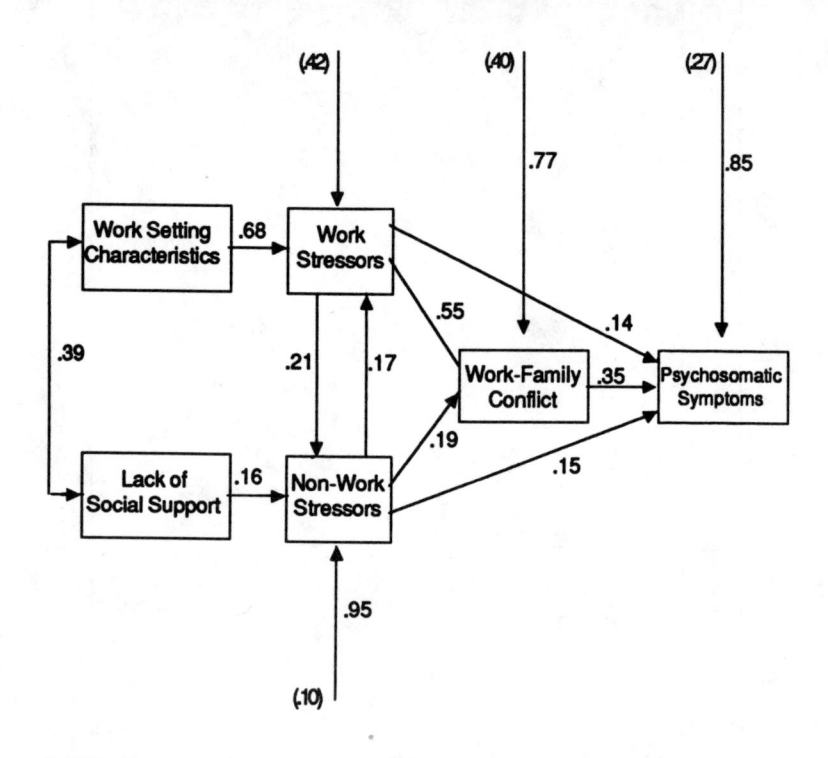

FIGURE 2   Path Analysis of Effects of Work-Family Conflict and Antecedent Variables on Psychosomatic Symptoms

significantly and directly related to psychosomatic symptoms; the first more strongly than the latter two. Both work and non-work stressors were significantly and directly related to work-family conflict, the former more than the latter. Work and non-work stressors were reciprocally related. The measure of work setting characteristics was significantly related to levels of experienced stressors at work. Finally, lack of social support was significantly related to levels of experienced non-work stressors.

Similar patterns were present in the other six path diagrams. Because of space limitation, only a summary of these relationships will be given here. All significant relationships shown in Figure 2 were present when Negative Affective States served as the outcome variable. All but one of the significant relationships shown in Figure 2 were present when Job Satisfaction, Psychological Burnout (MBI) and Cherniss-based Work Alienation served as outcome variables. There was no relationship between the measure of non-work stressors and these outcome variables. All but two of the significant relationships shown in Figure 2 were present when intention to turnover was the outcome variable. There was no relationship between work-family conflict and intention to turnover, nor between levels of experienced non-work stressors and intention to turnover. Finally, two of the significant relationships present in Figure 2 were absent when self-reported physical health and lifestyle behaviors was the outcome variable. There was no direct relationship between work stressors and physical health and lifestyle, and no relationship between non-work stressors and work-family conflict.

Explanator Power of the Model

The explanatory power of the model varied for particular outcome variables. The greatest amount of explained variance was observed with the Cherniss-based measure of work alienation (56%), followed in turn by psychological burnout (50%), job satisfaction (31%), psychosomatic symptoms and negative feeling states (27%), intention to turnover (16%), and physical health and lifestyle behaviors (12%).

DISCUSSION

The present research examined antecedents and consequences of work-family conflict in a sample of men and women in police work. Although the measure of work-family conflict was developed before Greenhaus and Beutell's review of the literature on work and family conflict (1985), it included time, strain and behavior-based sources of work-family conflict. It should be noted, however, that the measure focused solely on the conflict or interference of work on the family, and not vice versa. That is, the measure emphasized ways in which work interfered with personal life and family functioning (one direction).

Let us first consider potential antecedents of work-family conflict (Table 2). Demographic characteristics were generally weakly related to work-family conflict. The two significant findings (married individuals reported greater work-family conflict; individuals with greater Type A characteristics reported more work-family conflict) were consistent with previously reported findings suggesting time-based conflicts. In addition police officers on shift-work reported greater work-family conflict, suggesting a time schedule incompatibility conflict. Finally, work-related variables (work setting characteristics, experienced work stressors) were more strongly related to work-family conflict than were non-work variables (lack of social support, non-work stressors), though all relationships reached statistical significance. This pattern may be the result of the exclusive emphasis given to the effect of work on family in the measure of work-family conflict used in the study.

As expected, work-family conflict was significantly related to a variety of individual outcomes of both a work and well-being nature (Table 3). These relationships were stronger for the satisfaction and emotional well-being measures than for the self-reported physical health measures. These findings are consistent with previously reported results (Greenhaus & Beutell, 1985) of the adverse consequences of work-family conflict. Work-family conflict appears to affect both work and individual well-being outcomes equally strongly. Since physical health is affected by a wide variety of individual characteristics, the relatively weak effects of work-family conflict in this regard is not surprising.

Let us now consider the usefulness of the research framework used in the study (Figures 1 and 2). There was a fairly consistent pattern of relationships across the seven analyses that were undertaken. Work-family conflict had significant and independent effects on six of the seven outcomes (not on intention to turnover). Experienced work stressors had significant and independent effects on six outcome variables (not on physical health and lifestyle behaviors). Experienced non-work stressors had significant independent effects on three outcomes (not on job satisfaction, intention to turnover, psychological burnout, or work alienation). Work variables had stronger effects than non-work variables. Non work variables had no effect on work-related outcomes (job satisfaction, intention to turnover). Intention to turnover and physical health, perhaps influenced by a number of variables not included in the research model (e.g., labor market conditions, age, heredity), showed the largest unexplained variance.

The research model employed in this study viewed work-family conflict as an intervening variable with antecedent causes and both personal and work consequences. The model emphasized the negative implications of work-family conflict because of our interest primarily in its dysfunctional and socially costly effects on well-being and health. The model presumes that work-family conflict leads to lower job satisfaction and greater psychosomatic symptomatology, and that work-family conflict is caused by events in both work and family.

The specific findings presented here indicate that work-family conflict does indeed have negative consequences (Table 3, Figure 2). In addition, work-family conflict generally had stronger effects than work or non-work stressors. In summary, the results support many of the important links implied by the causal order shown in Figure 1.

Interestingly work and non-work stressors had significant effects on each other, i.e., results supported a dual-causality model. Then findings are consistent with notions of spill-over effects of experiences in work or family life, and vice versa.

The results of the path analyses must be treated with caution. One can never be sure that all relevant variables have been included. There may also be other research models consistent with the data. That is, there may be other theoretically plausible, causal configurations of the same variables that could explain their correlation equally well. Other concerns include correlated method variance among the self-report variables (Table 4) and the use of measures with only moderate levels of reliability. Still, it seems reasonable to suggest that the model received enough support to warrant confirmation or disconfirmation in further research.

Future research in the work-family area must include comprehensive models or frameworks so that a wide variety of relationships (and concepts) can be considered simultaneously. The present study represents a start in this direction. It is also critical that the measure of work-family conflict include bi-directional influences of one on the other, both male and female participants since gender differences appear to be strong (Burke & Greenglass, 1987), and a variety of occupations (Nieva, 1985). In addition, future research should examine potential positive influences of work and family roles as well as conflict. Finally, without longitudinal research, we are unable to determine the potential reciprocal effects among variables in more comprehensive models (Gutek, Repetti & Silver, 1988).

REFERENCES

Bortner, R.W. & Rosenman, R.H. (1967). The measurement of pattern A behavior. *Journal of Chronic Diseases, 20*, 525-533.

Bortner, R.W. (1969). A short rating scale as a potential measure of pattern A behavior. *Journal of Chronic Diseases, 22*, 87-91.

Burke, R.J. & Greenglass, E.R.(1987). Work and family. In C.L. Cooper & I.T. Robertson (Eds.), *International review of industrial and organizational Psychology* (pp. 273-320). New York: John Wiley.

Burke, R.J., Weir, T., & DuWors, R.E. (1979). Type A behavior of administrators' and wives' reports of marital satisfaction and well-being. *Journal of Applied Psychology, 64*, 57-65.

Cherniss, C. (1980). *Professional burnout in human service organizations*. New York: Praeger.

Cobb, S., Brooks, G.W., Kasl, S.V., & Connelly, W.E. (1966). The health of people changing jobs: A description of a longitudinal study. *American Journal of Public Health, 59*, 1476-1481.

Greenhaus, J.H., & Beutell, N.J. (1985). Sources of conflict between work and family roles. *Academy of Management Review, 10*, 76-88.

Greenhaus, J.H., & Parasurawan, S. (1987). A work-nonwork interactive perspective of stress and its consequences. In J.M. Ivancevich and D.C. Ganster (Eds.), *Job stress: From theory to suggestion* (pp. 37-60). New York: Haworth Press.

Gutek, B.A., Repetti, R.L., & Silver, D.L. (1988). Non-work roles and stress and work. In C.L. Cooper & R. Payne (Eds.), *Causes, coping and consequences of stress and work* (pp.141-174). New York: John Wiley.

Holmes, T.H., & Rahe, R.H. (1969). The Social Readjustment Rating Scale. *Journal of Psychosomatic Research, 11*, 213-218.

Holohan, C.K., & Gilbert, L.A. (1979). Conflict between major life roles: Women and men in dual-career couples. *Human Relations, 32*, 451-457.

Kanter, R.M. (1977). *Work and family in the United States: A critical review and agenda for research and policy*. New York: Russell Sage Foundation.

Koppelman, R.E., Greenhaus, J.D., & Connelly, T.F. (1983). A model of work, family, and interrole conflict: A construct validation study. *Organizational Behavior and Human Performance, 32*, 198-215.

Maslach, C., & Jackson, S.E. (1981). The measurement of experienced burnout. *Journal of Occupational Behavior, 2*, 99-113.

Nieva, V.F. (1985). Work and family linkages. In L. Larwood, A.H. Stromberg & B.A. Gutek (Eds.), *Women and work: An annual review* (Vol. 1) (pp. 162-190). Beverley Hills, CA: Sage Publications.

Quinn, R.P., & Shepard, L.J. (1974). *The 1972 Quality of Employment Survey*. Ann Arbor, MI: Survey Research Center, Institute for Social Research.

Van Sell, M. (1984). *A model for research on work-non-work conflict*. Paper presented at the Annual Meeting of The Academy of Management, Boston, MA (August).

Managerial Conflict Resolution Styles:
Work and Home Differences

Joan Mills
Florida International University, College of Business Administration
North Miami Campus, North Miami, FL 33181

Leonard H. Chusmir
Florida International University, College of Business Administration
Tamiami Trail, Miami, FL 33199

This study examined the conflict styles of 221 managers (113 males and 108 females) at three different organizational levels. Analyses of the data were conducted for both the home and work environments to see how managers resolve conflict in these two situations. Results show that managers at different levels varied substantially in their preferred method of resolving conflict at work. Further, they often changed their method of resolution when faced with conflict at home. Preferred conflict resolution styles adopted by managers at work did not necessarily match what some term the most effective; resolution styles at home were different and much "better."

Many social science writers and researchers see work and family roles as strongly interrelated. When the roles become incompatible in some way, work/family conflict occurs, especially when participation in one role detracts from the other (Greenhaus & Beutell, 1985). A consistent theme is that men and women workers cannot easily separate their work and family lives since both roles are so interdependent (Greenhaus & Parasuraman, 1986; Voydanoff, 1987, 1988). In an extensive review of the literature, Greenhaus and Beutell (1985) cited 24 recent studies that link the two worlds of work and family with inter-role conflict. It generally is accepted, therefore, that workers face conflict in both roles. However, few studies have examined how the resulting conflict is resolved and none looked exclusively at conflict resolution styles used by managers in both work and family roles.

The purpose of the present study is to examine the conflict styles of managers both at home and at work to see how they resolve conflict in each of the situations.

Authors' Note: Address reprint request and inquiries to the second author.
©1988 Select Press

Greenhaus and Beutell (1985) contended that "despite the blurring of work and family activities [behaviors] in some situations, work and family roles still have distinct norms and requirements that may be incompatible with one another" (p. 77). Under some circumstances the two worlds require different behaviors. Indeed, role theory also would predict different behaviors at work and at home since it states that the behavior of individuals changes as the occupied role changes (Sone, 1982). Workers occupy two different roles, each involving different situational expectations, and each likely requires different styles to resolve conflict.

Conflict resolution at work is a topic of growing importance (Lippitt, 1982; Rahim, 1981; Thomas & Schmidt, 1976). According to the American Management Association, managers spend about 24 percent of their time handling conflict, and rate conflict management equal to or more important than the basic management functions of planning, communication, motivation, and decision making (Thomas & Schmidt, 1976). Conflict at home—unavoidable among married couples—has equally serious implications for the family (Yelsma & Brown, 1985).

A conceptual scheme for classifying the styles or modes of conflict resolution was first introduced by Blake and Mouton (1964), and later modified by Thomas and Kilmann (1974). The modified version describes styles of managing conflict based on two basic dimensions: concern for self (assertiveness) and for others (cooperativeness). A combination of the two dimensions results in five different resolution modes: avoidance, collaboration, compromise, competing, or accommodating (Thomas, 1976). Avoidance does not address the conflict: Collaboration attempts to find some solution which fully satisfies both persons: Compromise finds some expedient, mutually-acceptable middle ground: Competing is a power-oriented style in which one tries to win one's own position at the other person's expense: Accommodating yields completely to another's point of view. The literature generally agrees that conflict in organizations may be functional or dysfunctional, but the method by which conflict is resolved can determine whether the outcome has a positive or negative effect on performance (Chan, 1981). Competing and avoidance modes were found to have a negative impact; collaboration a very high positive impact; and compromise and accommodating an inconsistent impact (Chan, 1981).

The most effective resolution styles are those which combine the assertive and cooperative dimensions, and therefore consider the rights and concerns of others as well as of self (Yelsma & Brown, 1985). The least effective are those modes that are uncooperative or unassertive and that try to defeat the other person or to avoid issues. Managers generally tend to rely most on those that are most effective, preferring compromise, collaboration, and accommodation styles to resolve conflict at work (Renwick, 1977; Zammuto, London & Rowland, 1979). They rely least on the ineffective styles of avoidance and competing. Revilla (1984) reported significant differences in resolution style preference due to management experience, with the more experienced managers being more competing, less compromising and more assertive than the less experienced administrators. Since more experienced managers likely have higher level positions than inexperienced managers, style of conflict resolution also may change depending on management level.

Social learning theory (Mischel, 1968) argues that behavior is highly specific to cues of the individual situation, and that individuals are not very consistent in their behavior over time and across situations. It rejects a generalized personality trait or disposition as a practical predictor of behavior. As applied to conflict resolution, social learning theory would posit that a manager's conflict resolution style likely would be predictable by the situation in which the manager is placed. On that basis, the preferred method of conflict resolution would change as the manager's hierarchical level changes, or as the situation (work versus home) changes, regardless of the individual's prior personal history. Based on that theory, we would expect widely-differing styles among managers, dependent upon various aspects of the conflict situation including such issues as stake in the conflict and common versus conflicting interests. Since both these issues likely differ by hierarchical rank, the present authors were lead to predict that managers' preferred conflict resolution styles will change due to hierarchical level as well as depending on whether the conflict needing resolution is at work at home. For that reason it was predicted that:

H-1. Hierarchical level is related to conflict resolution modes used by managers at work.

H-2. There are significant differences in conflict resolution modes used at home by managers to resolve disputes with spouses and/or significant others as compared to those used at work.

METHODS

Subjects

Data were obtained on 221 managers (113 males and 108 females) employed in Greater Miami, Florida. Students who work full time but who attend college part time were asked to get permission from their work organizations to test non-student employees. Subjects in these work places then voluntarily agreed to participate in the study. Because women hold a disproportionately low percentage of managerial positions, and because we wanted to test a reasonably balanced subject group, tests were conducted in 10 different organizations covering three occupational groups to obtain a sufficiently large number of both male and female subjects in all three hierarchical levels. The three occupational groups and number of subjects were as follows: Banking and mortgage (75); not-for-profit (73); and industry (73).

Subjects averaged 37 years of age and had been with their present organization 8 years. About 46% of the subjects reported that they held low-level management positions; 38% middle-level management positions, and 16% top-level positions.

Research Instruments

An unsigned survey questionnaire administered on-site contained demographic information as well as two Thomas-Kilmann Conflict Mode Instruments, identical in form but with different instructions. The Thomas-Kilmann instrument is a forced-choice, 30-item questionnaire designed to measure the five conflict resolution styles described above (Kilmann & Thomas, 1977; Thomas & Kilmann, 1974). The instrument also measures specific intentions for handling conflict rather than style of conflict management. Research shows the instrument to be more reliable than earlier questionnaires and convergent with similar concepts measured by other instruments (Thomas & Kilmann, 1978). Kilmann and Thomas (1977) reported coefficient alpha reliabilities for the instrument to be in the moderate range with .71, .65, .58, .62, and .43 for the competing, collaborating, compromising, avoiding, and accommodating scales respectively. The average internal consistency coefficient for the instrument was .60, as compared to .45 and .55 for the Lawrence-Lorsch and Hall conflict measures. Cronbach's alpha coefficients averaged .53 in the present sample, with .74, .36, .51, .47, and .59 for the competing, collaborating, compromising, avoiding and accommodating scales respectively. Additional empirical support for the instrument and theory has been reported by Ruble and Thomas (1976) and Cosier and Ruble (1981).

One set of instructions asks subjects to consider situations at work (not at home) in which their wishes differed from those of another person. The second set of instructions asked subjects to forget about work and to think about situations in their personal life. They were asked to think about those times "when you find your wishes differing from those of your spouse (if you're married), or from your significant or relevant other (if you're not married)."

Data were also obtained on subjects' organizational position and tenure, sex, age, education, marital status, number of children living at home, number of siblings and birth order.

RESULTS

Analysis of the data revealed that both hypotheses were supported. As predicted in Hypothesis 1, hierarchical level was related to conflict resolution styles used by managers at work. And, as predicted in Hypothesis 2, when controlling for management level, managers did change their resolution styles when settling disputes at home with spouses. Details of at-work and at-home differences in results are presented below in separately-labeled sections.

Table 1 presents the means, standard deviations, and correlations among the conflict resolution modes and demographic variables. As would be expected from conflict theory, the five conflict resolution modes were negatively related to one another in both work and home environments. The negative correlations among modes is characteristic of an Ipsative instrument, where a higher score on one mode means a corresponding decrease across scores of the other modes. Correlations between corresponding work and home conflict scores were all positively related, suggesting some consistency in style from one environment to the other when not controlling for hierarchical level or other variables.

At work: Table 1 also shows some significant relationships between specific conflict resolution modes at work and hierarchical level, as predicted by Hypothesis 1. Specifically, use of the competing mode at work was positively linked to hierarchical level, with that style being used more frequently as managers rise from lower to higher levels within the organization. An opposite relationship was found for compromising mode, which was negatively related to rank. Higher level managers were less apt to compromise than lower level rank managers. In addition, conflict resolution modes used by managers at work were connected with some of the other variables in the study. Not surprisingly, men were slightly more likely to compete at work ($r=.16$, $p<.01$) and women were more likely to compromise ($r=-.14$, $p<.05$). For both genders, older managers tended to collaborate more than younger managers ($r=.18$, $p<.01$). Although not shown in Table 1, number of brothers was negatively linked with compromising style ($r=-.14$, $p<.05$); and number of sisters was negatively correlated with competing style ($r=-.15$, $p<.05$). All other variables were not significantly related to any of the resolution modes with the exception of tenure, which generally followed the same patterns as age.

At home: Neither hierarchical level nor sex were significantly related to conflict resolution mode. The older the managers, however, the

TABLE 1 Means, Standard Deviations, and Correlations Among Variables (n=221)

Variables	Means	S.D.	1	2	3	4	5	6	7	8	9	10	11	12	13
1 Work Competing	5.31	3.02													
2 Work Collaborating	6.58	2.09	-.08												
3 Work Compromising	6.69	2.35	-.29***	-.30***											
4 Work Avoiding	6.28	2.25	-.33***	-.33***	-.16*										
5 Work Accommodating	4.93	2.53	-.54***	-.13*	-.15*	-.06									
6 Home Competing	3.49	2.97	.39***	-.07	-.19**	-.11	-.11								
7 Home Collaborating	6.95	2.56	.10	.37***	-.25***	-.10	-.12	-.10							
8 Home Compromising	6.51	6.33	-.03	.00	.23***	-.10	-.08	.00	-.12						
9 Home Avoiding	6.14	2.29	-.22**	-.09	-.04	.26***	.13	-.45***	-.33***	-.09					
10 Home Accommodating	7.21	2.31	-.17**	.03	.00	.01	.23***	-.53***	-.27***	-.05	.16*				
11 Hierarchical Level	1.71	.73	.18**	.11	-.14*	-.04	-.13	-.04	-.01	-.08	.09	.10			
12 Sex	1.51	.50	.16**	.12	-.14*	.12	-.10	.02	.10	-.12	.03	.03	.26***		
13 Age	37.21	8.58	-.03	.18**	-.05	-.03	-.02	-.05	-.06	-.05	.15*	.12	.18**	.16*	

*p<.05; **p<.01; ***p<.001.

more likely they were to use the avoiding style of conflict resolution (r=15, p<.05). Although not shown in Table 1, as education level increased, so did the use of accommodating style (r=15, p<.05).

Work-home comparisons: Paired t-tests of work and home conflict scores for the three levels of management were analyzed with results revealing significant differences (see Table 2). At all levels, managers differed substantially in use of the competing and accommodating modes in resolving conflict at work and home (p<.001); low level managers differed in use of the collaborating mode (p<.01)—partially confirming Hypothesis 2. Note that positive t-values shown in Table 2 indicate that home scores are larger than work scores. Negative t-values indicate that home scores are larger than work scores. Data analysis shows that managers at all organizational levels tended to use more of the competitive mode at work than at home. With the accommodative style, the opposite was true. Managers at all levels used this mode less frequently at work than at home. Low-level managers collaborated less at work than at home, while mid-level managers compromised more at work than at home.

Table 3 reports the priority of conflict resolution modes at work and at home by hierarchical level based on pairwise t-tests of mean differences. Tied ranks reflect non-significant differences (p<.05). Low-level managers in the work environment preferred compromising and avoiding (rank 1.5) over collaborating (rank 3) and competing and accommodating (rank 4.5). At home, the same level managers preferred compromising, accommodating, collaborating, and avoiding (rank 2.5) modes more than the competing (rank 5) mode. Mid-level managers at work preferred compromising, avoiding, and collaborating (rank 2) modes of settling conflict more than accommodating and competing (rank 4.5) modes. At home, however, they preferred accommodating and collaborating (rank 1.5) modes, more than avoiding and compromising (rank 3.5) modes, and more than competing (rank 5). Top-level managers at work differed from other managers in having a greater preference for competing, which tied with collaborating, avoiding and compromising (rank 2.5). Accommodating (rank 5) was their least-preferred mode at work. At home, however, they preferred accommodating and collaborating (rank 1.5), more than avoiding and compromising (rank 3.5), and more than competing (rank 5).

A stepwise multiple discriminate analysis was performed on the entire sample, with the conflict modes and demographic variables and hierarchical level as the grouping variable. The purpose of the discriminate analysis was to determine the linear combination of variables that best discriminates among (or separates) the three hierarchical groups

TABLE 2 Paired t-Tests of Mean Difference (Work-Home) Conflict Resolution Modes By Hierarchical Level

Dependent Variables

		Competing			Collaborating			Compromising			Avoiding			Accommodating		
		(W)	(H)	(T)	(W)	(H)	(T)	(W)	(H)	(T)	(W)	(H)	(T)	(W)	(H)	(T)
Low-Level	Means	4.83	3.63	3.84***	6.28	6.95	-3.15**	6.93	7.13	-.22	6.38	5.87	1.80	5.35	7.03	-5.70***
(n=101)	S.D.	2.88	3.12		2.00	2.31		2.15	9.08		2.48	2.39		2.59	2.32	
Mid-Level	Means	5.42	3.36	5.45***	6.86	6.98	-.38	6.76	6.04	3.19**	6.23	6.39	-.53	4.56	7.21	-8.43***
(n=84)	S.D.	3.06	2.80		1.93	2.40		2.31	1.88		2.06	2.24		2.34	2.18	
Top-Level	Means	6.42	3.42	5.76***	6.75	6.89	-.25	5.86	5.89	-.11	6.14	6.33	-.56	4.61	7.72	-5.98***
(n=36)	S.D.	3.07	2.98		2.59	3.50		2.82	2.39		2.03	2.06		2.72	2.56	
Total	Means	5.31	3.49	8.16***	6.57	6.95	-2.11*	6.69	6.51	.43	6.28	6.14	.73	4.93	7.21	-11.31***
(n=221)	S.D.	3.02	2.97		2.09	2.56		2.35	6.33		2.25	2.29		2.53	2.31	

Positive t-values indicate that work scores are larger than home scores. Negative t-values indicate that home scores are larger than work scores.
*p<.05; **p<.01; ***p<.001.

TABLE 3   Rank Order of Means of Preferred Conflict Resolution Modes At Work and At Home[a] By Hierarchical Level

	Competing	Collaborating	Compromising	Avoiding	Accommodating
Low-Level (n=101)					
At Work	4.5	3.0	1.5	1.5	4.5
At Home	5.0	2.5	2.5	2.5	2.5
Mid-Level (n=84)					
At Work	4.5	2.0	2.0	2.0	4.5
At Home	5.0	1.5	3.5	3.5	1.5
Top-Level (n=36)					
At Work	2.5	2.5	2.5	2.5	5.0
At Home	5.0	1.5	3.5	3.5	1.5
Total (n=221)					
At Work	4.5	2.0	2.0	2.0	4.5
At Home	5.0	2.0	2.0	4.0	2.0

[a]Tied ranks are based on non-significant (p>.05) differences between means.

(low-level managers, mid-level managers, and top-level managers). Mahalanobis' distance (Norusis, 1982) was the criterion for variable selection in the stepwise procedure. The discriminate analysis resulted in two canonical discriminate functions among the three groups. The first discriminant function (x^2=118.51, p<.001), which explained 84% of the total discriminating power, had positive pooled within-groups correlations with education (.51), job type (.42), sex (.32), live alone (.30), marital status (.26), age (.22), competing mode at work (.22) and accommodating mode at home (.11). Additionally, the first discriminant function had negative pooled within-groups correlations with accommodating mode at work (-.15), number of siblings (-.14), compromising mode at home (-.11), and avoiding mode at home (-.07). The groups with positive centroids were top-level managers (1.24) and mid-level managers (.45) and the group with a negative centroid was low-level managers (-.81). These results indicate that compared to the other two groups, top-level managers were more educated, managed people rather than projects, tended to be male, not living alone, were married or divorced rather than single, and preferred the competing mode at work and an accommodating mode at home. Compared to the other groups, low level managers reported greater preference for an accommodating mode at work, compromising and avoiding modes at home, and had more siblings.

The second discriminate function was not significant ($x^2=22.68$, $p=.36$). In total, 59% of the grouped cases were correctly classified by the discriminate functions. The classification of low-level managers (69.5%) and top-level managers (61.8%), was superior to the classification of mid-level managers (44.9%).

DISCUSSION

Results showing rank order of preferred modes indicated that managers in this study at different levels in the organization varied substantially in their preferred method of resolving conflict at work. In addition, they often changed their method of resolution when faced with conflict at home. Preferred conflict resolution styles adopted by the managers at work did not necessarily match what some experts term the most effective. Top level managers were the least consistent users of "best" resolution styles: Low level and mid level managers were somewhat better, confirming earlier findings of Revilla (1984).

Managers at all three hierarchical ranks chose more effective styles for resolving conflict at home, being more careful of the rights and concerns of their family than of their employees. Significant differences in selection of conflict resolution behaviors in work and family situations lend support to the idea that work/family behavior may be partially independent, as previous writers (Greenhaus & Beutell, 1985; Sone, 1982) suggested but did not test.

At work, the top level managers chose the competing style most often, but at home they more often resolved conflict with their spouse or significant other by using the accommodating or collaborating modes. At work, the mid-level managers most often used different approaches than top level managers, with compromising, avoiding and collaborating styles as their favorite choice. At home, however, they too usually switched styles, choosing both accommodating and collaborating styles of conflict resolution. Low level managers at work preferred compromising and avoidance to resolve conflict. At home they preferred collaborating and accommodating while avoiding competing.

One implication of these findings is that testing of conflict resolution styles for social science research, clinical or organizational purposes should specify resolution in the specific environment rather than a more generalized approach. It seems clear that managers in this study did not have a single style that they use both at home and at work. It is likely that subjects in any role or situation would adopt a behavior congruent with that role or situation. Questionnaires, therefore, that measure behavior or attitudes but do not specify the environment could be misleading.

Position power appears to offer a good possible explanation for choice of conflict resolution mode by managers at work. Because top level managers have the highest level of position power, they may be less at risk in adopting a conflict resolution style that is uncooperative (competing), and have little reason to be unassertive (avoiding). Low level managers, on the other hand, have the least position power of the three ranks, and may find that they have little choice but to compromise or avoid the conflict. Making "waves" could be dysfunctional at that level. Mid level managers, a little more secure in their position power—and perhaps a little more mature in management experience—add collaborating (a combination of assertive and cooperative styles) to their resolution repertoire, increasing their chances for effective resolution (Yelsma & Brown, 1985).

Power also may play a role in explaining why managers—particularly those at the highest level—commonly use the competing style at work, but switch to the accommodative style at home. Managers occupy a legitimate source of power at work, especially with subordinates, and have the authority needed for a competitive conflict resolution style. At home, since both marital partners usually hold relatively equal rank and power, the managers' authority no longer exists, and a less competitive strategy may be more acceptable. Power, therefore, may be the key situational ingredient that helps determine conflict behavior in both work and family roles. At work, power often is determined by hierarchical position. At home, power and subsequent behavior may be impacted by a number of factors including a traditional versus nontraditional view of gender and feminism, spousal age or education, and/or prior socialization. When the balance of power shifts from relatively equal to domination by either partner, the conflict resolution style used by the dominant and submissive partner likely will change accordingly.

One might logically assume that as a manager gains rank in an organization, he or she ought to have gained more experience in resolving conflict effectively. The top level manager should be more knowledgeable and well educated as to so-called "best" managerial behaviors. It may be difficult, therefore, to understand why top level managers consistently appear to resolve conflict at work using the "least effective" mode. At that level, they should know the difference between "good" and "bad," and, in fact, results of this study show that they did use the better style at home. In addition to the "power position" explanation offered earlier, other possible reasons for this apparent contradiction in logic include: 1) Cooperation may take more time. Top level managers may be so burdened with major decision-making situations they feel overloaded and cannot devote the time needed for more cooperative conflict resolution modes. 2) They may actually do less resolving of conflict than managers at the low or mid levels, since most popular management writers agree that it is best to resolve conflict at the lowest possible level in the organization. Although most conflict may be resolved at lower levels, unresolved conflict or conflict among higher level persons occasionally reaches the top. A cooperative mode may not work for these unresolved conflicts.

Conflict resolution training at work needs to consider the level of power. Trainers may concentrate on resolving conflict using different strategies based on the specific conflict situation as well as position level. Each of the five strategies may be more effective than others in different situations (Hart, 1981; Rahim, 1986). Training and development workshops may increase the use of effective contingent selection. In the same way, family counseling and therapy may be used to reduce any differences between preferred and effective conflict resolution strategies at home.

One limitation of this study is that results were based on a self-report measurement of preferences or intentions. Actual behavior in field settings might be more desirable to help eliminate the possibility that actual behavior may not follow the same direction as intended behavior. Some results may be an artifact of the social desirability biases sometimes found when using self-report instruments. However, there was significant reporting of less desirable behavior. Another limitation was that because of the difficulty of finding enough female managers in any one organization to test a representative selection of both male and female managers, results were based on a convenience sample composed of volunteers in several organizations. Future research should be considered to overcome those limitations.

REFERENCES

Blake, R. R., & Mouton, J.S. (1964). *The managerial grid.* Houston, Texas: Gulf Publishing.

Chan, M. (1981). Intergroup conflict and conflict management in the R & D divisions of four aerospace companies. (Doctoral dissertation, University of California, Los Angeles, 1981). *Dissertation Abstracts International, 42* (4), 1767-A.

Cosier, R.A., & Ruble, T.L. (1981). Research on conflict-handling behavior: An experimental approach. *Academy of Management Journal, 24,* 816-831.

Greenhaus, J.H., & Beutell, N.J. (1985). Sources of conflict between work and family roles. *Academy of Management Review, 10,* 76-88.

Greenhaus, J.H., & Parasuraman, S. (1986). Vocational and organizational behavior 1985: A review. *Journal of Vocational Behavior, 29,* 115-176.

Hart, L.B. (1981). *Learning from conflict*. Reading, MA: Addison-Wesley.
Kilmann, R.H., & Thomas, K.W. (1977). Developing a forced-choice measure of conflict-handling behavior: The "MODE" instrument. *Educational and Psychological Measurement, 37*, 309-325.
Lippitt, G.L. (1982). Managing conflict in today's organizations. *Training and Development Journal, 36*, 66-72.
Mischel, W. (1968) *Personality and assessment*. New York: Wiley.
Norusis, M.J. (1982). *SPSS introductory guide: Basic statistics and operations*. New York: McGraw Hill Book Company.
Rahim, M.A. (1981). Organizational behavior courses for graduate students in business administration: Views from the tower and battlefield. *Psychological Reports, 49*, 583-592.
Rahim, M.A. (1986). Referent role and styles of handling interpersonal conflict, *The Journal of Social Psychology, 126*, 79-86.
Renwick, P. (1977). The effects of sex differences on the perception and management of superior-subordinate conflict: An exploratory study. *Organizational Behavior and Human Performance, 19*, 403-415.
Revilla, V.A. (1984). Conflict management styles of men and women administrators in higher education. (Doctoral dissertation, University of Pittsburgh, 1984.) *Dissertation Abstracts International, 45*(6). 1601-A.
Ruble, T.L., & Thomas, K.W. (1976). Support for a two-dimensional model of conflict behavior. *Organizational Behavior & Human Performance, 16*, 143-155.
Sone, P.G. (1982). The effects of gender on mangers' resolution of superior-subordinate conflict. (Doctoral dissertation, Arizona State University, 1981). *Dissertation Abstracts International, 42*(11), 4914-A.
Thomas, K.W. (1976). Conflict and conflict management. In M.D. Dunnette (Ed.), *Handbook of industrial and organizational psychology* (pp. 273-320). Chicago: Rand-McNally.
Thomas, K.W., & Schmidt, W.H. (1976). A survey of managerial interests with respect to conflict. *Academy of Management Journal, 19*, 315-318.
Thomas, K.W., & Kilmann, R.H. (1974). *Thomas-Kilmann Conflict Mode Instrument*. Tuxedo, NY: Xicom.
Thomas, K.W., & Kilmann, R.H. (1978). Comparison of four instruments measuring conflict behavior. *Psychological Reports, 42*, 1139-1145.
Voydanoff, P. (1987). *Work and family life*. Newbury Park, CA: Sage.
Voydanoff, P. (1988). Work role characteristics, family structure demands, and work/family conflict. *Journal of Marriage and the Family, 50*, 749-761.
Yelsma, P., & Brown, C.T. (1985). Gender roles, biological sex, and predisposition to conflict management. *Sex Roles, 12*, 731-745.
Zammuto, R., London, M., & Rowland, K.M. (1979). Effects of sex on commitment and conflict resolution. *Journal of Applied Psychology, 64*, 227-231.

A Gender-Role Perspective on Role Conflict, Work Stress and Social Support

Esther R. Greenglass
Kaye-Lee Pantony
Ronald J. Burke

*Department of Psychology, York University
Downsview, Ontario, Canada M3J 1P3*

The present study assesses sex differences in role conflict in a sample of female and male teachers using Holahan and Gilbert's (1979) six role conflict scales which measure role conflict between professional and familial roles. Relationships among role conflict, work stress and social support were also examined in women and men as were the psychological consequences of role conflict. Results indicated that role conflict was higher in women than in men. Significant correlations between role conflict and work stress and social support, primarily in women, suggested a greater interdependence between work and family spheres in women. Implications of the results are discussed from a gender-role perspective.

Recent investigations of health and well-being increasingly are focusing on multiple social roles and the ways in which individuals manage the responsibilities associated with them. Responsibility for multiple roles opens the door to interrole conflict involving potentially incompatible demands on the individual which elicit strain. According to Sarbin and Allen (1968), a role theoretical analysis of the dual-worker family structure suggests that a potential source of stress may stem from role conflict. Employed women face demands which stem from emotional and practical considerations associated with the dual role. When women take on employment, they take on the role of employee, while maintaining their traditional roles of housewife and mother. To the extent that there is an increase in stress associated with their employment, role conflict in women should also increase. Although the number of husbands partici-

---

Authors' Notes: Grateful acknowledgement is due to York University for funding this project.

Gratitude is expressed to Mirka Ondrack and the Institute of Social Research for the data analyses.

©1988 Select Press

pating in housework has recently increased, married women continue to be responsible for most household tasks regardless of their employment status (Stein, 1984).

Ample data attest to the role conflict experienced by women. For example, Beutell and Greenhaus (1983) found that 79 of their 115 married students experienced at least one conflict between home and nonhome roles (i.e., among the roles of spouse, parent, worker). In a study of female managers from a variety of spheres, including corporate, educational and public service institutions, Greenglass (1985) examined the relationship between role conflict and various symptoms of stress. A forced-choice question asked respondents to indicate the ways job and family interfered with each other by checking the relevant ones in a list of nine different kinds of interference. Role conflict involving worker vs. parent and worker vs. spousal roles was assessed using Holahan and Gilbert's (1979) role conflict scales. Psychological measures of stress included job anxiety (Spielberger et al., 1970), depression, and irritation (Caplan et al., 1975). Results of the study suggest that a substantial proportion of employed married women are experiencing conflict between work and family roles. This is due in part to rigid work schedules and work overload. The same study found that the higher the number of reported interferences between job and family life, the greater the woman's depression, irritation and anxiety. Thus, role conflict would appear to have deleterious psychological consequences.

Given that role conflict generates stress, how then does the individual cope with it? A growing body of literature has documented the importance of the assistance provided by the "natural" support system in helping an individual negotiate personal crises (Cassel, 1974; Cobb, 1976). The quality of social attachments can influence psychological well-being as a buffer against stress (Andrews et al., 1978; Wilcox, 1981).

Support both at work and at home is important in reducing stress and conflict. For example, previous research suggests that social support may be effective in reducing stress such as when a supportive boss may make work situations less stressful (Roskies & Lazarus, 1980). And, there tends to be agreement that whether a husband supports his wife's employment is critical to her experience of marital and job conflict (Holahan & Gilbert, 1979; Berkowitz & Perkins, 1984).

According to House and Wells (1978), social support consists of frequent interactions, strong and positive feelings and the availability of emotional and instrumental support when needed. There are substantial grounds for believing that women would not only tend to perceive greater social support both in the work and family domains but also that they would be better able to utilize support in reducing their role conflict.

Females, more than males, may be able to express a wide range of emotions including fear and sadness in interpersonal situations. Given differences in learned sex-role expectations regarding the sharing of personal problems, males may be at a disadvantage in requesting assistance. Males appear less likely to be able to use emotions interpersonally (Allen & Haccoun, 1976). There are also sex-linked norms regarding the disclosure of problems to others—females self disclose more often than males (Rubin, Hill, Peplau, & Dunkel-Schetter, 1980). Thus, it is expected that social support, both at work and outside work, would more likely be related to lower role conflict in women than in men.

In light of the pressures on women to perform in a dual role, work and family spheres should be interrelated to a greater extent in women than in men. Men, on the other hand, receive support and encouragement to separate work and family spheres through socialization and the structuring of the work environment. In addition, being able to regard one's spouse (and not oneself) as being primarily responsible for the home would reinforce the separation of these spheres.

The present study was designed to assess sex differences in role conflict in male and female teachers using Holahan and Gilbert's (1979) six role conflict scales which measure, among other things, role conflict between the role of professional and those of parent and spouse. Related objectives were to examine the relationship among work stress, social support and role conflict as well as the psychological consequences of role conflict in women and in men. It is hypothesized that women, compared to men, will report higher role conflict. Role conflict in both women and men should be associated with deleterious psychological consequences such as increased anxiety and depression. Given the greater interdependence of work and family domains in women, role conflict should be positively associated with work stressors and negatively associated with social support in women only.

METHOD

Respondents

Respondents were 556 women and men employed within a school board in a large Canadian City. While respondents tended to be mainly teachers, they were also department heads, vice principals, and principals. Results of t-tests on means significant at the .05 level or higher indicated that males, compared to females, spent more years teaching (6.17 for males vs. 5.52 for females), had more students per class (26.00 for males vs. 23.90 for females) and were older (44.80 in males vs. 43.40 in females). While more women (60%) were full-time teachers than men (47%), more men (14%) than women (.4%) were principals. One-third of the male and female samples were represented at the three levels of school—elementary, junior high school and secondary schools.

More men (93.6%) were married and living with their spouse than women (80.8%) and more women (14.0%) than men (4.0%) were separated or divorced. On the average, respondents had two children. Only respondents with children were included in the study because the conceptual focus of the research involved work and the family.

Procedure

Data were collected using a mail-out questionnaire. Questionnaires were sent to teachers, department heads, vice principals and principals within a single school board at their schools. Completed questionnaires were then mailed back to a university address in a stamped self-addressed envelope. In total, 2189 questionnaires were sent out and 833 were returned, yielding a response rate of 38%.[1] Of 833 respondents, 556 reported having children. The final sample included these 556 respondents, 229 women and 327 men.

Measures

Role Conflict. Six areas of role conflict were assessed using scales developed by Holahan and Gilbert (1979). These include conflict between various roles such as Professional vs. Self, Professional vs. Spouse, Professional vs. Parent, Spouse vs. Parent, Parent vs. Self, and Spouse vs. Self. Each measure was based on either 3 or 4 items. Sample items are: "Putting yourself first in terms of your work versus your spouse putting himself/herself first in terms of his/her work" and "Giving priority to your family versus giving priority to yourself." Respondents answered in terms of how much internal conflict was caused by each item on a 5-point scale from "causes no internal conflict" to causes "high internal conflict."

Work Stress. The work-setting stress measure, developed by Burke et al. (1984) was based on eight work-setting characteristics: Poor Orientation, Work Load, Lack of Stimulation, Narrow Client Contacts, Lack of Autonomy, Unclear Institutional Goals, Poor Supervision, and Social Isolation. Examples of items used to assess work-setting stress are "My duties are such that I spend a lot of time working alone" (Social Isolation); "I don't have much freedom or control in my job—rules and regulations tell me what I can and can't do" (Lack of Autonomy). Respondents were asked to answer by indicating on a 7-point scale how strongly they agreed or disagreed with each statement.

---

[1]*The response rate obtained in this study may have been a function of the time of year in which the questionnaires were sent out, namely, in late spring. The rush to complete grading in schools at this time along with teacher preparation for summer vacation are factors that would likely make response rates lower at this time. Thus, little opportunity was available to increase the response rate with subsequent follow-up.*

Another measure of stress, "Sources of Stress," was identified by Cherniss (1980) and developed by Burke et al. (1984). "Sources of Stress" include Doubts about Competence; Problems with Students; Bureaucratic Interference; Lack of Stimulation and Fulfillment, and Lack of Collegiality. Examples of some of these items are: "When I began my present job there was a time in which I felt I was falling short" (Doubts about Competence) and "I often feel in a rut on my job" (Lack of Stimulation and Fulfillment). Respondents had to answer by indicating on a 7-point scale how strongly they agreed or disagreed with each statement.

Social Support. Social support from three sources, supervisor, co-workers and spouse, friends and relatives, was measured using adaptations of the scales employed by Caplan et al. (1975). Each subscale consisted of nine 4-point Likert-scaled items. The types of social support assessed by these scales are illustrated by the following items: "How much does each of these people go out of their way to do things to make your work life easier for you? How much is each of the following people willing to listen to your work-related problems? How much useful feedback do you get from each of these people?" Respondents answered these items in terms of support received from "your immediate supervisor," "other people at work," and "your spouse, friends and relatives."

Outcome Measures

Job Satisfaction was assessed by five items combined into a single score (Quinn & Shepard, 1974). An item from this scale is: "If you were free to go into any type of job you wanted, what would your choice be?" Respondents were asked to check one of the following response alternatives: "I would want the job I now have; I would want to retire and not work at all; I would prefer some other job to the job I now have."

Absenteeism was measured by four items which were combined into a single score (Quinn & Shepard, 1974). A sample item is "How many days of scheduled work have you missed in the past two weeks?" Respondents were asked to check one of the following alternatives:" "None; One day only, Two days only; Three or more days."

Respondents' depression, anxiety and somatization were assessed using the Hopkins Symptom Checklist (Derogatis et al., 1979). Each was based on composite measures involving at least seven items. Respondents indicated whether or not they had been diagnosed as having each of six different disease entitites: high blood pressure, diabetes, ulcers, migraine headaches, coronary heart disease and asthma/allergies. A composite measure of physical health was created based on frequencies with which respondents reported these diseases.

Marital Satisfaction was measured by a scale developed by Orden and Bradburn (1968) in which respondents were asked to indicate how

TABLE 1   Reliability of Composite Measures

Measures	Number of Items	α
Maslach Burnout Inventory	22	.70
Role Conflict		
Professional vs. Self	4	.80
Professional vs. Parent	4.	.79
Professional vs. Spouse	4.	.74
Parent vs. Spouse	3	.73
Parent vs. Self	3	.82
Spouse vs. Self	4	.66
Work-Setting Stress	8	.69
Additional Sources of Stress	5	.65
Social Support		
Boss Support	3	.95
Co-Worker Support	3	.92
Family/Friends Support	3	.89
Outcomes		
Job Satisfaction	5	.84
Absenteeism	4	.64
Depression	11	.84
Anxiety	7	.61
Somatization	12	.73
Marital Satisfaction	11	.80

frequently they had undertaken each of nine positive or pleasant activities with their spouse (or partner). They also indicated how frequently they had disagreed with their spouse in nine different areas during the past few weeks. The marital satisfaction score included a weighing of the positive minus the negative scores. An example of a positive activity was, "Had a good laugh together or shared a joke." A negative activity included disagreeing about "in-laws." Respondents were asked to check "yes" to each item that applied to them during the past few weeks.

RESULTS

Table 1 reports the internal consistency ratings for the composite measures.

Role Conflict

Table 2 presents t-tests on all of the role conflict measures between women and men. On every role conflict scale with the exception of Spouse vs. Self, women reported greater role conflict. Thus, women reported more role conflict not only between professional and family roles, but also between themselves as a self-actualized person and their professional and parental roles, as well as more total role conflict.

TABLE 2 T-tests on Mean Role Conflict[a] Scores for Female vs. Male Teachers

Variable	Females X̄	SD	N	Males X̄	SD	N	t
Professional vs. Self	8.63	4.08	163	7.65	3.43	231	-2.50*
Professional vs. Parent	8.86	4.17	131	7.15	3.29	200	-3.95***
Professional vs. Spouse	7.02	3.30	151	6.29	2.57	201	-1.26*
Parent vs. Spouse	5.96	3.17	109	4.65	2.21	165	-3.77***
Parent vs. Self	7.63	3.33	175	6.00	2.72	262	-5.38***
Spouse vs. Self	6.48	3.14	124	5.90	2.27	175	-1.76
Total Role Conflict	2.25	1.06	215	1.80	.82	314	-5.24***

[a] Role conflict was assessed on a scale where 1 = causes no internal conflict and 5 = high internal conflict.

*$p < .05$; ***$p < .001$.

Other Effects

T-tests conducted on measures of psychological and physical well-being indicated only two significant findings: women were more depressed than men (t= -3.37, df=534, p<.001) and also experienced more migraine headaches (t=4.02, df=507, p<.001). Further results indicated that while women were significantly higher than men on job satisfaction (t=3.08, df=517, p<.01), they did not differ significantly from their male counterparts on either absenteeism or marital satisfaction. No significant sex differences were found on either of the work stress measures or on any of the social support measures.

Role Conflict Relationships

Correlations were computed between role conflict scores and two sources of work stress, separately in women and men (see Table 3). Results were that in women, all of the role conflicts correlated significantly with both work setting stress as well as with sources of stress. In men, there were fewer significant correlations between role conflict and work stress. For example, nonsignificant relationships tended to be found between role conflict involving the role of husband and work stress.

Correlations computed between role conflict scores, job satisfaction, marital satisfaction and absenteeism showed significantly negative relationships for both women and men only for marital satisfaction. As role

TABLE 3   Correlations Between Work Stress and Role Conflict in Females and Males

	Work Setting Females	Work Setting Males	Additional Sources of Stress Females	Additional Sources of Stress Males
Professional vs. Self	.36***	.17**	.32***	.18**
Professional vs. Parent	.32***	.17*	.19*	.20**
Spouse vs. Parent	.25**	.07	.21*	.07
Spouse vs. Self	.35***	.06	.24**	.09
Parent vs. Self	.27**	.15*	.23**	.26***
Professional vs. Spouse	.33***	.12	.22**	.14*
Total Role Conflict	.28***	.16**	.26***	.22***

*$p < .05$; **$p < .01$; ***$p < .001$.

conflict increased, marital satisfaction decreased for the total sample. Job satisfaction was negatively related to all measures of role conflict in women. Only two significant relationships were observed for men — Parent vs. Self conflict and total role conflict were significantly negatively related to job satisfaction in men (see Table 4).

In general, absenteeism did not relate significantly to role conflict except for Spouse vs. Self conflict which correlated positively with absenteeism only in women ($r=.25$, $df=106$, $p<.01$).

While role conflict was positively related to depression, anxiety and somatization in women and men, there was little evidence that role

TABLE 4   Correlations Between Role Conflict, Job Satisfaction, and Marital Satisfaction in Females and Males

	Job Satisfaction Females	Job Satisfaction Males	Marital Satisfaction Females	Marital Satisfaction Males
Professional vs. Self	-.36***	-.07	-.44***	-.31***
Professional vs. Parent	-.27**	-.11	-.47***	-.26***
Spouse vs. Parent	-.27**	-.04	-.39***	-.17*
Spouse vs. Self	-.34***	-.12	-.57***	-.27***
Parent vs. Self	-.21**	-.18**	-.48***	-.32***
Professional vs. Spouse	-.38***	.01	-.51***	-.34***
Total Role Conflict	-.28***	-.14**	-.55***	-.36***

*$p < .05$; **$p < .01$; ***$p < .001$.

TABLE 5 Correlations Between Role Conflict, Depression, Anxiety, and Somatization

	Depression		Anxiety		Somatization	
	Females	Males	Females	Males	Females	Males
Professional vs. Self	.32***	.26***	.18**	.24***	.17*	.21***
Professional vs. Parent	.29***	.16*	.17*	.12*	.24**	.12
Spouse vs. Parent	.26**	.10	.13	.03	.09	.14*
Spouse vs. Self	.27**	.32***	.32***	.19**	.20*	.18**
Parent vs. Self	.25***	.35***	.10	.33***	.18**	.29***
Professional vs. Spouse	.27***	.27***	.21**	.25***	.20**	.25***
Total Role Conflict	.31***	.33***	.22***	.24***	.27***	.22***

*$p < .05$; **$p < .01$; ***$p < .001$.

conflict related significantly to total physical health (see Table 5). The relationship between social support and role conflict appeared to involve gender. Significantly negative relationships were observed between boss support and role conflict and between support from friends and family and role conflict predominantly in women (see Table 6).

TABLE 6 Correlations Between Role Conflict and Supervisor, Co-Worker and Family and Friend Support in Females and Males

	Supervisor		Social Support Peers		Family and Friend	
	Females	Males	Females	Males	Females	Male
Professional vs. Self	-.16*'	-.10	-.11	-.05	-.22**	-.07
Professional vs. Parent	-.22**	-.05	-.01	.02	-.22**	-.04
Spouse vs. Parent	-.20*	.01	-.08	-.01	-.30***	.07
Spouse vs. Self	-.20*	-.08	-.17*	-.12	-.20*	-.22**
Parent vs. Self	-.19**	-.07	-.10	-.09	-.30***	-.08
Professional vs. Spouse	-.19**	-.02	-.14*	.01	-.25***	-.10
Total Role Conflict	-.11	-.13**	-.09	-.13**	-.25***	-.25***

*$p < .05$; **$p < .01$; ***$p < .001$.

DISCUSSION

As predicted earlier, results of the present study indicated that women experienced significantly greater role conflict than men. Women had more role conflict not only between their familial roles (those of wife and mother), but also between their work role and each of their familial roles. These results are in line with data reported by Chassin et al. (1985) in their study of dual-worker couples with preschool children. They reported evidence suggesting that men in these couples may be faced with less inter-role conflict than women. Their data suggest that for women in dual-worker couples the inter-role conflict consists of a "trade-off" between the independence, freedom and "glamour" of the worker role and the sensitivity and warmth seen as appropriate to the wife and mother roles.

Such role conflict stems partly from stereotypes regarding appropriate feminine gender-role behaviour. For example, Pines and Solomon (1978) found conflict, in the eyes of college students, between the worker role and the feminine gender role. As Haynes et al. (1980) suggest, the dual role of employment and raising a family places excessive demands on women. The greater role conflict reported by women may have resulted in their experiencing more migraine headaches and more depression than men—results also reported by Cortis (1973) and Price (1970).

While women and men may have suffered more, psychologically and interpersonally when they had high role conflict, the woman's life was disrupted more as a result of high role conflict. The whole sample appeared to experience greater depression, anxiety, and somatization as well as greater dissatisfaction with their marriage when role conflict was high. However, it was mainly women who also experienced greater job dissatisfaction and absenteeism.

Women were also significantly more likely than men to be dissatisfied with their jobs when they experienced conflict between familial roles or between their work role and their roles as spouse and self as a self-actualized person. These results are in line with those of previous research in which stress resulting from the conflict between job and family responsibilities was related to a higher incidence of irritation, anxiety, and depression in managerial women (Greenglass, 1985).

Evidence from this study suggests that job stress was directly related to the woman's experience of role conflict while for men, this tended to be the case less often. Despite findings of lack of significant sex differences in work stressors, role conflict in men, specifically between the role of husband and those of father, teacher and self tended to be unrelated to job stress. Instead of experiencing conflict between these roles, men may be prioritizing roles. As Chassin et al. (1985) have noted, men indicated that they had trouble simultaneously enacting the roles of husband and father and as a result, the husband role went unfulfilled more often. The apparent independence of work and family in men parallels the typical organizational pattern which separates the two spheres. This may be due to a fear that "rational" task-centered relationships would be undermined by the "emotional" character of the family (Burke & Greenglass, 1987).

The association of social support with lesser role conflict (in women) parallels results of other research in which social support was effective in reducing stress (Roskies & Lazarus, 1980). Given the emphasis in female socialization on interdependence, the ability to relate meaningfully to others in interpersonal relationships (Greenglass, 1982), women should be better able to utilize support from others in lessening their role conflict.

Women reported more job satisfaction than men. Job satisfaction in women may depend on whether the job is male- or female- dominated. In jobs that tend to be dominated by men such as management, women often share common negative experiences such as feelings of isolation, lack of social support from male colleagues, and sex discrimination (Kanter, 1977). These would lead to high dissatisfaction with one's work. However, women tend to predominate in teaching (Statistics Canada, 1986). And, women in predominantly female jobs tend to be more satisfied with their work than their female counterparts in male-dominated spheres (Greenfeld, Greiner & Wood, 1980). Greater job satisfaction in women may be due to a greater opportunity for camaraderie from others and access to a support system.

REFERENCES

Allen, J.G., & Haccoun, D. (1976). Sex differences in emotionality: A multidimensional approach. *Human Relations, 8*, 711-722.

Andrews, G., Tennant, C., Newson, D., & Schonell, M. (1978). The relation of social factors to physical and psychiatric illness. *American Journal of Epidemiology, 108*, 27-35.

Berkowitz, A., & Perkins, H.W. (1984). Stress among farm women: Work and family as interacting systems. *Journal of Marriage and the Family, 46*, 161-165.

Beutell, N.J., & Greenhaus, J.H. (1983). Integration of home and nonhome roles: Women's conflict and coping behaviour. *Journal of Applied Psychology, 68*, 43-48.

Burke, R.J., & Greenglass, E.R. (1987). Work and family (Chapter 9). In C.L. Cooper and I.T. Robertson (Eds.), *International Review of Industrial and Organizational Psychology*. New York: Wiley.

Caplan, R.D., Cobb, S., French, J.R.P., Harrison, R.V., & Pinneau, S.R. (1975). *Job demands and worker health*. U.S. Dept. of Health, Education and Welfare, HEW Publication No. (NIOSH) 75-160.

Cassel, J. (1974). Psychosocial formulations. *International Journal of Health Services, 4*, 471-482.

Chassin, L., Zeiss, A., Cooper, K., & Reaven, J. (1985). Role perceptions, self-role congruence and marital satisfaction in dual-worker couples with preschool children. *Social Psychology Quarterly, 48*, 301-311.

Cobb, S. (1976). Social support as a moderator of life stress. *Psychosomatic Medicine, 38*, 300-314.

Cortis, G.A. (1973). The assessment of a group of teachers in relation to earlier career experience. *Educational Review, 25*, 112-123.

Derogatis, L.R., Lipman, R.S., Rickels, K., Uhlenhuth, E.H., & Cori, L. (1979). The Hopkins Symptom Checklist (HSCL): A self report symptom inventory. *Behavioural Science, 19*, 1-15.

Greenfeld, S., Greiner, L., & Wood, M.M. (1980). The "Feminine Mystique" in male dominated jobs. A comparison of attitudes and background factors of women in male-dominated versus female-dominated jobs. *Journal of Vocational Behaviour, 17*, 291-309.

Greenglass, E.R. (1985). Psychological implications of sex bias in the workplace. *Academic Psychology Bulletin, 7*, 227-240.

Greenglass, E.R. (1982). *A world of difference: Gender roles in perspective.* Toronto: Wiley.

Haynes, S., Feinleib, M., & Kannel, W.B. (1980). The relationship of psychosocial factors to coronary heart disease in the Framingham study III. Eight year incidence of coronary heart disease. *American Journal of Epidemiology, III*, 37-58.

House, J.S., & Wells, J.A. (1978). Occupational stress, social support, and health. In A. McLean, G. Black & M. Colligan, (Eds.), *Reducing occupational stress*. U.S. Department of Health, Education and Welfare Publication No. 78-140.

Holahan, C.K., & Gilbert, L.A. (1979). Conflict between major life roles: Women and men in dual career couples. *Human Relations, 32*, 451-467.

Jourard, S.M. (1961). Self disclosure patterns in British and American college females. *Journal of Social Psychology, 54*, 315-320.

Jourard, S.M., & Richman, P. (1963). Disclosure output and input. *Merrill/Palmer Quarterly*, 141-148.

Kanter, R.M. (1977). *Men and women of the corporation.* New York: Basic Books.

Morrison, D.F. (1976). *Multivariate statistical methods.* (Second Edition). New York: McGraw Hill.

Orden, S.R., & Bradburn, N.M. (1969). Working wives and marriage happiness. *American Journal of Sociology, 74*, 392-407.

Pines, M., & Solomon, D.(1978). *The social psychological double bind of the competent woman: Sex role and mental health stereotypes.* Paper presented at the Western Psychological Association, San Fransisco.

Price, L.W. (1970). *Organizational stress and job satisfaction in public high school teachers*, Ph.D. thesis (Stanford University), *Dissertation Abstracts International, 31*, (11-A), 5727-5728.

Quinn, R.P., & Shepard, L.J. (1974). *The 1972 Quality of Employment Survey.* Ann Arbor, MI: Survey Research Center, Institute for Social Research.

Roskies, E., & Lazarus, R.S. (1980). Coping theory and the teaching of coping skills. In P.O. Davidson & F.M. Davidson (Eds.), *Behavioral medicine:Changing health and life style* (pp. 38-69). New York: Brunner Mazel.

Rubin, Z., Hill, C.T., Peplau, L., & Dunkel-Schetter, C. (1980). Self-disclosure in couples. *Journal of Marriage and Family, 42*, 305-318.

Sarbin, T., & Allen, L. (1968). Role theory. In G. Lindzey & E. Aronson (Eds.), *The handbook of social psychology.* Reading, MA: Addison-Wesley.

Statistics Canada (1986). *Characteristics of teachers in public elementary and secondary schools, 1984-85.* Ministry of Supply & Services, Canada.

Stein, P.J. (1984). Men in families. In [special issue] Women and the family: Two decades of change. *Marriage and Family Review, 7*, 143-162.

Wilcox, B.L. (1981). Social support, life stress, and psychological adjustment: A test of the buffering hypothesis. *American Journal of Community Psychology, 9*, 371-386.

Burning Out in Medicine:
A Comparison of Husbands and Wives in Dual-Career Couples

Dafna N. Izraeli
Department of Sociology, Bar-Ilan University
Ramat-Gan, Israel 52100

This study examines spouse differences in burnout (in the sense of energy depletion) and burnout's correlates among 126 dual-career physician couples in Israel. The study found that burnout was more strongly associated with doubts about success in work performance for men than for women. Contrary to prediction, the study did not find that women were more burned out than men; nor was burnout more strongly associated with work-family conflict, with the feeling of having interfered with spouse's career or with the need for achievement/dominance and work involvement, in women than in men. Burnout, furthermore, was not greater in husbands whose status was lower than that of their wives. A serendipidous finding was that husbands who support their wives in both their domestic and professional careers are less burned out than those who do not. The discussion suggests that the way in which men's occupational roles are institutionalized constrain them from adjusting better to the new demands created by dual-career marriages.

Social scientists have traditionally studied family and work as separate, independent and unrelated spheres. In a review of the field, Burke and Greenglass (1987, p. 273) note that "while there is a plethora of information on each of these domains, little research attention has been directed to understanding the reciprocal relationship between them." The growth in women's labor force participation and the decline of the full-time homemaker role are among the factors that spurred researchers to pay

---

Author's Note: I wish to express my gratitude to Dahlia Etzion, whose work on burnout informed this study; to Dov Eden for his insightful and constructive critique; to Judy Lorber, whose skillful editing made the paper more readable; to Diane Margolis for her comments; and to Tiva Hirshman for her assistance in preparing the data.

©1988 Select Press

greater attention to the interdependence of family and work. Dual-career families provide a particularly revealing example of the contemporary dilemma faced by increasing numbers of couples. This is the need to juggle two jobs and two work schedules and simultaneously maintain a harmonious family life.

Women's entry into high status, male-dominated occupations, led to the growth in the number of dual-career families. This term was coined by Rapoport and Rapoport (1969, p. 3) to describe those families in which both partners are employed full time in the sort of "jobs which are highly salient personally, have a developmental sequence, and require a high degree of commitment." Early researchers of the dual-career family envisioned that the joint labor-market participation of husbands and wives engaged in "greedy occupations" would result in more symmetrical or egalitarian relationships between the spouses (Rapoport & Rapoport, 1969; Young & Willmott, 1973). Hunt and Hunt (1982), however, claim that the strain of having to cope with simultaneous demands of work and family roles will ultimately force couples to choose between commitment to work and a childless marriage or combining work and family at the expense of one spouse's foregoing a high-status career. What has become clear, is, that despite the great promise inherent in this new form of partnership, the potentially high cost in work overload and burnout, places a great burden on the family system (Gerber, 1983; Hertz, 1986).

The present study is about burnout in dual-career couples. Burnout has been defined as a "state of physical, emotional and mental exhaustion, which occurs as a result of long-term involvement in situations that are emotionally demanding" (Pines & Aronson, 1981). It is a result of energy depletion caused by continuous daily pressures, rather than by major life events (Etzion, 1987a), pressures with which the individual fails to cope effectively.

Reviewing a decade of her research on the subject, Etzion (1987a) concludes that both in the United States and in Israel, "across every profession, women tend to be more burned out than men." Wives tend to burn out more than husbands (Pines, 1987). Attempts to examine gender differences in burnout, however, have suffered from the lack of controls for key variables associated with burnout which are differentially distributed among men and women in the general population. For example, women generally do not fill the same jobs or the same hierarchical ranks as men and have less access to job-related rewards such as high income, social status, autonomy and opportunities for advancement. Employed men are more likely than employed women to be married, to have children and a spouse who can manage domestic responsibilities.

In a pioneering study, Etzion (1987b) compared 29 women and men in Israel who held middle-management positions and who were matched on age, seniority, and managerial level. She found that the women were more burned out and that success and influence on the job were associated with failure and dissatisfaction in private life for women, but not for men. She explains these findings as women's response to the "subtle every-day pressures of misfit stemming from being a minority in non-traditional situations, living with the incongruence between a feminine self-image and a managerial job that is defined as masculine and experiencing unresolved career/family conflict." In the Etzion study, 98 percent of the men but only 65 percent of the women were married. Being unmarried in Israel, especially for a woman, is a mark of failure (Hazleton, 1977), no matter how professionally successful she is.

In the present study of burnout in dual-career couples, the subjects are practising medical physicians married to each other and sharing the same household. This unusual sample makes it possible to compare men and women who have made a similar and intensive investment in professional training, who work in the same occupation, although not necessarily in the same specialization, and who share the same household. Couples working in the same profession represent an increasingly common social phenomenon (Lorber, 1984). This is a consequence of the increase in women in traditionally male professions and the fact that the training stage for the profession coincides with the mating stage in personal life.

The hypotheses tested in this study have been supported repeatedly in research and are congruent with commonly held beliefs about men and women in high-status careers. Most dual-career couple role-strain research focuses on the wife, assuming that because she is the one adding a primary role, she is also the one most affected by this new form of work-family linkage. The strain induced by the overlap and contradictions in her dual set of roles as career women and wife/mother/housekeeper has been well documented in previous research (Berman, Sacks & Lief, 1975; Bryson, Bryson & Johnson, 1978; Hall, 1972; Herman & Gyellstrom, 1977; Holahan & Gilbert, 1979; Johnson & Johnson, 1977; Rapoport & Rapoport, 1969; Yogev, 1981) found that these continuous, daily stresses result in women being more burned out than men. This is our first hypothesis.

1. *Women are more burned out than men.* The care of the home and children is at the essence of the traditional wife-mother role. Even when women work outside the home, they remain primarily responsible for the care of both the children and the home. They spend more hours doing both than their spouses (Meissner, 1985; Peres & Katz, 1984; Pleck & Staines, 1982). In addition, women in time-consuming and demanding jobs often experience guilt and self-recrimination for compromising their obliga-

tions as wives and mothers, according to Etzion and Blitz (1985). The double burden combined with the guilt results in greater home/work conflict for women and ultimately in greater burnout. Home/work conflict is less likely to be a stressor for men since, as Pleck (1977) has noted, social norms legitimize the spillover of work into family life for men, but not for women.

Our second hypothesis, therefore, is:

2. *Burnout is more strongly associated with work-family conflict for women than it is for men.* Being supportive of her husband's work career is a proverbial part of the traditional female role. Normative expectations are internalized during early socialization. A survey of how a representative national sample of 17 year old girls in Israel perceived the role performance of the ideal woman found that 41 percent indicated the women's successful performance in helping her husband as very important, compared to 27 percent who specified her successful performance in an occupation as very important (Bar-Yosef, Bloom & Levy 1976). The demands of the husband's career are often a major determinant of the wife's occupational decisions (Papanek, 1975; Mortimer, 1978). The arrangement, however, is not symmetrical: husbands who support their wives' careers are lauded as the praiseworthy exceptions rather than the rule.

Our third hypothesis, therefore is:

3. *Burnout is more strongly associated with the feeling of having interfered with spouse's career for women than it is for men.* In his process model of burning out, Cherniss (1980) views "doubts about competence" as an important stressor for professionals in general. Work, however, remains a more central aspect of masculine than of feminine self identity. There is evidence, furthermore, that perceived failure in work-related activities is more strongly associated with burnout among men than among women (Etzion, 1987a). For example, in a study of school administrators, Tung (1980) found that men were more bothered than women by such role-based stressors as feeling that they have too little authority to carry out their responsibilities, knowing they can't get information needed to carry out their job, and thinking they will not be able to satisfy the conflicting demands of their superiors.

Our fourth hypothesis, therefore, is:

4. *Burnout is more strongly associated with doubts about success in work performance for men than it is for women.* A women's employment outside the home is more accepted today as legitimate and even as providing a welcome source of additional income for the family (Bernard, 1984). This is provided, however, she is able to "balance" her double burden. This feat often entails constraining her ambition, limiting her

commitment to work and suppressing her need for achievement. A number of studies (Bailyn, 1987; Beutell, 1986; Etzion, 1988) show that women who are highly involved in their work or who attach high importance to success in career are more likely to experience conflict or burnout. Holahan and Gilbert (1979) found that career aspirations in dual-career couples were positively correlated with role conflict for women but negatively correlated with role conflict for men.

Our fifth hypothesis, therefore is:

5. *Burnout is more strongly associated with the need for achievement and dominance and with work involvement for women than it is for men.*

A major source of strain in a dual career marriage is the potential for competition between husband and wife over status. Problems arise when women break the "one step behind rule" (Bernard, 1974) or surpass their husbands in salary and status (Cooper, 1982). A number of studies report that success in dual-career marriages depends on the husband's earning more than his wife and the wife's treating her work as secondary (Poloma, 1972; Rapoport & Rapoport, 1969). A situation in which the wife's income or occupational status is greater than that of her husband is incongruent with social norms and can be a severe source of strain, especially for the husband. Since those engaged in the same occupation are familiar with its culture and its symbols of status, occupational prestige in physician couples is easily compared and highly visible. This makes incongruence potentially more problematic than among couples engaged in very different types of occupations.

Our sixth hypothesis, therefore, is:

6. *Burnout is greater for husbands whose status is lower than that of their wives compared to husbands whose status is higher than that of their wives.*

METHODS

Sample

An attempt was made to include the total Israeli population of practising medical doctors (excluding dentists), under age 69 who were married to each other and living in the same household. The privacy act prevented our getting official access to the names of medical couples through the medical association or any other source, so we had no way of knowing the exact size of the population. The original list of 300 couples was taken from the 1979-1980 directory of the Israel medical association, the last year in which the directory was updated and was complete. All identical family names of doctors living at the same address with a male and female first name were assumed to be married couples. (Women in Israel rarely fail to adopt their husbands' surname). Additional names were drawn from the list of current recipients of the official publication of the Israel medical association. More names, especially of younger couples, were received through informal channels from all the major medical schools and teaching hospitals in the country and a few additional names were supplied by respondents. The fact that each supplemental source included names which we already had, reassured us that we had covered the field fairly well.

Of the original 400 couples, there were about 100 in which either one or both spouses were deceased, critically ill, retired, emigrated from Israel, temporarily on extended leave out of the country, divorced, or new immigrants who did not know Hebrew well enough to answer. These were excluded from the sample. About 20 refused to answer because they were too busy; 30 said they had returned the completed questionnaire but we had not received it, and four of these sent a second questionnaire. We were unable to make telephone contact with about 50 couples from the 1979-80 list to whom we had sent questionnaires but who had not replied and whose names were not listed either in the phonebook or with telephone information. We have no information about their eligibility for inclusion, whether they received the questionnaire or even if they still exist. About 50 promised by telephone that they would reply but we did not receive their replies. Two questionnaires were not included because a reply was received from only the wife. An additional 11 completed questionnaires were excluded from this analysis because at least one of the spouses was over age 68. The final sample consisted of 126 couples which is 53 percent of those known to have received the questionnaire who met the criteria for participation.

Procedure

A total of 800 questionnaires were sent to 400 couples, an identical, but separate one for each spouse. A self-addressed and stamped return envelope was included. Couples wishing to receive a summary of the findings were asked to include their names and address: over 80 percent did so, which gave us some indication of who had replied. Questionnaires were followed by two reminders: a postcard and then a telephone call.

RESULTS

Dependent Variable

In his study of burnout as a theoretical construct, Ezrachi (1985) found "energy depletion" to be its major component. In this study, *burnout* was measured with an index adapted from Ezrachi (1985) and constructed from two items which relate to exhaustion or feelings of energy depletion. Respondents were asked:"When you think of yourself at work in the last while how often do you experience the following: 'I am full of energy.'"

"I feel like my batteries are running low."

Response range: 1 (very infrequently) to 5 (very frequently) (Cronbach's alpha = .64).

Independent Variables

Work-family conflict was measured by a four item index taken in part from Beutell and Greenhaus (1982). Respondents were asked how often the following statements apply to them: "My family life disturbs me in meeting the goals in my work." "My responsibility to the home and family make it difficult for me to devote all the time I would like to my work." "My work hours conflict with my family life." "I feel guilty that maybe my child(ren) lose(s) something because of my career." Response range: 1 (very infrequently) to 5 (very frequently) (Cronbach's alpha = .76).

Two additional individual items taken from Peres and Katz (1984) measured the positive aspects of combining work and family with the following statements: "My work helps me to be a better spouse." "My children rather benefit from my work—I am able to give more to them." Response range was from 1 (very infrequently) to 5 (very frequently).

Interference with spouse's career was measured by the following question: "How would you rate your contribution to your spouse's career?" Response range was from 1 (I contributed a great deal) to 5 (I interfered a great deal).

Doubts about success in work performance was measured by three individual items. Respondents were asked to what extent they were troubled by the following: "I don't have enough influence over the activities and decisions in the organization." "I don't have enough skills to cope with my job in the way I would like to." "The feeling that I have to prove myself all the time." Response range was from 1 (not at all) to 5 (a very great deal).

Need for dominance and achievement was measured using a 12-item version of the Steers and Braunstein (1976) 16 item Manifest Needs Questionnaire which measures need for achievement, for autonomy, for affiliation, and for dominance. A factor analysis resulted in a somewhat different factor structure than that found by Steers and Braunstein and in a different factor structure for men and women. Achievement and dominance items were mixed into one factor. An index of need for dominance/achievement was constructed from the four items common to the first factor for both men and women. These included: "I find myself organizing and directing the activities of others." "I strive to be 'in command' when I am working in a group." "I take moderate risks and stick my neck out to get ahead at work." "I try to perform better than my co-workers." Respondents were asked to what extent each of these statements describes their behavior at work. Response range was 1 (not at all) to 5 (very much) (Cronbach's alpha = .69).

Work involvement was used as an additional indicator of willingness to invest in the job. It was measured by a three-item index which included: "The most important things I do are related to my job." "My greatest pleasure in life comes from my job." "Things related to my work continue to occupy me even after work hours." Response range was 1 (not at all) to 5 (a great extent) (Cronbach's alpha = .68).

Status competition was measured along four different dimensions. For each, two groups were created—one in which the husband was superior to his wife and the other in which he was inferior to her. For each dimension couples equal in status were not included in the analysis. The four dimensions included: contribution to family income (contributes more/less than his wife); place of work (he in hospital, she not/ she in hospital, he not); husband's self-rating of his occupational status (higher/lower than that of wife), status of medical specialization (husband's specialization higher/lower than that of his wife). A three point measure of medical specialization status was constructed on the basis of a combination of the following criteria: length of training; whether it is surgical, internal or other; extent to which it is performed in a hospital setting; the likelihood of having to cope with emergencies, which according to Freidson (1970), is a major source of power for a hospital department. The criteria are not mutually exclusive and expert judges were used to classify the 35 different specializations.

Characteristics of the sample. The mean age of the sample was 45 years for women, with a range of 26-44; 47 for men with a range of 28-64 years. Eighty two percent of the women and 88 percent of the men had completed a specialization in medicine: mean years of seniority in the specialization was 12.6 for women, 13.3 for men. Forty-eight percent of the women and 67 percent of the men were employed in hospitals: an additional 37 and 21 percent respectively were employed in clinics of one of the health funds. With only rare exceptions, all hospitals in Israel are publicly owned and operated whether by the government or the Histadrut (Israel Federation of Labor) health fund. Since private medicine has been almost nonexistent until recently, the major source of status is based more on occupational prestige and reputation than on income. Thus the husbands' and wives' relative contribution to family income was very similar: 56 percent and 44 percent respectively. The couples had an average of two children; only 6 percent had no children. The average age at birth of first child for women was 27, the maximum age was 31 years.

TABLE 1 Paired Comparison of Doctors by Sex (n=252)[a]

Variable	Women x	Women sd	Men x	Men sd	t(pairs)
Home-work conflict: index	2.46	0.91	2.26	0.91	2.22*
Better parent	2.77	1.30	2.50	1.29	2.01*
Better spouse	2.74	1.43	2.52	2.37	1.73ns
Need for achievement/dominance	3.19	0.81	3.64	0.69	5.15**
Work involvement	3.48	0.72	3.76	0.63	3.46
Worry about work performance:					
Insufficient influence	2.89	1.12	2.92	1.15	0.27ns
Insufficient skills	2.10	1.02	1.91	0.99	2.09*
Need to prove myself	2.63	1.33	2.48	1.11	1.07ns
Contribution to spouse's career	2.20	0.75	2.20	0.80	0.44ns
Housework (hours daily)	2.14	1.23	1.33	0.94	7.05**
Professional work (hours daily)	7.61	1.99	9.07	2.00	6.78**
Burnout (energy depletion)	2.27	0.83	2.31	0.84	0.30ns

Key: response range for all measures 1 (low) - 5 (high)
[a] Because of missing values, the n varies slightly for each variable.
*p < .05; **p < .01

For 98 percent of the women and 97 percent of the men, this was the first marriage.

The professional workload of the women was less than that of the men. Fewer of them were in specializations involving frequent emergencies or night work, and they worked at their jobs fewer hours a day ($\bar{x}$ = 7.6 hours for women and 9.1 for men). They were less likely to hold a second job (31 percent held a second job compared to 48 percent of the men). They did after work home calls or hospital night shifts less often (61 percent made such calls less than once in two weeks or not at all, compared to 38 percent of the men). On the other hand, the domestic workload of the women was greater than that of the men. According to self-reports, women daily spent an average of 2.7 hours on childcare compared to 1.6 hours for men; 2.2 hours on domestic work compared to 1.1 hours for men and 1.1 hours on various tasks for the family outside the home compared to 1.0 hours for men. In total, women spent six hours and men 3.7 hours a day on family work. We found that the women in this study experienced

TABLE 2 Pearson Correlations of the Principal Variables with Burnout by Sex (n=115)

Variable	Women r	Men r	Fischer's r to z
Home-work conflict: index	-.03	.18*	1.73*
Better parent	-.15*	-.02	
Better spouse	-.20*	-.20*	
Need for achievement/dominance	-.31**	-.21*	
Work involvement	-.23**	-.19*	
Worry about work performance:			
Insufficient influence	-.02	.21**	1.81*
Insufficient skills	.02	.14°	
Need to prove myself	-.04	.20**	1.94*
Contribution to spouse career	.09	-.27**	1.35°
Housework (% of total done by couple)	.06	-.27**	2.40**

*$p < .05$; **$p < .01$; °marginal result: $.05 > p < .10$

greater home/work conflict, but felt more strongly than their husbands that their children benefit from their working. They were more worried than the men about having insufficient skills and had less need for achievement/dominance and less work involvement. On all other items, gender differences were not significant. The men and women physicians did not feel differently about the contribution their careers made to their role as spouses, about the extent to which they interfered with their spouses' careers, about having insufficient influence to do a good job, or about needing to constantly prove themselves. (See Table 1). Contrary to prediction, we found that women are not more burned out than men. Hypothesis 1 was not supported.

Contrary to prediction, the correlation between burnout and home/work conflict was not stronger for women. In fact, the correlation was statistically significant for men, but not for women, and the difference between the correlations was statistically significant. Burnout was negatively correlated for men and for women with feelings that the work role enabled the respondent to be a better spouse. With regard to feeling that the work role enabled respondent to be a better parent, the negative correlation with burnout was statistically significant for women, but not for men. The difference between the two correlations was not significant. Hypothesis 2 was not supported.

Contrary to our prediction in hypothesis 3, the correlation between interference with spouse career and burnout was stronger for the men than for the women. The importance for the husband of feeling supportive of his wife's career was also indicated in the previous finding where husbands who believed that their careers helped them to be better spouses (but not necessarily better fathers) were less burned out than those who did not believe this to be the case. Hypothesis 3 was not supported.

For the men, worry about having insufficient influence and about having constantly to prove oneself was associated with burnout, as predicted by hypothesis 4. For both measures, the gender difference in the strength of the correlations was significant. Worrying about having insufficient skill, however, was not a significant source of burnout for the men. Hypothesis 4 was partially supported.

Contrary to hypothesis 5, the need for dominance/achievement and work involvement were negatively correlated with burnout for women and men alike. The finding suggests that women do not pay a higher price for being non-traditional in their ambition and orientation to work, and that perhaps the contrary is the case. Hypothesis 5 was not supported.

None of the four measures of status competition produced a significant difference in burnout between men in the inferior position and men in the superior position. Men who contributed less than their wives to the family income, who did not work in a hospital while their wives did, or who rated their own occupational status as lower than that of their wives, were not more burned out than men in the superior position. For only one of the four measures, the prestige of the medical specialization, was the difference in the direction predicted and approaching significance. The lack of significance in this case may be due to small sample size and to the variance among men in the inferior situation. Hypothesis 6 was not supported.

DISCUSSION

Of the six hypotheses tested in this study, only one received partial support. Self-doubts about work performance seemed to have a stronger negative impact on the men than on the women. As for the remaining five, husbands whose status was inferior to that of their wives were not more burned out than those whose status was superior. In less than eight percent of the couples, however, was the husband inferior to his wife on any one of the three objective status measures, (see Table 3), and only one husband was inferior on more than one dimension. It is possible that the potential impact of status incongruence was mitigated by the fact that incongruence along one dimension was compensated for by congruence on other dimensions. There was not one husband in the sample whose status was consistently lower than that of his wife.

TABLE 3 Burnout—Comparison of Male Doctors by Status Relative to their Wives

Variable	Superior n	x	sd	Inferior n	x	sd	t
Family income	57	2.28	.81	7	2.36	0.80	0.24ns
Place of work	28	2.45	.85	10	2.25	1.28	0.53ns
Self rating of status	29	2.64	.81	21	2.33	0.97	1.18ns
Medical specialty	35	2.28	.91	9	2.60	0.55	1.26ns

The wives were not more burned out than their husbands. The women who were more achievement oriented and involved in their work were less burned out than those who were less so. Although the women experienced greater home/work conflict, its association with burnout was not significant; nor was the association significant between burnout and the contribution the women felt they had made to their husbands' careers.

A possible explanation for the lack of association between home/work conflict and burnout among women may be that women doctors are initially a self-selected, non-traditional group. This is evidenced by the choice of career and the willingness to make such a heavy investment in professional training. Women doctors' early goals make them different from women in many other male dominated occupations, such as managers, who frequently begin their careers without the clear intention of becoming managers (Adler & Izraeli, 1988; Gross & Trask, 1976; Kanter, 1977). Women managers tend to invest fewer years in professional training, and usually become managers after 10-15 years of employment and when their children are no longer infants. In this sample, 82 percent of the women had specialized beyond the basic medical degree, 88 percent had continued to work full time even when their children were small, 89 percent felt strongly that it is the men's obligation to care for the children as much as it is the women's, but only 46 percent considered their own careers to be as or more important than that of their husbands. Even though the women actually devoted more hours to both childcare and housework than their husbands, their career behavior and attitudes suggest that they explicitly expected husbands' support.

The most interesting single result of the study is the unexpected correlation for men between home/work conflict and burnout—a truly serendipidous finding. The fact that for the men, burnout was more strongly associated with being a good spouse than with being a good parent, suggests that the source of the stress is the relationship between the husband and wife. This interpretation is reinforced by the significant correlation found between burnout and husband's feeling that he has interfered with his wife's career. Taken together, the results suggested that feeling helpful to his spouse was a significant ingredient in a husband's level of burnout.

This unanticipated finding led us to search the data for additional evidence to support the argument that a husband's support of his wife affects his well-being. We examined the impact on burnout of the time husbands said they spent on housework. The assumption was that women perceive husbands' participation in housework as a more direct help to themselves than participation in childcare or out of home errands. When the proportion of time a husband spent on housework out of the total time thus spent by the couple was calculated, the result was a negative correlation for men between burnout and the proportion of hours spent on housework ($r = -.27^{**}$). In other words, the men who were more helpful at home were also less burned out. (The correlation between burnout and proportion of housework done by women was not significant; $r = .06$).

We also had indirect data about husbands' perceived rights regarding their wives' careers. Respondents were asked to indicate the extent of their agreement with the statement: "A woman who refuses to give up her job in order to move with her husband to another place will be responsible if the marriage breaks down." The more men (but not women) agreed with the statement the higher their level of burnout ($r = .25^{**}$).

The results are even more surprising when we consider that the questions about burnout related specifically to work. The significance of the wife's satisfaction for the husband's well-being at work has also been suggested by studies of male executives in multinational corporations (Guest & Williams, 1973 and Izraeli, Banai & Zeira, 1980). Successful performance of male executives was found to be influenced by the adjustment of their wives to the foreign environment. The conflicts the male doctors experienced in relation to their wives and their wives' careers appear to spill over and affect their experiences at work. Combined, these findings suggest that men pay a high price for lack of support to their wives both in the domestic and in the work domain.

In a study of men and women shopfloor labor union representatives (Izraeli & Poraz, 1980), we had found that the male industrial blue-collar workers claimed their union role interfered more strongly with their family lives than did the women. We interpreted this unexpected result as the outcome of self-selection. Women who felt that the union role interfered with family life were less likely to become candidates for a union representative position or to continue in office once elected. Men, on the other hand, were aware of the conflict their union role created for their family role, but could more readily ignore it and the imposition their union activities made on their respective families and were less likely to be deterred by it from union activity.

There is some evidence that among dual career couples these social norms may not operate to the same extent. When a man is married to a woman of equal or higher occupational status, his failure to meet the expectations associated with the spouse/father role is more difficult to ignore or legitimate. Greenhaus and Kopelman (1981), for example, found that men whose wives were employed in managerial/professional positions experienced more intense home/work conflict than men whose wives were employed in nonmanagerial/nonprofessional positions. Furthermore, in such cases, the wife is less likely to be supportive of his non-involvement in domestic chores, since it may have important implications for her own occupational involvements and achievements. The association between home/work conflict and burnout among the male doctors in this study seems to reflect the wear and tear of feeling that one is not living up to the standards the couple has set for itself (Hall & Hall, 1980).

In the classic "doctor family," the doctor's wife "is able to offer her husband both active and passive kinds of support that not only nurture and revitalize his career ambitions but also ensure that he is untroubled and unhampered in his quest for career success" (Fowlkes, 1980, p. 8). Medical training socializes doctors to perceive their "specialness" and to expect special consideration from family members (Gerber, 1983). Women, however, bring to their training, expectations internalized during an earlier period in their lives. They enter the profession aware of the potential conflicts it will involve for them. They are better prepared, both psychologically and practically, than are men, for undertaking domestic responsibilities and for coping with home/work conflicts. Consequently when it occurs, they are less burned out by it. Social norms permit, perhaps even compel, women to find practical solutions and develop effective strategies for coping with home/work conflict. They are more likely than men to include family considerations in their career decisions. For example, as noted in the description of the sample, the women in this study were more likely than their husbands to be in specializations which permitted greater control over their time and involved fewer emergencies. They worked at their jobs fewer hours a day and were less likely to hold a second job or make after-work home calls. Taken together, these gender differences are in keeping with the normative expectations that women compromise their careers to achieve a balance between the two important domains in their lives.

Not so, for the man. Rosin (1987) observes that "in contrast to the official sanction women have received for entering the traditionally male world of work, men have received virtually no societal encouragement to expand their domestic participation." Employers have not modified their expectations of men in recognition of the fact that they no longer have homemaking wives. The requisites for professional career success retain a rigid time schedule providing a disincentive for men to temper their investments in accordance with the demands and expectations of other roles. The narrowing of the marital age gap between men and women (Central Bureau of Statistics, 1987, p. 99), part of the trend toward more egalitarian relationships, means that at time of marriage both are likely to be in the career building stage of their respective careers. The traditional solution for career building male professionals, namely, to expect their families to adapt to the demands and contingencies of the medical role (Gerber, 1983) is problematic for doctors who are married to doctors. Husbands' burnout in this study may be the result of a lack of fit between the demands or expectations emanating from the physician's role partner at home and those of his role partners at work and the difficulty in finding an effective solution. While the findings of this study are highly unusual, they reflect strains that are deepening in the traditional pattern of husband-wife relations. Greater symmetry in husbands' and wives' roles at home appears to improve the person-environment fit and its positive effects on husband's well-being appear to spill over into the workplace.

Despite the dramatically different demands and expectations for men arising from changes in the roles of the women with whom they live and work, few studies have investigated the career and personal outcomes of these developments for men (Gilbert, 1986; Rosin, 1987). In concluding their review of the literature, Burke and Greenglass (1987) observe that "while there is an abundant literature on the role of the wife as a supportive other to the husband, rarely did [does] one find studies on the role of the husband as a support to his wife in the housewife role." The present study suggests that in a dual-career marriage, the husband's support to his wife, both in the housewife and the professional role, not only assists the wife but also has important payoffs for the husband.

REFERENCES

Adler, N.J., & Izraeli, D.N. (1988). Women in management worldwide. In N.J. Adler and D.N. Izraeli (Eds.), *Women in management worldwide*. New York: M.E. Sharpe.

Bailyn, L. (1987). Experiencing technical work: A comparison of male and female engineers. *Human Relations, 40,* 299-312.

Bar-Yosef, R., Bloom, A., & Levy, Z. (1976). *Role Ideology of Young Israeli Women*. Work and Welfare Research Institute. Hebrew University, Jerusalem.

Berman, E., Sacks, S., & Lief, H. (1975). The two-professional marriage: New conflict syndrome. *Journal of Sex and Marital Therapy, 1,* 242-253.

Bernard, J. (1974). *The Future of Motherhood*. New York: Penguin.

Bernard, J. (1984). The good provider role: Its rise and fall. In P. Voydanoff (Ed.), *Work and family: Changing roles of men and women*. Palo Alto, CA: Mayfield.

Beutell, N.K. (1986). Conflict between work-family and student-family roles: Some sources and consequences. In J. Burke and E.R. Greenglass (Eds.), Work and family.

Beutell, N.K. & Greenhaus, J.H. (1982). Interrole conflict among married women: The influence of husband and wife characteristics on conflict and coping behavior. *Journal of Vocational Behavior, 2,* 99-110

Bryson, R., Bryson, J., Johnson, M. (1978). Family size, satisfaction, and productivity in dual-career couples. *Psychology of Women Quarterly, 3,* 67-77.

Burke, R. J., & Greenglass, E.R. (1987). Work and family. In C.L. Cooper and I. Robertson (Eds.), *International Review of Industrial and Organization Psychology* (pp. 273-320). New York: John Wiley.

Central Bureau of Statistics (1987). *Statistical Abstract of Israel:* Vital statistics. Jerusalem.

Cherniss, C. 1980. *Professional Burnout in Human Service Organizations*. New York: Praeger.

Cooper, C.L. (1982). *Executive Families Under Stress*. New Jersey: Prentice Hall.

Etzion, D. (1987a). *Burnout the hidden agenda of human distress*. (Working paper no. 930/87). Tel Aviv University, The Israel Institute for Business Research.

Etzion, D. (1988b). Burning out in management: A comparison of women and men in matched organizational positions. *Israel Social Science Review: A Multidisciplinary Journal*.

Etzion, D. (1988). Burnout and work/nonwork success in male and female engineers: A matched pairs comparison. *Human Resource Management Journal, 5,* 147-163

Etzion, D., & Blitz, T. (1985). Life and work factors affecting the burning out of women in management positions. Paper presented at the Conference of the Israeli Sociological Society, February.

Ezrachi, Y. (1985). *Burnout in managerial and command positions: A construct validation of a concept*. Unpublished Doctoral Dissertation (Hebrew). Tel Aviv University, Israel.

Fowlkes, M.R. (1980). *Behind every successful man: Wives of medicine and academe*. New York: Columbia University Press.

Freidson, E. (1970). *Profession of medicine*. New York: Dodd, Mead & Co.

Gerber, L.A. (1983). *Married to their careers: Career and family dilemmas in doctors' lives*. New York: Tavistock Publications.

Gilbert, L.A. (1986). *Men in dual career families: Current realities and future prospects*. Hillsdale, New Jersey: Lawrence Erlbaum Assocs.

Greenhaus, J.H,. & Kopelman, R.E. (1981). Conflict between work and nonwork roles: Implications for the career planning process. *Human Resource Planning, 4*, 1-10

Gross, N.E., & Trask, A.E. (1976). *The Sex factor and the management of schools*. New York: Wiley.

Guest, D., & Williams, R. (1973). How home affects work. *New Society, 9*, 14-19.

Hall, D.T. (1972). A model of coping with role conflict: The role behavior of college educated women. *Administrative Science Quarterly, 17*, 471-486.

Hall, D.T., & Hall, F.S. (1980). Stress and the two career couple. In C.L. Cooper and R. Payne (Eds.), *Current concerns in occupational stress*. New York: Wiley.

Hazleton, L. (1977). *Israeli women: The reality behind the myths*. New York: Simon and Schuster.

Herman, J.B., & Gyllstrom, K.K. (1977). Working men and women: Inter- and intra-role conflict. *Psychology of Women Quarterly, 1*, 319-333.

Hertz, R. (1986). *More equal than others: Women and men in dual-career marriages*. Berkeley: University of California Press.

Holahan, C.K., & Gilbert, L.A. (1979). Conflict between major life roles: Women and men in dual career couples. *Human Relations, 32*, 451-467.

Hunt, J.G., & Hunt, L.L. (1982). Dual career families: Vanguard of the future or residue of the past? In J. Aldous (Ed.), *Two Paychecks: Life in Dual-earner Families*. Beverly Hills, CA: Sage.

Izraeli, D.N., & Poraz, A. (1980). *Women and men as shopstewards*. Research report (Hebrew). Institute for Research into Work and Society (Hebrew). Tel Aviv University, Israel.

Izraeli, D.N., Banai, M., & Zeira, Y. (1980). Women executives in subsidiaries of multinational corporations. *California Management Review, 22*, 53-64.

Johnson, C.L,. & Johnson, F.A. (1977). Attitudes toward parenting in dual-career families. *American Journal of Psychiatry, 134*, 391-395.

Kanter, R.M. (1977) *Men and women of the corporation*. New York: Basic Books.

Lorber, J. (1984). *Women physicians: Careers status and power*. New York: Tavistock Publications.

Meissner, M. (1985). The domestic economy—half of Canada's work: Now you see it, now you don't. In M. Safir, M.T. Mednick, D. Izraeli, & J. Bernard (Eds.), *Women's worlds: From the new scholarship*. New York: Praeger.

Mortimer, J., Hall, R. & Hill, R. (1978). Husband's occupational attributes as constraints on wives' employment. *Sociology of Work and Occupations, 5*, 285-313.

Papanek, H. (1975). Men, women, work: Reflections on the two-person career. *American Journal of Sociology, 78*, 852-872.

Peres, Y., & Katz, R. (1984). *The employed mother and her family*. Research Report. (Hebrew) Ministry of Labor and Welfare, Jerusalem.

Peres, Y., & Katz, R. (1981). Stability and centrality: The nuclear family in modern Israel. *Social Forces, 59*, 687-704.

Pines, A. (1987). Burnout in marriage: A comparison between Israel and the United States. *Israel Social Science Research, 5*, 60-75.

Pines, A., & Aronson, E. with Kafry, D. (1981). *Burnout: From tedium to personal growth*. New York: Free Press.

Poloma, M.M. (1972). Role conflict and the married professional women. In C. Safilios-Rothschild (Ed.), *Toward a sociology of women* (pp. 187-198). Lexington, MA: Xerox College.

Pleck, J.H. (1977). The work-family role system. *Social Problems, 24,* 417-427.

Pleck, J.H. & Staines, G.L. (1982). Work schedules and work-family conflict in two-earner couples. In J. Aldous (Ed.), *Two paychecks: Life in dual-earner families.* Beverly Hills, CA: Sage.

Rosin, H.M. (1987). Professional and personal consequences for men of dual income marriages: Organizational and policy implications. Paper presented at the European Congress of Industrial Relations, Herzlia, Israel.

Rapoport, R., & Rapoport, R. (1969). The dual-career family: A variant pattern and social change. *Human Relations, 22,* 3-30.

Steers, R.M., & Braunstein, D.N. (1976). A behaviorally-based measure of manifest needs in work settings. *Journal of Vocational Behavior, 9,* 251-266.

Tung, R.L. (1980). Comparative analysis of the occupational stress profiles of male versus female administrators. *Journal of Vocational Behavior, 17,* 344-355.

Yogev, S. (1981). Do professional women have egalitarian marital relationships? *Journal of Marriage and the Family, 43,* 865-871.

Young, M., & Willmott, P. (1973). *The symmetrical family—A study of work and leisure in the London region.* Boston: Routledge & Kegan Paul.

Mexican-American Professional Women: Role Satisfaction Differences in Single and Multiple Role Lifestyles

Ruth E. Zambrana
UCLA School of Social Welfare, 405 Hilgard Avenue
Los Angeles, CA 90024

Sandra Frith
UCLA Institute for Social Science Research, Los Angeles, CA 90024

The purpose of this paper is to examine the relationship between life role status and the level of personal and professional role satisfaction among 170 Mexican-American professional women. The data were derived from a national survey of Hispanic professional women. The results indicated that role status and responsibility and control in the workplace significantly contribute to personal satisfaction.

Professional Mexican-American women represent a growing population which is vastly underrepresented in the social science literature. Although 15% of all Hispanic women are in professional occupational categories, only 10% of these are of Mexican origin. Little information is available on professional Mexican-American women, particularly with respect to the relationship between multiple roles and personal and professional satisfaction. The major purpose of this paper is to examine this relationship. A secondary focus is to compare selected work and family characteristics and differing lifestyle roles.

Among Hispanic women, generally, increasing attention has been directed at understanding the diversity among the sub-ethnic groups in this community by age, socio-economic status, educational level and ethnic group of origin (Chacon, 1982; Escobedo, 1982; Tienda &Ortiz, 1986). The professional group of Hispanic women is of interest for two reasons: (1) there is a tremendous gap in knowledge in the general social science literature with regard to Hispanic professional women; and (2) they

---

Authors' Notes: The data reported in this paper were collected by the National Network of Hispanic Women (NNHW). We express our gratitude to NNHW for permission to use their data. The first author also acknowledges the support of a UCLA Faculty Career Development Award during the Fall Quarter while this manuscript was being prepared.

©1988 Select Press

possess special and different characteristics relative to other U.S. women. Specific to the latter reason, they are younger; tend to marry younger; have more children earlier; are more likely to be urban; are more likely to divorce or separate; and have higher reported stress in higher education settings (Davis, Haub, & Willette, 1983). A focus on Hispanic women's experiences, particularly their improved occupational status, is critical for two main reasons: to compensate for their regular omission from empirical research and theoretical discussions regarding women and to empirically document the nature of their experiences (Smith, 1983).

The relationship between family and work roles and its influence on physical and mental well-being has been a topic of interest in the last 20 years as increased numbers of women have entered the work force. The increase in labor force participation of professional women is the result of numerous influences: a declining birth rate, higher educational attainment, increased orientation toward a career, financial necessities, changing life styles, and legislative and policy changes (Wallace, 1982).

A major focus of research has been on how women manage multiple roles with particular reference to consequent role strain and role conflict (Johnson & Johnson, 1980; Thompson, 1980; Houseknecht & Macke, 1981). Several authors have identified factors which facilitate or hinder the combining of work and family roles. These include number and ages of children (Iglehart, 1979; Gordon & Kammeyer, 1982; McLaughlin, 1982), availability of social support resources such as childcare and domestic work assistance, role satisfaction, and the relationship between employment, health and mental well-being (Woods and Hulka, 1979; Waldron, 1980; Froberg, et al., 1986.)

Closely related to these areas of investigation has been the examination of how such factors as marital status, number of children, perceived health status, age, social participation, education and income contribute to role and life satisfaction. However, the racial and ethnic comparisons have been predominately between non-professional Black and White women (Freudiger & Almquist, 1985; Kandel et al., 1985).

A limited number of empirical studies on the changing role of Hispanic women have begun to document issues related to the management of roles. These include factors which contribute to paid employment, the role of the husband in assistance with domestic and childcare responsibilities (see e.g., Cooney, 1975; Baca-Zinn, 1980; Ybarra, 1982a, 1982b; Ybarra & Arce, 1981; Hurst & Zambrana, 1982), and most recently how paid employment and household responsibilities influence psychological well-being among Mexican-American women (Krause & Markides, 1985). While the focus of these studies has not been specifically on professional women, they assessed some of the factors which may contribute to fulfilling multiple roles among this population. McNeely (1987) in his review of the literature on professional satisfaction among women was unable to identify any on Hispanic professional women. Since this group of professional women has not been systematically studied, it is expected that their experiences in managing family roles may be predominantly influenced by cultural values and norms, whereas their experiences in work roles may be more similar to professional women in general.

There has been limited exploration on the specific factors which contribute to professional and personal satisfaction in the career paths of professional women. This is partly a result of the fact that only recently have large numbers of women entered professional careers. Personal and professional satisfaction are related to individual and situational factors. Many professional women, due to their lack of traditional family and societal support systems, have remained single or married and not had children (Astin, 1969; Bailyn, 1978). Several studies on dual-career families have shown that the husband's career takes precedence over the wife's (Bryson & Bryson, 1978). On the other hand, specific studies on professional women suggest that salary, sense of control, autonomy and age contribute to professional satisfaction (Betz & Fitzgerald, 1987).

The data on managing the home-work roles and the satisfaction with these roles and overall satisfaction suggest relative differences in role satisfaction by type and number of roles. Some studies have found that the management of multiple roles is detrimental to the health and well being of the women due to role overload and strain (e.g., Bailyn, 1978; Johnson & Johnson, 1980; Hewlett, 1986). Others have shown that the occupant of multiple roles experiences positive effects and satisfaction (Thoits, 1982; Verbrugge, 1986; Muller, 1986a,b). The model guiding current research suggests that marital status, attitudes toward work and perceived satisfaction with role configurations are major determinants of psychological and physical well-being (Hoffman, 1979; Thompson, 1980; Hodson, 1985; Waldron & Herald, 1986). In this study, there was an opportunity to test the relationship between life role status and perceived personal and professional satisfaction on a relatively homogeneous group of Mexican-American professional women.

METHOD

Sample

The data reported here were collected by a mail-out survey, conducted in 1985, to a group of Hispanic managerial and entrepreneurial women whose names appeared on a membership list of a national Hispanic women's professional organization. The overall response rate was 45.1%. Women who owned their own businesses and who were not of Mexican descent were eliminated from the present analyses since previous research has indicated differences in the situational context of managerial-entrepreneurial women as well as Hispanic sub-group ethnic differences. In addition, although the survey included several other Hispanic origin subgroups (Puerto Ricans, Cubans, and Central and South Americans), the number of respondents in each of these ethnic subgroups were too small to allow for subgroup comparative analyses. The study sample consisted of 170 professional women of Mexican descent who constituted the largest subgroup of respondents in this study.

Subgroups

The major focus of this study was to explore potential differences in personal and professional satisfaction among Mexican-American women in differing lifestyle roles. Therefore, a typology of role status groups was developed that would allow categorization on an exclusive and exhaustive basis. Since prior research has suggested that role status is a determinant of personal and professional satisfaction, the sample was parsed into 4 subgroups (Freudiger & Almquist, 1985; Froberg et al., 1986; Betz & Fitzgerald, 1987).

These operational definitions are outlined in Chart 1. A respondent could be categorized into one of four groups based upon responses to three items in the demographic section of the questionaire: 1) "Marital Status?" 2) "Do you have any children?" and 3) "Do you have any step-children?" The four role status groups are: single (defined as one role) work only (W); work and partner (WP); work and maternal role (WM) and three roles which include work, partner and maternal role (WPM). Although both Groups WP and WM could be considered a "two role" category, the distinction between them was maintained because recent findings suggest the possibility of unique differences in role satisfaction in Group WP members, who are career couples without children. Thus, the goal was to preserve qualitative as well as quantitative differences among role status groups.

Demographics

A description of the respondent's background characteristics is provided in Table 1. The mean age of the respondents was 37.2 years. Within the role status groups, the WP Group (Partner Only was the youngest ($\overline{X}$=32.4) while the WM Group (Children Only) was the oldest ($\overline{X}$=40.9). The standard deviation for age did not exceed 7.9 years. With respect to place of birth, the overwhelming majority were born in the United States (93%).

CHART 1 Operational Definitions by Role Status

Group	Name	Description	
Work (W)	One Role/Single	Marital Status:	Single-Never Married Separated Widowed
		Children:	None
Work & Partner (WP)	Two Roles/ Partner Only	Marital Status:	Single-Living with Partner Married-Not Living with Spouse (assumed not to be separated) Married-Living with Spouse
		Children:	None
Work & Mother (WM)	Two Roles/ Children Only	Marital Status:	Single-Never Married Married-Not Living with Spouse (assumed to be separated) Separated Divorced Widowed
		Children:	Yes
Work, Partner, & Mother (WPM)	Three Roles/ Children & Partner	Marital Status:	Single-Living with Partner Married-Living with Partner
		Children:	Yes

The sample was a highly educated group when compared to national norms for Hispanic women. The mean number of years of school completed was 18 for the study sample compared to 12.8 for all women, and 8.9 for Mexican-American women (U.S. Congressional Research Service, 1983). The modal category of education, aggregated for the Mexican-American sample, as well as for each role status group, was completion of post-bachelor's degree work. Only nineteen percent of the sample reported some college education or less. The WP Group was least likely to have completed postgraduate degrees (41%), whereas 54% of the W Group had completed a post graduate degree.

Two questions on income were included in the survey—respondent income and spouse/partner income (if applicable). Respondent rather than household income is reported in Table 1. The sample income is considerably above the national norms for Hispanic women, as well as for women as a whole. The median income category was in the $30,000 to $39,000 per annum range.

The distribution on the work sector variable revealed that the majority of the respondents held positions in the corporate sector (42.6%) and only 12.4% were in public community type organizations. The position

TABLE 1 Sample Characteristics by Role Status

	Role Status Group				
Variable	(W) Single (n=47)	(WP) Partner Only (n=22)	(WM) Children Only (n=30)	(WPM) Partner & Children (n=71)	Total Sample (170)
Age (Mean)	35.0	32.4	40.9	38.6	37.2
	SD=7.9	SD=4.0	SD=7.3	SD=7.9	SD=7.8
Education					
High school/ some college	8.7%	4.5%	26.7%	26.7%	19.0%
College	28.3	45.5	16.7	21.1	25.4
Post Grad/Deg.	54.3	40.9	43.3	42.3	45.5
Other	8.7	9.1	13.3	9.9	10.1
Personal Income					
10-19,999	10.9%	4.5%	10.3%	7.1%	8.3%
20-29,999	19.5	40.9	13.7	24.0	23.2
30-39,999	37.0	36.4	31.0	33.8	34.6
Over 40,000	32.6	18.2	45.0	35.0	33.9
Work Sector					
Corporate	42.6%	50.0%	36.7%	42.3%	42.4%
Higher Education	21.3	27.3	23.3	29.6	25.9
Public-Government	27.7	18.2	23.3	12.7	19.4
Public-Community	8.5	4.5	16.7	15.5	12.4
Position Level					
Entry Staff	2.2%	4.8%	—	4.3%	3.0%
Middle Staff	11.1	23.8	10.3	17.4	15.2
Senior Staff	13.3	28.6	10.3	11.6	14.0
Entry Management	17.8	19.0	17.2	5.8	12.8
Middle Management	22.2	9.5	31.0	39.1	29.3
Senior Management	11.1	14.3	6.9	8.7	9.8
Executive	20.0	—	13.8	2.9	9.1
CEO	2.2	—	10.3	10.1	6.7
Budget Responsibility					
None	19.6%	36.4%	20.7%	20.6%	22.4%
Under $50,000	17.4	18.2	10.3	23.5	18.8
50-149,999	10.9	13.6	3.4	11.8	10.3
150-299,999	15.2	—	13.8	13.2	12.1
300-499,999	13.0	—	17.2	7.4	9.7
500-Million	13.0	13.6	6.9	13.2	12.1
One Million +	10.9	18.2	27.6	10.3	14.5

level variable clearly showed that 80% of the respondents were in middle to senior level positions. The level of budget responsibility among respondents varied, but over 50% of respondents managed budgets between $150,000- $1 million.

Instrument

The instrument consisted of 109 items of the following types: Closed-ended questions with Likert type response options, multiple choice or items which involved ranking and two open-ended items. The open-ended questions were: "What is your occupation?" and "What is the title of your position?" The questionnaire contained the following sections: general socio-demographic characteristics, current employment status, work history, management of multiple roles, physical and emotional health, and personal and professional satisfaction. Data reported in this paper were obtained from the socio-demographic, current employment status, multiple roles and personal and professional satisfaction sections.

Analyses

Preliminary analyses included viewing the four study groups on a selection of socio-demographic characteristics and work and family related variables. Depending upon the nature of the dependent variable, either univariate anovas, student's t or chi square analysis was performed. Next, responses to the overall satisfaction items, personal and professional, were examined using one way analysis of covariance followed by Newman-Keuls tests.

RESULTS

Selected Family and Work Variables by Role Status

Table 2 presents a summary of selected family and work variables by role status. One item in the survey asked respondents to rank order a list of five categories of life values from highest (1) to lowest (5). Mean scores for each item were computed, and significant group differences were found. First, the group with work, mother, and partner roles (WPM) differed from all others in assigning highest priority to "Work and Career Goals." "Personal Development," a focus on the individual, was the second highest ranked item for single respondents with no children (W). For Groups WP, WM and WPM, this item was ranked third. Not surprisingly, "Marriage/Family Life" was the highest ranked item for Group WPM, who were significantly different from Groups W, WP and WM (p ≤ .05). Single respondents with no children (Group W) ranked this item third. Finally, although there were significant differences among groups in the ranking of "Social Life and Entertainment," all groups ranked it lower than the previous three life value categories. Group W rated it

TABLE 2 Selected Work and Family Characteristics by Role Status

Variable	(W) Single (n=47)	(WP) Partner Only (n=22)	(WM) Children Only (n=30)	(WPM) Partner & Children (n=71)
Ranking of Life Priorities (1 = Highest)				
Work/Career Goals	1.65 (1)[d]	1.86 (1)	1.50 (1)	2.04 (2)*[a]
Personal Development	1.85 (2)	2.27 (3)	2.44 (3)	2.61 (3)*[a]
Marriage/Family Life	2.93 (3)	1.95 (2)	2.29 (2)	1.49 (1)*[a]
Social Life/Entertainment	3.85 (4)	3.95 (4)	3.90 (4)	4.14 (4) *[a]
Rating of Job Stress (1=least / 5=most)	3.96	3.82	3.62	3.59[a]
Hours Worked Per Week				
Mean	50.36	50.41	50.75	48.99[a]
SD	7.18	9.06	9.55	9.27
Percent Who Have Taken a Leave of Absence from Work	12.8	18.2	33.3	52.9*[b]
Factors Ranked Highest in Choice of a new Job				
Work Gives Sense of Accomplishment	2.95 (1)[d]	3.13 (1)	3.21 (2)	2.88 (1)[a]
Independent/Autonomy	3.37 (3)	4.00 (4)	3.43 (3)	3.39 (2)[a]
Higher Income	3.18 (2)	3.41 (2)	3.07 (1)	3.48 (3)[a]
Opportunity for Advancement	3.47 (4)	3.77 (3)	3.75 (4)	4.17 (4)[a]
Rating of Extent Work Role Interferes with Role as Parent (1=least / 5=most)	NA	NA	2.61	2.92*[c]
SD			0.63	0.65
Rating of Extent Parent Role Interferes with Work (1=least / 5=most)	NA	NA	2.21	2.39[c]
SD			0.74	0.81
Rating of Difficulty of Balance Role as Partner and Professional (1=least / 5=most)	NA	2.81	NA	2.99[c]
SD		1.12		1.11

*$p \leq .05$.
[a] One way Anova; [b] Chi square; [c] t-test; [d] Group rank.

highest while Group WPM rated it lowest. On the basis of these results there is an indication that, among respondents with children and a partner (WPM), the first priority is home and the family. All other groups ranked work/career goals highest.

Descriptive information was also obtained on work-related variables such as perceived level of stress, work leaves and job factors related to choice of job. Perception of job stress did not differ significantly among the four groups, with all groups perceiving their work as at least moderately stressful. Significant differences were found between role status groups and taking a leave of absence from work (p .05). Groups WM and WPM reported having taken a leave substantially more often than Groups W and WP.

Three questions were asked regarding the management of partner, parent and professional roles which indirectly explored potential multiple role conflict. Those with partners, with or without children, were asked to rate the difficulty in balancing the professional and partner roles. Findings indicated no significant differences between Groups WP and WPM.

Those with children, with or without partners, were asked to rate the extent of work interference with their role as a parent and vice versa. Group WPM reported significantly more interference of work with parent role than did Group WM. However, the two groups did not differ significantly in their reporting of parent role interference in the work place.

Personal and Professional Satisfaction

A number of variables which have a strong correlation with professional and personal satisfaction have been reported in the literature. As such, analyses should control for as many of these correlates as possible. Three of these variables were available for inclusion as covariates: 1) Age of the respondent; 2) position level (thought to be related to sense of personal control); and 3) professional responsibility was operationalized as the budget dollar amount for which there was direct responsibility. Results of the analyses are summarized in Table 3.

With respect to professional satisfaction, the role status main effect, adjusted for the covariates, was not significant. However, professional satisfaction was found to be highly related to age, as indicated by its significance as a covariate. Thus, the presence or absence of partners and/or children (role status) did not appear to be an instrumental factor in the level of professional satisfaction.

Results of personal satisfaction were significant for both the main effect and two of the covariates, budget responsibility and position level. Neuman-Keul's post hoc tests revealed that Groups W, WP and WPM had significantly higher personal satisfaction scores than Group WM. Per-

TABLE 3 Analysis of Covariance for Personal and Professional Satisfaction

Source	SS	df	MS	F
Professional Satisfaction				
Covariates	7.17	3	2.39	2.64*
Age	3.44	1	3.44	3.81*
Budget Responsibility	0.42	1	0.42	0.46
Position Level	0.38	1	0.38	0.42
Main Effect				
Role Status	1.47	3	0.49	0.54
Error	135.62	150	0.90	
Personal Satisfaction				
Covariates	5.92	3	1.97	2.36*
Age	0.13	1	0.13	0.16
Budget Responsibility	5.29	1	5.29	6.33*
Position Level	3.16	1	3.16	3.79*
Main Effect				
Role Status	19.71	3	6.57	7.86*
Error	125.39	150	0.84	

*p .05.

sonal satisfaction was highest for Group WP ($\overline{X}$=4.27), those with partners but no children, and lowest ($\overline{X}$=3.27) for those with children but no partners (Group WM). Thus, personal satisfaction, but not professional satisfaction, appears to be influenced by role status. While age appears to be a strong intervening variable in professional satisfaction (r=0.21, p .05), the same cannot be said for personal satisfaction (r=-0.03). Budget responsibilities (r=0.12, p .05) and position level (r=0.15, p =.05) were significant covariates in the personal satisfaction analyses.

DISCUSSION

The characteristics of the respondents in the study reflect the attributes of a highly mobile professional group of women. As a result, their particular socioeconomic characteristics are best viewed within a historical cohort framework. In many respects, the respondents reflect young, urban professionals, members of the baby boom generation with college educations and high paying jobs. They were also beneficiaries of cultural and political changes in the 1970's which provided educational and occupational opportunities for all women (Wallace, 1982; Hammond, 1986; Romero & Garza, 1986).

The findings suggest the following relationships for Mexican-American professional women: 1) Role status group does play a part in personal but not professional satisfaction; 2) age is positively and highly related to professional satisfaction, independent of role status; 3) the extent to which women hold responsibility and have control in the workplace is related to personal satisfaction, independent of role status; 4) having children affects both short and long term absences from work; 5) when both a partner and children are in place, family life takes precedence over work and career goals; 6) economic factors in the choice of jobs is extremely important for those raising children alone, and 7) career roles have a tendency to interfere most with parent roles for those having both a partner and children.

The findings of this study lend some support to existing literature on factors which facilitate the management of multiple roles and suggest relationships of role statuses to personal and professional satisfaction. Several authors have found that women with small children in the home have greater levels of psychological distress (Nathanson, 1980; Krause & Markides, 1985). Thus, those areas which have been identified as causing more psychological distress, such as lack of assistance with childcare and housework, are not as powerful among these women due to either their having no children or older children. Apparently their high income level may permit them the option to use other resources to assist with these household responsibilites. Interestingly, although over half (60%) of the women reported that work interfered with their parenting role, it did not seem to affect their overall satisfaction.

The differences reported were by role status group. The single respondents were more likely to report higher work related stress, a higher priority on work career goals and personal development. These data substantiate the findings of Kandel et al. (1985), who found that single working respondents had higher levels of occupational stress. These single respondents may also represent a high-achieving, career oriented group who tend to be single and childless by choice (Astin, 1969). Thus for this group, career achievements at a relatively young age may contribute to professional satisfaction. For this group of women both societal gender expectations and cultural normative expectations may contribute to lower levels of personal satisfaction. It may also be that divorced and separated women who are currently single are seeking to resolve relationship issues with prior partners. These competing hypotheses need to be empirically tested.

A surprising finding was the high personal satisfaction among the women with partners only. This group was characterized by high priority in work-career and family life and the highest levels of personal satisfaction. This group of professional women may represent a unique subsample of highly committed professional women who tend to remain childless. In a recent study on attitudes regarding childlessness, Huber and Spitze (1983) concluded that there has been a reduction in social pressure to have children. This group may be experiencing the greatest personal satisfaction due to the opportunity to select a culturally divergent lifestyle.

Single mothers with children (divorced or separated) seemed to report the least personal satisfaction, and ranked work/career as highest priority. Furthermore, income was a major factor in choice of a new job. The factors which contribute to lower personal satisfaction may be related to their parenting responsibilities which hinder their extra-professional activities and other personal development activities. On the other hand, these women may also represent a group of career-oriented women whose marriage was disrupted by their priority on work/career development as reflected by their having the highest percent (45%) earning over $40,000. The literature on dual career marriages has shown the difficulties in managing work and home roles (Bryson & Bryson, 1978; Hewlett, 1986).

The data on women with most complex role configuration (worker, partner and parent) exhibited the lowest rating of job stress, the highest priority on marriage/family life, and the highest percentage of taking a leave of absence from work. They experienced relatively high levels of personal satisfaction which may be related to their age, having older children, and their economic and career stability. These data substantiate other studies which found that multiple role occupants experienced high role satisfaction (Thoits, 1982; Verbrugge, 1986; Muller, 1986a).

CONCLUDING COMMENTS

The study underlines the theoretical importance of developing typologies which differentiate number and types of roles This provides a more accurate assessment of personal and professional satisfaction among women. The major departures from existing models of analysis for understanding the management of multiple roles in this study were in three areas: (1) the assessment of both personal and professional satisfaction by role set; (2) control for occupational status and income levels; and (3) categories of distinct and mutually exclusive roles at a specific point in time. The inclusion of these additional parameters have clear implications for future studies. Replications need to modify the typology to account for differences in type of work, number and ages of children, socio-economic status and race and ethnicity.

The complexity of role management is related to a host of coping responses and societal and cultural prescriptions which do not lend themselves easily to measurement. Our typology provided a framework for testing and comparing across groups. However, it did not permit an in-depth study of the multifaceted aspects of the interplay of ethnicity, cultural and professional status.

Several studies have suggested that Hispanic and other racial-ethnic groups of professional women experience many conflicts and obstacles in their personal and professional lives. These include racism, tokenism, sexism, isolation and cultural conflicts. These constitute psychological and social barriers which represent the "costs" of professionalism in dominant culture institutions (Geiselman, 1979; Center for the Study, Education and Advancement of Women, 1983). The coping mechanisms used to balance work, family and parenting roles and their relationship to personal and professional satisfaction is another important area for future research.

Future research studies also need to examine the career paths of Hispanic professional women and how they vary not only from dominant culture women but also how they vary within Hispanic sub-ethnic groups. For Mexican-American women specifically, future studies need to examine the educational and career trajectories and identify those factors which contribute to their occupational mobility. Possible contributing factors which necessitate more in-depth analysis are their experiences in the workplace, and the types of stressors and the types of social supports (family and organizational) available in the different settings which impede or facilitate their upward mobility.

Studies of professional women have yet to rank order comparisons of professional and personal satisfaction among these role status groups. Yet, studies on non-professional women suggest differences by class and ethnicity. The present study was an attempt to evaluate the personal and professional dimensions of satisfaction in a related group of Mexican-American women. Thus, future research should involve cross-disciplinary efforts with systematic controls. This is an area where there has been limited attention.

REFERENCES

Astin, H. (1969). *The woman doctorate in America*. New York: Russell Sage Foundation.

Baca-Zinn, M. (1980). Employment and education of Mexican-American women: The interplay of modernity and ethnicity in eight families. *Harvard Educational Review, Women in Education, Part II*, (50).

Bailyn, L. (1978). Accomodation of work to family. In R. and R. Rapaport (Eds.), *Working Couples* (pp. 159-174). New York: Harper and Row.

Betz, N.E., & Fitzgerald, L.F. (1987). *The career psychology of women*. London: Academic Press.

Bryson, J.B., & Bryson, R. (Eds.). (1978). Dual career couples. *Psychology of Women Quarterly, 3* (special issue), 1-120.

Chacon, M. (1982). *Chicanas in postsecondary education*. Stanford, CA: Center for Research on Women, Stanford University.

Cooney, R.S. (1975). Changing labor force participation of Mexican-American wives: A comparison with Anglos and Blacks. *Social Science Quarterly*, (September), 252-261.

Davis, G., Haub, C., & Willette, J. (1983). U.S. Hispanics: Changing in the face of America. *Population Bulletin*. Washington, DC: Population Reference Bureau, Inc., *38*, (3).

Escobeda, T. (Ed.). (1982). Chicana issues. *Hispanic Journal of Behavioral Sciences, 4*, (2).

Freudiger, D., & Almquist, E. (1985). Sources of life satisfaction: The different worlds of black women and white women. In *Black working women debunking the myths: A multidisciplinary approach* (pp. 93-118). Proceedings of a research conference to examine the status of black working women in the United States. Berkeley, CA: Center for the Study, Education and Advancement of Women, University of California, Berkeley.

Froberg, D., Gjerdingen, D., & Preston, M. (1986). Multiple roles and women's mental and physical health: What have we learned? *Women and Health, 11*(2), 79-96.

Geiselman, L.A. (1979). *Proceedings of the Conference on the Minority Woman in America: Professionalism at what cost?* University of California, San Francisco, March 16-18.

Gordon, H.A., & Kammeyer, K.C. (1982). The gainful employment of women with small children. *Journal of Marriage and the Family, 44*, 407-419.

Hammond, J.L. (1986). Yuppies. *Public Opinion Quarterly, 50*, 487-501.

Hewlett, S.A. (1986). *A lesser life: The myth of women's liberation in America*. New York: William Morrow.

Hodson, R. (1985). Workers' comparisons and job satisfaction. *Social Science Quarterly, 66* (2), 266-280.

Hoffman, L.W. (1979). Maternal employment: 1979. *American Psychologist, 34*, 859-865.

Houseknecht, S.K., & Macke, A.S. (1981). Combining marriage and career: The marital adjustment of professional women. *Journal of Marriage and the Family, 43*, 651-661.

Huber, J., & Spitze, G. (1983). *Stratification: Children, housework and jobs*. New York: Academy Press.

Hurst, M., & Zambrana, R.E. (1982). Child care and working mothers in Puerto Rican families (pp. 113-124). *Annals of Political and Social Science*. Special Volume on The Young Child and Social Policy, (461), May.

Iglehart, A.P. (1979). *Married women and work*. Lexington, MA: Lexington Books and D.C. Heath & Co.

Johnson, C.L., & Johnson, F.A. (1980). Parenthood, marriage and careers: Situational constraints and role strain (pp. 143-161). In F. Pepitone-Rockwell (Ed.), *Dual-Career Couples*.

Kandel, D.B., Davies, M., & Raveis, U.H. (1985). The stressfulness of daily social roles for women: Marital, occupational and household roles. *Journal of Health and Social Behavior, 26*, 64-78.

Krause, N., & Markides, K.S. (1985). Employment and psychological well-being in Mexican-American women. *Journal of Health and Social Behavior, 26* (1), 15-26.

McLaughlin, S.D. (1982). Differential patterns of female labor-force participation surrounding the first birth. *Journal of Marriage and the Family, 44*, 407-419.

McNeely, R.L. (1987). *Predictors of job statisfaction among three racial/ethnic groups of professional female human service workers* (unpublished manuscript).

Muller, C. (1986a). Health and health care of employee women and homemakers: Family factors. *Women and Health, 11*(1), 7-26.

Muller, C. (1986b). Health and health care of employed adults: Occupation and gender. *Women and Health, 11* (1), 27-46.

Nathanson, C.A. (1980). Social roles and health status among women: The significance of employment. *Social Sciences and Medicine, 14A*, 463-471.

Romero, G.L., & Garza, R.T. (1986). Attributions for the occupational success/failure of ethnic minority and nonminority women. *Sex Roles, 14*, 445-452.

Smith, E. J. (1983). Issues in racial minorities career behavior (pp. 161-222). In W.B. Walsh & S.H. Osiprow (Eds.), *Handbook of Vocational Psychology*. Hillsdale, NJ: Lawrence Erlbaum.

Tienda, M., & Ortiz, V. (1976). Hispanicity and the 1980 census. *Social Science Quarterly, 1* (67) (March), 3-20.

Thoits, P.A. (1982). Conceptual, methodological, and theoretical problems in studying social support as a buffer against life stress. *Journal of Health and Social Behavior, 23* (2), 145-159.

Thompson, E. (1980). The value of employment to mothers of young children. *Journal of Marriage and the Family, 42*, 551-565.

U.S. Congressional Research Service (1983). *The Hispanic Population of the United States: An overview*. Washington, DC: U.S.Government Printing Office.

Verbrugge, L.M. (1986). Role burdens and physical health of women and men. *Women and Health, 11* (1), 47-77.

Waldron, I. (1980). Employment and women's health: An analysis of causal relationships (Review article). *International Journal of Health Services, 10*, 435-454.

Waldron, I., & Herald, J. (1986). Employment, attitudes toward employment, and women's health. *Women and Health, 11* (1), 79-98.

Wallace, P.A. (Ed.). (1982). *Women in the workplace*. Boston, MA: Auburn House.

Woods, N.F., & Hulka, B.S. (1979). Symptom reports and illness behavior among employed women and homemakers. *Journal of Community Health, 5* (1), 36-45.

Ybarra, L. (1982a). Marital decision-making and the role of machismo in the Chicano family. *DeColores*, Special issue on the family (6), 32-47.

Ybarra, L. (1982b). When wives work: The impact of the Chicano family. *Journal of Marriage and the Family, 44*, 169-177.

Ybarra, L., & Arce, C.H. (1981).*Gender linked division of labor among Chicano couples: An assessment of husband's participation in household chores*. (Unpublished manuscript).

Japanese and American Housewives' Attitudes Toward Employment of Women

John W. Engel

Department of Human Resources, University of Hawaii, 2515 Campus Road, Honolulu, Hawaii 96822

This study compares attitudes toward women's employment held by over 200 Japanese and American housewives. Neither Japanese nor American housewives believe very strongly that they can be happy as full-time housewives. They agree that mothers of infants and pre-schoolers should not be employed outside the home. Japanese housewives tend to believe more strongly that a wife/mother's employment has harmful effects on marriage and child development. They also believe more strongly that a wife/mother should not be employed when her husband wants her home, or when there is a school-aged or teenage child in the family. American housewives tend to believe more strongly that women are capable of handling both homemaking and career responsibilities. Findings are discussed in terms of cultural traditions and change.

In recent years, the world's economic center of gravity shifted to Pacific rim nations, and Japan became the world's wealthiest nation. According to Jack Vliet, Executive Vice President and Chief Investment Officer of brokerage firm Dean Witter Reynolds, Japan experienced or engineered "the most awesome rise in international economic power in modern history" and "in the coming decades Japan's financial power will dominate the world" (1988, p. 3).

What role do Japanese women play in this rise in economic power and wealth? Surely women's direct involvement in the labor force has made a contribution, though women's employment is not nearly as common in Japan as it is in America. Another major factor in growth of Japanese wealth relates to savings and investment. The average Japanese family saves much more of its income than does the average American family. According to traditional Japanese ideals, the Japanese housewife is responsible for the family's financial management. Indeed, the Japanese housewife has been described as "the world's best financial manager" by American financial columnist Sylvia Porter (1981).

Author's Note: An earlier version of this paper was presented at the annual conference of the National Council on Family Relations, Detroit, November 5, 1986. This work was supported by the Hawaii Institute of Tropical Agriculture and Human Resources, Journal Series No. 3251.

©1988 Select Press

Japanese housewives are often viewed as paragons of housewifery, homemaking and domestic arts. Traditionally, Japanese girls were educated to be "good wives and wise mothers." According to Baron Kikuchi (1909, cited by Smith, 1983), a former Minister of Education and President of both Tokyo and Kyoto Universities, a "good wife and wise mother" should be prepared "to help (her working man), for the common interests of the house, and as her share of duty to the state, by sympathy and encouragement, by relieving him of anxieties at home, managing household affairs, looking after the household economy, and, above all, tending the old people and bringing up the children in a fit and proper manner." While many women in traditional Japan did work outside the home, in agriculture and textile industries, the cultural ideal encouraged women to be housewives, that is, "good wives and wise mothers" (Smith, 1983). Traditional ideals continue to be taught in modern Japan, in social studies text books (Lewis & Lewis, 1977), and in compulsory home economics courses (Keiko, 1982).

The Japanese family life cycle has changed dramatically since World War II (Kumagai, 1984), with implications for women's careers in family and employment. While nearly all Japanese women marry, the typical Japanese woman marries later (when she is in her mid or late 20's) and has more time to develop a career than did her predecessors. On the average, Japanese women have their first child one year after marriage and their last child two years later. As a result of relatively short child bearing/rearing periods, contemporary Japanese women also have more time for career development. One might expect corresponding changes in behaviors and values related to women's employment and housewifery. Research carried out in 1982 by the Japanese government (Prime Minister's Office) found that 71 percent of women still believed that "the husband should work outside and the wife should take care of the family and home" (Imai et al., 1985). On the other hand, Kieko (1982) reported that the majority of one sample of female college graduates desired to work prior to the birth of their first child and then again after the child is "older." Thus, at least for some Japanese women, the absence of (presumably dependent) children is a condition that qualifies attitudes toward women's employment. Additional research is needed that specifies more clearly the context and conditions in which women live and work, including the ages of dependent children and attitudes of husbands.

In America also, traditional ideals encouraged women to be housewives and homemakers. However, in recent years, American women have joined the work force in record numbers and attitudes toward women's roles have changed substantially.

Age of dependent children is an important factor that influences labor force participation rates of mothers (Voydanoff, 1987). Mothers of younger children tend to be employed outside the home less than are mothers of older children. In 1950, only 18 percent of mothers with children under the age of 18 were employed outside the home (Waldman, 1983). By 1985, the majority of American mothers, 54 percent of mothers with children under 6 years of age, and 68 percent of mothers with children 6 to 17 years of age were employed outside the home (Hayghe, 1986).

American attitudes toward women's employment have changed dramatically over the years, from negative to positive. Recent surveys tend to find that the majority of contemporary American men and women have positive attitudes towards the general idea of women's employment (Kahn and Crosby, 1985). However, attitudes have been found to be less positive when the focus is on maternal (as opposed to women in general) employment and when mothers are thought to have dependent children of various ages (Engel, 1978).

While Japanese women are commonly assumed to be more traditional/conservative and homogeneous in their attitudes than American women (e.g., O'Reilly, 1983), there are no direct empirical comparisons of Japanese and American attitudes toward women's employment in the literature. This study was designed to test the above assumptions about differences and explore the work/family attitudes of Japanese housewives as compared with a similar sample of American housewives.

METHOD

Subjects and Procedure

The sample consisted of Japanese (N = 136) and American (N = 75) full-time housewives. Japanese and American tourists in Hawaii were approached and asked to fill out a short questionnaire in the presence of a researcher/interviewer. Less than five percent of both groups refused to cooperate. The questionnaires of full-time housewives were selected for analysis. Both groups could be characterized as "middle-class," by American standards, though class differentiation in Japan is controversial. The Japanese women averaged 35 years of age, the American women 36. The Japanese had an average of 13.2 years of education compared with 13.6 for the Americans. While the Japanese women had on the average 1.3 children, the American women had 2.1. Japanese women reported an average household size of 3.5 compared with 3.3 for the American women.

Questionnaire

A questionnaire was designed to assess beliefs and attitudes related to women's roles in work and family life. It included items used in previous research (e.g., Engel, 1978, 1986), that were designed to reflect potential attitude qualifying variables such as age of children and husband's attitude. Items used a Likert scale response format: strongly agree to strongly disagree. After pretesting on American subjects, the English version of the questionnaire was translated into Japanese. The two language versions were pretested and "back translated" (Brislin, 1980) for equivalency and revised accordingly.

RESULTS AND DISCUSSION

The results of comparisons of Japanese and American housewives' attitudes toward women's employment are summarized in Table 1. Differences between means were found to be significant ($p < .05$) in 8 out of 11 comparisons.

While Japanese and American groups did not differ significantly in their beliefs regarding whether they could be happy as full-time housewives (item 1), there was a general tendency for the Japanese to be "uncertain" (mean = 3.35) and the Americans to "agree" (mean = 3.57) that they could be happy as housewives. Japanese responses (SD = .93) to item 1 varied significantly ($F(74,131) = 1.71$, $p < .01$) less than did American responses (SD = 1.22), suggesting that Japanese housewives are more homogeneous in their attitudes related to this issue than are American housewives.

In effect, neither group believed strongly that they could be happy as housewives. This could be interpreted as an indication of dissatisfaction among housewives in both countries. Such an interpretation would be consistent with Lebra's (1984) observation of some devaluation of housewifery in Japan, and Andre's (1981) assessment of housewifery in America. Additional research is needed to explore further how women, both Japanese and American, feel about their current work/family roles, and to identify factors related to variation in satisfaction or "happiness" with those roles. Dissatisfaction with the housewife role may suggest additional changes in women's roles in the future in both Japanese and American societies.

While both Japanese and American groups believed that women are capable of handling both home and career (item 2), American housewives agreed more strongly with this item than did Japanese housewives. It could be that American women were more influenced by the idea popular in America during the 1970's and early 1980's that women "could have it all." It may also be that American women see more women around them who are indeed successfully combining work and family life. Although both groups tended to be uncertain whether "difficulties are likely to arise in marital adjustment when the wife is employed outside the home" (item

TABLE 1 Japanese and American Housewives' Attitudes toward Women's Employment

Attitude	Japanese (n = 136) Mean	American (n = 75) Mean	t
1. I could be happy as a full-time housewife.	3.35	3.57	1.38
2. Women are capable of handling both home and career.	3.58	3.99	3.32**
3. Difficulties are likey to arise in marital adjustment when the wife is employed outside the home.	3.36	2.96	-2.63**
4. Married women should be home having or raising children, instead of being employed outside the home.	2.68	2.26	-2.61**
5. Maternal employment is likely to have harmful effects on children's development.	3.11	2.66	-3.06**
6-11. *Given that a family has adequate financial support, a wife/mother should not work outside the home.*			
6. ... when there is an infant in the family.	4.12	4.07	-0.40
7. ... when there is a preschool-age child in the family.	3.67	3.65	-0.14
8. ....when there is a school-age child in the family.	3.49	3.13	-2.42*
9. ... when there is a teenage child in the family.	3.55	2.80	-5.37***
10. ... when husband wants her home.	3.79	3.07	-4.79***
11. ... when she doesn't want to work outside the home.	3.68	4.28	-5.49***

Note. Means were calculated from Likert scale scores, i.e., 1 = "strongly disagree," 2 = "disagree," 3 = "uncertain," 4 = "agree," and 5 = "strongly agree."

*$p < .05$, **$p < .01$, ***$p < .001$.

3), Japanese housewives agreed with this statement significantly more than did American housewives.

Japanese housewives tended to believe significantly more than American housewives that women belong in the home caring for children. While American housewives tended to disagree, Japanese housewives tended to be uncertain whether "married women should be home, having or raising children, instead of being employed outside the home" (item 4).

Similarly, while both groups tended to be uncertain about whether maternal employment has harmful effects on child development (item 5), Japanese housewives believed this significantly more than did American housewives. It could be that some respondents were uncertain because this item did not differentiate between children of different ages. The results on the following items should help to clarify this question.

Both Japanese and American groups agreed that mothers should not work outside the home when there is an infant (item 6) or a preschool-age child (item 7) in the family. No significant differences were found between Japanese and American groups on this item. Additional research is needed to explore the basis for such sentiments, to determine for example whether subjects believe that quality childcare services can not be substituted for biological mothering during this age range without hurting the child.

Both groups tended to be more uncertain about whether mothers should work outside the home when there is a school-age (item 8) or teenage (item 9) child in the family. Additional research is needed to explore whether school-aged and older children are believed to be no longer vulnerable to potential harmful effects related to maternal employment. Japanese subjects tended to believe significantly more than did American subjects that mothers should not work outside the home when there is a school-age or teenage child in the family.

Japanese housewives tended to agree significantly more than American housewives that wives should not work outside the home when their husbands want them home (item 10). The Japanese response to this item is consistent with traditional Japanese laws that gave men authority over women; and customs wherein women were expected to obey three men in their lifetimes, first their fathers, then their husbands, and finally their oldest sons (Smith, 1983). On the other hand, it is surprising that the American sample did not reject this idea more strongly, given America's liberation movement and previous research carried out in the late 1970's showing an increasing tendency for unmarried college students to reject husbands' authority over wives' employment related decisions (Engel, 1978). Related to this issue, it appears that American housewives are not very "liberated," despite being more so than Japanese housewives. Japanese responses (SD = .87) to this item varied significantly ($F(74,132)$ = 1.69, $p < .01$) less than did American responses (SD = 1.13), suggesting that Japanese housewives are more homogeneous in their attitudes related to issues of husband authority than are American housewives. The mean tendency to be "uncertain" and the greater variance of American housewives' responses may be a reflection of continuing liberation of American women from male dominance.

While both Japanese and American groups agreed that a wife/mother should not work outside the home when she doesn't want to (item 11), Japanese housewives agreed with this item significantly less than did American housewives. Considering America's traditional emphasis on freedom, individualism and self-determination, it is not surprising that American women would feel strongly that personal preference is an important consideration in whether or not a woman works outside the home. That this would be considered less important by Japanese subjects is consistent with traditional Japanese emphasis on duty and responsibility to the family. Japanese housewives appeared to be less homogeneous than American housewives in attitudes related to individualism and self-determination. Japanese responses (SD = .91) to item 11 varied significantly more ($F(130,74) = 1.99$, $p < .01$) than did American responses (SD = .65). This might indicate some controversy and change among Japanese housewives towards greater individualism.

Generalizations from this study should take into account the various limitations in the data. There can be no surety that the women sampled in this study represent all housewives in either Japan or America. Additional research is needed that expands the sampling to include part-time and full-time working women as well, and that differentiates groups according to work motivation.

Sex differences have been found in American attitudes toward women's employment (Engel, 1978, 1980). Research is needed that explores whether similar sex differences exist in Japan and how potential differences affect women and family life.

The research strategy used in this study assumes exposure to different cultures to be equivalent to different treatments, and depends upon control of extraneous variables (Campbell & Stanley, 1966). Of particular concern in cross-cultural research are comparability of instruments and comparability of samples. Every effort was made to insure that the English and Japanese versions of the questionnaire were equivalent, and equivalency was confirmed through "back translations" (Brislin, 1980). Similarly, every effort was made to insure that the Japanese and American samples were equivalent and that extraneous variables were controlled. The two samples were essentially equivalent in age, education and social class. American housewives reported more children while Japanese housewives reported larger household sizes.

The smaller number of children and larger household size reported by Japanese housewives can be explained in terms of more caring for elders within the family context, according to Japanese traditions. Despite evidence that there is a growing trend towards more nuclear family structures in Japan, the majority (74% in 1980) of elderly live with relatives, usually in their children's families (Kumagai, 1984). Thus it appears that there is more of a tendency for Japanese than American families to live in 3 generation households. One can only speculate whether such contextual factors influence attitudes toward women's employment. Housewives who have responsibilities for the care of elders, as well as husband and children, probably have less time for career development than those who are only responsible for childrearing. Further, it appears that definitions (which include role expectations) of housewife differ by culture. In this case, a Japanese definition of housewife would include responsibilities to family elders that would not be included in an American definition of housewife.

CONCLUSION

In summary, neither Japanese nor American housewives were found to believe very strongly that they can be happy as full-time housewives. Both groups agreed that a mother should not be employed outside the home when there is an infant or pre-school child in the family. In comparison with American housewives, Japanese housewives tended to believe more strongly that a wife/mother's employment would have harmful effects on marriage and child development, that married women should be home rearing children instead of working outside the home, and that a wife/mother should not be employed when there is a school-aged or teenage child in the family, or when a husband wants her home. American housewives tended to believe more strongly that women are capable of handling both homemaking and career responsibilities, and that a woman's personal preference should be an important consideration in whether or not she works outside the home. While the data provide evidence that Japanese housewives are indeed more conservative than American housewives in their views and attitudes toward women's employment, the data also suggest that Japanese housewives are uncertain about some of their traditional values. Their uncertainty may be an indication of controversy and change in Japanese society.

REFERENCES

Andre, R. (1981). *Homemakers: The forgotten workers.* Chicago: University of Chicago Press.
Brislin, R. W. (1980). Translation and content analysis of oral and written materials. In H. C. Triandis & J. W. Berry (Eds.), *Handbook of cross-cultural psychology* (Vol. 2). Boston: Allyn & Bacon.
Campbell, D. T., & Stanley, J. C. (1966). *Experimental and quasi-experimental designs for research.* Chicago: Rand McNally.
Engel, J. W. (1978). Changing attitudes toward the dual work/home roles of women (Doctoral dissertation, University of Minnesota). *Dissertation Abstracts International,* 3045B.
Engel, J. W. (1980). Sex differences in attitudes toward dual work/home roles of women. Paper presented at the *Annual Conference of the Western Psychological Association,* Honolulu.
Engel, J. W. (1986). Chinese and Japanese American student attitudes toward male/female roles. *Family Perspective, 20*(3), 196-206.
Hayghe, H. (1986, February). Rise in mothers' labor force activity includes those with infants. *Monthly Labor Review,* 34-45.
Imai, K., Kato, S., Maruyama, Y., Nakamura, K., Oshima, M., Senzaki, C., & Watanabe, T. (1985). Attitude of university graduates toward vocation and family. Paper distributed by the *Committee for Status of Women,* Japanese Association of University Women, Tokyo.
Kahn, W., & Crosby, F. (1985). Discriminating between attitudes and discriminatory behaviors. In L. Larwood, A. H. Stromberg, & B. A. Gutek (Eds.), *Women and work: An annual review* (pp. 215-238). Beverly Hills: Sage Publications.
Kieko, H. (1982). Japanese women in transition. *Japan Quarterly, 29,* 311-318.
Kikuchi, D. (1909). *Japanese education.* London: John Murray, Publ.
Kumagai, F. (1984). The life cycle of the Japanese family. *Journal of Marriage and the Family, 46*(1), 191-194.
Lebra, T. S. (1984). *Japanese women.* Honolulu: University of Hawaii Press.
Lewis, D. M., & Lewis, H. S. (1977). Socialization for marital roles and household task preference through Japanese first year social studies workbooks. Paper presented at the *Annual Conference of the North Central Sociological Association.*
O'Reilly, J. (1983, August 1). Women: A separate sphere. *Time,* pp. 66-69.
Porter, S. (1981, April 5). The world's best financial manager. *Honolulu Star Bulletin,* p. B-11.
Smith, R. J. (1983). Making village women into "good wives and wise mothers" in prewar Japan. *Journal of Family History, 8*(1), 70-84.
Vliet, J. V. (1988, Summer). The awesome power of Japan. *Money Talk,* p. 3.
Voydanoff, P. (1987). *Work and family life.* Beverly Hills: Sage Publications.
Waldman, E. (1983, December). Labor force statistics from a family perspective. *Monthly Labor Review,* 16-20.

Mothers Working Outside of the Home: Attitudes of Fathers and Mothers in Three Cultures

Patsy Skeen
Ligaya Palang Paguio
*Department of Child and Family Development
University of Georgia, Athens, GA 30602*

Bryan E. Robinson
*Department of Child and Family Development,
University of North Carolina at Charlotte, Charlotte, NC 28223*

James E. Deal
*Department of Psychology
University of Virginia, Charlottesville, VA 22904*

This study examined the differences in attitudes of 172 American, 140 Brazilian, and 142 Filipino parents concerning mothers working outside and inside the home. Results showed that American fathers reflected ambivalent and traditional views in that they were less favorable than Brazilian and Filipino fathers for mothers to work outside and inside the home. Among the mothers, the American sample were less favorable to work inside the home than the Brazilian and Filipino mothers. When couples of each culture were compared, American wives were more favorable to work outside of the home and less favorable to work inside the home than their husbands. No significant differences were found between the Brazilian and Filipino fathers and mothers and between couples of each of these cultures in their attitudes towards mothers working inside and outside the home. Implications of these findings are discussed.

Introduction

The role of women in many cultures has recently been changing. Whether or not husband and wife agree about the wife's role can either be a source of tension or positive support for their relationship. It is important to describe how husband and wife actually view the role of women and to

©1988 Select Press

understand how cultural values and behaviors might impact on their views. Therefore, cross cultural studies are important to understand these changing phenomena.

Traditionally, married American, Brazilian, and Filipino women stayed in the home and performed housework and childcare while husbands worked outside of the home and were responsible for the family's economic support (Saffioti, 1978; Smith, 1963; Sroufe & Cooper, 1988; Szanton, 1982). In the United States, because of economic reasons and the changing values and aspirations among women to pursue careers outside of the home, the trend of mothers working outside of the home has increased. The increase of women in the work force is also observed in Brazil (Saffioti, 1976; Schmink, 1986) and in the Philippines (Eviota, 1982; Fox, 1963).

Whether wives work or not has an impact on all the family members. In the United States, findings indicate that employed mothers when compared to housewives, have more positive images, are slightly favored in their mental health, set higher standards of mothering, and are more positive toward parental activities and about their children (Hoffman & Nye, 1974; Krause, 1984; Ritchie, 1982; Smith, 1981). Ideally, employed mothers prefer that girls be more confident, aggressive, and well-adjusted than nonemployed mothers (Paguio, Skeen, & Robinson, 1987). Daughters of working mothers tend to have more positive images of women and are more self-sufficient and less dependent when compared with other girls (Barahal, 1978; Zambrana, Hurst, & Hite, 1979). Also, maternal employment is associated with paternal involvement in child care (Barnett & Baruch, 1988). This has a positive effect on the cognitive functioning of their children (Radin, 1988). Furthermore, Scanzoni (1972) suggests that two-earner families compared to one-earner families, have more tendencies for marital cohesion as a result of sharing duties and decision making as well as expressing empathy, companionship, and affection. In Brazil, Norris (1985) reveals that lower-income earning women in couple-headed households appear to have more egalitarian relationships with their partners than do the nonemployed housewives. In addition, the employed compared to nonemployed mothers have more support groups in terms of resources for the family.

Although there have been few studies conducted on husband's attitude of his wife's working outside of the home, it can be concluded from these studies that the husband's attitude is important. In the United States, husband's attitude towards wife's employment has an effect on the psychological well-being of both husband and wife (Ulbrich, 1988). Working-class husbands seem to be more bound to traditional family life and role orientations than do middle class husbands (Rainwater, 1984).

Findings also suggest that attitudes toward wife's employment are more liberal among younger men and that husbands are more likely to oppose wife's employment if her education or earnings are low than if her education or earnings are high (Ulbrich, 1988).

Findings of a Philippine study reveals that although seventy-five per cent of husbands representing twelve regions of the country approve of their wives working outside of the home, there is a consensus among husbands that most women are better off in the home than in a job or profession and that people think less of a man if his wife works (Bulatao, 1978). Norris (1985) asserts that among Brazilian low-income families, husbands are opposed to their wives working outside of the home because of strong traditional values. The machismo is seen as dominant in the Brazilian and Filipino culture (Bulatao, 1978; Brandao, 1983; Rossi & Todd-Mancillas, 1987).

There is a need to explore this area more in order to understand this phenomena. It is particularly important to look at a family unit and compare views of husband and wife rather than groups of husbands and wives. The present study examined the differences in attitudes of American, Brazilian, and Filipino fathers and mothers from intact families concerning mothers working outside and inside the home. Based on previous findings which indicate that American husbands' and wives' views are in flux and that Filipino and Brazilian husbands are more traditional than their American counterparts, we hypothesized that the Brazilian and Filipino groups would demonstrate more traditional views than would the groups from the United States.

METHOD

Subjects

Data were collected from 172 parents in Southwest Virgina in the United States, aged 28 through 70 (M = 43.6 fathers, 38.9 mothers), from 140 parents in Northeast Coast Bahia in Brazil, aged 29 through 67 (M = 47 fathers, 41.4 mothers), and from 142 parents in Northern Mindanao in the Philippines, aged 20 through 77 (M = 45.3 fathers, 40.8 mothers). All regions were rural and middle class. Subjects were parents of children aged 11 to 18. The mean number of children among the American, Brazilian and Filipino samples were 1.5, 4.5, and 3.2, respectively.

Ninety-seven per cent of the American fathers were employed (30% white-collar, 70% blue-collar) and 47% of the American mothers were employed (48% white-collar, 52% blue-collar). All of the Brazilian fathers were employed (10% white-collar, 90% blue-collar) and 45% of the Brazilian mothers were employed (10% white-collar, 90% blue-

TABLE 1 Questionnaire of Father's and Mother's Attitude Concerning Mothers Working Inside and Outside the Home

Work Items	Home Items
A woman should also work away from home.	I would rather work at home than away from it.
I think a modern woman should be involved in work away from home.	I enjoy searching for new ideas related into my job at home.
It is a woman's right to choose to work away from home.	A woman's personal and professional fulfillment can occur only at home.
Working outside the home dignifies a woman.	Only dissatisfied mothers work outside the home.
I like working outside the home.	I prefer working at home rather than away.
I look for new ideas related to my job away from home.	Most women working away from home do so only because of tradition.
Working away from home enhances a woman's personal fulfillment.	Home is the only suitable place for a woman to work.
I am very interested in working away from home.	I think the modern woman should be more concerned with her chores at home.
Most women who work away from home do so because they enjoy it.	A woman's major concern for working away from home is financial advantages.

collar) while the Filipino sample included 92% employed fathers (24% white-collar, 76% blue-collar) and 55% employed mothers (53% white-collar, 47% blue-collar).

Instrument

The questionnaire used to measure attitudes was based on the instrument used by Pasquali & Callegari, 1978 (see Table 1). There is no validity and reliability data for the instrument but the investigators find this instrument appropriate for the study. The work and home items each contain nine statements. Each statement is presented in conjunction with a seven-option Likert-type scale with values ranging from "disagree very strongly" to "agree very strongly." A high score reflects a favorable attitude towards work outside and inside the home and a low score means an unfavorable attitude.

Procedure

The Brazilian instrument was translated into Portuguese by an educator who had a masters degree in early childhood from a noted university in the United States and who was trained by the investigators. The Filipino instrument was in English, as that language is the medium of instruction in the Philippines and the parents in this group had at least completed high school. The English language is understood and spoken quite fluently by educated Filipinos.

The subjects were randomly selected from the entire population qualified to participate in the study through their children who attended public schools in each area. The criteria for selection of participants were those from intact families, parents of children ages 11 to 18, and middle class. Children were asked to have their parents complete the questionnaire with instructions for the parents to call teachers if assistance was needed. Parents were told that participation was voluntary and their identity would be kept anonymous. The parents were asked not to discuss their responses until they had completed the instruments. Upon completion of the instruments each parent put his or her questionnaire in an envelope and sealed the envelope. The children returned the envelopes to their teacher, who noted their return on the roll book and gave the sealed envelopes to the investigators. As many as three follow up letters were sent to parents who had not returned their questionnaire via their children. The return rate was 90, 86, and 85 per cent for the American, Brazilian, and Filipino samples, respectively.

RESULTS

Fathers' Attitudes

The attitudes of American, Brazilian, and Filipino fathers concerning their wives working outside of the home were determined. Results of analysis of variance (Table 2) showed significant differences of responses among the three groups, $F(2,177) = 5.82$, $p < .01$. Duncan's Multiple Range Test showed that the American fathers scored significantly lower (more unfavorable; $M = 33.7$, $p<.01$) than the Brazilian ($M = 39.7$) and Filipino fathers ($M = 37.3$). No significant differences were found between the Brazilian and Filipino fathers.

The attitudes of the fathers concerning their wives working in the home were also computed. Results of analysis of variance showed significant differences of responses among the three groups, $F(2,180) = 16.04$, $p<.0001$. Interestingly, the Duncan's Multiple Range Test showed that the American fathers scored significantly lower (had more unfavorable atti-

TABLE 2 Mothers' and Fathers' Attitudes Towards Mothers Working Inside and Outside the Home

	American	Brazilian	Filipino	F	p
Fathers					
Work Items	33.7	39.7	37.3	5.82	.01
Home Items	35.8	42.1	40.3	16.04	.0001
Mothers					
Work Items	37.0	41.1	39.5	1.31	.27
Home Items	34.4	39.3	39.5	14.32	.0001

tudes; M = 35.8, P<.05) than the two groups. No significant differences were found between the Brazilian (M = 42.1) and Filipino fathers (M = 40.3).

Mothers' Attitudes

The attitudes of the mothers from the three cultures concerning working outside of the home were compared. The results of analysis of variance (Table 2) showed no significant differences of responses among the American, Brazilian, and Filipino mothers (M = 37.0, 41.1, and 39.5, respectively).

In addition, the mothers' responses to their attitudes concerning working inside the home were compared. As expected, the results of analysis of variance showed significant differences among their responses, $F(2,199) = 14.32$, $p<.0001$. The Duncan Multiple Range Test showed that the American mothers scored significantly lower (more unfavorable; M = 34.4, p<.001) than the Brazilian (M = 39.3) and Filipino (M = 39.5) mothers. No significant differences were found between the Brazilian and Filipino mothers.

Fathers and Mothers in Each Culture

Differences of responses of couples in each culture were determined. Results of t-tests showed that American fathers and mothers significantly differed in their responses regarding mothers working outside the home, $t = 3.4$, $p<.001$, and inside the home, $t = 3.2$, $p<.01$. Mothers scored (M = 33.6) in their attitudes toward work outside the home and scored significantly lower (less favorable; M = 33.5) than fathers (M = 37.5) in their attitudes toward work inside the home.

No significant differences were found between Brazilian fathers and mothers, and Filipino fathers and mothers in their responses to the work and home items.

DISCUSSION

Among the fathers, the American sample seem to show ambivalence in their responses. They were less agreeable than the Brazilian and Filipino fathers towards their wives working outside of the home but yet, they were less agreeable than the two groups of fathers towards their wives working at home. This ambivalence may reflect changes in working family dynamics and concomitant difficulty in adapting to both societal and family demands in the United States.

In underdeveloped countries working mothers become more an issue of survival than of social significance. Among developing countries, for example, the housewife's income is likely to be an important addition to the material support of the family. It is an important contribution to survival and improved quality of life (Schmink, 1986; Neher, 1982). The American sample in this study included rural, intact, and middle class families; in which case the husband's income may be adequate to support the family. Their wives do not have to work and if they do it is to attain a higher standard of living or for personal satisfaction.

A clearer view was shown when American fathers' responses were compared with their wives. They were less agreeable for their wives to work outside of the home and more agreeable for them to stay at home. Results of this study contradicted what was expected. It was hypothesized that American fathers would be less traditional than their Brazilian and Filipino counterparts. These findings suggest that American fathers have not yet resolved the issue of what role or roles are appropriate for women.

American men may still be trying to sort through the multiplexity of roles now deemed appropriate for women as a result of the women's movement in the United States. Men may also be trying to understand how the roles of men and women should fit together. Further, the American fathers might have wanted their wives to work outside of the home early in marriage but with the presence of children, their viewpoints might have changed. Additionally, the American sample is from a rural community. Perhaps, this particular group still holds traditional values.

As predicted, the American mothers were less agreeable than the Brazilian and Filipino mothers to staying at home. The same view was expressed when their responses were compared with their husbands. They were more favorable to work outside of the home. This is consistent with studies showing more American mothers wanting to join the labor force for personal and professional satisfaction as well as for financial considerations (Rubin, 1979; Veroff, Douvan, & Kulka, 1981). In the United States, the proportion of married women, living with their husbands, in the labor force doubled between 1950 and 1978, from 25.2% to 55.4%; the proportion for 1990 is estimated to reach 66.7% (Bernard, 1984).

A closer look at the cultural values and changing sex roles in each culture may explain some of the views reflected in this study. There is greater variability of views concerning the role of women expressed by the American sample than the other two groups. Disagreement and polarity of views are evident among the American group. Although sex roles are rapidly changing in the American society, there are those who still hold traditional views (Giele, 1984). On the other hand, similarity of views are seen in the Brazilian and Filipino groups. Although there is some movement of change in these two cultures, there is still a universal acceptance of specified roles for men and women (Eviota, 1982; Brandao, 1983).

It is important to mention that working inside and outside the home may not mean the same in these cultures. In the Philippines, working outside of the home is sometimes prestigious to a middle class mother because it means she has a college education. Education is not only a status symbol but seen as a way of gaining greater socioeconomic upward mobility (Bulatao, 1975; Bunge, 1984). Consequently, being a working wife somehow enhances the image of her husband (Arceo-Ortega, 1963). Also, in the Philippines and Brazil, domestic help is available at an affordable cost unlike in the United States where the cost of domestic help is higher. However, labor saving devices are available in most middle class American households. So, while American housewives have to deal with choosing, maintaining and repairing household appliances, the Filipino and Brazilian housewives are faced with hiring, training, and supervision of housemaids.

CONCLUSIONS

In summary, the study examined the differences in attitudes of American, Brazilian, and Filipino fathers and mothers concerning mothers working outside and inside the home. The American fathers reflected ambivalent and more traditional views than their Brazilian and Filipino counterparts. Among the mothers, the American sample expressed less traditional views than the Brazilian and Filipino mothers. Between couples of each culture, the American wives were more favorable to work outside the home and less favorable to work inside the home than their husbands.

More studies are needed to explore in depth the attitudes of fathers, why they hold the attitudes they do and the impact working mothers have on their marital relationships. Families in different sections of the population, of varying socioeconomic backgrounds and in various stages of family life, may vary in their attitudes concerning mothers working inside and outside the home. In addition, if the trend of working mothers continues to increase worldwide, information concerning the impact of culture and tradition on the role of women will be valuable in understanding changing family life.

REFERENCES

Arceo-Ortega, A. (1963). A career-housewife in the Philippines. In B. E. Ward (Ed.), *Women in the new Asia*. Netherlands: Arbeiderspers, Armsterdam.

Barahal, R. M. (1978). A comparison of parent-infant attachment and interaction patterns in day-care and non-day-care family groups. *Dissertation Abstract International, 38,* 5639.

Barnett, R. C., & Baruch (1988). Correlates of father's participation in family work. In P. Bronstein & C. P. Cowan (Eds.), *Fatherhood today*. New York: Wiley.

Bernard, J. (1984). The good-provider role: Its rise and fall. In P. Voydanoff (Ed.), *Work & family*. Palo Alto, CA: Mayfield.

Brandao, M. A. (1983). Brazil: Machismo and the new middle classes. In O. Harris (Ed.), *Latin American women*. London: Expedite Graphic.

Bulatao, R. A. (1975). *The value of children*. Honolulu, HI: University Press of Hawaii.

Bulatao, R. A. (1978). The double standard in sex roles. *Philippine Sociological Review, 26,* 201-223.

Bunge, F. M. (1984). *Philippines, a country study*. Washington, DC: US Government Printing Office.

Eviota, E. U. (1982). Philippines. In R. Jahan (Ed.), *Women in Asia*. London: Expedite Graphic.

Fox, R. (1963). Men and women in the Philippines. In B. E. Ward (Ed.), *Women in the new Asia*. Netherlands: Arbeiderspers, Armsterdam.

Giele, J. Z. (1984). Changing sex roles and family structure. In P. Voydanoff (Ed.), *Work & family*. Palo Alto, CA: Mayfield.

Hoffman, L. W., & Nye, F. I. (1974). *Working mothers*. San Fransisco, CA: Jossey Bass.

Krause, N. (1984). Employment outside the home and women's psychological well-being. *Social Psychiatry, 19,* 41-48.

Neher, C. D. (1982). Sex roles in the Philippines: The ambiguous Cebuana. In P. V. Esterik (Ed.), *Women in Southeast Asia*, Dekalb, IL: Northern Illinois University Center for Southeast Asian Studies.

Norris, W. P. (1985). *The social networks of impoverished Brazilian women: Work patterns and household structure in urban squatter settlements*. East Lansing, MI: Office of Women in International Development, Michigan State University.

Paguio, L. P., Skeen, P., & Robinson, B. (1987). Perceptions of the ideal child among employed and nonemployed American and Filipino mothers. *Perceptual and Motor Skills, 65,* 707-711.

Pasquali, L., & Callegari, A. I. (1978). Working mothers and daughters' sex-role identification in Brazil. *Child Development, 49,* 902-905.

Radin, N. (1988). Primary caregiving fathers of long duration. In P. Bronstein & C. P. Cowan (Eds.), *Fatherhood today*. New York: Wiley.

Rainwater, L. (1984). Mother's contribution to the family money economy in Europe and the United States. In P. Voydanoff (Ed.), *Work & family*. Palo Alto, CA: Mayfield.

Richie, J. (1982). Child-rearing practices and attitudes of working and full-time mothers. *Women's Studies International Forum, 5*, 419-425.

Rossi, A. M., & Todd-Mancillas, W. R. (1987). Machismo as a factor affecting the use of power and communication in the managing of personal disputes: Brazilian versus American male managers. *Journal of Social Behavior and Personality, 2*, 93-104.

Rubin, L. B. (1979). *Women of a certain age: The mid-life search for self*. New York: Harper & Row.

Saffioti, H. I. B. (1976). Relationships of sex and social class in Brazil. In J. Nash & H. I. Safa (Eds.), *Sex and class in Latin America*. New York: Praeger.

Saffioti, H. I. B. (1978). *Women in class society*. New York: Monthly Review.

Scanzoni, J. (1972). *Sexual bargaining*. Englewood Cliffs, NJ: Prentice-Hall.

Schmink, M. (1986). Women and urban industrial development in Brazil. In J. Nash & H. Safa (Eds.). *Women and change in Latin America*. South Hadley, MA: Bergin & Garvey.

Smith, E. J. (1981). The working mother: A critique of the research. *Journal of Vocational Behavior, 19*, 191-211.

Smith, T. L. (1963). *Brazil*. Kingsport, TN: Kingsport Press.

Sroufe, L. A., & Cooper, R. G. (1988). *Child development*. New York: Alfred A. Knopf.

Szanton, M. C. B. (1982). Women and men in Iloilo, Philippines: 1903 - 1970. In P. V. Esterik (Ed.), *Women of Southeast Asia*. Dekalb, IL: Northern Illinois University Center for Southeast Asian Studies.

Ulbrich, P. (1988). The determinants of depression in two-income marriages. *Journal of Marriage and Family, 50*, 121-131.

Veroff, J., Douvan, E., & Kulka, R. (1981). *The inner Americans: A self-portrait from 1957 to 1976*. New York: Basic Books.

Zambrana, R. E., Hurst, M., & Hite, R. L. (1979). The working mother in contemporary perspective: A review of the literature. *Pediatrics, 64*, 862-870.

Selected Bibliography on Work and Family

Elizabeth B. Goldsmith
Teryl A. Walters

Department of Home and Family Life
The Florida State University, Tallahassee, FL 32306

This bibliography is a selection of publications on work and family. In preparing a bibliography on work and family, we were confronted with the dilemma of what to include and exclude. Several areas are conceptually related to the topic of work and family: stress, burn-out, role overload, role conflict, dual-career, dual earner, division of labor, etc. There are many published works in each of these areas. We decided to include in our list only those publications which addressed the work and family interchange. To prepare the comprehensive bibliography, the following sources were consulted:

1. Reference and bibliography lists from three major sources: *Work and family life* (Voydanoff, 1987); *Lifeprints: New patterns of love and work for today's women* (Baruch, Barnett, and Rivers, 1982); and *Work and family* (Burke & Greenglass, 1987).

2. Reference suggestions by experts in the work and family field.

3. Reference lists of published materials (articles, books, and government publications) on work and family that were available to us.

Due to space and time considerations we decided to present a sample of the available resources. The following criteria were used to select the references presented:

1. Include professional references only—no strictly popular materials.

2. Exclude papers presented in professional meetings.

3. Exclude non-English works.

4. Exclude all masters theses and doctoral dissertations.

The final list includes 315 published works, over half of which (56%) were published since 1980.

Authors' Note: The bibliographic search was supported in part by a grant from the American Association of University Women Educational Foundation to Elizabeth Goldsmith. Teryl Walters was a research assistant on that project.

©1988 Select Press

SELECTED BIBLIOGRAPHY ON WORK AND FAMILY

Aldous, J. (1978). *Family careers: Developmental change in families.* New York: John Wiley.

Aldous, J. (1981). From dual-earner to dual-career families and back again. *Journal of Family Issues, 2,* 115-125.

Aldous, J. (Ed.). (1982). *Two paychecks: Life in dual earner families.* Beverly Hills, CA: Sage Publications.

Andrews, F.M., & Withey, S.B. (1976). *Social indicators of well-being: American's perceptions of life quality.* New York: Plenum.

Angrist, S.S., Lave, J.R., & Michelsen, R. (1976). How working mothers manage: Socioeconomic differences in work, child care, and household tasks. *Social Science Quarterly, 56,* 631-637.

Appley, M.H., & Trumbull, R. (Eds.). (1986). *Dynamics of Stress.* New York: Plenum Press.

Atkinson, H. (1985). *Women and fatigue.* New York: G.P. Putnam's Sons.

Axel, H. (1985). *Corporations and families: Changing practices and perspectives.* New York: Conference Board.

Baden, L. (1970). *Work and family: An annotated bibliography, 1978-1980.* Boston: Wheelock College Center for Parenting Studies.

Bailyn, L. (1970). Career and family orientation of husbands and wives in relation to marital happiness. *Human Relations, 23,* 97-113.

Bailyn, L., & Lynch, J.T. (1983). Engineering as a life long career: Its meaning, its satisfaction, its difficulties. *Journal of Occupational Behavior, 4,* 263-283.

Banner, D.K. (1974). The nature of the work-leisure relationship. *Omega, 2,* 181-195.

Barnes, L.B., & Hirshorn, S.A. (1976). Transferring power in the family business. *Harvard Business Review, 54* (4), 105-114.

Barnett, R.C., & Baruch, G.K. (1985). Women's involvement in multiple roles and psychological distress. *Journal of Personality and Social Psychology, 49,* 135-145.

Bartolome, F., & Evans, P.L. (1979). Professional lives versus private lives—shifting patterns of managerial commitment. *Organization Dynamics, 7* (4), 2-29.

Bartolome, F., & Evans, P.L. (1980). Must success cost so much? *Harvard Business Review, 58* (2),137-148.

Baruch, G.K., Barnett, R., & Rivers, C. (1982). *Lifeprints: New patterns of love and work for today's women.* New York: McGraw-Hill.

Baruch, G.K., Biener, L., & Barnett, R.C. (1985). *Women and gender in research on stress.* (Working Paper). Wellesley, MA: Center for Research on Women.

Baxandall, R., Gordon, L., & Reverby, S. (Eds.). (1976). *America's working women: A documentary history—1600 to the present.* New York: Vintage Books.

Bebbington, A.C. (1973). The function of stress in the establishment of the dual-career family. *Journal of Marriage and the Family, 35,* 530-537.

Becker, M.A., & Byrne, D. (1984). Type A behavior and daily activities of young married couples. *Journal of Applied Social Psychology, 14,* 82-88.

Beckman, F.J., & Houser, B.B. (1979). The more you have, the more you do: The relationship between wife's employment, sex role attitudes and household behavior. *Psychology of Women Quarterly, 4,* 160-174.

Beehr, T.A., & Bhagat, R.S. (Eds.). (1985). *Human stress and cognition in organizations.* New York: John Wiley.

Berheide, C., Berk, S., & Berk, R. (1976). Household work in the suburbs: The job and its participants. *Pacific Sociological Review, 19*, 491-581.

Bernard, J. (1972). *The future of the family.* New York: World Publishing.

Best, F. (1978). Preferences on worklife scheduling and work-leisure tradeoffs. *Monthly Labor Review, 101*, 31-37.

Best, F. (1980). *Flexible life scheduling.* New York: Praeger.

Beutell, N.J. (1986). *Conflict between work-family and student-family roles: Some sources and consequences.* (Working Paper). South Orange, NJ: Seton Hall University, W. Paul Stillman School of Business, Division of Research.

Beutell, N.J., & Greenhaus, J.H. (1983). Integration of home and nonhome roles: Women's conflict and coping behavior. *Journal of Applied Psychology, 68*, 43-48.

Biderman, A.D., & Drury, T.F. (Eds.). (1976). *Measuring work quality for social reporting.* New York: Russell Sage Foundation.

Bird, C. (1979). *The two-paycheck marriage.* New York: Rawson, Wade Publishers, Inc..

Bird, G.W., Bird, G.A., & Scruggs, M. (1984). Determinants of family task sharing: A study of husbands and wives. *Journal of Marriage and the Family, 46*, 345-355.

Bloom, D.E. (1986). Women and work. *American Demographics, 8* (9), 24-30.

Blotnick, S. (1985). *Otherwise engaged: The private lives of successful career women.* New York: Facts on File Publications.

Bodin, J., & Mitelman, B. (1983). *Mothers who work: Strategies for coping.* New York: Ballentine Books.

Bohen, H., & Viveros-Long, A. (1981). *Balancing jobs and family life.* Philadelphia: Temple University Press.

Booth, A. (1977). Wife's employment and husband's stress: A replication and refutation. *Journal of Marriage and the Family, 39*, 645-650.

Borman, K.M., Quarm, D., and Gideonse, S. (Eds.). (1984). *Women in the workplace: Effects on families.* Norwood, NJ: Ablex.

Boss, P.G., McCubbin, H.I., & Lester, G. (1979). The corporate executive wife's coping patterns in response to routine husband/father absence. *Family Process, 18*, 79-86.

Boulding, E. (1976). Familial constraints on women's work roles. *Signs, 1*, 95-118.

Brett, J.M. (1982). Job transfer and well-being. *Journal of Applied Psychology, 67*, 450-463.

Brinkerhoff, M.B. (Ed.). (1984). *Family and work: Comparative convergences.* Westport, CT: Greenwood.

Brody, E. (1985). Parent care as a normative family stress. *Gerontologist, 25*, 19-29.

Bryson, J.B., & Bryson, R.A. (Eds.). (1978). Dual career couples (Special issue). *Psychology of Women Quarterly, 3.*

Burden, D.S. (1986). Single parents and the work setting: The impact of multiple job/homelife responsibilities. *Family Relations, 35*, 37-43.

Burden, D., & Googins, B. (1987). *Balancing work and family stress in corporations.* Boston: Boston University School of Social Work.

Burke, R.J. (1980). How work and the family affect each other. *Canadian Training Methods: The Human Element, 9*, 12-14.

Burke, R.J. (1982). Impact of occupational demands on nonwork experiences of senior administrators. *Journal of Psychology, 112*, 195-211.

Burke, R.J. (1986). Occupational and life stress and the family: Conceptual frameworks and research findings. *International Review of Applied Psychology, 35*, 347-369.

Burke, R.J., & Greenglass, E.R. (1987). *Work and family* (Working Paper). Ontario: York University.

Burke, R.J., & Weir, T. (1975). Receiving and giving help with work and nonwork-related problems. *Journal of Business Adminstration, 6*, 59-78.

Burke, R.J., & Weir, T. (1976). Relationships of wives' employment status to husband, wife and pair satisfaction and performance. *Journal of Marriage and the Family, 38*, 279-287.

Burke, R.J., & Weir, T. (1977). Marital helping relationships: The moderators between stress and well-being. *Journal of Psychology, 95*, 121-130.

Burke, R.J., & Weir, T. (1977). Why good managers make lousy fathers. *Canadian Business, 50*, 51-54.

Burke, R.J., & Weir, T. (1980). The type A experience: Occupational and life demands, satisfaction and well-being. *Journal of Human Stress, 6*, 28-38.

Burke, R.J., & Weir, T. (1981). Impact of occupational demands on non-work experiences. *Group and Organization Studies, 6*, 472-485.

Burke, R.J., Weir, T., & DuWors, R. F. (1980). Work demands on administrators and spouse well-being. *Human Relations, 33*, 253-278.

Caplan, G., & Killilea, M. (Eds.). (1976). *Support systems and mutual help*. New York: Grune and Stratton.

Clark, R.A., Nye, F.I., & Gecas, V. (1978). Work involvement and marital role performance. *Journal of Marriage and the Family, 40*, 9-22.

Collins, R.H. (1979). Why do women work? *Graduate Woman, 73* (5), 12-13.

Cooke, R.A., & Rousseau, D.M. (1984). Stress and strain from family roles and work-role expectations. *Journal of Applied Psychology, 69*, 252-260.

Cooper, C. (Ed.). (1983). *Stress research*, New York: John Wiley & Sons.

Cooper, C.L. (1981). *How male and female managers keep their pressure out of their homes*. Englewood Cliffs, NJ: Prentice-Hall.

Cooper, C.L., & Payne, R. (Eds.). (1978). *Stress at work*. New York: Wiley.

Cooper, C.L., & Payne, R. (Eds.). (1980). *Current concerns in occupational stress*. New York: John Wiley.

Corfman, E. (Ed.). (1979). *Families today* (Vol. 1). Bethesda, MD: National Institute of Mental Health.

Crouter, A.C. (1984). Spillover from family to work: The neglected side of the work-family interface. *Human Relations, 37*, 425-442.

Davis, L.E., & Cherns, A.B. (Eds.). (1975). *The quality of working life* (Vol. 1). New York: Free Press.

Derr, C.B. (Ed.). (1980). *Work, family and career*. New York: Praeger.

Dohrenwend, B., & Dohrenwend, B.S. (1974). *Stressful life events: Their nature and effects*. New York: John Wiley & Sons.

Dougherty, K., Howrigan, G., Lein, L, & Weiss, H. (1977). *Work and the American family* (Working Family Project). Chicago: National Parent Teachers Association.

Duncan, G.J. (1984). *Years of poverty, years of plenty*. Ann Arbor, MI: Institute for Social Research.

Elman, M.R., & Gilbert, L.A. (1984). Coping strategies for role conflict in married professional women with children. *Family Relations, 33*, 317-327.

England, P., & Farkas, G. (1986). *Households, employment, and gender: A social, economic, and demographic view*. New York: Aldine Publishing Co.

Evans, P., & Bartolome, F. (1984). The changing picture of the relationship between career and family. *Journal of Occupational Behavior, 5*, 9-21.

Farmer, H.S., & Bohn, M.J. (1970). Home-career conflict reduction and the level of career interest in women. *Journal of Counseling Psychology, 17*, 228-232.

Feinstein, K.W. (Ed.). (1979). *Working women and families.* Beverly Hills, CA: Sage Publications.

Feldman, M., & Feldman, H. (1975). The family life cycle: Some suggestions for recycling. *Journal of Marriage and the Family, 37,* 277-284.

Ferber, M., & Huber, J. (1979). Husbands, wives, and careers. *Journal of Marriage and the Family, 41,* 315-325.

Ferguson, K. (1984). *The feminist case against bureaucracy.* Philadelphia: Temple University Press.

Finch, J. (1983). *Married to the job: Wive's incorporation in men's work.* Boston: Allen & Unwin.

Finn, P. (1981). The effects of shift work on the lives of employees. *Monthly Labor Review, 104* (10) 31-34.

Fogarty, M.P., Rapoport, R., & Rapoport, R.N. (1971). *Sex, career, and family.* London: Allen & Unwin.

Forisha, B., & Goldman, F. (Eds.). (1981). *Outsiders on the inside.* Englewood Cliffs, NJ: Prentice Hall.

Foster, M.A., Wallston, B.S., & Berger, M. (1980). Feminist orientation and job-seeking behavior among dual-career couples. *Sex Roles, 6,* 59-65.

Freudenberger, H.J. (1980). *Burn-out: The high cost of high achievement.* Garden City, NY: Anchor Press.

Gaylord, M. (1979, May). Relocation and the corporate family: Unexplored issues. *Social Work, 24,* 186-191.

Gerson, K. (1983). Changing family structure and the position of women. *American Planning Association Journal, 49,* 138-148.

Goebel, K., & Hennon, C.B. (1984). Husband-wife division of labour and quality of family life. *Journal of Consumer Studies and Home Economics, 8,* 61-72.

Goldsmith, E. (in press). Is the workplace a haven or a jungle? [Review of *To love & work: A systemic interlocking of family, workplace, and career*]. *Contemporary Psychology.*

Goldsmith, E. (1989). *Family involvement, work involvement, role overload, and fatigue: Professional men vs. professional women* (Working Paper). Tallahassee: Florida State University.

Goode, W.J. (1960). A theory of role strain. *American Sociological Review, 25,* 483-496.

Gould, S., & Werbel, J.D. (1983). Work involvement: A comparison of dual wage earner and single wage earner families. *Journal of Applied Psychology, 68,* 313-319.

Gray, J.D. (1983). The married professional woman: An examination of her role conflicts and coping strategies. *Psychology of Women Quarterly, 7,* 235-243.

Greenglass, E.R. (1982). *A world of difference: Gender roles in perspective.* Toronto: John Wiley.

Greenhaus, J.H., & Beutell, N.J. (1985). Sources of conflict between work and family roles. *Academy of Management Review, 10,* 76-88.

Greenhaus, J.H., & Kopelman, R. E. (1981). Conflict between work and nonwork roles: Implications for the career planning process. *Human Resource Planning, 4,* 1-10.

Greiff, B.S., & Munter, P.K. (1980). *Trade-offs: Executive, family and organizational life.* New York: Mentor.

Groat, H.T., Workman, R.L., & Neal, A.G. (1976). Labor force participation and family formation. *Demography, 13,* 115-125.

Guest, D., & Williams, R. (1973). How home affects work. *New Society, 9,* 14-19.

Hackman, R.J., & Lawler, E.E., III. (1971). Employee reactions to job characteristics. *Journal of Applied Psychology, 55,* 259-286.

Hall, D.T. (1972). A model of coping with role conflict: The role behavior of college educated women. *Administrative Science Quarterly, 17*, 471-486.

Hall, D.T., & Hall, F.S. (1979). *The two-career couple.* Reading, MA: Addison-Wesley.

Hall, F.S., & Hall, D.T. (1978). Dual careers—how do couples and companies cope with problems? *Organizational Dynamics, 6* (4), 55-77.

Hall, R., Gardner, C.W., Perl, M.S., Stickney, S., & Pfefferbaum, B. (1979, April). The professional burn-out syndrome. *Psychiatric Opinion,* 12-17.

Harrison, A., & Minor, J. (1978). Interrole conflict, coping strategies and satisfaction among black working wives. *Journal of Marriage and the Family, 40,* 799-805.

Hauenstein, L.S. (Principal investigator), & Blehar, M.C. (Author). (1980). Married women: Work and family. *Families Today* (Vol. 1). Rockville, MD: US Department of Health, Education and Welfare, National Institute of Mental Health.

Hayes, C.D., & Kamerman, S.B. (Eds.). (1983). *Children of working parents.* Washington, DC: National Academy Press.

Hayghe, H. (1981). Husbands and wives as earners: An analysis of family data. *Monthly Labor Review, 104* (2), 46-53.

Haynes, S.G., & Feinleib, M. (1980). Women, work and coronary heart disease. *American Journal of Public Health, 70,* 133-141.

Heckman, H.A., Bryson, R., & Bryson, J.B. (1977). Problems of professional couples: A content analysis. *Journal of Marriage and the Family, 39,* 323-330.

Hedges, J.N. (1977). Flexible schedules: Problems and issues. *Monthly Labor Review, 100* (2), 62-65.

Hedges, J.N., & Taylor, D.E. (1980). Recent trends in worktime: Hours edge downward. *Monthly Labor Review, 103* (3), 3-11.

Hendrix, W., Steel, R., & Schultz, S. (1987). Job stress and life stress: Their causes and consequences. *Journal of Social Behavior and Personality, 2* (3), 291-302.

Hewlett, S.A. (1986). *A lesser life: The myth of women's liberation in America.* New York: Morrow.

Hill, M.D. (1979). Faculty sex composition and job satisfaction of academic women. *International Journal of Women's Studies, 7* (2), 178-188.

Hill, M.S. (1979). The wage effects of marital status and children. *Journal of Human Resources, 14,* 579-593.

Hiller, D.V., & Philliber, W.W. (1982). Predicting marital and career success among dual-worker couples. *Journal of Marriage and the Family, 42,* 53-62.

Hiller, D.V., & Philliber, W.W. (1986). The division of labor in contemporary marriage: Expectations, perceptions and performance. *Social Problems, 33,* 191-201.

Hirschlein, B.M., & Braun, W.J. (Eds.). (1982). *Families and work.* Stillwater, OK: Oklahoma State University Press.

Hobfoll, S. (1986). *Stress, social support and women.* Washington, DC: Hemisphere.

Hofferth, S.L. (1984). Long-term economic consequences for women of delayed childbearing and reduced family size. *Demography, 42,* 141-155.

Hoffman, L. (1974). Fear of success in males and females, 1965-71. *Journal of Consulting and Clinical Psychology, 42,* 353-358.

Hoffman, L.W. (1979). Changes in family roles, socialization, and sex differences. *American Psychologist, 32,* 644-657.

Hoffman, L., & Nye, F. (Ed.). (1975). *Working mothers.* San Francisco: Jossey Bass.

Holahan, C.K., & Gilbert, L.A. (1979). Conflict between major life roles: Women and men in dual career couples. *Human Relations, 32,* 451-467.

Holmstrom, L.L. (1973). *The two-career family.* Cambridge, MA: Schenkman.

Hood, J.C. (1983). *Becoming a two-job family.* New York: Praeger.

Hopkins, J., & White, P. (1978). The dual-career couple: Constraints and supports. *Family Coordinator, 27,* 253-259.

House, J.S. (1981). *Work, stress, and social support.* Reading, MA: Addison-Wesley.

House, J.S. (1987). Chronic stress and chronic disease in life and work: Conceptual and methodological issues. *Work and Stress, 1,* 129-134.

Hudis, P.M. (1976). Commitment to work and to family: Marital status differences in women's earning. *Journal of Marriage and the Family, 38:* 267-278.

Hunt, J.G., & Hunt, L.L. (1977). Dilemmas and contradictions of status: The case of the dual-career family. *Social Problems, 24,* 407-416.

Igodan, O.C., & Newcomb, L.H. (1986, Spring). Are you experiencing burnout? *Journal of Extension, 24,* 4-7.

Jackson, S.E., & Maslach, C. (1982). After-effects of job related stress: Families as victims. *Journal of Occupational Behavior, 3,* 63-77.

Jackson, S.E., Zedeck, S., & Summers, E. (1985). Family life disruptions: Effects of job-induced structural and emotional interference. *Academy of Management Journal, 28,* 574-586.

Jacobson, A., & Lawhon, T. (1983). An important connection: Work and family. *Illinois Teacher of Home Economics, 26,* 89-91.

Jick, T.D., & Mitz, L.F. (1985). Sex differences in work stress. *Academy of Management Review, 10,* 408-420.

Johnson, B.L. (1980). Marital and family characteristics of the labor force, March 1979. *Monthly Labor Review, 103* (4), 48-52.

Johnson, B.L., & Waldman, E. (1981). Marital and family patterns of the labor force. *Monthly Labor Review, 104* (10), 36-38.

Johnson, C.L., & Johnson, F.A. (1977). Attitudes toward parenting in dual-career couples. *American Journal of Psychiatry, 134,* 391-395..

Johnson, F.A., & Johnson, C.L. (1976). Role strain in high commitment career women. *Journal of American Academy of Psychoanalysis, 4,* 13-16.

Jones, A.P., & Butler, M.C. (1980). A role transition approach to the stress of organizationally induced family role disruption. *Journal of Marriage and the Family, 42,* 367-376.

Jones, W., & Jones, R. (1980). *Two careers, one marriage.* New York: AMACOM.

Kabanoff, B. (1980). Work and nonwork: A review of models, methods, and findings. *Psychological Bulletin, 88,* 60-77.

Kamerman, S.B., & Hayes, C.D. (Eds.). (1982). *Families that work: Children in a changing world.* Washington, DC: National Academy Press.

Kanter, R.M. (1977). *Men and women of the corporation.* New York: Basic Books.

Kanter, R.M. (1977). *Work and family in the United States: A critical review and agenda for research and policy.* New York: Russell Sage Foundation.

Kanter, R.M. (1983, May). Productivity and the quality of life. *J.C. Penney Forum,* 14-16.

Katz, M.H., & Piotrkowski, C.S. (1983). Correlates of family role strain among employed black women. *Family Relations, 32,* 331-339.

Keith, P.M., & Schafer, R.B. (1980). Role strain and depression in two-job families. *Family Relations, 29,* 483-488.

Kelly, R.F., & Voydanoff, P. (1985). Work/family role strain among employed parents. *Family Relations, 34,* 367-374.

Kessler, R.C., & McRae, J.A. (1982). The effect of wives' employment on the mental health of married men and women. *American Sociological Review, 47,* 216-227.

King, W. L., & Hautaluoma, J. E. (1987). Comparison of job satisfaction, life satisfaction, and performance of overeducated and other workers. *Journal of Social Psychology, 127,* 421-433.

Kingston, P.W., & Nock, S.L. (1985). Consequences of the family work day. *Journal of Marriage and the Family, 47,* 619-629.

Kingston, P.W., & Nock, S.L. (1987). Time together among dual-earner couples. *American Sociological Review, 52,* 391-400.

Kon, I. (1975). Women at work: Equality with a difference? *International Social Science Journal, 27,* 655-665.

Kopelman, R.E., Greenhaus, J.H., & Connolly, T.F. (1983). A model of work, family, and interrole conflict: A construct validation study. *Organization Behavior and Human Performance, 32,* 198-215.

Kramerman, S.B., & Hayes, C.D. (1982). *Families that work: Children in a changing world.* Washington, D.C: National Academy Press.

Lamb, M.E. (Ed.). (1986). *The father's role: Applied perspectives.* New York: Wiley-Interscience.

Larwood, L., Stromberg, A.H., & Gutek, B.A. (Eds.). (1985). *Women and work: An annual review.* Beverly Hills, CA: Sage Publications.

Lee, M.D. (1985). Probing behavioral patterns of structuring daily life. *Human Relations, 38,* 457-476.

Lee, M.D., & Kanungo, R.N. (1984). *Management of work and personal life.* New York: Praeger.

Lee, R.A. (1983). Flextime and conjugal roles. *Journal of Occupational Behavior, 5,* 297-315.

Lein, L. (1979). Male participation in home life: Impact of social supports and breadwinner responsibility on the allocation of tasks. *Family Coordinator, 28,* 489-495.

Lein, L, Durham, M., Pratt, M., Schudson, M., Thomas, R., & Weiss, H. (1974). *Final report: Work and family life* (National Institute of Education Project No1. 3-33094). Cambridge, MA: Center for the Study of Public Policy.

Levinger, G., & Moles, O.C. (Eds.). (1979). *Divorce and separation: Context, causes and consequences.* New York: Basic Books.

Levitan, S.A. (Ed.). (1971). *Blue collar workers: A symposium on Middle America.* New York: McGraw-Hill.

Lodahl, T. & Kejner, M. (1965). The definition and measurement of job involvement. *Journal of Applied Psychology, 49,* 24-33.

Lopata, H.Z. (Ed.). (1980). *Research in the interweave of social roles: Women and men* (Vol. 1). Greenwich, CT: JAI Press.

Lopata, H.Z., & Norr, K.F. (1980). Changing commitments of American women to work and family roles. *Social Security Bulletin, 43* (6), 3-14.

Lopata, H.Z., & Pleck, J.H. (Eds.). (1983). *Research in the interweave of social roles: Families and jobs* (Vol. 3). Greenwich, CT: JAI Press.

Louis Harris & Associates. (1981). *Families at work: Strengths and strains* (American Family Report). Minneapolis, MN: General Mills.

Machlowitz, M. (1980). *Workaholics: Living with them, working with them.* New York: Mentor.

Mahoney, T.A. (1978). The rearranged work week. *California Management Review, 20* (4), 31-39.

Marks, S.R. (1977). Multiple roles and role strain: Some notes on human energy, time, and commitment. *American Sociological Review, 42*, 921-936.

Martin, T.W., Berry, K.J., & Jacobsen, R.B. (1975). The impact of dual-career marriages on female professional careers: An empirical test of a Parsonian hypothesis. *Journal of Marriage and the Family, 37*, 734-742.

Maslach, C. (1976, September). Burned-out. *Human Behavior*, 16-18.

McCubbin, H.I., Dahl, B.B., & Hunter, E.J. (Eds.). (1976). *Families in the military system.* Beverly Hills, CA: Sage Publications.

Miller, J., & Garrison, H.H. (1982). Sex roles: The division of labor at home and in the workplace. *Annual Review of Sociology, 8*, 237-262.

Miller, J., Schooler, C., Kohn, M., & Miller, K. (1979). Women and work: The psychological effects of occupational conditions. *American Journal of Sociology, 85*, 66-94.

Moore, K.A., & Hofferth, S.L. (1979). Effects of women's employment on marriage: Formation, stability and roles. *Marriage and Family Review, 2* (2), 1, 27-36.

Moris, A.H. (1979). Are women their own worst enemies? *Graduate Woman, 73* (5), 26-27.

Mortimer, J.T. (1976). Social class, work and the family: Some implications of the father's occupation for familial relations and sons' career decisions. *Journal of Marriage and the Family, 38*, 241-256.

Myrdal, A., & Klein, V. (1956). *Women's two roles.* London: Routledge & Kegan Paul (reprinted in 1968).

National Institute of Mental Health. (1979). *Families today: A research sampler on families and children* (DHEW Publication No. ADM 79-815). Washington, DC: Government Printing Office.

Near, J.P., Rice, R.W., & Hunt, R.G. (1980). The job satisfaction/life satisfaction relationship: A review of empirical research. *Basic and Applied Social Psychology, 1*, 37-64.

Near, J.P., Rice, R.W., & Hunt, R.G. (1980). The relationship between work and nonwork domains: A review of empirical research. *Academy of Management Review, 5*, 415-429.

Neff, W. (1985). *Work and human behavior.* New York: Aldine Publishing Co.

Nollen, S.D. (1979). Does flextime improve productivity? *Harvard Business Review, 57* (5), 12-22.

Nollen, S.D. (1982). *New work schedules in practice.* New York: Van Nostrand Reinhold.

Nowack, K.M. (1987). Health habits, type A behavior and job burnout. *Work and Stress, 1*, 135-142.

Nye, F.I., & Hoffman, L.W. (Eds.). (1963). *The employed mother in America.* Chicago: Rand McNally.

Oakley, A. (1972). Are husbands good housewives? *New Society, 112*, 377-379.

Oakley, A. (1975). *The sociology of housework.* New York: Pantheon.

Oakley, A. (1976). *Woman's work: The housewife, past and present.* New York: Vintage Books.

Oppenheimer, V.K. (1982). *Work and the family: A study in social demography.* New York: Academic.

Orden, S.R., & Bradburn, N.M. (1969). Working wives and marriage happiness. *American Journal of Sociology, 74*, 392-407.

Orpen, C. (1981). Work and nonwork satisfaction: A causal-correlational analysis. *Journal of Applied Psychology, 4*, 530-532.

Osherson, S., & Dill, D. (1983). Varying work and family choices: Their impact on men's work satisfaction. *Journal of Marriage and the Family, 45*, 339-346.

O'Toole, J. (Ed.). (1974). *Work and the quality of life.* Cambridge, MA: M.I.T. Press.

Papanek, H. (1973). Men, women, and work: Reflections on the two-person career. *American Journal of Sociology, 78,* 852-872.

Paulson, N. (1982). Change in family income position: The effect of wife's labor force participation. *Sociological Focus, 15,* 77-91.

Peterson, S.S., Richardson, J.M., & Kreuter, G.V. (Eds.). (1978). *The two career family: Issues and alternatives.* Washington, DC: University Press of America.

Philliber, W.W., & Hiller, D.V. (1983). Relative occupational attainments of spouses and later changes in marriage and wife's work experience. *Journal of Marriage and the Family, 45,* 161-170.

Pietromonaco, P.R., Manis, J., & Frohardt-Lane, K. (1986). Psychological consequences of multiple social roles. *Psychology of Women Quarterly, 10,* 373-382.

Pines, A., & Kafry, D. (1981). The experience of tedium in three generations of professional women. *Sex Roles, 7,* 117-134.

Piotrkowski, C.S. (1978). *Work and the family system.* New York: The Free Press.

Pleck, E. (1976). Two worlds in one: Work and family. *Journal of Social History, 10,* 178-195.

Pleck, J.H. (1977). The work-family role system. *Social Problems, 24,* 417-427.

Pleck, J.H. (1978). *The work-family role system.* New York: The Free Press.

Pleck, J.H. (1979). Men's family work: Three perspectives and some new data. *Family Coordinator, 28,* 481-488.

Pleck, J.H. (1985). *Working wives/working husbands.* Beverly Hills, CA: Sage Publications, Inc.

Pleck, J.H. (Principal investigator), & Corfman, E. (Author). (1980). *Married men: Work and family.* Rockville, MD: US Department of Health, Education, and Welfare.

Pleck, J., & Lang, L. (1978). *Men's family role: Its nature and consequences.* Wellesley, MA: Wellesley College Center for Research on Women.

Pleck, J.H., & Staines, G.L. (1985). Work schedules and family life in two-earner couples. *Journal of Family Issues, 6,* 61-82.

Pleck, J.H., Staines, G.L., & Lang, L. (1980). Conflicts between work and family life. *Monthly Labor Review, 103* (3), 29-32.

Poloma, M.M., & Garland, T.N. (1971). The married professional woman: A study in the tolerance of domestication. *Journal of Marriage and the Family, 33,* 531-540.

Poloma, M.M., Pendleton, B.F., & Garland, T.N. (1981). Reconsidering the dual career marriage. *Journal of Family Issues, 2,* 205-224.

Pond, S.B., & Green, S.B. (1983). The relationship between job and marriage satisfaction within and between spouses. *Journal of Occupational Behavior, 4,* 145-155.

Poor, R. (Ed.). (1972). *4 days, 40 hours: Reporting a revolution in work and leisure.* London: Pan Books.

Portner, J. (1978). *Impacts of work on the family.* Minneapolis, MN: Minnesota Council on Family Relations.

Preston, S., & Richards, A.T. (1975). The influence of women's work opportunities on marriage rates. *Demography, 12,* 209-222.

Quinn, R.P., & Staines, G.L. (1977). *The 1977 quality of employment survey.* Ann Arbor, MI: Institute for Social Research.

Quint, H.H., & Cantor, M. (1980). *Men, women, and issues in American history* (Vols. I and II). Homewood: The Dorsey Press.

Rank, M.R. (1982). Determinants of conjugal influence in wives' employment decision making. *Journal of Marriage and the Family, 42*, 591-604.

Rapoport, R., & Rapoport, R.N. (1965). Work and family in modern society. *American Sociological Review, 30*, 381-394.

Rapoport, R., & Rapoport, R.N. (1969). The dual-career family: A variant pattern and social change. *Human Relations, 22*, 3-29.

Rapoport, R., & Rapoport, R.N. (1971). *Dual-career families*. Baltimore: Penguin Books.

Rapoport, R., Rapoport, R.N., & Thiessen, V. (1974). Couple symmetry and enjoyment. *Journal of Marriage and the Family, 36*, 588-591.

Rapoport, R., & Rapoport, R.N. (1976). *Dual-career families re-examined: New integrations of work and family*. New York: Harper and Row.

Rapoport, R., & Rapoport, R.N. (Eds.). (1978). *Working couples*. New York: Harper & Row.

Rapoport, R.N., & Rapoport, R. (1978). Dual-career families: Progress and prospects. *Marriage and Family Review, 15*, 1-12.

Reilly, M.D. (1982). Working wives and convenience consumption. *Journal of Consumer Research, 8*, 407-418.

Renshaw, J.R. (1976). An exploration of the dynamics of the overlapping worlds of work and family. *Family Process, 15*, 143-165.

Reskin, B., & Hartmann, H. (Eds.). (1986). *Women's work, men's work: Sex segregation on the job*. Washington, D.C.: National Academy Press.

Rexroat, C. (1985). Women's work expectations and labor-market experience in early and middle family life-cycle stages. *Journal of Marriage and the Family, 47*, 131-142.

Rice, G.D. (1979). *Dual career marriage: Conflict and treatment*. New York: The Free Press.

Rice, R.W. (1982). *Work and family: A selected inventory of propositions* (Technical Report 82-11). Buffalo: Department of Psychology, State University of New York, Buffalo.

Rice, R.W. (1983). *Work and family: A bibliography* (Technical Report 83-12). Buffalo: Department of Psychology, State University of New York, Buffalo.

Rice, R.W., Near, J.P., & Hunt, R.G. (1980). The job-satisfaction life-satisfaction relationship: A review of empirical research. *Basic and Applied Social Psychology, 1*, 37-64.

Ridley, C.A. (1973). Exploring the impact of work satisfaction and involvement on marital interaction when both partners are employed. *Journal of Marriage and the Family, 35*, 229-237.

Ritzer, G. (1977). *Working, conflict, and change*. Englewook Cliffs, NJ: Prentice-Hall.

Ronen, S. (1984). *Alternative work schedules: Selecting, implementing and evaluating*. Homewood, IL: Dow Jones-Irwin.

Roper Organization. (1974). *The Virginia Slims American Women's Opinion Poll. Vol 3: A survey of the attitudes of women on marriage, divorce, the family and America's changing sexual morality*. New York: Roper Organization.

Rosenfeld, R.A. (1979). Women's occupational careers. *Sociology of Work and Occupations, 6*, 283-311.

Rousseau, D. (1978). The relationship of work to non-work. *Journal of Applied Psychology, 63*, 513-517.

Rowland, V.T., & Nickols, S.Y. (1985, Spring). How is the time spent? *Journal of Extension, 23*, 13-16.

Safilios-Rothschild, C. (Ed.). (1972). *Toward a sociology of women*. Lexington, MA: Xerox.

Safilios-Rothschild, C. (1976). Dual linkages between the occupational and family systems: A macrosociological analysis. *Signs, 1,* 51-60.

Sarason, I., & Johnson, J. (1979). Life stress, organizational stress and job satisfaction. *Psychological Reports, 44,* 70-75.

Scanzoni, J. (1980). Contemporary marriage types: A research note. *Journal of Family Issues, 1,* 125-140.

Schanninger, C.M., & Allen, C.T. (1981). Wife's occupational status as a consumer behavior construct. *Journal of Consumer Research, 8,* 189-196.

Schultz, J.B., & Henderson, C. (1985). Family satisfaction and job performance: Implications for career development. *Journal of Career Development, 12,* 33-47.

Seidenberg, R. (1973). *Corporate wives—corporate casualities.* New York: AMACOM.

Sekaran, U. (1982). An investigation of the career salience of men and women in dual-career families. *Journal of Vocational Behavior, 20,* 111-119.

Shostak, A., & Gomberg, W. (Eds.). (1964). *Blue-collar world: Studies of the American worker,* Englewood Cliffs, NJ: Prentice Hall.

Skinner, D.A. (1980). Dual-career family stress and coping: A literature review. *Family Relations, 29,* 43-51.

Smulders, P.G.W. (1983). Personal, nonwork and work characteristics in male and female absence behavior. *Journal of Occupational Behavior, 4,* 285-295.

Spector, P.E. (1987). Interactive effects of perceived control and job stressors on affective reactions and health outcomes for clerical workers. *Work and Stress, 1,* 155-162.

Spitze, G. (1984). The effect of family migration on wives' employment: How long does it last? *Social Science Quarterly, 65,* 21-36.

Spitze, G., & South, S.J. (1985). Women's employment, time expenditure, and divorce. *Journal of Family Issues, 6,* 307-329.

Staines, G. L. (1980). Spillover versus compensation: A review of the literature on the relationship between work and nonwork. *Human Relations, 33,* 111-129.

Staines, G.L., & Pleck, J.H. (1983). *The impact of work schedules on the family.* Ann Arbor, MI: The University of Michigan (The Institute of Social Research).

Staines, G.L., & Pleck, J.H. (1984). Nonstandard work schedules and family life. *Journal of Applied Psychology, 69,* 515-523.

Staines, G.L., & Pleck, J.H. (1986). Work schedule flexibility and family life. *Journal of Occupational Behavior, 7,* 147-153.

Staines, G.L., Pottick, K.J., & Fudge, D.A. (1986). Wives' employment and husbands' attitudes towards work and life. *Journal of Applied Psychology, 71,* 118-128.

Steers, R.M., & Rhodes, S.R. (1978). Major influences on employee attendance: A process model. *Journal of Applied Psychology, 63,* 391-407.

Stewart, A. J., & Salt, P. (1981). Life stress, life styles, depression, and illness in adult women. *Journal of Personality and Social Psychology, 40,* 1067-1069.

St. John-Parsons, D. (1978). Continuous dual-career families. *Psychology of Women Quarterly, 3,* 30-42.

St. Pierre, T.W. (1984). Addressing work and family issues among extension personnel. *Journal of Home Economics, 76,* 42-47.

Strasser, S. (1982). *A history of American housework.* New York: Pantheon.

Strober, M.H. (1977). Wives' labor force behavior and family consumption patterns. *American Economic Review, 67,* 410-417.

Strober, M.H., & Weinberg, C.B. (1980). Strategies used by working and non-working wives to reduce time pressures. *Journal of Consumer Research, 6,* 338-348.

Stromberg, A.H., & Harkess, S. (1978). *Women working.* Palo Alto, CA: Mayfield.

Sussman, M.B., & Cogswell, B.E. (1971). Family influences on job movement. *Human Relations, 24,* 477-487.

Suter, L.E., & Miller, H.P. (1973). Income differences between men and career women. *American Journal of Sociology, 78,* 962-974.

Swart, J.C. (1979). Flextime's debit and credit option. *Harvard Business Review, 57* (1), 10-12.

Talbot, N. (Ed.). (1976). *Raising children in modern America.* Boston: Little Brown.

Tetenbaum, T.J., Lighter, J., & Travis, M. (1981). Educators' attitudes toward working mothers. *Journal of Educational Psychology, 73,* 369-375.

Thoresen, R., & Goldsmith, E. (1987). The relationship between army families' financial well-being and depression, general well-being, and marital satisfaction. *Journal of Social Psychology, 127* (5), 545-547.

Tognoli, J. (1979). The flight from domestic space: Men's roles in the household. *Family Coordinator, 28,* 599-607.

Townsend, B. (1985). Working women. *American Demographics, 7* (1), 4-7.

Turner, C. (1971). Dual work households and marital dissolution. *Human Relations, 24,* 535-548.

Ulrich, D., & Dunne, H. (1986). *To love & work: A systemic interlocking of family, workplace, and career.* New York: Brunner/Mazel Publishers.

Van Maanen, J. (Ed.). (1974). *New perspectives in organizational careers.* New York: Wiley International.

Van Meter, M.J.S., & Agronow, S.J. (1982). The stress of multiple roles: The case for role strain among married college women. *Family Relations, 31,* 131-138.

Van Velsor, E.V., & O'Rand, A.M. (1984). Family life cycle, work career patterns. *Journal of Marriage and the Family, 46,* 365-373.

Verbrugge, L.M. (1983). Multiple roles and physical health of women and men. *Journal of Health and Social Behavior, 24,* 16-30.

Veroff, J., & Feld, S. (1970). *Marriage and work in America.* New York: Van Nostrand Reinhold.

Vicino, F.L., & Bass, B.M. (1978). Life space variables and managerial success. *Journal of Applied Psychology, 63,* 81-88.

Vocational Education Work and Family Institute. (1983). *Study of work-family issues in Minnesota.* St. Paul, MN: Minnesota Department of Education, Vocational Technical Division.

Voydanoff, P. (1980). *The implications of work-family relationships for productivity.* Scarsdale, NY: Work in America Institute.

Voydanoff, P. (1984). Economic distress and families: Policy issues. *Journal of Family Issues, 5,* 273-288.

Voydanoff, P. (1984). *Work and family: Changing roles of men and women.* Palo Alto, CA: Mayfield Publishing Co.

Voydanoff, P. (1987). *Work and family life.* Newbury Park, CA: Sage Publications, Inc.

Voydanoff, P., & Kelly, R.F. (1984). Determinants of work-related family problems among employed parents. *Journal of Marriage and the Family, 46,* 881-892.

Voydanoff, P., & Majka, L.C. (in press). *Families and economic distress: Coping strategies and social policy.* Beverly Hills, CA: Sage Publications.

Waite, L.J. (1980). Working wives and the family life cycle. *American Journal of Sociology, 86*, 272-294.

Waite, L.J., Haggstrom, G.W., & Kanouse, D.E. (1985). Changes in the employment activities of new parents. *American Sociological Review, 50*, 263-272.

Walker, K. (1970). *Time-use patterns for household work related to homemakers' employment.* US Department of Agriculture, Agricultural Research Service.

Walker, K.E., & Woods, M.E. (1976). *Time-use: A measure of household production of family goods and services.* Washington, DC: Center for the Family, American Home Economics Association.

Warr, P., & Parry, G. (1982). Paid employment and women's psychological well-being. *Psychological Bulletin, 91*, 498-516.

Weber, J.A., Cadwalader, D., Good, R., & Braun, B. (1986, Spring). The balancing act. *Journal of Extension, 24*, 17-20.

Weingarten, K. (1978). The employment patterns of professional couples and their distribution of involvement in the family. *Psychology of Women Quarterly, 3*, 43-52.

White, W.L. (1978). *A systems response to staff burn-out.* Rockville, MD: HCS.

Williams, J.H. (1987). *Psychology of women: Behavior in a biosocial context.* New York: W.W.Norton & Company.

Winter, D.G. (1973). *The power motive.* New York: Free Press.

Winter, D.G., Stewart, A.J., & McClelland, D.C. (1977). Husband's motives and wife's career level. *Journal of Personality and Social Psychology, 35*, 159-166.

Work and family: A changing dynamic. (1986). (Product Code 45 LSDR - 37). Rockville, MD: Bureau of National Affairs.

Yogev, S. (1981). Do professional women have egalitarian relationships? *Journal of Marriage and the Family, 43*, 865-871.

Yogev, S. (1982). Are professional women overworked: Objective versus subjective perception of role loads. *Journal of Occupational Psychology, 55*, 165-169.

Yogev, S., & Brett, J. (1985). Patterns of work and family involvement among single and dual-earner couples. *Journal of Applied Psychology, 70*, 754-768.

Yogev, S., & Brett, J. (1985). Perceptions of division of housework and child care and marital satisfaction. *Journal of Marriage and the Family, 47*, 609-618.

Zimmerman, K.W., Skinner, D.A., & Birner, R. (1980). Career involvement and job satisfaction as related to job strain and marital satisfaction of teachers and their spouses. *Home Economics Research Journal, 8*, 421-427.

Index of Names

Aberle 2, 17
Adams 193, 194, 202
Adler, N.J. 340, 344
Adolf, B. 285, 286
Agronow, S.J. 395
Ainlay, S. 207, 212, 224
Albrecht, K. 75, 90
Aldous, J. 4, 17, 33, 41, 133, 243, 247, 345, 346, 384
Allen, C.T. 394
Allen, J.G. 317, 319, 327
Allen, L. 328
Allen, V.L. 225
Almquist, E. 350, 360
Alvarez, W.F. 114, 131,132
Anderson, A. 206, 225
Anderson, S. 112
Anderson-Kulman, R.E. 131, 186, 189
Andre, R. 366, 371
Andres, D. 66, 69, 87
Andrews, F.A. 64, 85
Andrews, F.M. 384
Andrews, G. 318, 327
Aneshensel, C.S. 176, 177, 178,189
Angrist, S.S. 384
Antonucci, C. 206, 207, 225
Antonucci, T. 224
Appley, M.H. 384
Araji, S.K. 267, 276
Arce, C.H. 361
Arceo-Ortega, A. 380, 381
Arnott, C.C. 266, 276
Aronson, E. 330, 328, 345
Astin, H. 357, 359
Astin, H.S. 267, 276
Atkinson, H. 384
Atkinson, T. 328
Axel, H. 9, 17, 384

Baca-Zinn, M. 359
Backman, E. 77, 90
Baden, L. 384
Bahr, H.M. 208, 224
Bailyn, L. 32, 38, 71, 75, 85, 161, 172, 173, 333, 344, 359, 384
Baker, L. 94, 111
Bakke, E.W. 192, 194, 203
Bales, R.F. 58, 60
Baltes, P. 225
Banai, M. 341, 345
Bandura, A. 162, 174

Bane, M.J. 48, 53
Banner, D.K. 384
Bar-Yosef, R. 332, 344
Barahal, R.M. 374, 381
Barker, R. 189
Barling, J. 27, 28, 35, 41, 44, 69, 75, 85
Barnes, L.B. 384
Barnett, R.C. 7, 17, 64, 76, 85, 114, 131, 176, 177, 178, 186, 189, 206, 224, 374, 381, 383, 384
Baron, A.S. 265, 276
Barrera, M., Jr. 207, 212, 224
Barrett, G.V. 137, 156
Bartolomè, F. 138, 327, 384, 386
Baruch, G.K. 7, 17, 64, 76, 85, 114, 131, 176, 177, 178, 186, 189, 206, 224, 374, 381, 383, 384
Baskam, R.B. 115, 132
Bass, B.M. 395
Batson, C. 104, 111
Baum-Baicker, C. 101, 102, 110
Baxandall, R. 384
Bayer, G. 91, 104, 105, 106, 107, 110
Bebbington, A.C. 164, 174, 384
Becker, G. 58, 60
Becker, M.A. 384
Beckman, F.J. 384
Bedelian, A.G. 29, 34, 43, 43, 64, 68, 90
Beehr, T.A. 384
Beehr, T.W. 42
Belcastro, P.A. 137, 155
Belcourt, M.L. 36, 41
Belle, D. 50, 53
Belsky, J. 75, 80, 85, 115, 131
Benin, M.H. 80, 85, 266, 276
Berardo, D.H. 172, 174, 267, 275, 276
Berger, M. 228, 247, 387
Bergermaier, R. 114, 132
Berheide, C. 69, 85, 385
Berk, R. 228, 247, 385
Berk, S. 57, 58, 60, 228, 247, 385
Berkowitz, A. 318, 327
Berlew, D.E. 38, 41
Berman, E. 331, 344
Berman, P.W. 87
Bernard, J. 78, 86, 228, 247, 332, 333, 344, 345, 379, 381, 385
Berry, J.W. 371
Berry, K.J. 391
Bersoff, D. 70, 86
Best, F. 385

Betz, N.E. 28, 41, 350, 359
Beutell, N. 99, 110
Beutell, N.J. 10, 18, 25, 26, 27, 32, 36, 37, 41, 42, 249, 250, 251, 255, 257, 263, 288, 289, 299, 300, 301, 303, 304, 312, 314, 327, 333, 335, 344, 385, 387
Bhagat, R. 62, 86
Bhagat, R.S. 42, 136, 155, 384
Bianchi, S. 2, 20, 69, 89
Biderman, A.D. 89, 385
Biener, L. 7, 17, 114, 131, 178, 186, 189, 206, 224, 384
Billings, A.G. 114, 115, 118, 119, 120, 132, 133
Bird, C. 385
Bird, G.A. 69, 86, 385
Bird, G.W. 69, 86, 385
Birner, R. 396
Black, G. 328
Blake, R.R. 304, 314
Blechman 14, 17
Blehar, M.C. 388
Blitz, T. 332, 344
Block 11, 17
Blood, R. 93, 110
Bloom, A. 332, 344
Bloom, D.E. 385
Blotnick, S. 385
Bode, J. 267, 276
Bodin, J. 385
Bohen, H. 9, 17, 385
Bohn, M.J. 386
Boles, A.J. 64, 78, 86, 87
Booth, A. 81, 86, 208, 224, 385
Bopp, M. , 94, 110
Borg, I. 114, 132
Borgatta, E.F. 14, 20
Borman, K.M. 20, 385
Bortner, R.W. 294, 301
Borwick, I. 94, 98, 99, 100, 108, 110
Boss, P.G. 385
Boukydis, D.F.Z. 86
Boulding, E. 385
Bowman, P.J. 11, 17
Bradburn, N.M. 81, 89, 321, 328, 391, 328
Bradshaw, P. 27, 41, 138, 136, 155
Brand, S. 21
Brandao, M.A. 375, 381
Brassard, J. 115, 117, 132
Braun, B. 396
Braun, W.J. 388
Braunstein, D.N. 335, 346
Bray, D.W. 136, 155
Brayfield, A.H. 89
Brazelton, T.B. 18
Brett, J.M. 131, 159, 161, 162, 165, 174, 385, 396
Briar, K.H. 194, 201, 203
Brief, A.P. 29, 41
Brigham, F.H., Jr. 21
Brim, O.G. 225
Brinkerhoff, M.B. 19, 21, 385
Brislin, R.W. 366, 369, 371
Brody, E. 14, 17, 385
Bronfenbrenner, U. 2, 18, 113, 114, 115, 132, 228, 247
Bronstein, P. 85, 89, 381
Brooks, G.W. 293, 301
Brown, C.T. 304, 313, 315
Brown, R. 86
Brownlee, H. 91
Bryson, J.B. 41, 267, 276, 331, 358, 344, 359, 385, 388
Bryson, R.A. 344, 359, 385, 388
Bryson, R.B. 30, 41, 276
Bulatao, R.A. 375, 380, 381
Bunge, F.M. 380, 381
Burden, D.S. 77, 86, 385
Burke, R.J. 25, 27, 36, 41, 75, 86, 136, 137, 138, 144, 154, 155, 156, 287, 301, 320, 321, 322, 327, 329, 343, 344, 383, 385, 386
Burr, W.R. 20, 41, 247, 248
Butler, J.K., Jr. 268, 270, 276, 277
Butler, M. 93, 111
Butler, M.C. 389
Buxton, M. 112
Byrne, D. 384

Cadwalader, D. 396
Cain, V. 279, 280, 286
Callegari, A.I. 376, 381
Campbell, D.T. 369, 371
Campbell, R.J. 136, 155
Cantor, M. 392
Cantrell, R.S. 268, 270, 276
Caplan, G. 193, 194, 203, 207, 212, 386
Caplan, R.D. 194, 203, 318, 321, 327
Carson, C.S. 49, 53
Cassel, J. 327
Catalano, R. 88
Cauble, A. 100, 111
Cauble, E. 193, 203
Chacko, T.I. 64, 86, 138, 156
Chacon, M. 347, 360
Champoux, J. E. 114, 132, 152, 156
Chan, M. 304, 314
Chassin, L. 326, 327
Cherniss, C. 292, 293, 301, 321, 332, 344
Cherns, A.B. 386
Chess, W.A. 136, 156
Chung, T. 112

Chung, Y.L. 252, 264
Chusmir, L.H. 266, 267, 274, 276, 303
Clark, R.A. 69, 86, 386
Clark, V.A. 177, 189
Cobb, S. 193, 201, 203, 207, 212, 224, 293, 301, 318, 327
Cochran, M.M. 117, 132
Cogswell, B.E. 395
Cohen, S. 35, 41, 165, 174, 225
Cohn, R.M. 193, 203
Coie, J.D. 86
Coleman 12, 18
Colligan, M. 328
Collins, R.H. 386
Comeau, J. 100, 111, 193, 203
Condran, J. 267, 276
Connelly, T.F. 25, 43, 99, 11, 298, 293, 302, 390
Connelly, W.E. 293, 301
Cooke, R.A. 36, 41, 62, 86, 92, 99, 110, 386
Cooney, R.S. 360
Cooper, C.L. 29, 41, 62, 86, 155, 301, 302, 327, 333, 344, 345, 386
Cooper, K. 327
Cooper, R.G. 374, 382
Corfman, E. 386, 392
Corson, W. 194, 204
Cortis 326
Cosier, R.A. 306, 314
Cotis, G.A. 328
Couch, A.S. 250, 251, 252, 257, 263
Coverman 12, 18
Cowan, C.P. 64, 68, 71, 74, 75, 76, 79, 80, 81, 85, 86, 89, 381
Cowan, P.A. 61, 64, 68, 71, 74, 75, 76, 79, 80, 81, 86
Coyne, J. 102, 111
Coysh, W.S. 64, 76, 86, 87
Crits-Christoph, P. 69, 78, 89, 130, 133, 163, 174
Crnic, K.A. 115, 132
Cronkite, R.C. 133
Croog, S.H. 192, 203
Crosby, F. 7, 18, 70, 85, 86, 136, 138, 156, 365, 371
Crouter, A.C. 2, 3, 13, 18, 20, 36, 41, 75, 81, 85, 87, 131, 132, 251, 254, 255, 257, 259, 263, 386
Cummings, L.L. 43
Curtis-Boles, 64, 86

Dachler, H.P. 138, 157
Dahl, B.B. 391
Daniels, A.K. 12, 18
Daniels, D. 113, 120, 131, 132

Darrow, C.N. 33, 43
Davidson, F.M. 328
Davidson, P.O. 328
Davies, M. 360
Davis, G., 360
Davis, L.E. 68, 88, 386
Dawis, R.V. 136, 157
Deal, J.E. 373
Dean, A. 180, 189
DeMunn, E. 92, 112
Denzin, N.K. 252, 263
Depner, C. 207, 224
Derogatis, L.R. 321, 328
Derr, C.B. 41, 386
Deszca, G. 136, 155
Dibona, P. 77, 90
Dickie 75
Dill, D. 391
Dizard, J. 75, 87
Doane, J. 100, 110
Dohrenwend, B.S. 386
Dooley, D. 88
Dougherty, K. 386
Douvan, E. 379, 382
Drury, T.F. 89, 385
Dubois, L.M. 249, 251, 257, 259, 263
Duncan, G.J. 48, 53, 386
Dunnette, M.D. 19, 315
Durham, M. 390
DuWors, R.F. 137, 155, 157, 301, 386
Dyer, W.G. 2, 18, 138, 156
Dytell, R.S. 175 176, 178, 179, 188, 189

Eichler, L. 87
Elder, G.H., Jr. 73, 87
Ellwood, D.T. 48, 53
Elman, M.R. 386
Engel, J.W. 363, 365, 368, 369, 371
Engelken, C. 93, 110
England, G.W. 136, 157
England, P. 58, 60, 64, 69, 90, 386
Ensel, W. 192, 203
Ensel, W.M. 176, 180, 189
Epstein, C.F. 30, 41
Escobeda, T. 360
Esterik, P.V. 381, 382
Etzion, D 62, 87, 330, 331, 332, 333, 344
Evans, P.L. 138, 327, 384, 386
Eviota, E.U. 374, 381
Eyland, A. 83, 87
Ezrachi, Y. 334, 344

Farkas, G. 58, 60, 228, 247, 386
Farmer, H.S. 386
Fawl, C.L. 187, 189
Featherman, D.L. 118, 133

Feinleib, M. 388
Feinstein, K.W. 387
Feld, S. 395
Feldman, H. 387
Feldman, M. 387
Felstehausen, G. 250, 251, 252, 257, 263
Fendrich, M. 74, 87
Ferber, M. 276, 387
Ferguson, K. 387
Fernandez, J. P. 229, 247
Ferree, M.M. 178, 189
Figley, C.R. 21
Finch, J. 14, 18, 387
Finlay, B. 256, 263
Finn, P. 279, 280, 286, 387
Finney, J.W. 133
Fioravanti, M. 77, 87
Fischer, C.S. 225
Fischer, J.L. 205, 209, 211, 224
Fischer, K.W. 83, 87
Fitzgerald, L.F. 28, 41, 350, 359
Florian 137, 144, 154
Foa, E.B. 211, 224
Foa, U.G. 211, 224
Fogarty, M.P. 387
Folkard, S. 279, 280, 286
Folkman, S. 72, 88
Ford, J.G. 94, 110
Forisha, B. 387
Foster, M. 228, 247
Foster, M.A. 387
Fowlkes, M.R. 342, 344
Fox, K.D., 76, 87
Fox, M.F. 64, 69, 87, 227, 247
Fox, R. 374, 381
Franks 9, 22
Freidson, E. 336, 344
French, J. 92, 111
French, Jr., J.R.P. 19, 193, 203, 327
Frerichs, R.R. 177, 189
Freudenberger, H.J. 387
Freudiger, D. 350, 360
Friedman, E. 94, 98, 102, 103, 106, 108, 110
Froberg, D., 350, 360
Frohardt-Lane, K. 392
Fuchs, R. 73, 87
Fudge, D.A. 34, 44, 394
Fuhr, R. 130, 133

Galinsky 3, 9, 18
Ganster, D.C. 301
Gardner, C.W. 388
Garfinkel 13, 18
Garland, T.N. 227, 248, 266, 277, 392
Garmezy, N. 89

Garrett, E. 64, 86
Garrison, H.H. 2, 19, 391
Garza, R.T. 356, 361
Gaylord, M. 387
Gecas, V. 69, 86, 386
Geiselman, L.A. 359, 360
Gelpi, B.C. 20
Gerber, L.A. 330, 342, 343, 344
Gerson, K. 206, 225, 267, 276, 387
Gerstein, L. 91, 104, 105, 106, 107, 110
Gerstel, N. 12, 18, 19
Geyer-Pestello, H.F. 177, 190
Gideonse, S. 20, 385
Giele, J.Z. 381
Gilbert, L.A. 3, 18, 35, 42, 99, 110, 139, 156, 289, 302, 318, 319, 320, 328, 331, 333, 342, 345, 386, 389
Gjerdingen, D. 360
Glick, P.C. 13, 20
Glosson, L.R. 250, 251, 252, 257, 263
Gocka, E.F. 166, 174
Godley, S.H. 144, 157
Goebel, K. 387
Gold, D. 66, 69, 87
Gold, R.S. 137, 155
Goldberg, H. 94, 110
Goldberg, I. 94, 110
Goldberg, W.A. 86
Goldman, F. 387
Goldsen, R.K. 269, 276
Goldsmith, E.B. 383
Gomberg, W. 18, 394
Gongla 14, 18
Gonyea, J.G. 14, 19
Good, R. 396
Goode, W.J. 68, 87, 387
Googins, B. 77, 86, 385
Gordon, H.A. 360
Gordon, L. 384
Gore, S. 35, 42, 193, 194, 201, 202, 203
Gottlieb, B 225
Gottlieb, B.H. 115, 132
Gottlieb, N. 112
Goudy, W.J. 69, 88
Gough, H.G. 77, 87
Gould, S. 28, 42, 387
Gove, W.R. 176, 177, 189
Goysh 64
Grady, K. 212, 225
Granrose, C.S. 32, 42
Grant, D.L. 136, 155
Green, G.B. 62, 75, 78, 90
Green, S.B. 89, 209, 224, 392
Greenberg, M.T. 115, 132
Greenglass, E.R. 136, 155, 287, 301, 318, 326, 327, 329, 343, 344, 383, 386,

Greenglass, E.R.(con't) 387
Greenhaus, J.H. 10, 23, 25, 26, 27, 28, 29,
    31, 32, 34, 36, 37, 38, 41, 42, 43, 99,
    110, 111, 249, 250, 251, 255, 257,
    263, 288, 289, 299, 300, 301, 302,
    303, 304, 312, 314, 318, 327, 335,
    342, 344, 345, 385, 387
Greiff, B.S. 387
Groat, H.T. 387
Gross, H.G. 12, 19
Gross, N. 26, 42
Gross, N.E. 340, 345
Grossman, F. 71, 87
Groves, D. 14, 18
Gueron, J. 51, 53
Guest, D. 138, 156, 341, 345, 387
Gupta, N. 31, 42, 249, 250, 251, 255, 256,
    259, 263
Gurman, A. 94, 110
Guss, T. 73, 90
Gutek, B.A. 11, 20, 251, 263, 287, 301,
    302, 371, 390
Gyllstrom, K.K. 249, 251, 257, 263, 331,
    345

Haas, L. 163, 174
Haccoun, D. 319, 327
Hackman, J.R. 44
Hackman, R.J. 165, 174, 387
Hafer, M. 144, 157
Haggstrom, G.W. 7, 22, 396
Hall, D.T. 28, 31, 32, 36, 37, 38, 39, 41,
    42, 79, 80, 98, 162, 165, 174, 206,
    224, 228, 248, 331, 342, 345, 388
Hall, F. S. 32, 42, 224, 342, 345, 388
Hall, R. 345, 388
Hall, R.H. 87
Hamilton, D. 104, 110
Hamilton, V. 42
Hammond, J.L. 356, 360
Hanlon, M.D. 193, 194, 196, 200, 203
Hanson, A.L. 137, 157
Hanson, S.L. 70, 88
Harburg, E. 178, 189
Hare, H. 104, 112
Harkess, S. 395
Harrell, A.M. 268, 270, 277
Harrell, J. 131, 132
Harris, L. 390
Harris, O. 381
Harrison, A. 388
Harrison, R.V. 193, 203, 327
Hart, L.B. 314, 315
Harter, S. 68, 87
Hartmann, H. 393
Hartmann, H.I. 78, 90

Hartsock, N.C.M. 20
Harvey, A.S. 87
Harvey, W. 112
Haub, C. 360
Hauenstein, L.S. 178, 189, 388
Hautaluoma, J.E. 390
Haw, M.A. 66, 69, 87
Hawkes, G.R. 3, 20, 163, 174
Hayes, C.D. 388, 389, 390
Hayghe, H. 365, 371, 388
Haynes, S.G. 388
Hazleton, L. 331, 345
Heckman, H.A. 388
Hedges, J.N. 388
Hefferan, C. 193, 203
Heinicke, C. 71, 87
Heming, G. 64, 86
Henderson, C. 249, 250, 251, 255, 256,
    257, 259, 264, 266, 277, 394
Henderson, C.R. 114, 132
Hendrix, W. 388
Hendrix, W.H. 62, 87
Hennon, C.B. 387
Herald, J. 349, 361
Herman, J.B. 249, 251, 257, 263, 331, 345
Hertz, R. 3, 18, 174, 330, 345
Herzberg, F. 30, 42, 137, 154, 156
Hess, B.B. 20
Hesse-Biber, S. 64, 69, 87, 227, 247
Hewlett, S.A. 9, 18, 349, 358, 360, 388
Hicks, M.W. 4, 17, 33, 41, 243, 247
Hill, C.T. 319, 328
Hill, M.D. 286, 388
Hill, M.S. 81, 88, 286, 388
Hill, R. 41, 49, 53, 100, 101, 110, 192, 200,
    203, 247, 248, 345
Hiller, D.V. 388, 392
Hirsch, B. 206, 207, 224, 225
Hirschlein, B.M. 388
Hirshorn, S.A. 384
Hite, R.L. 374, 382
Hobfoll, S.E. 189, 190, 388
Hodson, R. 349, 360
Hofferth, S. 2, 20
Hofferth, S.L. 388, 391
Hofffman, C. 14, 17
Hoffman, L.W. 2, 4, 8, 18, 69, 73, 88, 131,
    132, 349, 360, 374, 381, 388, 391
Hoffman, M. 104, 110
Holahan, C.J. 115, 119, 120, 132
Holahan, C.K. 35, 42, 99, 110, 139, 156,
    289, 302, 317, 318, 319, 320, 328,
    331, 333, 345, 389
Hollister, R.G. 50, 51, 54
Holmes, T.H. 29, 42, 302
Holmstrom, L.L. 267, 277, 391

Holtgraves, M. 91
Hood, J.C. 8, 13, , 18, 88, 389
Hooyman, N.R. 14, 19
Hopkins, J. 389
Horn, J. 104, 111
Horowitz 14, 18
House, J.S. 19, 35, 42, 92, 111, 192, 203, 206, 207, 225, 389
Houseknecht, S.K. 75, 88, 266, 277, 360
Houser, B.B. 384
Howrigan, G. 386
Huber, J. 72, 90, 358, 360, 387
Hudis, P.M. 389
Hughes, M. 176, 189
Hulin, C.L. 136, 157
Hulka, B.S. 361
Hunt, J.G. 8, 19, 330, 345, 389
Hunt, L.L. 330, 345, 389
Hunt, R.G. 64, 78, 89, 90, 138, 157, 161, 391, 393
Hunter, E.J. 391
Hurst, M. 360, 374, 382
Huston, T.L. 80, 88

Iglehart, A.P. 360
Igodan, O.C. 389
Ihinger-Tallman, M. 92, 111
Ilchman, A.S. 9, 18
Imai, K. 364, 371
Imig, D. 102, 110
Imig, G. 102, 110
Iris, B. 137, 156
Irwin, R.D. 248
Israel, B.A. 210, 225
Ivancevich, J.M. 29, 42, 301
Izraeli, D.N. 329, 340, 341, 344, 345

Jackson, S.E. 27, 42, 114, 133, 136, 137, 139, 141, 142, 144, 154, 156, 157, 161, 174, 293, 302, 389
Jacobsen, R.B. 391
Jacobson, A. 389
Jahan, R. 381
James, L.R. 166, 174
Jankowski, J. 91
Jayaratne, S. 136, 137, 138, 144, 154, 156
Jenkins, C.D. Jr. 249, 250, 251, 255, 256, 259, 263
Jenkins, D. 31, 42
Jick, T.D. 252. 263, 389
Johnsen, P.T. 17
Johnson, B.L. 193, 203, 389
Johnson, C.L. 345, 349, 360, 389
Johnson, D.R. 81, 86
Johnson, F.A. 345, 349, 360, 389
Johnson, J. 394

Johnson, J.H. 29, 30, 42
Johnson, M.F. 41, 331, 334
Jolly, E.A. 207, 225
Jones, A. 93, 111
Jones, A.P. 389
Jones R. 389
Jones, W. 389
Journard, S.M. 328
Joy, C. 100, 111, 193, 203
Juster, F.T. 228, 247

Kabanoff, B. 19, 389
Kafry, D. 392
Kagan, J. 187, 190
Kahn, A.J. 9, 19
Kahn, L. 206, 225
Kahn, R.L. 25, 26, 42
Kahn, W. 365, 371
Kamarch, T. 165, 174
Kamerman, S.B. 9, 18, 19, 388, 389
Kammeyer, K.C. 360
Kamo, Y. 14, 19
Kandel, D.B. 357, 360
Kanner, A. 102, 111
Kanner, A.D. 72, 88
Kanouse, D.E. 7, 22, 396
Kanter, R.M. 4, 19, 30, 42, 58, 60, 92, 93, 111, 114, 133, 136, 228, 247, 287, 302, 327, 328, 340, 345, 389
Kanungo, R.N. 87, 89, 390
Karoly, P. 22
Kasarda, J.D. 48, 54
Kasl, S. 193, 201, 203
Kasl, S.V. 178, 189, 293, 301
Kato, S. 371
Katz, M.H. 130, 133, 389
Katz, R. 331, 335, 345
Keenan, A. 36, 43
Keith 69, 74
Keith, P.M. 69, 74, 88, 172, 174, 249, 250, 251, 255, 257, 259, 263, 389
Kejner, M. 162, 165, 174, 390
Kellerman, H. 88
Kelly, R.F. 6, 19, 45, 47, 48, 49, 50, 54, 75, 81, 88, 229, 247, 248, 249, 250, 251, 254, 255, 256, 257, 259, 264, 390
Kemper, P. 54
Kemper, T.D. 78, 88, 138, 156
Kendall, L.N. 136,157
Kessler, R.C. 36, 42, 74, 88, 114, 133, 176, 178, 189, 190, 390
Kew, S. 90
Khan, G.B. 285, 286
Kieko, H. 371
Kikuchi, B. 364

INDEX OF NAMES

Kikuchi, D. 371
Killilea, M. 21, 224, 386
Kilmann, R.H. 304, 306, 315
Kilpatrick, A. 266, 277
King, W.L. 328, 390
Kingston, P.W. 8, 9, 19, 20, 55, 174, 390
Kleban, M.H.. 17
Klein, E.B. 33, 43
Klein, V. 391
Kline, M. 61, 75, 88
Knaub, P. 92, 111
Kniskern, D. 94, 110
Kohn, M. 391
Kohn, M.L. 114, 133
Komarovsky, M. 75, 88
Kon, I. 390
Kopelman, R.E. 25, 43, 99, 111, 288, 289, 302, 342, 345, 387, 390
Korman, A.K. 34, 43, 69, 88
Korman, R.W. 34, 43
Kormanski, C. 101, 111
Kornhauser, A.W. 137, 156
Kramerman, S.B. 390
Krause, N. 70, 88, 177, 190
Krause, N.E 357, 360, 374, 381
Krausz, S.L. 187, 190
Kreuter, G.V. 392
Kulka, R. 379, 382
Kumagai, F. 369, 371
Kumka, D.S. 157
Kunkel, D.A. 135, 136, 156
Kunkel-Schetter, C. 328
Kuo, W. 192, 203

LaBier, D. 34, 43
Ladd, L. 73, 90
Ladewig, B.H. 206, 225
Lamb, M.E. 19, 390
Landerman, L.R. 19
Lane, D.M. 268, 277
Lang, L. 25, 34, 43, 249, 250, 251, 255, 263, 392
Lang, M.E. 80, 85
Langner 179, 190
Lapsley, H. 83, 87
LaRocco, J. 92, 111
LaRocco, J.M. 19
Larrick, D. 13, 21
Larson, J.H. 194, 201, 203
Larwood, L. 20, 302, 371, 390
Lasch, C. 104, 111
Launier, R. 36, 43
Lave, J.R. 384
Lawhon, T. 389
Lawler, E.E. 165, 174
Lawler, E.E., III. 387

Lazaro 137
Lazarus, R. 102, 111
Lazarus, R.S. 29, 36, 43, 72, 88, 318, 327, 328
Lazzari, R. 77, 87
Lebra, T. S. 366, 371
Lee, M.D. 87, 89, 156, 390
Lee, R.A. 9, 18, 19, 390
Lein, L. 8, 19, 386, 390
Leslie, E. 164, 172, 174
Leslie, G. 174
Leslie, G.R. 174, 267, 275, 276
Leslie, L. 206, 212, 225
Lester, G. 385
Levine, J. 187, 190
Levine, M.F. 68, 88
Levine, S. 192, 203
Levinger, G. 390
Levinson, D.J. 33, 43
Levinson, H. 103, 111
Levinson, M.H. 43
Levitan, S.A. 390
Levy, Z. 332, 344
Lewis, D.M. 364, 371
Lewis, H.S. 364, 371
Lewis, J. 93, 94, 111
Lewis, M. 93, 94, 111
Lewis, R.A. 77, 90
Licht, B.G. 267, 276
Licht, M.H. 276
Lichtenstein, S. 268, 277
Liebman, R. 94, 111
Lief, H. 331, 344
Liem, J.H. 73, 74, 88
Liem, R. 73, 74, 88
Lighter, J. 395
Lin, N., 189, 192, 203
Lindenthal, J.J. 192, 203
Lindholm, S. 62, 86, 136, 155
Lindzey, G. 263, 328
Lippitt, G.L 304, 315
Lipson, A. 192, 203
Liss, M.B. 285, 286
Lloyd, C. 78, 88
Locke E.A. 19, 136, 137, 156
Lodahl, T. 162, 165, 174, 390
Lofquist, L.H. 135, 136, 157
London, M. 43, 315
Lopata, H. 174, 192, 203
Lopata, H.Z. 390
Lorber, J. 331, 345
Lorence, J., 135, 157
Lupri, E. 12, 19
Lynch, J.T. 384

Maanen, J.V. 263

Machlowitz, M. 390
Macke, A.S. 75, 88, 266, 277, 360
Madans, J.H. 176, 190
Mahoney, T.A. 390
Majka, L.C. 13, 17, 21, 54
Manis, J. 392
Maret, E. 256, 263
Markides, K.S. 357, 360
Marks, S.R. 391
Marques, T.E. 268, 277
Marshall, J. 29, 41
Martin, J.K. 70, 88
Martin, T.N. 62, 64, 68, 88
Martin, T.W. 391
Maruyama, Y. 371
Maslach, C. 27, 42, 114, 133, 136, 137, 139, 141, 142, 144, 154, 156, 157, 293, 302, 389, 391
Mason, C. 83, 87
Mason, W.S. 26, 42
Matteson, M.T. 29, 42
Matthews, K. 104, 111
Maurice, M. 280, 286
Mausner, B. 137, 156
Maynard, R. 54
Mayseless, O.B. 115, 133
McClelland, D.C. 396
McCrae, J.A. 114, 133, 176, 189
McCubbin, H. 100, 111, 193, 194, 200, 203
McCubbin, H. E. 203
McCubbin, H.I. 21, 385, 391
McDaniel, S. 94, 110, 112
McEachern, A.W. 26, 42
McGee, G.W. 62, 90
McGee, W. 206, 225
McHale, S.M. 80, 88
McKee, B. 33, 43
McLanahan 13, 18
McLaughlin, S.D. 7, 19, 361
McLean, A. 328
McMichael, A.J. 19
McNeely, R.L. 361
McQuaid, S. 62, 86
McQuaid, S.J 136, 155
McRae, J.A., Jr. 74, 88, 390
Mednick, M.T. 345
Meissner, M. 331, 345
Mermelstein, R. 165, 174
Metzen, E.J. 76, 89
Michaels, G.Y. 86
Michelsen, R. 384
Miller, H.P. 395
Miller, J. 2, 19
Miller, J. 391
Miller, J.J. 120, 132

Miller, J.V. 266, 277
Miller, K. 391
Miller, W.B. 86
Mills, J. 303
Milman, L. 111
Minor, J. 388
Minors, D.S. 279, 280, 286
Minton, C. 187, 190
Minuchin, S. 94, 95, 111
Mirowsky, J. 72, 90
Mischel, W. 305, 315
Mitchell, E. 207, 212, 225
Mitchell, R. 225
Mitelman, B. 385
Mitz, L.F. 389
Model, S. 88
Moen, P. 3, 4, 10, 64, 69, 72, 88, 193, 194, 200, 201, 202, 203
Moles, O.C. 390
Mone, E.M. 43
Monroe, S.M. 206, 208, 225
Montgomery, R.J.V. 14, 19, 20
Moon, M. 78, 86
Moore, K. 69, 72, 75, 89
Moore, K.A. 2, 20, 391
Moore, L.L. 41
Moos, B.S. 113, 114, 115, 118, 119, 120, 130, 131, 132,
Moos, R.H. 207, 225
Morgan, J.N. 280, 286
Moris, A.H. 391
Morrison, D.F. 328
Mortimer, J.T. 3, 4, 11, 20, 75, 89, 135, 157, 332, 345, 391
Mosier, K. 135
Mossholder, K.W. 28, 34, 42, 43
Mouton, J.S. 304, 314
Moynihan, D. P. 54
Muller, C. 349, 358, 361
Mumola, D.E. 10, 20
Munter, P.K. 387
Murphy, D. 92, 111
Murphy, K. R. 268, 277
Murray, M.A. 328
Mussen, N.P. 87
Myers, D. 94, 111
Myers, J.K. 192, 203
Myrdal, A. 391

Naegele, K. 2, 17
Nakamura, C.Y. 251, 263
Nakamura, K. 371
Napoli, A. 179, 189
Nash, J. 382
Nathanson, C.A. 357, 361
Neal, A.G. 387

Neale, M.S. 9, 22
Near, J.P. 64, 78, 89, 90, 138, 157, 161, 391, 393
Neckerman, K. 49, 54
Needle, R. 100, 111, 193
Neff, W. 391
Neher, C.D. 379, 381
Netter, J. 248
Newcomb, L.H. 389
Newman, L.F. 86
Newson, D. 327
Newton, T.J. 36, 43
Nicholson, W. 194, 204
Nickols, S.Y. 76, 87, 89, 393
Nicola, J.S. 3, 20, 163, 174
Niemi, B. 78, 88
Nienstedt, B.C. 80, 85, 266, 276
Nieva, V.F. 3, 11, 20, 70, 89, 136, 157, 251, 263, 301, 302
Nock, S.L. 8, 19, 174, 390
Nollen, S.D. 391
Norr, K.F. 390
Norris, W.P. 374, 375, 381
Norton, A.J. 13, 20
Norusis, M.J. 311, 315
Nougaim, K. 162, 174
Novack, C.C. 20
Nowack, K.M. 137, 157, 391
Nuckolls 202
Nye, F.I. 2, 20, 41, 69, 86, 88, 132, 224, 247, 248, 374, 381, 386, 388, 391

O'Connor, P. 75, 90
O'Rand, A.M. 395
O'Reilly, J. 365, 371
O'Toole, J. 392
Oakley, A. 391
Olson, D.H. 174
Ooms, T. 21
Oppenheimer, V.K. 391
Orden, S.R. 81, 89, 321, 328, 391
Orpen, C. 89, 391
Orthner, D.K. 6, 20, 228, 229, 248, 266, 277
Ortiz, V. 361
Osherson, S. 391
Oshima, M. 371
Osiprow, S.H. 361
Oskamp, S. 133
Osmond, M.W. 4, 17, 33, 41, 243, 247
Ouchi, W. 247, 248
Ovalle, N.K., II 62, 87

Paguio, L.P. 374, 381
Pahl, J.J. 157, 138
Pahl, R.E. 157, 138

Palkovitz, R. 86
Pallack, S.M 133
Paludi, M.A. 131, 186, 189
Papanek, H. 3. 20, 332, 345, 392
Parasuraman, S. 28, 29, 32, 35, 36, 42, 43, 289, 301, 303, 314
Pardine, P., 179, 189
Parke, R. 88
Parry, G. 73, 90, 396
Parsons, T. 58, 60
Pasquali, L. 376, 381
Patterson, G. 73, 89, 112
Patterson, J. 100, 102, 111, 193, 203
Patterson, J.J. 50, 54
Patton, M.O. 254, 263
Paulson, N. 392
Payne, R. 302, 345, 386
Payton-Miyazaki, M. 89
Pearce, D. 13, 20
Pearlin, L.I. 36, 43, 176, 177, 178, 189, 190
Pedersen, F.R. 87
Pedhazer, E.J. 234, 248
Pendleton, B.F. 388
Peplau, L. 319, 328
Peres, Y. 331, 335, 345
Perkins, H.W. 318, 327
Perl, M.S. 388
Perry-Jenkins, M. 3, 13, 18, 20, 75, 85, 131
Peterson, S.S. 388
Pett, M.A. 14, 20
Pfeffer, J. 172, 174
Pfefferbaum, B. 388
Philliber, W.W. 388, 392
Pierre, J.H. 251, 257, 263
Pietromonaco, P.R. 392
Pines, A. 330, 345, 392
Pines, M. 326. 327. 328
Pinneau, S. 192, 193, 200, 204, 327
Piotrkowski, C.S. 3, 4, 8, 20, 69, 70, 71, 72, 78, 89, 114, 130, 133, 138, 163, 174, 389, 392
Pistrang, N. 66, 69, 72, 89
Pittman, J.F. 6, 20, 229, 248, 266, 277
Pleck, J.H. 8, 9, 20, 25, 26, 30, 43, 44, 71, 75, 78, 79, 80, 89, 90, 114, 133, 161, 162, 172, 174, 176, 186, 190, 206, 222, 225, 227, 228, 246, 248, 249, 250, 251, 255, 263, 285, 286, 331, 332, 346, 390, 392, 394
Plutchik, R. 88
Poloma, M.M. 227, 248, 226, 277, 333, 346, 392
Pond, S.B. 75, 78, 89, 392
Poor, R. 392
Poraz, A. 341, 345
Porter, S. 363, 371

Portner, J. 392
Pottick, K.J. 34, 44, 394
Powell, D.R. 192, 201, 204
Powers, E.A. 69, 88
Pratt, M. 390
Preister, S. 21
Presser, H. 279, 280, 285, 286
Preston, M. 360
Preston, S. 392
Price, L.W. 326, 328
Price, R.H. 36, 42, 179, 190
Price-Bonham, S. 92, 111, 174
Pruett, K.D. 73, 89

Quarm, D. 385
Quinn, R. 25, 42
Quinn, R.P. 293, 302, 321, 328, 392
Quint, H.H. 392

Rabinowitz, S. 28, 32, 42, 43, 228, 248
Rachlin, 3, 18
Radin, N. 73, 89, 374, 381
Ragozin, A.S. 115, 132
Rahe, R.H. 29, 42, 302
Rahim, M.A. 304, 314, 315
Rainwater, L. 374, 382
Rallings, E.M. 2, 20, 248
Rank, M.R. 393
Rapoport, R. 3, 4, 8, 21, 30, 31, 35, 43, 70, 78, 89, 90, 163, 174, 247, 266, 274, 275, 277, 330, 331, 333, 346, 359, 387, 393
Rapoport, R.N. 3, 4, 8, 21, 30, 31, 35, 43, 70, 78, 83, 90, 89, 90, 247, 266, 274, 275, 277, 330, 331, 333, 359, 387, 393
Rau, M.T. 207, 223, 225
Raveis, U.H. 360
Reaven, J. 327
Regan, M.C. 266, 268, 269, 275, 277
Reichler, M.L. 78, 88, 138, 156
Reilly, M.D. 393
Reiss, I.L. 41, 247, 248
Renshaw, J.R. 393
Renwick, P. 305, 315
Repetti, R.L. 71, 72, 89, 114, 115, 133, 301, 302
Reskin, B. 393
Reverby, S. 384
Revilla, V.A. 312, 315
Rexroat, C. 393
Rhodes, S.R. 394
Rice, D.G. 228, 248, 393
Rice, R.W. 64, 78, 89, 90, 138, 157, 391, 393
Richards, A.T. 392
Richards, C.B. 180, 190

Richardson, J.M. 392
Richie, J. 382
Richman, P. 328
Richter, J. 28, 29, 36, 37, 42, 43
Ridley, C.A. 69, 71, 90, 131, 132, 393
Rigger, T.F. 144, 154, 157
Ritzer, G. 393
Rivers, C. 383, 384
Robbins, C.A. 19
Robertson, I.T. 137, 155, 301, 327
Robinson, B. 373, 374, 381
Robinson, N.M. 115, 132
Rodgers, R.H. 165, 174
Rodman, H. 11, 12, 13, 21
Roland, H.E. , 266, 268, 269, 275, 277
Rollings, 10, 20
Romero, G.L. 356, 361
Ronen, S. 393, 79, 90
Rose, K. 285, 286
Rose, S.M. 208, 225
Rosenbaum, A. 28, 41
Rosenberg, M. 180, 190, 269, 276
Rosenfeld, R.A. 393
Rosenman, R. 104, 111
Rosenman, R.H. 294, 301
Rosenthal, R.A. 25, 42
Rosin, H.M. 343, 346
Roskies, E. 318, 327, 328
Rosman, B. 94, 111
Ross, C. 58, 60
Ross, C.E. 12, 21, 72, 90
Ross, I. E. 136, 157
Ross, J. 172, 174
Rossi, A. 71, 77, 78, 90
Rossi, A.M. 375, 382
Rousseau, D.M. 36, 41, 62, 86, 92, 99, 110, 386, 393
Rovine, M. 80, 85
Rowland, K.M. 315
Rowland, V.T. 393
Royce, J. 103, 111
Rubin, L.B. 379, 382
Rubin, Z. 319, 328
Ruble, T.L. 306, 314, 315
Russell, C. 73, 90
Russell, C.S. 174
Rustad, M. 80, 89
Rutter, M. 89

Sacks, S. 331, 344
Safa, H.I. 382
Saffioti, H.I.B. 374, 382
Safilios-Rothschild, C. 11, 12, 13, 73, 90, 346, 393
Safir, M. 345
Salomon, I. 39, 43

Salt, P. 176, 190, 394
Sanders, G. 156
Sarason, I. G. 29, 42, 394
Sarbin, T. 317, 328
Sarri, R.C. 13, 21
Sawhill, I.V 2, 20
Scanzoni, J. 4, 12, 13, 21, 33, 43, 374, 382, 394
Schafer, R.B. 74, 88, 172, 174, 249, 250, 251, 255, 257, 259, 263, 389
Schanninger, C.M. 394
Schein, E.H. 31, 33, 43, 44, 247, 248
Schermerhorn, J.R., Jr. 62, 64, 68, 88
Schervish, P. 11, 21
Schmidt, W.H. 304, 315
Schmink, M. 374, 379, 382
Schmitt, N. 64, 68, 90
Schneewind, K.A. 114, 131, 133
Schneider, B. 138, 157
Schonell, M. 327
Schooler, C. 36, 43, 114, 133, 391
Schoonover, C.B. 14, 17
Schudson, M. 390
Schuler, R.S. 29, 41, 137, 156
Schultz, J.B. 249, 250, 251, 252, 255, 256, 257, 259, 264, 266, 277, 394
Schultz, S. 388
Schulz, R. 207, 223, 225
Schwab, D.P. 40, 43
Schwab, R.L. 137, 156
Schwartzberg, N.S. 175, 176, 178, 179, 188, 189
Scruggs, M. 385
Seccombe, K. 256, 264
Seers, A. 62, 90
Segovis, J. 62, 86, 136, 155
Seidenberg, R. 394
Sekaran, U. 25, 30, 31, 43, 65, 69, 73, 75, 90, 139, 157, 394
Senzaki, C. 371
Serey, T.T. 62, 90
Shaefer, C. 102, 111
Shamir, B. 39, 43
Shaw, L.B. 70, 90
Shearer, J. 136, 155
Shehan, C.L. 186, 190, 172, 174, 267, 275, 276
Shepard, L.J. 75, 90, 293, 302, 321, 328
Shinn, M. 137, 156
Short, M.J. 180, 190
Shostak, A. 18, 394
Shulman, N. 206, 225
Silver, D.L. 287, 301, 302
Simeone, R. 192, 203
Simpson, I.H. 64, 69, 90
Singh, B.K. 166, 174

Skeen, P. 373, 374, 381
Skinner, D.A. 3, 21, 394, 396
Slovic, P., 268, 277
Smith, C.A. 64, 89
Smith, D. 112
Smith, E.J. 361, 382
Smith, P.C. 136, 157
Smith, R.J. 371
Smith, S.J. 28, 43
Smith, T.L. 364, 368, 374, 382
Smulders, P.G.W. 394
Snoek, J.D. 25, 42
Snyderman, B. 137, 156
Soliman, P. 115, 133
Sollie, D.L 205, 209, 224
Sone, P.G. 304, 312, 315
Sorell, G. 209, 224
Sorensen 3, 4, 11
South, S.J. 394
Spain, D. 2, 20, 69, 89
Spanier, G.B. 77, 90
Spector, P.E. 394
Spencer, B.A. 268, 277
Spitze, G. 12, 21, 58, 60, 358, 360, 394
Sprenkle, D.H. 174
Sroufe, L.A. 374, 382
St. John-Parsons, D. 394
St. Pierre, T.W. 394
Stack, C. 49, 54
Stackel, L. 92, 92, 111
Stafford, F.P. 228, 247
Stafford, R. 77, 90
Stahl, M.J. 268, 270, 277
Staines, G.L. 21, 25, 30, 34, 43, 44, 75, 90, 114, 133, 157, 249, 250, 251, 255, 263, 285, 286, 331, 346, 392, 394
Stanley, J.C. 369, 371
Stanton, M. 94, 111
Statham, A. 13, 21
Statuto, C.M. 3, 21
Staw, B.M. 43
Steel, R. 388
Steers, R.M. 335, 346, 394
Steffan, J.J. 22
Stein, P.J. 71, 90, 318, 328
Steinmetz, S.K. 89
Stevens, G. 118, 133
Stewart, A.J. 176, 190, 394, 396
Stickney, S. 388
Stoller, E.P. 14, 21
Strasser, S. 394
Strecher, V. 19
Streilitz, A. 78, 90
Strober, M.H. 20, 394
Stromberg, A.H. 20, 302, 371, 390, 395
Stueve, C. 206, 225

Stull, D.E. 14, 20
Style, C.B. 176, 189
Suchet, M. 28, 35, 44
Suchman, E.A. 269, 276
Suls, J. 156
Summers, E. 136, 156, 161, 174, 389
Sussman, M.B. 20, 86, 89, 395
Suter, L.E. 395
Suttle, J.L. 44
Swart, J.C. 395
Sweeney, J.J. 9, 18
Syme, S.L. 225
Szanton, M.C.B. 374, 382
Szinovacz, M.E. 2, 8, 21, 71, 77, 81, 90

Talbot, N. 395
Taylor, D.E. 388
Taylor, J.C. 68, 88
Tennant, C. 327
Tetenbaum, T.J. 395
Thoits, P. 93, 112
Thoits, P.A. 176, 177, 190, 349, 358, 361
Thomas, C.S. 192, 203
Thomas, K.W. 304, 306, 315
Thomas, R. 390
Thomas, S. 75, 90
Thompson, E. 349, 361
Tienda, M. 361
Tietjen, A.M. 193, 194, 200, 202, 204
Todd, T. 94, 111
Todd-Mancillas, W.R. 375, 382
Tognoli, J. 395
Tolsdorf, C. 207, 210, 225
Townsend, B. 395
Trask, A.E. 340, 345
Travis, M. 395
Treiman, D.J. 78, 90
Triandis, H.C. 371
Trickett, E. 207, 212, 225
Trivers, R. 104, 112
Troxler, R.G. 62, 87
Trumbull, R. 384
Tudor, J. 177, 189
Tung, R.L. 332, 346
Turner, C. 395

Ulbrich, P. 374, 375, 382
Unger, D.G. 192, 201, 202, 204
Ursprung, A.W. 144, 154, 157

Van de Vliert, E. 225
Van Maanen, J. 31, 44, 173, 395
Van Meter, M.J.S. 395
Van Sell, M. 29, 41, 289, 302
Van Velsor, E.V. 395
Vanfossen, B.E. 176, 177, 180, 187, 190

Vaughn-Cole, B. 14, 20
Verbrugge, L.M. 176, 190, 349, 358, 361, 395
Veroff, J. 379, 382, 395
Vicino, F.L. 395
Viscusi, W.K. 49, 54
Viveros-Long, A. 9, 17, 385
Vliet, J.V. 363, 371
Voydanoff, P. 1, 2, 3, 5, 6, 7, 8, 9, 10, 11, 12, 13, 14, 17, 19, 20, 21, 23, 24, 25, 33, 34, 35, 37, 40, 44, 45, 46, 54, 73, 75, 81, 88, 90, 114, 133, 192, 204, 206, 222, 225, 229, 248, 249, 250, 251, 254, 255, 256, 257, 259, 264, 266, 277, 303, 315, 344, 365, 371, 381, 382, 383

Wagner, B. 92, 112
Waite, L.J. 7, 22, 396
Waldman, E. 365, 371, 389
Waldron, I. 349, 361
Walker, J. 280, 286
Walker, K.E. 396
Wallace, P.A. 356, 361
Wallston, B.S. 228, 247, 387
Walsh, W.B. 361
Walters, T. A. 383
Warburton, D.M. 42
Ward, B.E. 381
Warr, P. 73, 90, 396
Wasserman, W. 234, 248
Watanabe, T. 371
Waterhouse, J. M. 279, 280, 286
Weber, J.A. 396
Weber, T. 94, 110, 112
Weeks, G. 94, 110
Weinberg, C.B. 394
Weingarten, K. 396
Weir, T. 27, 75, 86, 136, 155, 156, 301, 386
Weiss, D.J. 136, 141, 142, 157
Weiss, H. 386, 390
Weiss, M.G. 285, 286
Weiss, R. 102, 112
Wells, J.A. 19
Werbel, J.D. 28, 42, 387
White, L. 75, 81, 86
White, P. 90, 389
White, W.L. 396
Wilcox, B.L. 318, 328
Wiley, D.L. 27, 44
Willette, J. 360
Williams, J.H. 396
Williams, R. 138, 156, 341, 345, 387
Williams, R.M., Jr. 269, 276
Willmott, P. 330, 346

Wills, T. 102, 112
Wills, T.A. 35, 41, 224, 225
Wilson, W.J. 46, 47, 48, 49, 54
Winickoff, S. 71, 87
Winnett, R.A. 9, 19
Winter, D.G. 396
Withey, S.B. 64, 85, 384
Wittig-Berman, U. 34, 43
Wolfe, D. 93, 110
Wolfe, D.M. 25, 42
Woods, M.E. 396
Woods, N.F. 361
Workman, R.L. 387
Wortman, C.B. 36, 42, 179, 190
Wynne, L. 94, 110, 112

Ybarra, L. 361
Yelsma, P. 304, 313, 315

Yogev, S. 69, 90, 159, 161, 162, 165, 174, 275, 277, 331, 346, 396
Yogman, M.W. 18
Young, M. 330, 346

Zambrana, R.E. 360, 374, 382
Zammuto, R. 305, 315
Zander, A. 136, 157
Zedeck, S. 63, 64, 71, 90, 135, 136, 156, 157, 161, 174, 268, 277, 389
Zeira, Y. 341, 345
Zeiss, A. 327
Zigler, E. 9, 22
Zimmerer, T.W. 268, 277
Zimmerman, K.W. 396
Zoloth, B. 78, 86
Zung, W.W.K. 180, 190
Zvonkovic, A.M. 73, 90

Index of Subjects

Absence from the home 27
Absenteeism 6, 36, 137, 255, 321, 323, 326
Accomplishment 4
Achievement 333
  need for 333, 335, 338, 339
Active vs. passive kinds of support 342
Activity 211, 212
Adolescent programs 244
Adult development 33
Advancement (see also Career advancement) 34, 35
AFDC 13
Affectionate behaviors 211, 212, 219, 223
Affective reactions to work 141
Affective responses 135
Affective states, negative 298
Age of dependent children 364
Aggression 293
Air Force 229, 231
Alienation 34
Alternative family lifestyles (see also Lifestyles) 279
Alternative occupational choices 279
American fathers, ambivalence towards working mothers 379
American housewives 368
American society, social and demographic changes 249
Anger 230, 293
Anxiety 321, 326
Attitudes
  homogeneous 366
  Japanese and American attitudes toward women's employment 365
  of American, Brazilian, and Filipino fathers on wives working outside of the home 377
  of the mothers towards maternal employment 378
  towards maternal employment, Brazil 375
  towards maternal employment, Philippines 375
  toward wife's employment and age of husband 375

Automation 11
Autonomy 4, 33
  lack of 320
Balance 243
Balancing jobs 83
Behavior-based conflict 25, 27, 250
Behavioral taxonomies 28
Benefits
  flexible 37
  for family 255
Birth 256
Blue-collar workers 341
Boredom 230
Boss support 325
Boundary 38
Burnout 135, 138, 141, 142, 152, 154, 292, 293, 296, 298, 330, 332, 333, 334, 339, 340, 341, 342
  and depersonalization, 147, 150
  and emotional distress of family members 147
  and emotional exhaustion, 147, 150
  and job satisfaction 154
  and performance 144
  and sense of personal accomplishment 147
  in human services sector 137

Care of elderly 15, 370
Career 31 (see also Job, Occupation, Work)
  accomplishments 25, 35
  advancement 265, 274
  alternatives 37
  anchor 33
  aspirations 265, 266, 268, 271, 272, 275, 333
  commitments 233
  decisions 272
  demands 206
  development 38, 167, 170, 108, 222, 364, 370
    initial development 222
  entry 205, 218
  family conflict (see Work/family conflict)
  growth 39
  impacts on relationships 224
  involvement 206, 209

411

Career (con't)
  meaning of 31
  orientation 25, 33, 34, 35
  paths 37
  responsibilities 363
  salience 69
  success 34, 35
  tracking 207
  women 265, 272
Caregiving 14
Carryover (see also Spillover) 255
Causal theory 57
Challenging job 39
Changes in household 194
Child development 2, 3, 363
Child rearing 12
Childbearing 7
Childcare (see also Day Care) 2, 9, 76, 78, 153, 167, 170, 172, 250, 257, 266, 272, 283, 284, 341, 364
  help with 170
  responsibilities 85
  services 368
  tasks 79
Childless marriage 330
Children 2, 153, 250, 283, 364
  adolescent 69
  age of 170, 176, 180, 257, 259, 262, 364
  behavior of 28
  leaving home 256
  number of 28, 167, 170, 176, 180, 262, 272
  preschool 69, 280, 326
  responsibility for 162
  school-aged and older 368
  young 80
Chores (see also Household tasks) 79
Civilian corporations 247
Clerical workers 6
Clinical methodology 29
Co-workers 321
College students 209
Comfort 211, 212
Commitment 208, 211, 217
  to work 330
Communication dynamics 153
Commuter marriage 8
Compensation models 5
Competition 32, 333
Conceptual map 63
Conceptual models 40
Conflict 32, 326, 333 (see also Work/family, conflict)
  in men 326
Consumption Cutbacks Scale 196

Contact 216
Control 159
Convergent methodology 252
Coping 30, 36, 262
  in crisis situations 200
  unemployed women 200
  with stress 327
Cornell Values Study 269
Corporate wife 75
Counseling 9
Couple relationship (see also Marital relationship) 65, 85
Couples 8
Creativity 33
Cross-cultural meanings of working outside of the home 380
Cross-cultural research 369
Cultural differences 365
Cultural ideal 364
Cultural values 380

Daily transition 24, 28, 29
Daughters
  of working mothers 374
Day care (see also Child care) 244
  Government and employer-sponsored 59
Death 251, 256
Decision modeling and lifestyle 27
Demographic variables 294
Demographic variables 252, 262
Demographics 151
Depersonalization 137, 141
Depression 175, 177, 179, 192, 293, 321, 326
  and employment status 178
  and irritation 318
  anxiety and somatization 324
  spending behavior during 194
  ties with self-esteem 68
Determination, 369
Disabled, elderly 14
Dissatisfaction 331
Division of household tasks (see Household tasks)
Division of responsibilities 57
Divorce 241, 251
Doctors 333
Domestic chores (see also Household tasks) 342
Domestic help, paid 169, 172, 380
Domestic work 337
Dominance 333
  male 368
  need for 335, 338, 339
Doubts about success 335

INDEX OF SUBJECTS

Dual-career couples (see also Dual-earner couples) 2, 24, 31, 35, 233, 241, 329, 331, 333, 342, 343
    definition 31
    ladders 37
    lifestyle 25
    partners with children 28
    role-strain 331
    two-career status 35
    with children 28
Dual-earner couples (see also Dual-career couples) 161, 262, 326
    families 3, 6, 31, 56, 317, 330
        vs. one-earner families
    with children 159
    marital satisfaction 64
Dual-income 31
Dual-role 319
Dysfunctional consequences 30

Early career 37
Earner status 199
Economic provider 6
Economic resources 3, 4, 193
Economic rewards 3
Economic support, spousal 266
Economy 11
Education
    in Philippines 380
    level of 383, 375
Effects of Unemployment Questionnaire 196
Elderly 14, 364
    care of 14, 15, 370
    disabled 14
Emotional exhaustion 137, 141
Emotional support (see also Support) 191, 212
    lack of 175
    of husband 275
Emotional well-being 300
Employed women (see also Women) 176
Employee Assistance Program 91
Employee counseling 37
Employee measures 140
Employee performance and spouse views 150
Employment (see also Career, Job, Occupation, Work) 13, 182
    and housework 85
    and well-being 70
    conditions 76
    men's 69
    policies 3
    rates 7

Employment (con't)
    status 175, 178
    status of spouse 262
    women 2, 24
Energy depletion 334
Energy management 251
Equity 223
Evaluation 211, 212
Excessive work time 250
Exchange of resources in a time of crisis 201
Exchange theory 56
Expansion theory 10

Failure 331
Families, working, middle class 178
Family
    adjustment to reduced income 194
    as resources for unemployed women 202
    aspirations 34
    career decisions 275
    changes 251, 256
    characteristics 24
    demands 6, 7
    definition of, Census Bureau 59
    effect of night shift work on 280
    experiences 136
    income 265, 271
    interactions 279
    involvement 167, 170
        effects on family 254
    obligations 176
    policy 59
    responsibilities 6, 35, 36
        and job satisfaction 76
    role stresses, and employment status 178
    roles 23, 24, 69, 175
        perceived stresses 178
        primacy of, wife and mother 176
        satisfaction 5, 138
        satisfaction with 76
        stability 13, 193
        stages 380
        stress from 175
    sociological theory 56
    stress 175, 181
        and emotional health 175
        and employment status 180, 183
        and psychological well-being 175, 180
        lack of task sharing 180
        self-esteem and depression 182

Family (cont.)
   structure 13, 15
      changes in 55
      demands 6
   support programs 244
   support systems 229, 254, 255, 257, 261
   system 330
   traditional family 245
   variables 230
   work day 8
Family development framework 10
Family life and affective reactions to work 152
Family life stages 76, 79, 81, 85, 162, 167, 170, 172
Family research, current work 3
Family Stress Scale 179
Family type 194
Family's financial management 363
Fatigue 250
Feminist ideology 59
Financial
   of women 173
   counseling 244
   hardship 194
   power 167
   support 191
   status, and women's decision to work 274
   stress, due to job loss 194
Flexibility 159, 251
   job 62, 250, 255
Flexible benefits 37
Flexible work schedules 9, 25, 39, 59
Food, spending for 201
Freedom, individualism 369
Friend exchanges 222
Friends 223, 321
   as resources for unemployed women 202
Friendships, effect of night shift work on 280

Gasoline expenditures 197
Gender 65, 85, 208, 214, 222, 325, 338
Gender differences (see also Sex differences) 77, 229, 233, 243, 244, 342
Gender roles (see also Sex roles) 207
   behavior 326
Gender-based research 16
Genes 104
Geographic mobility 3, 5, 8, 9
Goals 340

Goods 211, 212
Guilt 34

Headaches 323, 326
Health 6, 176, 293, 296, 299, 300, 321
Holahan and Gilbert's (1979) six role conflict scales 317
Home/work conflict (see also Work/family, conflict) 332, 338, 339, 340, 342
Homemaker 329
Homemaking (see also Housewifery) 363
Hopefulness 230
Hopkins Symptom Checklist 321
Hours of family work 170
Hours worked per day 167, 170, 250
Household spending, as function of earner status 202
Household tasks 12, 78, 167, 170, 179, 172, 228, 266, 271, 272, 275, 341
   division 8, 77, 80, 254, 255, 261, 266
   help with 170
   lowering standards 256
   men's involvement in 78
Housewifery (see also Homemaking) 364
Housewifery in Japan 366
Housewives 66, 177, 178, 366, 370
   American 368
   income, importance of in developing countries 379
   role 343
Housework (see also Household tasks) 78, 167, 170, 179, 172, 341
   help with 170
Human ecology 228
Husband's
   approval 265, 271
   assistance with the household 265
   attitude toward maternal employment 266
   career involvement 206
   financial support of the family 267
   level of burnout 341
   support of his wife's career 206

Income 3, 34
   adequacy 245, 250
   family adjustment to reduced income 194
   inadequacy 250
   levels 245, 251, 255
   perceived adequacy of family income 233, 241
Individual, in context 64
Individualism 369
Insomnia 293
Instrumental behaviors 212, 220, 223

INDEX OF SUBJECTS

Inter-role conflict 317, 326
Interdependence 23, 36
Interference with spouse's career 335
Interpersonal communications 147
Irritation 326
Israel 332, 333

Japan 363
Japanese and American attitudes toward women's employment 365
Japanese housewives 364, 368
Jealousy 32
Job (see also Career, Occupation, Work)
    and quality of family life 136
    anxiety 318
    burnout 137
    characteristics 4, 24
    commitment 6, 227, 228, 231, 233, 234, 240, 241, 242, 246, 247
    demands 136
    dissatisfaction (see also Job satisfaction) 30, 36, 326
    high level of 243
    involvement 34, 69, 76
    loss and men's self-evaluation 73
    part-time 251, 369
    performance 6, 34, 259
    satisfaction 2, 4, 5, 30, 63, 64, 70, 77, 78, 135, 136, 138, 141, 154, 251, 268, 272, 275, 279, 293, 296, 298, 300, 321, 323, 327
        and burnout 142, 154
        and quality of family life 136
        and pay and promotion 136
        and self-confidence 137
        and working conditions 154
        antecedents of 136
        components and family variables, extrinsic, intrinsic 151
        intrinsic and extrinsic 141, 152
        lack of research on 136
        lowered 327
        women's 78
    stress 5, 62, 136, 326, 327
        and spousal well-being 136
    structural characteristics 5
    tension 6
    versus career priority 33

Kin (see also Family, Relatives) 220
    and friend networks 213
    exchanges 222
    network 208

Labor force participation 6

Labor saving devices 380
Langner 22-item screening scale 179
Leisure 4
Liberation movement 368
Life events (see also Life stages) 254
Life research progress 55
Life satisfactions 63
Life setting characteristics 290
Life stages 66, 68, 208
    and parental satisfaction 70
    effects 206
    family 76, 79, 81, 85, 162, 167, 170, 172
    transition to parenthood 80, 81
    trends 83
Life style behaviors 293
Life styles 293, 296
    behaviors 299
    integration 33
    orientation 266, 267, 272, 273
    patterns 271, 272, 279
Lodahl and Kejner scale 165
Longitudinal research 66, 83

Machismo 375
Male dominance 368
Male values 227
Managerial competence 33
Managerial women 326
Managers, male 167
Manufacturing jobs 11
Marital (see also Marriage)
    adjustment 206
    cohesion 374
    communications 28
    counseling 244
    problems 257
    quality 33, 246
    relationship 2, 138, 243, 246
    satisfaction 2, 5, 32, 33, 62, 64, 69, 70, 79, 82, 233, 237, 240, 241, 242, 243, 244, 246, 268, 272, 275, 321, 323, 326
        and father's participation in household work 76
        and men's employment time 69
    solidarity 78
    stress 176
        and work outside the home 70
Marital
    support services 244
Marriage 363
    affective quality of 176
    childless 330
    enrichment 244
    less stressed marriages 246

Marriage (con't)
    quality of the workers' marriage 62
    spousal domestic support 266
    spousal employment 233
    spousal or family satisfaction with an employee's job 138
    spousal reports of problems 135
    spousal support 251, 266, 273
        effect on women's career decisions 267
    spouse 321
    spouse ratings 144
    spouse's happiness with own job and happiness with employee's job 145
Maslach Burnout Inventory 141, 293
Maternal employment (see also Mothers, Wives, Women, Work) 2, 365
    and cognitive functioning of children 374
    and egalitarian spousal relationships 374
    and marital relationship 380
    and paternal involvement in child care 374
    and psychological well-being 374
    father's ambivalence towards 379
    in underdeveloped countries 379
    maternal employment and child development 69
    variability of views 380
Maternity leaves 59
Mating stage 331
Measurement (see Methodology)
Measures, work restructuring 164
Mental health 6
Methodology 63, 66, 252, 301
    convergent 252
    diverse 40
    longitudinal research 66, 83
    multiple data collection methods 252
    multiple regression equations 83
    multiple regression model 61
    research methods 251, 252
    research traditions 63
    self-report research 274
    self-report questionnaire data 251
    structural equation models 294
Middle class husbands 374
Middle-management 331
Migraine headaches 326
Military population 247
Minnesota Satisfaction Questionnaire 141

Models, work and family 63
Moderator effects 78
Money (see also Economic resources and Financial power) 211, 251
Money management (see also Financial management)
Morale 231
Motherhood, effects of 176
Mothers (see also Maternal employment, Wives, Women)
    cross-cultural attitudes of fathers and mothers 373
    employed vs. unemployed 175
Motivations for seeking employment 84
Moving 256
Multiple data collection methods 252
Multiple regression equations 83
Multiple regression model 61

Need for achievement 333
Need for dominance and achievement 335, 338, 339
Negative affective states 298
Network size 210, 214
Network sector 214, 220, 222
Night shift work 30, 279, 284, 337
    and time pressures on young marrieds 280
    camaraderie and loyalty within the work group 280
    childcare concerns 280, 284
    drawbacks 280
    effect on friendships 280
    escape from or avoidance of obligations and tensions 285
    financial incentives 284
    general attitudes toward 281
    interference with family life 280
    job opportunities 284
    level of enjoyment 281
    motivations for 279, 281
    satisfaction with 284
    social concerns 282
Night shift workers
    and children 283
    assignment to an afternoon shift 250
    attitudes toward their work 279
    childcare 284
        provided by relatives 280
    family relationships 283
    past research 280
    time spent with families 280
    time spent with family members 285
Non-work stressors 290, 292, 296, 299
Nonchallenge 183
Nontraditional work 245

Nonwork 36
Number of earners, and spending for foods 201

Occupation (see also Carreer, Job, Work) 167, 170, 171
    control of one's time 173
Occupational
    choices 279
    segregation 15
    status 251, 342
        wife's higher than husband's 251
    success 4, 33
Organizational commitment (see also Job commitment and Work commitment) 137
    environment 241
        quality of 232
    settings 36
    supportiveness 233, 237, 240, 244
        perceptions of 246
    variables 230
Organization's responsibilities 36
Overall gives/receives 218
Overtime, frequency of 250
Overload 175, 177

Paid domestic help 169, 172, 380
Paid work 79
Parent-child relationships 10
Parental leaves 9
Parental status 233
Parental stress, and work outside the home 70
Parenting (see also Children) 69
    attitudes 69
    competence 69
    roles 83
    satisfaction 64, 69, 70
    stress 62
        and father's participation in household work 76
    transition to parenthood 80, 81
Parents as providers of social support 192
Part-time jobs 251, 369
Path models 233
Patriarchal ideology 59
Patterns of family work 78
Pensions 13
Person-environment fit 343
Personal accomplishment 141
Personal adjustment 232
Personal and family lives 227
Personal growth 255
Personal hardiness (see also Health) 29
Personal satisfactions 79

Personal variables 230
Personnel policies 9
    family-oriented 9, 15, 16
Physical disability 13
Physical illness 179
Police officers' job burnout 27
Policy issues 9
Positive and negative emotions 230
Poverty cycle 201
Power 34
Power relations 57
Powerlessness 34
Pregnancy 7
Preschool children 326
Pride 4
Primary role 331
Productivity 3
Professionalism 31
Professionals 163, 167
Profit 213, 220
Promotions 35
Provider role 12
Psychological characteristics 5
Psychological disturbance 175, 179
Psychological health, of married women 176
Psychological interfaces 10
Psychological meaning of work 65
Psychological well-being 161
    of employed wives 177
Psychosomatic symptoms 293, 296

Quality of Employment Survey 250
Quality of family life 3, 4, 5, 6, 8, 9, 14, 138
Quality of life 24, 161
Quality of organizational environment 232
Quality of work environment 34

Reciprocal causality 84
Recognition 34
Relationship contact 211
Relationships
    new 251
    quality 75
Relationships (cont.)
    strained affiliative relationships 34
    supportive 35
    symmetrical, egalitarian 330
Relatives (see Family and Kin) 321
Relocation 35, 39
    assistance 9, 37
    programs 9

Research methods (see also Methodology) 251, 252
Research traditions 63
Residence 233
Resource allocation, timing of 201
Resource management 192
  within households 201
Resources, exchange in interpersonal relationships 211
Responsibility 4
  for children 162
Restructuring
  and occupation 173
  of work to accommodate family needs 159
  men 166, 167
    and paid help 167
  relationship between spouses 171
  women 166, 170, 172
Role, wife-mother role 331
  agreement about the wife's role 373
Role conflict 10, 25, 34, 56, 245, 269, 318, 319, 320, 322, 323, 324, 326, 333
  and role of mother 177
  intensity of 26
  inter-role conflict 317, 326
Role conflict scales 319
Role expectations 222, 370
Role precedence 26
Role pressures 27
  multiple role pressures 25
Role strain 10, 5, 81
Role strain theory 10
Role theory 56
Roles 205, 208, 222, 317, 365
  multiple roles 7, 10
  multiple life roles 24
  of women, in different cultures 373
  worker/earner 11, 12, 15, 16
Rosenberg self-esteem scale 180

Salaries and status 333
Satisfaction with life (see also Life satisfaction) 232
Satisfaction measures 28
Schedule conflicts 250, 254, 256
Schedule flexibility (see also Work schedules) 285
Scheduling 3, 5
  school schedules 15
School administrators 332
Scope of Assistance Scale 196

Second job 337
Security 33, 230
Self-concept 255 (see also Self-esteem)
Self-doubts 339
Self-efficacy 159, 162, 167, 169, 170, 172
Self-esteem 29, 35, 62, 64, 66, 68, 77, 80, 175, 176, 179
  men's 69
  mothers with young children 81
  wives' 68
Self-report questionnaire data 251
Self-report research 274
Self identity, feminine 332
Sense of "fit" 231
Sequential staging 7
Sex differences (see also Gender differences) 139, 171, 208, 219, 222, 228, 241, 246, 257, 262, 319, 330, 339
Sex roles 208, 332, 380
  changing sex roles 380
  expectations 319
  socialization 227
  well-being 78
Sex-typed jobs 227
Shared decision making 374
Shared jobs 251
Shift work (see Night shift work)
Shift workers (see Night shift workers)
Simultaneous staging 7
Single parent families 6, 10, 13, 14, 15
Single-earner spouses, marital satisfaction 64
Sleeping difficulties 27
Social isolation 320
Social roles
  interactions between (see also Roles) 177
  stress of 177
Social support (see also Support) 24, 29, 35, 191, 192, 194, 207, 229, 272, 292, 318, 319, 321
  as protection against adverse effects of unemployment 192, 193
  definition of 192
  government agencies 193
Social access 255
Social life 279
Social isolation 39
Social networks 192, 200, 205, 206, 207, 210, 218, 222, 224
  function 205
  interaction with for unemployed women 200
Social norms 173
Social Security 13
Social stratification 3

INDEX OF SUBJECTS

Social variables 230
Socialization, female 327
Societal demands 379
Socio-emotional character 327
Socioeconomic background 380
Socioeconomic resources 3
Socioeconomic status 233, 237
Sociological theory 58
Sole earner families 194, 197, 199, 200, 201, 202
    special needs of 202
Somatization 321, 326
Source of assistance
    and seeking behavior 201
    for unemployed women 199
Sources of assistance 199
Specialization 339, 342
Spending reductions 194
Spending for foods 201
Spillover from family to job 4, 152, 255, 257, 260, 332
Split shift schedules of parents (see also Work Schedules) 280
Spouse-employee relationships 147
Status competition 336, 339
Status incongruence 339
Stereotypes 332
Strain 317, 222, 331
Strain-based conflicts 25, 27, 250, 255, 261
Strategies to reduce work-family conflict 251
Stress 24, 25, 29, 30, 36, 39, 61, 138, 207, 244, 255, 318, 323
    as related to unemployment 29, 193
    support as stress reducer 191
Stressors 300, 332
    magnitude of 175
Structural equation models 294
Structural interfaces 10
Success 333
Supervisor 321
Support 343
    active vs. passive 342
    environment 242
    financial or informational 191
    from friends 223
    from spouse for one's work 76
    groups 374
    networks 241
    spousal 6
    types 199
        and number of earners 200
        for unemployed women 200
Supportive relationships 35
Supports, instrumental and affective 224

Symmetry 343

Tax credits 16
Teachers 317, 319
Teaching 327
Technical-functional competence 33
Tension (see also Stress) 13, 62
Theory 57
Time 251
    availability 12
    demands 25
    management skills 251
    management strategies 254, 262
    shortages. 250
    spent with family 145
Time management strategies and methods for coping with conflicts 256
Time-based conflicts 25, 27, 255, 261, 299
Tradeoffs 266, 326
Traditional family 245
Traditional sex role stereotypes, violation of 172
Traditional sex roles 171
Traditional values, and opposition to wife's employment 375
Transfer payments 13
Transfer policies 9
Travel 5, 170
    extensive time 39
    frequency of travel 167
Triangulation 252
Turnover 6, 136, 137, 293, 296, 299, 300
Two-earner families (see also Dual-earner couples and Dual-career families)
Two-factor theory of work motivation 30
Type A Behavior 294
Type A characteristics 299

Unemployed women (see also Unemployment) 2
    assistance from friends 197
    informational and emotional support from friends 199
    assistance from relatives 197
    emotional and financial support from parents 199
    assistance-seeking behavior 201
    effects on total family system 202
    interaction between family and friendship networks 194
    reduced expenditures for food 197

Unemployed women (con't)
    resource management of 191
    social network assistance 201
    social support 191
Unemployment 2, 3, 4, 10, 191
    adjustment to reduced incomes, uncertain financial futures 193
    and economic deprivation 193
    as crisis event 192
    effect on consumption patterns 191
    length of time 201
    women 191
        in single earner vs. multiple-earner families 194, 197, 199, 200, 201, 202
Unemployment insurance 13, 16
Unions 341
University women, lifestyle patterns 265
Unpaid work 10, 12, 15
Utilities expenditures 197

Values, male 227

Weekends 5
Welfare 13, 16
Well-being 63, 66, 68, 206, 343
    family 61
    individual 61, 64, 70
    marital 64, 70
    of employed wives 177
    parental 61, 64, 70
    partners 65
    psychological 161
Wife abuse 28
Wife-mother role 331
Wives (see also Maternal employment and Women)
    employment and marital happiness 58
Wives (cont.)
    support, marital satisfaction 7
    unemployment, and economic distress on family life 192
Women (see also Maternal employment, Unemployed women, Wives)
    employment 2, 24, 364
        changes over time 364
        impact on family members 374
    financial considerations 379
    full-time working 369
    labor force participation 6, 329
    motivations to work, personal 379
    professional satisfaction 379
    restructuring, and husbands' work 170

Women (con't)
    role conflict 327
    roles 365
    unemployment, research on 192
Work (see also Career, Job, Occupation, Night Shift Work) 23
    alienation 293, 298
    characteristics 161
    choices
        affect on later well-being 68
        couple's pattern 65
    colleagues 223
    conditions 169
    effects on family 5, 145
    environment, quality of 34
        effect on spouse 160
    experiences, impact on family life 139
    extra hours 167, 170, 172
    hours 35, 173
    involvement 38, 68, 170, 172, 333, 336, 338, 339
    meaning of 68, 82, 85
        men's involvement 28
    nontraditional work 245
    outcomes 296
    outside the home 249
    overload 310, 318
    patterns, study of 65
        differences and well-being 79
    performance 335, 339
    physical or psychological demands 250
    psychological meaning of 65
    restructuring 161
    roles 3, 5, 6, 7, 8, 24, 205, 208
        structural 3
        Worker-earner role 11, 12, 15, 16
    schedules (see also Flexibility, work schedules) 37, 318
    stress 62, 206, 290, 320, 327
    stressors 292, 296, 300, 319, 326
    variables 167
Work/family
    conflict 3, 5, 6, 7, 24. 25. 37, 249, 250, 251, 257, 265, 296, 299, 300, 331, 335
        antecedents and consequences 289, 292, 295
        connections between 55, 58
        consequences of 293
        dynamics 32
        in night shift workers 285
        joint effects 8
        management of, by restructuring work 171

Work/family (con't)
   model of 290
   family integration 62
   interactions 30
   interchange literature 191
   interface 2, 9, 11, 13, 227, 230, 242, 245, 249, 254, 255, 262, 331
   life cycle 7
   organization
   research
      economists 57
      historical perspective 56
   responsiveness to families 232
   roles 205, 228
      allocation 7
   strain 5, 81
   spillover 30, 259
   systems 10

Work setting characteristics 206, 290, 292
Work-at-home programs 39
Work-well-being connections 84
Work/home relationship, quality of 138
Worker-earner role 11, 12, 15, 16
Working mothers (see Maternal employment)
Working-class husbands 374
Workplace 327

Young adults 205, 207

Zung scale 180

NOTES

NOTES

NOTES

NOTES

NOTES

NOTES

NOTES

NOTES

NOTES